June 20–22, 2012
Newark, New Jersey, USA

**Association for
Computing Machinery**

Advancing Computing as a Science & Profession

SACMAT'12

Proceedings of the 17th ACM Symposium on

Access Control Models and Technologies

Sponsored by:
ACM SIGSAC

Association for Computing Machinery

Advancing Computing as a Science & Profession

The Association for Computing Machinery
2 Penn Plaza, Suite 701
New York, New York 10121-0701

Notice to Past Authors of ACM-Published Articles

ISBN: 978-1-4503-1295-0 (Digital)

ISBN: 978-1-4503-1735-1 (Print)

Additional copies may be ordered prepaid from:

ACM Order Department
PO Box 30777
New York, NY 10087-0777, USA

Phone: 1-800-342-6626 (USA and Canada)
+1-212-626-0500 (Global)
Fax: +1-212-944-1318
E-mail: acmhelp@acm.org
Hours of Operation: 8:30 am – 4:30 pm ET

Printed in the USA

Foreword

It is our great pleasure to welcome you to the *17th ACM Symposium on Access Control Models and Technologies (SACMAT 2012)*. This year's symposium continues its tradition of being the premier forum for presentation of research results on leading edge issues of access control, including models, systems, applications, and theory.

73 papers have been submitted from a variety of countries around the world. Submissions were anonymous; each paper has been reviewed by at least three reviewers who are experts in the field. Extensive online discussions took place to make the selections for the symposium. The program committee finally accepted 19 papers that cover a variety of topics, including RBAC, role mining, privacy, access control policies and models, and access control for mobile devices. The program again contains a demo session with five demos covering topics such as risk aggregation for RBAC, assured information sharing, policy enforcement and access control for business processes. In addition the program includes a panel on Emerging Trends around Big Data Analytics and Security, and keynote talks by Ruby Lee and Ravi Sandhu. We hope that these proceedings will serve as a valuable reference for security researchers and developers.

Putting together *SACMAT 2012* was a team effort. First of all, we would like to thank the authors for submitting to the symposium, the keynote speakers for graciously accepting our invitation, the demo presenters and panelists for contributing to the program. We are grateful to the program committee members and external reviewers for their efforts in reviewing the papers and their engagement in online discussions during the review process. Special thanks go to Jorge Lobo and Mahesh Tripunitara (Panels Chairs), Andreas Schaad (Demonstrations Chair), Dongwan Shin (Webmaster), Lujo Bauer (Publicity Chair) and Mohamed Shehab (Proceedings Chair) for their help in organizing and publicizing the symposium. We also thank the members of the steering committee and especially its chair, Gail-Joon Ahn, for providing valuable advice and support. Many thanks also go to the local arrangements chairs, Soon Ae Chun and Reza Curtmola.

We would like to thank our sponsor, ACM SIGSAC, for their continued support of this symposium. We would also like to acknowledge Rutgers Business School for providing the meeting space and valuable donations.

We hope that you will find this program interesting and that the symposium will provide you with a valuable opportunity to share ideas with other researchers and practitioners from institutions around the world.

Vijay Atluri
SACMAT'12 General Co-Chair
Rutgers University, USA

Axel Kern
SACMAT'12 Program Chair
Beta Systems Software AG, Germany

Jaideep Vaidya
SACMAT'12 General Co-Chair
Rutgers University, USA

Murat Kantarcioglu
SACMAT'12 Program Chair
University of Texas in Dallas, USA

Table of Contents

Demo Session
Session Chair: Andreas Schaad *(SAP AG)*

Session 4: Privacy
Session Chair: Murat Kantarcioglu *(University of Texas at Dallas)*

Session 5: Role-Based Access Control
Session Chair: Axel Kern *(Beta Systems Software AG)*

Session 6: Access Control Policies

Session Chair: James Joshi *(University of Pittsburgh)*

17th ACM Symposium on Access Control Models and Technologies (SACMAT 2012)

General Co-Chairs: Vijay Atluri (Rutgers University, US A)
Jaideep Vaidya (Rutgers University, USA)

Program Co-Chairs: Axel Kern (Beta Systems Software AG, Germany)
Murat Kantarcioglu (University of Texas at Dallas, USA)

Panels Co-Chairs: Jorge Lobo (IBM, USA)
Mahesh Tripunitara (University of Waterloo, Canada)

Proceedings Chair: Mohamed Shehab (University of North Carolina at Charlotte, USA)

Demonstration Chair: Andreas Schaad (SAP Labs, Germany)

Local Arrangements Co-Chairs: Soon Ae Chun (City University of New York, USA)
Reza Curtmola (New Jersey Institute of Technology, USA)

Publicity Chair: Lujo Bauer (Carnegie Mellon University, USA)

Treasurers: Jaideep Vaidya (Rutgers University, USA)
Basit Shafiq (Rutgers University, USA)

Webmaster: Dongwan Shin (New Mexico Tech, USA)

Steering Committee Chair: Gail-Joon Ahn (Arizona State University, USA)

Steering Committee: Axel Kern (Beta Systems Software AG, Germany)
Bhavani Thuraisingham (University of Texas at Dallas, USA)
Indrakshi Ray (Colorado State University, USA)
Ninghui Li (Purdue University, USA)
James Joshi (University of Pittsburgh, USA)

Program Committee: Gail-Joon Ahn (Arizona State University, USA)
Vijay Atluri (Rutgers University, USA)
Steve Barker (King's College, London University, UK)
Lujo Bauer (Carnegie Mellon University, USA)
Elisa Bertino (Purdue University, USA)
Ruth Breu (University of Innsbruck, Austria)
Mustafa Canim (IBM, USA)
Barbara Carminati (University of Insubria, Italy)
Jason Crampton (Royal Holloway, University of London, UK)
Wenliang Du (Syracuse University, USA)
David M. Eyers (University of Cambridge, UK)
Elena Ferrari (University of Insubria at Como, Italy)
Philip Fong (University of Calgary, Canada)

SACMAT 2012 Sponsor & Supporter

Sponsor:

Supporter: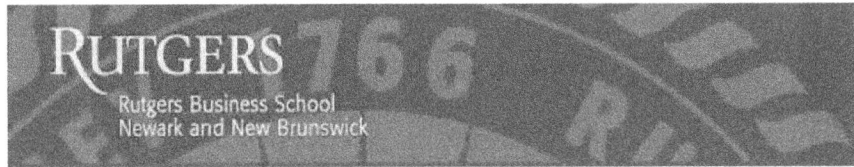

Hardware-enhanced Access Control
in Cloud Computing

Ruby B. Lee

Dept. of Electrical Engineering, Princeton University

Princeton, NJ

rblee@princeton.edu

Abstract:

Future trustworthy computer systems should provide built-in support for at least the cornerstone security properties of confidentiality, integrity and availability. Access control can help significantly towards achieving this. However, in today's computing landscape, traditional access control implemented only in software may be either insufficient or non-optimal. We discuss some of these situations. Furthermore, fine-grained access control and usage control mechanisms implemented in software are themselves subject to attack, and may impose heavy performance overheads. Can new hardware architecture improve the security achievable by software mechanisms for access control and usage control? If so, what types of hardware support are most useful while retaining the flexibility of software protection mechanisms? What can software do, to help hardware achieve the best results?

With the trend towards Cloud Computing, we discuss how new hardware architectural features for cloud servers can help protect the confidentiality and integrity of a cloud customer's code and data in his leased Virtual Machines -- even when the powerful underlying hypervisor may be compromised [1,2]. This uses a new, non-bypassable form of hardware access control. Without requiring new hardware, we can also leverage the hardware trend towards manycore chips, and the already available hardware virtualization features, to enhance Cloud Security – but with a few restrictions and some new software support [3,4]. In general, we would like to motivate collaborations between the software security and the hardware architecture communities to explore software-hardware co-design for security [5]. What comes *beyond access control* in cloud computing and mobile computing ecosystems? The goal is to design future trustworthy systems that provide security protections, at the levels needed, when needed, even with malware in the system.

Categories and Subject Descriptors: C.2.0 General (security and protection); D.4.6 Software: Security & Protection (K.6.5): Access controls

Keywords: Cloud Computing; Hardware Security; Virtualization; Security Architecture; Hardware-Software Co-design

References:

[1] Jakub Szefer and Ruby B. Lee, "Architectural Support for Hypervisor-Secure Virtualization," in Proceedings of the International Conference on Architectural Support for Programming Languages and Operating Systems (ASPLOS), March 2012.

[2] Jakub Szefer and Ruby B. Lee, "A Case for Hardware Protection of Guest VMs from Compromised Hypervisors in Cloud Computing," in Proceedings of the Second International Workshop on Security and Privacy in Cloud Computing (SPCC), June 2011.

[3] Jakub Szefer, Eric Keller, Ruby B. Lee, and Jennifer Rexford, "Eliminating the Hypervisor Attack Surface for a More Secure Cloud," in Proceedings of the Conference on Computer and Communications Security (CCS), October 2011.

[4] Eric Keller, Jakub Szefer, Jennifer Rexford, and Ruby B. Lee, "NoHype: Virtualized cloud infrastructure without the virtualization," in Proceedings of the International Symposium on Computer Architecture (ISCA), pages 350-357, June 2010.

[5] David Champagne and Ruby B. Lee, "Scalable Architectural Support for Trusted Software", IEEE International Symposium on High-Performance Computer Architecture (HPCA), Jan. 2010.

Speaker's Biography:

Ruby B. Lee is the Forrest G. Hamrick Professor in Engineering and Professor of Electrical Engineering with an affiliated appointment in Computer Science at Princeton University. She is the Director of the Princeton Architecture Lab for Multimedia and Security (PALMS). Her current research interests are in secure cloud computing, security-aware computer architecture, trustworthy hardware that does not leak information through side channels, secure manycore architecture, secure sensor nets, mobile security and security verification of hardware-software security architectures.

Prior to Princeton, Lee served as chief architect at Hewlett-Packard for processor architecture, multimedia architecture and security architecture. She was a founding architect of HP's PA-RISC architecture and instrumental in the initial design of several generations of PA-RISC processors for HP's business and technical computer product lines. She pioneered adding data-parallelism support for multimedia in microprocessors and enabling ubiquitous real-time multimedia in commodity computers. She was co-leader of an Intel-HP architecture team for 64-bit Intel processor systems. She led the security architecture team for enterprise and e-commerce security for HP before coming to Princeton. Lee is an ACM Fellow and an IEEE Fellow. She holds over 120 U.S. and international patents and has published numerous papers, with best paper awards in different fields. Lee is often asked to serve on national committees for improving cyber security research; she was a co-leader of the National Cyber Leap Year Summit (2009) and co-author of the earlier National Academies' study mandated by Congress to improve cyber security research in the U.S. Her undergraduate degree is from Cornell and her M.S. (CS) and Ph.D. (EE) degrees are from Stanford.

SACMAT'12, June 20–22, 2012, Newark, New Jersey, USA.
ACM 978-1-4503- 1295-0/12/06.

MOSES: Supporting Operation Modes on Smartphones

Giovanni Russello
Department of Computer
Science
University of Auckland
Auckland, New Zealand
g.russello@auckland.ac.nz

Mauro Conti
Università di Padova,
Padova, Italy
conti@math.unipd.it

Bruno Crispo
Università di Trento
Trento, Italy
crispo@disi.unitn.it

Earlence Fernandes
Vrije Universiteit Amsterdam
The Netherlands
earlence@cs.vu.nl

ABSTRACT

Smartphones are very effective tools for increasing the productivity of business users. With their increasing computational power and storage capacity, smartphones allow end users to perform several tasks and be always updated while on the move. As a consequence, end users require that their personal smartphones are connected to their work IT infrastructure. Companies are willing to support employee-owned smartphones because of the increase in productivity of their employees. However, smartphone security mechanisms have been discovered to offer very limited protection against malicious applications that can leak data stored on them. This poses a serious threat to sensitive corporate data. In this paper we present MOSES, a policy-based framework for enforcing software isolation of applications and data on the Android platform. In MOSES, it is possible to define distinct *security profiles* within a single smartphone. Each security profile is associated with a set of policies that control the access to applications and data. One of the main characteristics of MOSES is the dynamic switching from one security profile to another.

Categories and Subject Descriptors

D.4.6 [**Operating Systems**]: Security and Protection—*access controls, information flow controls*

Keywords

Android Security Extension, Separation of Modes, Light Virtualisation

1. INTRODUCTION

The total smartphone sales by the end of 2011 reached almost half a billion worldwide. Analysts expect that these figures will double by 2015 [7]. Of these, 100 million are sold only in the US, where smartphone penetration will overtake feature phone penetration by the end of 2011. Almost half of the new smartphones (43%)

are equipped with Android OS [3]. These few statistics are enough to show how popular and pervasive smartphones are becoming and the important role of Android in this market.

Such rapid growth is mostly justified by the fact that these mobile platforms are open to any third party to develop new applications and services. Consumers can easily download and install applications via well known distribution points like the Android Market. This openness has thus created plenty of new business opportunity. At the same time, however, it has raised some new security concerns. Recently, several cases of privacy-abusing applications have hit the media [5, 1]. Given the popularity of platforms such as Android, it is not a surprise that this is a growing trend. Only in the first half of 2011, between half a million to a million Android users have installed malware-contaminated applications in their smartphones [4].

1.1 Motivations

With their increasing computational power and storage capacity, smartphones allow end users to perform several tasks while being on the move. As a consequence, end users require that their personal smartphones are connected to their work IT infrastructure. Companies are willing to support employee-owned smartphones because of the increase in productivity of their employees and avoiding the need for them to carry around several devices (i.e. at least one for work, and one for private computing). Several device manufacturers are even following this trend by producing smartphones able to handle two SIMs (Subscriber Identification Modules) at the same time.

However, because users can install third-party applications on their smartphones, several security concerns may arise. For instance, malicious applications may access emails, SMS and MMS messages stored in the smartphone containing company confidential data. This poses serious security concerns to sensitive corporate data, especially when the standard security mechanisms offered by the platform are not sufficient to protect the users from such attacks.

One possible solution to this problem is to compartmentalize the phone, by keeping applications and data related to work separated from recreational applications and private/personal data. Within the same device, separate *security environments* might exist: one security environment could be only restricted to sensitive/corporate data and trusted applications; a second security environment could be used for entertainment where third-party games and popular applications could be installed. As long as applications from the second environment are not able to access data of the first environment the risk of leakage of sensitive information can be greatly reduced.

Such a solution could be implemented by means of virtualisation technologies where different instances of an OS can run separately on the same device. Although virtualisation is quite effective when deployed in full-fledged devices (PC and servers), it is still too resource demanding for embedded systems such as smartphones. Another approach that is less resource demanding is para-virtualisation. Unlikely full virtualisation where the guest OS is not aware of running in a virtualised environment, in para-virtualisation it is necessary to modify the guest OS to boost performance. Para-virtualisation for smartphones is currently in development and several solutions exist (e.g., Trango, VirtualLogix, L4 microkernel [30], L4Android [21, 16]). However, all the virtualisation solutions suffer from having a coarse grained approach (i.e. the virtualised environments are completely separated, even when this might be a limitation for interaction). Furthermore, the switch among the environments takes a significant amount time and battery.

1.2 Contributions

In this paper, we propose a *light virtualisation* solution for Android phones. We named our solution **MOSES** (MOde-of-uses SEparation for Smartphones). MOSES is a policy-based framework for enforcing software isolation of applications and data. In MOSES, it is possible to define distinct *security profiles* within a single smartphone. Each security profile is associated with a set of policies that control the access to applications and data. One of the main characteristics of MOSES is the dynamic switching from one security profile to another. Each profile is associated with a context as well. Through the smartphones sensors, MOSES is able to detect changes in context and to dynamically switch to the security profile associated with the current context. We have implemented MOSES and performed several performance tests. The results of our experiments show that MOSES overhead is minimal and not noticeable to the end user.

The rest of this paper is organised as follows. Section 2 provides an overview of the security framework of standard Android. In Section 3, we describe an application scenario to better illustrate the problem that we are addressing in this paper. Section 4 presents the architectural details of MOSES. Section 5 is focused on the main concept of our approach that is the separation of security profiles. The management of MOSES and security profiles are described in Section 6. To demonstrate the effectiveness of MOSES, we revisit our application scenario in Section 7. We have implemented MOSES and the evaluation of its performances is analysed in Section 8. In Section 9, we review existing approaches that aim at extending the security mechanism of the Android platform. Finally, Section 10 provides our concluding remarks and highlights future research directions.

2. ANDROID SECURITY

Google Android is a Linux-based mobile platform developed by the Open Handset Alliance (OHA) [2]. Most of the Android applications are programmed in Java and compiled into a custom byte-code that is run by the Dalvik Virtual Machine (DVM). In particular, each Android application is executed in its own address space and in a separate DVM. Android applications are built combining any of the following four basic components. *Activities* represent a user interface; *Services* execute background processes; *Broadcast Receivers* are mailboxes for communications within components of the same application or belonging to different applications; *Content Providers* store and share application's data. Application components communicate through messages called *Intents*.

Focusing on security, Android combines two levels of enforcement [18, 29]: at the Linux system level and the application framework level. At the Linux system level Android is a multi-process system. During installation, an application is assigned with a unique Linux user identifier (UID) and a group identifier (GID). Thus, in the Android OS each application is executed as a different user process within its own, isolated, address space.

At the application framework level, Android provides access control through the Inter-Component Communication (ICC) reference monitor. The reference monitor provides Mandatory Access Control (MAC) enforcement on how applications access the components. In the simplest form, protected features are assigned with unique security labels—*permissions*. Protected features may include protected application components and system services (e.g. Bluetooth). To make the use of protected features, the developer of an application must declare the required permissions in its package manifest file: AndroidManifest.xml.

As an example, consider an application that needs to monitor incoming SMS messages, AndroidManifest.xml included in the application's package would specify: <uses-permission android:name= "android.permission.RECEIVE_SMS"/>. Permissions declared in the package manifest are granted at the installation time and can not be modified later. Each permission definition specifies a protection level which can be: normal (automatically granted), dangerous (requires the user confirmation), signature (requesting application must be signed with the same key as the application declaring the permission), or signature or system (granted to packages signed with the system key).

3. EXPLANATORY SCENARIO AND REQUIREMENTS

In this section, we present an application scenario that will be used throughout the rest of this paper to demonstrate the capabilities of MOSES. Moreover, we list a set of requirements drawn from the application scenario that will be used for comparing our approach with existing ones.

More and more companies nowadays provide mobile versions of their desktop applications. Studies have shown that allowing access to enterprise services with smartphones increase employees' productivity [25]. An increasing number of companies are even embracing the BYOD: Bring Your Own Device policy [6], leveraging the employee's smartphone to provide mobile access to company's applications.

Wise Inc. is one of such enterprises. Wise Inc.'s employees have to install on their smartphone GroupMoveApp, a document collaboration application for Android allowing employees to view, edit, and share company files from their smartphone. GroupMoveApp can store files on the local SD and it uses a remote repository for synchronising files. Wise Inc. decided to use a repository service from Smart Inc., a cloud-based company that provides a very reliable infrastructure for a fraction of the cost of developing its own solution.

From this simple scenario, we can identify the following security requirements.

- R1: All the company files stored on the smartphone have to be accessed only by the GroupMoveApp (or any other application allowed by Wise Inc.). Any applications installed by the employee and not authorised by Wise Inc. should not be able to access company files.

- R2: Company files can only be sent to the repository managed by Smart Inc. For instance, the user should not be able to use GroupMoveApp in a way such that the storage operation is hijacked to a destination different from Smart Inc. Similarly, if the employee uses DropBox (i.e. an application different from GroupMoveApp) for the backup of her own files, she should not be able to drop company files in DropBox.

- R3: At the same time, to protect the employee's privacy from Wise Inc., any personal files stored in the smartphone should not be accessible to GroupMoveApp and/or stored in the repository of Smart Inc.

- R4: Applications should not be able to use permissions not granted to them by exploiting other application permissions. For instance, GroupMoveApp may get infected by malware that tries to send company files to a malicious server by using the internet permission of the GroupMoveApp. The malware should not be able to send the company files to another server on the internet.

- R5: Finally, all the isolation features should be enforced on a context-based mode. As an example, the phone might not be allowed to run gaming applications during working hours, while it could be allowed to do so in other contexts. Similarly, an application should be allowed to access some specific data only under specific circumstances. For instance, when on the train the employee should not access very sensitive company data. This is to prevent other passengers from possibly reading it. As another example, the use of some applications (e.g. games) might be restricted under several circumstances (e.g. low battery).

The security mechanism offered by standard Android is not adequate to satisfy the requirements listed above. For instance, if the user grants an application the permission to access the local SD storage and internet then that application can read any file in the SD and send it to any server (thus violating requirements R1, R2, and R3). It is well-known that standard Android security is vulnerable to privilege spreading attacks [17], where an unprivileged application exploits the permissions of privileged applications (in clear violation of our requirement R4). Things in standard Android are even worse. Applications can export services that other applications can use without the user being aware of this. Given the open approach taken by Google that allows developers to create applications for the Android Market by just paying a very small fee ($25), designing colluding applications, that, on purpose provide to other applications their own permissions, is becoming increasingly popular [11, 28, 22, 14]. Finally, in Android there is no notion of dis/enabling applications or accessing data based on the notion of context. The user can start any application and accessing any files at any time and in any place (violating requirement R5)[1].

In the literature, several approaches have been proposed that satisfy some of the above requirements. However, to the best of our knowledge none is able to satisfy all of the requirements at once. Finally, it is important to realise that the aim of this work is not to protect the corporate data from an employee that is actively engaged in leaking sensitive data. In the rest of this paper, we assume the smartphone user is not willing to behave maliciously, for

instance by installing on her smartphone a rogue application for intentionally leaking sensitive corporate data.

In the following section, we present MOSES, our Android security extension for data and application isolation which is able to satisfy all the above requirements.

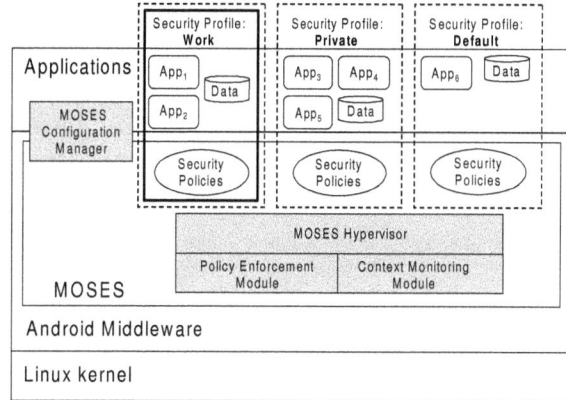

Figure 1: MOSES Overview.

4. MOSES

In this section, we provide details about MOSES system model and architecture.

4.1 System Model

Figure 1 provides an overview of MOSES. The MOSES framework is implemented within the Android middleware and rewrites/extends some of its modules. The main concept in MOSES is that of a **Security Profile** (SP). An SP represents an operation mode that can be used as a logical isolation unit that contains: applications, data and a set of *security policies*. Through the enforcement of the security policies associated with an SP, MOSES guarantees that applications within that SP can access only the data within the same SP. MOSES achieves this fine-grained level of enforcement by means of data tainting implemented in the **Policy Enforcement Module** (PEM). More details on this will be provided later. Here it suffices to say that the data within a given SP is tainted with the SP name. The security policies specified in that SP enforce the constraint that applications can only access data tainted with the label of the same SP name. For instance, in Figure 1 the data in the "Work" SP is tainted with the label "Work". The security policies of the "Work" SP grant access to the data only to applications contained in the same SP.

MOSES supports several SP instances within the same device. By default, the "Default" SP is always present in MOSES. This SP can be used for containing newly installed applications that are not associated with any SP, or for data that is not tainted with any label. A user can create new SPs and associate data and applications to the profile by means of the **MOSES Configuration Manager** (MCM). The user can use the MCM to edit the settings of existing ones. However, an SP can also require special credentials to be edited. For instance, the "Work" SP in Figure 1 is a special profile that the user owning the smartphone cannot edit. This profile has been created by the IT administrator of the company for which the user of the smartphone works (e.g., Wise Inc.). In this way, the company can make sure through MOSES that only the applications in the SP "Work" are allowed to access the company data. There is no limit

---

[1]R5 is partially addressable with Android 4.0, where it is possible to enable/disable the camera according to time and location through the Device Admin API.

5

to the number of different SPs that MOSES can support. However, for sake of simplicity, in the rest of this paper we consider only two profiles in the phone: "Work" and "Private". As we already said above, the "Work" SP is used for accessing work-related data through company-approved applications. The "Private" SP is used by the user for accessing private information such as emails and SMS messages from family and friends. Also, in "Private" SP the user can install her preferred applications and games.

Activations and deactivations of SP instances are executed by the **MOSES Hypervisor** (MH). When an SP is activated, the MH loads the security policies of the SP in the **Policy Enforcement Module** (PEM). When an application requests access to a piece of information, the PEM grants access only if a security policy in the SP grants such request. A user can switch manually from one SP to another. However, MOSES provides a more advanced mechanism where contextual information is used for automatically switching SP. In MOSES, SPs may be associated with context information (for instance location and time). When a given context is detected then the MH activates the respective SP. The context is detected through the **Context Monitor System** (CMS). For instance, the "Work" SP can be activated only during working hours and within the office facilities. Only outside the working environment, the employee is allowed to access applications and data within her private profile.

Context can be also used for automatically labelling data and applications. For instance, if a new contact is added to the phone contact list, the context and the current profile of the phone can be used to determine which label to use for tagging the new contact. Similarly for a new application that is installed to the phone.

On the other hand, a label associated with the data together with the current profile of the phone can be used to determine the behaviour of the phone. For instance, if the user receives a SMS from a private contact while the current SP is "Work" then instead of presenting directly the SMS to the user, MOSES can buffer the SMS and present the SMS only when the SP changes to "Private".

4.2 Architecture

In this section, we describe in more detail the internal components of each of the modules within the MOSES architecture. The components of each module are depicted in Figure 2.

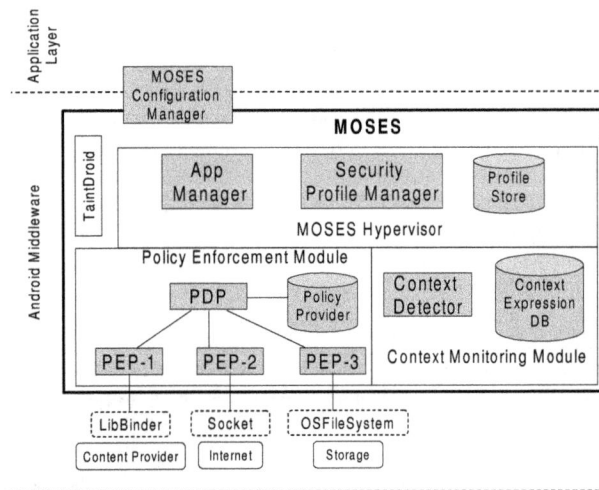

Figure 2: MOSES Architecture.

The MOSES Hypervisor (MH) represents the core module in MOSES. Within the MH, the **Security Profile Manager** is responsible for activating and deactivating the different SP instances defined in the **Profile Store**. The Profile Store obtains SP instances from the user either through the MOSES Configuration Manager or from authorised third-parties via SMS, MMS and Bluetooth. The SP switching can be done manually by the user or automatically by detecting the context in which the user is. In this latter case, the Security Profile Manager receives context information through the Context Monitoring Module (CMM). In the CMM, the **Context Detector** monitors the actual context by means of the smartphone sensors. Context in MOSES is defined as a boolean expression on the values generated by sensors. Context expressions associated with the SP instances contained in the Profile Store are stored in the **Context Expression DB**. Periodically, the Context Detector samples the different sensors and checks whether any context expression is satisfied. When a context expression is satisfied, the Context Detector notifies the Security Profile Manager that a new context has become active. If the new context is associated with an SP different from the one that is currently active, the Security Profile Manager makes active the corresponding SP. If no SP is associated with the new context, no changes are required.

The switching of SP consists in executing the following steps. Firstly, the Security Profile Manager notifies the **App Manager** to disable all the applications associated with the current SP. If applications are still active then the App Manager forces them to terminate. Secondly, the Security Profile Manger disables the set of security policies of the current SP that are stored in the **Policy Provider** (a component of the Policy Enforcement Module). Thirdly, the set of security policies associated with the new SP are enabled in the Policy Provider. Finally, the Security Profile Manager retrieves the list of applications of the new SP and notifies the App Manager to enable them.

The enforcement of the security policies happens within the Policy Enforcement Module (PEM). When an application requests access to a resource, the **Policy Enforcement Point** (PEP) intercepts such a request. The PEP collects information about application UID, the resource being accessed and the type of operation. The PEP forwards this information to the **Policy Decision Point** (PDP). The PDP uses the information received by the PEP to evaluate the security policies relevant to the request stored in the Policy Provider. Based on the evaluation of the policies, the PDP might decide either to allow or disallow the request. The PDP informs the PEP of the decision and then it is the responsibility of the PEP to take the necessary actions for the enforcement of such a decision.

In Android, several components are responsible for mediating access requests of applications to the device resources. Therefore, we need to connect several PEPs with these components within the Android Middleware to intercept such requests and to enforce the PDP decisions. The PEP-1 is connected with the `LibBinder` module for intercepting requests to access simple resources, such as device ID (IMEI), phone number and location data, as well as complex data such as user's calendar and contact entries.

In the `LibBinder`, we intercept the standard cursor from where we extract the `CursorWindow`. The `CursorWindow` provides methods that can be used for modifying the data contained in the cursor. Using the `CursorWindow` allows us to filter out from the cursor data only part of the information. In this way, our enforcement mechanism achieves a fine-grained filter capability. For instance, if a work application retrieves the contact entries from the contact provider, all the private contact entries can be filter out from the data contained in the `CursorWindow` before it is returned to the application.

Other PEPs are connected with some classes of the Java Framework Library (JFL) in the Dalvik Virtual Machine. In particular, the PEP-2 is connected with the `Socket` class for controlling network traffic even if sent over an encrypted socket (SSL). In the `Socket` class, we have modified the `socket.open(address)` method to inspect the address to where the data is sent. In this way, we can restrict the use of only authorised addresses or substitute the address specified by the application with an address defined by the user. By modifying the `sendStream()` method, we are able to intercept the data before it is sent and perform some actions, such as filtering or substitutions. Finally, for capturing operations on the file system, such as reading and writing on the local storage, the PEP-3 is connected with the `OSFileSystem` class.

5. REALISING SECURITY PROFILE ISOLATION

A central notion in MOSES is that of an SP (Security Profile) representing our unit of isolation to separate execution of applications and data accesses. This isolation is achieved by (i) separation of application executions, (ii) enforcement of security policies for accessing data, and (iii) dynamic adaptation through context. In the following, we provide details of each of these features.

5.1 Application Activity Separation

Separation of application executions is achieved by means of the App Manager component contained in the MH (shown in Figure 2). Each SP contains the list of applications that are allowed execute when the SP is active. To provide an immediate feedback to the user about which applications she is allowed to launch under a given SP, we have modified the Android `PackageManagerService` to display in the App Launcher only the applications defined in the active SP.

The App Manager is also responsible for terminating the applications associated with the SP that is being deactivated. If a process is not at the top of the Activity Stack, then the process will be just killed. Otherwise, if the process is the one in foreground, the App Manager launches a "decoy" activity which forces the previous activity to be pushed to run in background. This, in turn, forces the execution of `onPause()` in the Activity lifecycle, which gives developers a chance to gracefully save the process state. We then terminate the process and the "decoy" as well.

```
1  PolicyName: allow to Requester Operation on Target
2              with scope SP-Name
3              [perform Action(param-list)]
4              [while Condition]
```

Figure 3: The syntax of the MOSES policy language.

5.2 Security Policies

To constrain applications to access only data defined for the active SP, we leverage a data tainting mechanism. The main idea is that data within an SP is tainted with the SP name. For tracking the data, we use the TaintDroid labelling framework. We have extended TaintDroid to be able to use as labels the SP names.[2] Each taint is represented as a 32-bit value used to define the control

---

[2] Actually with our modifications of TaintDroid any labels can be used to taint data. For instance, it is possible to specify different labels for tainting data with different levels of sensitivity. For sake of simplicity, in this work we require that data is tainted with at least an SP name.

group, the taint label, and some extra information used for history based inspection. The control group is used to specify whether the data is coming from a system resource such as the GPS provider by means of the "SYSTEM_SENT" tag. Also the control group can be used to specify that the label associated with a data can be set as a consequence of a policy evaluation. This is particular useful if the taint of data needs to be augmented with labels to keep track of all the applications that have received the data.

We have developed the MOSES policy language for specifying security policies. Here we briefly introduce the syntax and semantics of the language. Afterwards, in Section 7 we will present more examples of security policies for our application scenario to demonstrate the power and flexibility of our approach.

Figure 3 shows the syntax of a MOSES policy. Policies are identified by a name and define what `Operation` a `Requester` application is allowed to execute on `Target` resources. In MOSES, a resource can represent system content providers, system service providers, and services exposed by other applications. The **with scope** clause controls whether the requesting application is accessing data within the scope of the given `SP-Name`. Finally, a policy can have two optional clauses: **perform** and **while**. The **perform** clause specifies actions that have to be performed if this policy is enforced. MOSES provides a set of libraries that can perform actions on the data (such as, filtering, anonymisation, generation of random values, data encryption) and on the values of the parameters of the requested operation. Depending on the nature of the action, this clause can be performed before the right is granted (i.e., checks on the parameters of the requested operation) or after the operation is performed (i.e., data filtering). The **while** clause contains a condition that is a boolean expression. For the system to grant the access right to the requester, the condition needs to be true at the time of policy evaluation. Moreover, if the operation is granted over a period of time it might be the case that over time the initial condition does not hold true. By means of the **while** clause, we can enforce that the access right will be valid while the condition holds true.

5.3 Dynamic Behaviour Through Context

One of the main contributions of MOSES compared to other similar approaches is the use of context for controlling the activation and deactivation of SPs. In MOSES, each SP is associated with one or several contexts. A context is defined as a boolean expression over data collected directly from the device physical sensors (such as GPS, clock, Bluetooth, etc.). A context expression can also be defined on *logical sensors*, that is functions that combine raw data from physical sensors to capture specific user behaviours, such as detecting when the user is running. For instance, a "Work" SP that should be activated when the user is performing job-related activities could be associated the following context expressions: *Work@Office*{(Time>8) AND (Time<18) AND (Location=OFFICE)} and *Work@Home*{(Time>18) AND (Time<24) AND (Location=HomeOffice) AND NOT (isWatchingFootballMatch)}.

When a new SP is stored in the Profile Store, the Security Profile Manager writes the SP's context expressions into the Context Expression DB. The context expressions are periodically evaluated by the Context Detector with data obtained by the different sensors. Whenever a context expression evaluates to true, the Context Detector retrieves the name of the SP associated with the context expression and notifies the Security Profile Manager for the SP activation.

6. SECURITY PROFILE MANAGEMENT

In this section, we describe how the SPs are managed in MOSES. The module responsible for SP management is the MOSES Configuration Manager. The internal components of this module are shown in Figure 4. The **Profile Manager App** is an application that allows the user to create an SP and modify existing ones. The application also allows the user to define and edit context expressions that later the user can associate with an SP. The Profile Manger App stores and retrieves the context expressions to and from the **ContextDef** content provider. When a new context definition is stored in ContextDef, a conflict check is performed to avoid that the new context definition is overlapping with the context definitions already stored in the ContextDef. As a matter of fact, if two or more context definitions overlap then it might be the case that in a given situation more than one SP needs to be activated. We decided to have here a very restrictive approach by avoiding that overlapping context definitions can be stored in the ContextDef. However, as part of our future research direction we will explore remediation strategies such as prioritising each SP to select the one with highest priority.

The **Profile Register** component is responsible for storing and retrieving the SP definitions. When a new SP is created, the Profile Register stores the SP definition in the Profile Store and it also registers the context expressions associated with the SP in the Context Expression DB. In this way, the new SP can be activated if the Context Detector evaluates to true the context expressions associated with it. In MOSES, each SP has assigned an *owner* that is the entity authorised to define and modify the SP. The owner of an SP can be the user of the device that creates her own SP. However, a user can deploy on her device SPs defined by third-parties. To protect the SP from unauthorised modification, we support several mechanisms for authenticating the SP owners, such as passwords, certificate, and biometric authentication.

SPs can also be edited/updated remotely. In this case, the requests are handled by the **Remote Manager** component. Edit/update Requests can be sent through SMS/MMS and/or Bluetooth. The authentication of remote requests can be performed through the SP owner's certificate. When a remote request for an update is made, first Authenticator verifies the validity of the certificate of the owner: the certificate includes the identity and the owner's public key, all these signed with the key of the certification authority. The trust architecture for remote management of SPs (via messages sent to the device) is organised as a Public Key Infrastructure (PKI). An incoming message containing a new version of a SP has to come with the certificate of the sender. A certificate can be transmitted in-band or just as an ID corresponding to a cached certificate in the **CertificateCache**. All certificates should be in the X.509 format. We use standard Java APIs to manipulate and verify certificates. The CA certificate is embedded in the system image at build time. All other certificates are cached in the `/data/moses/certificates` directory. The algorithm used for signature is SHA1 with RSA and a 2048-bit RSA public key. For all the algorithms, we use the BouncyCastle APIs – as done by Android itself. After the authentication phase completes successfully, the Remote Manager uses the Profile Register component to store the SP definition in the Profile Store and register the context expressions in the Context Expression DB.

7. APPLICATION SCENARIO, REVISITED

In this appendix, we present the MOSES policies used in application scenario presented in Section 3 when MOSES is used.

The listing in Figure 5 shows the MOSES policies defined for the

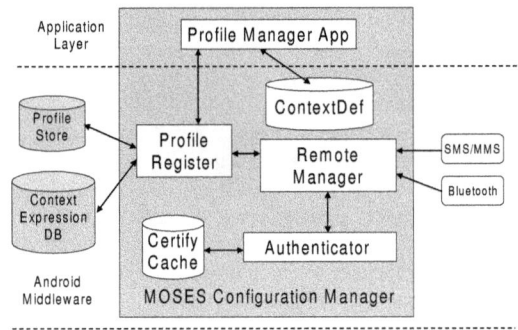

Figure 4: MOSES Configuration Manager.

```
1  WorkP1: allow to GMA ANY on ANY
2      with scope ''Work''
3      while context.isActual(''WorkOffice'')
4
5  WorkP2: allow to GMA Send on Internet
6      with scope ''Work''
7      perform sendOnlyTo(''www.smartinc.com'')
8
9  WorkP3: allow to GMA Read on ANY
10     with scope ''Work''
11     while location.isActual(''COMMUTING'') and
12         !ANY.level(''VerySensitive'')
```

Figure 5: The MOSES policies defined in the "Work" SP for the GroupMoveApp.

GroupMoveApp. In particular, the policy `WorkP1` specifies that the GroupMoveApp (identified in the policies as `GMA`) can perform any operations on any work data (line 2) while the user is in her office (captured in line 3 by the **while** clause). The policy `WorkP2` enforces that the application sends over the Internet work data and it can connect only to the url specified in the `sendOnlyTo` action in the **perform** clause (line 7). The policy `WorkP3` authorises the GroupMoveApp to read work data while the actual location of the user is on a train or a bus (line 11) as long as the sensitivity level of the data is not very high (line 12).

In the following, we discuss how MOSES addresses the requirements listed in Section 3. To guarantee that only applications authorised by Wise Inc. are authorised to access work data, as for requirement R1, the "Work" SP has to contain for each authorised application MOSES policies similar to `WorkP1`. MOSES implements by default a negative authorisation policy meaning that if no MOSES policy exists for a given application then the system does not authorise any operations on any resources coming from that application. If a MOSES policy exists then the **with scope** clause has to be satisfied. This clause makes sure that each authorised application accesses data associated with the same SP (by means of the tagging mechanism). As for the protection of the employee's privacy (requirement R3), MOSES policies defined in the "Work" SP will grant access to applications only to data tagged with the label `"Work"`. In this way, any employee's private data will be not accessible to any Wise Inc. applications. By means of the `sendOnlyTo` action in the **perform** clause, policies are able to enforce restrictions on where the data is being sent, thus satisfying requirement R2. This mechanism is also effective in the event the GroupMoveApp gets infected by a malware application that tries to exploit the GroupMoveApp permission to send data over the Internet. The malware could try to open a socket to send the work data to another server. However, policy `WorkP2` will prevent such an action from happening because the action on the **perform** clause will not be satisfied and the operation will not be permitted (satisfying requirement R4). Finally, in MOSES contextual information plays a fundamental role. Context information is used for controlling the activation and deactivation of the SPs. Moreover, as shown in policies `WorkP1` and `WorkP3`, context can be used for granting access rights though the evaluation of MOSES policies.

8. MOSES PERFORMANCE EVALUATION

In this section, we will present the results of our testing to measure the overheads introduced by MOSES. Since the time overhead is a central concern of user experience, we evaluate the time overhead introduced by our security extensions compared to a standard Android system. At the same time, we understand that MOSES also brings overhead in terms of battery consumption. In the following, we concentrate on evaluating time overhead and battery consumption of the two main aspects introduced by MOSES: namely Security Profile switches and enforcement of MOSES policies.

All the experiments were run on the Samsung Nexus S phone with the 2.3.4 version of Android i.e. stock and modified platforms are based on the same version. To obtain time overheads we used a call to `System.nanoTime()` before and after measured event and compute the difference between the measured values.

8.1 Security Profile Switch Overhead

We recall here the steps executed during a Security Profile (SP) switch. Firstly, the Security Profile Manager notifies the App Manager to disable all the applications associated with the current SP. If applications are still active then the App Manager forces them to terminate. Secondly, the Security Profile Manger disables the set of MOSES policies of the current SP that are stored in the Policy Provider. Thirdly, the set of MOSES policies associated with the new SP are enabled in the Policy Provider. Finally, the Security Profile Manager retrieves the list of applications of the new SP and notifies the App Manager to enable them.

To measure the time overhead of an SP switch, we devised the following experiment. We created two SPs, namely "Work" and "Private". Each SP is associated with 100 MOSES policies and four applications (that are just dumb activities used to fire up a Linux process). The test forces the system to execute 100 SP switches. Between each switch, the four applications are started. We measured the time that MOSES requires for completing the switch, namely from the instant the Security Profile Manager notifies the App Manager to disable the applications till the App Manager enables the applications associated with the new SP. The results are shown in Figure 6 (where the x-axis represent the 100 switches). As we can see, except for few outliers, the switching time is less than one second.

To measure the power consumption for the SP switching, we executed the same experiment we performed for time measurement of SP switches. Only this time we executed the switches over a period of 1 hour (resulting in 2400 SP switches). At the start of the experiment the battery was at a full charge level. After the experiment was concluded, the level of the charge dropped to 77%. This means each SP switch consumes 0.009% of a full battery.

8.2 MOSES Policy Enforcement Overhead

The second set of experiments aim at measuring the overhead in terms of time and battery consumption of the policy enforcement in MOSES. MOSES policies are enforced when applications request access to data. To measure the time overhead, we run an application that performed 100 read operations on GPS data. We first execute the application on stock Android, to measure the average time of a

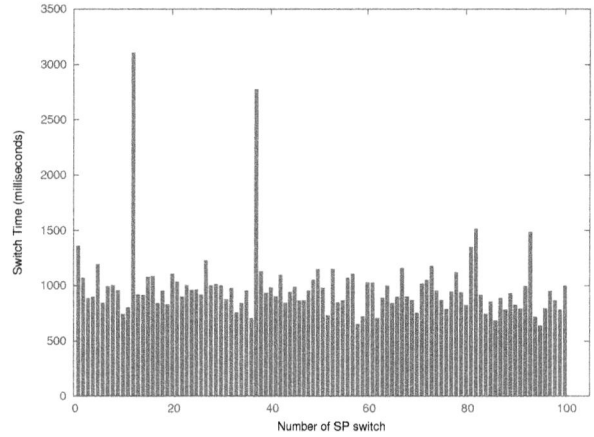

Figure 6: Time for Security Profile switching.

single GPS read operation. Then we execute the same application, but this time MOSES is activated. To be able to access the GPS data, the MOSES policy `TestP1`, shown in Figure 7 is enabled in the Policy Provider in the "Private" SP.

```
1  TestP1: allow to TestApp Read on GPS
2        with scope ''Private''
```

Figure 7: The MOSES policy defined for the TestApp in "Private" SP to read the GPS data.

We run several tests with MOSES enabled, each time increasing the number of MOSES policies present in the Policy Provider from 10 to 100. However, in each configuration we make sure that the `TestP1` is always the last to be evaluated resulting in the worst case scenario. The result are shown in Table 1. As we can see, the average time for accessing the data is around 1 millisecond in stock Android. When MOSES is enabled, the average time for the read operation increases from 3 (in the case of only 10 MOSES policies) to almost 10 milliseconds (in the case of 100 MOSES policies). We can conclude that the time overhead introduced by MOSES does not affect the user's experience.

Configuration	Average Time (ms)
Stock Android	1.071
MOSES-10	3.134
MOSES-20	3.813
MOSES-30	4.970
MOSES-40	5.615
MOSES-50	6.122
MOSES-60	7.205
MOSES-70	7.613
MOSES-80	7.621
MOSES-90	8.451
MOSES-100	9.658

Table 1: Performance of GPS reading operations with stock Android and with the "Private" SP activated.

The last set of experiments focus on the impact that the enforcement of MOSES policies has on the battery consumption. In order to have a tangible battery consumption we run the following experiment. We execute on stock Android the `TestApp` application to perform GPS read operations every 10 seconds over a period of 5 hours. At the start of the experiment, the battery was fully charged.

At the end of the 5 hours the percentage drop was 13%. After recharging the battery, we run again the same experiment, this time with the MOSES-100 configuration enabled (100 MOSES policies in the Policy Provider with the `TestP1` policy at the bottom). At the end of the 5 hours, the percentage drop was 17%. It should be noted that executing read operations every 10 second results in 1800 reads over a period of 5 hours. The percentage of battery consumption for a single operation in stock Android is 0.007% while with the MOSES enforcement mechanism it is around 0.010%.

From the above analysis, we can conclude that the overhead introduced in terms of time and battery consumption is negligible.

9. RELATED WORK

In this section, we provide an overview of the related work in the area, which is smartphone security: with focus on the Android system. In particular, in Section 9.1, we describe other research efforts in providing enhanced security mechanisms to the Android platform. In Section 9.2 we discuss solutions that could be used to solve (even though: only to some extent, partially, and in a non efficient way), the problem we address.

9.1 Security Approaches

In Android, at installation time users grant applications the permissions requested in the manifest file. Android supports an all-or-nothing approach, meaning that the user has to either grant all the permissions specified in the manifest or abort the installation of the application. Moreover, once an application is installed, the only way to revoke a permission is to completely uninstall the application.

To circumvent this coarse-grained approach, several solutions have been proposed to allow the user to manage in a more fine-grained way application permissions even during runtime. Saint [24] is a policy-based application management system that controls application permissions at install time and during runtime. Saint aims at controlling how applications interact with each other. Clearly, Saint is not aimed at solving the problems identified in our scenario. As a matter of fact, Saint policies can help in ensuring that applications authorised by the company are not invoked by user's applications (partially addressing requirement R1). However, Saint policies cannot prevent a user's application from accessing sensitive company data because there is no mechanism that facilitates distinguishing between private and work data. Finally in Saint, access rights cannot be granted on the basis of the actual context of the user since there is no way of defining context in the Saint policies.

Context information plays a pivotal role in the approaches presented by Nauman et al. [23] and Conti et al. [13]. Here, context is used to trigger rules at runtime, that, to some extent can also be used to enforce security properties. Bai et al. [8] has further extended this approach to support a UCON security model. Although these approaches can satisfy our requirement R5, none of them are able to guarantee that only company-authorised applications access company data (R1), to control the dissemination of the data (R2), protect the privacy of the users (R3), and protect the system from malicious spreading of permissions (R4).

More recent papers [9, 31] concentrate on the protection of the user's private data (satisfying only R3). MockDroid [9] is a system which can limit the access of the installed applications to the data by filtering out information. For instance, an application querying the contacts' provider may receive no results even if the provider is not empty. This approach is more refined in TISSA [31] where users are able to define the accuracy level of the information revealed to the application by means of privacy levels. In TISSA, it is

possible to define four privacy levels: *trusted, empty, anonymised or bogus*. For instance, *anonymised* means that the information is somehow anonymised while *Bogus* means that fake information is forged for the requesting application. Unfortunately, both the approaches do not solve the problem of privilege spreading. For instance, if an application that has a *trusted* privacy level (thus accessing real data) is infected with malware then the malware can access the real data as well, clearly violating requirement R4.

TaintDroid [17] proposes dynamic taint analysis to control how data flows between applications. TaintDroid is capable of tracking sources of specific tainted data. In TaintDroid, taints are statically associated with predefined data sources, such as the contact book, SMS messages, the phone number, the device identifier (IMEI), etc. TaintDroid limits the flow of tainted data by tracking the taints in the outbound network connections (satisfying requirements R2 and R4). However, TaintDroid is not capable of enforcing separation of operation modes. For instance, TaintDroid would treat private and work contacts as the same type (because they are tainted with the same taint) applying the same policy. Therefore it is not possible to have in TaintDroid corporate applications that can only access corporate data. The same holds true for private applications (thus violating requirements R1 and R3). Similar conclusions can be drawn for Paranoid Android [26]. Paranoid Android proposes tainting of data for runtime checks. In Paranoid Android security analysis is executed by a trusted remote server, which hosts the replicas of smart phones in virtual environments. However, this approach has a severe impact on the device performance since execution traces have to be continuously sent to the remote servers. Finally, both approaches do not consider contextual information for switching between different operation modes and for enforcing context-based security policies (violating requirement R5).

QUIRE [15] provides a lightweight provenance system that prevents the confused deputy attacks where a malicious application abuses the interfaces of a trusted application to perform an unauthorised operation (R4). QUIRE addresses the problem by tracing RPC chains to establish if all callers in the chain have the necessary privileges to execute the call. Tracing is realised by modifying the Android native RPCs. This however has the drawback that QUIRE's approach is not transparent to application developers. They need to rewrite their existing applications. Furthermore, QUIRE does not support separation of operation modes, meaning that applications can access both corporate and private data, in violation of requirements R1 and R3.

A solution similar to ours is AppFence [20]. By using TaintDroid's tainting capability, AppFence provides additional mechanisms to shadow sensitive data and to block exfiltration, that is the unauthorised leakage of data via network access (R2). Shadowing allows only data anonymisation and does not support other transformations over sensitive data. In principle, AppFence could be modified to support separation of operation modes as in our approach. However, there are no means for capturing context information to be used for enabling/disabling different operation modes (violating R5).

XManDroid [11] performs runtime monitoring and analysis of communications between applications by monitoring the ICC traffic and validates whether an ICC call can potentially lead to a spreading of privileges according to a desired system policy. This can be used to avoid that malware code exploits the privileges of other applications (satisfying R4) to perform unauthorised operations. The main limitation of this approach is that it cannot be used to control communication channels established outside the ICC framework, such as Internet communications (in violation of requirement R2). The main shortcoming of XManDroid is that it does not support separation of operation modes and context information to drive the enforcement of policies (in contrast with requirements R1, R3, and R5).

YAASE [27] is an Android security extension aiming at protecting the Android users from both confuse deputy and privilege escalation attacks. YAASE uses the data tainting capability of TaintDroid to limit application access to the resources declared in the manifest file. Similarly to XManDroid, YAASE is able to avoid that malware exploit other applications' privileges to perform unauthorised access (satisfying R4). In addition to this, YAASE is also able to control data flow outside the ICC framework (satisfying R2). However, YAASE is not designed for separating operation modes and to use context information to adapt the enforcement of policies (violating requirements R1, R3, and R5).

Finally we come to TrustDroid [12]. TrustDroid is an Android security framework that most closely matches MOSES security enhancements. TrustDroid provides separation of operation modes by "colouring" applications and data. The underlying security policy is that applications can access only data of the same colours. The separation of operation modes is supported by representing an operation mode with a colour, satisfying requirements R1, R2, and R3. Applications are statically assigned to a colour at installation time. The assignment of colours to data is somehow very constrained: when an application writes data then the data is automatically assigned the same colour of the application. TrustDroid supports basic context-based policies, such as preventing Internet access by private applications while an employee is connected to the company's network (partially satisfying R5). One of the main limitations in TrustDroid is that the security policies are very coarse-grained. Applications can read and write data of the same colour. It is not possible to enforce more fine-grained policies where some applications can only read data, while others can have a full set of rights. For instance, if we consider a scenario of micro-payments: only one application should be able to both read and modify the actual balance, while all the other applications should only be able to read the balance. Finally, TrustDroid does not perform extra checks to avoid malware that is able to use legitimate applications' permissions to send data over the internet to an adversary server (in violation of requirement R4).

9.2 Heavy separation of Operation Modes

Virtualisation provides environments that are isolated from each other, and that are indistinguishable from the "bare" hardware, from the OS point of view. The hypervisor is responsible for guaranteeing such isolation and for coordinating the activities of the virtual machines. Hence, at the same time virtualisation can: (i) increase security, while (ii) reducing the cost of deployment of applications (the hardware is shared in a secure way).

Similar security motivations, together with a higher usability (see also the motivation of our work in Section 1.1) is pushing virtualisation techniques into the smartphone scenario. In fact, several virtualisation solutions have been already proposed for smartphones [19], and they have been also already considered from security point of view: e.g. with their proposal as a tool for rootkit detection [10]. However, virtualisation does not come for free, and it is a particular demanding task for resource-constrained devices like smartphones (e.g. in terms of battery) [30]. In particular, in [30] the authors evaluate the overhead due to the virtualisation on a smartphone by comparing (using typical smartphone apps): (i) L4Linux (a para-virtualised Linux on top of L4 microkernel) with (ii) the native Linux performance. The authors conclude that while in some specific cases the overhead might be acceptable in terms of delay, it is also "use case dependent" (system call triggering more kernel activities has worst performances). Furthermore, for some system calls it has been observed an execution time is 30 times slower than the one on native Linux.

Virtualisation techniques have been recently also adapted to run a mainstream OS like Android. For example, the L4Android [21, 16] project combined L4Linux and Google modifications of the Linux kernel to enable a smartphone to run Android on top of a microkernel. However, even in this scenario, the pros and cons are inherited from the ones of virtualisation. In fact, while virtualisation is the perfect solution for our requirements R1 and R3, it cannot address requirement R2 (where isolation is not enough to describe the constraints of the operation mode of an application), it cannot address requirement R4 (isolation does not avoid confused deputy attack leveraged via applications belonging to the same environment), and it does not address requirement R5 (the actual environment running at a given time cannot be automatically defined via a context specification).

The proposal of systems like MOSES are hence motivated: from one side, by the need of virtualisation features on smartphones; from the other side, by the need to have a virtualisation that is efficient in terms of time, and energy overhead—which are still main issues for resource-constrained devices like smartphones.

10. CONCLUSIONS AND FUTURE WORK

In this paper, we have presented MOSES: a policy-based framework for Android that enables the separation and isolation of applications and data. Crucial in MOSES is the notion of security profiles. Each security profile represents a unit of isolation enforcing that applications can only access data of the same security profile. One of the innovative aspects introduced by MOSES is the dynamic switching from one security profile to another. Through the smartphones sensors, MOSES is able to detect changes in context and to dynamically switch to the security profile associated with the current context.

One of our main concerns was the impact on the smartphone user's experience when MOSES is used. In this respect, we implemented MOSES and analysed the overhead in terms of time and battery consumption introduced by MOSES. The results of our experiments show that MOSES overhead is minimal and not noticeable to the end user.

As future work, we are currently expanding the functionality of MOSES to enable the protection of data within a given security profile in case the user loses the smartphone. One possibility is to introduce encryption capabilities linked to the user's identity. Another option is to use the Mobile Trusted Module to validate the current context of the smartphone to decrypt the data only in a trusted environment. Another direction of future research is the distribution of security profiles and security policies. We are aware that the average smartphone user is not IT-minded. Specifying security profiles and policies could be a daunting task for most of the normal users. Our idea is to have third parties to create security profiles with different levels of security and make them available on the Android Market. Users can then install the security profile that matches their security needs and further customise it if needed.

11. REFERENCES

[1] Android malware steals info from one million phone owners. http://nakedsecurity.sophos.com/2010/07/29/android_malware_steals_info_million_phone_owners/.
[2] Android Project. http://www.android.com.
[3] Gartner says android to command nearly half of worldwide smartphone operating system market by year-end 2012.

http://www.gartner.com/it/page.jsp?id=1622614.

[4] Mobile app malware menace grows. http://www.theregister.co.uk/2011/08/04/mobile_malware_trends/.

[5] These 26 Android Apps Will Steal Your Phone's Information. http://www.businessinsider.com/up_to_120000_android_phones_have_been_infected_with_malware_2011_5.

[6] Unisys establishes a bring your own device (byod) policy. http://www.insecureaboutsecurity.com/2011/03/14/unisys_establishes_a_bring_your_own_device_byod_policy/.

[7] Worldwide smartphone market expected to grow 55of one billion in 2015. http://www.idc.com/getdoc.jsp?containerId=prUS22871611.

[8] Guangdong Bai, Liang Gu, Tao Feng, Yao Guo, and Xiangqun Chen. Context-aware usage control for android. In *Proc. SecureComm 2010*, pages 326–343, 2010.

[9] Alastair R Beresford, Andrew Rice, and Nicholas Skehin. MockDroid: trading privacy for application functionality on smartphones. In *Proc. HotMobile '11*, 2011.

[10] Jeffrey Bickford, Ryan O'Hare, Arati Baliga, Vinod Ganapathy, and Liviu Iftode. Rootkits on smart phones: Attacks, implications and opportunities. In *Proceedings of HotMobile 2010*, 2010.

[11] Sven Bugiel, Lucas Davi, Alexandra Dmitrienko, Thomas Fischer, and Ahmad-Reza Sadeghi. Xmandroid: A new android evolution to mitigate privilege escalation attacks. Technical report, Technische Universität Darmstadt, D-64293 Darmstadt, Germany, June 2011. Available at: http://www.informatik.tu-darmstadt.de/fileadmin/user_upload/Group_TRUST/PubsPDF/xmandroid.pdf.

[12] Sven Bugiel, Lucas Davi, Alexandra Dmitrienko, Stephan Heuser, Ahmad-Reza Sadeghi, and Bhargava Shastry. Practical and lightweight domain isolation on android. In *Proceedings of the 1st ACM workshop on Security and privacy in smartphones and mobile devices*, SPSM '11, pages 51–62, 2011.

[13] Mauro Conti, Vu Thien Nga Nguyen, and Bruno Crispo. Crepe: context-related policy enforcement for android. In *Proceedings of the 13th international conference on Information security*, ISC'10, pages 331–345, Berlin, Heidelberg, 2011. Springer-Verlag.

[14] Lucas Davi, Alexandra Dmitrienko, Ahmad-Reza Sadeghi, and Marcel Winandy. Privilege escalation attacks on android. In *Proceedings of the 13th international conference on Information security*, ISC'10, pages 346–360, 2011.

[15] Michael Dietz, Shashi Shekhar, Yuliy Pisetsky, Anhei Shu, and Dan S. Wallach. Quire: Lightweight provenance for smart phone operating systems. In *20th USENIX Security Symposium*, 2011.

[16] Technische Universitat Dresden and University of Technology Berlin. L4android.

[17] William Enck, Peter Gilbert, Byung-Gon Chun, Landon P. Cox, Jaeyeon Jung, Patrick McDaniel, and Anmol N. Sheth. TaintDroid: an information-flow tracking system for realtime privacy monitoring on smartphones. In *Proceedings of OSDI 2010*, October 2010.

[18] William Enck, Machigar Ongtang, and Patrick McDaniel. Understanding android security. *IEEE Security and Privacy*, 7(1):50–57, 2009.

[19] Nancy Gohring. VMWare Shows off Mobile Virtualization on Android. Internet Article, February 2011.

[20] Peter Hornyack, Seungyeop Han, Jaeyeon Jung, Stuart Schechter, and David Wetherall. These aren't the droids you're looking for": Retroffiting android to protect data from imperious applications. In *18th ACM Conference on Computer and Communications Security (CCS'11)*, CCS 2011, 2011.

[21] Matthias Lange, Steffen Liebergeld, Adam Lackorzynski, Alexander Warg, and Michael Peter. L4android: a generic operating system framework for secure smartphones. In *Proceedings of the 1st ACM workshop on Security and privacy in smartphones and mobile devices*, SPSM '11, pages 39–50, New York, NY, USA, 2011. ACM.

[22] Anthony Lineberry, David Luke Richardson, and Tim Wyatt. These aren't the permissions you're looking, 2010. Available at: http://dtors.files.wordpress.com/2010/08/blackhat-2010-slides.pdf.

[23] Mohammad Nauman, Sohail Khan, and Xinwen Zhang. Apex: extending android permission model and enforcement with user-defined runtime constraints. In *Proc. ASIACCS '10*, pages 328–332, 2010.

[24] Machigar Ongtang, Stephen McLaughlin, William Enck, , and Patrick McDaniel. Semantically rich application-centric security in android. In *Proc. ACSAC '09*, pages 73–82, 2009.

[25] SYBASE White Paper. Are Your Sales Reps Missing Important Sales Opportunities? http://m.sybase.com/files/White_Papers/Solutions_SAP_Reps.pdf.

[26] Georgios Portokalidis, Philip Homburg, Kostas Anagnostakis, and Herbert Bos. Paranoid android: versatile protection for smartphones. In *Proceedings of the 26th Annual Computer Security Applications Conference*, ACSAC '10, pages 347–356, 2010.

[27] Giovanni Russello, Bruno Crispo, Earlence Fernandes, and Yuri Zhauniarovich. Yaase: Yet another android security extension. In *SocialCom/PASSAT*, pages 1033–1040. IEEE, 2011.

[28] Roman Schlegel, Kehuan Zhang, Xiaoyong Zhou, Mehool Intwala, Apu Kapadia, and XiaoFeng Wang. Soundcomber: A stealthy and context-aware sound trojan for smartphones. In *Proceedings of the 18th Annual Network & Distributed System Security Symposium*, NDSS '11, pages 17–33, 2011.

[29] Asaf Shabtai, Yuval Fledel, Uri Kanonov, Yuval Elovici, Shlomi Dolev, and Chanan Glezer. Google android: A comprehensive security assessment. *IEEE Security and Privacy*, 8:35–44, 2010.

[30] Yang Xu, Felix Bruns, Elizabeth Gonzalez, Shadi Traboulsi, Klaus Mott, and Attila Bilgic. Performance evaluation of para-virtualization on modern mobile phone platform. In *Proceedings of the International Conference on Computer, Electrical, and Systems Science, and Engineering*, 2010.

[31] Yajin Zhou, Xinwen Zhang, Xuxian Jiang, and V.W. Freeh. Taming Information-Stealing Smartphone Applications (on Android). In *Proc. TRUST 2011*, 2011.

Android Permissions: A Perspective Combining Risks and Benefits

Bhaskar Sarma, Ninghui Li, Chris Gates, Rahul Potharaju, Cristina Nita-Rotaru
Department of Computer Science and CERIAS, Purdue University
305 N. University Street, West Lafayette, Indiana 47907-2107
{bsarma, ninghui, gates2, rpothara, crisn}@cs.purdue.edu

Ian Molloy
IBM Research TJ Watson
Hawthorne, NY, USA
molloyim@us.ibm.com

ABSTRACT

The phenomenal growth of the Android platform in the past few years has made it a lucrative target of malicious application (app) developers. There are numerous instances of malware apps that send premium rate SMS messages, track users' private data, or apps that, even if not characterized as malware, conduct questionable actions affecting the user's privacy or costing them money. In this paper, we investigate the feasibility of using both the permissions an app requests, the category of the app, and what permissions are requested by other apps in the same category to better inform users whether the risks of installing an app is commensurate with its expected benefit. Existing approaches consider only the risks of the permissions requested by an app and ignore both the benefits and what permissions are requested by other apps, thus having a limited effect. We propose several risk signals that and evaluate them using two datasets, one consists of 158,062 Android apps from the Android Market, and another consists of 121 malicious apps. We demonstrate the effectiveness of our proposal through extensive data analysis.

Categories and Subject Descriptors

D.4.6 [**OPERATING SYSTEMS**]: Security and Protection, Access controls; K.6.5 [**MANAGEMENT OF COMPUTING AND INFORMATION SYSTEMS**]: Security and Protection, Invasive software

General Terms

Security, Measurement

Keywords

Android, Malware

1. INTRODUCTION

As mobile devices become increasingly popular for personal and business use it is becoming increasingly more important to provide users with the ability to understand and control the benefit and risk of running apps on these devices. Mobile devices contain both traditional types of private data, such as contacts, email, and credit card numbers, and new types of resources, including accurate geolocation, audio recording, and making phone calls or sending premium SMS messages, all while maintaining constant internet connectivity on high speed wireless networks. Because of this shift in computing, a compromise can lead to greater exposure of personal information as well as direct financial impact. Mobile phones are increasingly being used for authentication at banks, as credit cards, e.g., Google Wallet, and to access corporate information remotely. At the same time, users seem to ignore potential problems, choosing to trust an app store to identify malware instead of evaluating risk on their own.

The Android platform has emerged as the fastest growing smartphone operating system being used by about 200 million devices, with around 700,000 devices being activated around the world daily. An increasing number of applications (or apps) are available for Android. The Google Android Market recently crossed more than 10 billion downloads. Such a wide user base coupled with ease of developing and sharing applications with the help of Android Market makes Android an attractive target for malicious application developers that seek personal gain while costing users' money and invading users' privacy. Indeed, recent events indicate an exponential increase in the number of malware for the Android system. Most of these malware are trojans that along with overt useful functionality perform covert malicious activities in the background. Examples of such malware activities include spyware that track users' private data and sending SMS to premium rate numbers.

To limit damages from security breaches, Google relies on the "principle of least privilege" and requires that an application request only for the most restrictive set of permissions for performing the task at hand. Android's current defense against malicious apps is to warn the user about permissions an app requires before an app is installed with the hope that the user will make the right decision. Specifically, Google's standard comment on malicious apps is: *"When installing an application, users see a screen that explains clearly what information and system resources the application has permission to access, such as a phone's GPS location. Users must explicitly approve this access in order to continue with the installation, and they may uninstall applications at any time. They can also view ratings and reviews to help decide which applications they choose to install. We consistently advise users to only install apps they trust."* This approach, however, is ineffective. The vast majority of Android apps require multiple permissions to execute. When a user sees essentially the same warning for almost every app, warnings quickly lose any effectiveness as the users are conditioned to ignore such warnings. There has been recent research [16] that confirms this ineffectiveness in the case of User Account Control (UAC), an attempt by Microsoft to protect its users in the context of Windows Vista that in some ways is similar to Android's approach. Motiee *et al.* [16] reported that 69% of the survey participants ignored the UAC dialog and proceeded directly to use the administrator account. Microsoft itself concedes that about 90% of the prompts are answered by "yes", suggesting that "users are responding out of habit due to the large number of prompts rather than focusing on the critical prompts and making confident decisions" [8].

Recently, risk signals based on the set of permissions an app requests have been proposed [7] as a mechanism to improve the existing warning mechanism for apps. Specifically, in [7], several rules that represent risky permissions are used to flag apps. However, such an approach is not very effective because it does not take into account the intended functionality of an app, that is, what the user expects the app to do, or what permissions are requested by other apps with similar functionality. While the potential risk of installing an app is best described by the set of permissions it requests, an approach using only permissions is insufficient because it does not capture the benefit offered by the application, or whether the risk is commensurate with the benefit. For example, SEND_SMS is a critical permission, as it enables an app to send out premium short messages, potentially costing the user money. While the permission can be used maliciously, it is also legitimately needed by certain communication applications—simply highlighting the fact that an app needs the permission is not effective. On the other hand, a game or a wallpaper app does not normally need to send short messages. If such an app requests the permission, then this represents an unusual risk not commensurate to its benefit.

In this paper, we focus on creating more effective risk signals about apps. An effective risk signal is a signal that: (1) has a simple semantic meaning that is easy to understand by both the users and the developers; (2) is triggered by a small percentage of apps; and (3) is triggered by many malicious apps. When a user observes that a risk signal is triggered by an app, understanding the reason helps the user make the decision whether to use the app. When a developer observes that her app triggered a risk signal, understanding the reason helps the developer to decide whether the app can be changed to not raise the signal.

Our approach takes into account both the benefit and the risk present with installing an app to create a more effective risk signal. Specifically, we propose to capture the benefit of an app by using the category and sub-category of the app. The Android Market currently divides apps into "Games" and "Applications", which are further divided into 8 and 26 sub-categories, respectively. We also propose a more effective way to capture risk by taking into account the occurrence of the permissions across apps with similar functionality. Our observation is that if a permission requested by an app is also requested by a large number of applications with similar functionality, then the permission is more likely to be needed and the risk associated with installing the app is smaller. On the other hand, if a permission requested by an app appears to be requested by a very small number of applications with similar func-

tionality, then the risk of allowing the permission by installing the app is higher.

As an example, one risk signal that we propose is what we call the Category-based Rare Critical Permission signal, denoted $CRCP(\theta)$. From Android's current list of 122 permissions, we choose 26 that we call critical permissions. For each app category, we call any critical permission that is requested by less than θ percent of apps in this category a θ-Rare Critical Permission (θ-RCP) in this category. Any app that requests one of the θ-RCP's in its category triggers the $CRCP(\theta)$ risk signal. We also consider the $RCP(\theta)$ signal, which is triggered when an app requests a critical permission that is requested by less than θ percent of all apps, and signals based on rare pair of permissions.

We envision such risk signals to be used as follows, using $CRCP(\theta)$ as an example. The Android Market's webpage for an app can indicate whether the app triggers $CRCP(\theta)$ for some standard values of θ. We could present them with the ability to select a category for the app other than its assigned category before installing it. This step of the user selecting the category is essentially identifying the potential benefit of installing the app. We may also give the user a choice to select a threshold for θ to display the $CRCP(\theta)$ signal. For each choice of (θ), it is also displayed what percentage of apps will trigger the signal for that (θ) so that the user has a better understanding of how (in)frequently this signal is triggered. Note that the $CRCP(\theta)$ signal is often triggered by more than θ percent of apps, because there is often more than one θ-RCP for a category, and requesting any one triggers the signal. The user is then warned if the app triggers the signal. As typical users have many apps to choose from for a certain task, users can choose to avoid apps that trigger the signal if it is raised for a small percentage (e.g., less than 10%) of apps. If the user is unable to select a category, then we can resort to the $RCP(\theta)$ signal. Such a risk signal indicates to the user when an application may be over provisioned, and thus represents excessive risk given the benefit they expect to receive.

We point out that our idea of utilizing category of apps and rarity of permissions can be deployed, even without the risk signal notion. For example, rather than showing all permissions requested by an app. The interface for showing permissions (both on Android market webpage and on the permission warning page shown to the user before the installation of an app) should sort the permissions by their frequency within its category (or over all apps when the category information is not available), list the least frequent first, and include the frequency together with each permission. The frequency can also be color coded, e.g., using red for the rarest permissions. Furthermore, the frequent permissions can be hidden by default (and available with a "show all" button).

In summary, the contributions of this paper are as follows:

- We introduce the notion of risk signals combining risks with benefits. This approach can provide a first line of defense in the case of downloading apps on Android platforms. It is applicable to other contexts such as Facebook applications and Chrome extensions as well.

- We propose a general formulation of risk signals exploiting rare critical permissions and rare pairs of critical permissions, as well as the category information of an app.

- We evaluate the effectiveness of our proposed risk signals by using two datasets. The first dataset consists of 158,062 Android apps and it was collected from Android market website in February 2011. The second dataset consists of 121 malicious apps and it was obtained from the Contagio Malware

Dump repository (http://www.contagiodump.blogspot.com). We show that our proposed risk signals, especially CRCP, are effective.

The rest of the paper is organized as follows. We present a description of the Android platform and the current warning mechanism in Section 2. Section 3 discusses the date sets that we have collected and certain characteristics about permissions in that data. In Section 4 we discuss how this data can be used to measure the risk that a certain app might introduce. We then present results of our finds for these risk signals in Section 5. We finish by discussing related work and concluding in Section 6 and 7.

2. ANDROID PLATFORM

In this section we provide an overview of the current defense mechanism provided by the Android platform and discuss its limitations.

2.1 Android Development Process

Android is an open source software stack for mobile devices that includes an operating system, an application framework, and core applications. The operating system relies on a kernel derived from the Linux kernel. The application framework consists of the Dalvik Virtual Machine that runs .dex files. Applications are written in Java using the Android SDK, compiled into .dex (Dalvik Executable), and packaged into .apk (Android package) archives for installation.

To be able to submit applications to the Android Market, an Android developer should obtain a publisher account. When submitting an Android application to the Android Market, each *.apk* binary is assigned a webpage on the Android Market. This webpage contains *meta-information* that keeps track of information pertaining to the application (name, category, version, size, prices) and its usage statistics (rating, number of installs, number of reviews).

2.2 Permissions in Android Platform

The current support provided by Android in addressing the problem of malware consist of sandboxing each application and warning the user about the permissions that the application requested. Specifically, each application runs as a separate process on a virtual machine of its own and by default does not have permissions to carry out actions or access resources which might have an adverse effect on the system or on other apps. For example, an application cannot send SMS, read contacts, or change system settings like Bluetooth, by default. However, an application can explicitly request these privileges through permissions.

When a user downloads an app through the Android Market, the user is taken through two screens. The first screen has information such as description, reviews, and screenshots of the app. The user has to select "Download" to move to the next screen. The second screen displays permissions requested by the application. Installing the application means granting the application all the requested permissions. The permissions are displayed under various categories to indicate their functionality. For example, permissions associated with messaging like READ_SMS and WRITE_SMS are grouped under the same category. A user can find out detailed information about a permission by clicking or tapping on it. This helps the user understand the potential risks of installing the application. For example, "FINE_LOCATION", a GPS-related permission, carries the following description "Access fine location sources such as the Global Positioning System on the phone, where available. Malicious applications can use this to determine where you are, and may consume additional battery power."

2.3 Limitations

Android's current permission warning approach has been very ineffective in curbing malicious applications. This is partly because the current mechanism of displaying permissions fails as an effective risk communication mechanism, as it warns the user about dangerous permission on almost all permissions. Many applications may have a legitimate need to access fine-grained GPS locations, for example, an application for reporting local weather can provide a benefit to the user by accessing their location. Many other applications use the FINE_LOCATION permission to provide a benefit to the user, hence the user will see the same warning again and again. Most of the time, the user will want to install the app despite this warning. This conditions users to ignore such warnings. When a malicious app comes along, a user has already been conditioned to ignore such information and most likely does not even look at the permissions.

Such effect has been discussed in the literature. In [13], Felt *et al.* analyzed 100 paid and 856 free Android applications, and found that "*Nearly all applications (93% of free and 82% of paid) ask for at least one 'Dangerous' permission, which indicates that users are accustomed to installing applications with Dangerous permissions. The INTERNET permission is so widely requested that users cannot consider its warning anomalous. Security guidelines or anti-virus programs that warn against installing applications with access to both the Internet and personal information are likely to fail because almost all applications with personal information also have INTERNET.*"

Felt *et al.* argued "*Warning science literature indicates that frequent warnings de-sensitize users, especially if most warnings do not lead to negative consequences [22, 15]. Users are therefore not likely to pay attention to or gain information from install-time permission prompts in these systems. Changes to these permission systems are necessary to reduce the number of permission warnings shown to users.*"

There is a parallel between the Android Model and Windows UAC prompt. Both are designed to inform the user of some potentially harmful action that is about to occur, in UAC's case that a process is trying to elevate it privileges in some way, and in Android's case that you are installing an app that will have all these elevated privileges. The difference is that UAC encourages the developer to work with fewer privileges since this will lead to a smoother user experience. However with Android there is no obvious feedback loop to the developer. An application requires the same effort to use if it requires one privilege or multiple, the only difference is the length of the permission list which is difficult to see on a small screen anyway.

While the ineffectiveness of the Android permission warning mechanism has been recognized, no effective solution has been proposed. In this paper, we aim at investigating how to improve the current state of the art in communicating risky permissions to the user.

3. DATASETS

In this section, we describe the two datasets we used in our study of Android app permissions. Below we describe the datasets and their characteristics.

3.1 Datasets Description

The "market dataset". The first dataset consists of 158,062 Android applications. We created this dataset during February 2011 by crawling the Android Market website and downloading the webpages for all the applications. We then extract the application package name, the category of the application, and the list of permissions that this application requests during installation. The Android Market divides apps into "Games" and "Applications", each of which is further divided into sub-categories. Back in February 2011, there were 6 sub-categories under Games and 24 sub-categories under "Applications". Since February 2011, Android market has created some new sub-categories, and currently the Android market has 34 sub-categories in total.

This dataset is more comprehensive and significantly larger than others that have been studied in the literature. For example, a dataset of 311 apps was used in [7], 940 was used in [11], and 1,100 was used in [6]. We expect that the vast majority of the apps in the market dataset to be benign; however, it may contain a very small percentage of malicious apps, as well as some apps that may be called grayware, as they may carry out questionable actions without sufficient user notification or approval.

The "malware dataset". The second dataset consists of 121 apps that are known to be malicious. We obtained this dataset from the Contagio Malware Dump (http://www.contagiodump.blogspot.com) repository. We downloaded all samples of malicious Android apps from the website, and obtained 180 Android Package (APK) files. However, there are duplicates in this dataset. After removing the duplicates, we are left with 121 samples. For each malware sample, we extracted the permissions requested using the AndroidManifest.xml file present inside the package file. For these malicious apps we do not have their category information. We call this the "malware dataset". This dataset is larger than other malicious Android datasets in the literature. As a comparison, 46 were used in [12], however these include malware for iOS, Android and Symbian platforms.

3.2 Frequently Requested Permissions

Table 1 shows the top-20 most frequently requested permissions by applications in the two datasets. We observe that overall malicious apps request more permissions than those in the market dataset. For some permissions, the percentages of malware apps requesting them are much higher than those in the market dataset. For example, SEND_SMS is requested by 64.46% of the malicious apps, but only 4.83% in the market dataset. This is probably due to the fact that many malicious apps use premium SMS messages to benefit financially. Also interesting is the fact that READ_HISTORY_BOOKMARKS is requested by 42.12% of the malicious apps, but none of the apps in our market dataset.

Another observation is that some permissions are requested by such a high percentage of apps in the market that warning that an app requests the permission is meaningless. We also observe that one Android permission often controls several different types of accesses, often with very different sensitivities. These observations lead us to argue that some of the Android permissions should be further divided. For example, it is clearly desirable to control the SEND_SMS permission, however, it is requested by 4.83% of apps in the market dataset. For apps in some categories, this ratio is much higher, because many apps have legitimate need to send SMS messages. We argue that premium-rate SMS messages should be controlled by a separate permission, as such messages incur much higher monetary costs to the user from normal SMS messages, and very few apps have legitimate reasons to send premium-rate SMS messages. For another example, the "READ_PHONE_STATE" permission is requested by 24.99% of apps in the market dataset and 80.99% in the malware dataset. This permission enables an app to get several kinds of information: including the phone number, the serial number of this phone, whether a call is active, the

Permission	Benign	Malicious
INTERNET	68.50 (1)	93.38 [1]
ACCESS_NETWORK_STATE	30.97 (2)	42.98 [8]
READ_PHONE_STATE	24.99 (3)	80.99 [2]
WRITE_EXTERNAL_STORAGE	24.14 (4)	59.50 [4]
ACCESS_COARSE_LOCATION	18.17 (5)	43.80 [7]
ACCESS_FINE_LOCATION	17.22 (6)	35.53 [12]
WAKE_LOCK	13.07 (7)	23.14 [18]
VIBRATE	12.84 (8)	23.14 [19]
ACCESS_WIFI_STATE	8.09 (9)	28.92 [16]
RECEIVE_BOOT_COMPLETED	7.99 (10)	23.14 [20]
READ_CONTACTS	7.50 (11)	47.11 [6]
GET_TASKS	5.32 (12)	5.78 [30]
CALL_PHONE	5.10 (13)	31.40 [14]
SEND_SMS	4.83 (14)	64.46 [3]
SET_WALLPAPER	4.75 (15)	30.57 [15]
CAMERA	4.35 (16)	5.78 [30]
GET_ACCOUNTS	4.31 (17)	4.95 [31]
RECEIVE_SMS	4.29 (18)	40.49 [10]
WRITE_SETTINGS	3.90 (19)	7.44 [27]
PROCESS_OUTGOING_CALLS	3.64 (20)	4.13[36]
READ_SMS	3.43 (21)	47.11 [5]
READ_HISTORY_BOOKMARKS	0 (113)	42.14 [9]
WRITE_HISTORY_BOOKMARKS	0(113)	37.19 [11]
WRITE_CONTACTS	1.99 (23)	32.23 [13]
MOUNT_UNMOUNT_FILESYSTEMS	1.25 (28)	26.44 [17]

Table 1: Table showing the top 20 most used permissions in the two datasets. 15 permissions occurred in both of top-20 lists. A total of 25 permissions are included. Column 2 shows the percentage (and ranking) of permissions in the market dataset, and column 3 shows the percentage (and ranking) in the malicious dataset.

number that call is connected to, and so on. It seems much more natural to separate these into different permissions.

Android tries to limit the number of permissions because having more of them simply lengthen the list of permission warning a user is going to see, further decreasing the usability of something that users are likely to ignore. However, with the risk signal approach we investigate in this paper, having more permissions does not lead to more meaningless warnings. In short, if one can devise effective risk signals based on permissions, then finer-grained permissions could be deployed, improving Android security.

4. RISK SIGNALS

In this section we describe the risk signals we propose for Android applications based on the permissions they request.

4.1 Design Goals for Risk Signals

When designing a risk signal two relevant measures are the **warning rate** which defines how often a user receives warnings generated by the risk signal and the **detection rate** which defines what percentage of malicious apps will trigger the signal. To avoid over-exposing users to warnings generated by risk signals, it is desirable that a risk signal has a low warning rate. To be effective at detecting malicious applications a risk signal should have a high detection rate. Moreover a risk signal should be easily understandable by end users.

Because there is no guarantee that the market data contains no malware, a warning rate of close to 0 is not necessarily desirable. At the same time the boundary between benign and malicious apps

Risk	Permission	Permission Allows	% market	% malware
Privacy	ACCESS_COARSE_LOCATION	access to coarse (e.g., Cell-ID, WiFi) location	18.17	43.80
	ACCESS_FINE_LOCATION	access to fine (e.g., GPS) location	17.22	35.53
	PROCESS_OUTGOING_CALLS	monitor, modify, or abort outgoing calls.	3.64	4.13
	READ_CALENDAR	read the user's calendar data.	0.64	0.82
	READ_CONTACTS	read the user's contacts data.	7.50	47.11
	READ_HISTORY_BOOKMARKS	read the user's browsing history and bookmarks.	0	42.14
	READ_PHONE_STATE	read only access to phone state.	24.99	80.99
	READ_SMS	read SMS messages.	3.43	47.11
	RECEIVE_MMS	monitor, record, or process MMS msgs	0.18	5.78
	RECEIVE_SMS	monitor, record, or process SMS msgs	4.29	40.49
	RECORD_AUDIO	record audio	1.91	4.13
	RECEIVE_WAP_PUSH	monitor incoming WAP messages	0.063	4.13
	READ_LOGS	read low-level log msgs	0.76	8.26
Monetary	CALL_PHONE	make a phone call w/o user's confirmation.	5.10	31.40
	INTERNET	open network sockets.	68.50	93.38
	SEND_SMS	send SMS messages.	4.83	64.46
Other	MOUNT_UNMOUNT_FILESYSTEMS	mount / unmount file sys for removable storage.	1.25	26.44
	WRITE_CALENDAR	write the user's calendar data.	0.49	2.47
	WRITE_CONTACTS	write the user's contacts data.	2.00	32.23
	WRITE_HISTORY_BOOKMARKS	write the user's browsing history and bookmarks.	0	37.19
	WRITE_SMS	write SMS messages.	3.10	22.31
	WRITE_EXTERNAL_STORAGE	write to external storage	24.14	59.50
Damage	NFC	perform I/O operations over NFC	0.006	0
	GET_ACCOUNTS	access the list of accounts in the Accounts Service	4.31	4.95
	BLUETOOTH	connect to paired bluetooth devices	0.57	4.95
	BLUETOOTH_ADMIN	discover and pair bluetooth devices	0.46	4.13

Table 2: Table displaying list of critical permissions

is blurred as many apps are unnecessarily over-privileged [11]. In this sense, raising warnings for such over-privileged apps is not a "false" positive; thus one should not equate the warning rate with the false positive rate in intrusion detection. On the other hand, an overly high warning rate is certainly undesirable because when users frequently see a warning, it becomes less effective. If a risk signal has a relative low warning rate (say, between 2% and 5%), then among every 100 apps the user investigates, on average between 2 to 5 of them raise the warning. As this is rare enough, and in the mobile platform market, a user often has choices among multiple competing apps with similar functionalities, then the user is likely to avoid these apps. In this paper, we generally restrict our warning rate to be in the range of 1% to 10%.

While we desire higher detection rate, one should be careful to assign too much weight when interpreting this rate in our analysis results. We are using a dataset of 121 malware apps. While this is the largest dataset in the literature we are aware of, it is difficult to argue that they are representative of all malware apps. More importantly, these malware apps were written when over-provisioning permissions were not punished. If approaches proposed in this paper are adopted in different forms, malware app authors may choose to request only the permissions absolutely necessary for the malicious task with the aim of avoiding detection. For example, from Table 1, we observe that 42.14% malicious apps request READ_HISTORY_BOOKMARKS, while no app in the market dataset does so. This leads to a trivial risk signal. However, it is difficult to argue that this will be effective for detecting future malware apps.

Rather than focusing only on the warning rate and the detection rate, we want to design risk signals that are more principled, in the sense that they could rule out apps with critical permissions that could potentially be abused. At the same time, we desire risk signals to have a relative low (between 1% and 10%) warning rate, and a relative high detection rate. Another property that we desire is that the risk signals should be easy for end users to understand. After all, no risk signal can be used to stop the installation of an app by itself. The ultimate decision lies with the end user. If the user can understand why a warning is raised, then there is higher chance that he can process the information accordingly.

Having an easy-to-understand risk signal also has the potential to benefit the overall eco-system of Android apps. The risk signal can be displayed on Android websites. If a small percentage of apps are identified as risky, and there is clear reason why, such as requesting a rare permission, this gives developers incentives to not request permissions the app can function without, since requiring too many permissions now reflects badly on an app. This creates a positive feedback loops as apps requesting fewer permissions will cause other apps that request many permissions to increasingly "stand out".

4.2 Permission Based Risk Signals

We consider two classes of risk signals: those that are created with some knowledge of signature of malicious apps, and those that do not use such knowledge.

Signals aware of malicious application signatures.

We consider risk signals that are constructed using the permissions of apps from both benign and malicious apps. For example, in our case the signals will be based on both the market and malicious apps datasets. We expect that risk signals in this category give the best tradeoffs between warning rate and detection rate. However, they run the risk of over fitting our particular malware dataset, which may not be representative of other yet undiscovered malware.

Support Vector Machines: Support Vector Machines (SVMs) [26] have gained significant popularity in the research community in the recent years. In its simplest linear form, an SVM is a hyperplane that separates a set of positive examples from a set of negative examples with maximum interclass distance, the *margin*. Our datasets, however, cause difficulty for the standard SVM algorithm, because the size of the market dataset is several order of magnitude larger than that of the malware dataset. There has been recent research [4] that indicated that when the training data sets with uneven class sizes were used, the standard support vector machine was undesirably biased towards the class with the large training size. Thus, we leverage the weighted variation of SVMs introduced by Huang et al. [14] due to the uneven nature of our datasets. Weighted SVMs can be expressed as an optimization problem:

$$\underset{w,b,\xi}{\text{minimize}} \quad \frac{1}{2}||w||^2 + C\sum_{i=1}^{l} s_i \xi_i$$
$$\text{subject to} \quad y_i(w \times \phi(x_i) + b) \geq 1 - \xi_i,$$
$$\xi \geq 0, \forall_i i = 1, 2, ..., l$$

where C is a parameter that is empirically selected and is taken for each training sample without discrimination, s_i is a weighting factor for the ith training sample. We leverage the SVM package called LibSVM [3] to carry out our analysis using the Weighted SVM variation and an RBF [23] kernel.

In order to run support vector machines we classify our data into two categories with labels, -1 for benign apps and 1 for malicious apps. Combining this data and using the permissions as features of this data, we are then able to use SVM to train and classify our datasets.

Signals oblivious of malicious application signatures.

Risk signals based only on apps from the Android market are more robust as they are not tuned to detect malicious apps in our particular dataset, and aim only at detecting apps that request too many permissions. Furthermore, we want a principled approach where the signals use only critical permissions so that such signals are more difficult to evade.

From Android's current list of 122 permissions, we choose 26 permissions that we call critical permissions. They are listed in Table 2. These 26 permissions were chosen because we believe they are critical for the security and privacy of end users. These permissions allow an app to infringe upon the privacy, cause monetary loss or damage otherwise. They were chosen before we conducted any experiments with the malware dataset. After conducting experiments, we realized that two of 26 permissions were very helpful in identifying malware apps in our dataset. They are READ_HISTORY_BOOKMARKS (requested by 42.14% of malware apps) and WRITE_HISTORY_BOOKMARKS (requested by 37.19% of malware apps); both are not requested at all in the market dataset. We feel that using these two permissions inflated our results. To avoid such a positive bias, in most experiments we remove these two from the critical set, and use the remaining 24 permissions. When we compare results from these two sets of critical permissions, we use P26 and P24 to differentiate them.

Rare Critical Permissions ($\#RCP(x) \geq \theta$). The first risk signal we consider is whether an app has a rare critical permission. We say that a critical permission is rare with respect to a threshold x if it occurs in less than x% of the Android Market applications. This signal is triggered by an app if it requests one or more rare criti-

cal permissions. One advantage of this signal is that the semantic meaning is very simple and easy to understand.

Rare Pairs of Critical Permissions ($\#RPCP(y) \geq \theta$). We consider a pair of critical permissions to be rare with respect to a threshold y if the individual permission's frequency is above threshold y but the frequency of occurrence of the two permissions as a pair is below y, and we define this as #RPCP(y). That is, we consider a pair of critical permissions to be rare if the permissions involved in the pair are themselves not rare (above threshold x) but their occurrence together in an app is rare (below threshold y).

Combination of RCP and RPCP ($\#RCP(x) + w * \#RPCP(y) \geq \theta$). In this signal we use a linear combination of #RCP(x) and #RPCP(y) to calculate a risk score, and then chose a threshold θ to determine whether the signal should classify an app as risky for our experiments. The value w can be viewed as representing the importance of rare pairs of critical permissions relative to rare critical permissions. We point out that while this is more general than the signal "#RCP(x) $\geq \theta$" and may give better results, it is more complicated for users to understand and for developers to take actions to avoid triggering the signal.

4.3 Permission and Benefit Based Risk Signal

We believe that taking into account the intended functionality or benefit provided by an app should result in an effective risk signal. We use category of an app to determine the intended benefit, because we hypothesize that apps in different categories often request different kinds of permissions. To test this hypothesis, we studied the percentages of applications requesting the SEND_SMS, FINE_LOCATION and READ_CONTACTS permission across the 30 categories in the market dataset, which is shown in Figure 1. As expected SEND_SMS and READ_CONTACTS are used the most in the Communication category, while FINE_LOCATION is used most frequently in Transportation, Travel, and Weather. The resulting graph supports our hypothesis.

We propose the Category-based Rare Critical Permission (CRCP) signal. We use CRCP(θ) to denote this signal, and it is defined as follows. For each category, we call any critical permission that is requested by less than θ percent of apps in this category a θ-Rare Critical Permission (θ-RCP) in this category. Any app that requests one of the θ-RCP's in its category triggers the CRCP(θ) risk signal. Similarly, we define the RCP(θ) signal to be triggered when an app requests a critical permission that is requested by less than θ percent of all apps.

The central idea behind the CRCP signal can be summarized as *comparing the intended functionality of an app (inferred from its category) with its actual functionality (obtained from its permission set) and reporting if there is any mismatch between the two.*

5. EXPERIMENTAL RESULTS

We evaluate the risk signals introduced in Section 4.2 using the market dataset and malware dataset and report the results here.

Analysis of Permission Based Risk signals. In order to get a baseline we first apply the only other mechanism that has been published to identify risk based on permissions, namely Kirin [7]. Kirin has several rules that dictate when an app is considered risky. We considered only 7 of the 9 rules in Kirin, because the other 2 rules refer to permissions that are no longer supported. Table 3 shows the result. It shows that at a 6.53% warning rate, Kirin has a 32.2% detection rate. We consider the warning rate acceptable; however, its ability to warn a user for malware in our dataset is low.

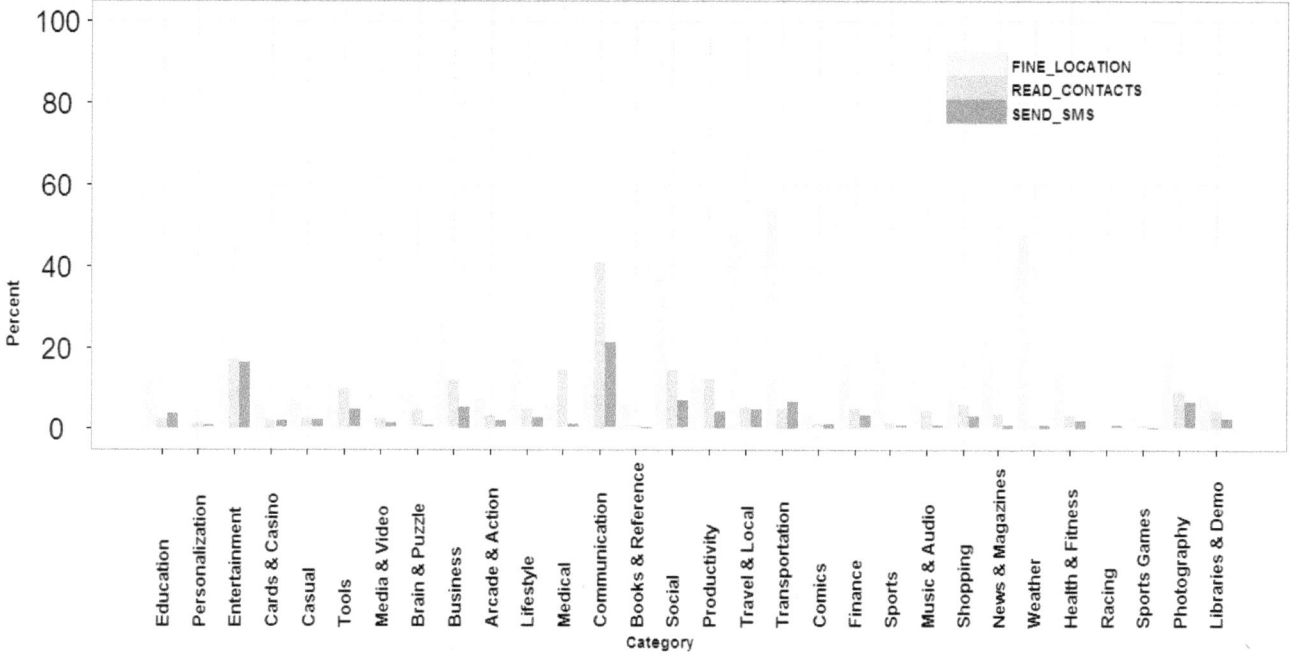

Figure 1: Graph showing percentage of applications using SEND_SMS, READ_CONTACTS and FINE_LOCATION across 30 categories

Rule	% malicious apps	% Android Market apps
SET_DEBUG_APP	0	0.01
READ_PHONE_STATE, RECORD_AUDIO, INTERNET	4.13 (5/121)	1.03
PROCESS_OUTGOING_CALLS, RECORD_AUDIO, INTERNET	0	0.08
ACCESS_FINE_LOCATION, INTERNET, RECEIVE_BOOT_COMPLETED	9.91 (12/121)	4.50
ACCESS_COARSE_LOCATION , INTERNET, RECEIVE_BOOT_COMPLETED	11.57 (14/121)	4.53
RECEIVE_SMS, WRITE_SMS	19 (23/121)	2.76
SEND_SMS, WRITE_SMS	20.66 (25/121)	2.87
Failing at least one rule	32.23 (39/121)	6.53

Table 3: Kirin results. The table shows for each rule in Kirin, the percent of malicious apps (out of 121) that fail the rule, and the percent of Android Market apps that fail it. The last row shows the percent of apps in each dataset failing at least one rule.

Figure 2 shows the ROC curves of using weighted SVM and seven other risk signals using rare critical permissions and rare pair of critical permissions. As can be seen, the SVM method unsurprisingly gives the best result. It is followed by the signal $\#RCP(2) + \#RPCP(1) \geq \theta$. Table 5 shows the numerical values of several data points for $\#RCP(\theta) \geq 1$, the simplest signal among the seven, and $\#RCP(2) + \#RPCP(1) \geq \theta$, the best performing one.

In the SVM method, we use 10-fold cross validation, which randomly selects parts of the data for training and the rest for testing, repeating this 10 times to get a reasonable result. We modified the standard libSVM code to also extract warning rate and detection rate for a given test. Due to the nature of our data we used weighted SVM, varying the weights for the malicious data set so that it had more significance in the training, adjusting these weights led to different trade-offs between the warning rate and the detection rate. For a very low warning rate of .05% we can can identify 50% percent of the malware. Using a different weight when training results in 71% detection rate and 2.4% warning rate.

We point out that while SVM outperforms other methods, this is expected for several reasons. First, SVM uses all permissions in its feature selection, as opposed to only the risky permissions, while all other signals use P24. Second, SVM is also trained on malware data. Finally, SVM is a sophisticated machine learning model. We view the sophistication of SVM as also its major disadvantage, as it is very difficult to explain to a user why a warning is raised, or to a developer how to avoid the warning signal.

In the first row in Table 5, we observe that for a θ of 2%, RCP has a warning rate of 6.36%, and a 52.90% detection rate, easily outperforming Kirin. That is, 6.26% apps in the market dataset request a critical permission (in P24) that is requested by less than 2% apps, and 52.90% of apps in the malware dataset does so.

The second row of Table 5 demonstrates the results of this approach for $\#RCP(2) + \#RPCP(1) \geq \theta$. Note that for $\theta = 2$, that is, the signal is raised is the when an app either requests a 2%-rare critical permission, or a pair of critical permissions that is 1%-rare, this method identifies 66.94% of malicious apps with relatively low warning rate of 7.62%.

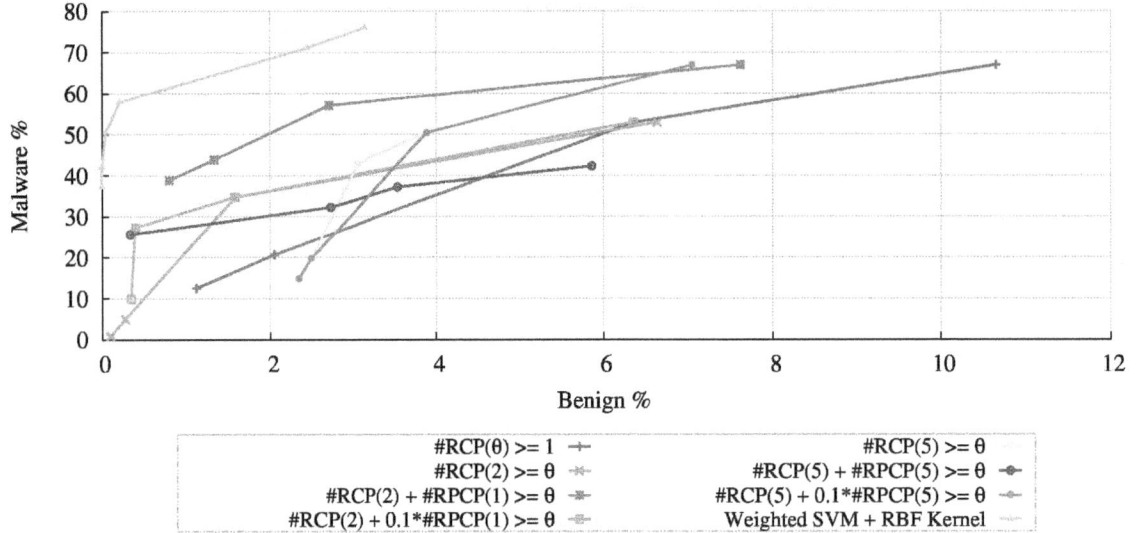

Figure 2: ROC curves for seven risk signals plus the SVM method. The X-axis is the warning rate, and the Y-axis is the detection rate.

	Android Market apps	Malicious apps (total 121)								
	Own category P26 / P24	All 30 cat.		At least 27 cat.		At least 25 cat.		At least 18 cat.		At least 1 cat. P26 / P24
		P26	P24	P26	P24	P26	P24	P26	P24	
$\theta = 1\%$	2.32	49.59	4.13	47.11	14.05	55.37	41.32	68.60	57.85	86.78
$\theta = 2\%$	4.90	60.33	30.57	62.81	51.23	66.11	55.38	74.38	68.59	88.42
$\theta = 3\%$	6.34	66.12	37.19	66.94	56.20	68.60	62.81	83.47	83.47	88.42
$\theta = 4\%$	8.12	71.07	44.62	70.24	60.33	80.99	80.99	83.47	83.47	88.42
$\theta = 5\%$	9.17	75.20	44.62	77.69	77.69	80.99	80.99	84.29	84.29	88.42

Table 4: Percentages of apps triggering the CRCP(θ) signal in their own category. It also shows the percentages of malware that trigger the signal for different number of categories.

Results for Benefit Adjusted Risk Signals.

The Benefit Adjusted Risk Signal works by taking into account the category of an app. Since the malicious apps did not come with a category we count the number of categories a malicious app is marked as risky in.

Table 4 shows the evaluation results of the CRCP(θ) signal, which is raised when an app requests a critical permission that is requested by less than $\theta\%$ apps in the category. The table has one row for each threshold. The second column shows the warning rate for Android Market Dataset apps. The remaining columns show the numbers of malware that trigger the risk signal in all 30, at least 27, at least 25, at least 18, and at least 1 categories of the Android Market. The label P26 indicates that the analysis results is using 26 critical permissions and P24 indicates usage of 24. A label "P26 / P24" indicates that the results of using either set of permissions are the same. We consider the percentages of malware classified as risky in at least 25 categories as an indicator of how successful the Benefit Adjusted Risk Signal would be in case we could determine the category of the malware accurately. We see a warning rate of 6.34% with a corresponding detection rate of 62.81%, which is an improvement over RCP's 6.36% warning rate and 52.89 detection rate, but is similar to the best non-category based risk signals. We also see a warning rate of 8.12% corresponds to a 80.99% detection

rate. This seems to suggest that at a slightly higher warning rate, this risk signal performs really well.

Discussion. There are several reasons why the distribution of a malware may be affected if it raises a risk signal for some categories, but not others. First, many malware apps try to impersonate a popular app, such as Angry Bird, which belongs to a particular category. Hence the category of these malware apps are limited to be the same as the original app, especially when users are asked to select the category. Second, to speed up propagation a malware may be uploaded in more than one categories. For many of these categories, a warning may be raised.

Moreover, even though the results of category-based approach are comparable to the category-independent signals using permission pairs, it has the advantage of being simpler, and easier to comprehend for both users and developers as to why an app triggers the signal. Taking all the above mentioned points we believe that CRCP approach is the most promising one in practice.

6. RELATED WORK

For malware detection, a detailed knowledge of application's characteristics is essential. To achieve this, static analysis involves various binary forensic techniques, including decompilation, decryption, pattern matching [24] and static system call analysis [21]. The common ground for all these techniques is that the code being analyzed is not executed. Hence, malware are generally filtered

Risk Signal	θ	AM%	Mal%	θ	AM%	Mal%	θ	AM%	Mal%	θ	AM%	Mal%
#RCP(θ) $\geq$ 1	5	12.93	83.47	2	6.36	52.89	1	2.05	20.66	0.5	1.12	12.40
#RCP(2) + #RPCP(1) $\geq \theta$	1	7.62	66.94	2	2.70	57.02	3	1.33	43.80	4	0.802	38.84

Table 5: Table showing the effect of various risk signals. The first column gives the description of the risk signal: #RCP(x) is whether an app requests a critical permission that is requested by no more than x% of Android Market apps. The second row shows percent of apps having risk scores above threshold θ using #RCP(2) + #RPCP(1) $\geq \theta$ to calculate risk score. In the table AM refers to the Android Market apps and Mal refers to malicious apps

through *signatures*. While this is a popular approach amongst many anti-virus vendors, this method cannot detect new malware whose signature does not exist in the database i.e. malicious code patterns have to be known in advance.

Felt *et al.* [9] use static analysis to determine whether an Android application is overprivileged. It classified an application as over-privileged if the application requested a permission which it never actually used. They apply their techniques to a set of 940 applications and find that about one-third are overprivileged. Their key observation was that developers are trying to follow least privilege but sometimes fail due to insufficient API documentation. Another work by the by Felt *et al.* [10] surveys applications (free and paid) from the Android Market. Their key observation was that 93% of free apps and 82% of paid apps request permissions that they deem as "dangerous". While this does not reveal much out of context, it demonstrates that users are accustomed to granting dangerous permissions to apps without much concern. Neither of these works actually attempt to detect or categorize malicious software.

Enck et al. [7] developed a system that examined risky permission combinations for determining whether the permissions declared by an application satisfy a certain global safety policy. This work manually specifies permission combinations such as WRITE_SMS and SEND_SMS, or FINE_LOCATION and IN-TERNET, that could be used by malicious apps, and then performs analysis on a dataset of apps to identify potentially malicious apps within that set. Another work by Enck et al. [6] makes an effort to decompile and analyze the source of applications to detect further leaks and usage of data.

Barrera *et al.* [2] present a methodology for the empirical analysis of permission-based security models using self-organizing maps. They apply their methodology to analyze the permission distribution of close to thousand applications. Their key observations were (i) the INTERNET permission is the most popular and hypothesized that most developers request this to request advertisements from remote servers, (ii) Location-based permissions are usually requested in pairs i.e. access to both fine and coarse locations is requested by applications in a majority of cases by developers and (iii) there are some categories of applications such as tools and messaging category where pairs of permissions are requested.

Au *et al.* [1] survey the permission systems of several popular smartphone operating systems and taxonimize them by the amount of control they give users, the amount of information they convey to users and the level of interactivity they require from users. Further, they discuss several problems associated with extracting permissions-based information from Android applications.

Dynamic Analysis: Another research direction in Android security is to use dynamic analysis. Portokalidis [19] propose a security solution where security checks are applied on remote security servers that host exact replicas of the phones in virtual environments. In their work, the servers are not subject to the constraints faced by smartphones and hence this allows multiple detection techniques to

be used simultaneously. They implemented a prototype and show the low data transfer requirements of their application.

Enck *et al.* [5] perform dynamic taint tracking of data in Android, and reveal to a user when an application may be trying to send sensitive data off the phone. This can handle privacy violations since it can determine when a privacy violation is most likely occurring while allowing benign access to that same data. However, there is a whole class of malicious apps that this will not defend against, namely security and monetary focused malware which send out spam or create premium SMS messages without accessing private information.

Security & Access Control: Research in this direction is geared towards furthering usable security associated with mobile phones by improving the fundamental security and access control models currently in use. This type of research entails introducing developer-centric tools [25] that enforce principle of least privilege, extending permission models and defining user-defined runtime constraints [17, 18] to limit application access and detecting applications with a malicious intent [5, 20].

Nauman et al. [17] present a policy enforcement framework for Android that allows a user to selectively grant permissions to applications as well as impose constraints on the usage of resources. They design an extended package installer that allows the user to set constraints dynamically at runtime. Ongtang [18] present an infrastructure that governs install-time permission assignment and their run-time use as dictated by application provider policy. Their system provides necessary utility for applications to assert and control the security decisions on the platform. Vidas [25] present a tool that aids developers in specifying a minimum set of permissions required for a given mobile application. Their tool analyzes application source code and automatically infers the minimal set of permissions required to run the application.

7. CONCLUSIONS

We have proposed the notion of using effective signals to improve Android security, and introduced risk signals combining information about the permissions requested by an app, the function category of an app, as well as what permissions other apps request. Through evaluation using two datasets, we demonstrate the effectiveness of our approach.

Acknowledgement

This paper is based upon work supported by the United States National Science Foundation under Grant No. 0905442.

8. REFERENCES

[1] K. Au, Y. Zhou, Z. Huang, P. Gill, and D. Lie. Short paper: a look at smartphone permission models. In *Proceedings of the 1st ACM workshop on Security and privacy in smartphones and mobile devices*, pages 63–68. ACM, 2011.

[2] D. Barrera, H. Kayacik, P. van Oorschot, and A. Somayaji. A methodology for empirical analysis of permission-based

security models and its application to android. In *Proceedings of the 17th ACM conference on Computer and communications security*, pages 73–84. ACM, 2010.

[3] C.-C. Chang and C.-J. Lin. LIBSVM: A library for support vector machines. *ACM Transactions on Intelligent Systems and Technology*, 2011. Software available at http://www.csie.ntu.edu.tw/~cjlin/libsvm.

[4] H. Chew, D. Crisp, R. Bogner, and C. Lim. Target detection in radar imagery using support vector machines with training size biasing. In *Proc. Int. Conf. on Control, Automation, Robotics, and Vision (ICARCV)*, 2000.

[5] W. Enck, P. Gilbert, B. Chun, L. Cox, J. Jung, P. McDaniel, and A. Sheth. Taintdroid: An information-flow tracking system for realtime privacy monitoring on smartphones. In *Proceedings of the 9th USENIX conference on Operating systems design and implementation*, pages 1–6. USENIX Association, 2010.

[6] W. Enck, D. Octeau, P. McDaniel, and S. Chaudhuri. A study of Android application security. In *Proceedings of the 20th USENIX conference on Security*, SEC'11, pages 21–21, Berkeley, CA, USA, 2011. USENIX Association.

[7] W. Enck, M. Ongtang, and P. McDaniel. On lightweight mobile phone application certification. In *Proceedings of the 16th ACM conference on Computer and communications security*, CCS '09, pages 235–245, New York, NY, USA, 2009. ACM.

[8] B. Fathi. Engineering windows 7 : User account control, October 2008. MSDN blog on User Account Control.

[9] A. Felt, E. Chin, S. Hanna, D. Song, and D. Wagner. Android permissions demystified. In *Proceedings of the 18th ACM conference on Computer and communications security*, pages 627–638. ACM, 2011.

[10] A. Felt, K. Greenwood, and D. Wagner. The effectiveness of application permissions. In *Proc. of the USENIX Conference on Web Application Development*, 2011.

[11] A. P. Felt, E. Chin, S. Hanna, D. Song, and D. Wagner. Android permissions demystified. In *Proceedings of the 18th ACM conference on Computer and communications security*, CCS '11, pages 627–638, New York, NY, USA, 2011. ACM.

[12] A. P. Felt, M. Finifter, E. Chin, S. Hanna, and D. Wagner. A survey of mobile malware in the wild. In *Proceedings of the 1st ACM workshop on Security and privacy in smartphones and mobile devices*, SPSM '11, pages 3–14, New York, NY, USA, 2011. ACM.

[13] A. P. Felt, K. Greenwood, and D. Wagner. The effectiveness of install-time permission systems for third-party applications. Technical Report UCB/EECS-2010-143, EECS Department, University of California, Berkeley, Dec 2010.

[14] Y. Huang and S. Du. Weighted support vector machine for classification with uneven training class sizes. In *Machine Learning and Cybernetics, 2005. Proceedings of 2005 International Conference on*. IEEE, 2005.

[15] W. A. Magat, W. K. Viscusi, and J. Huber. Consumer processing of hazard warning information. *Journal of Risk and Uncertainty*, 1(2):201–32, June 1988.

[16] S. Motiee, K. Hawkey, and K. Beznosov. Do windows users follow the principle of least privilege?: investigating user account control practices. In *Proceedings of the Sixth Symposium on Usable Privacy and Security*. ACM, 2010.

[17] M. Nauman, S. Khan, and X. Zhang. Apex: Extending android permission model and enforcement with user-defined runtime constraints. In *Proceedings of the 5th ACM Symposium on Information, Computer and Communications Security*, pages 328–332. ACM, 2010.

[18] M. Ongtang, S. McLaughlin, W. Enck, and P. McDaniel. Semantically rich application-centric security in android. In *Computer Security Applications Conference, 2009. ACSAC'09. Annual*, pages 340–349. Ieee, 2009.

[19] G. Portokalidis, P. Homburg, K. Anagnostakis, and H. Bos. Paranoid android: versatile protection for smartphones. In *Proceedings of the 26th Annual Computer Security Applications Conference*, pages 347–356. ACM, 2010.

[20] R. Potharaju, A. Newell, C. Nita-Rotaru, and X. Zhang. Plagiarizing smartphone applications: Attack strategies and defense. Springer, 2012.

[21] A. Schmidt, J. Clausen, A. Camtepe, and S. Albayrak. Detecting symbian os malware through static function call analysis. In *Malicious and Unwanted Software (MALWARE), 2009 4th International Conference on*, pages 15–22. IEEE, 2009.

[22] D. W. Stewart and I. M. Martin. Intended and unintended consequences of warning messages: A review and synthesis of empirical research. *Journal of Public Policy Marketing*, 13(1):1–19, 1994.

[23] J. Suykens and J. Vandewalle. Least squares support vector machine classifiers. *Neural processing letters*, 1999.

[24] P. Szor. *The art of computer virus research and defense*. Addison-Wesley Professional, 2005.

[25] T. Vidas, N. Christin, and L. Cranor. Curbing android permission creep. In *Proceedings of the Web*, volume 2, 2011.

[26] T. Zhang. An introduction to support vector machines and other kernel-based learning methods. *AI Magazine*, 2001.

Policy-by-Example for Online Social Networks

Gorrell P. Cheek, Mohamed Shehab
College of Computing and Informatics
University of North Carolina at Charlotte
Charlotte, NC 28223, USA
{gcheek, mshehab}@uncc.edu

ABSTRACT

We introduce two approaches for improving privacy policy management in online social networks. First, we introduce a mechanism using proven clustering techniques that assists users in grouping their friends for group based policy management approaches. Second, we introduce a policy management approach that leverages a user's memory and opinion of their friends to set policies for other similar friends. We refer to this new approach as Same-As Policy Management. To demonstrate the effectiveness of our policy management improvements, we implemented a prototype Facebook application and conducted an extensive user study. Leveraging proven clustering techniques, we demonstrated a 23% reduction in friend grouping time. In addition, we demonstrated considerable reductions in policy authoring time using Same-As Policy Management over traditional group based policy management approaches. Finally, we presented user perceptions of both improvements, which are very encouraging.

Categories and Subject Descriptors

D.4.6 [**Security and Protection**]: Access Controls; H.5.3 [**Information Interfaces and Presentation**]: Group and Organizational Interfaces

General Terms

Security, Human Factors

Keywords

Policy, Access Control, Grouping, Privacy, Social Network

1. INTRODUCTION

Social networking sites are experiencing tremendous adoption and growth. The internet and online social networks, in particular, are a part of most people's lives. eMarketer[1] reports that in 2011, nearly 150 million US internet users will

[1] http://www.eMarketer.com

interface with at least one social networking site per month. eMarketer also reports that in 2011, 90% of internet users ages 18-24 and 82% of internet users ages 25-34 will interact with at least one social networking site per month. This trend is increasing for all age groups. As the young population ages, they will continue to leverage social media in their daily lives. In addition, new generations will come to adopt the internet and online social networks. These technologies have become and will continue to be a vital component of our social fabric which we depend on to communicate, interact and socialize.

Not only are there a tremendous amount of users online, there is also a tremendous amount of user profile data and content online. For example, on Facebook[2], there are over 30 billion pieces of content shared each month. New content is being added every day; an average Facebook user generates over 90 pieces of content each month. This large amount of content coupled with the significant number of users online makes maintaining appropriate levels of privacy very challenging.

There have been numerous studies concerning privacy in the online world [4, 15, 18]. A number of conclusions can be drawn from these studies. First, there are varying levels of privacy controls, depending on the online site. For example, some sites make available user profile data to the internet with no ability to restrict access. While other sites limit user profile viewing to just trusted friends. Other studies introduce the notion of the privacy paradox, the relationship between individual privacy intentions to disclose their personal information and their actual behavior [21]. Individuals voice concerns over the lack of adequate controls around their privacy information while freely providing their personal data. Other research concludes that individuals lack appropriate information to make informed privacy decisions [2]. More over, when there is adequate information, short-term benefits are often opted over long-term privacy. However, contrary to common belief, people are concerned about privacy [1, 9]. But, most are not doing anything about it. This can be attributed to many things, e.g., the lack of privacy controls available to the user, the complexity of using the controls [26] and the burden associated with managing these controls for large sets of users.

We believe that additional tools need to be placed in the hands of the user to aid them in managing their privacy. Our research is focused in two areas. First, we aim to assist users in grouping their large friend sets for privacy policy management purposes. Next, we aim to provide an improved ap-

[2] http://www.facebook.com/press/info.php?statistics

proach for managing access to user profile data and content in online social networks. Our contribution is three-fold:

- We introduce a user assisted friend grouping mechanism that enhances traditional group based policy management approaches. Assisted Friend Grouping leverages proven clustering techniques to aid users in grouping their friends more efficiently. Our approach has demonstrated promising results in assisting users in efficiently grouping and setting expressive policies for their friends. In addition, user perceptions are encouraging.

- We introduce a policy management approach for online social networks that leverages a user's memory and opinion of their friends to set policies for other similar friends, which we refer to as Same-As Policy Management. Using a visual policy editor that takes advantage of friend recognition and minimal task interruptions, Same-As Policy Management demonstrated improved performance and user perceptions over traditional group based policy management approaches.

- We implemented a prototype Facebook application and conducted an extensive user study evaluating our improvements to privacy policy management in online social networks.

The rest of the paper is organized as follows: In Section 2, we provide a brief background of role/group based access control. Section 3 details our two improvements to privacy policy management in online social networks: Assisted Friend Grouping and Same-As Policy Management. Our user study design is described in Section 4 with the results and discussion detailed in Sections 5 and 6, respectively. Finally, we wrap up the paper with related work and conclusions.

2. BACKGROUND

Current social networking platforms offer a simple policy management approach. Security aware users are able to specify policies for their profile objects. For example, my work colleague is restricted from seeing my photos. But, my trusted best friend from school may access all my information. Facebook provides an optional mechanism that allows users to create custom *lists* to organize friends and set privacy restrictions. Similarly, Google+ allows users to create *Circles* of friends, such as family, acquaintances, etc., where the user can apply policies based on these *Circles*. Facebook also recently announced *smart lists* which automatically group friends who live near by or attend the same school. However, managing access for hundreds of *friends* is still a very difficult and burdensome task [17]. In addition, security unaware users typically follow an open and permissive default policy. As a result, the potential for unwanted information leakage is great [23]. We believe that current capabilities to manage access to user profile information on today's social networking platforms are inadequate.

One approach that has been taken to alleviate the burden of managing access permissions for large sets of *friends* is the implementation of a role based access control model (RBAC) [10, 25, 24]. Role based access control provides a level of abstraction with the introduction of a role between the subject and the object permission. A role is a container with a functional meaning, for example, a specific

job within an enterprise. Permissions to objects are assigned to roles and subjects are assigned to roles. Role members are granted objective permissions associated with the role(s) in which they belong. See Figure 1. This level of abstraction alleviates the burden of managing large numbers of subject to objective permissions assignments. For the purposes of discussion, we will use the term *group* as to be synonymous with the term *role*, with the understanding that traditionally *roles* have subjects and objects permission assignments and *groups* traditionally only have subject assignments.

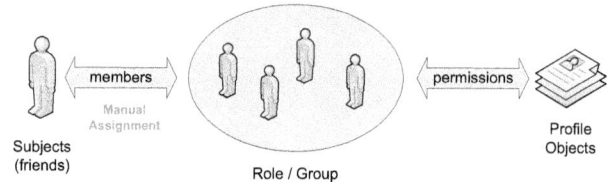

Figure 1: Role Based Access Control

Traditional RBAC can be leveraged within social networks. Often, people's relationships drive privacy decisions. People like to specify groups for their friend relationships, in which they then can set privacy policies [13, 22]. We refer to this approach as group based policy management. However, populating relationship groups can be very time consuming and burdensome to the user [14]. We introduce a group based policy management model that assists users in placing their subjects (or *friends*) into relationship groups. Our approach leverages proven clustering techniques to aid the user in grouping their friends more efficiently. In addition, we provide a mechanism to set friend-level exceptions within group policies. Our model is referred to as the Assisted Friend Grouping Model.

A shortcoming of the group based policy management approach is that the user's attention (mental model) is focused in multiple areas. For example, a user must first focus on the friend's relationship in order to group them appropriately. Next, the user must change focus to the group in order to set the group-level policy. Finally, the user must switch focus back to the friend in order to set any friend-level exceptions for each group policy. We introduce an approach that overcomes this weakness. Our model leverages users' memory and opinion of their friends to set policies for other similar friends. Studies have shown that users perform more efficiently using recognition based approaches that have minimal task interruptions [7, 12]. Using our visual policy editor, a user selects a representative friend (Same-As Example Friend), assigns appropriate object permissions to this friend and then associates other similar friends to the same policy. Our model is called Same-As Policy Management.

3. POLICY-BY-EXAMPLE

Our Policy-By-Example framework is made up of two access control models: Assisted Friend Grouping and Same-As Policy Management. We implemented both models as a prototype Facebook application. The details of which are discussed in the following sections.

3.1 Assisted Friend Grouping

Group based policy management allows users to populate groups based on relationship and assign object permissions to the groups, refer to Figure 1. Assisted Friend Grouping extends this model in two areas: 1) provides the user with assistance in grouping their friends, and 2) provides the user the ability to set friend-level exceptions within the group policy. See Figure 2.

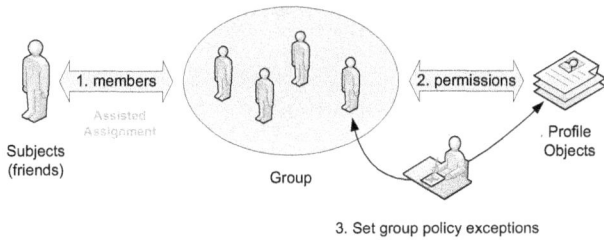

Figure 2: Assisted Friend Grouping Model

For the purposes of our prototype Facebook application, we predefined 10 relationship groups: Family, Close Friends, Graduate School, Under Graduate School, High School, Work, I do not know, Friends of Friend, Community and Other. These groups where carefully selected, in part, from the work of Jones et al. [14]. They postulate that users group their friends, for controlling privacy, based on six criteria: Social Circles, Tie Strength, Temporal Episodes, Geographical Locations, Functional Roles and Organizational Boundaries. Our friend relationship groups were selected to reflect these criteria.

Within our prototype, each friend is presented to the user in the center of a friend grouping page, refer to Figure 3. The user is asked to select, for each friend, the group that best represents their relationship. They can either "drag" the friend to the appropriate relationship group on the page. Or, the user can click the representative relationship group name. To assist users in populating their relationship groups, we leverage the Clasuet Newman Moore (CNM) network clustering algorithm [5]. This clustering algorithm analyzes and detects community structure in networks by optimizing their modularity. Our prototype clusters the user's social network graph creating CNM clusters (or groups) of friends. During friend grouping, we present the friends to the user in CNM group order as recommendations. For example, Bob has 50 friends and clustering his social network graph using CNM produces five clusters. We present to Bob, as recommendations for grouping, all the friends of one CNM group before presenting the friends of each subsequent CNM group. The premise is that CNM groups roughly align with user defined friend populated relationship groups.

By presenting friends in the order they potentially will be grouped, the friend grouping time can be vastly reduced. The user's mental model is focused on roughly one relationship at a time, e.g., work colleagues. The user can quickly ascertain that the stream of friends being presented are all work colleagues and can be placed in the *Work* group. This approach reduces the number of "mental task switches" the user must perform between multiple relationship groups. After all the friends are grouped, the user sets the group policy by setting permissions that allow or deny access to the user's profile objects, e.g., email address, photos, etc. Finally, we provide the user the ability to set friend-level exceptions for each group policy. For example, a group policy may deny access to the user's email address except for group mem-

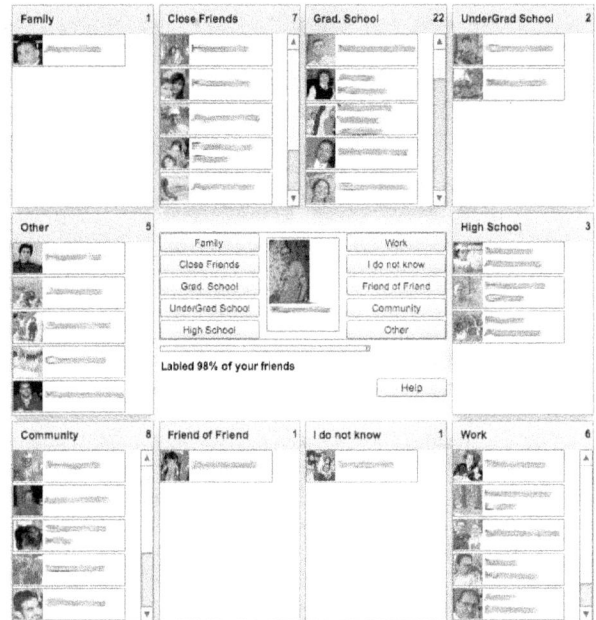

Figure 3: Friend Grouping

ber *Alice*. Most social networking platforms also provide a policy exception setting capability.

3.2 Same-As Policy Management

In group based policy management, the user must first group their friends. After which, they must select group permissions (setting the group policy). Finally, friend-level exceptions to the group policy are set. A user's attention (mental model) is focused in multiple areas. Whereas, in Same-As Policy Management, the user's attention is focused on a specific friend. The user leverages their memory and opinion of a friend to set policies for other like friends. In essence, we use a friend recognition approach, with minimal task interruptions, to aid the user in setting policies. A representative friend is selected (Same-As Example Friend), profile object permissions are assigned to this example friend and other similar friends (Same-As Friends) are associated with the same set of object permissions. Figure 4 illustrates our model; the Same-As Example Friend is depicted in front of the user's other similar friends who have been assigned the same set of object permissions.

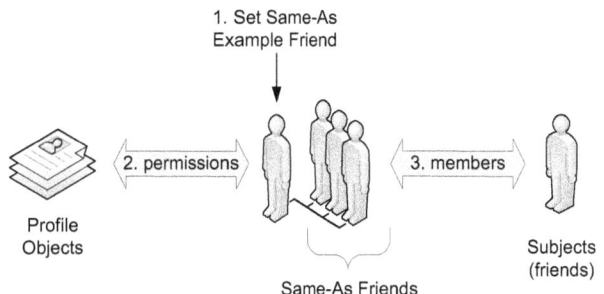

Figure 4: Same-As Policy Management Model

First, the user selects a friend (Same-As Example Friend)

that is representative of a subset of their friend set. The notion is that we all have subsets of friends that have similar levels of trust. The user selects one easy to remember friend from each subset as its respective representative.

Second, using our visual policy editor, the user assigns the appropriate object level permissions for each object within their profile to this Same-As Example Friend. For the purposes of our prototype Facebook application, we presented three profile object categories: *Albums*, *About Me* and *Education and Work*. Within each profile object category, objects of the same family are presented. For example, *About Me* includes Birthday, Status, Current City, email, etc., as indicated in Figure 5. The user can allow or deny access to any object or object category by simply clicking on the object or object category. For example, if the user doesn't want the Same-As Example Friend to have access to a specific photo album, they merely click on that album and the object permission is set to deny. The selected photo album will be grayed out. Or, for example, if the user doesn't want to allow access to any of their education and work information, they click on the object category *Education and Work* and the entire object category will be grayed out, thus effectively setting the permissions to deny for each profile object within that category. Any permutation of permissions is allowed.

Third, after the permissions are set for the Same-As Example Friend, other like or similar friends (Same-As Friends) are assigned to the policy. The visual policy editor presents to the user their friend set, where the user can associate a friend to an already defined Same-As Example Friend. Or, the user can designate a friend as a new Same-As Example Friend, thereby setting a new policy which would be assigned to other similar friends. This process repeats itself for the user's entire friend set.

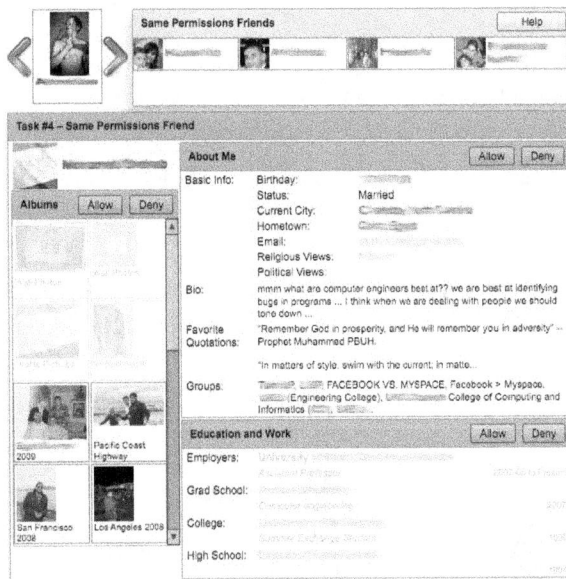

Figure 5: Visual Policy Editor (Blurred for Paper Anonymity Purposes)

3.3 Prototype Architecture

We implemented a prototype of our Assisted Friend Grouping Model and our Same-As Policy Management Model. The prototype is implemented as a Facebook application called PolicyMngr[3]. The application is hosted on our server. The back-end is based on PHP and MySQL. The client-side was implemented using Adobe Flex as a flash application. Upon installing the application, REST like Facebook APIs and Facebook Query Language are used to retrieve the user's profile and social connections. The collected data is transmitted over secure HTTPS based APIs to our server and stored in a MySQL database. The application builds the participant's social graph, which is clustered using the CNM implementation provided by the Flare Toolkit Library[4]. The application implements several additional functionalities, including user grouping, group policy specification, Same-As policy specification and survey tools.

4. USER STUDY

In designing our user study[5], we set out to answer the following research questions:

Q1. Can proven clustering techniques assist users in grouping their friends more efficiently?

Q2. What are users' perceptions of assisted friend grouping techniques?

Q3. Will a policy management approach based on leveraging a user's memory and perception of their friends outperform traditional group based policy management approaches?

Q4. Will users' perceptions of a policy management approach based on leveraging a user's memory and perception of their friends be higher than traditional group based policy management approaches?

4.1 Design

In order to answer these research questions, we built four tasks and two surveys into our Policy-By-Example prototype. The first three tasks and the first survey were designed to evaluate traditional group based policy management and our Assisted Friend Grouping Model. The fourth task and the second survey were designed to evaluate our Same-As Policy Management Model. See Table 1.

Table 1: User Study Tasks

Group Based Policy Management	
Task 1	Group friends
Task 2	Set group policy
Task 3	Review and possibly set friend-level exceptions to group policy
Survey 1	Complete a brief survey for Tasks 1-3
Same-As Policy Management	
Task 4	Set permissions for friends using another friend's permissions as the model/example
Survey 2	Complete a brief survey for Task 4

In the first task (Task 1), the user is instructed to place 50 of their randomly selected friends into the ten predefined

---

[3]https://apps.facebook.com/policymngr/
[4]http://flare.prefuse.org
[5]Approved IRB Protocol #11-08-01

groups. We divided the user participants into two groups, namely *Not Assisted* and *Assisted*. For the Not Assisted population, the 50 friends were presented to the user for grouping in random order. For the Assisted population, the 50 friends were presented to the user for grouping in CNM group order, as described in Section 3.1. Friends were presented to the user for grouping based on clustering the user's social graph using the CNM algorithm. We measured the grouping time for both populations. After the user placed their friends into groups, they were asked to select access permissions for each group (Task 2). Allow/Deny permissions were selected for each profile object and/or profile object category. Finally in Task 3, the user was asked to review and possibly select friend-level exceptions to the group policy that was set in Task 2.

Upon completion of Tasks 1, 2 and 3, the user was asked to complete the first survey. The initial part of the survey collected basic demographic information summarized in Section 4.2. In the remaining portion of the survey, the user responded to questions designed to capture their perceptions of group based policy management, both the Not Assisted and Assisted friend grouping approaches. The question responses are on a Likert-scale of 1 (Strongly Disagree) to 7 (Strongly Agree). Each question is designed to capture the user's perceptions in the following areas:

Ease of Use: The user needs to be able to manage their policies in an easy, intuitive and effective way such that they have a consistent experience. Complex and laborious policy management mechanisms can lead to ineffective policies.

Readability: Not only does a policy management solution have to be easy to use, it must be decipherable. The core component of any access control mechanism is the policy which governs the access. The policy not only must be available and visible to the user, but it also must be readable. Policies that are complex and difficult to understand are more likely to be misconfigured resulting in unintended consequences, e.g., data leakage.

Flexibility: Policy management mechanisms must be flexible to accommodate the user's needs and intentions. Effective policy management must create a balance between coarse grained and fine grained access control. Traditionally, coarse grained access control provides few options to the end user. On the other hand, fine grained access control, although extremely flexible in that it provides lots of options and capabilities, is traditionally overwhelming and complex. A balance between too little flexibility and an overly burdensome policy management mechanism is needed.

The fourth task was designed to evaluate our Same-As Policy Management Model, as described in Section 3.2. The user was instructed, for a subset of their friends (50 randomly chosen ones), to select a Same-As Example Friend, set appropriate profile object permissions for this example friend and assign the policy to appropriate like or similar friends. This step was repeated as necessary, i.e., for as many unique policies the user would like to assign for their friend set. We measured the total time to complete Task 4. After completing Task 4, the user completed a second survey identical to the first survey excluding the demographic questions.

4.2 Participants

We recruited our user study participants from the student and staff population of the university community and from

Amazon Mechanical Turk[6]. Amazon Mechanical Turk is a crowd sourcing marketplace that pairs *Requesters* of work and *Workers*. Requesters formulate work into Human Intelligent Tasks (HIT) which are individual tasks that workers complete. We set up our prototype Facebook application as a HIT. This included all four tasks and the two surveys, as described in Section 4.1. To better control the quality of the recruited participants, we mandated that each worker have a 95% HIT approval rating, or better. A HIT took approximately 10-15 minutes to complete, for which each worker was paid a fee of $1.50. A total of 101 users successfully completed the user study. We used the total time spent to complete the study as a measure to remove 5% of the outlying users who had an absolute Z-Score value greater than three.

That left 96 participants in our study, 77 male and 19 female. Most of our user participants were young, fairly well educated and active Facebook users. 67% were between the ages of 18 to 25. 74% had between two and four years of college. Almost 83% used Facebook daily. In addition, as part of the demographics portion of our survey, we collected Westin privacy sentiment information summarized below with definitions of *Unconcerned*, *Pragmatist* and *Fundamentalist* provided by [16]:

Unconcerned Users: 13.5% of our user study population. *This group does not know what the "privacy fuss" is all about, supports the benefits of most organizational programs over warnings about privacy abuse, has little problem with supplying their personal information to government authorities or businesses, and sees no need for creating another government bureaucracy (a Federal Big Brother) to protect someone's privacy.*

Pragmatists: 62.5% of our user study population. *This group weighs the value to them and society of various business or government programs calling for personal information, examines the relevance and social propriety of the information sought, wants to know the potential risks to privacy or security of their information, looks to see whether fair information practices are being widely enough observed, and then decides whether they will agree or disagree with specific information activities - with their trust in the particular industry or company involved being a critical decisional factor.*

Fundamentalists: 24% of our user study population. *This group sees privacy as an especially high value, rejects the claims of many organizations to need or be entitled to get personal information for their business or governmental programs, thinks more individuals should simply refuse to give out information they are asked for, and favors enactment of strong federal and state laws to secure privacy rights and control organizational discretion.*

5. STUDY RESULTS

The next two subsections detail our user study results for the Assisted Friend Grouping Model and Same-As Policy Management.

5.1 Assisted Friend Grouping

In evaluating our Assisted Friend Grouping Model, we set out to show that CNM will aid in grouping users' friends more efficiently for group based policy management approaches.

---

[6]https://www.mturk.com/

Our hypothesis is that CNM clusters roughly align with user defined friend relationship groups.In the example illustrated in Figure 6, CNM partitions the user's social graph into distinct clusters, as depicted by the large circles. The user also categorizes their friends into user defined relationship groups, i.e., Family, Graduate School, etc. Figure 6 illustrates that there is overlap and agreement between the CNM clusters and the user defined relationship groups. We leverage this alignment by presenting friends to the user for grouping based on cluster/relationship order. By presenting friends in this manner, the user's mental model is focused on one relationship at a time. This approach results in fewer "mental task switches" between multiple relationship groups and thus improved friend grouping times.

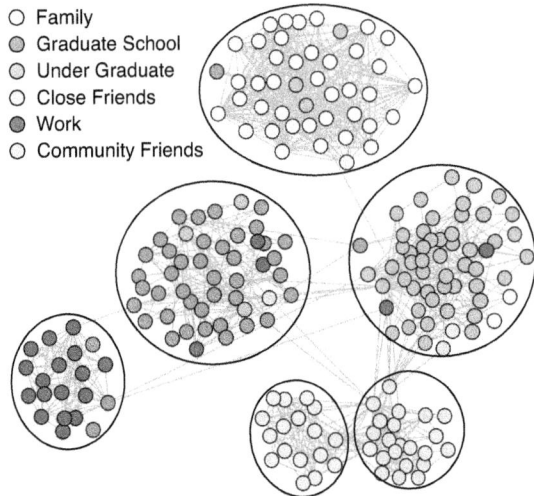

Figure 6: Example Cluster/Group Alignment

We used the Adjusted Rand Index to measure the agreement between CNM clusters and user defined relationship groups [11]. The Adjusted Rand Index compares the predicated labels (CNM clusters) with the actual labels (user defined relationship groups) and produces an index between 0 and 1, where 0 indicates no overlap and 1 is complete agreement or overlap. The Adjusted Rand Index, in general form, can be described as $\frac{Index - ExpectedIndex}{MaxIndex - ExpectedIndex}$. We clustered users' social graphs who were Not Assisted in grouping their friends, i.e., we presented their friend set for grouping in random order. We compared the clusters generated by CNM and the populated groups defined by the user. We found, that on average, users populated 6.4 relationship groups. Overall, our results showed an average Adjusted Rand Index of 0.653. This demonstrates that there is overlap and a level of alignment between CNM clusters and user defined relationship groups. In looking just at Unconcerned Users, we saw a higher level of alignment (Adjusted Rand Index = 0.784).

We also wanted to determine if presenting friends in CNM group order would influence the user in how they grouped their friends. We compared the Assisted friend grouping population with those that were Not Assisted. Using a Welch Two-Sample T-Test, we found no statistical significance between the two populations ($p = 0.224$). Refer to the Adjusted Rand Index section of Table 2 and Figure 7(a), where error bars show one standard deviation above and be-

low the mean. Our Assisted Friend Grouping Model does not bias the user, i.e., the user would produce the same groups and populate those groups with the same friends either using our Assisted Friend Grouping approach or not.

Table 2: Not Assisted vs. Assisted Friend Grouping

Measure	Not Assisted (μ, σ)	Assisted (μ, σ)	p-value
Adjusted Rand Index			
Unconcerned	(0.784, 0.10)	(0.731, 0.13)	0.383
Pragmatist	(0.654, 0.12)	(0.696, 0.15)	0.183
Fundamentalist	(0.631, 0.13)	(0.634, 0.18)	0.761
All	(0.653, 0.12)	(0.692, 0.15)	0.224
Grouping Time (seconds)			
Unconcerned	(124.1, 75.7)	(125.4, 70.5)	0.85
Pragmatist	(180.9, 105.48)	(150.4, 59.31)	0.012
Fundamentalist	(220.4, 90.36)	(171.8, 69.82)	0.026
All	(185.8, 102.8)	(150.6, 61.84)	0.038
User Perceptions (7 point Likert-scale)			
Ease of Use	(5.08, 1.54)	(5.70, 1.53)	0.041
Readability	(5.52, 1.65)	(5.57, 1.51)	0.861
Flexibility	(4.39, 1.33)	(4.49, 1.07)	0.681

Next, we set out to measure the time it took a user to populate their relationship groups. We measured the time it took a user to group 50 of their friends presented in random order (Not Assisted). We compared that with the time it took the same user to group 50 of their friends presented in CNM group order (Assisted), as described in Section 3.1. For Unconcerned Users, there was no statistical significance between Not Assisted and Assisted ($p = 0.85$). However, we did see statistical significance between the other categories of users: Pragmatists ($p = 0.012$), Fundamentalists ($p = 0.026$) and the population as a whole ($p = 0.038$). Overall, using CNM, we saw a 23% reduction in time that it took a user to group 50 of their friends, 150.6 seconds (Assisted) versus 185.8 seconds (Not Assisted). Refer to the Grouping Time section of Table 2 and Figure 7(b). One factor for this reduction in time is that the user's mental model is focused on one relationship group at a time, which enables the user to quickly group most family members, for example, before grouping the next set of friends. Fewer "mental task switches" between relationship groups are required thus reducing the overall friend grouping time. It is also interesting to note, although not entirely surprising, that Fundamentalists took longer, on average, to group their friends than Pragmatists and Unconcerned Users. One possible reason that Fundamentalists took more time may be because they apply more scrutiny as they group their friends.

We also measured users' perceptions of the Not Assisted and Assisted friend grouping approaches, as described in Section 4.1. A T-Test was used to compared the Not Assisted and Assisted populations. We found no statistical significance in the areas of Readability ($p = 0.861$) and Flexibility ($p = 0.681$). This would be expected because the policy management approaches for Not Assisted and Assisted are visibly the same with the only difference being the order in which friends are presented. However, we do see statistical significance in the area of Ease of Use ($p = 0.041$), Not Assisted averaged 5.08 and Assisted averaged 5.70 on a 7 point Likert-scale. Refer to the User Perceptions section of

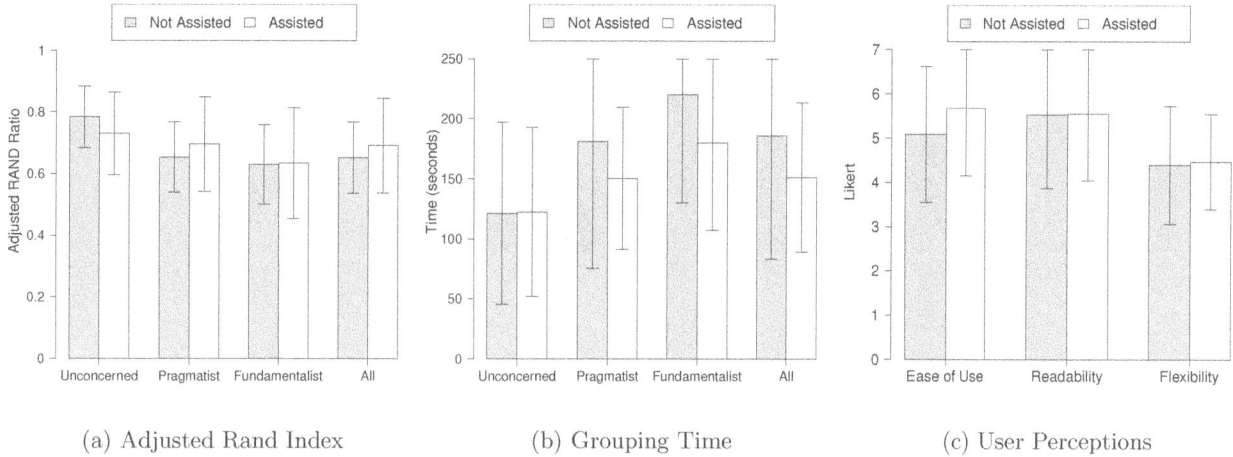

(a) Adjusted Rand Index   (b) Grouping Time   (c) User Perceptions

Figure 7: Not Assisted vs. Assisted Friend Grouping

Table 2 and Figure 7(c). Users found grouping their friends leveraging CNM easier than not having the assistance of CNM.

5.2 Same-As Policy Management

We compared the policy authoring times between Group Based Policy Management (hereafter referred to as Group Based) and Same-As Policy Management (hereafter referred to Same-As). Our results are summarized in the Policy Authoring Time section of Table 3 and illustrated in Figure 8(a). In analyzing these results, we found that there is statistical significance across all user categories, i.e., Unconcerned Users ($p = 0.036$), Pragmatists ($p < 0.001$) and Fundamentalists ($p =< 0.001$). Overall, Same-As outperformed Group Based in policy authoring time. Across the board, we observed more than a two-fold decrease in the amount of time it took a user to author their policy. One factor attributing to this reduction is the steps involved in authoring a policy. Group Based approaches have three distinct steps: 1) group friends, 2) set group policy and 3) assign friend-level exceptions to the group policy. Using this approach, the user first focuses on the friend's relationship in order to group them appropriately. Next, the user switches their attention to the group in order to set the group policy. Finally, the user switches their attention back to the friend in order to set any friend-level exceptions to the group policy. Whereas, using our Same-As approach and visual policy editor, the user simply leverages their memory and opinion of a friend to set policies for other similar friends. As a result, users can author policies in less time and thus ease the burden associated with managing their online privacy settings.

Not only are users able to set their policies more rapidly using Same-As, they are also setting more conservative policies, policies that are less permissive. We examined the *openness* of each user's policy, where Policy Openness is defined as:

DEFINITION 1. *(Policy Openness) The probability of a user permitting a friend access to a specific profile object.* $O(u, o) = \frac{|Allow(f,o)|}{|F_u|}$, *where* $Allow(f, o) \subseteq F_u$ *is the set of friends of user u who are allowed access to profile object o and F_u is the friend set of u.*

Table 3: Group Based vs. Same-As

Measure	Group Based (μ, σ)	Same-As (μ, σ)	p-value
Policy Authoring Time (seconds)			
Unconcerned	(338.9, 206.3)	(149.2, 77.9)	0.036
Pragmatist	(402.9, 193.1)	(181.9, 131.3)	< 0.001
Fundamentalist	(418.5, 134.4)	(180.4, 74.5)	< 0.001
All	(401.2, 185.8)	(179.7, 121.7)	< 0.001
Policy Openness (see Definition 1)			
Unconcerned	(0.827, 0.235)	(0.748, 0.264)	0.596
Pragmatist	(0.946, 0.163)	(0.843, 0.283)	0.006
Fundamentalist	(0.869, 0.338)	(0.751, 0.166)	0.022
All	(0.927, 0.202)	(0.823, 0.269)	0.002

We measured Policy Openness relative to a user's profile object (i.e., email address) and found, for Unconcerned Users, no statistical significance between Group Based and Same-As ($p = 0.596$). Unconcerned Users have "little problem with supplying their personal information" to others in either approach. However, we do see statistical significance between Group Based and Same-As for Pragmatists ($p = 0.006$), Fundamentalists ($p = 0.022$) and for the population as a whole ($p = 0.002$). Our findings are summarized in the Policy Openness section of Table 3 and Figure 8(b). Using Group Based, users associate the policy with a group. Whereas, using Same-As, users associate the policy with a friend and in doing so have the friend in the forefront of their mind. This allows users to be more selective and careful in assigning permissions. Users are thinking of people, not groups. In addition, as would be expected, our results show that Fundamentalists write more conservative policies than Pragmatists and Unconcerned Users.

Overall, users found Same-As easier to use than Group Based, 5.97 versus 5.38 on a 7 point Likert-scale, where 7 is Strongly Agree. We found statistical significance in our comparison ($p = 0.007$). Refer to Ease of Use section of Table 4 and Figure 9(a). Using Same-As over Group Based, we observed statistical significance and improved Ease of Use ratings for Unconcerned Users ($p = 0.045$) and Pragmatists ($p = 0.008$). We attribute the improved ratings to reasons

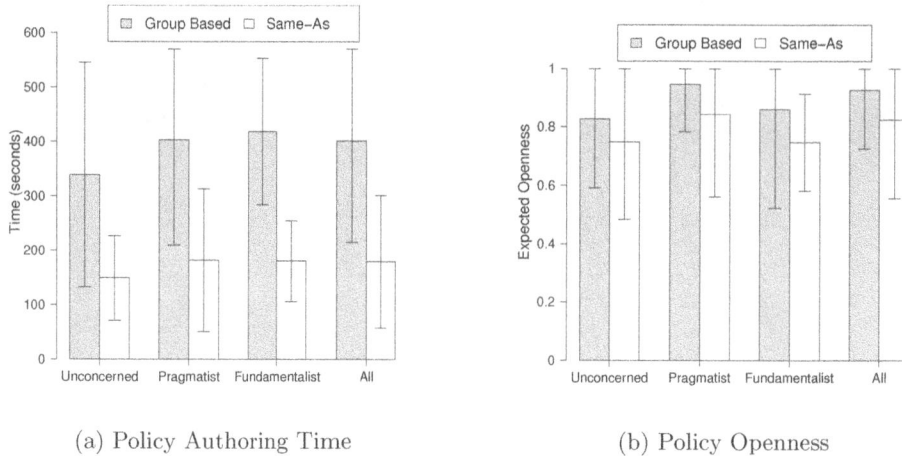

(a) Policy Authoring Time

(b) Policy Openness

Figure 8: Group Based vs. Same-As Policy Management

similar to what was discussed with regard to the reduction in policy authoring time: reduced number of steps for authoring policies, our visual policy editor and consistent focus with limited memory interruption. However, from an Ease of Use perspective, there was no statistical significance for Fundamentalists ($p = 0.604$). One possible reason is that fundamentalists are very concerned about privacy and may consider privacy "hard" to attain regardless of the approach. Also, it is interesting to note that Unconcerned Users averaged Ease of Use ratings higher than Pragmatists and Fundamentalists. Unconcerned Users don't necessarily care much about privacy and appreciate mechanisms that are easier. Fundamentalists find privacy to be "hard" regardless of approach and Pragmatists fall somewhere in the middle.

Table 4: Gp Based vs. Same-As – User Perceptions

Measure	Group Based (μ, σ)	Same-As (μ, σ)	p-value
Ease of Use (7 point Likert-scale)			
Unconcerned	(6.32, 0.47)	(6.88, 0.42)	0.045
Pragmatist	(5.37, 1.49)	(6.01, 1.45)	0.008
Fundamentalist	(4.86, 1.99)	(5.26, 2.07)	0.604
All	(5.38, 1.55)	(5.97, 1.54)	0.007
Readability (7 point Likert-scale)			
Unconcerned	(5.01, 0.48)	(6.80, 0.18)	< 0.001
Pragmatist	(4.49, 1.17)	(5.73, 1.34)	< 0.001
Fundamentalist	(3.81, 1.45)	(5.02, 1.82)	0.035
All	(4.44, 1.21)	(5.71, 1.42)	< 0.001
Flexibility (7 point Likert-scale)			
Unconcerned	(6.53, 0.48)	(6.70, 0.33)	0.505
Pragmatist	(5.55, 1.55)	(5.74, 1.44)	0.437
Fundamentalist	(4.99, 1.84)	(5.34, 1.99)	0.614
All	(5.55, 1.58)	(5.76, 1.51)	0.336

Users found Same-As to be substantially more readable than Group Based. There is statistical significance across all user categories. Refer to the Readability section of Table 4 and Figure 9(b). We attribute these high ratings to the simplicity of the Same-As approach. Users could easily

understand who had access to what profile object. Users found the organization of the information on the screen to be decipherable and ease to read. Using Same-As and leveraging our visual policy editor, a user need only to recall their opinions of their friends in order to set access control policies. This was accomplished all on one screen. Whereas, the Group Based approach was more complex with multiple steps and screens.

In evaluating Flexibility, on average, users gave relatively high ratings to both Group Based and Same-As, 5.55 for Group Based and 5.76 for Same-As. However, we found no statistical significance between the two populations ($p = 0.336$). Refer to the Flexibility section of Table 4 and Figure 9(c). In access control terms, both Group Based and Same-As have the same expressive power. That is, users can compose policies of the same granularity with either Group Based or Same-As. Group Based allows finer grained policies with the inclusion of friend-level exceptions to group policies. Same-As inherently has this capability.

6. DISCUSSION

Complex and laborious policy management mechanisms can lead to ineffective policies and compromises of information. Group based policy management is an improvement which provides a level of abstraction to the user (i.e., group) that allows them to manage permissions of large friend sets easier. However, this approach has some limitations, one being the ability to set fine grained access control policies. Introducing the capability to set friend-level exceptions to group policies overcomes this limitation. By doing so, users have the ability to set more expressive access control policies. Another shortcoming of group based policy management approaches is the burden associated with populating relationship groups for large friends sets. Our Assisted friend grouping model alleviates this burden by reducing the amount of time it takes to populate friend groups. User perceptions of our approach are encouraging. Providing tools in the hands of the user, which assist them in managing access to their profile objects, translates into more effective privacy management.

Same-As Policy Management further improves upon group

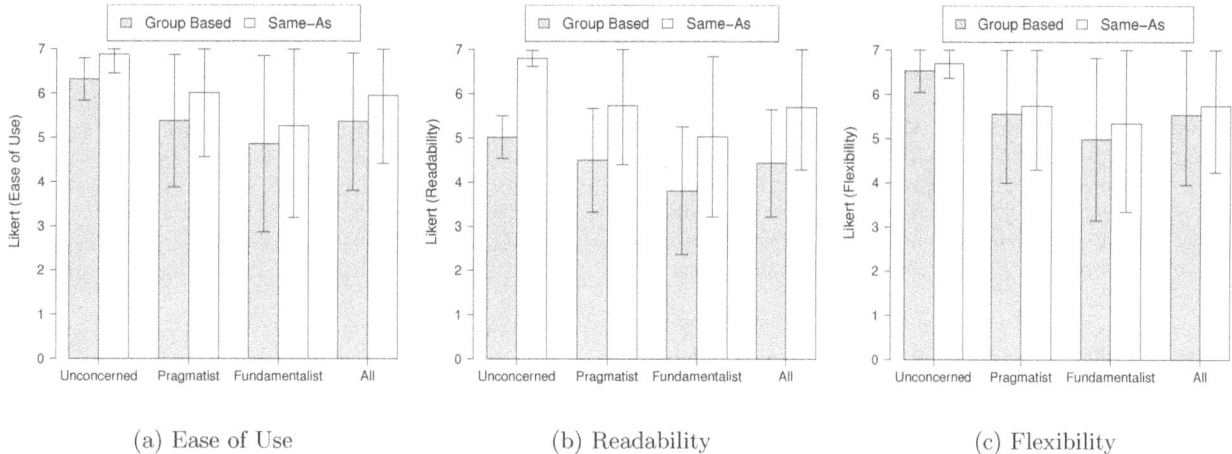

(a) Ease of Use   (b) Readability   (c) Flexibility

Figure 9: Group Based vs. Same-As Policy Management – User Perceptions

based policy management. It provides the same level of expressive power for setting fine grained policies. But, doing it in a way that is easier for the user to manage and intuitively easier to comprehend. Using our visual policy editor, users can compose readable policies that are not complex and difficult to understand. In addition, users can compose these policies in about half the time it takes traditional group based policy management approaches. Policy management becomes less of a laborious and tedious task and results in more properly configured and maintained policies, which leads to improved privacy. In addition, Same-As Policy Management results in more conservative policies, which ultimately provide better levels of protection. Same-As Policy Management keeps users more informed, improves the adoption and accuracy of access control policies and, ultimately, improves user security.

There are areas of opportunity with our research. For Assisted Friend Grouping, our prototype Facebook application cannot accommodate friends being placed into more than one relationship group. Currently, our approach recommends a friend be placed in the "best" group. Clearly, there are examples where we would expect a friend to be in multiple groups, e.g., Alice, my sister (*Family Group*), went to the same college (*Undergraduate School Group*) as I did. This is a limitation of our implementation and an area for further research.

Our user study participants were comprised of students and staff that we recruited from the university community and from *Workers* from Amazon Mechanical Turk, as described in Section 4.2. By leveraging a crowd sourcing marketplace, like Amazon Mechanical Turk, there is the possible element of a self-selection bias. Also, we presented to our participants, the Group Based Policy Management tasks followed by the Same-As Policy Management tasks. An improved approach would have been to present the tasks in random order.

7. RELATED WORK

Yuksel et al. [27] propose an approach to managing privacy in online social networks that is based on the grouping of friends, with the assumption that friends share the same

information with other group members. They use standard clustering techniques, as we do. In addition, they survey the users by asking them questions that would reveal their willingness to share information with others in their social network. Yuksel et al. take this survey data to further refine their grouping approach. This is an interesting approach. However, they provide little empirical data that would demonstrate its feasibility and effectiveness.

Jones et al. [14] investigate users' rationales for grouping friends, for privacy management purposes, within online social networks. They identify six criteria, which we leverage in choosing our predefined relationship groups. In addition, they evaluate the similarity of these criteria to the output of standard clustering techniques of users' friends. Their work supports our notion that standard clustering techniques can assist users in placing friends into groups analogous with privacy intentions. However, these mechanisms are not 100% accurate. We provide a mechanism that allows users to set exceptions to the grouping output of the automated clustering. By doing so, we can set more expressive policies based on users' intentions.

Mazzia et al. [20] introduce a policy visualization tool which displays privacy settings for user specific subgroups of friends within social networks. Besmer et al. [3] analyze the impacts of community information on access control policy decisions within social networks. Lipford [19] et al. compare two different approaches for representing social network privacy policies. They conclude that there are few differences in user performance. However, each has its strengths over the other. Many other studies have shown the benefits of recognition based approaches in aiding in memory recall [7, 8] and the ill effects of work/task interruption [12, 6]. Same-As Policy Management leverages concentrated memory recognition of friends using a visual policy editor to manage privacy in online social networks.

8. CONCLUSION

In this paper, we introduced two approaches to improving privacy policy management in online social networks. First, we presented an approach, leveraging proven clustering techniques, that assists users in grouping their friends for policy management purposes. Our approach demonstrated reduced grouping times and improvements in ease of use over traditional group based policy management approaches. Second, we introduced Same-As Policy Management, which leverages a user's memory and opinion of their friends to set policies for other similar friends. Our visual policy editor uses friend recognition and minimal task interruption to obtain substantial reductions in policy authoring times. In addition, Same-As Policy Management was positively perceived by users over traditional group based policy management approaches.

9. ACKNOWLEDGEMENTS

This research was partially supported by grants from the National Science Foundation (NSF-CNS-0831360, NSF-CNS-1117411) and a Google Research Award.

10. REFERENCES

[1] A. Acquisti and R. Gross. Imagined communities: Awareness, information sharing, and privacy on the facebook. In *Privacy Enhancing Technologies*, pages 36–58, 2006.

[2] A. Acquisti and J. Grossklags. Privacy and rationality in individual decision making. *IEEE Security and Privacy*, 3(1):26–33, 2005.

[3] A. Besmer, J. Watson, and H. R. Lipford. The impact of social navigation on privacy policy configuration. In *SOUPS*, 2010.

[4] J. Bonneau and S. Preibusch. The privacy jungle: On the market for data protection in social networks. In *The Eighth Workshop on the Economics of Information Security (WEIS 2009)*, 2009.

[5] A. Clauset, M. E. J. Newman, and C. Moore. Finding community structure in very large networks. *Physical Review E*, pages 1– 6, 2004.

[6] E. Cutrell, M. Czerwinski, and E. Horvitz. Notification, disruption, and memory: Effects of messaging interruptions on memory and performance. pages 263–269. IOS Press, 2001.

[7] R. Dhamija and A. Perrig. Deja vu: A user study using images for authentication. In *Proceedings of the 9th conference on USENIX Security Symposium - Volume 9*, pages 4–4, Berkeley, CA, USA, 2000. USENIX Association.

[8] P. Dunphy, A. P. Heiner, and N. Asokan. A closer look at recognition-based graphical passwords on mobile devices. In *Proceedings of the Sixth Symposium on Usable Privacy and Security*, page 1. ACM, 2010.

[9] C. Dwyer, S. R. Hiltz, and K. Passerini. Trust and privacy concern within social networking sites: A comparison of facebook and myspace. In *Proceedings of the Thirteenth Americas Conference on Information Systems (AMCIS 2007)*, 2007. Paper 339.

[10] D. Ferraiolo and R. Kuhn. Role-based access control. In *In 15th NIST-NCSC National Computer Security Conference*, pages 554–563, 1992.

[11] L. Hubert and P. Arabie. Comparing partitions. *Journal of classification*, 2(1):193–218, 1985.

[12] S. T. Iqbal and B. P. Bailey. Investigating the effectiveness of mental workload as a predictor of opportune moments for interruption. In *CHI '05 extended abstracts on Human factors in computing systems*, CHI EA '05, pages 1489–1492, New York, NY, USA, 2005. ACM.

[13] Q. Jones, S. A. Grandhi, S. Whittaker, K. Chivakula, and L. Terveen. Putting systems into place: a qualitative study of design requirements for location-aware community systems. In *In Proceedings of CSCW*, pages 202–211. ACM, 2004.

[14] S. Jones and E. O'Neill. Feasibility of structural network clustering for group-based privacy control in social networks. In *SOUPS*, 2010.

[15] H. Krasnova, O. Günther, S. Spiekermann, and K. Koroleva. Privacy concerns and identity in online social networks. *Identity in the Information Society*, 2:39–63, 2009.

[16] P. Kumaraguru and L. F. Cranor. Privacy indexes: A survey of westin's studies. *ISRI Tech. Report*, 2005.

[17] S. Lederer, J. I. Hong, A. K. Dey, and J. A. Landay. Personal privacy through understanding and action: five pitfalls for designers. *Personal and Ubiquitous Computing*, 8(6):440–454, 2004.

[18] K. Lewis, J. Kaufman, and N. Christakis. The taste for privacy: An analysis of college student privacy settings in an online social network. *Journal of Computer-Mediated Communication*, 14(1), 2008.

[19] H. R. Lipford, J. Watson, M. Whitney, K. Froiland, and R. W. Reeder. Visual vs. compact: a comparison of privacy policy interfaces. In *CHI*, 2010.

[20] A. Mazzia, K. LeFevre, and E. Adar. The PViz Comprehension Tool for Social Network Privacy Settings. Technical Report CSE-TR-570-11, University of Michigan, April 2011.

[21] P. A. Norberg, D. R. Horne, and D. A. Horne. The Privacy Paradox: Personal Information Disclosure Intentions versus Behaviors. *Journal of Consumer Affairs*, 2007.

[22] J. S. Olson, J. Grudin, and E. Horvitz. A study of preferences for sharing and privacy. In *CHI Extended Abstracts*, pages 1985–1988, 2005.

[23] PCWorld. Google buzz criticized for disclosing gmail contacts. http://www.pcworld.com/businesscenter/article/189081, February 2010.

[24] R. Sandhu, D. Ferraiolo, and R. Kuhn. The nist model for role-based access control: Towards a unified standard. In *In Proceedings of the fifth ACM workshop on Role-based access control*, pages 47–63, 2000.

[25] R. S. Sandhu, E. J. Coyne, H. L. Feinstein, and C. E. Youman. Role-based access control models. *IEEE Computer*, 29(2):38–47, 1996.

[26] K. Strater and H. R. Lipford. Strategies and struggles with privacy in an online social networking community. In *Proceedings of the 22nd British HCI Group Annual Conference on People and Computers: Culture, Creativity, Interaction - Volume 1*, BCS-HCI '08, pages 111–119, Swinton, UK, UK, 2008. British Computer Society.

[27] A. S. Yuksel, M. E. Yuksel, and A. H. Zaim. An approach for protecting privacy on social networks. In *Proceedings of 5th International Conference on Systems and Networks Communications*, Washington, DC, USA, 2010. IEEE Computer Society.

Ensuring Authorization Privileges for Cascading User Obligations

Omar Chowdhury
The University of Texas at San Antonio
ochowdhu@cs.utsa.edu

Murillo Pontual
The University of Texas at San Antonio
mpontual@cs.utsa.edu

William H. Winsborough
The University of Texas at San Antonio
wwinsborough@acm.org

Ting Yu
North Carolina State University
tyu@ncsu.edu

Keith Irwin
Winston-Salem State University
irwinke@wssu.edu

Jianwei Niu
The University of Texas at San Antonio
niu@cs.utsa.edu

ABSTRACT

User obligations are actions that the human users are required to perform in some future time. These are common in many practical access control and privacy and can depend on and affect the authorization state. Consequently, a user can incur an obligation that she is not authorized to perform which may hamper the usability of a system. To mitigate this problem, previous work introduced a property of the authorization state, *accountability*, which requires that all the obligatory actions to be authorized when they are attempted. Although, existing work provides a specific and tractable decision procedure for a variation of the accountability property, it makes a simplified assumption that no *cascading obligations* may happen, *i.e.*, obligatory actions cannot further incur obligations. This is a strong assumption which reduces the expressive power of past models, and thus cannot support many obligation scenarios in practical security and privacy policies. In this work, we precisely specify the strong accountability property in the presence of cascading obligations and prove that deciding it is NP-hard. We provide for several special yet practical cases of cascading obligations (*i.e.*, repetitive, finite cascading, *etc.*) a tractable decision procedure for accountability. Our experimental results illustrate that supporting such special cases is feasible in practice.

Categories and Subject Descriptors

K.6.5 [**Management of Computing and Information Systems**]: Security and Protection

General Terms

Security, Theory

Keywords

Obligations, RBAC, Cascading Obligations, Authorization, Accountability

1. INTRODUCTION

Many access control and privacy policies contain some notion of actions that are *required* to be performed by a system or its users in some future time. Such required actions can be naturally modeled as obligations. Consider the following paraphrased regulation excerpt from section §164.524 of the Health Insurance Privacy and Accountability Act (HIPAA) [11]. A covered entity must respond to a request for access no later than 30 days after receipt of the request of the patient. As we can see from the regulation, the action of the covered entity is required when he receives a request from the patient. When we use obligations to capture this notion of required actions, we need a proper framework and mechanisms by which obligations can be managed efficiently.

The notion of obligations is not new. Several researchers [3, 4,6,13,15–17,19,25,26] have proposed frameworks for modeling and managing obligations. The majority of the existing work [3,4,6,15,19,25,26] focuses on policy specification languages for obligations rather than efficient management of obligations [3,7,10,12,14,18,21]. Even for works on the management of obligations, they mainly consider *system obligations*. Our goal is to address technical issues for efficient management of *user obligations*. A user (resp., system) obligation is an action that is to be carried out by a user (resp., the system) in some future time. Managing user obligations is challenging as system obligations can be assumed to be always fulfilled whereas this is often not the case for user obligations. More generally, we consider user obligations that can require authorization and can also alter the authorization state of the system. As a user obligation is an action, it is subjected to the authorization requirements imposed by the security policy of the system. We also consider that each of the user obligations has a time interval (*e.g.*, 30 days, *etc.*) which represents the alloted time window at which the obligation should be performed. Such intervals help detect obligation violation.

When managing user obligations that depend on and can affect authorization, we have to consider the case in which users can incur obligations that they are not authorized to perform. Otherwise, when an obligation goes unfulfilled, it is difficult to know if it is due to insufficient authorization or lack of diligence from the user. When it is ensured that all the obligatory actions are authorized, any obligation violation will only be caused due to user negligence. Irwin *et al.* [12] introduce a property of the authorization state and the current obligation pool, *accountability*, that tries to ensure that all the obligatory actions are authorized in some part of their stipulated time interval. They consider two variations of the accountability property (*i.e.*, *strong accountability* and *weak accountability*) based on when in the time intervals the obligatory actions should be authorized.

Irwin *et al.* [12] propose to maintain the accountability property as an invariant of the system. They propose to use the reference monitor of the system for maintaining accountability by denying actions that violate accountability. Extending the work of Irwin *et al.* [12], Pontual *et al.* [20] show that for an obligation system using mini-RBAC [23,24] and mini-ARBAC [23,24] as its authorization model, strong accountability can be decided in polynomial time whereas deciding weak accountability is co-NP complete. They also provide empirical evaluations for showing that a reference monitor can maintain the strong accountability property efficiently. They partition possible actions into two disjoint sets, *discretionary* and *obligatory* and only allow discretionary actions to incur further obligations. By doing this, they disallow *cascading obligations*.

The assumption of disallowing cascading obligations is restrictive. It significantly reduces the expressive power of the obligation model they use. For instance, consider the following scenario. When a sales assistant submits a purchase order, the clerk incurs an obligation to issue a check in the amount identified in the purchase order. As soon as the clerk issues the check, the manager incurs an obligation that requires him to check the consistency of the purchase order. If the purchase order is consistent and the manager approves it, then the accountant incurs another obligation to approve the check. Now, this situation can be easily modeled with cascading obligations, but it cannot be modeled by the obligation model of Pontual *et al.* [20]. Thus, one of the principal goals of this paper is to provide a concrete model in which the policy writers can specify cascading obligations easily. Furthermore, we also present a decision procedure which can be used to decide the strong accountability[1] property efficiently for special but practical cases of cascading obligations in the model.

The abstract obligation model that Irwin *et al.* [12] and Pontual *et al.* [20] use, allows specification of cascading obligations. However, their concrete model does not support the specification of cascading obligations. We adopt the concrete model of Pontual *et al.* [20] that uses mini-RBAC and mini-ARBAC as its authorization model and augment it in a way that cascading obligations can be specified. Furthermore, existing work [12, 20] does not discuss how to specify the user (obligatee) who incurs the new obligation when a user takes an action (obligatory or discretionary). We present several proposals for specifying the obligatee in a policy. The enhancement to the obligation model and proposals for obligatee selection comprise our *first contribution*.

The specification for strong accountability presented by Pontual *et al.* [20] also takes advantage of the assumption that cascading obligations are not allowed. Our *second contribution* is to precisely specify the strong accountability property in presence of cascading obligations. There are two possible interpretations of strong accountability when

considering cascading obligations. We define both interpretations, *existential* and *universal*, and give motivations for choosing the existential interpretation.

Our *third contribution* is to present a theorem which states that deciding accountability in presence of cascading obligations is in general NP-hard. We then consider several special cases which makes the problem tractable. We then provide a polynomial time algorithm (polynomial in the size of the policy, the size of the current obligation pool, and the new obligations to be considered) that can decide strong accountability for special cases of cascading obligations. This is our *fourth contribution*.

We then present empirical evaluations of the accountability decision procedure allowing special cases of cascading obligations. Our empirical evaluations show that strong accountability can be efficiently decided for these special cases of cascading obligations. This is our *final contribution*.

Section 2 reviews the background materials. Section 3 discusses the necessary enhancement of the obligation model to specify cascading obligations. Our main technical contribution is presented in section 4. It presents the refined definition of strong accountability, the complexity of deciding strong accountability, special cases that make deciding accountability feasible, and an algorithm for deciding strong accountability under these assumptions. Section 5 explains our input instance generation and presents empirical evaluation results. Related works are discussed in section 6. Section 7 discusses our future work and concludes.

2. BACKGROUND

In this section, we first summarize the restricted variation of the role-based access control (RBAC) and administrative role-based access control (ARBAC) model, mini-RBAC [23, 24] and mini-ARBAC [23, 24], respectively. We then discuss the obligation model presented by Pontual *et al.* [20] that uses mini-RBAC and mini-ARBAC as its authorization model.

2.1 mini-RBAC and mini-ARBAC

In the context of studying the role reachability problem, Sasturkar *et al.* [23] introduced mini-RBAC and mini-ARBAC which are simplified variations of the widely used RBAC [9] and ARBAC97 [22] model, respectively. The variation of mini-RBAC and mini-ARBAC model we use excludes sessions, role hierarchies, static mutual exclusion of roles, conditional revocation, changes to the permission-role assignment, and role administration operations. We use mini-RBAC and mini-ARBAC due its similarities with the widely popular RBAC and ARBAC model. We refer interested reader to [23, 24] for a more detailed presentation.

DEFINITION 1 (MINI-RBAC MODEL). *A mini-RBAC model γ is a tuple $\langle U, R, P, UA, PA \rangle$ in which U, R, and P represents the finite set of users, roles, and permissions, respectively. Each element of P is a pair $\langle a, o \rangle$ where a represents an action and o denotes an object. The formal type of a and o will be given later. $UA \subseteq U \times R$, denotes the set of user-role assignment and $PA \subseteq R \times P$, denotes the set of permission-role assignment.*

DEFINITION 2 (MINI-ARBAC POLICY). *A mini-ARBAC policy Φ is a pair $\langle CA, CR \rangle$ in which CA and CR denotes the set of can_assign and can_revoke rules, respectively. The following is the formal type of $CA \subseteq R \times C \times R$ in which*

---

[1]We only consider strong accountability in this work due to the complexity results of weak accountability.

C represents the set of all possible pre-conditions. Each *can_assign* rule $\langle r_a, c, r_t \rangle \in CA$ specifies that a user in role r_a is authorized to grant a target user the target role r_t provided that the target user satisfies the pre-condition c. A pre-condition c is a conjunction of positive and negative role memberships. The formal type of CR is $CR \subseteq R \times R$. Each $\langle r_a, r_t \rangle \in CR$ represents that a user in role r_a can revoke the r_t role from another user.

2.2 Obligation Model

We now summarize the obligation model proposed by Pontual *et al.* [20]. Note that, we augment this model for supporting cascading obligations in section 3. We use $U \subseteq \mathcal{U}$ to denote the finite set of users in the system at any given point of time. We use u possibly with subscripts to represents users. The finite set of objects in the system is denoted by $O \subseteq \mathcal{O}$. We use o with possibly subscripts to range over the elements of O. Note that, the universes $\mathcal{U}$ and $\mathcal{O}$ are countably infinite as we want to model systems of finite but unbounded sizes. For supporting administrative actions, we have $U \subseteq O$. The set of possible actions in the system is given by $\mathcal{A}$. The formal type of $\mathcal{A}$ is given below.

We denote a system state with $s = \langle U, O, t, \gamma, B \rangle$ where $t \in \mathcal{T}$ denotes the current system time, $\gamma \in \Gamma^2$ represents the mini-RBAC authorization state, and $B \subseteq \mathcal{B}$ represents the current pool of obligations. Obligations in the system has the form $b = \langle u, a, \vec{o}, t_s, t_e \rangle$, the universe of which, $\mathcal{B}$ has the formal type $\mathcal{U} \times \mathcal{A} \times \mathcal{O}^* \times \mathcal{T} \times \mathcal{T}$ [3]. For an obligation $b = \langle u, a, \vec{o}, t_s, t_e \rangle$, $[t_s, t_e]$ denotes the interval in which the obligation should be performed. Moreover, we require that $t_s < t_e$. We use $b.u$, $b.a$, and $b.o^*$, respectively, to denote the user, the actions, and the object(s) of the obligation b.

We consider two types of actions, namely, *discretionary* and *obligatory*. The system views them uniformly as events. The universe of discretionary action $\mathcal{D}$ has the formal type $\mathcal{U} \times \mathcal{A} \times \mathcal{O}^*$. Thus, the universe of all possible events is $\mathcal{E} = \mathcal{D} \cup \mathcal{B}$. Each action $a \in \mathcal{A}$ has the formal type $(\mathcal{U} \times \mathcal{O}^*) \to (\mathcal{FP}(\mathcal{U}) \times \mathcal{FP}(\mathcal{O}) \times \Gamma) \to (\mathcal{FP}(\mathcal{U}) \times \mathcal{FP}(\mathcal{O}) \times \Gamma)$ [4]. Actions can add or remove users and objects and can also alter the authorization state. Thus, for a given user u and object(s) $\vec{o}$, the action $a(u, \vec{o})$ is a mapping that that maps the current set of users, objects, and the current authorization state to a new set of users, objects, and authorization state.

Each action in our system is regulated by a fixed set of positive, policy rules $\mathcal{P}$. Each policy rule $p \in \mathcal{P}$ has the form $p = a(u, \vec{o}) \leftarrow cond(u, \vec{o}, a) : F_{obl}(s, u, \vec{o})$. This represents that a user u is authorized to perform an action a that is applied to object(s) $\vec{o}$, when the predicate $cond(u, \vec{o}, a)$ is satisfied in the current authorization state γ (denoted by $\gamma \vDash cond(u, \vec{o}, a)$) and this in turn incurs a set of obligations (possibly empty) for u or some other users. The predicate *cond* represents the authorization requirements imposed by the policy rule. $F_{obl}(s, u, \vec{o})$ is a function that takes as input s, u, and $\vec{o}$ and returns a set of obligations (possibly empty) when the policy rule p is used to authorize the action a. For a policy rule $p \in \mathcal{P}$ of form $p = a(u, \vec{o}) \leftarrow cond(u, \vec{o}, a) : F_{obl}(s, u, \vec{o})$, when $a \in \mathcal{B}$ and the $F_{obl}(s, u, \vec{o})$ is not empty, we call the obligatory action a, a *cascading obligation*. We

also require that for each action, there is at least one policy rule that governs that action.

Recall that, we consider actions that can alter the authorization state of the system. Based on whether an action alters the authorization, we classify the actions in two possible categories, namely, *administrative* and *non-administrative*. An action a is called administrative (denoted by $a \in$ administrative) when it has the form $grant(u, \vec{o})$ or $revoke(u, \vec{o})$ and called non-administrative, otherwise.

Now, we turn our attention to how state transition occurs in the obligation system. We use $s \xrightarrow{\langle e, p \rangle} s'$ to denote the transition from state s to state s' when event e takes place and is authorized using the policy rule p. When e is of form $\langle u, a, \vec{o} \rangle$, we require that $u \in s.U$ and $\vec{o} \in s.O^*$. Furthermore, for each state s of the form $\langle U, O, t, \gamma, B \rangle$, the transition relation ensures that $\forall b \in s.B \cdot (b.u \in s.U) \wedge (b.\vec{o} \in s.O^*)$ and $s.U = s.\gamma.U$ holds. We first formalize what it means that the current authorization state γ satisfies the $cond(u, \vec{o}, a)$ predicate of a policy rule p (definition 3). We then formally specify the transition relation of the system.

DEFINITION 3. *For all $u \in \mathcal{U}$ and $\vec{o} \in \mathcal{O}^*$, $\gamma \vDash cond(u, \vec{o}, a)$ if and only if the following holds.*

$$(\exists r).(((u, r) \in \gamma.UA) \wedge$$
$$(i) \quad [a \notin \text{administrative} \to (\langle r, \langle a, \vec{o} \rangle \rangle \in \gamma.PA)] \wedge$$
$$(ii) \quad (\forall u_t, r_t).[a = grant \wedge \vec{o} = \langle u_t, r_t \rangle \to$$
$$(\exists c).((\langle r, c, r_t \rangle \in \Phi.CA) \wedge (u_t \vDash_\gamma c))] \wedge$$
$$(iii) \quad (\forall u_t, r_t).[a = revoke \wedge \vec{o} = \langle u_t, r_t \rangle \to$$
$$(\exists c).(((\langle r, c, r_t \rangle \in \Phi.CR) \wedge (u_t \vDash_\gamma c))])$$

DEFINITION 4 (TRANSITION RELATION). *Given any sequence of event/policy-rule pairs, $\langle e, p \rangle_{0..k}$ [5], and any sequence of system states $s_{0..k+1}$, the relation $\longrightarrow \subseteq \mathcal{S} \times (\mathcal{E} \times \mathcal{P})^+ \times \mathcal{S}$ is defined inductively on $k \in \mathbb{N}$ as follows:*

(1) $s_k \xrightarrow{\langle e, p \rangle_k} s_{k+1}$ holds if and only if, letting $p_k = a(u, \vec{o}) \leftarrow cond(u, \vec{o}, a) : F_{obl}(s, u, \vec{o})$, we have $s_k.\gamma \vDash cond(e_k.u, e_k.\vec{o}, e_k.a)$, and $s_{k+1} = \langle U'', O'', t'', \gamma'', B'' \rangle$, in which $\langle U'', O'', \gamma'' \rangle = a(u, \vec{o})(s_k.U, s_k.O, s_k.\gamma)$, $B'' = (s_k.B - \{e\}) \cup F_{obl}(s_k, e_k.u, e_k.\vec{o})$ when $e_k \in \mathcal{B}$, and $B'' = s_k.B \cup F_{obl}(s_k, e_k.u, e_k.\vec{o})$ otherwise. t'' denotes the system time when a is completed.

(2) $s_0 \xrightarrow{\langle e, p \rangle_{0..k}} s_{k+1}$ if and only if there exists $s_k \in \mathcal{S}$ such that $s_0 \xrightarrow{\langle e, p \rangle_{0..k-1}} s_k$ and $s_k \xrightarrow{\langle e, p \rangle_k} s_{k+1}$.

3. ENHANCEMENT OF THE MODEL

In this section, we extend the obligation model of Pontual *et al.* [20] to facilitate the specification and analysis of accountability in presence of cascading obligations.

3.1 Time Interval of the Incurred Obligation

In the previous obligation model [20], when a discretionary action a is taken at time t and it causes an obligation b to be incurred, the time interval of b depends on the time t. Thus, the time interval of b is calculated using a fixed offset from t and the interval size of b. Let us assume the fixed offset is δ

---

[2]Γ here denotes the set of abstract authorization states.

[3]$\mathcal{O}^*$ is the Cartesian product of zero or more copies of $\mathcal{O}$.

[4]$\mathcal{FP}(\mathcal{X}) = \{X \subset \mathcal{X} | X \text{ is finite}\}$ denotes the set of finite subsets of the given set $\mathcal{X}$.

[5]Notation: We use $s_{0..j}$ to denote the sequence $s_0, s_1, \ldots, s_j$ where $j \in \mathbb{N}$, and for $\ell \in \mathbb{N}$, $\ell \leq j$, $s_{0..\ell}$ denotes the prefix of $s_{0..j}$ and when $\ell < j$ the prefix is *proper*. Similarly, $\langle e, p \rangle_{0..j}$ denotes $\langle e_0, p_0 \rangle, \langle e_1, p_1 \rangle, \ldots, \langle e_j, p_j \rangle$.

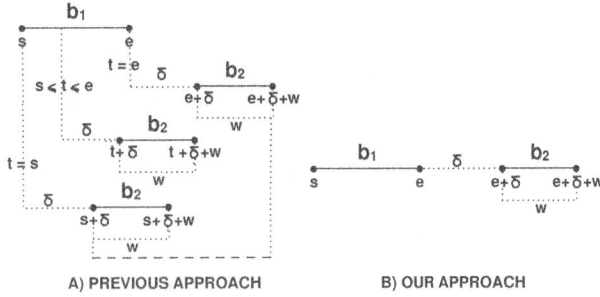

Figure 1: Time Interval of the Incurred Obligation.

and the interval size of b is w. So, the time interval of b will be $[t+\delta, t+\delta+w]$. Now, consider the case where an obligation b_1 with time interval $[s,e]$ incurs another obligation b_2. The time t at which b_1 can possibly be performed can be any value between s and e, inclusive. Thus, we have several possible intervals for b_2 considering each possible values of t (see figure 1(a)). For deciding strong accountability, we have to check whether b_2 is authorized in each of the possible time intervals. One possibility is to consider the interval $[s+\delta, e+\delta+w]$ to be the time interval of b_2, as all the possible time intervals are inside this interval. However, when b_1 is performed (we know t) we get b_2's original time interval and have to shrink the large time interval $[s+\delta, e+\delta+w]$ appropriately with respect to t. When we use this approach, it will yield runtime overhead for managing obligations and accountability will be less likely to hold due to increasingly large obligation time intervals.

To mitigate this problem, we assume that b_2's time interval will be at a fixed distance $\delta \in \mathbb{N}$ from the time interval of b_1 (see figure 1(b)). We assume δ is measured from the end time of b_1's interval. Thus, b_2's stipulated time interval in our approach will be $[e+\delta, e+\delta+w]$. This approach will ensure that the cascading obligation's time interval is fixed. For a discretionary action incurring an obligation, we replace e with t, the time at which the action is performed. Thus, in our model obligations have the form $b = \langle u, a, \vec{o}, t_s, t_e, \delta, w \rangle$. In section 4.4.2, we further augment our obligations to contain one additional field (repetition). We also extend the notion of the transition relation to allow cascading obligations.

3.2 Selection of Obligatee

We now present some strategies by which a user who incurs obligations, can be specified in the policy. When a user executes an action, this can generate other obligations to the user who initiated the action, or for other users. The user who incurs an obligation is called an *obligatee*. Existing work [12, 20] does not discuss how obligatees are specified in the policy. To allow the specification of obligatees, we extend the policy rules to include an extra field called "obligatee". Thus, policies now have the following form: $p = a(u, \vec{o}) \leftarrow cond(u, \vec{o}, a) : F_{obl}(obligatee, s, u, \vec{o}, \delta, w)$. Note that, F_{obl} function returns a set of obligations and is guaranteed to terminate in a constant time.

Explicit User: In this strategy, the obligatee is hard-coded in the policy rule.

EXAMPLE 5 (EXPLICIT USER). *Let us consider the following policy rule, $p_0 : check(u, log) \leftarrow (u \in manager) : F_{obl}(Bob, s, u, log, \delta = 10, w = 5)$. This rule authorizes a user*

in the role of manager to check the log and it will incur an obligation[6] for Bob.

Self, Target, and Explicit User: In this strategy, the obligatee field can contain "Self", "Target", or an explicit user. When a policy rule's obligatee field contains "Self", it represents that the user who initiates the action, authorized by the current policy, will incur the associated obligations.

EXAMPLE 6 (SELF). *Let us consider a policy rule, $p_1 : grant(u, \langle u_t, programmer \rangle) \leftarrow ((u \in manager) \wedge (u_t \in employee)) : F_{obl}(Self, s, u, \langle u_t, programmer \rangle, \delta = 10, w = 5)$. This rule authorizes a user u in the role of manager to grant a new role programmer to a target user u_t in the role of employee and this will incur an obligation for u. Let us consider that manager Bob grants the employee Alice the role programmer. This will generate a new obligation for Bob.*

On the other hand, whenever the policy rule is authorizing an administrative action and the obligatee field of that policy rule contains "Target", it signifies that the target of the original administrative action authorized by this policy would incur the obligations specified by it.

EXAMPLE 7 (TARGET). *Let us consider a policy rule, $p_2 : grant(u, \langle u_t, programmer \rangle) \leftarrow ((u \in manager) \wedge (u_t \in employee)) : F_{obl}(Target, s, u, \langle u_t, programmer \rangle, \delta = 10, w = 5)$. The policy rule p_2 is similar to p_1 except it incurs an obligation for the target. As in the previous example, when Bob grants the role programmer to Alice, Alice will incur an obligation as she is the target of the action.*

Role Expression: In this approach, the obligatee field can contain a boolean role expression. Each literal in the boolean expression is either a positive or a negative role membership test. The system can select a user to be the obligatee provided that the user satisfies the role expression when the original action is performed. A comprehensive example of this strategy is presented in appendix A.

In the current work, we use the "Self, Target, and Explicit User" scheme to specify the obligatee. Although this approach is not the most general strategy to specify an obligatee, our accountability decision procedure requires every obligation to have an individual user statically associated with it. However, in the "Role expression" scheme multiple users can satisfy the role expression specified in the obligation policy rule. Thus, we have two possible interpretations of strong accountability. One of which says that the newly incurred obligation will maintain accountability if at least one of the users satisfying the role expression is authorized to perform the obligation during its whole time interval. The other interpretation requires that every user who satisfies the role expression must be authorized to perform the obligation during its whole time interval. Although both of the interpretations have practical utility, the choice of interpretation will influence the time complexity of the accountability decision procedure. We leave the adoption of the role expression scheme for specifying the obligatee as a future work.

4. STRONG ACCOUNTABILITY

When considering user obligations that depend on and affect authorization, we can have a situation where a user can

---

[6]The action associated with the obligation will be specified in the body of the F_{obl} function. For clarity, we do not show the body of the F_{obl} function.

incur obligations which she is not authorized to fulfill. However, without any preemptive approach, the obligatee will realize the absence of proper authorization in the time she attempts the obligation. This can hinder the proper functioning of the system. To mitigate this, Irwin *et al.* [12] introduced a property of the authorization state and the current obligation pool, accountability, that ensures that all the obligatory actions are authorized in some part of their time interval. Based on when they are supposed to be authorized in their time intervals, they introduced two variations of the accountability property, weak and strong. Pontual *et al.* [20] have shown that deciding weak accountability is co-NP complete for a model using mini-RBAC and mini-ARBAC, whereas deciding strong accountability is polynomial. Due to its high complexity, we do not consider weak accountability. Roughly, strong accountability requires that as long as prior obligations have been performed in their stipulated time interval, each obligatory action must be authorized no matter what policy rules are used to authorize the other obligations and no matter when they are performed in their time interval.

In this section, we first present the definition of strong accountability presented by Pontual *et al.* [20]. As mentioned before, their definition of strong accountability does not take into account cascading obligations. We call their notion of the property *restricted strong accountability*. We then refine their notion of the property and give a recursive definition of it considering the presence of cascading obligations. We go on to show that deciding strong accountability in presence of cascading obligations in general is NP-hard. We then consider some special cases of cascading obligations and give a tractable decision procedure for deciding strong accountability in their presence.

4.1 Restricted Strong Accountability

Roughly stated, under the assumption that all previous obligations have been fulfilled in their time interval, strong accountability property requires that each obligation be authorized throughout its entire time interval, no matter when during that interval the other obligations are scheduled, and no matter which policy rules are used to authorize them.

Given a pool of obligations B, a *schedule* of B is a sequence $b_{0..n}$ that enumerates B, for $n = |B| - 1$ (including the possibility that B may be countably infinite). A schedule of B is *valid* if for all i and j, if $0 \le i < j \le n$, then $b_i.\text{start} \le b_j.\text{end}$. This prevents scheduling b_i before b_j if $b_j.\text{end} < b_i.\text{start}$. Given a system state s_0, and a policy $\mathcal{P}$, a proper prefix $b_{0..j}$ of a schedule $b_{0..n}$ for B is *authorized by* policy-rule sequence $p_{0..j} \subseteq \mathcal{P}^*$ if there exists s_{j+1} such that $s_0 \xrightarrow{\langle b, p \rangle_{0..j}} s_{j+1}$.

DEFINITION 8 (RESTRICTED STRONG ACCOUNTABILITY). *Given a state $s_0 \in \mathcal{S}$ and a policy $\mathcal{P}$, we say that s_0 is strongly accountable (denoted by $RStrongAccountable(s_0, \mathcal{P})$) if for every valid schedule, $b_{0..n}$, every proper prefix of it, $b_{0..k}$, for every policy-rule sequence $p_{0..k} \subseteq \mathcal{P}^*$ and every state s_{k+1} such that $s_0 \xrightarrow{\langle b, p \rangle_{0..k}} s_{k+1}$, there exists a policy rule p_{k+1} and a state s_{k+2} such that $s_{k+1} \xrightarrow{\langle b, p \rangle_{k+1}} s_{k+2}$.*

4.2 Unrestricted Strong Accountability

In this section, we provide a formal specification of the strongly accountability property with cascading obligations. The strong accountability definition presented by Pontual *et*

al. [20] disallowed cascading obligation. We extend their model to allow them. We define three auxiliary functions that will be used in the definition of strong accountability.

DEFINITION 9 (Ψ FUNCTION). *Ψ is a function that takes as input an obligation $\hat{b}$ and a fixed set of policy rules $\mathcal{P}$ and returns a set of sets of obligations $\hat{B}$ in which each element represents a set of obligations that $\hat{b}$ can incur according to the F_{obl} function of a policy rule authorizing it. The formal specification and the type of Ψ are precisely shown below.*

$$\Psi : B \times \mathcal{FP}(\mathcal{P}) \to \mathcal{FP}(\mathcal{FP}(B))$$
$$\Psi(b = (u, a, \vec{o}, t_s, t_e, \delta, w), \mathcal{P}) =$$
$$\Big\{ F_{obl}(obligatee, s, u, \vec{o}, \delta, w) \mid p = (a(u, \vec{o}) \leftarrow cond(u, \vec{o}, a) :$$
$$F_{obl}(obligatee, s, u, \vec{o}, \delta, w)) \wedge (p \in \mathcal{P}) \Big\}$$

DEFINITION 10 (Π FUNCTION). *Π is a function that takes as input a set of obligations $\bar{B}$ and a fixed set of policy rules $\mathcal{P}$ and returns a set of sets of obligations $\tilde{B}$ in which each element is a possible set of obligations that all the obligations of $\bar{B}$ can incur. In short, $\tilde{B}$ is the set containing all possible combination of obligations that $\bar{B}$ can incur. The formal specification of Π and its type are shown below.*

$$\Pi : \mathcal{FP}(B) \times \mathcal{FP}(\mathcal{P}) \to \mathcal{FP}(\mathcal{FP}(B))$$
$$\Pi(b_{1...n} = (u_{1...n}, a_{1...n}, \vec{o}_{1...n}, t_{s_{1...n}}, t_{e_{1...n}}, \delta_{1...n}, w_{1...n}), \mathcal{P})$$
$$= \{ \mathcal{B} \subseteq \mathcal{B} | \forall i \in 1 \dots n. \Psi(b_i, \mathcal{P}) \ne \varnothing \to \exists f \in \Psi(b_i, \mathcal{P}).f \subseteq BB \}$$

DEFINITION 11 (Ξ FUNCTION). *Ξ is a function that takes as input a set of sets of obligations and a set of policy rules and applies Π to each of set of obligations and then combines the results. This allows us to find the set of all possible sets of obligations generated by a given set of possible obligations. For simplicity in later definitions, we also include in the output sets, the original sets which generated those obligations.*

$$\Xi : \mathcal{FP}(\mathcal{FP}(B)) \times \mathcal{FP}(\mathcal{P}) \to \mathcal{FP}(\mathcal{FP}(B))$$
$$\Xi(\tilde{B}, \mathcal{P}) = \{ \forall \bar{B} \in \tilde{B}, \bigcup_{B \in \Pi(\bar{B})} B \cup \bar{B} \}$$

Note that, each action a in our system can be authorized by multiple policy rules. Each of the policy rules authorizing a can incur different obligations. Furthermore, it can be the case that among different possible obligations incurred due to a, some of them maintain accountability and some of them do not. Provided that the policy allows infinite cascading obligations and a is authorized by multiple policy rules, each of which incurs different obligations, then all possible obligations incurred due to a can be modeled as a tree (possibly infinite). Based on this, we can have two interpretations of strong accountability, *existential* and *universal*. The existential interpretation requires that there exists a single path in the tree in which all the obligatory actions maintain accountability when added to the current pool of obligations. The universal interpretation is the dual and requires that all the paths in the tree maintain strong accountability. We think the universal interpretation is too strong. As a result of which, we use the existential interpretation of the strong accountability property and define it just below. However, the following definition can be extended to express the universal interpretation of strong accountability.

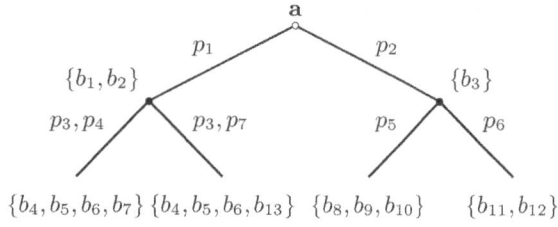

Figure 2: Possible obligations incurred by action a

In the example (in figure 2), let us consider the current accountable pool of obligations is B. We want to know whether performing a would maintain accountability. Let us consider that a can be authorized by policy rule p_1 or p_2. When a is authorized using p_1, it incurs obligations b_1 and b_2. However, when p_2 is used to authorize a, it incurs obligation b_3. Then, b_1 can be authorized by p_3 and b_2 can be authorized by either p_4 or p_7 and so on. In the existential interpretation, if one of the following sets is accountable then adding a would maintain accountability: $B \cup \{b_1, b_2, b_4, b_5, b_6, b_7\}$, $B \cup \{b_1, b_2, b_4, b_5, b_6, b_{13}\}$, $B \cup \{b_3, b_8, b_9, b_{10}\}$, and $B \cup \{b_3, b_{11}, b_{12}\}$. The universal interpretation requires all the above sets to be accountable.

In order to formalize this, we need to first define the set of possible future sets of obligations using the Ξ function. In particular, we wish to define a series of sets of sets of obligations. We will define $\Xi^0(\tilde{B}) = \tilde{B}$ and for all integers $i > 0$, we define $\Xi^i(\tilde{B}) = \Xi(\Xi^{i-1}(\tilde{B}))$. Further, we define $\Xi^\infty = \lim_{i \to \infty} \Xi^i$. Thus, given a starting set of obligations B, we can define the set of all sets of possible obligations which can arise from B as $\Xi^\infty(\{B\})$. Note that this is a countable, but possibly infinite, set of countable, but possibly infinite, sets of obligations. Because we are allowing for potentially infinitely cascading obligations, this is necessary.

DEFINITION 12 (STRONG ACCOUNTABILITY). *Given a state $s_1 \in \mathcal{S}$, in which $s_1.B$ is a strongly accountable pool of obligations, a policy $\mathcal{P}$, a set of new obligations B_c that can generate cascading obligations, we say that the state s (where $s.B := s_1.B \cup B_c$) is existentially strongly accountable (denoted by $StrongAccountable(s, \mathcal{P})$) if and only if*

$$\exists B'_c \in \Xi^\infty(s.B, \mathcal{P}).RStrongAccountable(s[B := B'_c \cup s.B], \mathcal{P})$$

4.3 Computational Complexity

This section discusses the computational complexity of deciding strong accountability in presence of cascading obligations. Prior work [12, 20] disallowed cascading obligations while deciding strong accountability. They give intuitive discussions about why deciding strong accountability in presence of cascading obligation is difficult. However, they did not present any theoretical results regarding this.

We have the following theorem which states that the strong accountability decision problem is NP-hard. We reduced the Hamiltonian path problem for graphs to the decision of unrestricted strong accountability property. We present a detailed proof of the theorem in the technical report [5].

THEOREM 13. *Given a strongly accountable pool of obligations B, a new obligation b, an initial authorization state γ, and a mini-ARBAC policy Φ that allows cascading obligations and also allows each action to be authorized by multiple policy rules, deciding whether $B \cup B_c \cup \{b\}$ is strongly accountable (either in existential or universal interpretation)*

is NP-hard in the size of B, γ, and Φ, where B_c is the set of cascading obligations incurred by b.

4.4 Special Cases of Cascading Obligation

As in section 4.3, deciding accountability in presence of cascading obligations is NP-hard. Our goal is to find certain special cases of cascading obligations for which the accountability decision is tractable. This section introduces two such special cases.

4.4.1 Finite Cascading Obligation

In this special case of cascading obligation, we consider that the policy is written in a way that the maximum number of new obligations incurred by a single obligation is bounded by a constant (see appendix A). Furthermore, we also consider that each action, object pair is authorized by only one policy rule. We also assume that the policy rules are free of cycles prohibiting infinite cascading. This can be achieved by a static checking for cycles in the policy.

4.4.2 Repetitive Obligation

Repetitive obligations occur recurrently after a fixed amount of time. A real life example of repetitive obligation can be found in the chapter 6803(a) of Gramm-Leach-Bliley Act (GLBA) [1]. According to the regulation, a financial institution must send a customer an annual privacy notice as long as the individual is a customer. Note that, we cannot specify repetitive obligations in our model directly. For this, we follow Ni *et al.* [18] to augment our obligations with an extra field that specifies the number of repetition (denoted by ρ). We allow both finite and infinite repetitive obligation. Now, let us consider an obligation $b = \{u, a, \vec{o}, t_s, t_e, \delta, \rho, w\}$. This obligation is considered to be infinite repetitive when $\rho = I$ or finite repetitive when $\rho \in \mathbb{N}$ and $\rho > 1$.

Finite Repetitive Obligations. This kind of obligation recurs finitely after a fixed amount of time. For instance, $b = \{Bob, check, log, t_s = 5, t_e = 8, \delta = 2, \rho = 3, w = 3\}$ will generate 3 obligations $\{Bob, check, log, 5, 8\}$, $\{Bob, check, log, 10, 13\}$, and $\{Bob, check, log, 15, 18\}$.

Infinite Repetitive Obligations. This kind of obligations on the other hand recurs indefinitely. For example, $b = \{Bob, check, log, t_s = 5, t_e = 8, \delta = 2, \rho = I, w = 3\}$ will generate the following infinite number of obligations: $\{Bob, check, log, 5, 8\}$, $\{Bob, check, log, 10, 13\}$, $\cdots$.

4.5 Algorithm

As deciding accountability in presence of cascading obligations is NP-hard, we simplify our accountability decision problem by imposing several restrictions on the problem. The restrictions are: (1) We consider each action, object pair is authorized by one policy rule, prohibiting disjunctive choices. (2) We require that the policy is free of cycles which prohibits obligations which incur an infinite number of new obligations. (3) We disallow role expressions to specify the obligatee of the new obligation. (4) We also disallow finite cascading obligations which incur repetitive obligations. (5) We also disallow repetitive obligations which incur non-repetitive cascading obligations.

Under restrictions, strong accountability can be decided in polynomial time of the policy size, number of obligations, and the number of new obligations that need to be considered. The algorithm (algorithm 1) decides whether adding an obligation to an accountable pool of obligations maintains accountability. The algorithm takes as input the accountable pool of obligations B (containing the finite cascading, finite repetitive, and infinite repetitive obligations), the current authorization state γ of the system, a mini-ARBAC policy Φ, and the new obligation b. It returns true when adding $B \cup \{b\} \cup B_c$ is strongly accountable where B_c is the new set of obligations incurred by b. Note that, the time complexity of the algorithm additionally depends on the type of the obligation to be added and the number of infinite repetitive obligations that need to be unrolled. The complexity of the algorithm is precisely described in appendix C.

In the algorithm 1, the new obligation b can either incur no new obligations, finite cascading obligations, finite repetitive obligations, or infinite repetitive obligations. Based on what kind of new obligation(s) b incurs, we have to take different course of actions. The main idea behind the algorithm is to unroll a finite amount of new obligations and use the non-incremental algorithm presented by Pontual *et al.* [20] to decide whether the original pool of obligation in addition with the new obligation and finitely unrolled obligation is strongly accountable. The way in which each type of obligation is unrolled is presented in the following discussion.

Algorithm 1 $StrongAccountableCascading\ (\gamma, \Phi, B, b)$

Input: A policy $\langle \gamma, \Phi \rangle$, a strongly accountable obligation set B, and a new obligation b that generates cascading obligations.
Output: returns **true** if addition of b to the system preserves strong accountability.
1: **if** $b.\rho = 1$ **then**
2:     $B_{final} := B \cup UnrollCascading(\gamma, \Phi, b)$;
3: **else if** $b.\rho = I$ **then**
4:     $B_{final} := B \cup \{b\}$;
5: **else**
6:     $B_{final} := B \cup UnrollFiniteRepetitive(\gamma, \Phi, b)$;
7:     $m := MaxEndTime(B_{final})$;
8:     $B_{final} := B_{final} \cup UnrollInfiniteRepetitive(\gamma, \Phi, B_{final}, m)$;
9: **for** each obligation $b^* \in B_{final}$ **do**
10:     **if** $b^*.a$ = grant or revoke **then**
11:         $InsertIntoDataStructure(b^*)$;
12: **for** each obligation $b^* \in B_{final}$ **do**
13:     **if** $Authorized\ (\gamma, \Phi, B_{final}, b^*)$ = **false then**
14:         **return false**
15: **return true**

Unrolling Finite Cascading Obligations. To unroll the chain of cascading obligations incurred by b, Algorithm 1 uses procedure *UnrollCascading* described in Algorithm 2. This procedure is an adapted breadth-first search algorithm. Recall that we disallow infinite cascading obligations which guarantees that the procedure *UnrollCascading* will terminate. Furthermore, we also impose the restriction that each action, object pair can be authorized by only one policy rule. Thus, the new obligations incurred by a fixed obligation will be finite and fixed. For this, we use the function Ψ (discussed in section 4.2) that takes an obligation b and set of policy rules and returns a set of set of obligations which can be possibly incurred by b. Due to the restriction above, the result of Ψ will be a single set of obligations B_f that can be incurred by b. The different fields of each obligation $\hat{b} \in B_f$ will depend of the fields of b and the policy rule that authorizes b.

Unrolling Finite Repetitive Obligations. When the new obligation we want to add (b) is a finite repetitive obligation ($b.\rho \in \mathbb{N}$ and $b.\rho > 1$), we use the procedure *Un-*

Algorithm 2 $UnrollCascading\ (\gamma, \Phi, b)$

Input: A policy $\langle \gamma, \Phi \rangle$ and a new obligation b.
Output: returns a set of cascading obligations B that is generated by b.
1: $B = \varnothing$;
2: $queue < obligation > q$;
3: q.push(b);
4: **while** $!q.empty()$ **do**
5:     $b = q.front()$; $B := B \cup \{b\}$;
6:     $q.pop()$; $B' := \Psi(b, \Phi)$;
7:     **for** each obligation $b^* \in B'$ **do**
8:         $q.push(b^*)$;
9: **return** B

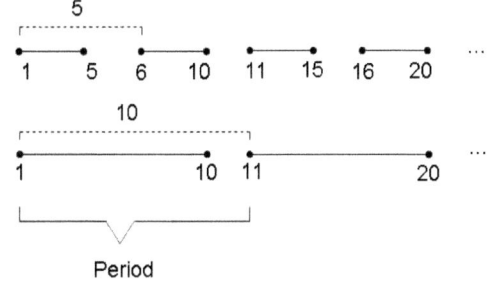

Figure 3: Computing Period of Infinite Repetitive

rollFiniteRepetitive described in Algorithm 3 to unroll it appropriately. We follow the procedure presented in appendix B to unroll finite repetitive obligations. Thus, for the obligation b, the procedure *UnrollFiniteRepetitive* clones b, varying only the time intervals of the new obligations based on $b.\delta$. The exact number of copies of b that are unrolled will depend on $b.\rho$.

Algorithm 3 $UnrollFiniteRepetitive\ (\gamma, \Phi, b)$

Input: A policy $\langle \gamma, \Phi \rangle$ and a finite repetitive obligation b.
Output: returns a set of unrolled obligations B that is generated by b.
1: $B = \varnothing$; $i := 1$;
2: **while** $i \leq b.\rho$ **do**
3:     $b_i := b$; $b_i.t_e := (b.w - b.\delta) \times i + b.t_s - b.\delta$;
4:     $b_i.t_s := b_i.t_e - w$; $B := B \cup \{b_i\}$; $i := i + 1$;
5: **return** B

Unrolling Infinite Repetitive Obligations. When the obligation we want to add (b) is an infinite repetitive obligation, Algorithm 1 uses procedure *UnrollInfiniteRepetitive*, described in algorithm 4, to unroll a finite amount of it. Let us consider $B_i \subseteq B$ is the set of infinite repetitive obligations. Note that, $b \in B_i$. First, we find the *overall period* of all the obligations in B_i at which the infinite repetitive obligations repeat themselves. In figure 3 we have two infinite repetitive obligations, $b_1 = \{u_1, a, o, t_s = 1, t_e = 5, \delta = 1, \rho = I, w = 4\}$ and $b_2 = \{u_1, a, o, t_s = 1, t_e = 10, \delta = 1, \rho = I, w = 9\}$. It is clear that after time 11, we see a pattern formed by the obligations, this is the overall period. The overall period is the least common multiple (LCM) of the periods of each $b_i \in B_i$. For each infinite repetitive obligation b_i, the period of b_i is given by $b_i.\delta + b_i.w$. Once the period is computed, we check to see whether the overall period is greater than the maximum end time of the finite obligations (repetitive or non-repetitive). If this is the case, we just need to unroll the infinite repetitive obligations three periods (to be safe). Otherwise, we unroll the infinite obligations until the maximum

---

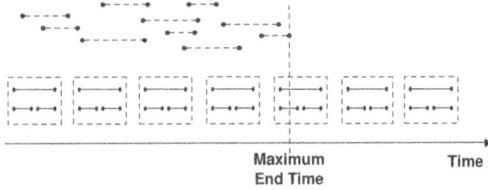

Figure 4: Unrolling Infinite Repetitive Obligations

time, and then we unroll two additional periods (figure 4). In the current pool of obligations let us assume that the only type of obligations present are the infinite repetitive obligations. When we have calculated the overall period of these infinite repetitive obligations, part of the authorization state influencing the permissibility of the infinite repetitive obligations, after each of these period should be equivalent to the authorization state before, if the system is accountable. If the authorization state is not necessarily equivalent, this will be revealed when the second repetition is analyzed. Thus, we do not need to analyze the infinite repetitive obligations beyond two repetitions. Similarly, when we have other types of obligations residing in the current pool of obligations, we can safely unroll the infinite repetitive obligations for two additional period after the maximum end time of the finite obligations and soundly decide accountability.

Algorithm 4 $UnrollInfiniteRepetitive\ (\gamma, \Phi, B, m)$

Input: A policy $\langle \gamma, \Phi \rangle$, a set of obligations, where $B_i \subseteq B$ is a set of infinite repetitive obligations, and m representing the last time point where a non-infinite obligation happens.

Output: returns a set of unrolled obligations B' that is generated by B.

1: $B' = \varnothing;\ period = LCM(B)$
2: **if** $period > m$ **then**
3:    $finalTime := period * 3;$
4: **else**
5:    $finalTime := (\lceil (m/period) \rceil + 2) \times period;$
6: **for** each obligation $b' \in B_i$ **do**
7:    $end := b'.t_e;$
8:    **while** $end <= finalTime$ **do**
9:       $b_i := b';\ b_i.t_e := (b'.w - b'.\delta) \times i + b'.t_s - b'.\delta;$
10:       $b_i.t_s := b_i.t_e - w;\ B' := B' \cup \{b_i\};\ end := b_i.t_e;$
11: **return** B'

We now briefly summarize the non-incremental algorithm for deciding strong accountability due to Pontual *et al.* [20] which we use as a procedure for deciding accountability in presence of special cases of cascading obligations. We refer readers to Pontual *et al.* [20] for a detailed presentation.

The non-incremental algorithm takes as input a set of obligations, an authorization state, and a mini-ARBAC policy and returns true when the set of obligations is strong accountable. For this, the algorithm inserts all the administrative obligations in the set to a modified interval search tree. Then it checks whether each of the obligation is authorized in its whole time interval. To do this, the algorithm inspects whether the user performing the obligation has the necessary roles in the whole time interval. For simplicity, let us consider the user u needs the role r to perform the obligation. Then, the algorithm checks whether u has role r in the current authorization state. If so, then it checks whether there is an obligation overlapping with the current obligation that revokes r. If not, then u is guaranteed to have role r in the whole time interval. In case, u currently does not have role r, then the algorithm checks whether there is a grant of the role r to u and no one is revoking it. If that

is the case, then u is guaranteed to have role r in the whole time interval.

5. EMPIRICAL EVALUATION

The goal of the empirical evaluations is to determine whether strong accountability can be decided efficiently for some special cases of cascading obligations. For those cases, our empirical evaluations illustrate that it is actually feasible to decide the strong accountability property.

The algorithm for deciding strong accountability for special cases of cascading obligations is implemented using C++ and compiled with g++ version 4.4.3. All experiments are performed using an Intel i7 2.0GHz computer with 6GB of memory running Ubuntu 11.10.

5.1 Input Instance Generation

As in the case for many security researchers, we do not have access to real life access control policies that contain obligations. Thus, we synthetically generate problem instances for our empirical evaluations. We believe the values of the different parameters we assume are appropriate for a medium sized organization.

In our experiments, we consider 1007 users, 1051 objects, and 551 roles. We also consider 53 types of actions, 2 of which are administrative (grant and revoke). We handcrafted a mini-RBAC and mini-ARBAC policy with 1251 permission assignment rules, 560 role assignment rules (maximum 5 pre-conditions in each), and 560 role revocation rules. Among the policy rules, 100 of them can incur new obligations. Each of which can incur a maximum of 10 new obligations totaling 1000 new cascading obligations.

To generate the obligations, we handcrafted 6 strongly accountable sets of obligations in which each set has 50 obligations. Each set has a different ratio of administrative to non-administrative obligations (rat). We then replicated each set of obligations for different users to obtain the desired number of obligations. Similarly, we generate the infinite and finite repetitive obligations, we use 6 sets of repetitive obligations that are strongly accountable. The execution times shown are the average of 100 runs of each experiment.

5.2 Empirical Results

Our accountability decision procedure takes as input an accountable pool of obligations B, the current authorization state γ, a mini-ARBAC policy Φ, and a new obligation b. It returns true when adding b and its associated new obligations maintain accountability. In these empirical evaluations, we consider cases where b can incur a finite amount of new obligations and can be finitely (infinitely) repetitive.

Finite Cascading Obligations.
In this case, we add an obligation to a strongly accountable set of obligations. This obligation in turn incurs 1000 new obligations. Then, the algorithm needs to decide whether these 1000 obligations along with the original strongly accountable obligation set is still strongly accountable. Figure 5 presents the results for the strong accountability algorithm for this case. Although the number of cascading obligations is fixed (1000) throughout this experiment, we vary the number of obligations by changing the number of pending obligations in the pool from 0 to 99000. We follow the same strategy for all the other cases.

The time required by the strong accountability algorithm grows roughly linearly in the number of obligations. In the

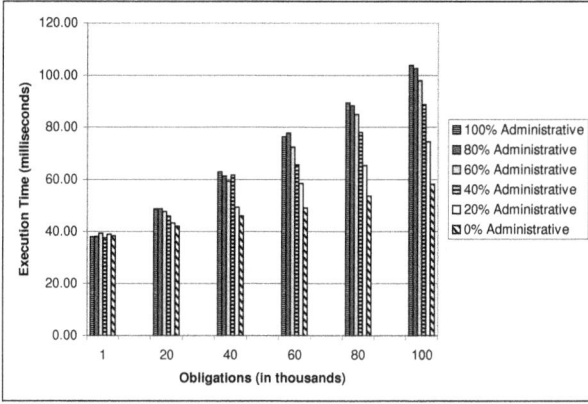

Figure 5: Finite Cascading Obligations.

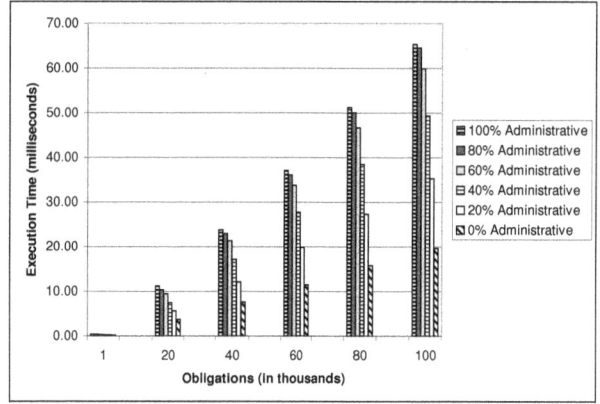

Figure 6: Infinite Repetitive Obligations.

worst case (99,000 administrative obligations plus 1000 finite cascading obligations), the algorithm runs in 103 milliseconds to determine that the set is strongly accountable. This is roughly two times slower than the non-incremental strong accountability algorithm presented by Pontual *et al.* [20] without cascading of obligations. This is due to the overhead of unfolding the cascading obligations (algorithm 3). As the algorithm must inspect every obligation following each administrative obligation, rat influences the execution time of the algorithm. In addition, we have also simulated (not shown) the same case when the original set of obligations have infinite repetitive obligations, in this case the worst execution time is still 103 milliseconds. This is due to the fact that the time of procedure *UnrollCascading* dominates the time of procedure *UnrollInfiniteRepetitive*.

Finite Repetitive Obligations.

In this experiment, we add a finite repetitive obligation to a strongly accountable obligation set. This new obligation repeats 1000 times ($\rho = 1000$). The algorithm decides whether the old set of obligations plus the 1000 copies of the repetitive obligation is strongly accountable. The execution time of the strong accountability algorithm grows roughly linearly in the number of obligations. In the worst case, the algorithm runs in 66 milliseconds to decide whether the set is strongly accountable. In general, if the number of obligations generated by the finite repetitive obligations is not too large (when compared with the original set), the time necessary to decide accountability is not affected by the addition of finite repetitive obligations. As algorithm 3 can unroll the repetitive obligations in a trivial way, the overhead of this procedure will be small provided that the number of repetition is small. In addition, we have also simulated (not shown) the same case when the original set of obligations have infinite repetitive obligations. The worst case execution time, for this case, is 66 milliseconds.

Infinite Repetitive Obligations.

In these experiments, we add an infinite repetitive obligation to a strongly accountable obligation set that already contains some infinite repetitive obligations. These infinite repetitive obligations together with b is cloned for a total of 519 times. Figure 6 shows the results for the strong accountability algorithm for this case. The execution time of the strong accountability algorithm grows roughly linearly in the number of obligations. In the worst case, the algorithm runs in 66 milliseconds.

6. RELATED WORK

Obligations have received a lot of attention from different researchers [3,4,6,7,10,12–19,21,25,26]. Some of them are interested in efficiently specifying obligatory requirements [3, 4,6,15,19,25,26] and others are interested in the management of obligations [3,7,10,12,14,18,21].

Ni *et al.* [18] presented a user obligation model based on an extended role based access control for privacy preserving data mining (PRBAC) [19]. Their model supports repeated obligations, cascading obligations, pre and post-obligations and also conditional obligations. In addition, they also present how to detect infinite obligation cascading in a policy. Their work is complimentary to ours, since we study the impact of different types of cascading obligations when deciding accountability.

Ali *et al.* [2] presented an enforcement mechanism for obligations in service oriented architectures. Their model supports repetitive obligations, conditional and pre-obligations, but do not support finite cascading obligations. Although their model is more expressive than ours, they assume that obligations have all the necessary permissions.

Elrakaiby *et al.* [8] borrow the concepts of Event Condition Action from the area of database to present an obligation model. It supports pre and post-obligations, on-going, and continuous obligations. Obligations can have relative or absolute deadlines. To cope with violations, conflicts, and lack of permissions, they adopt a set of strategies such as sanctions for users that violate obligations, cancellation of obligations, delay of obligations, and re-compensation for users that fulfill their obligations. In contrast, we use accountability to detect violations before they occur.

Li *et al.* [14] extended XACML [26] to support a richer notion of obligations. They view obligations as state machines and can express pre-obligations, post-obligations, statefulobligations, *etc.* However, they do not consider obligations requiring authorizations and in turn do not concentrate on deciding accountability. In this sense, our view of managing obligations is different than theirs.

7. CONCLUSION AND FUTURE WORK

In current work, we have refined the notion of strong accountability due to Irwin *et al.* [12] to allow cascading obligations. We also enhance the obligation model used by Pontual *et al.* [20] to support the specification of cascading obligations. We present several proposals to specify the obligatee in the policy. We then show that deciding accountability in general is NP-hard. Thus, we consider several simplifications for which the strong accountability decision becomes tractable. We provide an algorithm, its complexity, and also present empirical evaluations of the algorithm. Our experiments show that accountability can be efficiently decided for special cases of cascading obligations.

We want to explore other approaches for obligatee specification and understand their impact on accountability decision. Furthermore, we want to explore how to specify different kinds of obligations, namely, negative obligations, stateful obligations, group obligations, *etc.*, in our model and also study their impact on accountability decision.

8. ACKNOWLEDGEMENT

Ting Yu is partially supported by NSF grant CNS-0716210. Jianwei Niu is partially supported by NSF grant CNS-0964710. We would like to thank the anonymous reviewers and Andreas Gampe for their helpful suggestions.

9. REFERENCES

[1] Senate banking committee, Gramm-Leach-Bliley Act, 1999. Public Law 106-102.

[2] M. Ali, L. Bussard, and U. Pinsdorf. Obligation Language and Framework to Enable Privacy-Aware SOA. In *Data Privacy Management and Autonomous Spontaneous Security*, volume 5939 of *Lecture Notes in Computer Science*, pages 18–32. Springer Berlin, Heidelberg, 2010.

[3] A. Barth, A. Datta, J. C. Mitchell, and H. Nissenbaum. Privacy and contextual integrity: Framework and applications. *Security and Privacy, IEEE Symposium on*, 0:184–198, 2006.

[4] C. Bettini, S. Jajodia, X. S. Wang, and D. Wijesekera. Provisions and obligations in policy rule management. *J. Netw. Syst. Manage.*, 11(3):351–372, 2003.

[5] O. Chowdhury, M. Pontual, W. H. Winsborough, T. Yu, K. Irwin, and J. Niu. Ensuring authorization privileges for cascading user obligations. Technical Report CS-TR-2012-005, UT San Antonio, 2012.

[6] D. Damianou, N. Dulay, E. Lupu, and M. Sloman. The Ponder Policy Specification Language. In *2nd International Workshop on Policies for Distributed Systems and Networks*, Bristol, UK, Jan. 2001. Springer-Verlag.

[7] D. J. Dougherty, K. Fisler, and S. Krishnamurthi. Obligations and their interaction with programs. In *Proceedings of the 12th European Symposium On Research In Computer Security, Dresden, Germany, September 24-26, Proceedings*, pages 375–389, 2007.

[8] Y. Elrakaiby, F. Cuppens, and N. Cuppens-Boulahia. Formal enforcement and management of obligation policies. *Data Knowl. Eng.*, 71:127–147, Jan. 2012.

[9] D. F. Ferraiolo, R. S. Sandhu, S. Gavrila, D. R. Kuhn, and R. Chandramouli. Proposed NIST standard for role-based access control. *ACM Transactions on Information and Systems Security*, pages 224–274, Aug. 2001.

[10] P. Gama and P. Ferreira. Obligation policies: An enforcement platform. In *6th IEEE International Workshop on Policies for Distributed Systems and Networks*, Stockholm, Sweden, June 2005. IEEE Computer Society.

[11] Health Resources and Services Administration. Health insurance portability and accountability act, 1996. Public Law 104-191.

[12] K. Irwin, T. Yu, and W. H. Winsborough. On the modeling and analysis of obligations. In *Proceedings of the 13th ACM conference on Computer and communications security*, pages 134–143, New York, NY, USA, 2006. ACM.

[13] A. J. I. Jones. On the relationship between permission and obligation. In *ICAIL '87*, New York, NY, USA. ACM.

[14] N. Li, H. Chen, and E. Bertino. On practical specification and enforcement of obligations. In *Proceedings of the second ACM conference on Data and application security and privacy*, 2012.

[15] M. J. May, C. A. Gunter, and I. Lee. Privacy APIs: Access control techniques to analyze and verify legal privacy policies. In *CSFW '06*, Washington, DC, USA, 2006. IEEE Computer Society.

[16] L. McCarty. Pemissions and obligations. In *Proceedings IJCAI-83*, 1983.

[17] N. H. Minsky and A. D. Lockman. Ensuring integrity by adding obligations to privileges. In *Proceedings of the 8th international conference on Software engineering*, pages 92–102, Los Alamitos, CA, USA, 1985. IEEE Computer Society Press.

[18] Q. Ni, E. Bertino, and J. Lobo. An obligation model bridging access control policies and privacy policies. In *SACMAT' 08*, New York, NY, USA. ACM.

[19] Q. Ni, A. Trombetta, E. Bertino, and J. Lobo. Privacy-aware role based access control. In *Proceedings of the SACMAT'07*, New York, NY, USA. ACM.

[20] M. Pontual, O. Chowdhury, W. Winsborough, T. Yu, and K. Irwin. Toward Practical Authorization Dependent User Obligation Systems. In *ASIACCS' 10*, pages 180–191. ACM Press, 2010.

[21] M. Pontual, O. Chowdhury, W. H. Winsborough, T. Yu, and K. Irwin. On the management of user obligations. SACMAT '11, New York, NY, USA. ACM.

[22] R. S. Sandhu, V. Bhamidipati, and Q. Munawer. The ARBAC97 model for role-based aministration of roles. *ACM Transactions on Information and Systems Security*, 2(1):105–135, Feb. 1999.

[23] A. Sasturkar, P. Yang, S. Stoller, and C. Ramakrishnan. Policy analysis for administrative role based access control. In *Computer Security Foundations Workshop, 2006. 19th IEEE*, 2006.

[24] S. D. Stoller, P. Yang, C. R. Ramakrishnan, and M. I. Gofman. Efficient policy analysis for administrative role based access control. In *CCS '07*, New York, NY, USA, 2007. ACM.

[25] A. Uszok, J. Bradshaw, R. Jeffers, N. Suri, P. Hayes, M. Breedy, L. Bunch, M. Johnson, S. Kulkarni, and J. Lott. Kaos policy and domain services: Toward a description-logic approach to policy representation, deconfliction, and enforcement. In *POLICY '03*, Washington, DC, USA, 2003. IEEE Computer Society.

[26] XACML TC. Oasis extensible access control markup language (xacml). *http://www.oasis-open.org/committees/xacml/*.

APPENDIX

A. CASCADING OBLIGATIONS EXAMPLE

Let us assume the following policy rules. Policy rule p_1 allows a registered user to submit a paper and this in turn creates an obligation for a user (obligatee) in role reviewer to submit the review of the paper. Rule p_2 authorizes a user in role reviewer to submit a review of a paper and it incurs an obligation for a user in the role PC_chair that requires him to make a decision on the paper. Rule p_3 authorizes a user in role PC_chair to submit a decision for a paper and it incurs an obligation for the same user submitting the decision to notify the corresponding author. Rule p_4 authorizes a user in the role PC_chair to notify the author of a paper. Now,

$p_1 : submit(u, paper) \leftarrow (u \in registeredUser) :$
$F_{obl}(reviewer, s, u, paper, 2 \, days, 1 \, week)$
$\{$

$\quad (Choose \, u_1 \, such \, that \, u_1 \in reviewer)$
$\quad \quad submitReview(u_1, \langle u, paper \rangle)$
$\}$
$p_2 : submitReview(u, \langle author, paper \rangle) \leftarrow (u \in reviewer) :$
$F_{obl}(PC\_Chair, s, u, \langle author, paper \rangle, 1 \, day, 1 \, day)$
$\{$

$\quad (Choose \, u_1 \, such \, that \, u_1 \in PC\_Chair)\{$
$\quad \quad submitDecision(u_1, \langle author, paper \rangle);$
$\quad \}$
$\}$
$p_3 : submitDecision(u, \langle author, paper \rangle) \leftarrow (u \in PC\_Chair) :$
$F_{obl}(Self, s, u, \langle author, paper \rangle, 1 \, day, 1 \, day)$
$\{$

$\quad notify(u, \langle author, paper \rangle)$
$\}$
$p_4 : notify(u, \langle author, paper \rangle) \leftarrow (u \in PC\_Chair) : \varnothing$

consider the following situation. The set of current users of the system is $\gamma.U = \{Alice, Bob, Carol\}$ and their current role assignments are $\gamma.UA = \{\langle Alice, registeredUser \rangle,$ $\langle Bob, reviewer \rangle, \langle Carol, PC\_Chair \rangle\}$. Let us assume Alice submits a paper on 07/01/2012 and according to p_1 Bob (in role reviewer) will get the following obligation $\langle Bob, submit-Review, \langle Alice, paper \rangle, 07/03/2012, 07/10/2012 \rangle$. According to p_2, this obligation in turn will incur the obligation $\langle Carol, submitDecision, \langle Alice, paper \rangle, 07/11/2012, 07/12/2012 \rangle$ for Carol (in role PC_chair). According to p_3 when Carol submits the decision, she incurs the obligation $\langle Carol, notify, \langle Alice, paper \rangle, 07/13/2012, 07/14/2012 \rangle$.

B. REPETITIVE OBLIGATIONS

Let us consider an obligation $b = \{u, a, \vec{o}, t_s, t_e, \delta, \rho, w\}$. This obligation is considered to be infinite repetitive when $\rho = I$ or finite repetitive when $\rho \in \mathbb{N}$ and $\rho > 1$. For finite and infinite repetition of the obligation the possible time intervals of the recurring obligation are the following.

- **Finite Repetitive:** $[t_s, t_e], [t_e + \delta, t_e + \delta + w], \cdots [t_s + (\rho - 1)(w + \delta), t_e + (\rho - 1)(w + \delta)]$.

- **Infinite Repetitive:** $[t_s, t_e], [t_e + \delta, t_e + \delta + w], \cdots [t_s + (n - 1)(w + \delta), t_e + (n - 1)(w + \delta)], \cdots$ where $n \in \mathbb{N}$.

C. COMPLEXITY ANALYSIS OF THE ALGORITHM

Let us consider the current pending pool of obligations is B where $|B| = n$. Moreover, let us consider $B_i \subseteq B$ denotes the set of infinite repetitive obligations in the current pending pool of obligations where $|B_i| = d$. Let us consider the number of policy rules Φ is k. (1) When the new obligation b we want to add incurs a finite number of cascading obligations, the number of finite cascading obligations due to b can be approximated by k. This is due to our restriction that our policies are free of cycles. Furthermore, let us consider that the number of times the infinite repetitive obligations are unrolled is α. Thus, the total number of obligations for which we need to check accountability in this case is $\eta_c = \alpha \times d + k + (n - d)$. Then, we check each of the η obligations are all authorized, which can be done using the non-incremental algorithm presented by Pontual *et al.* [20] in $\mathcal{O}(k\eta_c^2 \times \log(\eta_c))$. (2) In the case b being a finite repetitive obligation, the number of times b needs to be unrolled is $b.\rho$. Let us denote it by m. Thus, the total number of obligations for which we need to check accountability in this case is $\eta_r = \alpha \times d + m + (n - d)$. The resulting complexity of the algorithm in this case will be $\mathcal{O}(k\eta_r^2 \times \log(\eta_r))$ (3) For the case, b is an infinite repetitive obligation, we have to compute the overall period of the obligations in B_i and b. Let, β denote the number of times the obligations in B_i and b needs to be unrolled. Thus, the total number of obligations for which we need to check accountability in this case is $\eta_i = \beta \times (d + 1) + (n - d)$. This results in a time complexity of $\mathcal{O}(k\eta_i^2 \times \log(\eta_i))$.

Generative Models for Access Control Policies: Applications to Role Mining Over Logs with Attribution

Ian Molloy, Youngja Park, Suresh Chari
IBM Research TJ Watson
Hawthorne, NY, USA
{molloyim, young_park, schari}@us.ibm.com

ABSTRACT

We consider a fundamentally new approach to role and policy mining: finding RBAC models which reflect the observed *usage* of entitlements and the *attributes* of users. Such policies are interpretable, i.e., there is a natural explanation of why a role is assigned to a user and are conservative from a security standpoint since they are based on actual usage. Further, such "generative" models provide many other benefits including reconciliation with policies based on entitlements, detection of provisioning errors, as well as the detection of anomalous behavior. Our contributions include defining the fundamental problem as extensions of the well-known role mining problem, as well as providing several new algorithms based on generative machine learning models. Our algorithms find models which are *causally* associated with actual usage of entitlements and any arbitrary combination of user attributes when such information is available. This is the most natural process to provision roles, thus addressing a key usability issue with existing role mining algorithms.

We have evaluated our approach on a large number of real life data sets, and our algorithms produce good role decompositions as measured by metrics such as *coverage, stability*, and *generality*. We compare our algorithms with traditional role mining algorithms by equating usage with entitlement. Results show that our algorithms improve on existing approaches including exact mining, approximate mining, and probabilistic algorithms; the results are more temporally stable than exact mining approaches, and are faster than probabilistic algorithms while removing artificial constraints such as the number of roles assigned to each user. Most importantly, we believe that these roles more accurately capture what users actually *do*, the essence of a role, which is not captured by traditional methods.

Categories and Subject Descriptors

D.4.6 [**Operating Systems**]: Security and Protection—*Access Controls*; H.2.8 [**Database Management**]: Database Applications—*Data Mining*

General Terms

Management, Security, Experimentation

Keywords

access control, RBAC, role mining, generative models

1. INTRODUCTION

Role based access control is a popular model for access control policy and is used widely as it provides a convenient way to specify entitlements corresponding to specific business function. Despite the emergence of alternatives such as ABAC, it still remains the model for access control in most frameworks. There has been considerable work [4,5,10,12,18–21] on the problem of decomposing a set of users and their entitlements into a set of role assignments to users and permissions to roles. Usability is one of the key challenges with current role mining algorithms: roles produced by these algorithms are simply an agglomeration of unrelated permissions, i.e., there is no rationale for why a user is assigned a given role.

This paper considers a fundamentally new approach to finding accurate and usable RBAC models: given data on *usage* of entitlements, we build a *generative* RBAC model, i.e., a model which best explains the observed usage pattern. In the resulting models, users who have the same entitlements but with different usage will, typically, have different roles. A natural example of this is a user who infrequently functions as a backup when the administrator is unavailable: they must have the same entitlements but clearly have distinct roles. Generative RBAC models are interpretable, i.e., there is a natural explanation of why a role is assigned to a user. Extending the definitions of the core role mining problem [19], we formally define the *generative role mining* problem as well as many variants, and provide efficient algorithms for these problems. An important variant is *attributive* generative models, i.e., models where the roles assigned to a user are causally correlated with user attributes [7, 12] (and their combinations) when such information is available. Attribution makes generative models even more usable: users are assigned roles based on their attributes and these roles are assigned to permissions based on usage patterns.

Besides usability, there are a number of other advantages of generative models. From a security standpoint, they are conservative: policy reflects actual usage, thereby reducing operational risk. Further, the roles imply the usage pattern which can be taken into account for risk analysis of assignments. Another use case is for policy reconciliation, i.e., reconciling the usage-based generative model with either intended high level policy or policies derived from entitlements. This yields considerable insight in how provisioned roles are used, e.g., the evolution of role definitions when users acting in certain roles begin to use some permissions more than others. Such analysis can also be used to identify entitlement provisioning errors such as unrevoked permissions (which are never used), as well as users who have attributes different from other users with the same entitlements, which could be a provisioning error. Finally, by comparing generative models across different time periods, we can analyze how usage patterns change and, in particular, detect anomalous changes in usage which may indicate insider attacks or malware controlled access. This paper focuses on the basic algorithms for generative models, and, in ongoing work, we are exploring these other applications.

The algorithms we present are based on generative machine learning techniques of *Latent Dirichlet Allocation (LDA)* [2] and *Author-Topic Model (ATM)* [16], which can be used to obtain a probabilistic assignment. We enhance this with a discretization procedure to convert the probabilistic assignment into actual binary permission to role and role to user assignments. These algorithms are very effective in performance and lead to generative role assignments which explain the observed usage. The models produced by the ATM based algorithm will result in roles which are causally correlated with user attributes such as department, work location, manager name, etc. Our work provides the most general framework for generating such models improving on the work of Frank et al. [7], which considers only a restricted model where a single attribute dictates the role assignment, and Molloy et al. [13], which doesn't directly handle role attribution. There are several variations of the core machine learning models which can all be similarly adapted to yield generative models. Our work can be seen as linking the problem of obtaining generative models to a class of machine learning models in the same vein as the work of Vaidya et al. [19] who link the basic role mining problem to Minimum Tiling and the Discrete Basic problems.

We have extensively validated our algorithms on a range of data sets. A very large data set with over 440 million access log records for about 50 different applications comes from monitoring access to source code repositories at a large IT company. We also validate our algorithms with several entitlement datasets which were used to test other role mining algorithms such as **firewall** and **apj** [4]. Our experiments validate the notion of generative models and attribution. Key conclusions are:

- Our algorithms generate assignments which provide excellent coverage of observed access logs and entitlement data. The coverage is better than comparable earlier algorithms for the entitlements.
- Our algorithms are very efficient and for entitlement data they perform about three orders of magnitude faster than comparable prior algorithms.
- The generative models from access logs are *stable*. We find that the RBAC models produced from different time periods are very similar.
- The attribution algorithms produce role decompositions with good coverage and these are causally tied to conjunctions and disjunctions of attributes.
- They produce good models as measured by traditional

criteria used on RBAC models, e.g., smaller RBAC state. They are also general and have no artificial constraints on the number of roles assigned to a user that some prior approaches have imposed.

Broadly, role mining algorithms can be classified into three categories: *exact optimization* [4, 12, 19, 20], *inexact optimizations* [10, 12, 13], and *probabilistic* [5, 7, 18]. Exact role mining algorithms attempt to find a decomposition which exactly represents the same level of access while optimizing some complexity function. There problems are typically NP-hard [11], and heuristic algorithms are presented. Compared to exact algorithms, the presented approaches result in fewer roles that are not over fit to the data, and are robust to noise. More importantly, exact role mining algorithms produce roles which are just blobs of permissions with no intuition of why these permissions are grouped into roles or assigned to users. Similarly, while *inexact optimization* attempt to relax the restrictions of exact mining algorithms and become robust to noise, they suffer the same problems with semantics, and inexact mining criteria are often too weak to be meaningful [13]. Since [5], several probabilistic role mining algorithms have been proposed, such as DDM and MAC, which are robust to noise in ways more sound than most inexact solutions. However, existing approaches [5,7,18] must place artificial constraints on the models to be efficiently evaluated. Our probabilistic approaches perform better without requiring such constraints.

2. GENERATIVE ROLE MINING

2.1 Problem Definition

To formally define generative role mining, we start with definitions from the role mining literature [10, 19], which defines role mining as the process of automatically transitioning from a non-RBAC system to an RBAC system [1].

Throughout this paper, we will use the following notation to define the inputs to the role mining problem.

- U is a set of users in the system.
- P is a set of permissions in the system.
- UP a binary user-permission mapping, $UP \subseteq U \times P$.

Further, we introduce the following notation to capture generative models and attribution.

- $USAGE$: $U \times P \mapsto \mathbb{Z}$, is a function mapping $(u, p) \in U \times P$ into the number of times u used p.
- $ATTR$, an optional mapping of users to attributes. Each user is typically mapped to a set of key value pairs to define various attributes, e.g., $U \times \mathbb{Z} \to \mathbb{Z}$.

Role mining algorithms compute a set of roles R and the following assignments:

- A permission assignment relation $PA \subseteq R \times P$
- A user assignment $UA \subseteq U \times R$

Given a set of n users, m permissions, and k roles, one can naturally define PA as a $k \times m$ binary matrix whose entry at position (i, j) is 1 if permission j is assigned to role i. Similarly, one can define UA as a $n \times k$ binary matrix. From the function $USAGE$, we define $GUPA$ (generative user permission assignment) as the $n \times m$ binary matrix where the entry (i, j) is 1 if $USAGE(i, j) > 0$, i.e., if the user i has used permission j. Note that $GUPA \subseteq UP$.

Using this we first define the distance of a given assignment. Given two binary matrices, A and B, $A - B$ denotes the binary matrix where the i, j entry is 1 if and only if $A_{i,j} = 1$ and $B_{i,j} = 0$. Also, $\odot$ is the element-wise matrix multiplication, and $\| A \|_1$ is the L_1 norm.

DEFINITION 1 (λ-DISTANCE). *Given UA and PA, we define the λ-distance, $\lambda > 0$, of this assignment to a given usage function USAGE as*

$$\| (GUPA - UA \times PA) \odot USAGE \|_1 + \lambda \times \| UA \times PA - GUPA \|_1$$

The first component gives the number of user actions that cannot be attributed to roles (i.e., under-assignments), and the second component gives the number of over-assignments. We weight each over assignment by a constant λ, which can be chosen based on particulars of the application. Traditional definitions of assignment distance can be obtained by making USAGE binary (0 or 1) and $\lambda = 1$, which measures the hamming distance between the matrices $UA \times PA$ and $GUPA$. Conservative security applications can assign large values of λ to prevent over-assignments. Other natural candidates for λ are the maximum or the mean of the usage function. The λ-distance metric emphasizes mining algorithms which produce good coverage of *used* permissions. The central thesis of this paper is that role mining algorithms should emphasize coverage of these used permissions and not on permissions which are rarely used. With the definition of the λ-distance, we can formally define the generative role mining problem.

DEFINITION 2 (GENERATIVE ROLE MINING). *Given a set of users U, permission P, usage function USAGE, λ parameter, and k, find a set of k roles, R, and corresponding UA and PA relations that minimize the λ-distance.*

Similar to Lu et al. [10], we define several variants, such as minimizing k where λ-distance $< \delta$, including the weighted structural complexity [12], i.e., the size of the UA and PA relations, etc. Since the underlying basic role mining problems can easily be reduced to their generative versions, all the generative mining problems remain NP-complete.

Alternatively, we can adopt the role mining framework of Frank et al. [5–7, 18], to define role mining in a probabilistic framework. Here, role mining is the problem of finding RBAC configurations that most likely produced the observed policy, i.e., maximize $\mathbf{Pr}[UP \mid UA, PA]$. For generative role mining, this simply becomes $\mathbf{Pr}[USAGE \mid UA, PA]$ for usage logs alone, and $\mathbf{Pr}[USAGE \mid UA, PA, ATTR]$ when user attributes are available.

2.2 Algorithms for Generative Role Mining

The generative role mining problem can be addressed using a greedy algorithm or a probabilistic approximation. In this section, we present a simple greedy algorithm for the λ-distance variant which is fast but produces a large number of (unstable). Later sections describe our machine learning algorithms that are more efficient and produce much better role assignments.

Our greedy algorithm is described in Figure 1. Similar to previous greedy solutions to role mining problems [10], we begin with a set of candidate roles and select a subset optimizing the λ-distance function. We make one simplifying assumption that users cannot be assigned roles that would authorize them for permissions they would not otherwise have, i.e., we do not allow over assigning permissions

to users. This makes our greedy algorithm strictly conservative. Simply, the algorithm begins with an empty set of roles, and adds roles one at a time from the set of candidate roles, $Cand$, such that the next role optimizes the λ-distance of the generative role mining problem. For our experiments, we use the FastMiner algorithm [20] to generate our set of candidate roles. The Score calculates the λ-distance, and for simplicity, we assume it will define UA such that there are no over-assignments, corresponding to $\lambda = \infty$.

Input: $USAGE$, the mapping from users and permissions to usage frequency counts; $Cand$, a set of candidate roles; k, the maximum number of roles to select; and λ, the lambda distance for the generative role mining
Output: R, an optimized subset of candidate roles $Cand$
Algorithm:
$R = \emptyset$
while $|R| < k$
$\quad r_i = \underset{r \in Cand}{\arg\max}\ \mathsf{Score}(USAGE, R \cup \{r\}, \lambda)$
$\quad R = R \cup \{r_i\}$
$\quad Cand = Cand \setminus \{r_i\}$
done
return R

Figure 1: Greedy algorithm for the generative role mining problem

2.3 Applications

Usage-based RBAC models define a conservative security policy since users are assigned only those permissions which they actually use and this reduces operational risk. Generative models also model exactly how users actually use the permissions. For instance generative models will distinguish the role of a backup to an administrator who has the same entitlements but only uses them occasionally. Besides these directly apparent benefits, generative role models have many interesting applications which we are investigating in ongoing work.

- **Policy Reconciliation**: Generative models can be used to reconcile with traditional RBAC models built from entitlements. This yields useful insights such as the evolution of role definitions when users begin to use some permissions more than others.
- **Identifying Policy Errors**: Generative models can be used to identify a number of errors in policies such as overprovisioned users as well as users who have different attributes than other users using the same permisions.
- **Anomaly Detection**: By comparing generative models across different periods of time, one can deduce changes in user behavior in terms of permission usage. This could flag anomalous behavior such as user who starts using an entirely new set of permissions.

3. RELATED WORK

The problem of role engineering was first proposed by Coyne [3] as a top-down approach to role modeling. Kuhlmann et al. [9] then proposed role engineering as a bottom-up data mining problem, leading to a tremendous amount of work on formally defining different role mining problems as constraint optimizations. Most of these define a complexity model for an RBAC state, and attempt to optimize this metric. For example, role minimization [4,10,19], the size of the user-assignment and permission-assignment relations [4,10], assignments including role hierarchies [21], etc. Molloy et al. [12] defined weighted structural complexity which subsumes many of these measures.

Another active area is the problem of mining with noisy data, most notably through probabilistic role mining algorithms. The disjoint decomposition model (DDM) [5], based on the infinite relational model [8], assigns each user to a *single* business role, and each permission to a single functional role. A two-layer role hierarchy connects business roles to technical roles, authorizing permissions to users. This model has the problem of significant under-assignment in some use cases. Multi-assignment clustering (MAC) [18] for binary relations removes the restriction of a single role for each user and permission. MAC assumes that each assignment (u, p) comes from either a signal or a noise distribution, and the signal allows each user to obtain a permission from multiple clusters it is assigned. To calculate the fitness of the data, called the risk, requires model evaluation for all cluster sets, which is exponential and must be constrained.

Finally, several recent works propose role mining algorithms with some attribution by connecting roles to user attributes. The MAC algorithm has since be extended to include user attributes [7] where the risk measure is weighted with a role's attribute compliance, the number of attributes shared by users assigned the role. The method given works for a single attribute type, such as the user's *title* or *job code*. Molloy et al. [13] use collective matrix factorization [17] to clean and preprocess the user-permission(UP) and user-attribute(UA) relations prior to role mining. Collective matrix factorization will produce a decomposition that shares a factor over the common dimension, i.e., $UA \approx A \times B^T$, $UP \approx B \times C^T$. The resulting factors are not boolean, and cannot be directly interpreted as roles. While we believe the techniques developed in this work can be applied to interpreting A, B, and C in the context of RBAC, we instead focus on applying the generative machine learning models.

We note that prior work does not consider the actions a user *actually* performs. While the problem of noise in entitlement data considers users who have been over-provisioned, it fails to address the problem of why a user is assigned a role. By directly mining on user access log data, role mining algorithms can more accurately determine which privileges are important to the tasks performed by the user, i.e., those used frequently versus those that may be provided in error or though temporary delegation.

4. MACHINE LEARNING MODELS

One of the key contributions of this paper is to adapt and formulate the problem of finding generative models and variants, to a family of techniques in machine learning. These generative machine learning models have been developed for unsupervised topic discovery in a large collection of documents, and attempt to explain how the observations (documents) were generated given certain hidden parameters. They learn the joint probability distribution between observations and latent parameters and then use Bayesian models to infer the parameters given these observations. This is conceptually close to the problem of explaining a set of observed logs by associating them with latent roles.

In this paper we focus on the application of two widely used generative models —Latent Dirichlet Allocation (LDA) and author-topic models (ATM) [2, 15]—to generative role mining. We translate the problem of finding latent roles to the problem of latent semantic analysis i.e. finding the latent topics in a collection of documents. These generative models are well suited for role mining applications since they require no manual labels and allow users to have multiple roles. We provide a few details of LDA and ATM models, and how we can apply them to role mining.

4.1 Latent Dirichlet Allocation (LDA)

LDA is a probabilistic generative model for collections of discrete data such as documents [2]. Each document in a corpus is modeled as a finite mixture over underlying set of topics, and each topic is, in turn, modeled as a probabilistic distribution over words. LDA assumes the following generative process for creating a document d in a corpus $\mathcal{D}$:

1. For each document d, a distribution over topics is sampled from a Dirichlet distribution, $\theta \sim Dir(\alpha)$.
2. For each word w in the document, a single topic, z, is selected according to the distribution, $Multinomial(\theta)$.
3. Finally, a word is chosen from a multinomial distribution over words specific to the topic, $p(w|z, \phi)$. ϕ is a matrix of word probabilities over topics which is to be estimated from the training data.

Note that LDA allows an arbitrary number of topics assigned to a document. For role mining, we can model each user's observed actions (document) as a finite mixture over an underlying set of roles (topics) which we can estimate using LDA.

4.2 Author-Topic Model (ATM)

Author-topic model (ATM) extends LDA by adding authors of the documents in the modeling process and aims to simultaneously model the content of documents and the interests of authors [15,16]. ATM assumes the following process to generate a document d: For each word in d, an author is randomly chosen. Then a topic is chosen from a multinomial distribution over topics specific to the author, and the word is generated from the selected topic. Therefore, a multi-author document inherits the mixture of probability distributions associated with each author, allowing the mixture weights for different topics to be determined by the document authors.

An author is represented by a multinomial distribution over topics, and each topic is represented as a probability distribution over words. Assume there are T topics and W words created by A authors in a text collection. The multinomial distribution over topics for each author is parameterized by Θ of size $T \times A$, where θ_{ta} represents the probability of assigning topic t to a word generated by author a. The multinomial distributions of topics over words are parameterized by Φ of size $W \times T$, where ϕ_{wt} represents the probability of generating word w from topic t.

Author-topic models can be adapted to role mining with explicit attribution. User attributes will be the authors and as before the documents are the observed usage and topics the roles. By learning the parameters of the model, we can extract the set of topics (roles) in a corpus ($USAGE$), and identify which topics (roles) are generated by which authors (user attributes).

5. GENERATIVE ROLE MODELS

This section describes how we apply LDA to identify an appropriate set of roles assigned to users. We first outline how to recast the *role mining* problem into topic discovery for a corpus of documents. As noted earlier, LDA produces a probability distribution θ over the topics for each user and a distribution ϕ from topics to words. We provide a *discretization* algorithm that transforms the probability distributions into discrete role and permission assignments, and henceafter call our algorithm dLDA.

5.1 Role Mining using LDA

The translation of role mining problem to topic discovery is fairly straightforward. We consider each *user* as a *document* in a corpus, and the individual *permissions* assigned to users as the *words* in documents. A user's usage count of a particular permission is treated as the number of times a word appeared in a document. Finally, *topics* correspond to the *roles* to assign to users. Thus, by using LDA, we are seeking an optimal set of *roles* which can explain the observed corpus of permissions used by all the users.

LDA takes as input two Dirichlet priors α and β for the distribution of documents over topics and the distribution of topics over words respectively; the number of iterations for parameter estimation; and the total number of topics, K, to discover from the given corpus. α defines a prior belief of seeing topic z in a document before any of its word counts was observed. Similarly, β describes a prior belief of seeing word w in a topic z before having observed any words of that topic. One can customize α and β to a specific corpus when domain knowledge on the data is available. In this work, we don't attempt to customize our algorithms towards individual data, and use a default value, 0.01, for both α and β throughout the experiments. Further, all results are obtained from 1,000 iterations of sampling. The total number of topics K is determined dynamically based on the number of documents, $|D|$, using $\sqrt{|D|}$. We note that, by using LDA, only the maximum number of roles a user can be assigned (K) needs to be determined in advance, and, there are no constraints on what or how many roles are assigned to a particular user, which is a significant improvement over prior approaches [5, 18].

5.2 Discretization of probability distribution

As described in Sec. 5.1, invoking LDA results in a set of k roles, and probability distributions θ and ϕ which map users into roles and roles into permissions respectively. For a user u, the distribution for u, θ_u, will be a probability distribution over the k roles, i.e., $\theta_{u,r}$ is the probability that user u will be in role r. Similarly, ϕ_r for a role r will define a distribution over the individual permissions. For role mining, we need to discretize these probability distributions to obtain binary assignments of roles to users and permissions to roles.

We observe that, in all cases, the distributions show a sharp drop-off after a few values and one can order the probability distributions for a particular user or role in decreasing order. Our discretization algorithm essentially goes through the probability vector finding an optimal point at which we stop assigning roles to users or permissions to roles. The objective of the discretization process is to find the optimal value t_i and ℓ_j for each user and role respectively, and assign the top t_i roles and the top ℓ_j permissions. Thus, the vectors $\vec{t}$ define the user-assignment, UA and $\vec{\ell}$ define the permission-assignment, PA, relations. Our discretization is *monotonic*, i.e., if $\theta_{u,r_1} \geq \theta_{u,r_2}$, then user u will be assigned role r_1 whenever he is assigned role r_2.

Finding the optimal values for each user and role depends on the desired optimization criteria. For example, the Hamming distance between $GUPA$ and $UA \times PA$ is the δ-consistency [10], which can be altered to weight over- and under-assignments differently, yielding more conservative solutions. Alternatively, the λ-distance can be used. Regardless, we assume a distance function $D(USAGE \parallel \vec{t}, \vec{\ell})$.

For each user role, we now have a linear set of candidate assignments, $O(k)$, down from $O(2^k)$ in MAC, however the entire search space is still large, i.e., $O(k^n m^k)$. We begin with an initial random assignment of the top roles to users and permissions to users, and use an annealing framework to iteratively converge towards an optimal assignment. To understand, imagine we know the optimal role assignments of all users and all but one role; we can perform a linear search to compute the missing value that optimizes the distance function. When not all values are optimal, we iteratively perform this optimization. While this may work well in practice, it often produces a local optima. The annealing framework allows controlled randomization that stabilizes over time. In deterministic annealing [14] we probabilistically accept an updated $\vec{t'}$ by drawing from a distribution
$$\mathbf{Pr}\left[\exp((D(USAGE \parallel \vec{t}, \vec{\ell}) - D(USAGE \parallel \vec{t'}, \vec{\ell}))/T)/\mathcal{Z}\right],$$
where $\mathcal{Z}$ is a normalization factor and T is the temperature. Initially T is high, resulting in a uniform, and it is slowly decreased to stabilize the samples. This process is executed by performing all calculations based on the previous iteration, such that the roles and users appear to update *simultaneously*. We can also use a simulated annealing framework where new samples $\vec{t'}$ are drawn proportional to $\exp(-D(USAGE \parallel \vec{t'}, \vec{\ell})/T)$. The algorithm is described in detail in Algorithm 1.

6. EVALUATION

We have evaluated our new generative algorithms on a large number of real life data sets including both access logs as well as purely entitlement data. On both types of data, our algorithms produce very good, stable role decompositions validating the concept of generative models. We have also compared our algorithms with prior role mining algorithms on a range of parameters, and, in almost all cases, our algorithms perform significantly better. This section describes the data sets and the evaluation results.

6.1 Data Set for Evaluation

The data sets we primarily use to validate our algorithms are a large number of access logs from a source code version control of a large IT company. These logs record all the commands issued by users of the control over a span of four years. The total number of access control records in this data is in excess of 440 million! The version control system stores in each log record the user key, the software product or application that was accessed, the name of the file resource and the action performed on the resource (e.g. FileCheckOut, FileCheckIn, etc.) as well as the start and end time and the result of the command. Table 1 provides a high level overview of the data set.

For the experiments, we selected the access logs of successfully completed actions and ignored failed or unautho-

Discretization($USAGE, \theta, \phi, \gamma, maxIter$)
Input:
$USAGE$: user-permission usage frequency relation
θ : probability distributions of users over roles
ϕ : probability distributions of roles over permissions
γ : temperature decreasing rate
$maxIter$: the maximum number of iterations
Output:
UA : binary assignments of users to roles
PA : binary assignments of roles to permissions

begin
    $\vec{t} \leftarrow \mathbb{Z}^k$ random initialization for UA;
    $\vec{\ell} \leftarrow \mathbb{Z}^m$ random initialization for PA;
    $T \leftarrow$ initial temperature ;
    $i \leftarrow 0$;
    while *not converged or* $i \leq maxIter$ **do**
        foreach *user u* **do**
            $\vec{t'} \leftarrow \vec{t}$;
            $t'_u \leftarrow [\max(0, t_u - \epsilon), \min(k, t_u + \epsilon)]$;
            if $D(USAGE \parallel \vec{t'}, \vec{\ell}) < D(USAGE \parallel \vec{t}, \vec{\ell})$ **then**
                Accept t'_u ;
            else
                Accept t'_u with probability
                $\mathbf{Pr}\left[\exp((D(USAGE \parallel \vec{t}, \vec{\ell}) - D(USAGE \parallel \vec{t'}, \vec{\ell}))/T)/\mathcal{Z}\right]$;
            end
        end
        ; /* Repeat for role-permission assignments */
        $\vec{t} \leftarrow \vec{t'}$;
        $\vec{\ell} \leftarrow \vec{\ell'}$;
        Update UA_i and PA_i *simultaneously*, all at once
        with recorded changes ;
        $T \leftarrow \gamma * T$;
    end
end

Algorithm 1: Simulated annealing discretization algorithm for converting probability distributions to binary role and permission assignments

total number of records	445,551,191
number of unique applications	50
number of unique actions	196
number of unique users	10,598

Table 1: Statistics of the access log data set

rized accesses. We divided the four year time period into six month slices and created generative RBAC models for each application and each six month time slice. In each time period, we only consider applications which meet a *minimum requirement* for the amount of data: the number of users using that application during the time period is at least 50.

We used the same data sets to evaluate our attribution algorithms using various user attributes that were obtained from the company's LDAP directory. The attributes we used in our evaluation were the employee's organization *division*, the *manager's name* (indicative of a particular group), if the user is a *manager or not*, and the user's *employment type* (e.g., "full-time", "part-time", or "contractor").

In addition to the above access control logs, we also use several datasets from more traditional applications of role mining. These include a number of static access control policies, some public, some proprietary. The public datasets are from HP Labs [4], in particular we focus on **firewall1**,

Dataset	Num. of Roles	MAC	dLDA
Firewall	15	16.1h	55s
Firewall	25	28.6h	88s
APJ	25	122.5h	529s
Customer	15	3.4h	37s

Table 2: Time comparison of dLDA and MAC

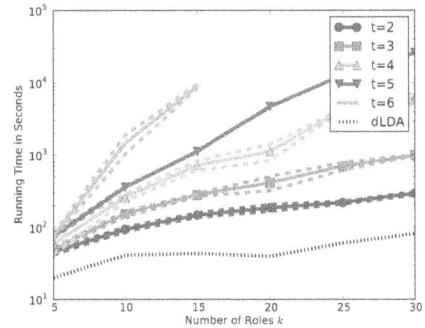

Figure 2: Performance comparison of dLDA ($t = k$) and MAC with different value of t (max roles per user). Note time is on a log scale.

a firewall policy, and **apj**, a Cisco firewall used to provision external users access to HP resources. We also use proprietary data sets, **customer**, which represent administrative access to various resources. The **customer** data sets also contain attribute information about users.

6.2 Role Mining Results

6.2.1 Performance

Our algorithms perform well on almost all data sets containing access logs or entitlements. For example, on a single application with 36M actions by 2050 users, our algorithm is able to produce a good stable decomposition in less than one hour. For the same application, the greedy algorithm, while faster, produces over 270K candidate roles, resulting in a slower pruning process. To compare with prior algorithms, we evaluate the performance on entitlement data against MAC, the only other state of the art probabilistic role mining algorithm. The biggest advantage of our algorithm is the *dramatic* performance improvements of several orders of magnitude. Table 2 compares running time of our algorithm with MAC over a range of datasets. We restricted the total number of roles to 25 and 15 since increasing this value will cause MAC to run unreasonably long. The key reason for the performance improvements is that MAC enumerates all possible assignments of k roles, i.e., $O(2^k)$, and then optimizes the assignment of permissions to the roles. Due to slow performance, MAC is often restricted to assign at most $t < k$ roles to each user. Figure 2 illustrates the impact on restricting the maximum number of roles on the running time of MAC compared to our LDA-based approach.

6.2.2 Coverage

A set of candidate roles can be measured by how well the roles enable the users to perform their tasks (i.e., *coverage*). Traditionally, this is measured by the Hamming distance

Start Date	Number of Applications				
	All	Coverage			
		$\geq 80\%$	$\geq 90\%$	$\geq 95\%$	$\geq 99\%$
2007-08-01	1	1	1	0	0
2008-02-01	6	6	6	6	1
2008-08-01	17	17	16	10	1
2009-02-01	21	21	20	12	1
2009-08-01	21	20	20	13	1
2010-02-01	18	17	16	10	1
2010-08-01	13	13	12	6	0

Table 3: Number of apps meeting minimum data requirements (six month windows).

App	Users	Perms	Roles	Assign.	Over	Uncov.
App 1	140	101	11	1654	0	7.63
App 2	143	100	11	1678	0	4.79
App 3	1530	122	39	17613	76	2.68
App 4	568	138	23	7875	1	6.39
App 5	214	116	14	2254	2	3.17
App 6	689	127	26	14722	31	4.12
App 7	98	92	9	1331	0	1.26
App 8	503	122	22	9530	0	1.39
App 9	52	104	7	1031	5	5.04
App 10	270	110	16	4372	23	6.89
App 11	93	69	9	815	1	4.65
App 12	157	107	12	1972	0	0.99
App 13	94	105	9	1169	6	3.84
App 14	64	66	8	931	2	4.52
App 15	246	121	15	3022	2	11.04

Table 4: Performance of dLDA for a six month time period beginning 01 Feb. 2009

between the input policy and the resulting role decomposition. When user access logs are taken into account, it can be better measured by the λ-distance, the percentage of the access logs that can be attributed to roles. Actions which users perform infrequently or performed by a small number of users may be exceptions, permissions directly assigned to the users, or delegation.

We compare the coverage of our generative models (dLDA) with our greedy algorithm and MAC across a number of application logs and six-month time windows drawn from the source code repository logs. Table 3 shows the number of applications in each time window, and the number of applications that achieve high levels of coverage from 80% to 99% using dLDA. As we can see, dLDA have very good coverage across most applications and time periods achieving the $\geq 90\%$ coverage level for almost all applications.

Table 4 shows more detailed performance for a specific time period across all applications. The names of each application have been anonymized. Note that our algorithm does produce a small number of over-assignments. The table presents the over-assignments and coverage instead of presenting the unified λ-distance. As can be seen, the specific results show even better coverage, with some applications more than 99%. A small number of applications, however, do not have good coverage due to insufficient data. See Appendix A. In general, we can increase the performance by increasing the size from which we draw usage data.

We have also compared our results with MAC and our greedy algorithm based on FastMiner to generate candidate roles. First, we produce a binary UP relation from the

$USAGE$ relation, such that we assign a user a permission if they used it at least once. The MAC algorithm is applied to the binary relation, and, using the $USAGE$ relation, we calculate the coverage as the λ-distance for $\lambda = 0$. For our greedy algorithm, we apply the FastMiner algorithm on the binary UP relation to produce a set of candidate roles. We then apply our greedy algorithm such that there are no over assignments. Note that the larger the candidate set of roles, the tighter we expect the coverage to be.

The results are shown in Table 5. We can clearly see that all three algorithms adequately cover the permission usage logs, but each has a trade off. Some assignments may have been used a small number of times by a small cluster of users, resulting in MAC defining a role for these assignments. Our generative approach did not recognize the infrequent usage as a role, resulting in slightly decreased coverage and more under assignments, but also fewer over assignments. Many infrequent operations are for sensitive operations, and should not be over assigned. We do find that the greedy algorithm outperforms both our generative role mining algorithm and MAC on coverage in the majority of the example datasets. This is not surprising, and we would expect any role mining algorithm that specifically optimizes a fitness function, such as WSC or λ-distance, will. However, it is not clear that the resulting roles are meaningful, and often represent infrequently used permissions. In the next section, we will illustrate that the roles from both MAC and our greedy algorithm produce roles that are unstable—they are over fit to the data observed in each six month time period and must undergo significant alterations in each time period to perform consistently.

6.2.3 Mining Entitlement Data

We have also compared our generative role mining algorithm with MAC on entitlement data. To mimic permission usage logs, we assign a default value, w to each user-permission pair, and then apply our generative role mining algorithm as usual. In Section 6.3 we discuss the impact of w. Here, we compare each algorithm's ability to reconstruct the original input user-permission relation and measure the normalized Hamming distance for varying values of k. For performance reasons, we restrict MAC to at most two roles per user. We later relaxed this restriction to three without a significant improvement. Due to the running time of MAC, we were not able to relax the restriction further. The final results for varying values of k are shown in Figure 3. This figure clearly illustrate the performance of our generative approach is comparable to MAC for entitlement data, and even outperforms MAC on the **Customer** dataset.

6.2.4 Stability

A crucial assumption in RBAC is that the permissions assigned to a role and the basic role structure should be largely static over time, while the users assigned to the roles (and implicitly how much the users use each role) may change over time. This reduces the administrative complexity, and underlies the intuition behind weighted structural complexity measures [12] used throughout the role mining literature [4, 10, 19]. We evaluate how well our log-based role mining algorithm produces static roles by measuring the stability or consistency of the permissions assigned to the role when mined from different time periods. For each six-month period, we run our dLDA algorithm to produce a set of roles,

		dLDA		MAC		Greedy	
Data	Assignments	Over	Uncovered (%)	Over	Uncovered (%)	Over	Uncovered (%)
App 8	9530	0	1.3	1306	0.4	0	0.2
App 9	1031	5	5.0	93	24.4	0	0.8
App 11	815	1	4.6	84	16.7	0	1.9
App 12	1972	0	0.9	251	0.5	0	0.2
App 14	931	2	4.5	119	19.4	0	1.4
App 16	489	1	7.7	69	1.1	0	4.8
App 17	309	0	11.8	23	7.1	0	7.5
App 18	3659	3	10.4	339	4.3	0	1.0
App 19	662	4	14.5	100	3.4	0	5.5
App 20	146	0	3.0	4	90.1	0	2.4
App 21	431	0	6.3	67	10.6	0	1.8
App 22	206	0	2.2	13	1.2	0	0.5
App 23	2738	5	2.8	277	1.7	0	0.5
App 24	568	1	7.6	73	08.9	0	1.5

Table 5: Comparison of the coverage and number of over assignments for the our generative role mining algorithm, MAC, and our greedy algorithm based on FastMiner. Our LDA-based approach produces very high coverage of the access logs, without the larger number of over assignments seen in MAC.

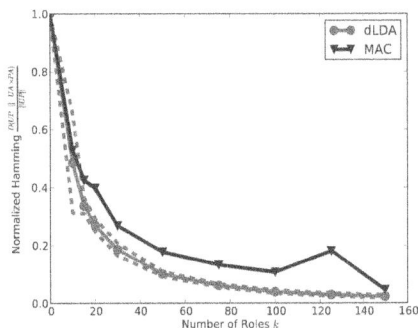

Figure 3: Hamming distance of dLDA ($w = 10$) and MAC with fixed number of roles on Customer.

and measure the stability as a maximal matching between roles in one set with roles in a second set as described independently by Molloy et al. [13] and Frank et al. [6]. By finding the closest one-to-one matching between the roles, we calculate how dissimilar the matched roles are using a distance function, such as the Jaccard distance. The more dissimilar, the less stable the roles are. We also compare the probabilistic algorithms against a more traditional role mining algorithm, FastMiner, when restricting FastMiner to the same fixed number of roles and applying our greedy algorithm to maximize the λ-distance.

Given n six-month time periods, we mine the roles in each time period, and calculate the dissimilarity for all n^2-1 role-set pairs. All scores are normalized for each role. The results are plotted as histograms indicating the overall performance of the algorithm for the given dataset, and a normal distribution is fitted to the data as shown in Figure 4. It can clearly be seen that the roles produced by our generative algorithm are more stable across all time periods, i.e., requiring few changes over a five year period. This is a key property the roles should have to ensure their adoption and continued use.

6.3 Impact of Parameters in dLDA

As described in Section 2, the generative role modeling algorithms take as input the weight or usage count of permissions by each user. Access logs provide accurate usage

information, enabling direct application of generative modeling to role mining. However, we note that this information may not be obtained in some situations. In the absence of this information, one can use a constant weight w or some arbitrary weights based on domain experts' knowledge on how often permissions are actually used by users. In this section, we discuss how different values of w would impact on the performance of our generative methods.

Intuitively, low values of w, say $w = 1$, don't yield good results for several reasons. Firstly, permissions which are assigned to few users are effectively ignored leading to poor coverage. Secondly, with small weights, the gap between a permission being used by a user and not being used at all is not significant. We have evaluated this with a number of values for w and, as intuition suggests, increasing w leads to better results but increasing beyond $w = 10$ does not improve performance. On a small number of experimental data sets, we observed erratic behavior for small values of w, as seen in Figure 5. To understand why low w values may be unstable, consider the following analogy: if a user is authorized to use a permission, but only uses it once, it's not a significant permission that defines a user's roles. Further, the significance between a user using a permission zero times or once is not significant. One can also observe that there is more variance in the resulting roles for low values of w, as seen in the **apj** dataset[1].

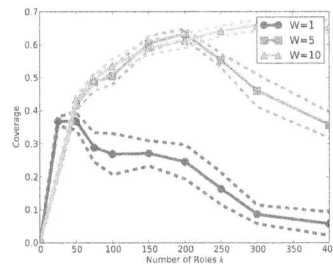

Figure 5: Impact of the permission weight, w, on role coverage.

---

[1]This also results in more local optima the discretization algorithm must avoid.

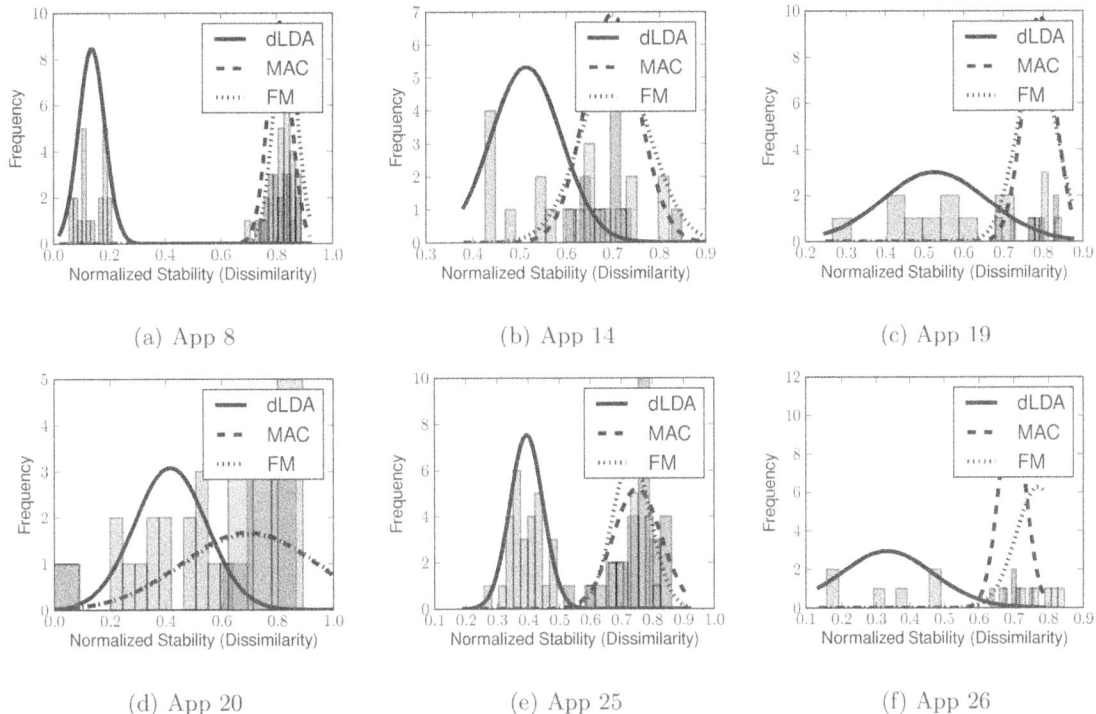

(a) App 8   (b) App 14   (c) App 19

(d) App 20   (e) App 25   (f) App 26

Figure 4: Stability of dLDA compared to MAC and our FM-based greedy algorithm. The y-axis denotes frequency of stability from pairs of roles from different time periods. Lower x-values are better.

7. ROLE ATTRIBUTION WITH ATM: MINING ABAC POLICIES

For role mining with explicit attribution, we use the Author-Topic model which extends the models of LDA. We assume that besides the user-permission data, we are also given a list of attribute values for each user. The goal is to find a role decomposition which is correlated with the attributes of the user. The translation of this problem to ATM is again straightforward: As before, the *words* are the individual permissions, the *documents* are the users (permissions assigned to the users). In addition, the *authors* are the attributes of the individual users.

Abstractly, applying this model to access control logs produces the following analogy describing their creation. First, an attribute, or set of attributes, are selected that define some job function of the user. From these attributes, we select a role through which the user will act, and will provision them the necessary permissions to function in the job. Finally, given the role (which is selected solely from the user's attributes), we select an action the user will perform. Succinctly, it is the attributes which entitle the user's to roles, and thus permissions.

ATM can thus be used to obtain a distribution from authors to topics, i.e., from the user attributes to the assigned roles, in addition to the distribution ϕ, from topics to words. This yields a role decomposition which has explicit attribution. As before, we will need to discretize these distributions to explicit role assignments for each user. For a given user, we average the probability distribution corresponding to the each of the attributes of this user. This yields a probability distribution over assigned roles which can be discretized as described in Section 5.2.

7.1 Preprocessing

Very crucial to the performance of ATM is the choice of relevant user attributes to use in the model, as well as cleansing the values of these attributes. First, attribute values need to be inspected to rationalize different values which are semantically the same (e.g., country = USA and country = US). Further, using all user attributes results in poor performance and greatly increase the time to fit the model to the data. A simple measure to identify relevant attributes is to discard any attribute value which is not assigned to more than a threshold number of users [7,13].

7.2 Allowing arbitrary attributes

In contrast to prior approaches [7], we want to allow any arbitrary number of attributes to imply a role. In particular, using the *kernel-trick* from machine learning, we precompute attributes which are boolean functions of the original attributes and use these as the authors in ATM. In our implementation, we use a few optimizations: Typically in the provisioning of entitlements, one *never* uses the negation of an attribute to provision roles. In the author-topic model, attributes will be selected uniformly, and any attributes may imply the assignment of a given role. As a result, role assignment through disjunction is provided "for free", Thus the only boolean functions we need to consider are only conjunctions as disjunctions arise naturally from the definition of the ATM. As a further optimization, we only consider conjunctions with at most three conjuncts since we believe that for larger conjuncts it is more natural to define a new attribute reflecting these larger conjunctions. This is not a limitation but simply a design choice. Ours is the first to allow for both disjunctions and conjunctions of attributes to imply permissions and roles.

App	LDA		AT Single		AT Conj.	
	Over	Uncov.	Over	Uncov.	Over	Uncov.
App 1	0	1.4	0	15.8	4	26.8
App 2	0	4.6	0	19.3	0	9.5
App 3	4	5.2	0	25.8	0	26.3
App 5	7	3.5	0	23.0	2	32.5
App 7	2	1.2	0	0.4	0	0.4
App 10	6	6.8	14	28.3	10	29.2
App 11	0	4.7	0	49.7	0	43.0
App 12	0	0.9	0	23.9	0	36.2
App 13	1	5.2	4	29.8	14	28.8
App 14	3	4.4	0	23.2	1	27.7
App 18	12	6.2	5	15.1	8	15.9
App 25	6	1.4	16	17.9	14	22.7

Table 6: Performance of Attribution based mining

7.3 Evaluation of ATM based mining

Evaluation on the same data sets shows that the ATM-based algorithm performs almost as well as the LDA-based algorithm. For the same coverage, the ATM based algorithm needs an additional number of roles. This is natural since the attribution requires a user to possess a set of attributes to be authorized a to a particular role which decreases the coverage of a given set of roles. This effect was also observed by Frank et al. [7], but is different from the net-positive effect observed by Molloy et al. [13] where fuzzy (non-boolean) relations are fit to the data.

Table 6 summarizes our results for attributive role mining. The table shows coverage using the simple LDA models, using just single attributes independently and with conjunction of two or more attributes given as new attributes. First the results show that attributive generative models including arbitrary combination of user attributes is feasible. As noted in the table, for the same number of overall roles the coverage decreases with single attributes and further with arbitrary combinations. This is an intuitive tradeoff between semantically meaningful roles, and fitness to the data. Some of the applications don't have very good coverage with attributes, and some explanations could be that the set of attributes we considered were not appropriate for that application or users' roles evolved in the time slice we evaluated, etc.

8. CONCLUSION

This paper proposed a new approach to producing usable RBAC models: mining roles from *usage* of permissions. Such models reflect the actual pattern of usage and are therefore interpretable and address one of the key challenges of role mining *i.e.* producing meaningful roles. Another key contribution of this paper is to relate role mining to a class of machine learning algorithms. We showed how to use generative machine learning models such as LDA and ATM for mining roles from both usage records as well as from entitlements. Extensive validation over large data sets shows that our algorithms are efficient and produce compact, stable decompositions and on many criteria do better than most prior algorithms. A key variant that we considered was mining roles causally related to user attributes and our algorithms thus yield very natural decompositions suitable for ABAC policies. Both our algorithms solve their problems in full generality and remove many constraints assumed in prior work. We believe that *generative* models and the machine learning techniques we outlined are very promising and will lead to many new applications of role mining.

Acknowledgment

We would like to thank Mario Frank for his comments and suggestions on an earlier draft of this paper.

9. REFERENCES

[1] ANSI. Role-based access control. Technical Report ANSI INCITS 359-2004, 2004.

[2] D. Blei, A. Ng, and M. Jordan. Latent dirichlet allocation. *J. Mach. Learning Research*, 3, 2003.

[3] E. J. Coyne. Role engineering. In *ACM RBAC*, 1995.

[4] A. Ene, W. Horne, N. Milosavljevic, P. Rao, R. Schreiber, and R. E. Tarjan. Fast exact and heuristic methods for role minimization problems. In *SACMAT*, 2008.

[5] M. Frank, D. A. Basin, and J. M. Buhmann. A class of probabilistic models for role engineering. In *CCS*, 2008.

[6] M. Frank, J. M. Buhmann, and D. Basin. On the definition of role mining. In *SACMAT*, 2010.

[7] M. Frank, A. Streich, D. Basin, and J. Buhmann. A probabilistic approach to hybrid role mining. In *CCS*, 2009.

[8] C. Kemp, J. B. Tenenbaum, T. L. Griffiths, T. Yamada, and N. Ueda. Learning systems of concepts with an infinite relational model. In *AAAI*, 2006.

[9] M. Kuhlmann, D. Shohat, and G. Schimpf. Role mining - revealing business roles for security administration using data mining technology. In *SACMAT*, 2003.

[10] H. Lu, J. Vaidya, and V. Atluri. Optimal boolean matrix decomposition: Application to role engineering. In *ICDE*, 2008.

[11] I. Molloy, H. Chen, T. Li, Q. Wang, N. Li, E. Bertino, S. Calo, and J. Lobo. Mining roles with multiple objectives. *TISSEC*, 13(4):36, Dec 2010.

[12] I. Molloy, H. Chen, T. Li, Q. Wang, N. Li, E. Bertino, S. B. Calo, and J. Lobo. Mining roles with semantic meanings. In *SACMAT*, 2008.

[13] I. Molloy, N. Li, J. Lobo, Y. A. Qi, and L. Dickens. Mining roles with noisy data. In *SACMAT*, 2010.

[14] K. Rose. Deterministic annealing for clustering, compression, classification, regression, and related optimization problems. *Proc. of the IEEE*, (86), 1998.

[15] M. Rosen-Zvi, C. Chemudugunta, T. Griffiths, P. Smyth, and M. Steyvers. Learning author-topic models from text corpora. *TOIS*, 28(1), 2010.

[16] M. Rosen-Zvi, T. Griffiths, M. Steyvers, and P. Smyth. The author-topic model for autors and documents. In *UAI*, 2004.

[17] A. P. Singh and G. J. Gordon. Relational learning via collective matrix factorization. In *KDD*, 2008.

[18] A. P. Streich, M. Frank, D. Basin, and J. M. Buhmann. Multi-assignment clustering for boolean data. In *ICML*, 2009.

[19] J. Vaidya, V. Atluri, and Q. Guo. The role mining problem: finding a minimal descriptive set of roles. In *SACMAT*, 2007.

[20] J. Vaidya, V. Atluri, and J. Warner. Roleminer: mining roles using subset enumeration. In *CCS*, 2006.

[21] D. Zhang, K. Ramamohanarao, and T. Ebringer. Role engineering using graph optimisation. In *SACMAT*, 2007.

APPENDIX

A. AMOUNT OF DATA

One potential shortcoming of the generative models is the amount of data that's required to sufficiently train a model. For highly active applications, for example, databases, this is unlikely to cause problems and within a short time interval most users should generate enough traffic to allow the models to be trained. Other applications are less active. This has several implications. The first is that the generative models cannot separate the actions produced by true roles, from background noise; the signal to noise ratio is too low. The result is the user-role and role-permission distributions more closely resemble a uniform distribution. The second result is that these learned models have more variation and variability, and are less stable.

To illustrate these observations, we plot the relationship between the average number of actions per user against the percentage of the access logs that cannot be attributed to the roles mined after applying the discretization process to the generative models after relaxing our data requirements to allow time periods with fewer users. We notice two properties. First, there is a statistically significant decrease in the number of uncovered actions as the number of actions per user increases. Second, we observe more variance in the number of uncovered actions when the number of actions per user is low. See Figure 6. These experiments provide some boundaries on the minimum number of actions required before mining may yield desirable results.

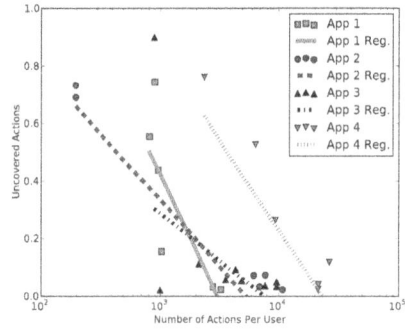

Figure 6: Coverage versus Quantity of Input Data

Algorithms for Mining Meaningful Roles*

Zhongyuan Xu
Department of Computer Science
Stony Brook University, USA
zhoxu@cs.stonybrook.edu

Scott D. Stoller
Department of Computer Science
Stony Brook University, USA
stoller@cs.stonybrook.edu

ABSTRACT

Role-based access control (RBAC) offers significant advantages over lower-level access control policy representations, such as access control lists (ACLs). However, the effort required for a large organization to migrate from ACLs to RBAC can be a significant obstacle to adoption of RBAC. Role mining algorithms partially automate the construction of an RBAC policy from an ACL policy and possibly other information, such as user attributes. These algorithms can significantly reduce the cost of migration to RBAC.

This paper proposes new algorithms for role mining. The algorithms can easily be used to optimize a variety of policy quality metrics, including metrics based on policy size, metrics based on interpretability of the roles with respect to user attribute data, and compound metrics that consider size and interpretability. The algorithms all begin with a phase that constructs a set of candidate roles. We consider two strategies for the second phase: start with an empty policy and repeatedly add candidate roles, or start with the entire set of candidate roles and repeatedly remove roles. In experiments with publicly available access control policies, we find that the elimination approach produces better results, and that, for a policy quality metric that reflects size and interpretability, our elimination algorithm achieves significantly better results than previous work.

Categories and Subject Descriptors: D.4.6 [**Operating Systems**]: Security and Protection—*Access Controls*; H.2.8 [**Database Management**]: Database Applications—*Data Mining*

Keywords: role mining, role-based access control

1. INTRODUCTION

Role-based access control (RBAC) offers significant advantages over lower-level access control policy representa-

*This work was supported in part by ONR under Grant N00014-07-1-0928, NSF under Grant CNS-0831298, and AFOSR under Grant FA0550-09-1-0481.

tions, such as access control lists (ACLs). However, the effort required for a large organization to migrate from ACLs to RBAC can be a significant obstacle to adoption of RBAC. Role mining algorithms partially automate the construction of an RBAC policy from an ACL policy and possibly other information, such as user attributes. These algorithms can significantly reduce the cost of migration to RBAC.

Several versions of the role mining problem have been proposed. The most widely studied versions involve finding a minimum-size RBAC policy consistent with (i.e., equivalent to) given ACLs. However, interpretability of roles is also crucial, because typically, a role produced by a role mining algorithm will be adopted by security administrators only if they can identify a reasonable interpretation of the role, in which case the role is said to be "meaningful". Indeed, researchers at HP Labs wrote that "the biggest barrier we have encountered to getting the results of role mining to be used in practice" is that "customers are unwilling to deploy roles that they can't understand." [3]. When data about attributes of users is available, it can be used to help identify meaningful roles. The general idea is that a role is meaningful if its set of members can be characterized by an expression involving user attributes. There are numerous reasonable variants of the definitions of policy size and interpretability, and different definitions may be appropriate in different contexts.

The main contribution of this paper is a role mining algorithm that can easily be used to optimize a variety of policy quality metrics—including metrics based on policy size, metrics based on interpretability of the roles with respect to user attribute data, and compound metrics that consider size and interpretability—and that achieves good results.

All of our algorithms begin with a phase that constructs a set of candidate roles. We consider two strategies for the second phase: start with an empty policy and repeatedly add candidate roles, or start with the entire set of candidate roles and repeatedly remove roles. In experiments with publicly available access control policies, we find that the elimination approach produces better results, and that, for a previously proposed policy quality metric that reflects size and interpretability, our elimination algorithm achieves significantly better results than previous work that aims to optimize that metric, even though our algorithm is not specifically tuned for that metric.

Other contributions of this paper include:

- an investigation of the effect of varying the order in which roles are considered for removal in the elimination algorithm;

- an algorithm for synthesizing user attribute data. The use of synthetic user attribute data in experiments is regrettable but currently unavoidable, due to the lack of publicly available real user attribute data.

2. PROBLEM DEFINITION

This section defines the role mining problems that we consider. Our definitions are similar to those in [9].

Policies and Policy Quality.

An *ACL policy* is a tuple $\langle U, P, UP \rangle$, where U is a set of users, P is a set of permissions, and $UP \subseteq U \times P$ is the user-permission assignment.

An *RBAC policy* is a tuple $\langle U, P, R, UA, PA, RH \rangle$, where R is a set of roles, $UA \subseteq U \times R$ is the user-role assignment, $PA \subseteq R \times P$ is the permission-role assignment, and $RH \subseteq R \times R$ is the role inheritance relation. Specifically, $\langle r, r' \rangle \in RH$ means that r is senior to r', hence all permissions of r' are also permissions of r, and all members of r are also members of r'.

An *RBAC policy with direct assignment* is a tuple $\langle U, P, R, UA, PA, RH, DA \rangle$, which is an RBAC policy extended with a direct user-permission assignment $DA \subseteq U \times P$. Allowing direct assignment of permissions to users provides more flexibility to handle anomalous permissions.

An RBAC policy is *consistent* with an ACL policy if $UA \circ PA = UP$, where $\circ$ is composition of relations. An RBAC policy with direct assignment is *consistent* with an ACL policy if $UA \circ PA \cup DA = UP$.

User-attribute data is a tuple $\langle A, f \rangle$, where A is a set of attributes, and f is a function such that $f(u, a)$ is the value of attribute a for user u. For simplicity, we assume that all attribute values are natural numbers.

A *policy quality metric* is a function from RBAC policies (or RBAC policies with direct assignment) to a totally-ordered set, such as the natural numbers. The ordering is chosen so that small values indicate high quality; this might seem counter-intuitive at first glance, but it is natural for metrics such as policy size. We define two basic policy quality metrics and then consider combinations of them.

Weighted Structural Complexity (WSC) is a generalization of policy size [9]. For an RBAC policy π of the above form, we define weighted structural complexity by $\mathrm{WSC}(\pi) = w_1|R| + w_2|UA| + w_3|PA| + w_4|RH|$, where $|s|$ is the size (cardinality) of set s, and the w_i are user-specified weights. For an RBAC policy with direct assignment, the definition is the same except with an additional summand $w_5|DA|$.

Interpretability is a policy quality metric measures how well the roles in the policy can be characterized (interpreted) in terms of user attributes. Specifically, we quantify policy interpretability as *attribute mismatch*, which measures how well the sets of members of the roles can be characterized using expressions over user attributes. An *attribute expression* e is a function from the set A of attributes to sets of values. A user u *satisfies* an attribute expression e iff $(\forall a \in A.\ f(u, a) \in e(a))$. For example, if $A = \{dept, level\}$, the function e with $e(dept) = \{\mathrm{CS}\}$ and $e(level) = \{2, 3\}$ is an attribute expression, which can be written with syntactic sugar as $dept \in \{\mathrm{CS}\} \wedge level \in \{2, 3\}$. We refer to the set $e(a)$ as the conjunct for attribute a. Let $[\![e]\!]$ denote the set of users that satisfy e. For an attribute expression e and a set U' of users, the *mismatch* of e and U', denoted $\mathrm{mismatch}(e, U')$, is the size of the symmetric difference of $[\![e]\!]$

and U', where the symmetric difference of sets s_1 and s_2 is $s_1 \ominus s_2 = (s_1 \setminus s_2) \cup (s_2 \setminus s_1)$. The *attribute mismatch* of a role r, denoted $\mathrm{AM}(r)$, is $\min_{e \in E} \mathrm{mismatch}(e, \mathrm{assignedU}(r))$, where E is the set of all attribute expressions, and $\mathrm{assignedU}(r) = \{u \mid \langle u, r \rangle \in UA\}$. The *attribute mismatch* of an RBAC policy π (with or without direct assignment) is $\mathrm{AM}(\pi) = \sum_{r \in R} \mathrm{AM}(r)$. We define policy interpretability INT as attribute mismatch, i.e., $\mathrm{INT}(\pi) = \mathrm{AM}(\pi)$.

Compound policy quality metrics take multiple aspects of policy quality into account. One approach is to combine multiple policy quality metrics using a weighted sum; however, the choice of weights may be difficult or arbitrary. We combine metrics by Cartesian product, with lexicographic ordering on the tuples. Let $\mathrm{INT\text{-}WSC}(\pi) = \langle \mathrm{INT}(\pi), \mathrm{WSC}(\pi) \rangle$ and $\mathrm{WSC\text{-}INT}(\pi) = \langle \mathrm{WSC}(\pi), \mathrm{INT}(\pi) \rangle$.

Role Mining from ACLs.

The problem of *role mining from ACLs* is: given an ACL policy π_a and a policy quality metric Q, find an RBAC policy π_r that is consistent with π_a and has the best quality, according to Q, among policies consistent with π_a. The problem of *role mining with direct assignment from ACLs* is the same except that π_r is an RBAC policy with direct assignment.

Role Mining from ACLs and User Attributes.

The problem of *role mining from ACLs and user attributes* (with or without direct assignment) is the same as for role mining from ACLs, except that the input also includes user-attribute data, which may be used in the policy quality metric.

Our algorithms produce RBAC policies in which role membership is always defined by explicit user-role assignment, even when the current membership of a role can be characterized exactly by an attribute expression. In practice, assigning users to roles fully automatically based on user attributes might be risky; requiring explicit user-role assignments by an administrator is safer. The administrator's effort can be reduced by an algorithm that suggests appropriate roles for new users, based on their attributes. For example, we can compute and store a best-fit attribute expression e_r for each role r, i.e., an attribute expression that minimizes the attribute mismatch for r. When a new user u is added to the access control system, the system suggests that u be made a member of the roles for which u satisfies the best-fit attribute expression, and it presents these suggested roles for u in descending order of the attribute mismatch. This allows good suggestions even in the presence of noise.

3. ALGORITHMS

This section presents our role mining algorithms. In general, they compute only approximate solutions to the role-mining problem: the generated RBAC policy is always consistent with the given ACL policy, but it does not always have the best possible quality. This is a common limitation of role mining algorithms, because computing an optimal solution is NP-hard for policy quality metrics of interest [9].

3.1 Elimination Algorithm

Our *elimination algorithm* has three phases. Phase 1, role generation, generates a candidate role hierarchy that contains all "interesting" candidate roles. Phase 2, role elim-

```
// Create initial roles.
1: InitRole ← ∅
2: permSets ← ⋃_{u∈U} {p ∈ P | ⟨u, p⟩ ∈ UP}
3: for ps in permSets \ {∅}
4:    r = new Role()
5:    InitRole ← InitRole ∪ {r}
6:    PA ← PA ∪ ({r} × ps)
7: end for

// Compute all intersections of initial roles.
8: R ← ∅
9: for r in InitRole
10:   InitRole ← InitRole \ {r}
11:   for r′ in InitRole
12:      P ← assignedP(r) ∩ assignedP(r′)
13:      if ¬empty(P) ∧ ∄r″ ∈ R. assignedP(r″) = P
14:         r″ = new Role()
15:         PA ← PA ∪ ({r″} × P)
16:         R ← R ∪ {r″}
17:      end if
18:   end for
19:   for r′ in R
20:      P ← assignedP(r) ∩ assignedP(r′)
21:      if ¬empty(P) ∧ ∄r″ ∈ R. assignedP(r″) = P
22:         r″ = new Role()
23:         PA ← PA ∪ ({r″} × P)
24:         R ← R ∪ {r″}
25:      end if
26:   end for
27:end for
28:R ← R ∪ InitRole
```

Figure 1: Role generation, step 1: compute candidate roles.

```
// Initialize variables. Assign users to roles.
1: UA ← ∅; RH ← ∅
2: for u in U
3:    P ← {p ∈ P | ⟨u, p⟩ ∈ UP}
4:    for r in R
5:       if authP(r) ⊆ P
6:          UA ← UA ∪ {⟨u, r⟩}
7:       end if
8:    end for
9: end for

// Add inheritance edges, and eliminate inherited
// permissions and members from UA and PA.
10:for r in R
11:   parents ← {r′ ∈ R | ⟨r, r′⟩ ∈ RH}   // parents of r
12:   for r′ in R \ {r}
13:      if authP(r′) ⊆ authP(r)
14:         ∧ ∀r″ ∈ parents. authP(r′) ⊈ authP(r″)
15:         RH ← RH ∪ {⟨r, r′⟩}
16:         for ⟨r, p⟩ in PA
17:            if p ∈ authP(r′)
18:               PA ← PA \ {⟨r, p⟩}
19:            end if
20:         end for
21:         for ⟨u, r′⟩ in UA
22:            if u ∈ assignedU(r)
23:               UA ← UA \ {⟨u, r′⟩}
24:            end if
25:         end for
26:         for r″ in parents
27:            if authP(r″) ⊈ authP(r′)
28:               RH ← RH \ {⟨r, r″⟩}
29:            end if
30:         end for
31:      end if
32:   end for
33:end for
```

Figure 2: Role generation, step 2: construct role hierarchy, based on R and PA from step 1.

ination, removes roles from the candidate role hierarchy if the removal preserves consistency with the given ACL policy and improves policy quality. Phase 3, role restoration, adds some removed roles back to the policy, if this improves policy quality.

Phase 1: Role Generation.

Our algorithm for role generation is based closely on CompleteMiner [14], although for increased scalability, we could easily substitute FastMiner [14] or the FP-Tree approach [5, 10]. Roles are characterized primarily by the set of permissions assigned to the role. An *initial role* has a set of permissions that contains all permissions assigned to some user. A *candidate role* has a set of permissions obtained by intersecting the permission sets of an arbitrary number of initial roles. As argued in [14], in the absence of other information on which to base the construction of candidate roles, this method generates all interesting candidate roles. Pseudo-code for this construction appears in Figure 1. It is essentially the same as the pseudo-code for CompleteMiner in [14]. It uses the functions assignedP(r) = {p ∈ P | ⟨r, p⟩ ∈ PA} and assignedU(r) = {u ∈ U | ⟨u, r⟩ ∈ UA}.

CompleteMiner does not produce a role hierarchy. Our algorithm computes a role inheritance relation with the maximum amount of inheritance: a candidate role r_p inherits from another role r_c whenever the permissions of r_p are a superset of the permissions of r_c. Furthermore, when that

inheritance relation is introduced, the permissions inherited by r_p from r_c are removed from the permissions explicitly assigned to r_p by PA, and the members inherited by r_c from r_p are removed from the members explicitly assigned to r_c by UA. Pseudo-code appears in Figure 2. It uses functions authP(r) = {p ∈ P | ∃r′ ∈ R. ⟨r, r′⟩ ∈ RH* ∧ ⟨r′, p⟩ ∈ PA} and authU(r) = {u ∈ U | ∃r′ ∈ R. ⟨r′, r⟩ ∈ RH* ∧ ⟨u, r′⟩ ∈ UA}, where RH^* is the reflective transitive closure of RH.

A role hierarchy has *full inheritance* if every two roles that can be related by the inheritance relation are related by it, i.e., ∀r, r′ ∈ R. authP(r) ⊇ authP(r′) ∧ authU(r) ⊆ authU(r′) ⟹ ⟨r, r′⟩ ∈ RH*. Guo *et al.* call this property *completeness* [4].

All of our algorithms generate RBAC policies with full inheritance. Although relaxing this requirement would allow our algorithms to achieve better policy quality in some cases, we impose this requirement, because in the absence of other information, all of these possible inheritance relationships are equally plausible, so removing any of them risks removing some that are semantically meaningful and desirable.

Phase 2: Role Elimination.

Roughly, the role elimination phase removes roles from the candidate role hierarchy if the removal preserves consistency with the given ACL policy and improves policy quality. When a role r is removed, the role hierarchy is adjusted to preserve inheritance relations between parents and children of r, and the user assignment and permission assignment are adjusted to explicitly assign to other roles the members and permissions that they previously inherited from r.

The order in which roles are considered for removal is important, because it may lead to different RBAC policies in the end. We control this ordering with a *role quality metric* Q_{role}, which maps roles to an ordered set, with the interpretation that large values denote high quality (note: this is opposite to the interpretation of the ordering for policy quality metrics). Low-quality roles are considered for removal first. The algorithm is parameterized by the choice of role quality metric. We consider three basic role quality metrics and then consider combinations of them.

Clustered size measures how well user permissions are clustered in the role. A first attempt at formulating such a metric might simply be the total number of UP pairs (i.e., elements of the UP relation) that are covered by the role, or, equivalently but with the metric normalized to be in the range $[0,1]$, the fraction of all UP pairs covered by the role. However, such a metric would give the same rating to a role r_1 that covers one permission for each of 10 users and a role r_2 that covers 5 permissions for each of 2 users, even though r_2 is preferable; for example, if all of the users have exactly 5 permissions, then the two users in r_2 would not need to belong to any other roles, while all of the users in r_1 would need to belong to other roles as well. To take this into account, we define the clustered size metric to equal the fraction of the permissions of the role's members that are covered by this role; formally,

$$\text{assignedUP}(r) = \{\langle u, p \rangle \in UP \mid u \in \text{assignedU}(r)$$
$$\wedge\, p \in \text{assignedP}(r)\}$$
$$\text{clsSz}(r) = |\text{assignedUP}(r)| \div |\{\langle u, p \rangle \in UP \mid u \in \text{assignedU}(r)\}|$$

The numerator considers assigned users and permissions, instead of authorized users and permissions, so that a role gets credit only for the UP pairs that it covers by itself, not for UP pairs covered by its ancestors or descendants.

Attribute fitness measures how well the set of members of a role can be characterized (interpreted) in terms of user attributes. It is based on attribute mismatch, defined in Section 2, normalized to be in the range $[0,1]$ and subtracted from 1 so that higher values of the metric indicate higher quality; formally, $\text{attrFit}(r) = 1 - \frac{\text{AM}(r)}{|\text{assignedU}(r)|}$.

Redundancy measures how many other roles also cover the UP pairs covered by a role. Removing a role with higher redundancy is less likely to prevent subsequent removal of other roles, so we eliminate roles with higher redundancy first. Values of the redundancy metric are pairs, with lexicographic order. The redundancy of role r is the negative of the minimum, over UP pairs $\langle u, p \rangle$ covered by r, of the number of other removable roles that cover $\langle u, p \rangle$ (we take the negative so that roles with more redundancy have lower quality and hence get considered for removed first).

$$\text{authUP}(r) = \{\langle u, p \rangle \in UP \mid u \in \text{authU}(r) \wedge p \in \text{authP}(r)\}$$
$$\text{redun}(\langle u, p \rangle) = |\{r \in R \mid \langle u, p \rangle \in \text{authUP}(r) \wedge \text{removable}(r)\}|$$
$$\text{redun}(r) = -\min_{\langle u, p \rangle \in \text{authUP}(r)}(\text{redun}(\langle u, p \rangle))$$

```
 1: π ← policy produced by role generation
 2: q ← Q_pol(π)
 3: workList ← list containing removable roles in π
 4: changed ← true
 5: while ¬empty(workList) ∧ changed
 6:     sort workList in ascending order by Q_role
 7:     changed ← false
 8:     for r in workList
 9:         if ¬removable(r)
10:             remove r from workList
11:         else
12:             π' ← removeRole(π, r)
13:             q' ← Q_pol(π')
14:             if q' < δq
15:                 π ← π'
16:                 q ← q'
17:                 changed ← true
18:                 remove r from workList
19:             end if
20:         end if
21:     end for
22: end while

function removeRole(π, r)
23: ⟨U, P, R, UA, PA, RH⟩ ← π
24: R ← R \ {r}
25: for ⟨r_1, r⟩ in RH
26:     RH ← RH \ {⟨r_1, r⟩}
27:     for ⟨r, r_2⟩ in RH
28:         if ⟨r_1, r_2⟩ ∉ RH*
29:             RH ← RH ∪ {⟨r_1, r_2⟩}
30:         end if
31:     end for
32:     for ⟨r, p⟩ in PA
33:         if p ∉ authP(r_1)
34:             PA ← PA ∪ {⟨r_1, p⟩}
35:         end if
36:     end for
37: end for
38: for ⟨r, r_2⟩ in RH
39:     RH ← RH \ {⟨r, r_2⟩}
40:     for ⟨r, u⟩ in UA
41:         if u ∉ authU(r_2)
42:             UA ← UA ∪ {⟨r_2, u⟩}
43:         end if
44:     end for
45: end for
46: return ⟨U, P, R, UA, PA, RH⟩
```

Figure 3: Role elimination.

Compound role quality metrics can be formed in the same ways as compound policy quality metrics, e.g., max(clsSz, attrFit).

Our algorithm may remove a role even if the removal worsens policy quality slightly. Specifically, we introduce a *quality change tolerance* δ, with $\delta \geq 1$, and we remove a role if the quality Q' of the RBAC policy resulting from the removal is related to the quality Q of the current RBAC policy by $Q' < \delta Q$ (recall that, for policy quality metrics, smaller values are better). Choosing $\delta > 1$ partially compensates for the fact that a purely greedy approach to policy quality improvement is not an optimal strategy.

Pseudo-code for role elimination appears in Figure 3. It is parameterized by a policy quality metric Q_{pol}, a role quality metric Q_{role}, and a quality change tolerance δ. A role is *removable* if every UP-pair covered by r is covered by at least one other role currently in the policy; formally,

$$\text{removable}(r) = \forall \langle u, p \rangle \in \text{authUP}(r). \exists r' \in R.$$
$$r' \neq r \wedge \langle u, p \rangle \in \text{authUP}(r')$$

A removable role can be removed while preserving consistency with the given ACL policy. The removeRole function removes a role r, adjusts the role hierarchy to preserve inheritance relations between parents and children of r, and adjusts the user assignment and permission assignment to explicitly assign to other roles the members and permissions that they previously inherited from r. The removability test in line 9 is necessary because a role that is initially removable might become unremovable, due to other removals. The quality of each role is computed only in line 6, immediately before sorting the worklist. Role quality metrics may change as roles are removed and hence are re-computed each time line 6 is executed.

Phase 3: Role Restoration.

Phase 3 restores removed roles when this improves policy quality. Specifically, it considers each removed role r, in the same order that the roles were removed, and restores r if this improves the policy quality. Pseudo-code to restore a role appears in Figure 4. It uses the relation $\prec$ defined by $r \prec r' = \text{authP}(r) \subset \text{authP}(r')$. It makes r a child of roles r' such that $r \prec r' \wedge \neg \exists r'' \in R. r \prec r'' \prec r'$, makes r a parent of roles r' such that $r' \prec r \wedge \neg \exists r'' \in R. r' \prec r'' \prec r$, and adjusts the permission assignment, user assignment, and inheritance relations of roles related to r to eliminate redundancy.

Direct User-Permission Assignment.

If direct user-permission assignment is allowed, we add a final phase that replaces roles with direct assignment if that improves policy quality. Pseudo-code appears in Figure 5; variable π initially contains the policy produced by phase 3, which contains no direct assignments, i.e., $DA = \emptyset$.

Determining Algorithm Parameters.

Different choices of role quality metric Q_{role} and quality change tolerance δ may give the best results for different datasets, so we enclose the algorithm in a loop that tries all combinations of the following values for those parameters and returns the result from the best combination: Q_{role} in $\{\langle \text{redun}, \text{clsSz} \rangle, \langle \max(\text{attrFit}, \text{clsSz}), \text{redun} \rangle\}$, and δ in $\{1, 1.001, 1.002\}$. We also experimented with $\text{sum}(\text{clsSz}, \text{attrFit})$ for Q_{role}, and with larger values for δ, but that did not improve the results.

3.2 Selection Algorithm

Our *selection algorithm* works in the opposite way as the elimination based algorithm. Specifically, it starts with an empty policy and repeatedly adds candidate roles to the policy. The selection algorithm is parameterized by a role quality metric. In phase 1, candidate roles are generated as in the elimination algorithm (see Figure 1). In phase 2, candidate roles are added to the RBAC policy in order of descending role quality, until the RBAC policy is consistent with the given ACL policy. Phase 3 performs pruning: for each role r in the policy in the reverse order that the roles

```
function restoreRole(π, r)
1:  ⟨U, P, R, UA, PA, RH⟩ ← π
2:  for r′ in R
3:      if r ≺ r′ ∧ ¬∃r″ ∈ R. r ≺ r″ ≺ r′
            // make r a child of r′
4:          assignedP(r′) ← assignedP(r′) \ authP(r)
5:          assignedU(r) ← assignedU(r) \ authU(r′)
6:          RH ← RH ∪ {⟨r′, r⟩}
7:          for r″ in R such that ⟨r′, r″⟩ ∈ RH   // children of r′
8:              if r″ ≺ r
                    // remove r″ as a child of r′. r″ will be
                    // a child of r and a grandchild of r′
9:                  RH ← RH \ {⟨r′, r″⟩}
10:             end if
11:         end for
12:     end if
13:     if r′ ≺ r ∧ ¬∃r″ ∈ R. r′ ≺ r″ ≺ r
            // make r a parent of r′
14:         assignedP(r) ← assignedP(r) \ authP(r′)
15:         assignedU(r′) ← assignedU(r′) \ authU(r)
16:         RH ← RH ∪ {⟨r, r′⟩}
17:         for r″ in R such that ⟨r″, r′⟩ ∈ RH // parents of r′
18:             if r ≺ r″
                    // remove r″ as a parent of r′. r″ will be
                    // a parent of r and a grandparent of r′
19:                 RH ← RH \ {⟨r″, r′⟩}
20:             end if
21:         end for
22:     end if
23: end for
24: R ← R ∪ {r}
25: return ⟨U, P, R, UA, PA, RH⟩
```

Figure 4: Restore role r to policy π.

```
1:  for r in R
2:      π₁ ← removeRole(r)
3:      π₂ ← π₁ with all UP pairs in the given ACL policy
              that are not covered in π₁ added to DA
4:      if Q_pol(π₂) < δQ_pol(π)
5:          π ← π₂
6:      end if
7:  end for
```

Figure 5: Create direct user-permission assignment.

were added, checks whether the role is removable, and if so, whether removing it improves policy quality, and if so, removes it.

3.3 Complete Algorithm

Our *complete algorithm* has two phases. Phase 1 generates a hierarchical RBAC policy in exactly the same way as the elimination algorithm. Phase 2 is role removal. While the elimination algorithm heuristically takes a greedy approach to removals, the complete algorithm considers all subsets of the set of removable roles, to find the set of removals that produces the policy with the highest quality.

To avoid explicitly storing the set of sets of removable roles that have been explored so far, our role removal algorithm is expressed as a recursive search. Removal of one role may prevent subsequent removal of another role, but removals commute in the sense that, if it is possible to remove r_1 and then remove r_2, then it is also possible to remove r_2 and

Dataset	$|U|$	$|P|$	$|UP|$	high-fit		low-fit	
				N_a	AF	N_a	AF
healthcare	46	46	1486	20	1	5	0.79
domino	79	231	730	20	1	12	0.48
emea	35	3046	7220	20	1	6	0.56
apj	2044	1146	6841	40	0.94	10	0.57
firewall-1	365	709	31951	40	0.997	15	0.58
firewall-2	325	590	36428	40	1	10	0.50
americas-small	3477	1587	105205	50	0.95	9	0.36

Figure 6: Information about datasets. N_a **is the number of attributes. AF is the attribute fit.**

then remove r_1, and these two sequences of removals lead to the same policy. To ensure that the algorithm does not unnecessarily explore the same removals in multiple orders, we impose an arbitrary ordering on the removable roles, by storing them in a list R_{rmv}, and the algorithm considers only sequences of removals consistent with that ordering; in other words, it considers sequences of removals that correspond to subsequences (not necessarily contiguous) of R_{rmv}. The algorithm is parameterized by a policy quality metric Q_{pol}. The algorithm is complete in the following sense: if Q_{pol} is WSC, then the complete algorithm computes a policy that minimizes WSC among policies consistent with the given ACL policy; for other policy quality metrics Q_{pol}, the complete algorithm computes a policy that minimizes Q_{pol} among policies that are consistent with the given ACL policy and have full inheritance.

4. DATASETS

We know of no publicly available real ACL policies with user attribute data, so we use publicly available real ACL policies, described next, together with synthetic user attribute data, generated as described below.

The ACL policies are listed in Figure 6. They originate from Hewlett-Packard (HP) Labs [3]. The healthcare dataset was obtained by HP Labs from the U.S. Veteran's Administration, which has developed a comprehensive list of the healthcare permissions that may be assigned to licensed or certified providers. The domino data is from a set of user and access profiles for a Lotus Domino server. americas-small is a network access control policy from Cisco firewalls used to manage external business partner's access to HP's network. apj and emea are similar but smaller datasets. HP Labs produced the firewall-1 and firewall-2 datasets based on analysis of network connectivity permitted by Checkpoint firewall rules.

Generation of User Attribute Data.

Molloy *et al.* provide summary information about non-public user attribute data and ACL policies from three customers [11]; we exploit this to make our synthetic attribute data have some approximately realistic characteristics. Based on the information in the paper, we construct the following distributions: (a) for each customer i, we fit an exponential distribution $card_i$ to the distribution of cardinalities of user attributes for that customer. (b) for each attribute of each customer, we fit a Zipf distribution to the distribution of values of that attribute (based on the information in [11, Figures 3-5]), to obtain a Zipf-distribution exponent for each attribute, and then we fit a Weibull distribution

$zipfExp$ to the resulting distribution of Zipf-distribution exponents. The individual Zipf-exponents obtained from our measurements of the charts in [11, Figures 3-5] have considerable uncertainty, due to the limited information in those charts, but these uncertainties might average out to some extent, making the parameters of the Weibull distribution $zipfExp$ somewhat more robust.

Our algorithm for generating user attribute data is parameterized by an ACL policy and the desired number N_a of attributes. The algorithm has two phases. Phase 1 generates user attribute data for each attribute separately, independent of the ACLs. Phase 2 modifies the user attribute data to improve its fit with the ACLs. In more detail, phase 1 starts by identifying the customer i in [11] for which the number of users is closest to the number $|U|$ of users in the given ACL policy, and then, for each of the desired attributes, select a cardinality c_a from $card_i$ and a Zipf-exponent s_a from $zipfExp$. Next, the value of attribute a for each user is selected from a Zipf distribution with c_a elements and exponent s_a. We take all attribute values to be natural numbers interpreted as ranks in the Zipf distribution (0 is the most common value, 1 is the second most common value, etc.).

Phase 2 tries to reduce the attribute mismatch for each permission. Let U_p denote the set of users with permission p, i.e., $U_p = \{u \in U \mid \langle u, p \rangle \in UP\}$. For each permission p, we first compute an attribute expression e_p representing the least superset of U_p expressible as an attribute expression; e_p is given by $e_p(a) = \{f(u, a) \mid u \in U_p\}$. e_p may be a very loose upper bound on U_p, so we convert it to a lower bound on U_p by repeatedly removing an attribute value from a conjunct of e_p until $[\![e_p]\!] \subseteq U_p$; in each iteration, we remove the attribute value with the largest value of the metric m, where, for a value v in the conjunct for attribute a

$$m(v, a) = \quad |\{u \in U \mid f(u, a) = v \land u \notin U_p\}| \\ - |\{u \in U \mid f(u, a) = v \land u \in U(p)\}|$$

Finally, we try to make the lower bound tighter as follows: for each user u in $U_p \setminus [\![e_p]\!]$, for each attribute a such that $f(u, a) \notin e_p(a)$, if adding $f(u, a)$ to $e_p(a)$ preserves the fact that $[\![e_p]\!] \subseteq U_p$, then add $f(u, a)$ to $e_p(a)$, otherwise try to modify f so that $f(u, a) \in e_p(a)$, by swapping the values of $f(u, a)$ and $f(u', a)$ for some other user u', provided the swap does not affect whether u' satisfies the attribute expressions already constructed for other permissions. Note that swapping values of attributes between users preserves the distribution of values of each attribute.

The *attribute fit* of the resulting attribute assignment is defined as $1 - \frac{1}{|UP|} \sum_{p \in P} \text{mismatch}([\![e_p]\!], U_p)$. For each dataset, we start with $N_a = 10$, generate user attribute data, and compute the attribute fit. If it is above 0.9, we stop, otherwise we increment the number of attributes by 10 and try again, until the attribute fit is above 0.9. We call the resulting user attribute data the *high-fit* user attribute data.

In practice, the available user attribute data will often have a lower attribute fit than 0.6, e.g., because some relevant user attributes are unavailable. Therefore, we also produce a version of the user attribute data with fewer attributes; specifically, we discard attributes one at a time, until the attribute fit drops below 0.6 (except we use a higher threshold of 0.8 for healthcare, otherwise N_a is very low). We call this the *low-fit* user attribute data.

Figure 6 contains information about the generated user

attribute data. Generation of user attribute data takes only a few minutes for small datasets, and it takes less than an hour for the largest dataset.

5. EXPERIMENTAL RESULTS

This section compares our algorithms with each other, compares the elimination algorithm (which is best among our algorithms) with prior work, and explores the effects of different policy quality metrics and role quality metrics.

Comparison of Elimination Algorithm with Hierarchical Miner and Graph Optimisation.

Figure 7 shows the WSC and interpretability (using the high-fit attribute data) of policies produced by the elimination algorithm and Hierarchical Miner (HM) [9] with policy quality metric WSC-INT and the WSC of policies produced Graph Optimisation (GO) [15] (modified slightly by Molloy *et al.* to use WSC as the policy quality metric). The weight vector for WSC contains all ones except that the weight for direct assignment is infinity (in other words, direct assignment is prohibited). In the comparison of eight role mining algorithms in [10] and the comparison of four role mining algorithms in [9], for this weight vector, the best WSC for every dataset is achieved by either HM or GO. *Figure 7 shows that the elimination algorithm achieves smaller or equal WSC than HM and GO on every dataset, while simultaneously achieving good policy interpretability* (Figure 11 shows that the elimination algorithm simultaneously achieves good results for both components of the policy quality metric). The WSC from HM and GO are 2.7% worse and 14.0% worse, respectively, averaged over the datasets, compared to the WSC from the elimination algorithm. The INT from HM is 46.3% worse, averaged over the datasets, compared to the INT from the elimination algorithm; this is not surprising, because HM does not consider user attributes or policy interpretability. The results for HM are computed from policies produced by HM that Molloy sent to us. The results for GO are from [9, Table VI] for all datasets except americas-small, which is not used in [9]; the results for GO for americas-small are from [10, Table 4].

On a PC with an Intel Core 2 Quad 2.66 GHz CPU (the processor has 4 cores, but our code is purely sequential), the elimination algorithm terminates in 30 seconds or less for all datasets except americas-small, which takes about 3.5 minutes. Running times for HM and GO are not reported in [15, 10, 9], and the implementations of HM and GO described in those papers are not publicly available. We fit curves to a graph of running time *vs.* $|UP|$ for the datasets in Figure 6 and found that a quadratic function fits well.

Figure 8 shows the result of our elimination algorithm when allowing direct assignments, with a WSC weight vector containing all ones. The results for HM are computed from policies producd by HM that Molloy sent us. The results for GO are from [9, Table VII] for all datasets except americas-small, which is not used in [9]; the results for GO for americas-small are from [10, Table 4]. The original GO does not consider direct assignment, but Molloy *et al.* extended GO to support it. *Figure 8 shows that the elimination algorithm achieves smaller WSC than HM and GO on every dataset, while simultaneously achieving good policy interpretability.* The WSC from HM and GO are 1.5% worse and 18.8% worse, respectively, averaged over the datasets, compared to the WSC from the elimination algorithm. The

Dataset	Elimination		HM		GO
	INT	WSC	INT	WSC	WSC
healthcare	14	144	16	149	168
domino	21	404	30	418	413
emea	32	3709	92	3795	3888
apj	392	4248	411	4282	4600
firewall-1	48	1385	59	1426	1543
firewall-2	7	945	7	945	960
americas-small	214	6330	324	6710	9721

Figure 7: Comparison of elimination algorithm with policy quality metric WSC-INT, Hierarchical Miner, and Graph Optimisation, when direct user-permission assignment is prohibited.

Dataset	Elimination		HM		GO
	INT	WSC	INT	WSC	WSC
healthcare	9	140	10	142	168
domino	7	371	9	379	413
emea	36	3644	39	3693	3888
apj	130	3827	164	3862	4600
firewall-1	17	1340	21	1349	1543
firewall-2	4	944	4	944	960
americas-small	182	6214	198	6468	9721

Figure 8: Comparison of elimination algorithm with policy quality metric WSC-INT, Hierarchical Miner, and Graph Optimisation, when direct user-permission assignment is permitted.

INT from HM is 15.2% worse, averaged over the datasets, compared to the INT from the elimination algorithm.

Comparison of Elimination Algorithm with Attribute Miner.

Among prior work on role mining that takes policy interpretability into account, the most closely related is Molloy *et al.*'s work on Attribute Miner [9]. Figure 9 compares the elimination algorithm (using the redundancy role quality metric and $\delta = 1.001$) with Attribute Miner [9]. Molloy *et al.*'s implementation of Attribute Miner is not publicly available, so the results for Attribute Miner are from our own implementation of it. Attribute Miner is designed to optimize the policy quality metric Weighted Structural Complexity with Attributes (WSCA) [9]. WSCA differs from WSC in how the size of the user-role assignment is measured. In WSC, it is simply $|UA|$ or equivalently $\sum_{r \in R} |U(r)|$, where $U(r)$ is the membership (assigned users) of role r. In WSCA, if $U(r)$ can be characterized exactly by an attribute expression $D(r)$, the size of $D(r)$ (i.e., the number of conjuncts) is used instead of $|U(r)|$; otherwise, the geometric mean of $|U(r)|$ and $|[\![B(r)]\!]|$ is used instead of $|U(r)|$, where $B(r)$ is the attribute expression that is the least upper bound for $U(r)$. We have some reservations about WSCA: (1) use of the geometric mean of $|U(r)|$ and $|[\![B(r)]\!]|$ seems unintuitive, since it does not directly measure either the size or the interpretability of the role; (2) WSCA is very sensitive to whether a role can be characterized exactly by an attribute expression—a small change to the input data can significantly change the WSCA associated with a role, because $|D(r)|$ is often much smaller than $|U(r)|$; (3) as discussed at the end of Section 2, it might be safer to use attribute expressions to suggest role membership than to define role

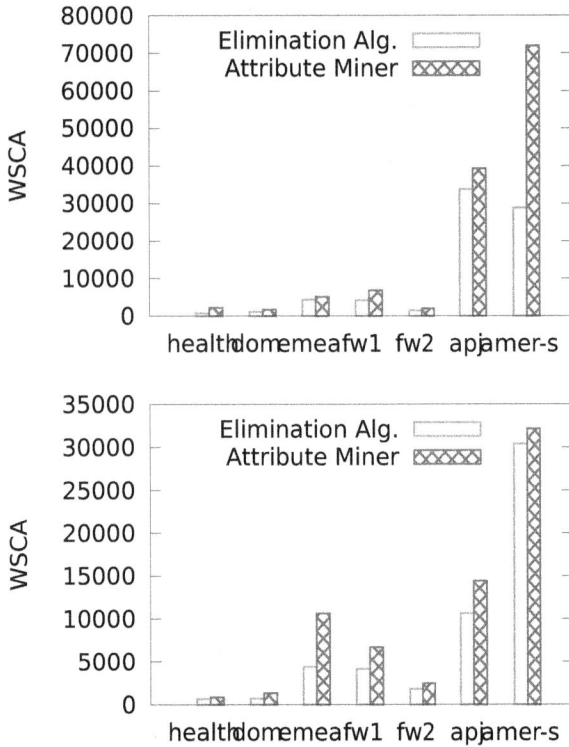

Figure 9: Comparison of elimination algorithm and Attribute Miner (AM). Names of datasets are abbreviated, e.g., fw1 abbreviates "firewall-1". The upper and lower graphs use the high-fit and low-fit user attribute data, respectively.

Figure 10: Results for elimination algorithm and selection algorithm, with policy quality metric INT-WSC. The clusters of points correspond, from left to right in the order they are connected, to the datasets in the following order: firewall-2 healthcare, domino, firewall-1, emea, americas-small, apj.

Comparison of Our Algorithms.

Figure 10 contains results for the elimination algorithm with the redundancy role quality metric and the selection algorithm with role quality metric max(attrFit, clsSz). We use INT-WSC as the policy quality metric for both algorithms. The weight vector for WSC contains all ones except that the weight for direct assignment is infinity (in other words, direct assignment is prohibited). Figure 10 shows that the elimination algorithm achieves the same or better results than the selection algorithm on both components of the policy quality metric for every dataset. We ran the complete algorithm on the smallest dataset, healthcare, with Q_{pol}=WSC. The result has WSC = 141, which is better than elimination algorithm (WSC = 144) and HM (WSC = 149). We started to run the complete algorithm on the second smallest dataset, domino, but we aborted it after 30 hours.

Effect of Policy Quality Metric in Elimination Algorithm.

Figure 11 compares the quality of policies produced by the elimination algorithm with policy quality metrics WSC-INT and INT-WSC, using the high-fit user attribute data. Recall that the elimination algorithm tries multiple role quality metrics Q_{role} and quality change tolerances δ; the tables also show the best combination of those parameters for each policy quality metric and each dataset. Surprisingly, for all of these datasets, it makes little or no difference whether priority is given to WSC or interpretability.

Effect of Role Quality Metric and Quality Change Tolerance in Elimination Algorithm.

We compared the results of the elimination algorithm with policy quality metric INT-WSC and four role quality metrics: redundancy, max(attrFit, clsSz), and the "reverse" of each of these, obtained by taking the negative of the value. The reverse orders exemplify a bad choice of role quality metric. We used $\delta = 1.0$ and policy quality metric WSC-INT with all four role quality metrics. Averaged over the datasets, using reverse-max(attrFit, clsSz) instead of max(attrFit, clsSz) worsens policy interpretability by 5.0% and WSC by 0.9%, and using reverse-redundancy instead of redundancy wors-

membership. Nevertheless, we use WSCA for this comparison, because Attribute Miner is designed to optimize WSCA and would probably fare poorly in a comparison based on INT-WSC.

Attribute Miner, as described in [9] uses attribute expressions that are conjunctions of positive literals over Boolean attributes. We implemented a generalized version of Attribute Miner that uses attribute expressions of the form described in Section 2. This involves straightforward changes to the code that computes least upper bounds and to the definition of the size of an attribute expression, which is used in the definition of WSCA [9, Definition 13] and in the definition of the cost of an attribute role [9, Table III]. We define the size of an attribute expression e to be $\sum_{a \in A} |e(a)|$. Attribute Miner takes user attribute data and a set of candidate roles as input; we generate the set of candidate roles using Phase 1 of the elimination algorithm.

Figure 9 shows that the elimination algorithm achieves better WSCA than Attribute Miner on every dataset. With the high-fit attribute data, Attribute Miner is 78% worse, averaged over the datasets, i.e., the average of the ratios of the WSCA values obtained using the two algorithms is 1.78; the median of the ratios is 1.38. With the low-fit attribute data Attribute Miner is 57% worse, averaged over the datasets, i.e., the average of the ratios of the WSCA values obtained using the two algorithms is 1.57; the median of the ratios is 1.36.

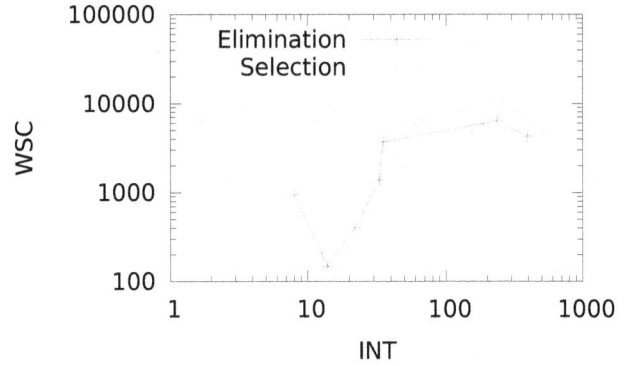

64

Dataset	WSC-INT				INT-WSC			
	INT	WSC	Q_{role}	δ	INT	WSC	Q_{role}	δ
healthcare	14	144	rdn	1.001	14	144	rdn	1.001
domino	21	404	max	1.001	21	404	max	1.001
emea	32	3709	max	1.000	32	3709	max	1.000
apj	392	4248	rdn	1.000	384	4331	rdn	1.002
firewall-1	48	1385	max	1.000	44	1419	max	1.003
firewall-2	7	945	max	1.000	7	945	max	1.000
amer-small	214	6330	max	1.000	180	6912	red	1.003

Figure 11: Comparison of two different policy quality metrics in elimination algorithm. "rdn" and "max" denote $\langle$redun, clsSz$\rangle$ and $\langle$max(attrFit, clsSz), redun$\rangle$, respectively.

ens policy interpretability by 3.9% and WSC by 1.0%. This shows that the order in which roles are considered for removal has a small but non-negligible effect.

We also compared the results of the elimination algorithm using all six combinations of the two role quality metrics and three quality change tolerances specified in Section 3. We found that the combination Q_{role} = redun and δ = 1.001 gives the best result or close to it—within 2% for WSC and interpretability—for every dataset in our experiments.

6. RELATED WORK

The literature on role mining is sizable, so we discuss only the most closely related work.

Vaidya et al.'s RoleMiner algorithm has two phases [14]. Phase 1 produces a set of candidate roles, each represented by a set of permissions. They give two algorithms for this: CompleteMiner, which we adopt as the first step in Phase 1 of our elimination algorithm, and FastMiner, which is similar to CompleteMiner but more scalable, because it considers only pairwise intersections of initial roles. Phase 2 prioritizes the candidate roles produced by Phase 1. The prioritized list of roles is the final result of the algorithm. The algorithm does not attempt to determine which candidate roles to include in such an RBAC policy, to produce a role inheritance relation, or to assign users to roles. In contrast, our algorithm addresses these issues in order to produce an RBAC policy. Vaidya et al. also developed algorithms for computing an RBAC policy with minimal $|R|$ that is consistent with a given ACL policy [13]. Lu et al. [7] present role mining algorithms that minimize either $|R|$ or $|UA| + |PA|$. None of these papers considers more general policy size metrics (such as WSC), role hierarchy, or interpretability of roles with respect to user attribute data.

Zhang et al.'s Graph Optimisation (GO) algorithm starts with each user's permission set as a candidate role, and repeatedly splits or merges roles when the transformation improves policy quality [15]. They do not consider interpretability of roles with respect to user attribute data. The data in Figures 7 and 8 show that the elimination algorithm achieves better WSC than GO does. The main reasons are: (1) GO performs role generation and role selection in a single phase, considering new candidate roles lazily according to a greedy heuristic, instead of eagerly generating all candidate roles in an initial phase; as a result, GO is faster, but it might fail to consider some useful roles; (2) it appears from the paper that GO does not explicitly control the order in

which roles are considered for splitting and merging; and (3) GO never tries to eliminate roles.

Ene et al.'s role mining algorithms aim to minimize either $|R|$ or $|UA| + |PA|$ [3]. They do not consider policy interpretability with respect to user attribute data. Molloy et al. generalized the algorithm that aims to minimize $|UA| + |PA|$ so that it aims to minimize WSC instead, and they found that the modified algorithm performs well when the weight vector corresponds to the algorithm's original metric (i.e., when WSC equals $|UA| + |PA|$) but performs worse than GO and HM with other weight vectors [9], including the weight vectors used in our experiments.

Li et al.'s Dynamic Miner [6, 10] has three phases. Phase 1 generates a set of candidate roles. Phase 2 selects candidate roles to include in the RBAC policy, adding them to the policy in descending order of the estimated decrease in WSC achieved by adding the role (it is an estimate because the user-role assignment and role hierarchy are not known yet). Phase 3 constructs the user-role assignment and role hierarchy. Our selection algorithm is similar to Dynamic Miner, but more general, because it is parameterized by the role quality metric that controls the order in which roles are considered for selection, and, more importantly, it allows the role quality metric to take the role hierarchy and user-role assignment into account, because they are computed during the role selection phase. Molloy et al. found that Dynamic Miner generally produces worse WSC than HM and GO [10]. This is consistent with our finding that the selection algorithm generally produces worse results than the elimination algorithm.

Molloy et al.'s Hierarchical Miner (HM) has two phases. Phase 1 uses formal concept analysis to create a candidate role hierarchy consistent with a given ACL policy; phase 1 of the elimination algorithm is equivalent to phase 1 of HM. Phase 2 eliminates roles, removes their inheritance edges, or replaces them with direct user-permission assignment when this preserves consistency with the given ACL policy and lowers the WSC. The elimination algorithm achieves slightly better results than HM in our experiments. We believe this is mainly because the elimination algorithm uses a role quality metric to control the order in which roles are considered; the order in which roles are considered in HM is not explicitly controlled and depends on implementation details of a hashset library [8]. The use of a quality change tolerance and a role restoration phase also help the elimination algorithm achieve better results. Although phase 1 of HM produces a candidate role hierarchy with full inheritance, phase 2 of HM does not preserve this property; we plan to experiment with allowing similar deviations from full inheritance in the elimination algorithm, which should allow better results for policy quality. HM does not consider policy interpretability with respect to user attribute data.

Molloy et al.'s Attribute Miner (AM) has two phases. Phase 1 produces a set of candidate normal roles and a set of candidate attribute roles (i.e., roles whose membership is defined by an attribute expression). Phase 2 greedily selects normal roles and attribute roles for inclusion in the policy in descending order of the role's benefit-to-cost ratio, which is an estimate of the role's effect on the policy's WSCA. The elimination algorithm is more flexible than AM, since it can easily be used with any policy quality metric, and it achieves significantly better results than AM even for AM's target policy quality metric, namely, WSCA. We believe the main reason for this is that the elimination approach (i.e., repeatedly remove roles) generally yields better results than the selection approach (i.e., repeatedly add roles), as we saw in the comparison of the elimination algorithm with our selection algorithm in Section 5, and as noted above in the discussion of Dynamic Miner.

Colantonio *et al.* propose two metrics to measure the interpretability of roles [1]. Their approach relies on an *activity tree*, describing the hierarchical structure of business activities (business processes), and an *organization unit tree*, describing the hierarchical structure of the organization. It also assumes knowledge of which permissions are required for each activity and of the assignment of users to organizational units. The *activity-spread* of a role measures the dispersion within the activity tree of the activities enabled by the role's permissions. The *organization-unit-spread* of a role measures the "dispersion" within the organization unit tree of the role's members. Roles with low activity-spread and low organization-unit-spread are considered to be more meaningful. These metrics are intuitively appealing and could be combined with metrics based on user attributes in our algorithms when the required information is available.

Colantonio *et al.* propose an approach to taking user attributes into account during role mining [2]. They first partition the set of users based on the values of selected attributes, and then perform role mining separately for each set of users in the partition (using the corresponding slice of the *UP* relation). Note that the role mining in the second step does not explicitly consider user attributes. They propose metrics that are used to select a set of attributes that provides the most meaningful partition of the users. Their paper does not consider metrics to directly evaluate the interpretability of the resulting roles or RBAC policies.

7. CONCLUSIONS AND FUTURE WORK

We presented a role mining algorithm, the elimination algorithm, that can easily be used to optimize a variety of policy quality metrics. In our experimental evaluation, using realistic datasets, it achieves equal or better results than previously proposed algorithms.

One direction for future work is to consider other metrics for policy interpretability, e.g., metrics that consider heterogeneity of users in different roles as well homogeneity of users in the same role [12]. Another direction is to improve scalability. We are exploring use of a scalable clustering algorithm or graph partitioning algorithm to decompose an ACL policy into subpolicies that can be role-mined separately; the metric that guides clustering or partitioning is designed to minimize policy quality loss due to the decomposition.

Acknowledgment.
We thank Ian Molloy for helpful comments and for sending us policies produced by Hierarchical Miner.

8. REFERENCES

[1] A. Colantonio, R. Di Pietro, A. Ocello, and N. V. Verde. A formal framework to elicit roles with business meaning in rbac systems. In *SACMAT '09: Proc. 14th ACM symposium on Access control models and technologies*, pages 85–94. ACM, 2009.

[2] A. Colantonio, R. Di Pietro, and N. V. Verde. A business-driven decomposition methodology for role mining. *Computers & Security*, 2012.

[3] A. Ene, W. G. Horne, N. Milosavljevic, P. Rao, R. Schreiber, and R. E. Tarjan. Fast exact and heuristic methods for role minimization problems. In *Proc. 13th ACM Symposium on Access Control Models and Technologies (SACMAT 2008)*, pages 1–10, 2008.

[4] Q. Guo, J. Vaidya, and V. Atluri. The role hierarchy mining problem: Discovery of optimal role hierarchies. In *Proc. 2008 Annual Computer Security Applications Conference (ACSAC '08)*, pages 237–246, 2008.

[5] J. Han, J. Pei, and Y. Yin. Mining frequent patterns without candidate generation. In *Proc. 2000 ACM SIGMOD International Conference on Management of Data (SIGMOD 2000)*, pages 1–12. ACM, 2000.

[6] N. Li, T. Li, I. Mollog, Q. Wang, E. Bertino, S. Calo, and J. Lobo. Role mining for engineering and optimizing role based access control systems. Technical Report 2007-60, CERIAS, Purdue University, November 2007.

[7] H. Lu, J. Vaidya, and V. Atluri. Optimal boolean matrix decomposition: Application to role engineering. In *Proc. 24th International Conference on Data Engineering (ICDE)*, pages 297–306, 2008.

[8] I. Molloy. Private communication, Dec. 2011.

[9] I. Molloy, H. Chen, T. Li, Q. Wang, N. Li, E. Bertino, S. B. Calo, and J. Lobo. Mining roles with multiple objectives. *ACM Trans. Inf. Syst. Secur.*, 13(4):36, 2010.

[10] I. Molloy, N. Li, T. Li, Z. Mao, Q. Wang, and J. Lobo. Evaluating role mining algorithms. In *Proc. 14th ACM Symposium on Access Control Models and Technologies (SACMAT 2009)*, pages 95–104, 2009.

[11] I. Molloy, J. Lobo, and S. Chari. Adversaries' holy grail: Access control analytics. In *Proc. First Workshop on Building Analysis Datasets and Gathering Experience Returns for Security (BADGERS 2011)*, pages 52–59, 2011.

[12] G. J. Szekely and M. L. Rizzo. Hierarchical clustering via joint between-within distances: Extending ward's minimum variance method. *J. Classification*, 22(2):151–183, 2005.

[13] J. Vaidya, V. Atluri, and Q. Guo. The role mining problem: Finding a minimal descriptive set of roles. In *Proc. 12th ACM Symposium on Access Control Models and Technologies (SACMAT 2007)*, pages 175–184, 2007.

[14] J. Vaidya, V. Atluri, and J. Warner. RoleMiner: Mining roles using subset enumeration. In *Proc. 13th ACM Conference on Computer and Communications Security (CCS 2006)*, pages 144–153, 2006.

[15] D. Zhang, K. Ramamohanarao, and T. Ebringer. Role engineering using graph optimisation. In *Proc. 12th ACM Symposium on Access Control Models and Technologies (SACMAT 2007)*, pages 139–144, 2007.

Panel

Emerging Trends around Big Data Analytics and Security

Organizer
Rafae Bhatti
Accenture Technology Labs
rafae@acm.org

Ryan LaSalle
Accenture Technology Labs
ryan.m.lasalle@accenture.com

Tim Grance
NIST
grance@nist.gov

Rob Bird
Red Lambda, Inc
rbird@redlambda.com

Elisa Bertino
Purdue University
bertino@cs.purdue.edu

ABSTRACT

This panel will discuss the interplay between key emerging security trends centered around big data analytics and security. With the explosion of big data and advent of cloud computing, data analytics has not only become prevalent but also a critical business need. Internet applications today consume vast amounts of data collected from heterogeneous big data repositories and provide meaningful insights from it. These include applications for business forecasting, investment and finance, healthcare and well-being, science and hi-tech, to name a few. Security and operational intelligence is one of the critical areas where big data analytics is expected to play a crucial role. Security analytics in a big data environment presents a unique set of challenges, not properly addressed by the existing security incident and event monitoring (or SIEM) systems that typically work with a limited set of traditional data sources (firewall, IDS, etc.) in an enterprise network. A big data environment presents both a great opportunity and a challenge due to the explosion and heterogeneity of the potential data sources that extend the boundary of analytics to social networks, real time streams and other forms of highly contextual data that is characterized by high volume and speed. In addition to meeting infrastructure challenges, there remain additional unaddressed issues, including but not limited to development of self-evolving threat ontologies, integrated network and application layer analytics, and detection of "low and slow" attacks. At the same time, security analytics requires a high degree of data assurance, where assurance implies that the data be trustworthy as well as managed in a privacy preserving manner. Our panelists represent individuals from industry, academia, and government who are at the forefront of big data security analytics. They will provide insights into these unique challenges, survey the emerging trends, and lay out a vision for future.

Categories and Subject Descriptors

D.4.6 [Software: Operating Systems] **Security and Protection**; H.2.4 [Database Management] **Systems** H.3.3 [**Information Search and Retrieval**]

Keywords

Big Data, Analytics, Security, Privacy

Panelists

[1] **Ryan LaSalle:** Ryan is the Senior Director of Cyber R&D at Accenture Technology Labs, Accenture's cross-industry research and development organization. As the lead for Accenture's Cyber Lab, Ryan's current role focuses on research that brings together the areas of analytics, knowledge discovery, and cyber-security/information assurance, with the goal of developing first-of-a-kind approaches to sharpening threat assessment methodologies and enhancing knowledge of successful responses. Ryan holds patents in human resource management, knowledge discovery and establishing trust between entities online. Ryan also serves as the lead architect for the Secure Enterprise Networks Consortium, an organization which includes of Accenture, CA, Cisco, Los Alamos National Lab and Sun/Oracle. The SEN-C works collaboratively with public sector agencies to research cyber defense and share industry leading practices. Ryan is a graduate of Princeton University, with a B.S. degree in Electrical Engineering.

[2] **Robert Bird**: Rob is the President, CTO, and Founder of Red Lambda. He leads research and development, cloud delivery platform, and customer service. He holds a European patent in holistic network management, and is the co-author of numerous pending- patents in unsupervised real-time learning and security intelligence in free-scale distributed systems. Mr. Bird was chosen to testify before the US House of Representatives as an expert witness

regarding the elimination of child pornography on the Internet and the mitigation of peer-to-peer (P2P) file-sharing. Mr. Bird is an active member of numerous security industry standards bodies and working groups, including IEEE, ACM, IETF NEA (Network Endpoint Assessment), SAAG (Security Area Advisory Group), OPSEC (Operational Security for IP Network Infrastructure) and MANET (Mobile Ad-Hoc Networks). He served as technical chair for conferences on Computational Intelligence for Security and Defense Applications, and Bio-inspired Computing for Defense and served as PI (Principal Investigator) of the NSF SBIR Grant "Red Lambda Neuro-Pattern Classification System." Mr. Bird holds a Bachelor of Science in Mathematics from the University of Florida.

[3] **Tim Grance**: Tim is a senior computer scientist in the Information Technology Laboratory at the National Institute of Standards and Technology in Gaithersburg, MD. He is the Program Manager for Cyber and Network Security (CNS) Program and exercises broad technical and programmatic oversight over the NIST CNS portfolio. This portfolio includes high profile projects such as the NIST Hash Competition, Cloud Computing, Security Content Automation Protocol (SCAP), Protocol Security (DNS, BGP, IPv6), Combinatorial Testing, and the National Vulnerability Database. He has extensive public and private experience in accounting, law enforcement, and computer security. He has written on diverse topics including incident handling, intrusion detection, privacy, metrics, contingency planning, forensics, and identity management. He was named in 2003 to the Fed 100 by Federal Computer Week as one of the most influential people in Information Technology for the US Government. He is also is a two time recipient of the US Department of Commerce's highest award—a Gold Medal, from the Secretary of Commerce.

[4] **Elisa Bertino:** Elisa is a professor in Computer Science and research director at CERIAS at Purdue University. Her research interests cover many areas in the fields of information security and database systems. Professor Bertino serves or has served on the editorial boards of several journals - many of which are related to security, such as the ACM Transactions on Information and System Security, the IEEE Security & Privacy Magazine, and IEEE Transactions on Dependable and Secure Computing. She is currently serving as program chair of the 36th International Conference on Very Large Data Bases (VLDB 2010).

Professor Bertino is a Fellow of the Institute of Electrical and Electronics Engineers and a Fellow of ACM. She received the IEEE Computer Society Technical Achievement award in 2002 for outstanding contributions to database systems and database security and advanced data management systems, and received the 2005 Tsutomu Kanai Award by the IEEE Computer Society for pioneering and innovative research contributions to secure distributed systems. She is currently serving in the IEEE Computer Society Board of Governors and as Chair of ACM SIGSAC.

Moderator

Rafae Bhatti: Rafae is a Research Manager in Cyber Security group at Accenture Technology Labs. His primary expertise is around data security and privacy. In his current role, Dr. Bhatti is helping develop Labs's strategic vision in this space for their clients worldwide. His research is focused on designing innovative solutions for security and privacy issues posed by emerging technology paradigms, in particular healthcare, cloud, and mobile applications, and developing points of view and technology assets around them. Prior to Accenture, he has worked at IBM Almaden Research Center and Oracle. His doctoral work has been cited by the OASIS industry consortium in connection with security standards such as RBAC and SAML. In other roles, he is also an author and part-time educator, and has a passion to share knowledge and engage with the community. He received a PhD in Computer Engineering from Purdue University in 2006.

The Authorization Leap from Rights to Attributes: Maturation or Chaos?

Ravi Sandhu
Institute for Cyber Security
University of Texas at San Antonio
San Antonio, Texas
ravi.sandhu@utsa.edu

ABSTRACT

The ongoing authorization leap from rights to attributes offers numerous compelling benefits. Decisions about user, subject, object and context attributes can be made relatively independently and with suitable decentralization appropriate for each attribute. Policies can be formulated by security architects to translate from attributes to rights. Dynamic elements can be built into these policies so the outcomes of access control decisions automatically adapt to changing local and global circumstances. On the benefits side this leap is a maturation of authorization matching the needs of emerging cyber technologies and systems. On the risks side devolving attribute management may lead to attributes of questionable provenance and value, with attendant possibility of new channels for social engineering and malware attacks. We argue that the potential benefits will lead to pervasive deployment of attribute-based access control (ABAC), and more generally attribute-based security. The cyber security research community has a responsibility to develop models, theories and systems which enable safe and chaos-free deployment of ABAC. This is the current grand challenge for access control researchers.

Categories and Subject Descriptors

D.4.6 [**Operating Systems**]: Security and Protection—Access controls; K.6.5 [**Management of Computing and Information Systems**]: Security and Protection

General Terms

Security, Privacy

Keywords

Authorization, Rights, Attributes

1. INTRODUCTION

Access control has been a central component of cyber security for over four decades, and will remain so for decades. Access control seeks answers to fundamental questions of cyber security: Who is authorized to access specific objects and in what mode (e.g., read, write)? Who determines overall policy for this purpose? In whose interests is such policy deployed? Where and how is this policy articulated? How do we comprehend and manage interactions between various policy components? Who controls and manages details of access by specific users to specific objects? How does access control policy evolve and adapt? How do we enforce access controls, especially in large distributed systems? How do we achieve adequate assurance regarding enforcement?

Researchers have developed dozens of access control models to address such questions. Only three have received meaningful practical traction: Discretionary Access Control (DAC) [5, 6], Lattice-Based Access Control (LBAC[1]) [1, 2] and Role-Based Access Control (RBAC) [3, 8]. Numerous others have been proposed and studied (too many to cite even a small sample) providing fundamental insights and theoretical understanding, and articulating interpretations and requirements of access control in new domains such as workflow systems, geospatial systems, digital rights management and social media. Nonetheless DAC, LBAC and RBAC remain the dominant paradigms in practice so far.

DAC, LBAC and RBAC have strong mathematical and intuitive foundations. The intuition underlying DAC is that the owner of a resource should control who can access that resource. LBAC seeks to enforce one-directional information flow in a lattice of security labels. The intuitive concept of RBAC is that access should be determined by function via the role abstraction, rather than by identity or clearance. RBAC is fundamentally different from DAC and LBAC in its deliberate lack of built-in policy. The overriding concept rather is mechanistic in requiring the primacy of a role as the unit that enables authorization. The actual function or purpose of each role is left unspecified.

DAC and LBAC emerged almost concurrently with the development of multi-user computers in the late 1960s and dominated access control for a quarter century. Although, nascent notion of roles had been used in commercial applications and access control products since the early 1970s, RBAC remained an amorphous concept and did not gain significant traction amongst researchers and practitioners until publication of the RBAC96 family of core RBAC models [8]. Since RBAC's emergence in the early to mid 1990s with solid conceptual and formal foundations, it has become the dominant form of access control in commercial systems.

2. FROM RBAC TO ABAC

Even though RBAC has been enthusiastically received and practised there has been an undercurrent of dissatisfaction

SACMAT'12, June 20–22, 2012, Newark, New Jersey, USA.
ACM 978-1-4503-1295-0/12/06.

---

[1]Equivalently known as Mandatory Access Control (MAC), Multi-Level Security (MLS) or BLP (Bell-LaPadula).

beginning almost contemporaneously with its success. Anecdotal evidence from the author's practitioner contacts indicates the common feeling, "We are using RBAC because there is nothing better at the moment." Researchers have been acutely aware of RBAC's shortcomings and have proposed a variety of incremental improvements. The major issues with RBAC include the following: role granularity is inadequate for fine-grained authorization leading to role explosion, explicit user-role and permission-role assignment by administrators is cumbersome, role design and engineering is difficult and expensive, adjustment based on local/global situational factors is difficult, and there is a proliferation of extensions to the core RBAC models.

Over the past decade ABAC has slowly but surely emerged as a strong candidate to supplant or supplement RBAC. Intuitively, an attribute is a property usually expressed as a name:value pair which can be associated with any entity in the system, including users, subjects, objects and contexts. Suitably defined attributes can represent security labels, clearances and classifications (LBAC), identities and access control lists (DAC) and roles (RBAC). Thereby ABAC supplements and subsumes rather than supplants these currently dominant models. Moreover any number of additional attributes such as location, time of day, strength of authentication, departmental affiliation, qualification, frequent flyer status, and so on, can be brought into play within the same extensible framework of attributes. Thus the proliferation of RBAC extensions might be unified by adding appropriate attributes within a common framework, solving many of these shortcomings of core RBAC. At the same time we should recognize that ABAC with its flexibility may further confound the problem of role design and engineering. Attribute engineering is likely to be a more complex activity, and a price we may need to pay for added flexibility.

Much as nascent RBAC concepts were around for decades before their formalization in 1996 [4], nascent ABAC notions have been around for a while. X.500, X.509, LDAP and XACML are familiar practitioner standards. In academic research ABAC models, such as [7, 9], have been proposed in specific contexts. The situation with ABAC today is analogous to that of RBAC in the early 1990s, as a promising but amorphous concept without authoritative conceptual and formal foundations. The persistence of ABAC notions, even in absence of such foundations, indicates its native appeal and suggests that ABAC will be with us for a very long time.

The core compelling value of ABAC is divide and conquer. Decisions about user, subject, object and context attributes can be made relatively independently and with suitable decentralization appropriate for each attribute. Policies can be formulated by security architects to translate from attributes to rights. Dynamic elements can be built into these policies so the outcomes of access control decisions automatically adapt to changing local and global circumstances. This is very much in line with the needs of emerging cyber systems and technologies. The core risk of ABAC lies in the potential chaos that can result from assembling multiple independent, and possibly conflicting, decisions predictably into a coherent whole. Moreover, attributes may have questionable provenance and value due to malfeasance by malicious users. Even well-meaning and diligent users can be led astray by phishing, social engineering and surreptitious malware. Surely ABAC will introduce new channels for such attacks. Is ABAC then a recipe for chaos?

3. THE GRAND CHALLENGE

In a nutshell, the grand challenge is how to garner the promised benefits of ABAC without engendering chaos? We believe this can happen only if we are able to develop rich and usable models and architectures for ABAC with strong conceptual and formal foundations. We need to do for ABAC what the RBAC96 model [8], the NIST standard [3] and their numerous extensions and enhancements did for RBAC.

Is there a guarantee that such ABAC models and architectures will be found? In science the only guarantee is in the finding. However, there are several reasons to believe that formulation of such ABAC models is well within our grasp. In particular, the innovative research and practical deployments inspired by the RBAC96 model over the past fifteen plus years give us a promising road map for ABAC. ABAC research can be more systematic and organized than was possible with RBAC, given our accumulated understanding of access control since the birth of RBAC. We are confident that an aggressive and coordinated research thrust in ABAC will achieve for ABAC at least what was achieved for RBAC via a rather ad hoc research agenda in its early days (mid to late 1990s).

We believe that practitioners will move to ABAC regardless of what the research community does, because the benefits are too compelling to bypass. Ad hoc efforts by practitioners to build ABAC systems are likely to lead to chaos rather than maturation. Hence the grand challenge!

Acknowledgments The author's work is partially supported by grants from AFOSR, NSF and the State of Texas.

4. REFERENCES

[1] D. Bell and L. LaPadula. Secure computer systems: Unified exposition and Multics interpretation. Technical report, Mitre, 1975.

[2] D. Denning. A lattice model of secure information flow. *Communications of the ACM*, 19(5):236–243, 1976.

[3] D. F. Ferraiolo, R. Sandhu, S. Gavrila, D. R. Kuhn, and R. Chandramouli. Proposed NIST standard for role-based access control. *ACM TISSEC*, 4(3):224–274, August 2001.

[4] L. Fuchs, G. Pernul, and R. Sandhu. Roles in information security: A survey and classification of the research area. *Comp. and Sec.*, 30(8):748 – 769, 2011.

[5] G. Graham and P. Denning. Protection – principles and practice. In *AFIPS Spring Joint Computer Conference*, pages 40:417–429, 1972.

[6] B. Lampson. Protection. In *5th Princeton Symposium on Information Science and Systems*, pages 437–443, 1971. Reprinted in *ACM Operating Systems Review* 8(1):18–24, 1974.

[7] J. Park and R. Sandhu. The UCON$_{ABC}$ usage control model. *ACM TISSEC*, 7(1):128–174, February 2004.

[8] R. Sandhu, E. Coyne, H. Feinstein, and C. Youman. Role-Based Access Control Models. *IEEE Computer*, pages 38–47, 1996.

[9] L. Wang, D. Wijesekera, and S. Jajodia. A logic-based framework for attribute based access control. In *ACM FMSE Workshop*, pages 45–55, 2004.

SCUTA: A Server-Side Access Control System for Web Applications

Xi Tan, Wenliang Du, Tongbo Luo, and Karthick D. Soundararaj
Dept. of Electrical Engineering & Computer Science, Syracuse University
Syracuse, New York, USA
xtan@syr.edu, wedu@syr.edu, toluo@syr.edu, d.s.karthick@gmail.com

ABSTRACT

The Web is playing a very important role in our lives, and is becoming an essential element of the computing infrastructure. Unfortunately, its importance makes it the preferred target of attacks. Web-based vulnerabilities now outnumber traditional computer security concerns. A recent study shows that over 80 percent of web sites have had at least one serious vulnerability. We believe that the Web's problems, to a large degree, are caused by the inadequacy of its underlying access control systems. To reduce the number of vulnerabilities, it is essential to provide web applications with better access control models that can adequately address the protection needs of the current Web.

As a part of the efforts to develop a better access control system for the Web, we focus on the server-side access control in this paper. We introduce a new concept called *subsession*, based on which, we have developed a ring-based access control system (called SCUTA) for web servers. SCUTA provides a fine-grained and backward-compatible access control mechanism for web applications. We have implemented SCUTA in PHP, and have conducted comprehensive case studies to evaluate its benefits.

Categories and Subject Descriptors

D.4.6 [**Security and Protection**]: Access controls

Keywords

Web security, Server-Side Access Control

1. INTRODUCTION

The Web has been growing at a rapid rate over the last 15 years. The first Google index (1998) already had 26 million pages, and by 2000 the Google index reached the one billion mark. On July 25, 2008, the one trillion milestone was reached [1]. As of May 2009, these web pages were hosted by over 109.5 million websites [2]. The Web is gradually becoming part of our lives. We do many things online, such as shopping, making friends, banking, reading news, sharing personal pictures, etc. As the most important application of the Internet infrastructure, the Web itself is becoming an essential part of the infrastructure. With such an important role the Web is playing, making sure that the Web is secure is becoming a priority for trustworthy computing.

Because of its ubiquity, the Web has become attackers' preferred target. Web-based vulnerabilities now outnumber traditional computer security concerns [3]. Cross-site scripting, cross-site request forgery, and SQL injection are among the most common attacks on web applications. A recent report shows that over 80 percent of websites *have had* at least one serious vulnerability, and the average number of serious vulnerabilities per website is 16.7 [4].

It is tempting to blame developers for these security problems, because it is indeed their mistakes that have caused the problems. However, when we look deeper, asking why the percentage of vulnerabilities is so abnormally high, we soon realize that something more fundamental in the Web is wrong. One of the fundamental problems is the Web's access control system, which, being sufficient for the earlier day's Web, becomes inadequate to address the protection needs of today's Web.

The Situations. The Web, initially designed for primarily serving static contents, has now evolved into a quite dynamic system, consisting of contents and requests from multiple sources, some more trustworthy than others. Let us look at some representative scenarios. The first is *untrusted contents*. Many web applications now include user-provided contents, such as blogs, comments, and feedbacks. These are third-party data, and are less trustworthy than the first-party contents generated by the web applications themselves. If not carefully handled, malicious code can be injected into these contents.

Second, many web applications include *client-side extensions*, i.e., they include links to third-party code or directly include third-party code in their web pages. Examples of client-side extensions include advertisements, Facebook applications, iGoogle's gadgets, etc. In Figure 1, both the iPad advertisement and the weather gadget are client-side extensions. Their contents, containing JavaScript code, can be very dangerous if they are vulnerable or malicious,

Third, some web applications include *server-side extensions*, which are developed by third parties. For example, Elgg is an open-source social network application. It was designed as an open framework, allowing others to extend its functionality. Elgg already has hundreds of third-party extensions. To use these extensions, the administrators of the `Elgg` server need to install them, essentially mixing them with `Elgg`'s first-party code. These contents can also be dangerous, if they are vulnerable or malicious.

What further complicates the above scenarios is the cross-origin requests. A cross-origin request is sent from a page of one origin to a server at a different origin. Cross-origin requests are becoming quite popular nowadays. For example, many web pages now contain small icons (e.g. Facebook icon) like those in Figure 1. Requests triggered by clicking these icons are generated by the page of `www.example.com`, but are sent to a different server. These cross-origin requests make it more convenient for users to share information among their accounts, especially their social-network accounts. Originally, cross-origin requests were only allowed for normal HTTP requests, not AJAX requests, due to obvious security concerns. Recently, however, as web technologies evolve, this restriction has been lifted to support better interactions among web applications via a protocol called Cross-Origin Resource Sharing [5]. All major browsers—Chrome, Firefox, IE and Safari—support cross-origin AJAX requests in their latest versions.

Threat Model. Our primary goal is to narrow the attack surface of web servers by enhancing server-side access control. In our threat model, attacks are launched by untrusted web contents against innocent users. We assume that an attacker does not attack browsers directly, but can make malicious same-origin requests by providing third party data (e.g. blogs) or malicious client extensions (e.g advertisements) on client side. An attacker can also issue cross-origin request forgery attack, or compromise a less secured website for attacking a more secured website by exploiting cross-origin AJAX requests between two websites. Moreover, it is still possible for attackers to trigger web servers to install malicious server-side extensions which may destroy its database and the whole server system.

Security Needs and Problems. To secure such a complex system and deal with sophisticated attacks in the threat Model, good access control at the system level is essential. Without it, application developers have to include complicated protection logic in their programs to deal with the risks caused by the scenarios and the threat Model described above. Mistakes in the implementations of the logic, or a lack of the implementation, can cause vulnerabilities.

The Web consists of two major components, the browser and the server; access control needs to be implemented at both places. At the browser side, the access control in the current Web is based on the Same-Origin Policy (SOP), which gives the same privileges to all contents from the same origin. Such a coarse granularity, which may have been sufficient for the nascent Web in its earlier days, cannot handle untrusted contents or client-side extensions well: although these contents come from the same origin, they are not equally trusted. The inadequacy of SOP has been pointed out by various studies, and several solutions have been proposed to provide finer granularity beyond SOP [6–12], including our earlier work ESCUDO [11], which separates the contents with different levels of trustworthiness, and mediates their actions based on trust levels.

On the server side, access control is primarily based on sessions. When a user logs into a web application, the server creates a dedicated session for this user, separating him/her from the other users. Sessions are implemented using ses-

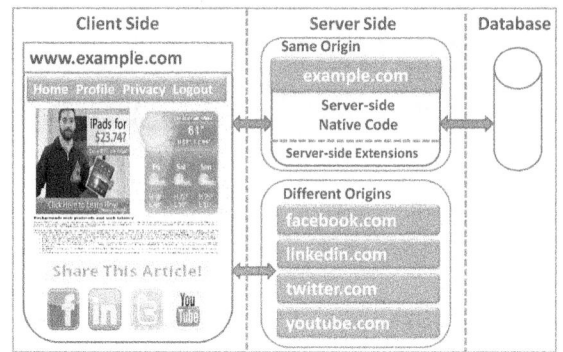

Figure 1: A web application example

sion cookies; as long as a request carries a session cookie, it will be given all the privileges associated with that session. *Namely, within each session, all requests are given the same privileges, regardless of whether they are initiated by first-party or third-party contents, from client-side or server-side extensions, or from another origin.* Therefore, the server is exposed to the threat model without appropriate access protection. We would like to use an example in Figure 2 to illustrate the problem of the session-based access control.

The web page in Figure 2 allows its users to initiate three requests—`ViewFriends`, `AddFriends`, and `DeleteFriends`—from three different regions. The protection needs on the three server-side scripts are quite different: `DeleteFriends` can only be invoked by the contents that are absolutely trustworthy (e.g., the code generated by the web application itself); `AddFriends` can be invoked by the contents from semi-trusted sources, such as the code from third parties with good reputations; `ViewFriends`, due to its read-only nature, can be exposed to less trustworthy contents.

Unfortunately, the current session-based access control at the web server cannot satisfy the above protection needs, neither can the existing browser-side access control solutions. Based on the current access control systems, it is very difficult to allow the three regions to access the same session, while preventing some of them from invoking certain server-side services. To achieve these two conflicting goals, applications have to implement their own ad hoc protection logic, such as asking users to confirm their actions, embedding tokens in hidden fields, etc.

The fundamental cause of the above problem is the granularity of a session: it is too coarse. The Web has become more and more complicated, and its client-side contents are no longer uniformly trusted, so requests initiated by these contents are not uniformly trusted either. Therefore, giving all the requests within the same session the same privileges cannot satisfy the protection needs of today's Web anymore. In order not to ask application developers to bear the complete responsibility of implementing those protection needs, we need a better server-side access control system.

Our Work and Contributions. The objective of our work is to develop a fine-grained server-side access control system, which can assign different privileges to the requests in the same session, based on their trustworthiness. We have

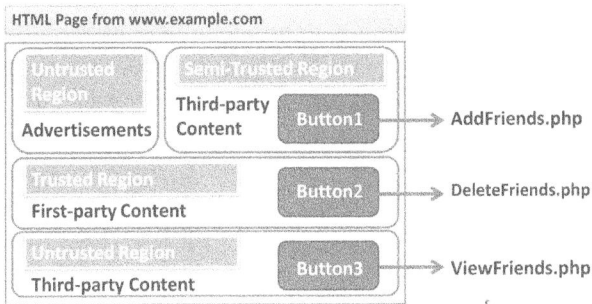

Figure 2: Diversified protection needs

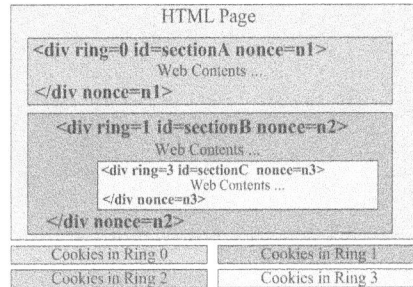

Figure 3: An Example of Escudo Configuration

developed a system called SCUTA [1], which is a novel and backward-compatible access control system for web application servers. Built upon the well-established ring model, SCUTA labels server-side data (tables in database) and programs (functions, classes, methods, or files) with rings, based on their protection needs. Programs in a lower-privileged ring cannot access data or code in a higher-privileged ring.

SCUTA divides a session into multiple *subsessions*, each mapped to a different ring. Requests from a more trustworthy region in a web page belong to a more privileged subsession. Requests belonging to subsession k are only allowed to access the server-side programs and data in ring k and above (numerically). With the subsession and ring mechanisms, server-side programs can differentiate the requests in the same session, based on the trustworthiness of their initiators, and thus provide access control at a finer granularity.

We believe that SCUTA is the first system approach that intends to enhance the session-based access control system of the web server. To demonstrate its effectiveness, we have implemented SCUTA in PHP, a widely adopted platform for web applications. We have conducted comprehensive case studies to demonstrate how SCUTA can be used to satisfy the diversified protection needs in web applications.

2. BACKGROUND: ESCUDO

The server-side access control scheme described in this paper depends on the ESCUDO [11] access control on the browser, because identifying request's subsessions needs the help from browsers, especially ESCUDO-enabled browsers. We give a brief summary of how ESCUDO works in this section. We also explain why ESCUDO alone is not sufficient to deal with the security problems in web applications.

The primary objective of ESCUDO is to allow web servers to convey the trustworthiness of their contents to browsers, so browsers can use this information as the basis for the client-side access control. This provides a finer granularity than the Same-Origin Policy (SOP).

ESCUDO introduces a `ring` concept, borrowed from the Hierarchical Protection Rings (HPR) access control model [13]. Rings in ESCUDO are labeled 0, ..., N, where N is application dependent. In the HPR model, higher numbered rings have less privileges than lower numbered rings, i.e., ring 0 is the highest-privileged ring.

Rings Assignment. Browser-side contents consist pri-

marily of two types: cookies and Document Object Model (DOM) elements. ESCUDO assigns a ring label to each cookie. Cookies that contain sensitive data should be put in a higher-privileged ring, and vice versa.

ESCUDO also assigns ring labels to DOM elements, using the HTML `<div>` tag and the `ring` attribute introduced by ESCUDO. This `ring` attribute assigns a ring label to all the DOM elements within the scope of the tag, which is the region enclosed by the `<div>` and `</div>` pairs (Figure 3 shows an example of ring assignment). ESCUDO ensures a *scoping rule:* the privileges of a node cannot exceed its parent's privileges, regardless of what ring label this new node has. Special attentions are taken to defend against the well-known *node-splitting attack* [14,15]. The `nonce` attribute in Figure 3 is intended for that purpose.

Limitation of Escudo. In terms of accessing sessions, ESCUDO only provides two choices: either allowing the client-side requests to access a specific session or not allowing the access, by putting the session ID cookies in those rings where the session access is allowed.

However, the binary decision is inadequate for today's web servers. As we have shown in Figure 2, to address the protection needs in that example, at least four levels of granularity are needed. ESCUDO can only support two levels: allowing all and denying all.

Despite its limitations, ESCUDO is an indispensable component in our proposed access control framework, because it not only helps to preserve the trust status from the server to the client, but also helps to ensure the integrity of the trust status at the browser. SCUTA relies on ESCUDO, and working together, they provide a more complete solution to the access control problems in web applications.

3. THE DESIGN OF SCUTA

In the current Web, the finest principal unit for server-side programs is *session*. When an HTTP request is received by a web server, the server identifies which session the request belongs to, and then gives the invoked server-side program all the privileges entitled to that session. As a consequence, all the server-side programs invoked in the same session share the same privileges. As explained earlier, this level of granularity is inadequate nowadays, because contents in today's web applications are not uniformly trusted anymore due to the mixture of advertisements, user inputs, third-party code and active contents, etc. Actions invoked by these unequally-trusted contents should not be given the same privileges, even if they belong to the same session. This calls for a granularity level finer than session.

---

[1]"Scuta" is the plural of the Latin word "scutum", meaning a large shield used by soldiers in ancient Rome.

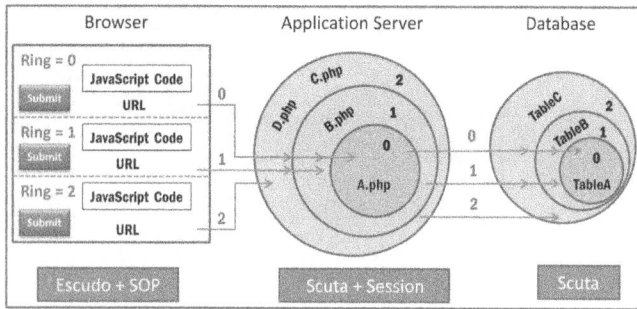

Figure 4: Server-Side Ring Mappings

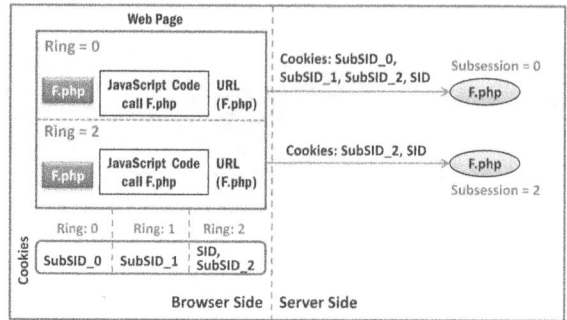

Figure 5: The Subsession mechanism

We have designed a novel server-side access control system called SCUTA, which provides a finer granularity than session. We describe the design of SCUTA in this section.

3.1 Subsessions

To achieve a finer granularity in access control, we divide a session into multiple *subsessions*, each identified by a subsession ID called SubSid. In the original web infrastructure, when a server-side program gets invoked, the server identifies which session the invocation belongs to, and then sets the corresponding running environment and protection. With the addition of SubSid, the server also identifies the subsession ID of the invocation.

Similar to sessions, subsessions are also implemented using cookies. In SCUTA, when a server creates a session ID, it also creates $N+1$ subsession IDs: SubSID_0, ..., SubSID_N, where $N+1$ is the total number of rings defined by the web application. These subsession IDs are sent to the browser as cookies, each marked with a different ring label: SubSID_K is marked with ring K. The following example shows a portion of the HTTP header generated by the server when a session is created (ESCUDO introduces a new header called Set-Ring to set the rings for cookies):

```
Set-Cookie: SID=pjdfbpnd228b2n; path=/
Set-Cookie: SubSID_0=gg5u1pc3inutmb
Set-Cookie: SubSID_1=h1d3vg4ep351qv
Set-Cookie: SubSID_2=n91n6kgiv05fe2
Set-Ring: SID=2
Set-Ring: SubSID_0=0
Set-Ring: SubSID_1=1
Set-Ring: SubSID_2=2
```

With ESCUDO's access control rules, contents in ring t can access the subsession cookies in rings t and above (numerically). Therefore, when an HTTP request is made in ring t from an ESCUDO-protected webpage, all the subsession cookies from rings t and above will be attached to the request; the server can use these cookies to decide that the request belongs to subsession t. Figure 5 depicts the subsession-identification process. In the figure, the server-side program F.php is invoked under two different scenarios: one by the contents (button, JavaScript code, or link) in ring 0, and the other in ring 2. With the help of ESCUDO, SCUTA can successfully identify the subsession IDs of these invocations.

It should be noted that the session ID (SID) is placed in the lowest-privileged ring (ring 2 in this example), allowing it to be carried by all requests, so servers can identify what session a request belongs to.

3.2 The SCUTA Ring Model

Using subsessions, servers can clearly tell from which ring a request is made, and thus know how trustworthy the request is. This is essential for access control, but we need something more: we need to allow web applications to assign privileges to each subsession. The ring model, used by ESCUDO to configure web pages, can be naturally applied to configure application servers. Figure 4 depicts an overall picture of this model in SCUTA.

To use ESCUDO for access control at the browser side, web applications need to generate a set of rings, and configure web pages using these rings. SCUTA uses the same set of rings, but instead of configuring web pages, it configures the server-side programs. Namely, SCUTA places server-side programs into different rings, based on their protection needs. The trustworthiness given to a particular ring in servers is the same as that in browsers. To avoid confusion, we use "ESCUDO ring" and "SCUTA ring" to refer to the ring configuration in web pages and at servers, respectively.

Once the server-side programs are labeled with SCUTA rings and the subsessions of HTTP requests are identified, SCUTA can conduct fine-grained access control on those requests. We have the following basic access rule:

DEFINITION 3.1. **Basic Access Rule:** *An HTTP request originating from* ESCUDO *ring t on the client side will be identified as belonging to subsession t; it is allowed to invoke the server-side programs in* SCUTA *ring w if $w \geq t$.*

The above rule does not only apply to the entry programs at the server side (e.g. DeleteFriends.php in Figure 2), it also applies to all the functions invoked during the execution of the programs. These functions include stand-alone functions, methods in classes, as well as scripts "invoked" via the include command in PHP. These functions are labeled with the ring information in a configuration file (see the implementation details in Section 4).

Using the ring-based access control in SCUTA, web applications can put their security-critical server-side programs in higher-privileged SCUTA rings, limiting their accesses only to the web-page contents in the corresponding ESCUDO rings. Since the less trustworthy web-page contents are put in less-privileged ESCUDO rings, even if they, due to security breaches, contain malicious code, forms, or URL links, they are prevented from accessing the security-critical programs placed in the higher-privileged SCUTA rings. For example, the security-critical DeleteFriends program in Figure 2 can be put in a high privileged SCUTA ring, such as ring 0.

Some functionalities of web applications are less security-critical, and they can be put into lower-privileged rings to allow broader access. For example, `ViewFriends` does not involve modification, so it is less security sensitive; if the web application wants to allow `ViewFriends` to be accessible by third-party JavaScript code, or even by requests from another origin (i.e. cross-origin request), they can simply put this program in the less-privileged SCUTA rings, allowing less-trustworthy client-side contents to invoke it.

Database Protection using Rings. SCUTA's ring-based access control also applies to databases. Namely, data in databases are also mapped to rings, such that a request in subsession t can only access the data in rings t and above. In particular, we label tables of databases with rings depending on the level of protection required by web applications. For example, in a social-network application, the profile table is usually security sensitive, so its access should be restricted to ring 0. To achieve that, we put the profile table in ring 0. For tables that are less security sensitive, we put them in the lower-privileged rings, allowing a broader access. The right side of Figure 4 depicts the ring configuration of databases.

SCUTA's ring configuration is not necessarily limited to the table level; it supports a much finer granularity. For example, SCUTA can label a table in a way, such that it is read-only in ring 3, but writable in ring 0; SCUTA can also label some columns of a table with one ring, while labeling other columns with another ring. Such a fine granularity provides a great flexibility to web applications. More sophisticated examples are given in Appendix B.

3.3 Cross-Ring Invocations

In real-world applications, cross-ring invocations are often desirable. There are two types: from lower to higher privileged rings and vice versa. We discuss how SCUTA supports these types of invocations.

From lower to higher privileged ring. As we have learned from many other ring-based access control systems, such as those in operating systems and 80x86 CPUs, disallowing invocations from lower to higher privileged rings tends to be over restrictive; in many cases, such an invocation needs to be supported. For example, in operating systems, user-level programs are basically running in a less privileged ring, but to access files, they need to invoke the code in the kernel (running in a higher privileged ring). That is a cross-ring execution. Operating systems support that with system calls, the essence of which is to support a controlled invocation from lower to higher privileged rings.

To support the similar kind of invocation, borrowing from operating systems, we introduce the *gate* concept in SCUTA. Its definition and rules are described in the following:

DEFINITION 3.2. **Gate Access Rule:** *A gate is a function labeled with the* **GATE** *keyword and a tuple* (R, W)*, where R is the ring that this function belongs to, and W is the threshold, representing the highest ring number (i.e. the least privileged ring) that is allowed to access this gate. Subsession t can invoke a gate function with the label (r, w) if $r \leq t \leq w$, i.e., the subsession is less privileged than ring r, but compared to the threshold w, t's privilege is sufficient.*

With gates, web developers can write "system calls" for their applications, providing a "gate" for the less privileged

code to invoke more privileged code, in a controlled fashion. For example, as in Figure 2, we may want to allow some third-party extensions in ESCUDO ring 1 to invoke the `DeleteFriends` function, as long as the user specifically grants the permission (i.e., the function will provides extra application-specific control to safe-guard the friend list). However, because of protection needs, the `Friend` table is stored in SCUTA ring 0, forcing the `DeleteFriends` function to be put in ring 0 as well, and denying invocation by the third-party JavaScript code (in ESCUDO ring 1). This dilemma can be solved using gates: we can keep the `Delete-Friends` function in ring 0, but label it as a gate, and assign $(0, 1)$ to it. Such a configuration allow code in rings 0 and 1 to invoke `DeleteFriends`, which will be executed in the context of SCUTA ring 0.

From higher to lower privileged ring. SCUTA allows code in higher-privileged rings to invoke that in lower-privileged rings. This is essential; for example, in Figure 2's example, the function `AddFriends` is in placed in SCUTA ring 1, but we do want the contents in ESCUDO ring 0 to invoke it. Obviously, allowing such an invocation brings risks, especially when the callees are not trustworthy. Putting a function in less privileged rings does not necessarily mean this function is less trustworthy (e.g. shared libraries are often put in the least privileged ring), but a less trustworthy function must be put in less privileged rings.

Many web applications also allows servers to import third-party code. For example, ELGG, a popular social-network application, provides an open framework to developers, who can develop interesting applications that can be added to ELGG. These third-party ELGG extensions may be buggy, or even malicious potentially. With SCUTA, they can be put in a less privileged ring. However, if the client-side contents in subsession 0 or the server-side code in ring 0 invokes these extensions, the execution will take the caller's privilege (i.e., ring 0). This becomes dangerous. Therefore, we have the following access rule:

DEFINITION 3.3. **Privilege Downgrading Rule.** *When a caller running in ring t invokes a function in a less privileged ring $w > t$, the effective subsession ID during the execution of this function is downgraded to w; the caller regains its effective subsession ID t after the function returns.*

3.4 Supporting Other Access Control Models

Discretionary Access Control. All access control models have their limitations, especially for simple models that are intended to address the generic needs; there will be security needs that cannot be covered. Therefore, a good access control model should provide primitives to enable the implementation of discretionary access control by applications.

SCUTA provides a primitive called `session_esubsid()`, which returns the effective subsession ID of the current execution. With this API, programs can enforce their application-specific security policies based on subsession IDs. For example, if a program wants to perform different tasks for different subsessions, it can do the following:

```
switch (session_esubsid()) {
  case 0: Do task A; break;
  case 1: Do task B; break;
  case 2: Do task C; break; }
```

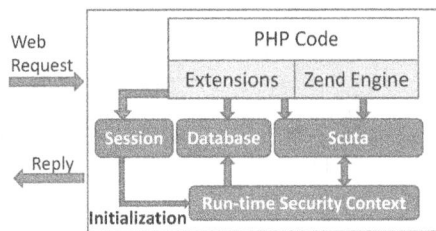

Figure 6: The Architecture of the Scuta System

Other Access Control Models. SCUTA chooses to enforce the multi-level ring model, because it intends to conduct access control based on trust, and trust, by natural, has multiple levels. As the Web evolves, needs for other models, such as multilateral models, may arise. We do believe that the subsession concept introduced by SCUTA can be adapted to serve as the basis for those models; obviously, the access control rules need to be redesigned if model changes. We will study other models in our future work.

4. IMPLEMENTATION OF SCUTA

4.1 The Architecture of the SCUTA System

SCUTA is a general model that can be implemented in various platforms, including PHP, Java Servlet, and ASP.NET. In this work, we choose the open-source PHP platform in our implementation. In order to implement SCUTA, we need to change the behavior of PHP to enforce the ring-based access control policy during the execution of PHP code. Normally, this requires a modification of the target system. However, the PHP architecture was designed for extensibility, allowing developers to add new or modify the existing functionalities.

The PHP architecture has two major components: core and extensions. The core focuses on setting up the running environment, file streams, error handling, etc, which are essential functionalities of PHP. Besides, the core provides an interface for loading additional functionalities (called *extensions*). It is these flexible extensions that make PHP one of the most popular choices for web applications. Most PHP functionalities familiar to developers are actually extensions. For example, the session and database-access mechanisms are all implemented as extensions.

At the center of the core lies a virtual machine, called the Zend Engine, which parses PHP scripts into opcodes, and then executes them. The Zend Engine was also designed for extensibility. It not only allows the overriding of its basic functionality, including compilation, execution, and error handling, but also allows developers to add new functionalities through a set of well-defined hooks [16]. Appendix A provides more details about these hooks.

PHP's extensible architecture makes it quite convenient to implement SCUTA in PHP. The implementation of SCUTA involves three PHP extensions: session, database, and Scuta. The first two are existing extensions that need to be modified, and the third one, SCUTA's access control engine, is a new extension created by us. These three extensions depend on a common security context, which serves as the basis for our access control. The main element of this security context is the *effective subsession ID*, which indicates the effective ring of the current execution. The session module initializes this security context, the database module uses the context,

while the Scuta module uses and updates this context. A high-level overview of the SCUTA system is depicted in Figure 6, and we will discuss these modules in details.

4.2 The SCUTA Access Control Module

The main access control engine of SCUTA is implemented as a PHP extension (called Scuta). Its primary goal is to enforce SCUTA's ring-based access control during the execution. SCUTA's access control is conducted at the function level, i.e., when a function is invoked, SCUTA needs to decide whether the invocation is allowed or not. To achieve this, we need to intercept function calls during the runtime.

The Scuta extension intercepts function calls using the hooks provided by the Zend Engine. As we mentioned before, the Zend Engine provides a number of hooks, allowing extensions to insert additional code at particular places. In our implementation, we mainly used two hooks: one on function entry, and the other on function exit. At the function entry point, the Scuta extension checks whether a function can be invoked; if not, it throws a fatal error, causing the program to terminate. If the invocation is allowed, the Scuta extension updates the security context, and then gives the control to the invoked function. When the function returns, the Scuta extension takes control again via the function-exit hook, and updates the security context.

The Ring Configuration File. We use a configuration file to map program directories, files, classes, class methods, and functions to rings. This configuration is loaded into a hash-table when the web server is started. During the runtime, for each function (or method), SCUTA can get all its information, including function name, class name (for methods only), file name, and directory name. SCUTA then searches for the ring information of this function from the hash-table in the following order: (1) use the function name or method name, (2) use the class name (only for methods), (3) use the file name, (4) use the directory name, and (5) if all fail, set the subsession to the least privileged ring (i.e., SCUTA's default setting).

Labeling server-side programs is done outside of the programs; therefore, setting the security policy in SCUTA is separated from the program logic, and achieved using "configuration", instead of "implementation".

4.3 The Session Module

In the web applications that use PHP's built-in session mechanism, the function `session_start()` needs to be called at the beginning of a program. If the session does not exist, i.e., the HTTP request does not contain a Session ID (SID) cookie, this function will generate an SID cookie, and set the cookie in the header of the reply. When the client gets the reply, it will store the SID cookie in the browser, and attach the cookie to the subsequent HTTP requests bound to the same server. When serving subsequent HTTP requests, `session_start()` will still be invoked, but now seeing the SID cookie, it will not create a new session; instead, it will resume the existing session identified by the SID, as well as loading the session data.

To implement the subsession mechanism, we modified the `session_start()` function in the session extension. We added two functionalities. First, when a new session is created, subsessions will be generated, and the subsession cookies will be sent to the browser, along with the session cookie. Details of this process are already given in Section 3.1. Second, when an HTTP request comes, carrying subsession IDs, `session_start()` identifies the request's subsession ID based on the subsession cookies carried by the request. Then the function initializes the runtime security context. Both functionalities are quite easy to implement. The modification only involves about 120 lines of code.

Backward compatibility issue. In our implementation, instead of using the standard `Set-Cookie` to set the subsession cookies, we decided to define a new header called `Set-CookieSub` for that purpose (only for setting the subsession cookies; the session cookie is still set using `Set-Cookie`). This is mainly for backward compatibility. In an ESCUDO-enabled browser, `Set-CookieSub` is equivalent to `Set-Cookie`. However, in a non-ESCUDO browser, the `Set-CookieSub` header will be ignored, so no subsession ID will be set as cookies on the browser side; therefore, requests from a non-ESCUDO browser will not attach any subsession ID. In this way, servers can tell whether a browser is ESCUDO-enabled or not. If not, the server will automatically assign the lowest-privileged subsession ID to the requests, and thus providing the minimal services to non-ESCUDO browsers.

4.4 The Database Modules

PHP-based web applications interact with databases using the APIs provided by several PHP extensions, such as `mysql` and `mysqli` for MySQL databases. In most web applications, PHP connects to databases through a single user account. We use `dbuser` to refer to this account in our discussions.

To enforce the ring-based access control in databases, we leverage the databases' built-in access control mechanism, which can grant different database-access privileges to different users. Our basic idea is to create several new user accounts, one for each ring, so we can use the database's user-based access control. In particular, in our MySQL implementation, for the `dbuser` account, we create accounts `dbuser_0`, `dbuser_1`, and `dbuser_2` (assuming there are only three rings), with `dbuser_t` corresponding to ring t. We then use MySQL's `GRANT` command to grant each `dbuser_t` the database-access privileges entitled to ring t. This is achieved by the database administrator from inside the database. For example, if we want to put `TableA` in ring 0, `TableB` in ring 1, and `TableC` in ring 2, we run the following `GRANT` commands:

```
GRANT ALL ON TableA TO dbuser_0;
GRANT ALL ON TableB TO dbuser_0;
GRANT ALL ON TableC TO dbuser_0;
GRANT ALL ON TableB TO dbuser_1;
GRANT ALL ON TableC TO dbuser_1;
GRANT ALL ON TableC TO dbuser_2;
```

`mysql_connect()` is an API in `mysql` extension used to establish a connection with database. This API requires a user name and a password. We modified `mysql_connect()`, so when a program wants to connect to the database using the `dbuser` account, we replace this account name with `dbuser_t`, where t is the effective subsession ID. Therefore, subsequent queries using this connection are bounded by the privileges assigned to `dbuser_t`, i.e., they can only access the tables in rings t and above; Similar changes are made in `mysql_pconnect()`. Moreover, many applications use `mysqli_connect()` of the `mysqli` extension to connect to the database. We thus made corresponding changes to `mysqli`. The total changes are less than 30 lines of code.

MySQL's `GRANT` command allows us to conduct access control at even finer levels, including table columns, type of database operations, etc. More details are given in Appendix B.

Configuration tool. To avoid mistakes caused by manually running the `GRANT` command, we created a configuration tool, allowing developers to specify the ring configuration in a file. The file will be loaded by MySQL when it starts, and the configuration tool will then turn the ring configuration into corresponding `GRANT` commands. The format of the configuration file is given in Appendix B.

5. CASE STUDIES AND EVALUATION

To evaluate how SCUTA helps secure web applications, we have conducted five case studies using several open-source web applications, including `Collabtive` (a web-based project management system), `Mediawiki` (a wiki system), and `PHP-Calendar` (a web calendar). We use `Collabtive` as the basis (Figure 7(a)), which has a holder for client-side extensions. We have developed three different extensions for the demonstration purpose: Alert (Figure 7(b)), FindMe (Figures 7(c)), and AddEvent (Figure 7(d)). The case studies are divided into two major categories: protecting same-origin requests and protecting cross-origin requests.

5.1 Protecting Same-Origin Requests

Case 1: Client-side extensions. To demonstrate the benefit of SCUTA, we created a client-side extension called Alert for `Collabtive` (Figure 7(b)). This extension primarily displays a user's upcoming project deadlines; session cookies need to be attached to its requests to get the user's project information. In the current Web, that means the extension is granted all the user's privileges and can do a lot of damages to the user. Extensions like this have become quite popular in the Web. Client-side extensions are often developed by third parties, so they are less trustworthy than the web application's first-party contents. If they are malicious or vulnerable, the entire web application becomes endangered.

Because of the needs for client-side extensions to execute JavaScript and access session cookies, most of the existing methods, such as iframe, character escaping, NoScript add-ons [17] and ESCUDO, cannot easily achieve the desirable protection when including client-side extensions. In fact, all these methods either disallow JavaScript or disallow the access to session cookies; none supports the Alert extension. Without an appropriate protection mechanism, most web sites have to resolve to code verification and examination, filtering out malicious and vulnerable extensions, a practice that is complicated and error-prone.

SCUTA provides an intuitive and systematic mechanism to protect web applications against malicious/vulnerable client-side extensions. Using SCUTA, we can place client-side extensions, if not fully trusted, in a lower privileged ESCUDO ring within web pages, and accordingly, place its required server-side functions in the same SCUTA ring. Meanwhile, we place all the sensitive server-side functions, such as delete, update and insert, in the higher privileged SCUTA rings. Therefore, the not-fully-trusted client-side extensions will be limited to access the less sensitive server-side programs,

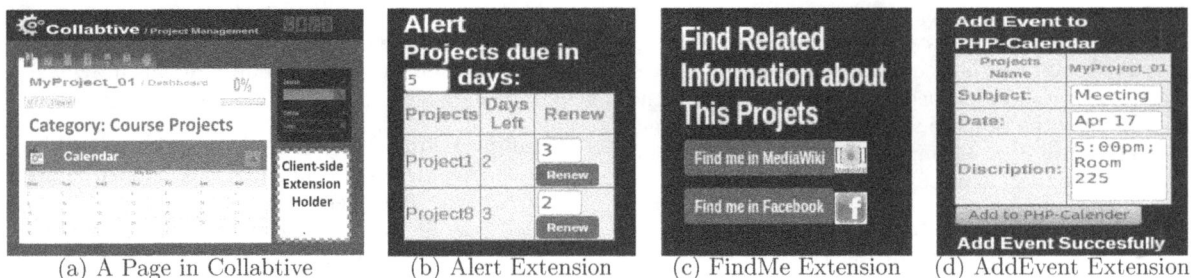

| (a) A Page in Collabtive | (b) Alert Extension | (c) FindMe Extension | (d) AddEvent Extension |

Figure 7: Collabtive and Its Client-Side Extensions

such as displaying and viewing functions. The damage is greatly limited if they are compromised.

In our demonstration in Figure 7(b), we put the Alert client-side extension in ESCUDO ring 3. To allow it to get the project deadline information, we place the read-only server-side function `display()` in SCUTA ring 3, while placing all the modification-involving functions in SCUTA ring 0. Therefore, if this extension is malicious, it can steal information, but cannot modify anything on the server side.

Case 2: Gate. Our Alert client-side extension in the previous case also has a `renew` button, which allows the user to postpone a project's deadline by at most a week. The extension needs to invoke some server-side function to modify project deadlines. The PHP function `add()` allows such a modification, but in addition to deadlines, it can also be used to modify many other aspects of projects (e.g., project titles). To prevent it from being invoked by untrusted client-side contents, this function is placed in SCUTA ring 0, essentially preventing the access by our Alert client-side extension. To solve this dilemma, we use Gate in SCUTA.

Gate is like system calls in operating systems, allowing lower-privileged code to invoke higher-privileged code, but in a controlled fashion. We created a Gate function called `renew()`, which calls `add()` to postpone project deadlines only, but before making the call, it verifies that the requested postpone duration is within a week. We place the Gate function `renew()` in SCUTA ring 0, but allowing accesses from subsession 3 (i.e. the threshold value in the gate specification is set to 3). Therefore, the Alert client-side extension, placed in ESCUDO ring 3, can invoke `renew()`, which runs in SCUTA ring 0 and can thus call `add()` to modify deadlines. Essentially, `renew()` provides a controlled access to the security-sensitive function `add()`.

Case 3: Server-side extensions. Server-side extensions of web applications are server-side programs developed by third parties. Examples of server-side extensions include `Elgg`'s social-network applications, third-party libraries, etc. These extensions are intended to extend the functionalities of web applications, and they are installed at the server side by web applications' administrators.

The current Web's security infrastructure is unable to deal with the risk introduced by server-side extensions, because these extensions, once installed, have the same privileges as the native code of web applications: they can directly manipulate databases, invoke the security-critical APIs, etc. This situation is dangerous if the extensions are vulnerable, or even worse, malicious.

In Figure 7(a), the functionality to display the category information was actually added by us. It sends an AJAX request to the server-side program `DisplayCat`, which fetches and returns the category information from the database. `DisplayCat` was also implemented by us (i.e., third-party developers), and was incorporated in `Collabtive` as a server-side extension. Because of our oversight, there was a SQL injection vulnerability in the code[2]. That is, a user, legitimate one, can intercept the AJAX request (e.g. using Firefox Add-ons), modify the value of its parameters using the SQL injection technique, and can thus cause `DisplayCat` to execute a malicious SQL statement. The situation will be more devastating if `DisplayCat` is malicious, because once triggered, it can run whatever PHP and SQL code it wants, essentially attacking `Collabtive` from the inside.

With SCUTA, we can reduce the risks caused by server-side extensions. This is done by placing the untrusted server-side extensions to less privileged rings (say ring K). When client-side requests or other server-side programs invoke a function in this extension, the function will be executed only with the privilege of ring K. In the example in Figure 7(a), the `DisplayCat` function is placed in ring 3. Since no database-update privileges or security-sensitive PHP functions are placed in ring 3, even if `DisplayCat` is vulnerable or malicious, and even if it is invoked from subsession 0, according to SCUTA's *privilege-downgrading rule*, it will be executed in the context of subsession 3; its damage is thus limited.

5.2 Protecting Cross-Origin Requests

A cross-origin (or cross-site) request is sent from a page of one origin to a server at a different origin. Cross-origin requests are becoming quite popular nowadays. We study how SCUTA can help secure these requests. There are two types of cross-origin requests: non-AJAX and AJAX.

Case 4: Cross-origin non-AJAX request. The non-AJAX type is typical cross-site HTTP requests. On one hand, cross-origin requests are widely used by web applications, but on the other hand, this type of requests are the culprit of the cross-site request forgery attack (CSRF).

To allow cross-origin requests while protecting against the CSRF attack, developers have to implement specific protection logic in their applications. A common practice is to embed secret tokens in web pages, which can only be attached to the requests from these pages (i.e., same-origin requests), not the cross-origin requests. At the sever side, web applications add extra program logic to check the existence of

---

[2]SQL injection vulnerability is one of the most common vulnerabilities in web applications [18].

the secret tokens. If developers miss a place, CSRF may be possible. Collabtive uses the secret-token approach, but unfortunately, it only places the checks in 6 out of the 16 server-side programs that need protection against the CSRF attack. MediaWiki has a similar situation. ESCUDO is also quite limited in protecting against CSRF, which directly denies cross-origin requests for sensitive sessions information.

SCUTA allows cross-origin requests to use sessions without becoming a victim of the CSRF attack. The basic idea is to only expose those CSRF-safe services to the cross-origin requests. CSRF-safe means that even if a request is forged, it can do no harm to the server. For example, the services that don't allow modifying anything on the server are CSRF-safe. Using SCUTA, developers can place those CSRF-safe services in the least-privileged ring. This ring is accessible to the cross-origin requests, because cross-origin requests are treated from the least-privileged subsession by ESCUDO. For those CSRF-unsafe services, developers must place them in the more privileged rings. If controlled accesses to these services are needed, we can use gates. Compared with the existing CSRF countermeasures, the protection achieved by SCUTA is simple and systematic.

Case 5: Cross-origin Ajax request. Due to security risks, making cross-origin requests using AJAX was initially disallowed by browsers based on the same-origin policy. Recently, however, to allow better interactions among web applications, this restriction has been lifted by almost all major browsers. A protocol called Cross-Origin Resource Sharing (CORS) [5] was introduced to support such type of requests. CORS uses HTTP's newly introduced Origin header to identify the origin of cross-origin requests; application servers can decide whether to allow the access from the specified origin.

We made an example in Figure 7(d), in which, users of Collabtive can add project-related events to their calendars at PHP-Calendar. The request, from Collabtive pages to the PHP-Calendar server, is a cross-origin AJAX request. To allow such a request, we need to add an origin-checking logic in the PHP-Calendar's AddEvent service, checking whether a cross-origin request is from Collabtive or not; if not, requests will be denied. Essentially, PHP-Calendar puts Collabtive on its trusted white-list for the AddEvent service.

Such a trust is too coarse-grained and risky: when putting Collabtive on its white-list, PHP-Calendar automatically delegates the trust to all the contents in the Collabtive's pages, regardless of whether they are Collabtive's first or third party contents. If those third-party contents are vulnerable or malicious, attackers can take advantage of the trust, and launch attacks on PHP-Calendar from Collabtive. Current Web systems cannot distinct where those cross-origin AJAX requests are initiated from.

SCUTA's subsession mechanism can achieve such a distinction, enabling web applications to conduct access control on cross-origin AJAX requests at a finer granularity than the current practice. In our case study, the EventAdd gadget is placed in ESCUDO ring 1. When it makes a cross-origin AJAX request to PHP-Calendar, it will be recognized by PHP-Calendar as belonging to subsession 1. The AddEvent function is placed in SCUTA ring 1 at the PHP-Calendar server, allowing the cross-origin access from the Collabtive's EventAdd gadget. If some untrusted contents on the same page try to access AddEvent, as long as Collabtive

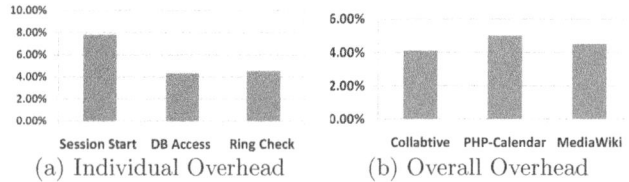

(a) Individual Overhead   (b) Overall Overhead

Figure 8: Performance Evaluation

puts these contents anywhere above ESCUDO ring 1, the access will be denied by SCUTA.

If PHP-Calendar trusts Collabtive less, it can map Collabtive's requests from ESCUDO ring K to subsession K+Δ, to downgrade cross-origin requests' privileges by Δ rings.

5.3 Performance Evaluation

To evaluate the performance of SCUTA, we measured the server-side execution overhead caused by SCUTA. We used an Apache benchmarking tool called ab in our experiment. The tool allows us to measure the processing time of each HTTP request. Network latency is already excluded in our measurement, as it has nothing to do with SCUTA.

We have designed two sets of experiments: The first set focuses on evaluating the overhead of individual operations that are affected by SCUTA. These operations involve session/subsession initialization, database access, and SCUTA ring check. Figure 8(a) indicates that the overhead on individual operations is quite small, especially for database access and SCUTA ring check (only around 4%); session-start needs to generate and verify subsession IDs, and the extra encryption/decryption causes more overhead (around 8%).

In the second set of experiments, we measured the overall execution overhead that SCUTA brings to real web applications. We used Collabtive, MediaWiki and PHP-Calendar, and plotted the results in Figure 8(b). The results show that the overall overhead caused by SCUTA is only about 4%.

6. RELATED WORK

The need for providing a fine-grained access control on the server-side of the web infrastructure has been well recognized by many researchers. A number of language-based approaches have been proposed in the past. Early language-based work focuses on enforcing confidentiality and integrity of web applications. They use static analysis methods to help enforce fine-grained security policies [19], or use dynamic tainting methods to detect vulnerabilities [20].

Recent language-based work starts to focus on enforcing fine-grained access control at the framework level. Chong et al. proposed a novel framework, called SIF [21], to build web applications. With SIF, explicit confidentiality and integrity policies can be given as a compile-time program annotation or as run-time user requirement. Compile-time and run-time checking will enforce these policies. Another language-based approach is called Capsules [22] by Krishnamurthy et al. This framework benefits from an object-capability language called Joe-E [23]. Capsules provides interfaces that expose limited, explicitly-specified privileges to application components. With Capsules, the web framework can enforce privilege separation and isolation of web applications, and thus restricts what each component of the application can do and quarantines buggy or compromised code.

The goal of SCUTA and the language-based approaches is the same, i.e., to achieve a fine-grained access control in web applications, but SCUTA takes a very different approach. SCUTA provides a new subsession primitive for web applications. Actually, SCUTA and the existing language-based approaches complement each other quite nicely. For instance, web developers can use SCUTA to map the programs to different subsessions, and then use the language approaches to further restrict the programs within each particular ring; the subsession concept can also be integrated into the security policies that are enforced by the language approaches.

In addition to the session-based architecture currently used by most web applications, researchers are also exploring other alternatives [24, 25]. SCUTA may not be directly applicable to those new architectures, but we believe that ideas similar to SCUTA may be used to provide a fine-grained access control in their security infrastructures.

7. CONCLUSION

To improve the security in web applications, we have designed SCUTA, a fine-grained access control system for web servers. SCUTA is based on the subsession concept which allow servers to distinguish more trustworthy HTTP requests from less trustworthy ones. Such a distinction can help servers enforce fine-grained access control. Based on subsessions, we have developed a ring-based access control model and implemented SCUTA in PHP. Using case studies, we have demonstrated that SCUTA can be used by web applications to satisfy a variety of protection needs, most of which are hard to satisfy, using the Web's current access control systems. In our future work, we plan to further develop configuration and automation tools to help users configure their web applications, and detect problems in their configuration.

8. REFERENCES

[1] J. Alpert and N. Jesse, "We knew the web was big..." The Official Google Blog. http://googleblog.blogspot.com/2008/07/we-knew-web-was-big.html, 2008.

[2] N. Intelligence, "Domain counts & internet statistics," http://www.domaintools.com/internet-statistics/, May 2009.

[3] S. Corp., "Symantec internet security threat report: Trends for july-december 2007 (executive summary)," Page 1–2, 2008.

[4] WhiteHat Security, "Whitehat website security statistic report, 10th edition," 2010.

[5] "Cross-origin resource sharing," URL: http://www.w3.org/TR/cors/, 2010.

[6] C. Jackson, A. Bortz, D. Boneh, and J. C. Mitchell, "Protecting browser state from web privacy attacks," in *WWW 2006*.

[7] B. Livshits and U. Erlingsson, "Using web application construction frameworks to protect against code injection attacks," in *PLAS 2007*.

[8] C. Karlof, U. Shankar, J. D. Tygar, and D. Wagner, "Dynamic pharming attacks and locked same-origin policies for web browsers," in *CCS 2007*.

[9] B. Parno, J. M. McCune, D. Wendlandt, D. G. Andersen, and A. Perrig, "CLAMP: Practical prevention of large-scale data leaks," in *Proc. IEEE Symposium on Security and Privacy*, Oakland, CA, May 2009.

[10] M. Dalton, C. Kozyrakis, and N. Zeldovich, "Nemesis: Preventing authentication & access control vulnerabilities in web applications," in *Proceedings of the Eighteenth Usenix Security Symposium (Usenix Security)*, Montreal, Canada, 2009.

[11] K. Jayaraman, W. Du, B. Rajagopalan, and S. J. Chapin, "Escudo: A fine-grained protection model for web browsers," in *Proceedings of the 30th International Conference on Distributed Computing Systems (ICDCS)*, Genoa, Italy, June 21-25 2010.

[12] K. Patil, X. Dong, X. Li, Z. Liang, and X. Jiang, "Towards fine-grained access control in javascript contexts," in *Proceedings of the 31st International Conference on Distributed Computing Systems (ICDCS)*, Minneapolis, Minnesota, USA, June 20-24 2011.

[13] M. D. Schroeder and J. H. Saltzer, "A hardware architecture for implementing protection rings," *Commun. ACM*, vol. 15, no. 3, pp. 157–170, 1972.

[14] T. Jim, N. Swamy, and M. Hicks, "Defeating script injection attacks with browser-enforced embedded policies," in *WWW 2007*.

[15] M. V. Gundy and H. Chen, "Noncespaces: Using randomization to enforce information flow tracking and thwart cross-site scripting attacks," in *Proceedings of the 16th Annual Network and Distributed System Security Symposium (NDSS)*, San Diego, CA, February 2009.

[16] G. Schlossnagle, *Advanced PHP Programming*. Sams, 2004.

[17] "Noscript add-ons," URL: https://addons.mozilla.org/en-US/firefox/addon/noscript/.

[18] OWASP, "The ten most critical web application security risks," http://www.owasp.org/index.php/File:OWASP_T10_-_2010_rc1.pdf, 2010.

[19] N. Jovanovic, C. Kruegel, and E. Kirda, "Pixy: A static analysis tool for detecting web application vulnerabilities," in *Proceedings of the IEEE Symposium on Security and Privacy*, 2006.

[20] W. Xu, V. N. Venkatakrishnan, R. Sekar, and I. V. Ramakrishnan, "A framework for building privacy-conscious composite web services," in *Proceedings of the 15th USENIX Security Symposium*, 2006.

[21] S. Chong, K. Vikram, and A. C. Myers, "Sif: enforcing confidentiality and integrity in web applications," in *Proceedings of 16th USENIX Security Symposium on USENIX Security Symposium*, 2007, pp. 1:1–1:16.

[22] A. Krishnamurthy, A. Mettler, and D. Wagner, "Fine-grained privilege separation for web applications," in *WWW*, 2010, pp. 551–560.

[23] A. Mettler, D. Wagner, and T. Close, "Joe-e: A security-oriented subset of java," in *17th Network and Distributed System Security Symposium*, 2010.

[24] C. Queinnec, "Inverting back the inversion of control or, continuations versus page-centric programming," in *Newsletter of ACM SIGPLAN Notices*, 2003.

[25] E. Cooper, S. Lindley, P. Wadler, and J. Yallop, "Links: Web programming without tiers," in *Proceedings of 5th International Symposium on Formal Methods for Components and Objects (FMCO)*, 2006, pp. 266–296.

APPENDIX

A. THE HOOKS OF ZEND ENGINE

The Zend Engine provides a number of hooks, allowing developers to insert their own logic into the compilation and execution process. We list some of its hooks in the following:

- `zend_compile_file`: compiler hook, used to add additional logic to the compilation process, or override the existing compilation process.

- `zend_execute`: execution hook, used to add additional logic to the execution process, or override the existing execution process.

- `statement_handler`: invoked after executing each single PHP statement, mainly used for debugging.

- `fcall_begin_handler`: invoked before the execution enters each single function.

- `fcall_end_handler`: invoked before the execution returns from a function.

- `startup`: invoked when the zend extension is loaded at server setup.

- `shutdown`: invoked when the zend extension is unloaded at server shutdown.

- `activate`: invoked at the beginning of each request.

- `deactivate`: invoked at the end of each request.

Let us take the `zend_compile_file` and `zend_execute` hooks as examples. Assuming that we want to include some extra logic before and after PHP compiles a function, we can do the following:

```
old_compile_file = zend_compile_file;
zend_compile_file = my_compile_file;

zend_op_array *my_compile_file()
{
    ... Our logic before compilation ...

    // run the original compilation process
    zend_op_array *op_array op_array = old_compile_file();

    ... Our logic after compilation ...
}
```

We can do similar things to the execution process, i.e., adding extra logic before and after a program is executed.

```
old_execute = zend_execute;
zend_execute = my_execute;

my_execute()
{
    ... Our logic before execution ...

    // run the original execution process
    old_execute();

    ... Our logic after execution ...
}
```

B. DATABASE RING CONFIGURATION

The `GRANT` command in MySQL assigns specific privileges to users. In our SCUTA implementation, we use this command to assign rings to database objects. To avoid mistakes caused by manually running the `GRANT` command, we let users write their ring configuration into a file using an intuitive format; we have created a configuration tool to automatically convert the configuration into a series of `GRANT` commands. The format of the configuration file is described in the following:

```
[USER]
    Ring:Operations:Table:Columns
```

With this configuration file, we can do access control on operations (e.g. SELECT, UPDATE, etc.), tables (e.g. Table A, Table B, etc.) and colums (e.g. Colum Name of Table A, Column Course of Table B, etc.).

We describe three examples of ring configuration and their corresponding `GRANT` commands.

Permission on tables. Assuming `TableA`, `TableB` and `TableC` can be accessed by dbuser. We would like to to place `TableA` in ring 0, `TableB` in ring 1, and `TableC` in ring 2. We have the following configuration file:

```
[dbuser]
    0:ALL:TableA:*
    1:ALL:TableB:*
    2:ALL:TableC:*
```

Because SCUTA supports hierarchical structure, if we place a table in ring k, the tables can also be accessed from rings 0 to k. Our tool converts the above configuration file into the following commands:

```
GRANT ALL ON TableA TO dbuser_0;
GRANT ALL ON TableB TO dbuser_0;
GRANT ALL ON TableC TO dbuser_0;
GRANT ALL ON TableB TO dbuser_1;
GRANT ALL ON TableC TO dbuser_1;
GRANT ALL ON TableC TO dbuser_2;
```

Permission on columns. Assuming `MyTable` can be accessed by dbuser. We would like to place its columns into different rings: columns `Deadline` and `Action` in ring 0, column `Profile` in ring 1, and column `Name` in ring 2. We have the following configuration file:

```
[dbuser]
    0:ALL:MyTable:Deadline, Action
    1:ALL:MyTable:Profile
    2:ALL:MyTable:Name
```

Our tool converts the above configuration file into the following commands:

```
GRANT ALL (Deadline, Action) ON MyTable TO dbuser_0;
GRANT ALL (Profile, Name) ON MyTable TO dbuser_0;
GRANT ALL (Profile, Name) ON MyTable TO dbuser_1;
GRANT ALL (Name) ON MyTable TO dbuser_2;
```

Permission on operations. Assuming `MyTable` can be accessed by `dbuser`, and it has a column called `Profile`. We would like to assign different operation privileges to this column: ring 2 can conduct `SELECT` only (i.e. read-only), ring 1 can additionally conduct `UPDATE`, and ring 0 can additionally conduct `DELETE` and `INSERT`. We have the following configuration file:

```
[dbuser]
    0:DELETE, INSERT:MyTable:Profile
    1:UPDATE:MyTable:Profile
    2:SELECT:MyTable:Profile
```

Our tool converts the above configuration file into the following commands:

```
GRANT DELETE (Profile) ON MyTable TO dbuser_0;
GRANT INSERT (Profile) ON MyTable TO dbuser_0;
GRANT UPDATE (Profile) ON MyTable TO dbuser_0;
GRANT SELECT (Profile) ON MyTable TO dbuser_0;
GRANT UPDATE (Profile) ON MyTable TO dbuser_1;
GRANT SELECT (Profile) ON MyTable TO dbuser_1;
GRANT SELECT (Profile) ON MyTable TO dbuser_2;
```

Graph-Based XACML Evaluation

Santiago Pina Ros*
University of Murcia
Murcia, Spain
santiago.pina1@um.es

Mario Lischka†
AGT Group (R&D) GmbH
Darmstadt, Germany
mlischka@agtgermany.com

Félix Gómez Mármol
NEC Laboratories Europe
NEC Europe Ltd.
Heidelberg, Germany
felix.gomez-marmol@neclab.eu

ABSTRACT

The amount of private information in the Internet is constantly increasing with the explosive growth of cloud computing and social networks. XACML is one of the most important standards for specifying access control policies for web services. The number of XACML policies grows really fast and evaluation processing time becomes longer. The XEngine approach proposes to rearrange the matching tree according to the attributes used in the target sections, but for speed reasons they only support equality of attribute values. For a fast termination the combining algorithms are transformed into a first applicable policy, which does not support obligations correctly.

In our approach all comparison functions defined in XACML as well as obligations are supported. In this paper we propose an optimization for XACML policies evaluation based on two tree structures. The first one, called Matching Tree, is created for a fast searching of applicable rules. The second one, called Combining Tree, is used for the evaluation of the applicable rules. Finally, we propose an exploring method for the Matching Tree based on the binary search algorithm. The experimental results show that our approach is orders of magnitude better than Sun PDP.

Categories and Subject Descriptors

D.4.6 [**Security and Protection**]: Access controls

General Terms

Performance

Keywords

XACML, Evaluation

---

*This paper is based on the authors work during an internship at NEC Laboratories Europe

†This paper is based on the authors work while being employed at NEC Laboratories Europe

1. INTRODUCTION AND MOTIVATION

OASIS eXtensible Access Control Language (XACML) [11, 12] is a widely deployed standard language for access control policy specifications. It follows an attribute based model to identify atomic authorization elements (e.g subject and resource). The rules encoded in XACML are evaluated against a given request by a component called Policy Decision Point (PDP). Once a policy is specified, it evolves by and by to address new requirements and becomes large both in content and number of cases covered. This causes issues in policy evaluation run-time. Due to this known problem, there is a line of research to effectively handle large number of rules and policies with varying number of attributes.

Among the various efforts on this field, XEngine [5, 6] represents the state-of-the-art for XACML based authorization decision. XEngine has performance gains in orders of magnitude compared to SUN XACML engine (Corp.). It employs efficient data structures and special pre-processing techniques to improve the evaluation. The key idea is to pre-process the target section of the hierarchy formed by policy sets, policies and rules, and take into account that the conditions of a rule are only evaluated in case all the attributes in the target sections along the path are matching with a given request.

It is important to note that these attributes may be evaluated in any order, as long as the correct condition is reached in the end, or, in case of XEngine, just the final decision of accept or deny. In contrast to the evaluation of the target sections of policy sets, policies and rules, whose numbers could increase dramatically in large organizations, the run-time of this approach is limited by the number of attributes Ids (a), and their values (v_a) used in the target sections. Thus, XEngine has an average runtime of $O(a * log(max(v_a)))$ but as some limitations and drawbacks:

- The normalization process described in XEngine does not support XACML obligations although they are a fundamental construct in XACML.

- XEngine supports equal functions, while complex functions and comparison functions are not supported.

- The internal data structure (i.e. multi-valued decision diagram) causes extreme memory consumption.

Motivated by these issues, an enhanced concept for evaluation is presented in this paper. While we focused on the first two points of the above list, the multi-value requests and policies are currently not supported.

2. RELATED WORK

Since XACML was standardized by OASIS in 2003, a striking number of research works have been done on XACML so far. Most of the research work has been focused on verification, modelling, analysis and testing of XACML policies [1, 4, 8, 13].

Some recently researches are focused in XACML optimization [6, 7, 10]. The proposals presented in [5, 6] and [7] constitute the current state of the art in XACML optimization. [7] is based on statistics of the past requests and its matched rules, which are categorized according to a clustering-based technique, and tries to reorder policies and rules according to the statistics results. This approach, however, has two main flaws: i) reordering of policies does not support obligations, as we will see in section 4, and ii) the statistic method does not improve the processing time when the access requests are not uniform.

XEngine [5, 6] focuses on improving the performance of the PDP by numericalization and normalization of the XACML Policies. In the implementation[1] *numericalization* is a hash function that converts every attribute type into integers and stored in a hash table with the objective of an efficient comparison. By doing like this, they achieve an improvement in performance, but are unable to handle any comparison functions. The *normalization*, in turn, converts every combining algorithm into a first applicable combining algorithm in order to build a flat policy structure from the original policies tree structure. Finally they build a tree with the numericalized and normalized policies for efficient processing of requests.

Our proposal has some similarities and differences with XEngine. The approaches are similar since both works try to achieve an improvement in the performance of the PDP using a tree data structure. Essentially both approaches build a decision path and store the matched rules at the end of the paths, but the differences are in the details. Since numericalization does not support comparison functions and our goal is to try to support most XACML specifications, we decided not to use it. For the same reason we also refused to use normalization, since reordering rules and policies does not support obligations, as mentioned before.

In our approach we build two types of trees, namely: Matching Tree and Combining Tree. The Matching Tree is similar to the tree built in XEngine without the numericalization process, and with different end nodes. As each edge in the tree is representing a concrete value[2], thus our approach does not support multi-valued requests or target sections.

The leaf nodes in XEngine are the normalized rules in a flat structure, while leaf nodes of a Matching Tree are actually Combining Trees. The latter consist basically of a structure that stores policies and rules preserving the original tree structure of the policy set. We will explain deeply the concepts of Matching Tree and Combining Tree in section 4.

3. PROBLEM STATEMENT

XEngine [5, 6] is based on the idea of using decision diagrams for a faster evaluation, and experimental results have shown that the approach provides a number of magnitude

---

[1]In [5, 6] all occuring attribute values are just enumerated.
[2] [5, 6] are using the combination of multi value rules.

faster evaluation compared to the SUN Reference Implementation (SUN RI).

The key idea is to transform the target matching of the policy sets, policies and rules into a decision diagram (DD). Decision Diagrams are widely used in verification tools, in particular, software systems used for hardware design. A DD is a directed acyclic graph, $G = (V, E)$, where the nodes V represent attributes (used in the target sections) and E represent the equality of the attributes in the request with a particular value. The edges are leading to the next attribute present in the target sections.

Binary decision diagrams (BDDs) have been studied extensively in the literature [2], and many variants [3], [9] have been introduced. A decision based on decision diagrams is obtained by combinations of variable assignments that lead to a terminal node in G.

The reason for the performance advantage of this approach is the limitation of the evaluation time by the length of the evaluation paths in the decision diagrams. In turn, the maximum length is limited by the number of attributes used in the various target sections and is not bound to the number of policy sets, policies and rules. In XEngine a technique called forwarding tables is used to find the correct edges in constant time. If the transformation is not used, some fast search algorithms are required to find the edge to the next node. While the general approach of XEngine is quite convincing, their decision diagrams lack support for several concepts:

- Incomplete list of attributes. In general, a subset of the attributes could lead to a decision. Yet, XEngine needs all the attributes to be able to reach a decision.

- Support of comparison functions. The domain approach especially causes problems if the value area is countable, but theoretically infinite (e.g. time of the request has to be larger than a specific date).

- Support of regular expressions match functions. As the algorithm for matching could not be transformed to a simple comparison, this functionality is not supported.

- Correct handling of DenyOverrides and PermitOverrides. In case the dominant effect does not determine the result, the correct set of obligations is not returned.

As one of our requirements has been to fully support the OASIS XACML 2.0 standard (having a clear view on how to support XACML 3.0 as well), we have carefully considered the aforementioned features in our solution.

4. IMPROVED CONCEPT OF GRAPH EVALUATION

In this section we will present an improved concept for XACML evaluation making use of a graph based on the attribute IDs of a policies tree. In Figure 1 a sample policy set, policies and rules are shown, which we will use to illustrate our concept. The hierarchical structure of this graph entails the inclusion of rules, policies and policy set (button up).

In our approach we are distinguishing between the search of the applicable rules for a request and the search of the correct effect in the applicable rules. Furthermore, we will show why this approach solves the limitations presented in

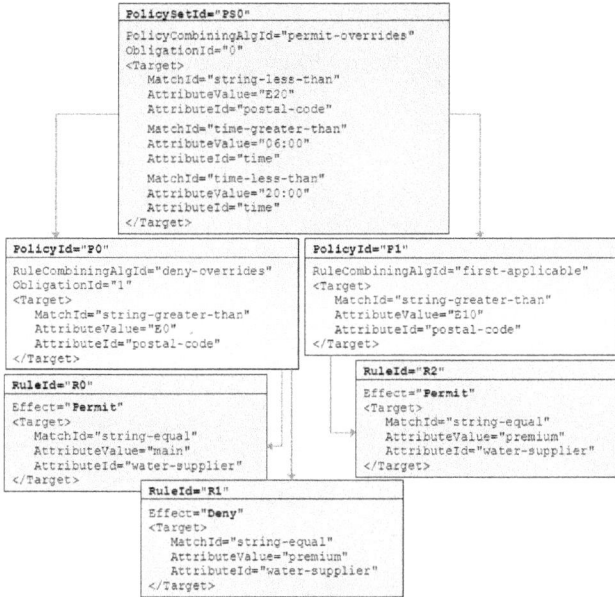

Figure 1: Example Policies Tree

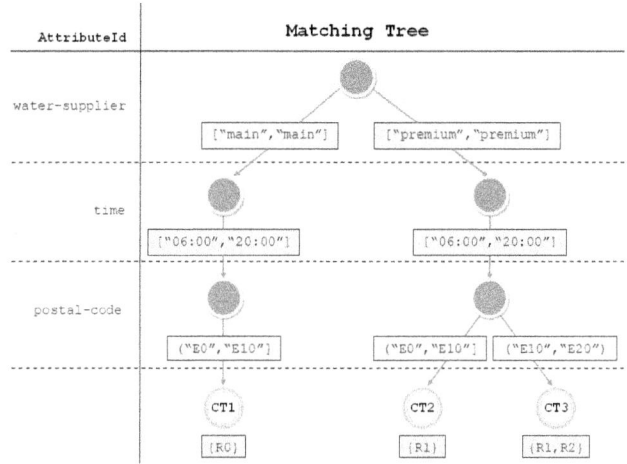

Figure 2: Corresponding Matching Tree

previous Section 3, in particular the correct support of obligations and all types of target matching functions.

In order to develop this separation we have created two data structures, namely: Matching Tree and Combining Tree.

The Matching Tree is used to find the applicable rules based on the values of the attributes in the various target sections. This tree has one level per different attribute Id, and the edges are represented by disjoint intervals of different comparable elements (e.g., ["SE10","SE20"], [5.3,7.8], [14:00, 15:30]). The evaluation of a request begins from the root node, it takes from the request the attribute value that corresponds to the attribute id of the current level, it searches the interval that contains such attribute value, and repeats the process with the node pointed by the selected interval. The evaluation is successful when a terminal node is reached, indicating that there is at least one rule whose target attributes are matching the request. When an attribute value taken from the request is not contained in any interval, there is no matching rule.

In Figure 2 we can see the Matching Tree built with the policies described in Figure 1. While the structure as such has been used in XEngine, we will discuss some optimizations regarding the sorting of the attributes in section 5.2. In the next sections the path (sequence of nodes) from the root node to a terminal node in the Matching Tree will be called the *MatchingPath* of this terminal node. In contrast to XEngine, each terminal node of the tree contains, in turn, a Combining Tree built with the rules that match with the path followed to reach this terminal node.

A Combining Tree is a structure based on the policies tree containing a subset of all the rules, where the targets of all the elements are empty, since a Combining Tree is built only with those rules which are actually applicable. This approach allows us to find the result of the request in a shorter time. In addition this structure preserves the original hierarchy of combining algorithms, which have to

be applied to the obligations also included in the combining tree.

Regarding the support of incomplete list of attributes and complex functions (regular expressions, etc), we have to create special edges that need a separate evaluation. In that case the evaluation can take multiple paths in the Matching Tree, and we have to merge all the Combining Trees belonging to each path. There is a similar problem with requests with multi-valued attributes, and the solution is to make a separate evaluation for each attribute value and merge all the resulting Combining Trees again.

4.1 Combining algorithms

For XEngine, the policy combining algorithms DenyOverrides and PermitOverrides are transformed into a FirstApplicable algorithm. This approach is only valid in the case where obligations are not used. In case the policy sets and their underlying policies contain obligations, then such solution is not longer valid, as the obligations of all evaluated policies or policy sets which have the same effect as the final decision have to be provided to the PEP [11, sec 7.14]. Let's assume a policy set applies DenyOverrides: if the resulting effect to the request is permit, then all underlying policies have to be evaluated and the evaluations have to check if there is an applicable rule with the effect deny. According to the standard, all obligations with the effect of the decision (i.e. Permit or Deny) have to be attached to the result, not only those of the first policy with the effect permit.

In case of incomplete attribute lists, usage comparison or regular expression functions, the evaluation is forked. Hence, multiple terminating nodes could be reached. This represents the case where multiple rules provide a result during the evaluation and policy combining has to be applied.

During the creation of the decision diagram, the original tree of policy sets and policies has to be examined and a Combining Tree is built with the rules of each terminating node. A Combining Tree preserves the tree structure of policy sets and policies, keeping the obligations and the combining algorithm of each node. In a Combining Tree the corresponding terminating nodes are rules, which can be reordered, assigning priorities to the rules with empty targets, in order to achieve a faster evaluation. If multiple terminat-

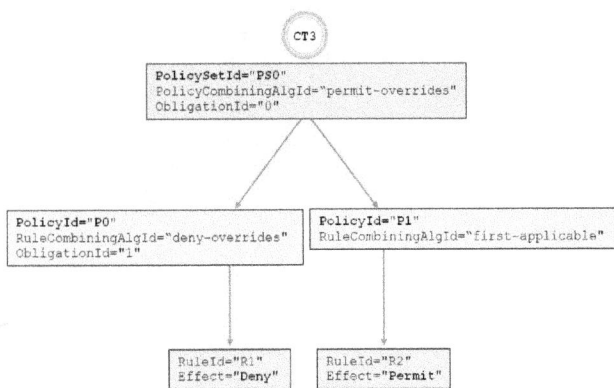

Figure 3: Example Combining Tree

ing nodes are reached during the evaluation, we will have to merge all Combining Trees.

4.1.1 Combining Tree

A Combining Tree (see Figure 3) is an auxiliary data structure based on the policies tree. It is essentially a subset of the tree without any target section. Initially one could think of reordering the policies or even changing the tree structure to a list with a special order of the rules, but if we want to preserve obligations, we have to keep the tree structure and the order of the policies. The policies have to be evaluated in the same order because otherwise the result could get a different obligation, and therefore the returned effect could be wrong.

Our goal is to keep all the applicable rules of a Matching Path in the corresponding leaf node. In order to preserve obligations we will create a Combining Tree with those applicable rules. At this point we should highlight that, as we can see in Figure 2, the same rule could be at the end of different Matching Paths, and subsequently, in different Combining Trees. As an example Figure 3 shows the Combining Tree CT3 of the Matching Tree shown in Figure 2

4.1.2 Rule Combining Algorithms

Since rules does not have obligations (at least in XACML 2.0; this is introduced in XACML 3.0 [12]), we can reorder them in the Combining Tree. The new order of the rules will depend on the combining algorithm of their parents in the Combining Tree. We will assign priorities to the rules in the original policies trees, to make it easier to build the Combining Tree with the sorted rules. When building a Combining Node referencing to a policy, its children rules will be added in descending order starting with the highest priority rule. The priorities are assigned as follows, depending on the rule combining algorithm:

- In case of a first-applicable combining algorithm, the priority is assigned to the rules in reverse order of the occurrence in the policy and increased each time, starting with priority 1.

- In case of a deny-overrides combining algorithm, all policies with the effect permit get the priority 1. The remainder rules with effect deny are assigned a priority in the reverse order of their occurrence in the policy.

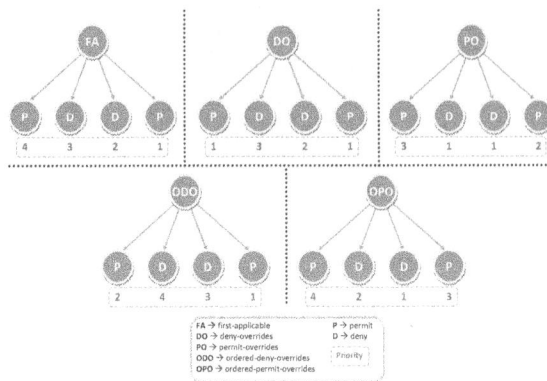

Figure 4: Priorities example

- In case it is ordered-deny-overrides combining algorithm, the priority to those rules with effect permit is again assigned in reverse order and increased by one each time starting with 1. Then those rules with effect deny are assigned in reverse order with a priority starting from the highest priority of the last permit rule plus one.

- In case of permit-overrides the assignment is done symmetrically (first rules with effect deny, then those with effect permit).

- In case of a ordered-permit-overrides combining algorithm, the priority to those rules with effect deny is again assigned in reverse order and increased by one each time starting with 1. Then those rules with effect permit are assigned in reverse order with a priority starting from the highest priority of the last deny rule plus one.

An example is shown in Figure 4 where the order of the leaf nodes correspond to the order in the containing policy, and the numbers are indicating the priority assigned based on the approach presented above.

4.2 XEngine comparison

XEngine represents the state-of-the-art for fast XACML based authorization decision, being currently, as far as we know, the fastest way to evaluate XACML policies. However, it also has some limitations. The main differences in the structures presented in this paper and the ones presented in XEngine are twofold:

- XEngine maps every attribute value to a numerical value and the PDD based in numerical intervals, while we build a Matching Tree with only one level per attribute value and the edges are represented with generic intervals.

- XEngine transforms the policies tree structure to a flat structure with the first-applicable combining algorithm. On the other hand we build Combining Trees, that preserve the tree structure and the combining algorithms.

In the following we present a qualitative comparison between XEngine and our approach.

4.2.1 Correctness

XEngine presents a formal proof of the correctness of Normalization, but since we do not modify the tree structure of the policy sets and policies it is easy to see that our approach find the correct solution. We separate the evaluation in two parts, first we search the applicable rules with the Matching Tree; once we have the applicable rules we create a Combining Tree preserving the original structure of the overall policy set, and we use the original algorithms to evaluate the request. So, we use the original structure, containing the applicable rules and we evaluate the response using the original algorithms, then the response must be the same. In this case both approaches are correct.

4.2.2 Support of comparison functions

Decision diagrams are optimized to support the check of equality of attribute values. In XEngine a range check is used for String values, but these ranges are determined by the values parsed in the policies. However, the request may contain additional values not yet known. Thus, the mapping to integer technique does not seem to be adequate.

The reason is simple, you can always find an string between any two given strings, but you can not find an integer between any two given integers. For example, you can not find any integer between 4 and 5, but given the string "x" and the string "y", with "x" < "y", ("x" +"a") is between "x" and "y". For that reason we can not find any bijective function from strings to integers.

A first approach is to find a bijective function from strings to a real number, but it present two problems:

- String comparison seems to be faster than most mapping functions, since you have to explore every char in the string.
- The precision of the mapping could be as much between 7 and 10 chars, due to the precision of doubles.

In order to solve this problem we use data-intervals. A data-interval is a structure similar to a numerical interval but composed by a different comparable data type. Intervals of dates, char, etc., are "natural", but we need to add two new values to the value set of each data type: left infinity, and right infinity.

They are ordered according to the attributes given in the target section and used for comparison. During the evaluation these lists are checked and whenever the attribute value given in the request is valid for a particular comparison, the corresponding edge has to be evaluated has well. As in the aforementioned case of missing attributes, it has to be determined whether this should be done in a concurrent or sequential fashion. As the lists are ordered according to the respective comparison operator, they are traversed until the first comparison fails.

In addition, some early experiments have indicated that computing the hash value of a string takes significantly more time than a string comparison.

Mapping String to Integer is a good idea, since Integer comparison is fast than String comparison, but as explained before we lost the String comparison functions support. So if String comparison functions are needed it is recommended to

choose the MatchingTree solution rather than the Decision Diagram solution.

4.2.3 Incomplete lists of attributes

Assuming a variety of different attributes used in the target sections, it is more than likely that not all known attribute Ids are used in a decision path. The order in which the attributes are checked, i.e. on which level they are present in the decision diagram, is arbitrary, or subject to further optimization strategies. At some point (due to the presence of the attribute in one target section and the absence in another target section) a special handling is necessary. In this case two paths have to be evaluated: the one which contains the attribute (assuming that the attribute is present in the request) and the one which does not introduce such attribute.

Whether this forked evaluation is done in a concurrent fashion or the open ends are stored for a sequential analysis has to be determined at a later stage. Both approaches introduce some coordination overhead. Obviously, empty target categories for subjects, resources or actions are handled in the same way.

Special edges built specifically for empty attributes IDs are needed to support empty targets sections in a decision diagram solution, but XEngine does not mention this case and cannot supports it.

4.2.4 Regular expression support

The use of regular expression in the target sections has to be handled in a similar way than comparisons. As there is no simple replacement for this function, the matching has to be evaluated. In case of a match, the respective edge has to be evaluated (concurrently or sequentially). Since the regular expression match operations are quite expensive computations, the attributes which are checked with this function should be moved to the end of the potential decision paths. For this reason a special edge has to be created for each match function. This way, an earlier missing or mismatching attribute might already terminate the evaluation before these nodes are reached.

Regular expression can not be mapped to a single integer value, so the numericalizarion method can not be applied to this kind of function and the regular expression has to be evaluated. On the other hand the Matching Tree creates a special edge for this kind of functions and fork the evaluation. This issue should be studied deeply in future work since both approaches seem to be computational expensive.

4.2.5 Indeterminate response support

In XACML specification is described the policy combining algorithms and the response of the evaluation of the algorithm can be deny or permit if the policy combining algorithm get an Indeterminate response evaluation a rule. This issue is not contemplated in flat structures of rules like the one used in XEngine, so it is needed preserve the tree structure if we want to give an adequate response in this cases.

4.2.6 Obligations handling

In the traditional evaluation like SUN PDP, a decision is reached on rule level and the result is sent up again. During this backtracking, the obligations specified in the traversed policy sets and policies have to be collected. This collection is then sent to the PEP as part of the result. During the creation of the decision diagram, the obligations specified in the policy sets and policies have to be tracked, and it has to be ensured that all obligations which are along a specific path are stored in the final node which also contains the condition to be evaluated. This way whenever a terminating node is reached, the related obligations just have to be sent with the result. In our solution we propose Combining Trees for the final evaluation of a request and, according to this approach, we can handle obligations with the algorithm of the XACML specification.

A solution with obligation support also needs to preserve the tree structure of the applicable rules, in order to collect the obligations once the result is found. The flat structure of rules and the reordering into first-applicable combining algorithms used in XEngine does not take into account the special cases where the none dominant result (i.e. deny in case of permit-overrides) is determined. Thus XEngine only provides the set of obligations related to the first applicable policy (set), instead of all the obligations of all policies evaluated according to [11,12] and done in our approach.

4.2.7 Multi-valued policies and requests

As we have previously mentioned, our approach supports requests with multi-valued attributes, but the Matching Tree does not support policies (or more precisely predicate path lists) with multi-valued attributes. This is due to the current concept in which each level of the Matching Tree represents a different attribute Id and the edges of the tree are disjoint intervals. Based on this, it is not possible to build an edge with an interval that match only with two given values. As part of our future working we are evaluating the idea of adding dedicated edges or sets of edges to support policies with multi-valued attributes.

On the other hand, XEngine support this characteristic with the use of several levels per attribute Id. This point could be important in some environments, so in this case the use of XEngine could be more interesting.

4.2.8 Processing time

An important goal of this paper is to reduce the processing time of evaluation and, as we will see in section 6, our approach is several times faster than SUN implementation. XEngine is also several time faster than SUN RI and two points lead us to think that XEngine could be faster than our approach:

- The use of Integer comparison is faster than the use of String comparison. and the numericalization process convert every String to Integer. This numericalization is done in XEngine by a mapping. Initial experiments indicated that hashing the attribute values of the request will void the advantage of integer comparison. Thus, we preserve the string values, also to support comparison and regular expression functions.

- XEngine transform every combining algorithm to first-applicable combining algorithm, and the response is found faster with this algorithm. Since obligations are not supported with this kind of transformation, we decided to preserve the correct combining algorithms in the Combining Tree.

So in environments were the speed is valued over functionality XEngine is more suitable, but in environments were

functionality is valued over speed our approach is more appropriate.

5. SOLUTION DETAILS

In this section we will describe the needed algorithms for building the Matching Tree and the Combining Tree, as well as the algorithms for a correct evaluation of these trees.

5.1 Preliminary concepts

Here we present some concepts and terms needed to better understand the aforementioned algorithms:

- Predicate ($P = (att, f, v)$): It is a tuple of the three elements, namely attribute id, function and attribute value, where the function could be any of the ones presented in the XACML specification. The function specifies if a request matches with the Predicates.

- PredicatePath ($PP = (P_1, \ldots, P_n)$): It is a list of Predicates. It is used to represent all the Predicates that a request has to satisfy for matching the target of a series of elements (policy sets, policies or rules). A request matches one PP iff the request matches $P_i \in PP \, \forall \, i \in [1, n]$.

- PredicatePathList ($PPL = (PP_1, \ldots, PP_n)$): It is a list of PredicatePaths. A request matches one PPL iff $\exists \, i \in [1, n]$ such that the request matches PP_i.

- IntervalPath ($IP = (I_1, \ldots, I_n)$): It is a list of Intervals of different data-types. This list contains exactly one interval for each different attribute Id.

- IntervalPathList ($IPL = (IP_1, \ldots, IP_n)$): It is a list of IntervalPaths.

- Element (E): One Element can represent a Rule, a Policy or a PolicySet and it conserves their properties (i.e. obligations, effect, etc).

- CombiningNode (CN): A CombiningNode is a node of the Combining Tree and it is defined by an Element E.

- CombiningNodeList ($CNL = (CN_1, \ldots, CN_n)$): It is a list of CombiningNodes. It is used to collect a complete branch where CN_1 is the root node, and CN_n is one leaf.

- Builder ($B = (CNL, IPL)$): It is an auxiliary structure used to collect information and to build both trees (Matching Tree and Combining Tree).

- BuilderList ($BL = (B_1, \ldots, B_n)$): A BuilderList is a list of Builders, and it is the starting point for building the Matching Tree.

- Node ($N = (leaf, CT, edges)$): N represents a node of the Matching Tree composed by three elements. *leaf* is a boolean value that indicates whether the node is a leaf or not. CT is the Combining Tree created with the rules that match with the path, and it is empty if the node is not a leaf. Finally *edges* represent a list with the edges of the node.

- Edge ($e = (I, N)$): The edges of the Matching Tree, e, represent the pair (I, N), where I is an interval and N is a node.

5.2 Transformation algorithm

Once we know the concepts used in the algorithms, we will describe some functions used that will help us to better understand the process of building both the Matching and the Combining Trees.

- extractPredicatePaths(E): this function, used in the line 6 of the algorithm 1, extracts a PPL from the target of the element E such that a request matches with the target iff the request matches with one of the $PP \in PPL$.

- addRestriction(I,P): this function, applied in the line 9 of the algorithm 2, adds the restriction extracted from the predicate P to the interval I (i.e. function $=$ (x < "E10") $\Rightarrow$ return $I \cap (-\infty,$ "E10")). If the function is a "complex function" (i.e. regular expression) it is attached to the interval and it has to be executed each time that you check if $x \in I$.

- sort(IP): as we know, each interval I in the interval-Path IP depends on one attribute id. Then we can find a bijective function $\mathcal{F}: IP \rightarrow AT$, where AT is the set of every attributesIds. If we have an order in AT then we can define an order in IP such that $I_1 < I_2 \Leftrightarrow \mathcal{F}(I_1) < \mathcal{F}(I_2); I_1 > I_2 \Leftrightarrow \mathcal{F}(I_1) > \mathcal{F}(I_2);$ and $I_1 = I_2 \Leftrightarrow \mathcal{F}(I_1) = \mathcal{F}(I_2)$. The order in AT has to be always the same regardless of the IP of the argument. How to order AT is a difficult question and we will present one possible order at the end of this subsection.

In the following lines we will describe 4 algorithms used for the construction of the Matching Tree and the Combining Tree. We can separate the algorithms in two principal functions, one collect the information used to build the trees and the second builds the tree using the collected information, So first we need an algorithm to extract the important information from the policies tree and store it in new structure. We want to use this structure to build the trees, so we will extract the relevant information of each rule and later we will add the rules one by one to the Matching Tree. Then we will store two things for each rule of the PolicySet in the structure BL:

- The list of IntervalPaths that a request has to satisfy for being applicable to that rule.

- The list of CombiningNodes built with the parents' policies.

We extract them using the recursive function extractPaths() described in Algorithm 1, that explores the policies tree and return the mentioned information. Once have all the information needed to build the Matching Tree and the Combining Tree we need an algorithm to add the rules into a given Matching Tree (starting empty) using this information. This algorithm is described in Algorithm 3, and for each node of the existing Matching Tree the function takes the interval information of the given rule and builds the correspondent edge and node. When the algorithm reach a terminal node the Combining Tree of the given rule is added. So once we have the information in the structure BL we have to add the rules one by one with this algorithm.

So the first step is to obtain the BL using the function extractPaths() described in Algorithm 1. The function calculates the BL starting from E, and using the information of CNL and PPL_0 that is relative to the parents of E. The algorithm explores the policies tree, it takes for each element the CNL and the PPL of its parents and joins them with its own CN and PPL. When the current element is a rule, we transform the PPL into an IPL with the function predicatesToInterval(), described in Algorithm 2, and return a new BL containing its B. When the current element is not a rule the algorithm calculate the BL of its children, and returns the union of them.

Algorithm 1: extractPaths() function

```
1   Input: PPL₀ = (PP₁,...,PPₙ);
2          CNL = (CN₁,...,CNₘ);
3          E, where E ∈ {'Rule','Policy','PolicySet'}
4   Output: {BL₀ = (B₁,...,Bₙ)}
5
6      PPL₁ ← extractPredicatePaths(E);
7
8      if (PPL₀ = ∅)
9          PPL₂ ← PPL₁;
10     if (PPL₁ = ∅)
11         PPL₂ ← PPL₀;
12
13     for each PPᵢ ∈ PPL₁
14         for each PPⱼ ∈ PPL₀
15             PPL₂.PPₙ₊₁ ← (PPᵢ ∪ PPⱼ);
16
17     CN.E ← E;
18     if (E =' Rule') {
19         CNL₁ ← CNL₀ ∪ (CN);
20         B.CNL ← CNL₁;
21         B.IPL ← predicatesToInterval(PPL₂);
22         BL₀ ← (B);
23         return BL₀;
24     } else {
25         CNL₁ ← CNL₀ ∪ (CN);
26         for each (child ∈ E.children) {
27             BL₁ ← extractPaths(PPL₂,CNL₁,child);
28             BL₀ ← BL₀ ∪ BL₁;
29         }
30         return BL₀;
31     }
```

Algorithm 2: predicatesToInterval() function

```
1   Input: PPL = (PP₁,...,PPₙ)
2   Output: IPL = (IP₁,...,IPₙ)
3
4      for each PPᵢ ∈ PPL {
5          for each (attributeId k)
6              Iₖ ← (-∞,+∞);
7
8          for each Pⱼ ∈ PPᵢ
9              I_{Pⱼ.attId} ← addRestriction(I_{Pⱼ.attId}, Pⱼ);
10
11         for each (attributeId k)
12             IPᵢ ← IPᵢ ∪ (Iₖ);
13
14         IPL ← IPL ∪ (IPᵢ);
15     }
16  return IPL;
```

The function predicatesToInterval(), described in the Algorithm 2, transforms a PPL to an IPL. For each predicate P of each PP, the algorithm adds the restriction established by the function of the predicate, to the interval associated to the attributeId of the predicate. Then it forms an IP with the intervals extracted form the PP. The result is the union of this IP in an IPL.

The function addNodes() (Algorithm 3) is a recursive algorithm that adds to the Matching Tree the corresponding nodes and edges, extracting the information from a sorted IntervalPath IP. If the current node is not terminal, the algorithm add a new edge to N built with the interval I_L; but since the intersection of the edge's intervals must be empty, we need to modify the current edges of N and add some news. For each $e \in N.edges$, such that $e.I \cap I_L \neq \emptyset$, we need to add the edge $e'.I \leftarrow e.I \cap I_L$, and then $e'.N$ will be the combination of $e.N$ and I_{L+1} using the function addNodes(). Once we have added the interval $e.I \cap I_L$ to a new edge, we need to modify the old edge $e.I \leftarrow e.I - (e.I \cap I_L)$. Finally we need to subtract to I_L every $e.I$ such that $e \in N.edges$, and add a new edge with the resulting interval I_L. When we reach a terminal node we have to merge the existing Combining Tree with the given CNL.

Algorithm 3: addNodes() function

```
1   Input: N, a node of the Matching Tree;
2          IP = (I_1, ..., I_n);
3          CNL = (CN_1, ..., CN_m);
4          L, depth level of N
5   Output: N'
6
7   if (L = n + 1) {
8       N'.leaf ← true;
9       N'.CT ← N.CT ∪ CNL;
10  } else {
11      N'.leaf ← false;
12
13      for each (edge e ∈ N.edges) {
14          e'.I ← e.I ∩ IP.I_L;
15          e'.N ← addNodes(e.N, IP, CNL, L + 1);
16          N'.edges ← N'.edges ∪ (e');
17          e.I ← e.I - e'.I;
18          N'.edges ← N'.edges ∪ (e);
19      }
20
21      for each (edge e ∈ N'.edges)
22          IP.I_L ← IP.I_L - e.I;
23
24      e'.I ← IP.I_L;
25      e'.N ← addNodes(∅, IP, CNL, L + 1);
26      N'.edges ← N'.edges ∪ (e');
27  }
28
29  return N';
```

Algorithm 4: Obtaining the Matching Tree

```
1   Input: RootPolicy
2   Output: MT, the Matching Tree
3
4   BL ← extractPaths(RootPolicy);
5
6   for each (B_i ∈ BL)
7       for each (IP_j ∈ B_i.IPL) {
8           sort(IP_j);
9           MT ← addNodes(MT, IP_j, B_i.CNL, 0);
10      }
11
12  return MT;
```

Finally, the Algorithm 4 builds the Matching Tree based on the above functions. The algorithm extracts the Predi-

catePathLists PPL and CombiningNodeList CNL of each rule starting from the root of the policies tree. Then it sorts every IntervalPath IP, as we will explain next, and adds each one with its corresponding CombiningNodeList CNL to the tree with the function addNodes() (algorithm 3).

As we commented before, we need to order the attributeIds. We propose to sort the attributeIds in increasing order by the complexity of the attributeIds. Thus, the algorithm should reach less "complex functions" during the search when a path is truncated. For calculating the complexity of an attributeId in the variable C=0, we take all the predicates that contain this attribute id an depending on the complexity of the functions we add a different value (equal→ C+= 1, compare→ C+= 10, regexp→ C+= 100). By this way the evaluation will do less unnecessary complex functions. This is just a first approach and it is a good point for optimize in future researches.

5.3 Evaluation Algorithm

Algorithm 5 shows how to obtain the appropriate Combining Tree corresponding to a given Request. It explores the Matching Tree obtained from algorithm 4 using a "depth-first search" and merging all the reached Combining Trees.

Finally, the resulting merged Combining Tree is evaluated against the Request according to the combining algorithms described in the XACML standard.

Algorithm 5: Obtaining the Combining Tree (getCombiningTree() function)

```
1   Input: Request; N, a node of the Matching Tree
2   Output: CT, the Combining Tree
3
4   if (N.leaf = true)
5       return N.CT;
6
7   for each (attribute att ∈ Request.Attributes)
8       for each (edge e_i ∈ N.edges)
9           if (att ∈ e_i.I) {
10              CT' ← getCombiningTree(Request, e_i.N);
11              CT ← CT' ∪ CT;
12          }
13
14  return CT;
```

5.4 Binary Search Evaluation Algorithm

With the aim of enhancing even more the evaluation processing time, it is possible to make some modifications in the data structures and in the evaluation algorithm. The first modification is to sort the list of edges of each node in the Matching Tree. To this end, we should have two lists: one with the special edges, and a sorted list with the interval edges. The second modification is to use a binary search algorithm in the evaluation algorithm for finding the correct edge in the interval edges. The main reasons for using this algorithm are:

- Intervals are disjoint, so an attribute can only be contained in one interval.

- Intervals have comparable data-type, so it is easy to sort the edges.

The new evaluation algorithm uses the method binarySearch(), as shown in algorithm 6. This method returns:

- The edge, extracted from `Edges`, whose interval contains the attribute.

- An empty edge if the attribute is not contained in any interval from `Edges`.

Algorithm 6: Obtaining the Combining Tree using binary search (`getCombiningTreeBS()` function)

```
1   Input: Request; N
2   Output: CT, the Combining Tree
3
4   if (N.leaf = true)
5      return N.CT;
6
7   for each (attribute att ∈ Request.Attributes) {
8      edge e ← binarySearch(att ∈ N.intervalEdges);
9      if (e ≠ ∅) {
10        CT' ← getCombiningTreeBS(Request, e.N);
11        CT ← CT' ∪ CT;
12     }
13     for each (edge e' ∈ N.specialEdges)
14        if (att ∈ e'.I) {
15           CT' ← getCombiningTreeBS(Request, e'.N);
16           CT ← CT' ∪ CT;
17        }
18  }
19
20  return CT;
```

6. EXPERIMENTAL COMPARISON

For an experimental examination of our approach we created several policy sets with a different amount of attribute IDs (ranging from 6 to 12) and different total number of policies (ranging from 20 to 400) each policy with 10 rules. The number of levels of each policy set depends on the number of policies contained, then the overall policy sets formed with 20 to 60 policies has 2 levels of depth, the policy sets composed with 80 to 200 policies has 3 levels of depth, and the ones with 220 to 400 policies has 4 levels of depth. A random mixture of combining algorithm has been used based on [14].

The targets of each policy set are composed by "equal functions" and "complex functions" such as string-greater-than, string-greater-or-equal, etc, the 70% are "equal functions" and the rest are "complex functions". Every combining algorithm is presented in each test set the same number of times, so each combining algorithm represents the 25% of the total number of combining algorithms. We did not include obligations in our experiments since the processing time is not affected by the obligations.

These testing sets have been generated in a similar way than those presented in [14]. The target attributes of synthetic policies used in the experiments of [5,6] only differentiate in their attribute values i.e. one attribute ID for subject, one for resource and one for action. Thus, the main effect of a faster evaluation is gained from the quick lookup of the matching attribute value.

The algorithms has been implemented in Java, using some auxiliar data structures (List, Hashtable, etc) available in Java framework. The PDP developed has been integrated in NEC XACML implementation, so during the experiments we have compared just evaluation time of the PDP in both implementations.

Each setup has been tested with the reference implementation (SUN), our simple solution (Tree), and our solution based on Binary Search (BsTree). As mentioned in section 4.2 our goal is to improve XEngine functions support but keeping faster than SUN PDP, as we do not targeted to improve XEngine speed an experimental comparison is not necessary at this point. For each experiment we measured the processing time of the given policy sets, required to evaluate 100 requests.

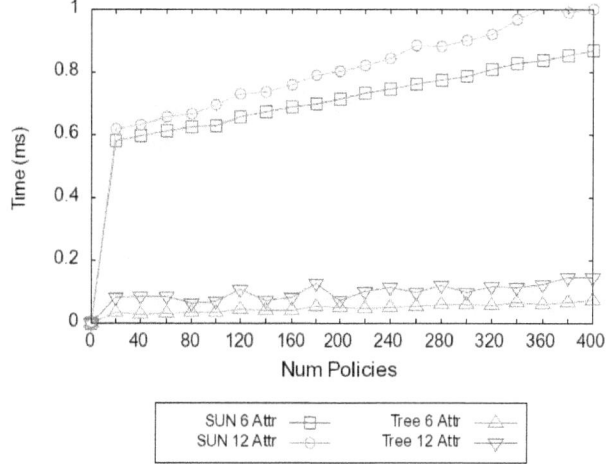

Figure 5: Comparison with SUN RI

The experimental results show that our first approach is one order of magnitude faster than Sun PDP, as shown in Figure 5. The problem is that the processing time of SUN and Tree growth linearly with the number of policies-rules. It is worth noticing that the growth rate of Tree is lower. this fact motives for our second approach: `Binary Search Evaluation Algorithm`, explained in the subsection 5.4.

The Figure 5 shows the comparison of the processing time of a request evaluation with the SUN implementation and the one of our first tree based approach for 6 and 12 different attribute IDs. The processing time with our approach is one order of magnitude faster than the SUN PDP. Due to the scale an increase of the processing time in our approach with a rising number of policies is barely notable. The evaluation time roughly doubles when we quadruple the number of policies. As discussed in Section 4 the number of levels of the Matching Tree is the number of different attribute IDs used in the policies represented by the tree; thus the processing time should increase significantly with the number of levels of the tree. In addition the Matching Tree becomes wider with the number of policies, because each policy adds new functions to the tree; then processing time should increase with the number of policies.

In Figure 6 we compare the processing time of a request evaluation of our different approaches. The processing time of the `Binary Search Evaluation Algorithm` is about two times faster than the simple approach. We assume that the fluctuation in the results is based on the preciseness of the measurement in combination with the tree structure we are utilizing to store the attribute values. Overall the processing time of the `Binary Search Evaluation Algorithm` grows logarithmically with the number of policies, while the result

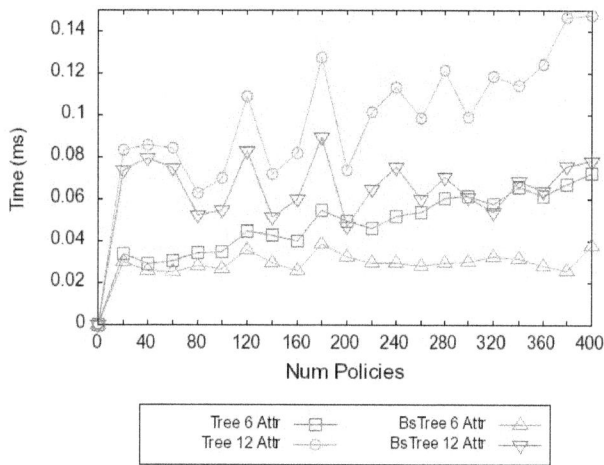

Figure 6: Comparing Tree and Binary Search

of the simple `Evaluation Algorithm` indicate a linear with the number of policies.

For real systems which concurrently receive a huge number of request, reducing the linear dependency on the number of policies to be evaluated to a logarithmical one has a large impact. Although the improvement of a binary search tree over the initial tree result shows quite some fluctuations, we can detect that the evaluation only took half the time. In real systems with a large number of requests, this is a notable improvement.

7. CONCLUSIONS AND FUTURE WORK

Nowadays XACML policies are used in a large number of applications and some of them receive a big amount of requests. These application could range from a web service, to an identity prover, or an application. Thus there is a general need for an high performance XACML PDP, independent of specific use case characteristics. Therefore instead of focusing of one particular scenario we utilized the generic set of test policies as presented in [14].

In this paper we presented an optimization of XACML policies evaluation which support most of the XACML specifications, while future work will include the support of multi-valued requests. We explained two new concepts: Matching Tree, based in XEngine tree, and Combining Tree. We built a new data structure with these concepts and presented two different evaluation algorithms over this structure. The first was a simple evaluation algorithm, while the second was an enhanced version based on a binary search. Finally we showed that our approach is orders of magnitudes better than SUN PDP but still being completely aligned with all features required by the XACML standard. Since our approach supports multi-valued requests, but not multi-valued policies, the future work is focusing on the support of multi-valued policies without increasing the memory utilization.

8. REFERENCES

[1] Dhiah Diehn I Abou-Tair, Stefan Berlik, and Udo Kelter. Enforcing Privacy by Means of an Ontology Driven XACML Framework. In *Proceedings of the Third International Symposium on Information Assurance and Security*, pages 279–284, Manchester, United Kingdom, 2007. IEEE Computer Society.

[2] Randal E Bryant. Graph-Based Algorithms for Boolean Function Manipulation. *IEEE Transactions on Computers*, C-35(8):677–691, 1986.

[3] M. Fujita, P. C. McGeer, and J. C.-Y. Yang. Multi-terminal binary decision diagrams: An efficient datastructure for matrix representation. *Form. Methods Syst. Des.*, 10(2-3):149–169, April 1997.

[4] Dan Lin, Prathima Rao, Elisa Bertino, and Jorge Lobo. An approach to evaluate policy similarity. *Proceedings of the 12th ACM symposium on Access control models and technologies SACMAT 07*, page 1, 2007.

[5] Alex X. Liu, Fei Chen, JeeHyun Hwang, and Tao Xie. Designing Fast and Scalable XACML Policy Evaluation Engines. *IEEE Transactions on Computers*, 60(12):1802–1817, December 2011.

[6] A.X. Liu, F. Chen, J.H. Hwang, and T. Xie. XEngine: A fast and scalable xacml policy evaluation engine. In *ACM SIGMETRICS Performance Evaluation Review*, volume 36, pages 265–276. ACM, 2008.

[7] Said Marouf, Mohamed Shehab, Anna Squicciarini, and Smitha Sundareswaran. Adaptive Reordering & Clustering Based Framework for Efficient XACML Policy Evaluation. *IEEE Transactions on Services Computing*, 4(4):300–313, October 2011.

[8] Pietro Mazzoleni, Bruno Crispo, Swaminathan Sivasubramanian, and Elisa Bertino. XACML Policy Integration Algorithms. *ACM Transactions on Information and System Security*, 11(1):1–29, 2008.

[9] Shin-ichi Minato. Zero-suppressed bdds for set manipulation in combinatorial problems. In *Proceedings of the 30th international Design Automation Conference*, DAC '93, pages 272–277, New York, NY, USA, 1993. ACM.

[10] Philip L Miseldine. Automated xacml policy reconfiguration for evaluation optimisation. *Proceedings of the fourth international workshop on Software engineering for secure systems SESS 08*, pages 1–8, 2008.

[11] OASIS. *eXtensible Access Control Markup Language (XACML) Version 2.0*, February 2005.

[12] OASIS. *eXtensible Access Control Markup Language (XACML) Version 3.0*, April 2009. Comittee Draft 1.

[13] Shariq Rizvi, Alberto Mendelzon, S Sudarshan, and Roy Pollock. Extending query rewriting techniques for fine-grained access control. In *Proceedings of the International Conference on Management of Data*, pages 551–562, 2004.

[14] Fatih Turkmen and Bruno Crispo. Performance evaluation of XACML PDP implementations. *Proceedings of the 2008 ACM workshop on Secure Web Services*, pages 37–44, 2008.

Optimal Workflow-aware Authorizations

David Basin [†]
basin@inf.ethz.ch

Samuel J. Burri [†,‡]
sbu@zurich.ibm.com

Günter Karjoth [‡]
gka@zurich.ibm.com

[†] ETH Zurich, Department of Computer Science, Switzerland
[‡] IBM Research – Zurich, Switzerland

ABSTRACT

Balancing protection and empowerment is a central problem when specifying authorizations. The principle of *least privilege*, the classical approach to balancing these two conflicting objectives, says that users shall only be authorized to execute the tasks necessary to complete their job. However, when there are multiple authorization policies satisfying least privilege, which one should be chosen?

In this paper, we model the tasks that users must execute as workflows, and the risk and cost associated with authorization policies and their administration. We then formulate the balancing of empowerment and protection as an optimization problem: finding a cost-minimizing authorization policy that allows a successful workflow execution. We show that finding an optimal solution for a role-based cost function is **NP**-complete. We support our results with a series of examples, which we also use to measure the performance of our prototype implementation.

Categories and Subject Descriptors

D.4.6 [**Operating Systems**]: Security and Protection—*Access controls*; K.6.5 [**Management of Computing and Information Systems**]: Security and Protection

General Terms

Performance, Security, Theory

Keywords

Authorizations, workflows, optimality, complexity

1. INTRODUCTION

Authorizations, which govern users' access to resources, have a dual nature: they express what actions may occur and must not occur. In this way, they empower users to execute job-relevant tasks while protecting the integrity and confidentiality of resources. The question naturally arises as to how to best balance protection and empowerment.

The classical answer to this question is the principle of *least privilege* [20], which says that users shall only be authorized to execute the tasks necessary to complete their job. However, in an environment where business processes require the execution of multiple tasks by different users, multiple authorization policies, representing different authorizations, may satisfy least privilege. Furthermore, the choice of an authorization policy may be influenced by the cost associated with the respective administrative change. Thus, although least privilege is a guiding principle, it does not provide the final answer to the question of how to best strike a balance between protection and empowerment.

In this paper, we present a new approach to answering this question by mapping authorization administration to an optimization problem. Specifically, we model business activities as tasks, structured as workflows. Authorizations then specify which users may execute which tasks. We distinguish authorizations with respect to two criteria: their dependency on the workflow's execution history and whether they can be administrated during workflow execution. In more detail, *history-dependent* authorizations constrain task executions based on past task executions. Examples are *Separation of Duty (SoD)* and *Binding of Duty (BoD)*. SoD, also known as Four-Eyes-Principle, aims at preventing fraud and errors by requiring a set of critical tasks to be executed by multiple users, whereas BoD requires a set of tasks to be executed by the same user to limit the exposure of sensitive data and to reuse knowledge. In contrast, the evaluation of *history-independent* authorizations is not influenced by the execution history. Examples of policy models for history-independent authorizations are access control lists (ACLs), the Bell-LaPadula (BLP) model [6], and Role-based Access Control (RBAC) [12] without sessions.

Administrable authorizations may change during workflow execution, *i.e.* the respective policy is edited to reflect organizational changes such as employees joining or leaving the company or being promoted. In contrast, *non-administrable* authorizations do not change during workflow execution. However, if they are history-dependent, then their evaluation may change during workflow execution, depending on who has previously executed which tasks.

In practice, *e.g.* [15], authorization policies for workflows often compose different (sub-)policies. We consider in this paper policies for history-dependent, non-administrable SoD and BoD constraints and policies for history-independent, administrable authorizations. In particular, we model the cost of changing from one history-independent authorization policy to another one by a binary function. This function may account for the cost of the administrative activity associated with the change, the cost of maintaining the new policy, and the risk associated with the new policy. We consider minimizing risk to be equivalent to maximizing protection.

Let W be a workflow, H an execution history corresponding to an instance of W, ϕ_n a non-administrable authorization policy, ϕ_a an administrable authorization policy, and cost a function as described above. We investigate the problem

$$\min_{\phi_a'} \left\{ \mathsf{cost}(\phi_a, \phi_a') \; \middle| \; \begin{array}{l} (\phi_a', \phi_n) \text{ allows a successful} \\ \text{completion of } W \text{ after } H \end{array} \right\} ,$$

where ϕ_a' ranges over all feasible, administrable authorization policies and (ϕ_a', ϕ_n) denotes the composition of ϕ_a' and ϕ_n. The requirement of "getting the job done" becomes the feasibility condition and cost serves as the objective function of the optimization problem. Hence, we reduce the question of how to balance empowerment and protection to the problem of finding an authorization policy that maximizes protection, minimizes the cost associated with the administrative change, and empowers users to do their job while satisfying the policy.

We proceed by formalizing workflows, their execution history, and authorization policies. Workflows, also known as business processes, provide a realistic abstraction for capturing what authorizations users need to get their work done, *i.e.* empowerment. As this paper's focus is not authorization-constrained workflows *per se*, we use the policy model that we previously developed in [3]. In the interest of keeping our formalization concise and not letting the complexity of deciding whether an authorization policy satisfies a workflow overshadow the optimization problem's complexity, we abstract from [3]'s process algebraic models and build directly on its graph-based approximations. Based on this formalization and a generic definition of a cost function, we formally define the optimization problem sketched above.

In a second step, we refine our generic cost function using roles and demonstrate the applicability of our general approach to a realistic scenario. The additional structure facilitates mapping our optimization problem to the well-established Integer Linear Programming Problem (**ILP**). A proof of our mapping's soundness and completeness enables us to use off-the-shelf software for **ILP** to compute the optimal authorization policy that allows a successful execution of a given workflow. We use a running example to illustrate our results and to measure the performance of our mapping's implementation.

Our main contribution is to generalize the decision problem of whether a given authorization policy allows a successful workflow execution to the notion of an *optimal* authorization policy that satisfies this property. Our approach provides considerable modeling freedom in terms of the notion of optimality used. For example, we may aim to minimize the cost associated with a policy change or maximize the protection resulting from the new policy. We thereby facilitate a fine-grained balancing of empowerment and protection with respect to various criteria. Moreover, we prove that finding a optimal, role-based authorization policy that allows a workflow execution is **NP**-complete. Finally, our work shows how well-established results from optimization theory can be applied to information security, in particular access control.

The remainder of this paper is structured as follows. In Section 2, we provide background on **ILP** and graph coloring. In Section 3, we formalize workflows and authorizations that constrain their execution. In Section 4, we first present the general problem of finding an optimal authorization policy that allows a workflow's execution. Afterward we refine this problem, assuming a role-based cost function. We present related work in Section 5 and conclude in Section 6. An extended version of this paper is available as a technical report [4].

2. BACKGROUND

We denote by $\mathbb{N}$ the set of natural numbers, by $\mathbb{Z}$ the set of integers, and by $\mathbb{R}$ the set of real numbers.

Let two sets Z_1 and Z_2 be given with $z_1 \in Z_1$ and $z_2 \in Z_2$. We may identify a function $\pi : Z_1 \to Z_2$ with its relation (graph) $\pi \subseteq Z_1 \times Z_2$. For example if $\pi(z_1) = z_2$ we equivalently write $(z_1, z_2) \in \pi$. Given a relation π we refer to π's *domain* as $\mathsf{dom}(\pi)$, to its *range* as $\mathsf{ran}(\pi)$, and to its *inverse* as π^{-1}.

2.1 Integer Linear Programming

Let $m, n \in \mathbb{N}$. We specify by $\mathbf{A} \in \mathbb{R}^{m \times n}$ an m by n *matrix* $\mathbf{A}$ of real numbers. Furthermore, $\mathbf{b} \in \mathbb{R}^m$ is a *(column) vector* composed of m real numbers. Let $\mathbf{A} \in \mathbb{R}^{m \times n}$, $\mathbf{b} \in \mathbb{R}^m$, $\mathbf{c} \in \mathbb{R}^n$, and $\mathbf{x} \in \mathbb{Z}^n$. For $i \in \{1, \dots, m\}$ and $j \in \{1, \dots, n\}$, we refer to $\mathbf{A}$'s ith row vector as $\mathbf{a}_i$ and a_{ij} is the jth element in $\mathbf{a}_i$. Correspondingly, b_i is $\mathbf{b}$'s ith element. Moreover, $\mathbf{Ax}$ denotes matrix-vector multiplication resulting in a vector $\mathbf{d} \in \mathbb{R}^m$ and $\mathbf{c}^{\mathrm{T}}\mathbf{x}$ denotes vector multiplication $\sum_{j=1}^{n} c_j x_j$, where $\mathbf{c}^{\mathrm{T}}$ is $\mathbf{c}$'s *transposed*. For $\mathbf{b}, \mathbf{d} \in \mathbb{R}^m$, we write $\mathbf{d} \leq \mathbf{b}$ if for all $i \in \{1, \dots, m\}$, $d_i \leq b_i$.

We now recall basic definitions from integer linear programming.

Definition 1 (Integer Linear Programming Problem **ILP**)

Input: $\mathbf{A} \in \mathbb{R}^{m \times n}$, $\mathbf{b} \in \mathbb{R}^m$, *and* $\mathbf{c} \in \mathbb{R}^n$, *for* $m, n \in \mathbb{N}$.

Output: $\min_{\mathbf{x} \in \mathbb{Z}^n} \{\mathbf{c}^{\mathrm{T}}\mathbf{x} \mid \mathbf{Ax} \leq \mathbf{b}\}$

or No *if the above set is empty.*

Let $\mathbf{A} \in \mathbb{R}^{m \times n}$, $\mathbf{b} \in \mathbb{R}^m$, and $\mathbf{c} \in \mathbb{R}^n$ be an **ILP**-instance, and let $i \in \{1, \dots, m\}$ and $j \in \{1, \dots, n\}$. We may refer to the output corresponding to the input $(\mathbf{A}, \mathbf{b}, \mathbf{c})$ as **ILP**$(\mathbf{A}, \mathbf{b}, \mathbf{c})$. A variable x_j is called a *decision variable* and $\mathbf{c}^{\mathrm{T}}\mathbf{x}$ is called the *objective function*. Note that $\mathbf{Ax} \leq \mathbf{b}$ can be decomposed into m inequalities of the form $\mathbf{a}_i\mathbf{x} = \sum_{j=1}^{n} a_{ij}x_j \leq b_i$, each called a *constraint*. If $\mathbf{x}$ satisfies $\mathbf{Ax} \leq \mathbf{b}$, *i.e.* $\mathbf{x}$ satisfies all m constraints, it is called a *feasible solution*. If there exists no feasible solution for a given **ILP**-instance, then the instance is *infeasible*. A feasible solution that minimizes the objective function with respect to all feasible solutions is an *optimal (feasible) solution*.

It is common practice to use shorthand notation for constraints. For example, the equality $\mathbf{a}_i\mathbf{x} = b_i$ is equivalent to the two constraints $\mathbf{a}_i\mathbf{x} \leq b_i$ and $-\mathbf{a}_i\mathbf{x} \leq -b_i$. If variables are not defined, they are implicitly assumed to be zero. For example, the constraint $a_{i1}x_1 + a_{i2}x_2 + a_{i3}x_3 \leq b_i$ is equivalent to $\mathbf{a}_i\mathbf{x} \leq b_i$ where $a_{i4} = \dots = a_{in} = 0$.

Integer linear programming is a specialization of linear programming in that decision variables assume only values

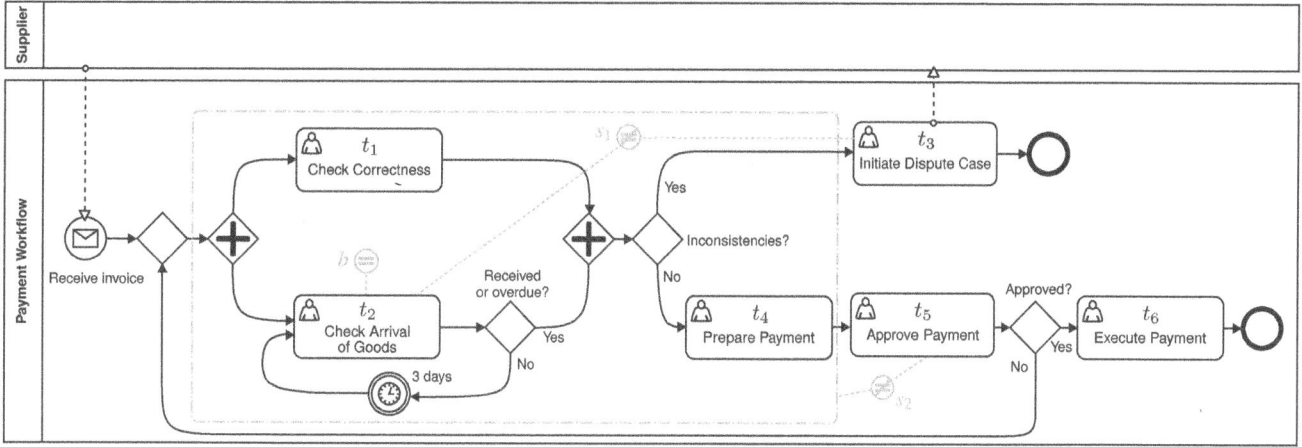

Figure 1: Payment workflow modeled in BPMN

from $\mathbb{Z}$ and not from $\mathbb{R}$. This is necessary for modeling situations where only a discrete set of states is possible. However, this restriction has substantial algorithmic implications that are outside the scope of this paper. We simply note that **ILP** is **NP**-complete [21].

2.2 Graph Coloring

We use the standard k-**Coloring** problem in Section 3.4 and briefly define it here.

A *graph* G is a tuple (V, E) where V is a set of *vertices* and $E \subseteq \{e \subseteq V \mid 2 = |e|\}$ is a set of 2-element subsets of V, called *edges*.

Definition 2 (k-**Coloring** Problem)

Input: *A graph $G = (V, E)$ and a $k \in \mathbb{N}$.*

Output: YES *if there exists a function*
          $\mathsf{col} : V \to \{1, \dots, k\}$ *such that for all*
          $\{v_1, v_2\} \in E$, $\mathsf{col}(v_1) \neq \mathsf{col}(v_2)$, *or*
          NO *otherwise.*

If an algorithm for this problem returns YES for a graph G and an integer k, then the respective function col is called a k-*coloring* of G. The k-**Coloring** problem is **NP**-complete [7].

3. AUTHORIZATION-CONSTRAINED WORKFLOWS

Our workflow terminology and formalization is based on [3] but adapted to suit our transformation of a workflow-aware authorization administration to an optimization problem.

A *task* is a basic unit of work and may be executed multiple times. A task execution is performed by a user and we call it a *task instance*. A *workflow* models the causal and temporal dependencies between a set of tasks, whose execution fulfills a business objective. We call the execution of a workflow a *workflow instance*.

At *design time*, a business expert designs a workflow using a modeling language such as the Business Process Modeling Notation (BPMN) [19] (see Figure 1 for an example). He may additionally specify history-dependent authorizations, such as SoD and BoD constraints, which are workflow-

specific. Orthogonal to this, a security expert defines authorizations that are independent of both the workflow and its execution history. At *run time*, the workflow specification is deployed to a *workflow engine*, which schedules and instantiates tasks according to the workflow's control-flow. For each task instance, the workflow engine determines the set of users who are authorized to execute it with respect to both the history-dependent and the history-independent authorizations. As motivated in the introduction, we assume that history-dependent authorizations are non-administrable whereas history-independent authorizations are administrable.

In this paper, we overapproximate a workflow's control-flow and assume that a workflow engine may eventually instantiate every task. This approximation imposes no constraints on the workflow design and is compatible with all standard workflow patterns [23]. We further comment on this design decision in Section 3.4.

3.1 Workflows

For the remainder of this paper, let $\mathcal{T}$ be a set of *tasks* and $\mathcal{U}$ a set of *users*. We model a workflow as a set of tasks $T \subseteq \mathcal{T}$, called a *workflow task set*. Furthermore, we model the execution of a task t by a user u, *i.e.* a task instance involving t and u, as a tuple (t, u) and call it an *execution event*. Let $\mathcal{X} = \mathcal{T} \times \mathcal{U}$ be the set of all execution events. Let T be the workflow task set modeling a workflow W. We model an instance of W as a set of execution events $H \subseteq T \times \mathcal{U}$, called a *workflow (execution) history*. Note that a workflow history does not store how many times a user u has executed a task t but only whether u has executed t. However, this is sufficient to decide whether the authorization policies that we introduce below are satisfied.

Example 1 As a running example, consider the BPMN [19] model of a payment workflow shown in Figure 1. This workflow is sketched in a report on the harmonization of electronic invoicing in the EU [11]. Ignoring the gray modeling elements for the moment, the workflow describes the tasks that a customer (organization) executes to process an invoice received by a supplier. Upon receipt of an invoice, a user checks whether the invoice is correct (t_1). In parallel, a user checks whether the goods corresponding to the invoice have arrived (t_2). If they have not arrived yet and their arrival is not overdue, the user waits for three days and checks again. Otherwise, the workflow proceeds. If inconsistencies have occurred, *i.e.* if the invoice is incorrect or the arrival is overdue, a user sends a dispute case (t_3) to the supplier and the workflow terminates. If no inconsistencies have occurred, a user prepares the payment (t_4). Afterward, the payment is either approved (t_5), issued (t_6), and the workflow terminates, or the payment is not approved (t_5) and the workflow loops back to the start.

The payment workflow corresponds to the workflow task set $\{t_1, \ldots, t_6\}$ and we consider the set of users $\mathcal{U} = \{$Alice, Bob, Claire, Dave, Emma, Fritz$\}$. Let $H_1 = \{(t_1, \text{Alice}), (t_2, \text{Bob}), (t_2, \text{Dave}), (t_4, \text{Claire}), (t_5, \text{Claire})\}$ and $H_2 = \{(t_1, \text{Alice}), (t_2, \text{Bob}), (t_4, \text{Dave}), (t_5, \text{Claire})\}$ be workflow histories. The workflow history H_1 says that Alice executed t_1, Bob executed t_2, *etc.* We return to these workflow histories below. ★

3.2 History-dependent Authorizations

We consider two kinds of history-dependent authorizations: Separation of Duty (SoD) and Binding of Duty (BoD) constraints. Both are commonplace in regulated environments, such as the financial industry, and also recommended by best-practice frameworks, *e.g.* [16], that give organizations guidance in complying with regulatory requirements.

Definition 3 *An* SoD *constraint s is a tuple (T_1, T_2), for two disjoint sets of tasks T_1 and T_2. A workflow history H satisfies s, written $H \models s$, if $\neg \exists u \in \mathcal{U}, t_1 \in T_1, t_2 \in T_2 \,.\, \{(t_1, u), (t_2, u)\} \subseteq H$.*

In other words, H satisfies s if there is no user in H who executes tasks from both T_1 and T_2. Thereby, s separates the duties associated with the tasks in T_1 from those in T_2.

Definition 4 *A* BoD *constraint b is a set of tasks T. A workflow history H satisfies b, written $H \models b$, if $|\{u \mid \exists t \in T \,.\, (t, u) \in H\}| \leq 1$.*

Informally, H satisfies b if there is not more than one user in H who executes the tasks in T. Thereby, b binds the duties associated with the tasks in T. Note that according to Definition 4, H satisfies b even if H contains no instance of a task in T. We aggregate SoD and BoD constraints in a history-dependent authorization policy, which we assume to be non-administrable, *i.e.* not edited during workflow execution.

Definition 5 *A (history-dependent) authorization policy ϕ is a tuple (S, B), for a set of SoD constraints S and a set of BoD constraints B. A workflow history H satisfies ϕ, written $H \models \phi$, if H satisfies every $s \in S$ and every $b \in B$.*

Example 2 We return to our running example. Consider again Figure 1, in particular the gray modeling elements. Using the visualization proposed in [3], we denote an SoD constraint (T_1, T_2) by identifying T_1 and T_2 with two dash-dotted boxes and link them with a dotted line and a node labeled with the symbol "$\neq$". Similarly, we visualize a BoD constraint b by identifying the respective set of tasks T with a dash-dotted box linked to a node labeled with the "$=$" symbol. If a set contains only one task, we omit the dash-dotted box and link the task directly to the respective node. Figure 1 shows the SoD constraints $s_1 = (\{t_2\}, \{t_3\})$ and $s_2 = (\{t_1, t_2, t_4\}, \{t_5\})$ and the BoD constraint $b = \{t_2\}$.

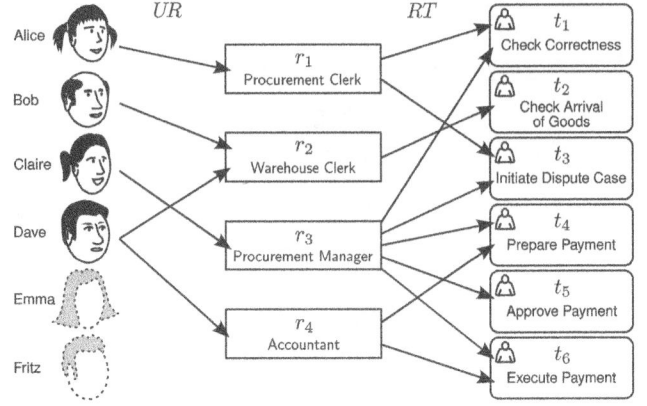

Figure 2: Initial RBAC policy

Our example authorization policy is thus $\phi = (\{s_1, s_2\}, \{b\})$. The SoD constraint s_1 ensures that a user cannot embezzle the received goods and later initiate a dispute case. Similarly, the constraint s_2 ensures that any user who approves a payment did not execute one of the preceding tasks. Therefore, the approval of a fraudulent payment requires the collusion of at least two users. The BoD constraint b requires that only one user checks whether the goods have arrived. This facilitates the reuse of knowledge and thereby increases efficiency if multiple checks are required.

Consider again the workflow histories H_1 and H_2 from Example 1. The history H_1 does not satisfy ϕ because the execution events (t_2, Bob) and (t_2, Dave) violate b (t_2 is executed by two different users) and (t_4, Claire) and (t_5, Claire) violate s_2 (t_4 and t_5 are executed by the same user). However, H_2 satisfies ϕ because it satisfies s_1, s_2, and b. ★

3.3 History-independent Authorizations

In the interest of keeping the forthcoming definitions independent of particular authorization models, we first formalize workflow-independent authorizations abstractly by a relation $UT \subseteq \mathcal{U} \times \mathcal{T}$, called a *user-task assignment*. Afterward, we refine UT using roles and use this additional structure when modeling the cost of changing UT. For the remainder of this paper, let $\mathcal{R}$ be a set of *roles*. We use the core idea of *Role-based Access Control (RBAC)* [12], namely the decomposition of UT into two relations.

Definition 6 *An RBAC policy is a tuple (UR, RT), where $UR \subseteq \mathcal{U} \times \mathcal{R}$ is a user-role assignment and $RT \subseteq \mathcal{R} \times \mathcal{T}$ is a role-task assignment.*

Given an RBAC policy (UR, RT), we can derive a user-task assignment UT by composing RT and UR with the composition operator "$\circ$". Formally, $UT = RT \circ UR = \{(u, t) \mid \exists r \in \mathcal{R}.(u, r) \in UR$ and $(r, t) \in RT\}$.

We use UT to define the workflow-independent assignment of users to tasks. Moreover, its domain $\mathsf{dom}(UT)$ also represents the set of *available* users and, conversely, $\mathcal{U} \setminus \mathsf{dom}(UT)$ is the set of *unavailable* users, *e.g.* those users who are not ready to work or are not part of the organization. We leave it up to an implementation to give these terms a concrete meaning.

Example 3 Figure 2 shows an RBAC policy (UR, RT) for the payment workflow. We refer to the role Procurement Clerk as r_1, Warehouse Clerk as r_2, Procurement Manager as r_3, and Accountant as r_4. The set of roles is thus $\mathcal{R} = \{r_1, r_2, r_3, r_4\}$ and the user-task assignment $UT = RT \circ UR$ contains, for example, the tuple (Alice, t_1). The set of available users is $\mathrm{dom}(UT) = \{\mathsf{Alice}, \mathsf{Bob}, \mathsf{Claire}, \mathsf{Dave}\}$, whereas Emma and Fritz are unavailable. ★

3.4 Allocation

Given a workflow and an authorization policy, we now formalize the existence of an allocation of users to the workflow's tasks that allows a successful execution of the workflow, satisfying the authorization policy.

Definition 7 *Let T be a workflow task set, H a workflow history, ϕ an authorization policy, and UT a user-task assignment. An allocation for T, H, ϕ, and UT is a (total) function* $\mathsf{alloc} : T \rightarrow \mathcal{U}$ *that satisfies:*

(1) $\mathsf{alloc}^{-1} \subseteq UT$ *and*

(2) $H \cup \mathsf{alloc} \models \phi$.

We write $\mathsf{alloc} \models (T, H, \phi, UT)$ if alloc is an allocation for T, H, ϕ, and UT and $\overset{\exists}{\models} (T, H, \phi, UT)$ if there exists an allocation alloc such that $\mathsf{alloc} \models (T, H, \phi, UT)$.

A workflow history is a record of past task instances and the users who executed them. An allocation defines for every future task instance the user who will be assigned to execute the respective task. Condition (1) requires that a user u is only allocated to a task t if u is authorized to execute t with respect to UT. Condition (2) requires that future task executions satisfy the history-dependent authorizations in ϕ, also accounting for past task instances. A consequence of Condition (2) is that there exists no allocation for T, H, ϕ, and UT, if $H \not\models \phi$. This is consistent with our notion that it is impossible to find an extension of a workflow history H that satisfies the history-dependent ϕ, if H does not satisfy ϕ.

The two conditions illustrate the fundamental difference between history-dependent and history-independent authorizations. Deciding whether a task execution is authorized with respect to a history-dependent authorization depends on past task instances. In contrast, deciding whether a task execution is authorized with respect to a history-independent authorization can be decided without knowing the workflow and its execution history. Hence, the two names.

An allocation instructs a workflow engine which users to assign to newly instantiated tasks. Condition (2) ensures that no matter which tasks are instantiated in the future, there is always a user who is authorized to execute them. Thus, the existence of an allocation guarantees that the workflow engine can execute the respective workflow instance to completion.

Example 4 Consider again our example with the workflow task set T and the workflow history H_2 from Example 1, the authorization policy ϕ from Example 2, and the user-task assignment UT from Example 3. The function $\mathsf{alloc} = \{(t_1, \mathsf{Alice}), (t_2, \mathsf{Bob}), (t_3, \mathsf{Alice}), (t_4, \mathsf{Dave}), (t_5, \mathsf{Claire}), (t_6, \mathsf{Dave})\}$ is an allocation for T, ϕ, UT, and H_2. ★

This example also illustrates that our overapproximation of a workflow's control-flow is reasonable, in particular when the workflow contains loops. Even though almost all tasks of the payment workflow have been executed in the workflow instance corresponding to H_2, a workflow engine may eventually schedule an instance of every task if the payment is not approved.

We now cast the existence of an allocation as a decision problem and analyze its complexity.

Definition 8 (Allocation Existence Problem **AEP**)

Input: *A workflow task set T, a workflow history H, an authorization policy ϕ, and a user-task assignment UT.*

Output: YES *if* $\overset{\exists}{\models} (T, H, \phi, UT)$ *or* No *otherwise.*

Lemma 1 **AEP** *is* **NP**-*complete.*

PROOF. Let a graph (V, E) and an integer k be an instance of the **NP**-complete k-**Coloring** problem, introduced in Section 2.2. In the following, we present a polynomial reduction to **AEP**. Let $T = V$, $H = \varnothing$, $\mathcal{U} = \{1, \dots, k\}$, and $UT = \mathcal{U} \times T$. For every $\{v_1, v_2\} \in E$, we add an SoD constraint $(\{v_1\}, \{v_2\})$ to the set of SoD constraints S and let $\phi = (S, \varnothing)$.

Suppose an algorithm for **AEP** finds an allocation alloc such that $\mathsf{alloc} \models (T, H, \phi, UT)$. We show that alloc is a k-coloring for (V, E). By our construction and Definition 7, $\mathsf{alloc} : V \rightarrow \{1, \dots, k\}$, *i.e.* alloc has the domain and range of a k-coloring for (V, E). Let $H' = H \cup \{(v, n) \mid \mathsf{alloc}(v) = n\}$. Consider an edge $\{v_1, v_2\} \in E$ and let s be the corresponding SoD constraint $(\{v_1\}, \{v_2\})$ in S. By condition (2) of Definition 7, $H' \models \phi$ and therefore $H' \models s$. It follows by Definition 3 that $\{u \mid \exists v \in \{v_1\}.(v, u) \in H'\} \cap \{u \mid \exists v \in \{v_2\}.(v, u) \in H'\} = \varnothing$. Because $(v_1, \mathsf{alloc}(v_1)) \in H'$ and $(v_2, \mathsf{alloc}(v_2)) \in H'$ by the definition of H' it follows that $\mathsf{alloc}(v_1) \neq \mathsf{alloc}(v_2)$. Hence, alloc is a k-coloring for (V, E).

Conversely, let $\mathsf{col} : V \rightarrow \{1, \dots, k\}$ be a k-coloring for (V, E). Because $UT = \{1, \dots, k\} \times V$, col satisfies Condition (1) of Definition 7. By our construction, $\mathsf{col} \models s$ for every $s \in S$. Because $B = \varnothing$ and $H = \varnothing$, it follows that $H \cup \mathsf{col} \models \phi$ by Definition 5, *i.e.* col satisfies Condition (2) of Definition 7. Hence, col is an allocation for (T, H, ϕ, UT) and **AEP** is **NP**-hard.

Given an instance (T, H, ϕ, UT) of **AEP** and a function $\mathsf{alloc} : T \rightarrow \mathcal{U}$, one can check in polynomial time whether $\mathsf{alloc} \models (T, H, \phi, UT)$ by verifying that alloc satisfies the two conditions of Definition 7. Hence, **AEP** is in **NP** and thereby **NP**-complete. ∎

We do not provide an algorithm for **AEP** here. Instead, we show in Section 4.2 how to use algorithms for problems that build on **AEP** to solve instances of **AEP**.

4. OPTIMAL ADMINISTRATIVE CHANGES

Our formal model for authorization-constrained workflows, in particular **AEP**, gives us a notion of empowerment that is required for achieving a business objective. We now investigate the counterpart of empowerment, namely protection, and the question of how to balance the two. Consider the following motivational example.

Example 5 Let UR_0 be the user-role assignment UR illustrated in Figure 2 and let RT be the corresponding role-task assignment. Furthermore, let $UT_0 = RT \circ UR_0$. We concluded in Example 4 that there exists an allocation for

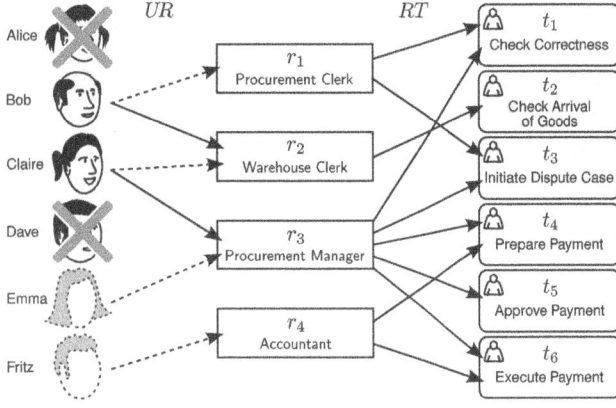

Figure 3: Changed RBAC policy

the workflow task set T, the workflow history H_2, the authorization policy ϕ, and UT_0 (called UT in Example 4). Suppose now that Alice and Dave become unavailable, say they went on holiday. The new RBAC policy (UR, RT) is illustrated in Figure 3, ignoring the dotted arrows for the moment. Note that RT did not change whereas $UR = UR_0 \setminus \{(\text{Alice}, r_1), (\text{Dave}, r_2), (\text{Dave}, r_4)\}$. As a result, we get the new user-task assignment $UT = RT \circ UR$.

It is easy to see that there exists no allocation for T, H_2, ϕ, and UT. Only Claire is authorized to execute t_1 and t_4 with respect to UT. However, the SoD constraint s_2 in ϕ does not authorize Claire to execute t_1 and t_4 because according to H_2 she has already executed t_5. ★

To overcome the situation illustrated in this example, we must change UT by assigning more roles to available users or making previously unavailable users available. However, this change should incur minimal cost.

In this section, we introduce a cost function that models the administrative cost of changing UT to UT' and the associated risks. We use this function to evaluate potential new user-task assignments and to find the optimal assignment UT' such that $\overset{\exists}{\models} (T, H_2, \phi, UT')$.

4.1 The General Problem

In the interest of keeping the general definition of the problem of balancing empowerment and protection independent of particular authorization models, we start with a generic definition of the cost function.

Definition 9 *For a totally ordered set C, a cost function is a partial function* $\mathsf{cost} : 2^{\mathcal{U} \times \mathcal{T}} \times 2^{\mathcal{U} \times \mathcal{T}} \to C$.

We use a cost function for two purposes. For two user-task assignments UT and UT'

1. $\mathsf{cost}(UT, UT')$ is the cost of changing UT to UT' and

2. $\mathsf{dom}(\mathsf{cost})$ defines the feasible changes, *i.e.* it is possible to change from UT to UT' if $(UT, UT') \in \mathsf{dom}(\mathsf{cost})$.

In this general setting, the cost of changing from a user-task assignment UT to a user-task assignment UT' can have many meanings and cost may satisfy different properties accordingly. We give a few examples of potential costs that may be modeled using cost. A concrete example for a role-based cost function follows in the next section.

Risk: By empowering users to execute tasks, a user-task assignment exposes the underlying resources to risks, such as fraud, errors, and data leakage. There exist various methodologies for performing a risk analysis [17, 5]. We consider them outside the scope of this paper and simply point out that the expected value computed by a quantitative risk analysis corresponds to a cost [17]. If the cost function encodes only risks, the value of $\mathsf{cost}(UT, UT')$ is independent of UT. Additionally, if the risk quantifies only the misuse of authorizations, it is reasonable to assume that $\mathsf{cost}(UT, \varnothing) \leq \mathsf{cost}(UT, UT')$ for all user-task assignments UT and UT'. In other words, empowering no user to execute a task entails the least risk, *i.e.* maximizing protection.

Administrative cost: The activities associated with changing an authorization policy are typically not for free. For example, recruiting a new employee, assigning her initial authorizations, and training her to use them appropriately may be costly [18]. Consequently, if cost encodes only administrative costs, it is reasonable to assume that $\mathsf{cost}(UT, UT) \leq \mathsf{cost}(UT, UT')$ for all user-task assignments UT and UT'. In other words, it costs the least to make no changes at all.

Maintenance cost: Maintaining an authorization policy may involve costs such as salaries and license fees required for task executions. Abstractly, a cost function only encoding maintenance costs behaves the same way as a cost function only encoding risk: it is cheapest to maintain an empty user-task assignment.

Using the existence of an allocation as the empowerment condition and a cost function as the measure of protection, we now reduce the question of how to balance empowerment and protection to an optimization problem.

Definition 10 (Optimal Workflow-aware Authorization Administration Problem **OWA**)

Input: *A cost function* cost, *a workflow task set T, a workflow history H, an authorization policy ϕ, and a user-task assignment UT.*

$$\text{Output: } \min_{UT'} \left\{ \mathsf{cost}(UT, UT') \;\middle|\; \begin{array}{l} \overset{\exists}{\models} (T, H, \phi, UT') \text{ and} \\ (UT, UT') \in \mathsf{dom}(\mathsf{cost}) \end{array} \right\}$$

or No *if the above set is empty.*

The Optimal Workflow-aware Authorization Administration Problem **OWA** asks for a user-task assignment that enables the successful completion of the given workflow instance and incurs minimal cost.

Note that instead of using the domain of the cost function as a predicate for feasible authorization policies, we could alternatively require cost to be a total function and define the cost of infeasible policies to be infinite. However, this would lead to two case distinctions in **OWA**: one for the case that there exists no feasible policy and one for the case that there exists no allocation.

Without any assumptions about the structure of the cost function, it is impossible to make statements about **OWA**'s runtime or space complexity. The refined cost function that we propose in the following chapter allows us to determine these complexities.

4.2 A Role-based Cost Function

To demonstrate the applicability of **OWA** to a realistic example, we refine **OWA** by decomposing user-task assignments into RBAC policies and assume the cost function to be role-based. For simplicity, we also assume that the totally ordered set C is $\mathbb{R}$. Specifically, we define the cost function in terms of the following auxiliary functions. For a role $r \in \mathcal{R}$:

- $\mathsf{risk}(r) \in \mathbb{R}$ models the risk associated with the assignment of a user to r,

- $\mathsf{add}(r) \in \mathbb{R}$ models the administrative cost of assigning a user to r,

- $\mathsf{rm}(r) \in \mathbb{R}$ models the administrative cost of removing a user's assignment from r, and

- $\mathsf{ma}(r) \in \mathbb{R}$ models the maintenance cost of having a user assigned to r.

Using these functions, we define the cost of changing a user-role assignment.

Definition 11 *Given the auxiliary functions* $\mathsf{risk}, \mathsf{add}, \mathsf{rm}, \mathsf{ma} : \mathcal{R} \to \mathbb{R}$, *a role cost function is a function* $\mathsf{costR} : 2^{\mathcal{U} \times \mathcal{R}} \times 2^{\mathcal{U} \times \mathcal{R}} \to \mathbb{R}$, *such that for two user-role assignments* UR *and* UR',

$$\mathsf{costR}(UR, UR') = \sum_{(u,r) \in UR'} (\mathsf{risk}(r) + \mathsf{ma}(r))$$
$$+ \sum_{(u,r) \in UR' \setminus UR} \mathsf{add}(r)$$
$$+ \sum_{(u,r) \in UR \setminus UR'} \mathsf{rm}(r)$$

A role cost function defines the cost of changing from UR to UR' simply as the sum of all the risk and maintenance costs associated with UR' and the administrative cost of adding and removing assignments when changing from UR to UR'. We assume that the auxiliary functions $\mathsf{risk}, \mathsf{add}, \mathsf{rm}$, and ma are total and hence costR is total too. Instead of using costR's domain to determine feasible user-role assignment changes, we define a *maximal user-role assignment* $UR^{\max} \subseteq \mathcal{U} \times \mathcal{R}$ and assume that every user-role assignment $UR \subseteq UR^{\max}$ is feasible.

Example 6 Table 1 lists the risk, maintenance, and administrative costs associated with the four roles of the payment workflow. We adopt the elementary approach that roles assigned to a large number of tasks represent more responsibility and are therefore more costly [14]. Let costR be the corresponding role cost function.

	risk	ma	add	rm
Procurement Clerk (r_1)	5	3	2	1
Warehouse Clerk (r_2)	3	3	2	1
Procurement Manager (r_3)	12	5	3	2
Accountant (r_4)	7	4	2	1

Table 1: Decomposition of the role cost function

Recall the RBAC policy (UR, RT) shown in Figure 3 and let the solid and dotted arrows between users and roles be the maximal user-role assignment $UR^{\max}$ for the payment workflow. For example, Emma is unavailable with respect to $UT = RT \circ UR$. Because $(\mathsf{Emma}, r_3) \in UR^{\max}$, we may change Emma's availability by assigning her to r_3, resulting

in the user-role assignment $UR' = UR \cup \{(\mathsf{Emma}, r_3)\}$. The administrative activity of assigning Emma to r_3 costs 3 and the overall risk and maintenance cost rises by $12 + 5$. Thus, $\mathsf{costR}(UR, UR') - \mathsf{costR}(UR, UR) = 3 + 12 + 5 = 20$. ★

Using costR and $UR^{\max}$, we now refine **OWA** to **ROWA**.

Definition 12 (Role-based Optimal Workflow-aware Authorization Administration Problem **ROWA**)

Input: A role cost function costR, a maximal user-role assignment UR^{max}, a workflow task set T, a workflow history H, an authorization policy ϕ, and an RBAC policy (UR, RT), such that $H \models \phi$.

Output: $\displaystyle\min_{UR' \subseteq UR^{max}} \{\mathsf{costR}(UR, UR') | \overset{\exists}{\models} (T, H, \phi, RT \circ UR')\}$

or No *if the above set is empty.*

We refer to the output corresponding to the **ROWA**-instance *rowa* as **ROWA**(*rowa*). In the following, we define a function ROWAtoILP that transforms a **ROWA**-instance to an **ILP**-instance. We specify the matrix $\mathbf{A}$ and the vectors $\mathbf{b}$, $\mathbf{c}$, and $\mathbf{x}$ indirectly by defining the respective (**ILP**) constraints and the cost function in terms of sums. Furthermore, we index decision variables with a superscript, which should not be mistaken for an exponent. We thereby simplify the forthcoming proofs. Transforming the constraints and variables to a matrix-vector form is straightforward and therefore not shown in detail.

Definition 13 *Let* $(\mathsf{costR}, UR^{max}, T, H, \phi, (UR, RT))$ *be a* **ROWA**-*instance, let* costR *be composed of the auxiliary functions* $\mathsf{risk}, \mathsf{add}, \mathsf{rm}$, *and* ma, *and let* $U = \mathrm{dom}(UR^{max})$ *and* $R = \mathrm{ran}(UR^{max})$. *The function* ROWAtoILP *transforms* $(\mathsf{costR}, UR^{max}, T, H, \phi, (UR, RT))$ *to an* **ILP**-*instance as follows:*

Decision variables:

$$x^{u,r}, x^{u,t} \in \mathbb{Z} \text{ for every } u \in U, r \in R, \text{ and } t \in T$$

Objective function:

$$\sum_{(u,r) \in U \times R} x^{u,r}(\mathsf{risk}(r) + \mathsf{ma}(r)) +$$
$$\sum_{(u,r) \in (U \times R) \setminus UR} x^{u,r} \mathsf{add}(r) +$$
$$\sum_{(u,r) \in UR} (1 - x^{u,r}) \mathsf{rm}(r)$$

Constraints:

(1) $\forall t \in T, u \in U . \sum_{\{r | (r,t) \in RT\}} x^{u,r} \geq x^{u,t}$

(2) $\forall t \in T . \sum_{u \in U} x^{u,t} = 1$

(3) $\forall t \in T . \sum_{\{u \in U | H \cup \{(u,t)\} \not\models \phi\}} x^{u,t} = 0$

(4) $\forall (T_1, T_2) \in S, t_1 \in T_1, t_2 \in T_2, u \in U . x^{u,t_1} + x^{u,t_2} \leq 1$

(5) $\forall T' \in B, t_1, t_2 \in T', u \in U . x^{u,t_1} = x^{u,t_2}$

(6) $\sum_{(u,r) \in (U \times R) \setminus UR^{max}} x^{u,r} = 0$

(7) $\forall u \in U, r \in R . x^{u,r} \geq 0 \text{ and } x^{u,r} \leq 1$

(8) $\forall u \in U, t \in T . x^{u,t} \geq 0 \text{ and } x^{u,t} \leq 1$

Consider a **ROWA**-instance composed of costR, $UR^{\max}$, T, H, ϕ, and (UR, RT), and let $(\mathbf{A}, \mathbf{b}, \mathbf{c})$ be the corresponding **ILP**-instance returned by ROWAtoILP. We refer to a constraint or a set of constraints i in Definition 13 as Ci. Next, we define a relation between feasible solutions of **ILP**-instances generated by ROWAtoILP, and user-role assignments and allocations for their corresponding **ROWA**-instances. Afterward, we use this relation to explain the constraints C1–C8 and we prove the soundness and completeness of ROWAtoILP.

Note that a feasible solution $\mathbf{x}$ for $(\mathbf{A}, \mathbf{b}, \mathbf{c})$ is composed of the decision variables $x^{u,r}$ and $x^{u,t}$, where u ranges over $\mathrm{dom}(UR^{\max})$, r over $\mathrm{ran}(UR^{\max})$, and t over T. Because $\mathbf{x}$ is a feasible solution, the decision variables satisfy all constraints listed in Definition 13, in particular C7 and C8. Therefore, the decision variables assume either the value 0 or 1.

Definition 14 *Let* $(\mathrm{costR}, UR^{max}, T, H, \phi, (UR, RT))$ *be a* **ROWA***-instance and* $(\mathbf{A}, \mathbf{b}, \mathbf{c})$ *the corresponding* **ILP***-instance returned by* ROWAtoILP*. Furthermore, let* $\mathbf{x}$ *be a feasible solution for* $(\mathbf{A}, \mathbf{b}, \mathbf{c})$, $U = \mathrm{dom}(UR^{max})$, *and* $R = \mathrm{ran}(UR^{max})$. *For a user-role assignment* UR' *and an allocation* alloc, *we say that* $\mathbf{x}$ *corresponds to* (UR', alloc), *written* $\mathbf{x} \sim (UR', \mathrm{alloc})$, *if*

(1) $UR' = \{(u, r) \in U \times R \mid x^{u,r} = 1\}$ *and*

(2) $\mathrm{alloc} = \{(t, u) \in T \times U \mid x^{u,t} = 1\}$.

In other words, the decision variables of the form $x^{u,r}$ determine UR' and those of the form $x^{u,t}$ determine alloc. More specifically, if $x^{u,r} = 1$, for a user u and a role r, then u is assigned to r in UR'. Moreover, for a user u and a task t, $x^{u,t} = 1$ implies that alloc maps t to u. Note that the correspondence relation $\sim$ uniquely determines a tuple (UR', alloc) given a vector $\mathbf{x}$ and *vice versa*.

We now informally describe the (**ILP**) constraints created by ROWAtoILP. We expand upon this in the proof of Lemma 2. C1 ensures that an allocation assigns a user u only to a task t if u is assigned to a role r that is assigned to t. C2 enforces that an allocation maps every task to exactly one user. C3 ensures that an allocation's assignments do not violate the given execution history. C4 and C5 enforce that an allocation satisfies the given SoD and BoD constraints, respectively. Finally, C6 restricts user-role assignments to subsets of the given maximal user-role assignment. C7 and C8 were already explained above.

The following lemma, which we prove in [4], establishes that ROWAtoILP is both sound and complete.

Lemma 2 *Let* $(\mathrm{costR}, UR^{max}, T, H, \phi, (UR, RT))$ *be a* **ROWA***-instance and* $(\mathbf{A}, \mathbf{b}, \mathbf{c})$ *the corresponding* **ILP***-instance returned by* ROWAtoILP*. Let* $\mathbf{x}$ *be a vector,* UR' *a user-role assignment, and* alloc *an allocation, such that* $\mathbf{x} \sim (UR', \mathrm{alloc})$.

- Soundness: *If* $\mathbf{x}$ *is a feasible solution for* $(\mathbf{A}, \mathbf{b}, \mathbf{c})$ *then* $UR' \subseteq UR^{max}$ *and* $\mathrm{alloc} \models (T, H, \phi, RT \circ UR')$.

- Completeness: *If* $UR' \subseteq UR^{max}$ *and* $\mathrm{alloc} \models (T, H, \phi, RT \circ UR')$ *then* $\mathbf{x}$ *is a feasible solution for* $(\mathbf{A}, \mathbf{b}, \mathbf{c})$.

Given the soundness and completeness of ROWAtoILP, we now show with Theorem 1 that ROWAtoILP and algorithms for **ILP** can be employed to solve **ROWA**-instances.

Theorem 1 *For every* **ROWA***-instance rowa,*

$$\mathbf{ROWA}(rowa) = \mathbf{ILP}(\mathrm{ROWAtoILP}(rowa)) .$$

PROOF. Let $(\mathrm{costR}, UR^{\max}, T, H, \phi, (UR, RT))$ be a **ROWA**-instance and $(\mathbf{A}, \mathbf{b}, \mathbf{c})$ be the corresponding **ILP**-instance returned by ROWAtoILP. Let $U = \mathrm{dom}(UR^{\max})$, $R = \mathrm{ran}(UR^{\max})$, $\phi = (S, B)$, and let costR be defined by the auxiliary functions risk, add, rm, and ma. Furthermore, let UR' be a user-role assignment, alloc an allocation, and $\mathbf{x}$ a vector such that $UR' \subseteq UR^{\max}$, $\mathrm{alloc} \models (T, H, \phi, RT \circ UR')$ and $\mathbf{x} \sim (UR', \mathrm{alloc})$. From Lemma 2 we have that $\mathbf{x}$ is a feasible solution for $(\mathbf{A}, \mathbf{b}, \mathbf{c})$.

As derived in Figure 4, it follows from Definitions 11, 13, and 14 that $\mathrm{costR}(UR, UR') = \mathbf{c}^{\mathrm{T}}\mathbf{x}$. Assume that UR' minimizes costR with respect to all user-role assignments $UR'' \subseteq UR^{\max}$ such that $\models^{\exists} (T, H, \phi, RT \circ UR'')$, *i.e.* $\mathrm{costR}(UR, UR') = \mathbf{ROWA}(\mathrm{costR}, UR^{\max}, T, H, \phi, (UR, RT))$. To derive a contradiction, assume that $\mathbf{ILP}(\mathbf{A}, \mathbf{b}, \mathbf{c}) \neq \mathrm{costR}(UR, UR')$. Because $\mathbf{x}$ is a feasible solution for $(\mathbf{A}, \mathbf{b}, \mathbf{c})$ and $\mathrm{costR}(UR, UR') = \mathbf{c}^{\mathrm{T}}\mathbf{x}$, there must exist a feasible solution $\mathbf{y}$ for $(\mathbf{A}, \mathbf{b}, \mathbf{c})$ such that $\mathrm{costR}(UR, UR') > \mathbf{c}^{\mathrm{T}}\mathbf{y}$. Let UR'' be a user-role assignment and alloc' an allocation such that $\mathbf{y} \sim (UR'', \mathrm{alloc}')$. It follows by Lemma 2 that $UR'' \subseteq UR^{\max}$ and $\mathrm{alloc}' \models (T, H, \phi, RT \circ UR'')$. As reasoned before, we have $\mathrm{costR}(UR, UR'') = \mathbf{c}^{\mathrm{T}}\mathbf{y}$ and therefore $\mathrm{costR}(UR, UR') > \mathrm{costR}(UR, UR'')$. However, this violates our minimality assumption for $\mathrm{costR}(UR, UR')$. Hence, $\mathbf{x}$ is an optimal solution for $(\mathbf{A}, \mathbf{b}, \mathbf{c})$ and the two outputs are equal. ∎

We now establish the space and runtime complexity of ROWAtoILP. Let $(\mathrm{costR}, UR^{\max}, T, H, \phi, (UR, RT))$ again be a **ROWA**-instance and $(\mathbf{A}, \mathbf{b}, \mathbf{c})$ the corresponding **ILP**-instance returned by ROWAtoILP. Furthermore, let $U = \mathrm{dom}(UR^{\max})$, $R = \mathrm{ran}(UR^{\max})$, and $\phi = (S, B)$. The **ILP**-instance $(\mathbf{A}, \mathbf{b}, \mathbf{c})$ ranges over $|U||R| + |U||T|$ decision variables, which corresponds to the same number of columns of the matrix $\mathbf{A}$. There are $|T||U|$ constraints of kind (1), $|T|$ constraints of kinds (2) and (3), $O(|S||T|^2|U|)$ constraints of kind (4), $O(|B||T|^2|U|)$ constraints of kind (5), there is one constraint of kind (6), $|U||R|$ constraints of kind (7), and $|U||T|$ constraints of kind (8). Thus, the total number of constraints is in $O(|U|(|T|^2(|S| + |B|) + |R| + |T|))$, corresponding to the same number of rows of $\mathbf{A}$. For the generation of constraints of kind (3), $H \cup \{(u, t)\} \not\models \phi$ must be computed for every task $t \in T$ and user $u \in U$. However, by Definitions 3, 4, and 5, this computation has a polynomial runtime complexity in the size of the **ROWA**-instance. Hence, ROWAtoILP is a polynomial reduction from **ROWA** to **ILP**.

Solving **ROWA** requires solving **AEP**, which is **NP**-complete by Lemma 1. Therefore, the following corollary is a direct consequence of Theorem 1 and the observation that ROWAtoILP is a polynomial reduction from **ROWA** to the **NP**-complete problem **ILP**.

Corollary 1 ROWA *is* **NP***-complete.*

We have thereby shown that finding an optimal RBAC policy that allows a successful completion of a given workflow instance is in the same complexity class as deciding whether the workflow instance can be successfully completed for a given RBAC policy. Furthermore, the polynomial reduction from **ROWA** to **ILP** enables us to solve **ROWA**-instances using well-established algorithms for **ILP**. An example follows in the next section.

Note that ROWAtoILP and an algorithm for **ILP** can also be used to solve **AEP**. Let (T, H, ϕ, UT) be an **AEP**-

$$\text{costR}(UR, UR') = \sum_{(u,r)\in UR'}(\text{risk}(r) + \text{ma}(r)) + \sum_{(u,r)\in UR'\setminus UR}\text{add}(r) + \sum_{(u,r)\in UR\setminus UR'}\text{rm}(r)$$

$$= \sum_{(u,r)\in UR'} 1\,(\text{risk}(r) + \text{ma}(r)) + \sum_{(u,r)\in (U\times R)\setminus UR'} 0\,(\text{risk}(r) + \text{ma}(r))$$
$$+ \sum_{(u,r)\in UR'\setminus UR} 1\,\text{add}(r) + \sum_{(u,r)\in ((U\times R)\setminus UR')\setminus UR} 0\,\text{add}(r)$$
$$+ \sum_{(u,r)\in UR\setminus UR'} 1\,\text{rm}(r) + \sum_{(u,r)\in UR\cap UR'} 0\,\text{rm}(r)$$

$$= \sum_{(u,r)\in U\times R} x^{u,r}(\text{risk}(r) + \text{ma}(r)) + \sum_{(u,r)\in (U\times R)\setminus UR} x^{u,r}\text{add}(r) + \sum_{(u,r)\in UR}(1 - x^{u,r})\text{rm}(r)$$

$$= \mathbf{c}^{\text{T}}\mathbf{x}$$

Figure 4: Equality of role cost function and objective function

instance. Using a set of roles R, we decompose UT into an RBAC policy (UR, RT) such that $RT \circ UR = UT$. Furthermore, let $UR^{\text{max}} = UR$, and costR be the role cost function composed of the auxiliary functions $\text{risk}(r) = \text{ma}(r) = 0$ and $\text{add}(r) = \text{rm}(r) = 1$, for all $r \in R$. $\mathbf{ROWA}(\text{costR}, UR^{\text{max}}, T, H, \phi, (UR, RT)) = 0$ if and only if $\models^{\exists} (T, H, \phi, UT)$. This follows from the observation that the minimal value of costR is 0, which is only possible for $\text{costR}(UR, UR) = 0$, implying that $\models^{\exists} (T, H, \phi, RT \circ UR)$.

4.3 Experimental Results

We return to our running example and demonstrate how off-the-shelf software can be used to solve **ROWA**-instances using our reduction to **ILP**. We implemented ROWAtoILP using the numerical software MATLAB [22].

Example 7 Recall the RBAC policy (UR, RT) shown in Figure 3 and our observation in Example 5 that there exists no allocation for T, H_2, ϕ, and $UT = UR \circ RT$. Furthermore, recall the role cost function costR and the maximal user-role assignment UR^{max} presented in Example 6.

Using our ROWAtoILP-implementation, we transform the **ROWA**-instance $(\text{costR}, UR^{\text{max}}, T, H, \phi, (UR, RT))$ to an **ILP**-instance $(\mathbf{A}, \mathbf{b}, \mathbf{c})$ and compute an optimal solution $\mathbf{x}$, which corresponds by Definition 14 to the user-role assignment $UR' = \{(\text{Bob}, r_2), (\text{Claire}, r_3), (\text{Emma}, r_3)\}$ and the allocation $\text{alloc} = \{(t_1, \text{Emma}), (t_2, \text{Bob}), (t_3, \text{Claire}), (t_4, \text{Emma}), (t_5, \text{Claire}), (t_6, \text{Claire})\}$. The cost of changing from UR to UR' is $\text{costR}(UR, UR') = 43$. Hence the optimal administrative change with respect to costR is to extend UR by assigning Emma to the role Procurement Manager (r_3). This empowers the users to complete the payment workflow, without violating ϕ and respecting the execution history H_2.

Suppose now that the risk exposure changes in that the risk associated with an assignment to role r_3 increases by 3 to 15. The other numbers in Table 1 remain unchanged. By running our program again, we see that this small change of cost results in a different optimal solution. The optimal user-role assignment is now $UR'' = \{(\text{Bob}, r_2), (\text{Bob}, r_2), (\text{Claire}, r_3), (\text{Fritz}, r_4)\}$, the respective allocation is $\text{alloc}' = \{(t_1, \text{Bob}), (t_2, \text{Bob}), (t_3, \text{Claire}), (t_4, \text{Fritz}), (t_5, \text{Claire}), (t_6, \text{Claire})\}$, and $\text{costR}(UR, UR'') = 46$. Because the risk associated with r_3 increased, it is now cheaper, i.e. less risky, to assign Bob additionally to the role Procurement Clerk (r_1) and Fritz to Accountant (r_4) instead of assigning Emma to the role Procurement Manager (r_3). ★

Computing optimal solutions for **ILP**-instances, such as the ones presented in the example above, takes about 100 milliseconds on a standard PC configuration.[1] We also experimented with larger, randomly generated maximal user-role assignments. On our test system, we observed an exponential increase of the running time in the size of the input, which is consistent with our complexity analysis of ROWAtoILP and Corollary 1. However, we did not investigate optimizations of our prototype implementation.

5. RELATED WORK

Crampton was the first to analyze the computational complexity of deciding for a given workflow whether an allocation of users to tasks exists such that an authorization policy is satisfied [9]. In [25], Wang and Li call this decision problem the *workflow satisfiability problem* and prove that it is **NP**-complete for their authorization model. **AEP** is an adaptation of the workflow satisfiability problem to our authorization model from [3] and serves as a building block for the definition of **OWA** and **ROWA**.

Most papers on authorization-constrained workflows implicitly assume that authorizations are non-administrable. One exception is the work on *delegation* in workflow systems. Building on and extending the seminal work of Atluri et al. [1], different delegation models for workflows have been proposed, e.g. [24]. Crampton and Khambhammettu [10] were the first to check if permitting a delegation request prevents the completion of a workflow instance. Another exception is the *workflow resiliency problem* introduced by Wang and Li [25], which asks whether a workflow can be executed successfully if a given number of users is unavailable. None of the above consider the *optimality* of authorization policies. They just provide algorithms to determine whether a given authorization policy satisfies a workflow, i.e. algorithms for the problem that we formalized as **AEP**.

Related work on SoD and BoD, e.g. [13], often uses the term *dynamic* for what we call *history-dependent* and *static* for *history-independent*. However, because we distinguish authorizations both with respect to their dependency on a workflow's execution history and with respect to whether they are administrable at run time, the term *dynamic* is not sufficiently refined. Hence, we avoid it.

The notion of risk has been introduced into authorization models to adapt authorizations to changing conditions. Methods to measure and quantify risks are given in [8, 17]. Aziz et al. use a risk semantics to transform policies with respect to operational, combinatorial, and conflict of interest risks with the goal of minimizing the risk associated with a

[1]Mac OS X, 2.5 GHz Intel Core 2 Duo, 2 GB RAM.

policy [2]. In contrast to our work, they change role-task assignments, leaving the user-role assignment, where changes occur in practice more frequently, untouched.

To quantify risk in role delegation, Han *et al.* consider the position of the role within the role hierarchy, the number of permissions gained, and also associate workflow instances with a risk based on the data they process [14]. However, risk is not linked to successful workflow termination. The cost drivers for authorization management identified by Casassa Mont *et al.* [18] provide further metrics for defining role cost functions.

6. CONCLUSION AND FUTURE WORK

We have presented the concept of a cost-minimizing authorization policy that empowers users to execute a given workflow. Our approach comes with considerable modeling freedom. For example, cost can model the risk associated with an authorization policy and hence the optimal policy maximizes protection. By first introducing the generic **OWA**-problem and later refining it to **ROWA**, we showed that our approach is both general and also applicable to concrete business scenarios. Furthermore, we presented a mapping from **ROWA** to the optimization problem **ILP**, which allows us to use of off-the-shelf software to solve **ROWA**.

The generality of our approach gives rise to many design decisions and consequently to various directions for future work. For example, other workflow authorization models provide different features than [3], *e.g.* support for delegation [10]. Similarly, user-task assignments can be refined based on different authorization models and our role-based cost function could be further refined to account for additional properties such as role hierarchies. Furthermore, the predicate whether an authorization change is feasible could account for additional properties such as time.

Meaningful risk metrics for authorization policies are a precondition for the effective use of our approach. We pointed to various methods for quantifying the risk associated with authorization policies. However, finding such metrics is challenging. This does not, of course, reduce the importance of such metrics and we see our results as providing additional evidence for their usefulness.

Acknowledgments. We thank Srdjan Marinovic and the anonymous reviewers for their helpful comments. This work was partially funded by the European Commission under the Seventh Framework Project "PoSecCo" (IST 257129).

7. REFERENCES

[1] V. Atluri, E. Bertino, E. Ferrari, and P. Mazzoleni. Supporting delegation in secure workflow management systems. In *Proc. of the Annual Working Conference on Data and Application Security*, pp. 190–202, 2003.

[2] B. Aziz, S. N. Foley, J. Herbert, and G. Swart. Reconfiguring role based access control policies using risk semantics. *J. High Speed Networks*, 15(3):261–273, 2006.

[3] D. Basin, S. J. Burri, and G. Karjoth. Obstruction-free authorization enforcement: Aligning security with business objectives. In *Proc. of the IEEE Computer Security Foundations Symposium (CSF '11)*, pp. 99–113 2011.

[4] D. Basin, S. J. Burri, and G. Karjoth. *Optimal Workflow-aware Authorizations*, IBM Research, RZ 3815, 2012.

[5] D. Basin, P. Schaller, and M. Schläpfer. *Applied Information Security*. Springer, 2011.

[6] D. E. Bell and L. J. LaPadula. *Secure computer systems: Mathematical foundations*, MTR-2547, The Mitre Corporation, 1973.

[7] G. Chartrand and P. Zhang. *Chromatic Graph Theory*. Chapman & Hall, 2008.

[8] P.-C. Cheng, P. Rohatgi, C. Keser, P. A. Karger, G. M. Wagner, and A. S. Reninger. Fuzzy multi-level security: An experiment on quantified risk-adaptive access control. In *Proc. of the IEEE Symposium on Security and Privacy (S&P '07)*, pp. 222–230, 2007.

[9] J. Crampton. A reference monitor for workflow systems with constrained task execution. In *Proc. of the ACM Symposium on Access Control Models and Technologies (SACMAT '05)*, pp. 38–47, 2005.

[10] J. Crampton and H. Khambhammettu. Delegation and satisfiability in workflow systems. In *Proc. of the ACM Symposium on Access Control Models and Technologies (SACMAT '08)*, pp. 31–40, 2008.

[11] European Union. *Final report of the expert group on e-invoicing.* `http://bit.ly/yvWtfQ`, 2009.

[12] D. F. Ferraiolo, R. S. Sandhu, S. I. Gavrila, D. R. Kuhn, and R. Chandramouli. Proposed NIST standard for Role-Based Access Control. *TISSEC*, 4(3):224–274, 2001.

[13] V. D. Gligor, S. I. Gavrila, and D. Ferraiolo. On the formal definition of separation-of-duty policies and their composition. *Proc. of the the IEEE Symposium on Security and Privacy (S&P '98)*, pp. 172–183, 1998.

[14] W. Han, Q. Ni, and H. Chen. Apply measurable risk to strengthen security of a role-based delegation supporting workflow system. In *Proc. of the IEEE International Symposium on Policies for Distributed Systems and Networks (POLICY '09)*, pp. 45–52, 2009.

[15] IBM. WebSphere Process Server (WPS), v 6.2, 2011.

[16] IT Governance Institute. *Control objectives for information and related technology (COBIT) 4.1*, 2005.

[17] I. Molloy, P.-C. Cheng, and P. Rohatgi. Trading in risk: using markets to improve access control. In *Proc. of the Workshop on New Security Paradigms (NSPW '08)*, pp. 107–125, 2008.

[18] M. C. Mont, Y. Beresnevichiene, D. Pym, and S. Shiu. Economics of identity and access management: Providing decision support for investments. In *Network Operations and Mgnt. Symposium Workshops*, pp. 134 –141, 2010.

[19] Object Management Group (OMG). Business Process Model and Notation (BPMN), v 2.0. 2011.

[20] J. Saltzer and M. Schroeder. The protection of information in computer systems. *Proc. of the IEEE*, pp. 1278–1308, 1975.

[21] A. Schrijver. *Theory of Linear and Integer Programming.* Wiley, 1998.

[22] The MathWorks. Matlab r2011b. 2012.

[23] W. M. P. van der Aalst, A. H. M. ter Hofstede, B. Kiepuszewski, and A. P. Barros. Workflow patterns. *Distributed and Parallel Databases*, 14(1):5–51, 2003.

[24] J. Wainer, A. Kumar, and P. Barthelmess. DW-RBAC: A formal security model of delegation and revocation in workflow systems. *Inf. Syst.*, 32(3):365–384, 2007.

[25] Q. Wang and N. Li. Satisfiability and resiliency in workflow authorization systems. *TISSEC*, 13(4):40, 2010.

[26] L. Zhang, A. Brodsky, and S. Jajodia. Toward information sharing: Benefit and risk access control (BARAC). In *Proc. of the IEEE International Workshop on Policies for Distributed Systems and Networks (POLICY '06)*, pp. 45–53, 2006.

Access Control for RDF Graphs using Abstract Models

Vassilis
Papakonstantinou
FORTH-ICS and
University of Crete
papv@ics.forth.gr

Maria Michou
maria.michou@gmail.com

Irini Fundulaki
FORTH-ICS
fundul@ics.forth.gr

Giorgos Flouris
FORTH-ICS
fgeo@ics.forth.gr

Grigoris Antoniou
FORTH-ICS and
University of Huddersfield
antoniou@ics.forth.gr

ABSTRACT

The Resource Description Framework (RDF) has become the defacto standard for representing information in the Semantic Web. Given the increasing amount of sensitive RDF data available on the Web, it becomes increasingly critical to guarantee secure access to this content. In this paper we advocate the use of an *abstract access control model* to ensure the selective exposure of RDF information. The model is defined by a set of *abstract operators* and *tokens*. Tokens are used to label RDF triples with access information. Abstract operators model RDF Schema inference rules and propagation of labels along the RDF Schema (RDFS) class and property hierarchies. In this way, the access label of a triple is a complex expression that involves the labels of the triples and the operators applied to obtain said label. Different applications can then adopt different *concrete access policies* that encode an assignment of the abstract tokens and operators to concrete (specific) values. Following this approach, changes in the interpretation of abstract tokens and operators can be easily implemented resulting in a very flexible mechanism that allows one to easily experiment with different concrete access policies (defined per context or user). To demonstrate the feasibility of the approach, we implemented our ideas on top of the MonetDB and PostgreSQL open source database systems. We conducted an initial set of experiments which showed that the overhead for using abstract expressions is roughly linear to the number of triples considered; performance is also affected by the characteristics of the dataset, such as the size and depth of class and property hierarchies as well as the considered concrete policy.

Categories and Subject Descriptors

H.1 [**Information Systems Applications**]; H.2.8 [**Database Applications**]

General Terms

Access Control Models

Keywords

Access Control, Abstract Model, RDF, Inference

1. INTRODUCTION

RDF [8] has established itself as a widely used standard for representing data in the Semantic Web. Several commercial and academic efforts, such as the W3C Linked Open Data initiative [19], target the development of RDF datasets. The popularity of the RDF data model [8] and the RDF Schema language (RDFS) [3] is due to the flexible and extensible representation of information under the form of *triples*. An RDF triple *(subject, property, object)* asserts the fact that *subject* is associated with *object* through *property*. A set of triples form an *RDF graph* that can be represented by a node and edge labeled directed graph. Nodes of the graph represent the *subject* and *object* components of triples (*resources*) connected by edges that model the *predicates* of triples. RDFS is used to add semantics to RDF triples, through the *inference rules* specified in the RDF Schema language [11] that entail new *implicit* triples.

The number of applications that publish and exchange possibly sensitive RDF data continuously increases in a large number of domains. In light of the sensitive nature of the available information, the issue of *securing* RDF content and *ensuring the selective exposure of information* to different classes of users is becoming all the more important.

In this paper we focus on the problem of providing secure access to RDF data taking into account RDFS *inference* and the *propagation of access labels* along the RDFS *class* and *property* hierarchies. In the case of inference a possible scenario is to consider that the label of an implied triple depends on the labels of its implying triples [9]. Propagated labels are useful when one wants to enforce the inheritance of labels along the RDFS class and property hierarchies (e.g., an application may consider that an instance should inherit the label of its class). This is a common approach in XML access control where the labels are inherited from a node to its children nodes in an XML tree.

The majority of the state of the art approaches for RDF access control [2, 7, 12, 13, 20] use *annotation models* where each triple is assigned a *concrete value* as access label that determines whether the triple is accessible or not. In these models the computation of the access label of a triple (via implication or propagation) is done in a fixed manner according to predefined semantics. For instance, an application may consider a concrete policy where the access label of a triple takes one of the values "public", "confidential", "secret" and "top-secret". The semantics of the application are hard-coded inside the policy specification: the policy considers that a triple gets the "public" access label if all its implying triples are labeled as "public". Consequently, when the initial assignment of the access labels to triples change, then the labels of all the implied triples in the dataset must be recomputed.

One possible solution to this problem is to store *how* the access label of a triple is computed. To do so, we advocate the use of an annotation model in which we *do not commit* to *(i)* a specific assignment of values to access labels of triples and *(ii)* predefined semantics for computing the access labels of the triples obtained through inference and propagation. Instead, we use an *abstract access control model* defined by *abstract tokens and operators*. In this way, the access label of a triple is an *abstract expression*, consisting of tokens and operators. This expression describes *how the access label of said triple is computed*. This is inspired by the approach advocated in *how provenance models* [10] for relational data provenance.

To determine the actual label of a triple associated with an abstract expression (i.e., in order to decide whether a triple is accessible or not), one should concretize the respective tokens and operators. This is done using a *concrete policy*, defined by the corresponding application. Using this policy, one can compute the value of the abstract expression, i.e., the concrete label associated with the triple in question. Based on the computed value and the semantics of the policy, one can decide whether the triple is accessible or not.

The main benefits of the proposed model are discussed below:

• When abstract models are considered, the abstract labels are computed only once at *annotation* time. The application can then adopt a concrete policy to serve its needs. The concrete labels of triples are only computed at query time (on a need-to-have basis). Hence applications can easily experiment with different concrete access policies without needing to recompute the access labels each time since only the value of an abstract expression needs to be computed. Similarly, our approach can support applications that dynamically adapt their policies, e.g., on a per-user basis.

• In standard annotation models, a change in the assigned access label of a triple would require a complete recomputation of the access labels of all triples obtained through propagation and inference. This must be done in order to ensure the correctness of annotations [14]. In the case of abstract models, the abstract expressions make explicit the tokens and operators involved in the computation of the complex label. Consequently, various types of changes (in both the dataset and in the associated authorizations) can be supported more efficiently that can lead to important gains especially when large datasets are considered. The present paper only lays the foundations for our abstract access control model and does not consider the problem of dynamically adapting the abstract labels in response to an update.

• The flexibility of the proposed model to handle different applications with diversified needs simplifies the maintenance of an access control-enhanced dataset. The abstract approach generalizes in a straightforward manner the existing RDF access control models that consider RDFS semantics since they can be considered as specific concretizations of the general model.

The main contributions of our work are:

1. The definition and use of an *abstract access control model* to provide secure access to RDF *triples*, that allows us to determine how the access label of a triple was computed. The abstract control model works on *triples* rather than *resources* (i.e., nodes in an RDF graph). This approach is motivated by the fact that the semantics in an RDF graph are not given by the resources themselves, but by their interconnections and relationships as expressed in triples. Thus, triples are the "first-class citizens" that comprise an RDF graph; triples can describe resources (e.g., the fact that a given resource is a class), whereas the opposite is not possible (e.g., resources cannot describe a subsumption relationship).

2. The *extension* of the standard *RDFS inference rules* in order to determine the access labels of implied triples, as well as the definition and formalization of *propagation rules*, that determine how access labels are propagated along the RDFS *class* and *property* hierarchies.

3. A first implementation of our ideas on top of the MonetDB and PostgreSQL open source RDBMSs and a preliminary set of experiments that show the computational properties of our approach.

The rest of this paper is structured as follows: in Section 2, we provide a motivating example that is used in the remainder of the paper. In Section 3, we describe the RDF, RDFS and SPARQL languages. In Section 4 we define the abstract access control model. Section 5 discusses how concrete policies can be defined. In Section 6 we discuss implementation issues and the conducted experiments. In Section 7 we describe related work, and conclude in Section 8.

2. MOTIVATING EXAMPLE

Figure 1 shows (in tabular form) a set of RDF triples (inspired by the FOAF ontology[1]) that we will use in this paper for illustration purposes. *Access control authorizations* are used to assign an *abstract access control token* to RDF triples, as specified by means of a *query*. We say that the triples returned from the evaluation of the query are *in the scope of the authorization*. In this paper we rely on authorizations that make use of the SPARQL [18] language to determine the RDF triples concerned by it.

Figure 2 shows a set of access authorizations defined for the set of RDF triples of Figure 1. In our work, we use *quadruples* to encode the access label of an RDF triple. We write (s, p, o, l) to denote that l is the access label assigned to triple (s, p, o). Quadruples are used to represent information such as time, trust, provenance among others. The approach we follow is similar to the named graphs concept discussed in [5].

---

[1]http://www.foaf-project.org/

	s	p	o
$t_1:$	*Student*	sc	*Person*
$t_2:$	*Person*	sc	*Agent*
$t_3:$	*&a*	type	*Student*
$t_4:$	*&a*	*firstName*	Alice
$t_5:$	*&a*	*lastName*	Smith
$t_6:$	*Agent*	type	class

Figure 1: RDF Triples

Figure 3 shows the RDF quadruples obtained by evaluating the authorizations of Figure 2 to the set of triples in Figure 1. For instance quadruples q_1, q_2 are obtained from the evaluation of authorization $\mathcal{A}_2$ that assigns to triples with predicate sc (triples t_1 and t_2) the abstract token at_2. Quadruple q_3 is obtained from the evaluation of authorization $\mathcal{A}_3$ that assigns to triples with predicate type and object *Student* the token at_3 (triple t_3). Authorization $\mathcal{A}_1$ assigns to triples with predicate *firstName* the access token at_1 (triple t_4) thus obtaining quadruple q_4. Quadruple q_6 is obtained by assigning token at_4 to triples with predicate type and *object* class through authorization $\mathcal{A}_4$ (triple t_6). Finally, authorization $\mathcal{A}_5$ assigns to triples with *object Person* access token at_5 (triple t_1) thereby obtaining quadruple q_7. Triple t_5 is not in the scope of any of the authorizations $\mathcal{A}_1 - \mathcal{A}_5$, so we assign to it the *default token* $\bot$ (quadruple q_5).

$\mathcal{A}_1:$	(CONSTRUCT	$\{?x\ firstName\ ?y\}$
	WHERE	$\{?x$ type *Student*$\}, at_1)$
$\mathcal{A}_2:$	(CONSTRUCT	$\{?x$ sc $?y\}, at_2)$
$\mathcal{A}_3:$	(CONSTRUCT	$\{?x$ type *Student*$\}, at_3)$
$\mathcal{A}_4:$	(CONSTRUCT	$\{?x$ type class$\}, at_4)$
$\mathcal{A}_5:$	(CONSTRUCT	$\{?x\ ?p\ Person\}, at_5)$

Figure 2: Access Control Authorizations

	s	p	o	l
$q_1:$	*Student*	sc	*Person*	at_2
$q_2:$	*Person*	sc	*Agent*	at_2
$q_3:$	*&a*	type	*Student*	at_3
$q_4:$	*&a*	*firstName*	Alice	at_1
$q_5:$	*&a*	*lastName*	Smith	$\bot$
$q_6:$	*Agent*	type	class	at_4
$q_7:$	*Student*	sc	*Person*	at_5

Figure 3: RDF Quadruples

Note that in our example each of the authorizations uses a different access token. Nevertheless, our model does not forbid different authorizations from using the same token. In addition, the same triple may obtain labels from different authorizations. This is the case for triple t_1 that is in the scope of authorizations $\mathcal{A}_2$ and $\mathcal{A}_5$, thereby obtaining quadruples q_1 and q_7 respectively.

In the above discussion we have not taken into account the RDFS inference rules [11] or the propagation of access

labels along the RDFS class and property hierarchies. RDFS inference rules compute *implied* triples from *explicit* ones. The RDFS inference rules that we consider in our work refer to the transitivity of *subClassOf* (sc), *subPropertyOf* (sp) and *type* (type) hierarchies. For instance, when applying transitivity for the RDFS sc and type hierarchies (i.e., a resource is an instance of all the superclasses of its class) for triples t_1 and t_3 shown in Figure 1 we obtain triple (&a, type, *Person*).

RDFS inference rules can be naturally extended for quadruples and the natural question that comes to mind in this case is *"what is the access label of the implied quadruple?"*. Consider for instance quadruples q_3 and q_1. The label of the implied quadruple (&a, type, *Person*, l) cannot be one of tokens at_3 or at_2 but a *composite* label that <u>involves both</u> tokens. We model the composite label of such an implied quadruple using the *abstract inference operator* denoted by $\odot$ that operates on the labels of its implying quadruples. Using $\odot$, said quadruple will be (&a, type, *Person*, $at_3 \odot at_2$) (q_{10} in Figure 4).

By applying the RDFS inference rules on the type and sc hierarchies in all possible ways, we obtain several quadruples, some of which are shown in Figure 4. Implicit quadruples may also be involved in inferences, resulting in more complex expressions. For example q_{11} is obtained from quadruples q_{10} and q_2. Quadruple q_{12} results from quadruples q_3 and q_9.

	s	p	o	l
$q_8:$	*Student*	sc	*Agent*	$at_2 \odot at_2$
$q_9:$	*Student*	sc	*Agent*	$at_5 \odot at_2$
$q_{10}:$	*&a*	type	*Person*	$at_3 \odot at_2$
$q_{11}:$	*&a*	type	*Agent*	$(at_3 \odot at_2) \odot at_2$
$q_{12}:$	*&a*	type	*Agent*	$at_3 \odot (at_5 \odot at_2)$

Figure 4: Implied Quadruples (Partial List)

The RDFS semantics associated with the class and property hierarchies cause several authors to consider the *propagation* of labels along such hierarchies [13]. For example, an application may require that a triple that defines an instantiation relation between an instance and a class, inherits the access label of the triple defining such class (an instance inherits the label(s) of its class). To support this feature, we define the abstract *unary propagation operator* denoted by $\otimes$.

Recall that in our framework we assign access labels to *triples* rather than *resources*, so the label of a class C is specified by the label of quadruple (C, type, class, l). Similarly, the label of an instance x of a class C is defined by quadruple (x, type, C, l). Under this understanding, quadruple q_6 should propagate its label (at_4) to all instances of *Agent*, thus obtaining the quadruple $q_{13} = $ (&a, type, *Agent*, $\otimes at_4$), which, in our example is the only propagated quadruple.

As explained above, our framework does not bound the abstract tokens (at_i), the default token ($\bot$) and the operators $\odot$ and $\otimes$ to concrete values. Instead, each application, depending on its needs defines a *concrete policy* that *maps* every abstract access token to a concrete value and specifies the concrete operators that implement the abstract ones. The concrete policy also specifies how conflicting labels are resolved and how the default access token should be treated by the concrete operators. This case arises when multiple quadruples that refer to the same triple exist but with different labels. In our example, the concrete policy might determine that the abstract tokens at_1, at_2 and at_3 are mapped to *true* whereas at_4 and at_5 to *false*. The policy semantics may specify that the label of an implied quadruple is *true* if and only if the labels of its implying quadruples are both *true* ($\odot$ is mapped to conjunction), and that the labels are propagated as such ($\otimes$ is mapped to identity). In the case of conflicting labels for a triple the application favors quadruples with the *false* label. In this scenario quadruples q_1, q_2, q_3, q_4 will get a *true* label, whereas q_6 and q_7 label *false*. Implied quadruples q_8, q_{10} and q_{11} will get a *true* label whereas q_9 and q_{12} the *false* label. Note that quadruples q_8 and q_9 refer to the same triple (*Student*, sc, *Agent*). According to the semantics of the policy the resulting quadruple will obtain label *false*. Last, quadruple q_{13} will get the *false* label since the propagation operator is mapped to identity and the label propagated is the *false* label (at_4).

3. PRELIMINARIES

3.1 RDF and RDF Schema

An RDF triple [8] is of the form (*subject*, *predicate*, *object*) and asserts the fact that *subject* is associated with *object* through *property*. We assume two disjoint and infinite sets $\mathbb{U}$, $\mathbb{L}$, denoting the URIs and literals respectively. Then set $\mathcal{T} = \mathbb{U} \times \mathbb{U} \times (\mathbb{U} \cup \mathbb{L})$ is the set of all RDF triples.

The RDF Schema (RDFS) language [3] provides a built-in vocabulary for asserting user-defined schemas in the RDF data model. For instance, RDFS names *rdfs:Class* (class) and *rdf:Property* (prop)[2] can be used to specify *class* and *property* types. These can be used as the object of an RDF triple. Furthermore, one can assert *instanceOf* relationships of resources with the RDF predicate *rdf:type* (type), whereas *subsumption* relationships among classes and properties are expressed with the RDFS *rdfs:subClassOf* (sc) and *rdfs:subPropertyOf* (sp) predicates respectively.

An *RDF Graph* $\mathcal{G}$ is defined as a *set of RDF data and schema triples*, i.e., $\mathcal{G} \subseteq \mathcal{T}$. In this work we consider graphs in which the sc and sp relations are *acyclic*. This assumption is introduced in order to avoid the repeated generation of new quadruples with new labels that can occur when cycles exist. Note that acyclicity holds in the large majority of RDF data used in real applications [24], and is a common assumption made for efficiency (e.g., query optimization [21]) in many RDF applications.

RDFS defines a set of *inference rules* [11] depicted in Table 1, which are used to compute the *closure* of an RDF graph $\mathcal{G}$, denoted by $Cn(\mathcal{G})$. Rules $\mathcal{R}_1$ and $\mathcal{R}_4$ discuss the transitivity of sp and sc properties resp., whereas $\mathcal{R}_2$ and $\mathcal{R}_3$ discuss the transitivity for the sc and sp relations and class and property instances.

3.2 SPARQL

SPARQL [18] is the official W3C recommendation for querying RDF graphs, and is based on the concept of matching patterns against the RDF graph. Thus, a SPARQL query determines the pattern to seek for, and the answer is the

---

[2]In parenthesis are the terms we use in this paper to refer to the RDFS built-in classes and properties.

$$\mathcal{R}_1 : \frac{(p, \text{ sp}, q), (q, \text{ sp}, r)}{(p, \text{ sp}, r)} \qquad \mathcal{R}_2 : \frac{(p, \text{ sp}, q), (x, p, y)}{(x, q, y)}$$

$$\mathcal{R}_3 : \frac{(x, \text{ sc}, y), (z, \text{ type}, x)}{(z, \text{ type}, y)} \qquad \mathcal{R}_4 : \frac{(x, \text{ sc}, y), (y, \text{ sc}, z)}{(x, \text{ sc}, z)}$$

Table 1: RDFS Inference Rules

part of the RDF graph that matches this pattern.

More specifically, SPARQL defines *triple patterns* which resemble an RDF triple, but may have a *variable* (prefixed with character ?) in any of the subject, predicate, or object positions in the RDF triple. Intuitively, triple patterns denote the triples in an RDF graph that have a specific form. SPARQL *graph patterns* are produced by combining triple patterns through the *join*, *optional* and *union* SPARQL operators. Graph patterns may contain filters, using the *filter* expression that specifies conditions on the triple patterns.

The SPARQL syntax follows the SQL select-from-where paradigm. The SPARQL queries we consider in our work use the CONSTRUCT clause, and return a single RDF graph (i.e., set of triples) specified by a graph pattern in the WHERE clause of the query. We choose this form of queries since in our framework we assign access labels to *triples* and not to nodes in the RDF graph. The graph pattern specified in the CONSTRUCT clause should also be included in the query's WHERE clause. For readability purposes only we have not included it in our authorization queries.

The interested reader can find a more detailed description of the semantics of the SPARQL language in [17]. Note that SPARQL does not support functionalities necessary for navigating the RDFS sc and sp property hierarchies. Consequently, to query the closure of the RDF graph, one must either compute it before hand (by applying the rules in Table 1) or evaluate it on the fly. In our work we focus on the computation of the access labels for the implied RDF triples and not on efficient ways of how to compute the closure of an RDF graph.

4. ABSTRACT ACCESS CONTROL MODEL

An *abstract access control model* is comprised of *abstract tokens* and *abstract operators*. Abstract tokens are assigned to RDF triples through *authorization rules*, whereas abstract operators describe *(i)* the computation of access labels for implied triples and *(ii)* the propagation of access labels along the RDFS class and property hierarchies. RDF triples are either annotated with tokens or with a complex expression that involves the tokens and operators of the abstract model.

In our work *annotated RDF triples* are represented as *quadruples*. A quadruple is of the form (s, p, o, l) where s, p, o are the *subject*, *property* and *object* of the triple and l is an *abstract access control expression*. Now we are ready to define the notion of *access control model*.

DEFINITION 4.1. *An abstract access control model $\mathcal{M}$ is a tuple $\mathcal{M} = \langle \mathcal{L}, \perp, \odot, \otimes \rangle$ where:*

- $\mathcal{L}$ *is the set of abstract access tokens*

- $\perp$ *is the default access token that is assigned to triples that are not in the scope of some authorization rule*

- $\odot$ *is the binary inference operator*

- $\otimes$ *is the unary propagation operator*

The access label of a quadruple is an expression that is defined over the abstract tokens in $\mathcal{L}$ and the inference and propagation operators.

4.1 Inference Operator

Implied triples are obtained from the application of RDFS inference rules [11] on an RDF graph. The inference rules shown in Table 2 extend those specified in Table 1 in a straightforward manner to take into account access labels. An implied triple is annotated by a complex expression that involves the labels of its implying triples associated through the binary *inference operator* $\odot$.

$$\mathcal{QR}_1 : \frac{(P, \mathsf{sp}, Q, al_1), (Q, \mathsf{sp}, R, al_2)}{(P, \mathsf{sp}, R, (al_1 \odot al_2))}$$

$$\mathcal{QR}_2 : \frac{(P, \mathsf{sp}, Q, al_1), (x, P, y, al_2)}{(x, Q, y, (al_1 \odot al_2))}$$

$$\mathcal{QR}_3 : \frac{(x, \mathsf{sc}, y, al_1), (z, \mathsf{type}, x, al_2)}{(z, \mathsf{type}, y, (al_1 \odot al_2))}$$

$$\mathcal{QR}_4 : \frac{(x, \mathsf{sc}, y, al_1), (y, \mathsf{sc}, z, al_2)}{(x, \mathsf{sc}, z, (al_1 \odot al_2))}$$

Table 2: RDFS Inference Rules on quadruples

In order for the inference operator $\odot$ to be compliant with its role of "composing" labels during inference, we require it to be commutative and associative. These properties are necessary, because the access label of an implicit triple should be uniquely determined by the access labels of the triples that imply it and not by the order of application of the inference rules. Note that we do not require the inference operator to be idempotent, since we might need to take into account multiple appearances of the same label. Formally:

DEFINITION 4.2. *The abstract inference operator, denoted by $\odot$, is a binary operator defined over abstract tokens from $\mathcal{L} \cup \{\bot\}$ with the following properties:*

$$
\begin{aligned}
al_1 \odot al_2 &= al_2 \odot al_1 && (Commutativity) \\
(al_1 \odot al_2) \odot al_3 &= al_1 \odot (al_2 \odot al_3) && (Associativity)
\end{aligned}
$$

EXAMPLE 4.1. *Consider rule $\mathcal{QR}_3$ from Table 2. When this rule is applied to quadruples $q_1 = (Student, \mathsf{sc}, Person, at_2)$ and $q_3 = (\&a, \mathsf{type}, Student, at_3)$ in Figure 3, we obtain quadruple $q_{10} = (\&a, \mathsf{type}, Person, (at_3 \odot at_2))$ shown in Figure 4.*

4.2 Propagation Operator

The idea of propagation of access labels is found in XML access control models. These models take into account the hierarchical nature of XML data and *propagate* labels to the descendants or ancestors of a node in an XML tree [25]. The propagation rules we advocate in our work *do not generate new triples* since this is the role of the inference rules discussed previously. They simply assign to *existing* triples new labels hence producing *new quadruples*. In this work we focus on *"downward"* propagation rules along the sc, sp and type hierarchies: the labels are propagated from the upper

$$\mathcal{QR}_5 : \frac{(x, \mathsf{type}, \mathsf{class}, al_1), (y, \mathsf{sc}, x, al_2), (y, \mathsf{type}, \mathsf{class}, al_3)}{(y, \mathsf{type}, \mathsf{class}, \otimes(al_1))}$$

$$\mathcal{QR}_6 : \frac{(x, \mathsf{type}, \mathsf{class}, al_1), (y, \mathsf{type}, x, al_2)}{(y, \mathsf{type}, x, \otimes(a_1))}$$

$$\mathcal{QR}_7 : \frac{(x, \mathsf{type}, \mathsf{prop}, al_1), (y, \mathsf{sp}, x, al_2), (y, \mathsf{type}, \mathsf{prop}, al_3)}{(y, \mathsf{type}, \mathsf{prop}, \otimes(al_1))}$$

$$\mathcal{QR}_8 : \frac{(P, \mathsf{type}, \mathsf{prop}, al_1), (x, P, y, al_2)}{(x, P, y, \otimes(al_1))}$$

Table 3: Propagation Rules

level of a hierarchy to the lower levels (e.g., from a class to its instances). It is straightforward to model propagation rules for the opposite direction.

We model the propagation of labels with the *abstract propagation operator*, denoted by $\otimes$. Currently, we consider the propagation of a *single label* and therefore $\otimes$ is a unary operator over abstract access expressions. Table 3 shows the propagation rules that we consider in our work. Note that this set of rules can change and adapt to the application needs, or be omitted altogether.

We require $\otimes$ to be idempotent so that multiple applications on the same label would not give new quadruples. Without this property, each of the propagation rules could be applied arbitrarily many times, each time producing a new quadruple: $(t, \otimes al)$, $(t, \otimes \otimes al)$, ..., $(t, \otimes \ldots \otimes al)$, ... We will hence obtain an infinite number of quadruples for the same triple.

DEFINITION 4.3. *The abstract propagation operator, denoted by $\otimes$, is a unary operator defined over labels, with the property:*

$$\otimes(\otimes(al)) = \otimes(al) \quad (Idempotence)$$

EXAMPLE 4.2. *$\mathcal{QR}_6$ shown in Table 3 states that the label of a class x (defined by quadruple $(x, \mathsf{type}, \mathsf{class}, al_1)$) is propagated to its instances (defined by quadruple $(y, \mathsf{type}, x, al_2)$), thereby obtaining quadruple $(y, \mathsf{type}, x, \otimes(al_1))$. When this rule is applied to the quadruples $q_{11} = (\&a, \mathsf{type}, Agent, (at_3 \odot at_2) \odot at_2)$ from Figure 4 and $q_6 = (Agent, \mathsf{type}, \mathsf{class}, at_4)$ from Figure 3 we obtain quadruple $q_{13} = (\&a, \mathsf{type}, Agent, \otimes at_4)$.*

4.3 Computing Abstract Expressions

Now consider an RDF graph $\mathcal{G}$ (i.e., set of triples) and a set of *authorization rules* that assign abstract access tokens to triples by means of SPARQL queries. In order to obtain the set of quadruples *(i)* we first evaluate the authorization rules on the triples in the input RDF graph; after this step, the triples that did not receive any label are annotated with the default access token ($\bot$); *(ii)* we then apply the *inference rules* on the resulting quadruples to obtain the *implied* ones along with their labels. Inference rules are applied until no new quadruples are produced; *(iii)* last the *propagation rules* are applied on the resulting quadruples to get the quadruples with propagated labels.

At the end of this process, the access label of any quadruple is of the form:

$$proplabel ::= \otimes aclabel \mid at_i$$

$$aclabel ::= at_i \mid aclabel \odot aclabel$$

where at_i is an abstract token from $\mathcal{L}$ or $\perp$.

5. CONCRETE POLICIES

As discussed in Section 2, in order for an application to determine the triples in an RDF graph that are accessible, it must assign specific values to the abstract tokens and operators. This is achieved through a *concrete policy* $\mathcal{P}$ that specifies *i*) the *concrete tokens*, *ii*) a mapping between the concrete and abstract tokens *iii*) the *concrete operators iv*) the *conflict resolution operator* and *v*) the *access function*.

A concrete policy is bound to a *fixed* set of *abstract tokens* from $\mathcal{L}$. The set of *concrete tokens* is denoted by $\mathcal{L_P}$; the *mapping* specifies how the abstract tokens from $\mathcal{L}$ are mapped to the concrete tokens in $\mathcal{L_P}$. Note that $\perp$ is a special token that does not belong in $\mathcal{L}$.

The *concrete operators* implement the abstract inference ($\odot$) and propagation ($\otimes$) operators and handle the default access token. The proposed implementations must respect the properties defined for the their abstract counterparts. The concrete operators are defined over the set $\mathcal{L_P} \cup \{\perp\}$ (i.e., they specify how to handle $\perp$ as well).

In our framework, it is possible that a triple is assigned several different concrete tokens through different quadruples, and/or the special value to which the default access token ($\perp$) is mapped. The *conflict resolution operator*, denoted by $\oplus$, is used to select the final concrete token of said triple. If $\perp$ is included in the set of tokens assigned to the triple, then, by definition, it should be ignored in the presence of other concrete tokens from $\mathcal{L_P}$. Formally, $\oplus$ is defined as a selection function over subsets of $\mathcal{L_P} \cup \{\perp\}$, such that, for any given $\mathcal{X} \in 2^{\mathcal{L_P} \cup \{\perp\}}$ it holds that:

- $\oplus \mathcal{X} \in \mathcal{X}$ if and only if $\mathcal{X} \neq \emptyset$.

- $\oplus \mathcal{X} = \perp$ if and only if $\mathcal{X} = \emptyset$ or $\mathcal{X} = \{\perp\}$.

The *access function*, denoted by *access*() is the final component of a concrete policy and determines whether a triple associated with a certain token is accessible or not. Note that, if a triple is associated with several different concrete tokens, then the conflict resolution operator should be applied first, in order to select one of the tokens for consideration by *access*(). Formally, *access*() is a function mapping each concrete token as well as $\perp$, to *allow* or *deny*, indicating that the corresponding triple is accessible or not respectively.

To visualize our approach we will use two reasonable, and rather simple, concrete policies, **C1** and **C2**. The former is based on boolean tokens, whereas the latter is based on numerical access levels. More specifically, in **C1**, the abstract tokens are mapped to boolean values: $\mathcal{L_P} = \{true, false\}$. A mapping determines how the values in $\mathcal{L}$ are mapped to $\mathcal{L_P}$ (any mapping would do – details are omitted). The abstract operator $\odot$ is mapped to the following operator:

$$al_1 \odot al_2 = \begin{cases} al_1 \wedge al_2 & \text{if } al_1 \text{ and } al_2 \text{ are different from } \perp \\ al_i & \text{if } al_i \neq \perp, al_j = \perp, i \neq j \\ \perp & \text{if } al_1 \text{ and } al_2 \text{ are equal to } \perp \end{cases}$$

where $\wedge$ is the standard boolean conjunction. The propagation operator is simply defined as $\otimes al = al$. The conflict resolution operator resolves conflicts in favor of *false* values:

$$\oplus \mathcal{X} = \begin{cases} false & \text{if } false \in \mathcal{X} \\ true & \text{if } false \notin \mathcal{X}, true \in \mathcal{X} \\ \perp & \text{if } false, true \notin \mathcal{X} \end{cases}$$

The access function assigns *"allow"* to *true* value (i.e., a quadruple with a *true* label is accessible), and *"deny"* to *false* value; triples with no label (i.e., triples assigned the special token $\perp$) are assigned the value *"deny"*.

The concrete policy **C2** uses positive integer values corresponding to increasing levels of confidentiality (i.e., *1* means minimum confidentiality). Thus, $\mathcal{L_P} = \mathcal{N}$. The mapping, as before, is irrelevant (any mapping from $\mathcal{L}$ to $\mathcal{L_P}$ would do). The operator $\odot$ is mapped to addition, ignoring $\perp$, i.e., $n \odot m = n + m$, $n \odot \perp = n$. The propagation operator is the identity: $\otimes al = al$. The conflict resolution operator selects the most restrictive (maximum) token, ignoring $\perp$: $\oplus \mathcal{X} = max(\mathcal{X} \setminus \{\perp\})$ when $\mathcal{X} \setminus \{\perp\} \neq \emptyset$, and $\oplus \mathcal{X} = \perp$ otherwise. The access function specifies that all quadruples whose confidentiality token is lower than a certain number (say *2*) are accessible (i.e., $access(n) = allow$ iff $n \leq 2$), and inaccessible otherwise (thus, e.g., $access(\perp) = deny$).

To handle cases where multiple users with different roles access the same dataset, one could define different concrete policies, or concrete policies with different access functions.

6. IMPLEMENTATION AND EVALUATION

6.1 Storage (Relational Schema)

The quadruples and the related access labels are stored in a relational schema, which uses three tables: $Map(value, id)$, $Quad(qid, s, p, o, prop, iop, label)$ and the auxiliary table $LabelStore(qid, qid\_uses)$. Table $Map(value, id)$ is used to map URIs and literals (*value* column) to unique identifiers (*id* column), in order to avoid an overhead during query evaluation.

Table $Quad(qid, s, p, o, prop, iop, label)$ stores the quadruples. More specifically, column *qid* stores the quadruple's unique identifier; columns *s*, *p*, *o* store the *id* from table *Map* to which the URI/literal of the subject (*s*), predicate (*p*) and object (*o*) of the corresponding triple are mapped to. Columns *prop* and *iop* take boolean values and are used to indicate whether $\otimes$ or $\odot$ respectively are used in the computation of the abstract label of the quad; *label* stores the access token of the quadruple (in case it is explicit), or is set to *null* to indicate that the label is a complex expression. In this case, the auxiliary table $LabelStore(qid, qid\_uses)$ is used to store the access label (discussed in detail below). In this paper we reported our experiences with a non-normalized schema where all quadruples are stored in a single table. We are studying a normalized version of the proposed schema that considers three tables: one for the explicit, one for the implied and one for the propagated quadruples. This schema takes into consideration the foreign and primary key constraints in the schema and preliminary experiments have shown that we can achieve better performance results since the underlying query optimizer takes into account the above constraints and optimizes the produced plans.

To understand the intuition behind the representation of labels, recall that a label can be obtained as follows:

1. directly through an authorization, in which case it is an abstract token;

2. indirectly, when the associated triple is not in the scope of any authorization, in which case it is the default access token $\bot$;

3. through an inference rule, in which case it is a complex expression of the form $al_1 \odot al_2$, where al_1, al_2 are the labels of the quadruples used to infer said quadruple;

4. through a propagation rule, in which case it is $\otimes al$ (al is the propagated label);

In Case (1) we set *prop* and *iop* to *false*, and store the access token in *label*. Case (2) is similar to the previous one except from the fact that *label* is set to $\bot$. In Case (3) the label of the quadruple is a complex expression, so we set *label = null*, and the *iop* flag to the value *true* (to indicate that $\odot$ is used in the expression). The labels involved in the inference (al_1,al_2) are stored using the table *LabelStore*: the first column (qid) keeps the qid of the quadruple whose complex label we want to store. qid_uses stores the qid of the quadruple that contributed to the label of the implied quadruple. More specifically, one tuple is added in *LabelStore* for each of the quadruples that imply said quadruple.

In *LabelStore* we store the *explicit* quadruples that contribute to the implication of the implicit ones. For example, consider q_8 in Figure 4; q_8 is an inferred quadruple, occurring from the application of the inference rule $\mathcal{QR}_4$ upon q_1, q_2. We store the fact that q_8 results from applying the $\odot$ operator upon the identifiers of q_1, q_2. Note that this is different from storing the fact that q_8 results from applying the $\odot$ operator upon at_2, at_2 (the labels for q_1, q_2). The former is useful because it allows finding in constant time all the explicit quadruples that are involved in an implicit one. We plan to exploit this feature in the future in order to improve performance when authorizations change (i.e., one or more authorizations are added, deleted or modified). In our example *LabelStore* would contain the tuples $(8, 1), (8, 2)$ where x is the identifier for quadruple q_x. Consider now quadruple q_{11} from Figure 4, which results from the application of inference rule $\mathcal{QR}_3$ upon q_3, q_8. Recall that in *LabelStore* we store the identifiers of the *explicit quadruples* used to obtain the implied quadruples. In this manner *LabelStore* will contain tuples $(11, 1), (11, 2)$ (for q_8) and $11, 3$ (for q_3). If we had followed a different approach in which we would record the identifiers of the contributing *implied* quadruples, then in order to retrieve all the labels that contributed to the label of said quadruple, additional joins with the *Quad* and *LabelStore* tables would be necessary. The approach we follow resolves this problem by eliminating this "nesting" of complex labels. The "unnesting" of labels occurs during the application of inference and propagation rules and helps avoiding recursive joins that would slow down the process of label (and query) evaluation.

Case (4) is handled in a manner similar to Case (3). Again, we store the operation used ($prop = true$, $iop = false$) and the fact that the label of the quad is complex (by setting *label = null*). *LabelStore* stores the quadruple whose label was propagated (as above).

6.2 Datasets and Access Policies

We used both real and synthetic datasets in our experiments. The real datasets used were the CIDOC [6] and the GO [1] ontologies. The CIDOC Conceptual Reference Model (CRM) provides definitions and a formal structure for describing the concepts and relations used in cultural heritage documentation. CIDOC contains 3282 triples that define 82 classes, 262 properties, 94 sc, 130 sp relations and 342 type relations. The ontology does not include any class or property instances. After the application of the inference and propagation rules, we obtain in total 3733 implicit and explicit quadruples. The Gene Ontology (GO) project is a bioinformatics initiative with the aim of standardizing the representation of genes and gene product attributes. GO consists of a controlled vocabulary of terms describing gene product characteristics and gene product annotation data. It contains 265355 explicit triples that define 35451 classes and only 5 properties. Similarly to CIDOC, GO does not have any class or property instances; it defines 55169 sc, no sp relations and 35451 type relations.

To produce the synthetic schemas for our experiments we used Powergen [23], which is the first synthetic RDFS schema generator that takes into account the morphological features that schemas frequently exhibit in reality [24] to produce realistic ontologies. We used the parameters of PowerGen to obtain ontologies with an increasing number of implied triples and different characteristics, in order to test the applicability of our approach in various cases. In particular, we produced 152 synthetic ontologies containing 100-1000 classes, 113-1635 properties, 124-50295 class instances and 110-1321 property instances. We also experimented with different depth for the sc and sp hierarchies of the input RDF schema (ranging from depth 4 to 8).

Since there is no standard benchmark for access control, we used our own custom set of authorizations. In a sense, all the authorizations and concrete policies we experimented with are synthetic. Our authorizations assigned access tokens to the sc, sp and type relations, and were defined in such a way that featured the assignment of multiple access tokens to the same triple, as well as the assignment of the same token to multiple triples.

6.3 Experiments

All experiments were conducted on a Dell OptiPlex 755 desktop with CPU Intel® Core^{TM}2 Duo CPU E8400 at 3.00GHz, 8 GB of memory and running Linux Ubuntu 2.6.35-31-generic x86_64. We used PostgreSQL 8.4.9 (a row-store) and MonetDB v11.3.3-Apr2011-SP1 (a column-store) as our RDBMS backends. MonetDB does not support recursive SQL and hence the implementation of entailment and propagation rules shown in Tables 2 and 3 is done with the use of stored procedures. To avoid issues with performance varying between different runs, we performed only cold-cache experiments.

For our work we conducted three experiments. EXPERIMENT 1 measures the time required to compute all the inferred and propagated quadruples (*annotation time*). EXPERIMENT 2 and EXPERIMENT 3 respectively consider the time required to compute for a concrete policy and a set of annotated quadruples, the concrete labels from the abstract ones (*evaluation time*). EXPERIMENT 2 and EXPERIMENT 3 differ in the following aspect: the former measures the time needed to compute the concrete values for all the datasets used in our experiments and for their integrality whereas the latter reports the time needed to compute the concrete values for a fraction of triples in a specific dataset. We set a timeout of 60 minutes, i.e., any experiment that ran for more than 60 minutes was stopped and is not included in the reported times.

The general observation from our experiments is that the annotation and evaluation times are roughly linear to the number of triples considered: the number of implied triples of the input for EXPERIMENT 1 and total triples for EXPERIMENT 2, and the fraction of the dataset for EXPERIMENT 3. Other factors affecting the time are the ontology's structure and the nature of the concrete policy used (for EXPERIMENTS 2 and 3), and, of course, the RDBMS backend (MonetDB is generally faster). However, some experiments (especially those involving PostgreSQL) gave poor results. This indicates that, despite the encouraging (linear) scaling properties of our approach, there is much room for improvement in terms of efficiency, using more efficient storage schemes for our abstract labels; this effort will be part of our future work. More details on the various experiments and the related results follow.

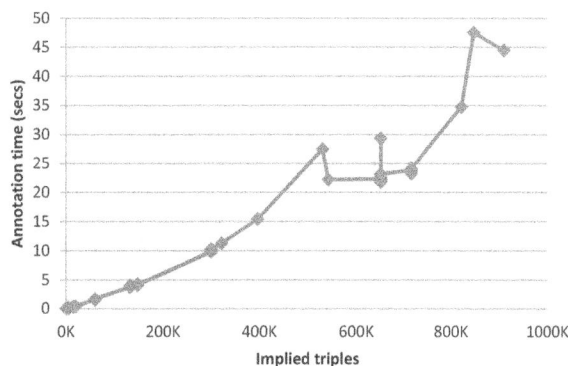

Figure 5a: EXPERIMENT 1 (**MonetDB**)

EXPERIMENT 1 measured the *annotation time*, that is the time needed to apply the inference and propagation rules in Tables 2 and 3 on a set of quadruples. This set was obtained from the application of the authorizations to the initial set of RDF triples; note that the time needed to assign these initial access tokens (using the authorizations) upon the existing triples is an offline process, so we omit it from our experiments.

Figures 5a and 5b show the annotation time for the synthetic schemas for MonetDB and PostgreSQL respectively and for the synthetic datasets only. The graphs show that the annotation time increases as the number of implied triples increases. This is an expected result since when the number of implied triples increases, the number of times the inference and propagation rules are applied also increases. The observed plunges are due to changes in the structure of the ontology and more specifically to the reduction of the depth of the class and property hierarchies (a PowerGen parameter). The implication of such a decrease is that even though the number of implicit triples increases, there are fewer recursive applications of the inference rules. With MonetDB we were able to annotate all synthetic schemas that we produced. However, PostgreSQL managed to compute the abstract expressions for schemas with up to 1000 classes, 1635 properties, 50167 class instances and 95 property instances before reaching the timeout.

Regarding the real datasets, in the case of CIDOC on-

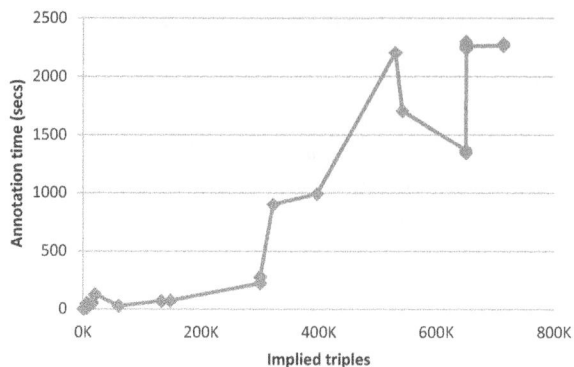

Figure 5b: EXPERIMENT 1 (**PostgreSQL**)

tology, the annotation process required 69ms and 4000ms for MonetDB and PostgreSQL respectively. On the other hand, the GO ontology required approximately 32sec and 844sec for MonetDB and PostgreSQL respectively. This result is due to the increased size of the GO ontology, as well as its large number of sc, sp and type relations that are involved in the inference rules that lead to a large number of inferred quadruples. More specifically, the CIDOC ontology produces only 549 new quadruples (using the inference and propagation rules), whereas GO produces 393699 inferred quadruples (almost twice the size of the original GO RDF graph).

EXPERIMENT 2 measured the time required to compute the concrete labels for all RDF quadruples of each dataset, under concrete policies similar to the ones discussed in Section 5. Figure 6 shows the related evaluation time for the synthetic datasets. We note, as expected, that the evaluation time increases linearly with respect to the total triples in the dataset and that MonetDB outperforms PostgreSQL for all synthetic datasets. Another interesting observation is that concrete policy **C2** is faster for both RDBMSs; this is explained by the fact that **C2** uses arithmetic operations which are implemented as built-in SQL functions, contrary to **C1**, which consists of logical operations that are implemented using custom SQL code.

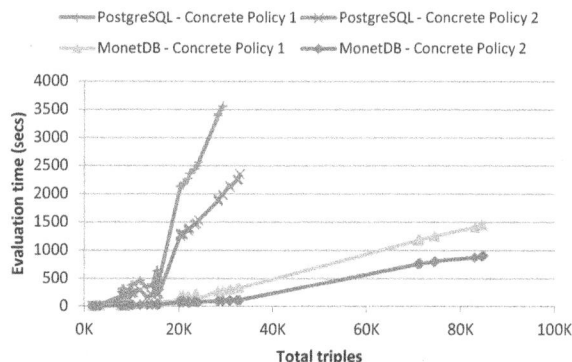

Figure 6: EXPERIMENT 2 (**MonetDB/PostgreSQL**)

The same observations can also be made for CIDOC, for which we need about 7775ms to evaluate the concrete access values for **C1** and 3923ms for **C2**. Unfortunately, we failed to compute the concrete access values for the quadruples in the case of the GO ontology, as the process exceeded our set timeout.

EXPERIMENT 3 measured the evaluation time for some of the quadruples in the chosen dataset, as a function of the fraction of the dataset considered. This is useful at query time, when the retrieved triples must be filtered to exclude non-accessible triples, and this includes the process of determining the concrete access token for said triples. In our experiments we consider the 10%, 30% and 50% of the total triples in the dataset. This experiment was done for the largest synthetic dataset for which all concrete labels were computed successfully (without a timeout) in EXPERIMENT 2. For MonetDB we used the dataset that contained 100 classes, 113 properties, 10028 class instances and 8706 property instances. The dataset we used for the experiment for PostgreSQL contained 1000 classes, 1635 properties, 1244 class and 704 property instances.

The results are shown in Figures 7a, 7b for MonetDB and PostgreSQL respectively.

Finally, our preliminary experimental results showed that our approach requires up to one order of magnitude more space to store triples with their final abstract label, compared to the standard approach of storing the computed concrete label.

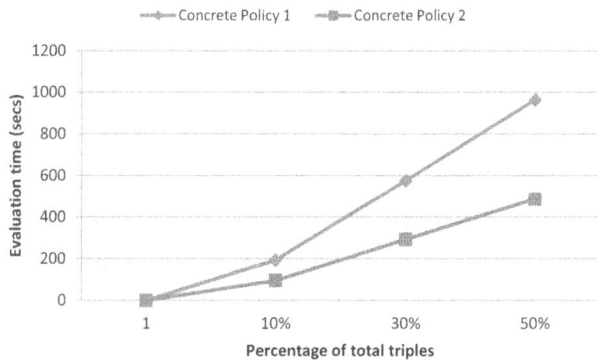

Figure 7a: EXPERIMENT 3 (**MonetDB**)

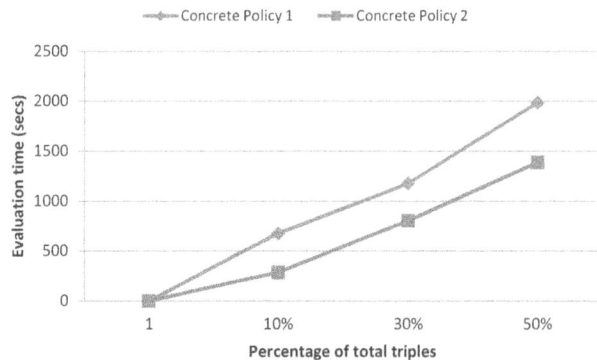

Figure 7b: EXPERIMENT 3 (**PostgreSQL**)

7. RELATED WORK

Despite the importance of the problem, there have been only a few works dealing with the problem of access control for RDF data and schema graphs, and most of them do not adequately consider the RDFS semantics. Moreover, to the best of our knowledge, none of the existing works consider abstract access control models; instead, they use an access control policy with fixed semantics, which implies that all access labels have to be recomputed following any change in the authorizations, in the dataset, or in the access control policy itself.

Jain et. al [12] use the notions of RDF security object that is equivalent to our notion of quadruple and access control authorizations but with limited expressivity, as they use simple RDF triple patterns rather than SPARQL queries. RDFS inference is supported but the approach does not consider propagation rules. Given a set of security objects, the authors produce a *security cover* which essentially amounts to resolving conflicts caused by ambiguous security labels. The computation of the labels of the implied triples is hard-coded (the label of the implied triple is the least upper bound of the labels of its implying triples). The conflict resolution strategy is also hard-coded and always resolves the conflict in favor of the security label which is the least upper bound of the involved ones. This comes in contrast with our approach where both strategies are defined by customizable concrete policies.

In Kim et. al [13], access control is defined at the level of nodes in the RDF graph (URIs and literals), rather than at the level of RDF triples as in our work and in Jain et. al. [12]. The authors focus on how to resolve conflicts that arise due to the implicit and explicit propagation of RDF authorizations for the RDFS class and property hierarchies and propose an efficient algorithm to identify conflicts and resolve them according to specific (fixed) semantics.

Authors in [15] discuss RDFS inference in the spirit of [12]. In this work, the access labels of triples are *logical expressions* involving *conjunction* (for RDFS inference) and *disjunction* (for conflict resolution). This approach is closer to ours since the access labels are logical expressions and not concrete values. Nevertheless, the expressions are again formulated with concrete, rather than abstract operators.

Our work can also be compared to works related to *annotated RDFS* [4, 22], where algebraic models are used. Authors in [4] annotate triples with algebraic terms following the line of research done in the context of provenance for relational databases [10] and develop an algebra of annotations for RDFS. They show that the proposed annotation algebra can be used for computing annotations of inferred triples that store information on belief, trust and temporal aspects of data among others. Work in [4] generalizes the work in [22], whose goal is to apply fuzzy logic to RDFS via an abstract model similar to [10]. In our work we also model the propagation of labels along the RDFS class and property hierarchies, and propose a unified framework for modeling access control for RDF graphs. Flouris et. al in [9] propose a commutative semiring to model the provenance of implied RDF triples. The approach we advocate in our work is similar to [9] as far as modeling the labels of implied triples is concerned. Authors in [16] showed that Named Graphs [5] alone cannot model the labels of implied quadruples, but a higher level construct is needed.

8. CONCLUSION

As more and more (potentially sensitive) data are being made available through the Web (e.g., as part of the Linked Open Data initiative [19]), the need for controlling access to such data becomes all the more important. This work addresses this problem for RDF graphs, by providing an open and customizable framework for defining access control policies which takes into account RDFS inference rules and propagation of access labels along the RDFS class and property hierarchies.

The main contribution, and the distinguishing feature of this work compared to existing frameworks for RDF access control, is the use of *abstract access control models*. The model uses abstract tokens and operators, the latter encode *inference* and *propagation* of labels along the RDFS *subclassOf* and *subpropertyOf* relations. The proposed model provides full support for RDFS inference rules (unlike existing frameworks that provide only partial or inadequate support) and propagation rules which are missing in most state of the art access control frameworks.

In our work, abstract tokens are used by authorizations to tag triples, and abstract operators express how the label was constructed, e.g., through the application of inference or propagation rules. To evaluate the label, each application provides its own *concrete policy* (concretization for said tokens and operators) and semantics which allows the application to decide whether a triple is accessible or not. The main advantage of our approach is its *flexibility*, caused by the fact that the access control label contains the information on how it was generated. We plan to exploit this fact as part of our future work, in order to support dynamic datasets, authorizations, requirements and access control semantics and simplify the maintenance of an access control-enhanced dataset. We believe that in a dynamic setting the efficiency of adapting the access labels during changes will justify the overhead imposed by the use of abstract labels.

We implemented our ideas on top of the MonetDB and PostgreSQL open source RDBMS. We also conducted a preliminary set of experiments that show the need for more efficient storage and indexing schemes to handle abstract expressions. This also involves identifying ways to address the problem of ontologies producing a large number of quads (through the inference and propagation rules).

Acknowledgments

The authors would like to thank E. Kostylev, Y. Theoharis, and G. Karvounarakis for helpful discussions on earlier versions of this work. We would also like to thank Stefan Manegold for his help with MonetDB. This work was partially supported by the European NoE PlanetData.

9. REFERENCES

[1] The Gene Ontology (GO). http://www.geneontology.org/.

[2] F. Abel, J. L. De Coi, N. Henze, A. Wolf Koesling, D. Krause, and D. Olmedilla. Enabling Advanced and Context-Dependent Access Control in RDF Stores. In *ISWC/ASWC*, 2007.

[3] D. Brickley and R.V. Guha. RDF Vocabulary Description Language 1.0: RDF Schema. www.w3.org/TR/2004/REC-rdf-schema-20040210, 2004.

[4] P. Buneman and E. V. Kostylev. Annotation algebras for RDFS. In *SWPM*, 2010.

[5] J. Carroll, C. Bizer, P. Hayes, and P. Stickler. Named graphs, provenance and trust. In *WWW*, 2005.

[6] CIDOC Conceptual Reference Model (CRM). http://www.cidoc-crm.org/, 2006. ISO 21127:2006.

[7] S. Dietzold and S. Auer. Access Control on RDF Triple Store from a Semantic Wiki Perspective. In *ESWC Workshop on Scripting for the Semantic Web*, 2006.

[8] B. McBride F. Manola, E. Miller. RDF Primer. www.w3.org/TR/rdf-primer, February 2004.

[9] G. Flouris, I. Fundulaki, P. Pediaditis, Y. Theoharis, and V. Christophides. Coloring RDF Triples to Capture Provenance. In *ISWC*, 2009.

[10] T. J. Green, G. Karvounarakis, and V. Tannen. Provenance semirings. In *PODS*, 2007.

[11] P. Hayes. RDF Semantics. www.w3.org/TR/rdf-mt, February 2004.

[12] A. Jain and C. Farkas. Secure Resource Description Framework. In *SACMAT*, 2006.

[13] J. Kim, K. Jung, and S. Park. An Introduction to Authorization Conflict Problem in RDF Access Control. In *KES*, 2008.

[14] M. Knechtel and R. Peñaloza. A Generic Approach for Correcting Access Restrictions to a Consequence. In *ESWC*, 2010.

[15] J. Lu, J. Wang, Y. Zhang, B. Zhou, Y. Li, and Z. Miao. An Inference Control Algorithm for RDF(S) Repository. In *PAISI*, 2007.

[16] P. Pediaditis, G. Flouris, I. Fundulaki, and V. Christophides. On Explicit Provenance Management in RDF/S Graphs. In *TaPP*, 2009.

[17] J. Pérez, M. Arenas, and C. Gutierrez. Semantics and complexity of SPARQL. *ACM TODS*, 34(3), 2009.

[18] E. Prud'hommeaux and A. Seaborne. SPARQL Query Language for RDF. www.w3.org/TR/rdf-sparql-query, January 2008.

[19] W3C Linking Open Data. esw.w3.org/topic/SweoIG/ TaskForces/CommunityProjects/LinkingOpenData.

[20] P. Reddivari, T. Finin, and A. Joshi. Policy-Based Access Control for an RDF Store. In *IJCAI Workshop on Semantic Web for Collaborative Knowledge Acquisition*, 2007.

[21] G. Serfiotis, I. Koffina, V. Christophides, and V. Tannen. Containment and minimization of rdf/s query patterns. In *ISWC*, 2005.

[22] U. Straccia, N. Lopes, G. Lukacsy, and A. Polleres. A General Framework for Representing and Reasoning with Annotated Semantic Web Data. In *AAAI*, 2010.

[23] Y. Theoharis, G. Georgakopoulos, and V. Christophides. PoweRGen: A Power-Law Based Generator of RDFS Schemas. *Information Systems*. Elsevier, 2011.

[24] Y. Theoharis, Y. Tzitzikas, D. Kotzinos, and V. Christophides. On Graph Features of Semantic Web Schemas. *TKDE*, 20(5), 2008.

[25] M. Garofalakis W. Fan, C.-Y. Chan. Secure XML Querying with Security Views. In *SIGMOD*, 2004.

A Cloud-based RDF Policy Engine
for Assured Information Sharing *

Tyrone Cadenhead, Vaibhav Khadilkar, Murat Kantarcioglu and
Bhavani Thuraisingham
The University of Texas at Dallas
800 W. Campbell Road, Richardson, TX 75080
{thc071000, vvk072000, muratk, bxt043000}@utdallas.edu

ABSTRACT

In this paper, we describe a general-purpose, scalable RDF
policy engine. The innovations in our work include seamless
support for a diverse set of security policies enforced by a
highly available and scalable policy engine designed using a
cloud-based platform. Our main goal is to demonstrate how
coalition agencies can share information stored in multiple
formats, through the enforcement of appropriate policies.

Categories and Subject Descriptors

D.4.6 [**Operating Systems**]: Security and Protection—*Access Control*; D.4.2 [**Operating Systems**]: Storage Management—*Secondary storage*

General Terms

Design, Security

Keywords

Assured Information Sharing, RDF Policies, Cloud Computing

1. INTRODUCTION

In today's digital age, numerous government agencies generate and store large amounts of data. The data originates from both, private and public collections, and may be used for intelligence gathering and tracking, such as surveillance data (*viz.* a private source), as well as news feeds (*viz.* a public source). The agencies collaborate and share their data for common goals. Any improper disclosure of data could result in litigations or losses to the parties involved. To mitigate the security risks of disclosure and to support large datasets, we describe a policy engine framework that

---

*This material is based upon work supported by The Air
Force Office of Scientific Research under Award No. FA-
9550-08-1-0260. We thank Dr. Robert Herklotz for his support.

uses the Resource Description Framework (RDF) [5] to store
data, as well as to define and store policies.

RDF is a W3C recommendation for the World Wide Web;
it can be used to provide interoperability and semantics for
both, the data and the policies, which can then be stored
side by side on the same platform. In addition, the advent of
cloud computing and the continuing movement toward the
software as a service (SaaS) paradigm has posed an increasing need for providing assured information sharing as a service in the cloud. These factors motivated us in developing a
policy engine framework that achieves high availability and
scalability while maintaining low setup and operation costs
to each agency for sharing its resources.

2. ARCHITECTURE

We used a three-tier approach in designing our architecture (see Figure 1). At the front-end, we have a user interface; the middle layer consists of our policy engine logic; and
at the backend, we have our data stores. We next define each
of the layers in our architecture. Then, we present details
of the current policy engines supported by our framework,
and finally, we provide a description of the novel features of
our implementation.

2.1 Modules in our Architecture

The **User Interface Layer** is exposed as a series of web
browser pages. We use a form-based Authentication pattern,
as well as a challenge-response test to distinguish legitimate
users from robots (which may pose as normal users). The
legitimate users are presented with a querying screen that
allows them to compose SPARQL queries once they have
been authenticated. Note that SPARQL [6] is a query language for RDF and is used for retrieving data from triple
stores. The SPARQL queries are validated and then sent
to our policy engine layer, which in turn returns a resultant
RDF graph that is then displayed on a web page.

The **Policy Engine Layer** first evaluates the user queries
against the stored data resources (which can be traditional
data, or provenance meta data). A data resource is characterized by a uniform resource identifier (URI), which connects to an actual RDF graph in the data storage layer. The
policy layer uses a factory object to create the underlying
policies. The factory exposes a policy through a consistent
interface, thus making it easy to extend our policy engine to
support other types of policies in the future. We currently
support access control, redaction, and information sharing
policies. To support traditional policies, we use SPARQL
queries to define views over resources where a view can be

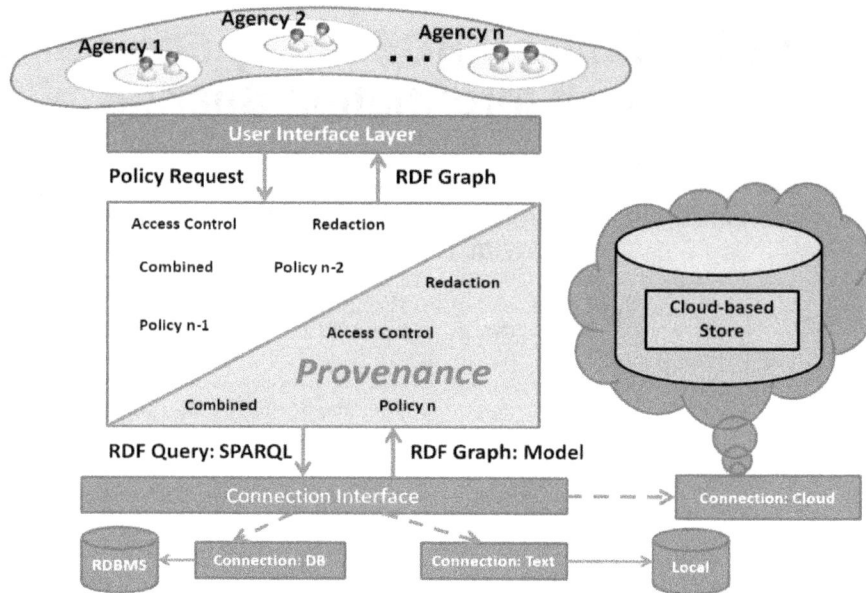

Figure 1: Architecture

associated with positive and negative authorizations. Provenance records the history of a piece of data item. However, provenance takes on a directed acyclic graph (DAG) structure, and as such requires its own policies [1]. Therefore, we support the use of regular expression SPARQL queries for access control policies [2], as well as redaction policies [3]. We have also implemented sharing policies over data and provenance that allow cooperating agencies to share information based on mutual agreements.

The **Data Layer** makes use of a connection factory, which acts as a facade for creating a connection object. A connection object takes as input, a URI, and returns a resultant RDF graph from any of the underlying storage subsystems. The connection factory thus ensures that the policy engine layer is independent of any data storage technology.

Our policy engine framework can be used as a key enabler in augmenting security for RDBMS's, as well as cloud-based systems. RDBMS's are developed with atomicity, concurrency and durability in mind, but are normally shipped with limited support for access control. A cloud storage layer allows the agencies to store and scale policies with finer levels of control over RDF resources. The cloud was developed with scalability and availability in mind, but access control was neglected. Our policy engine can be configured to complement policies in a RDBMS system with an entry point for supporting security policies over cloud-based backends.

2.2 Policy Engines

A policy is defined by an interface, which allows the implementation of the logic of each policy. A policy engine takes as input, a user's credentials and an agency's resource (which is a URI that dereferences an agency's resource in the data layer). It then evaluates the underlying logic of the policy before returning a new RDF graph (or model) to the user interface layer. An agency requires more than one type of policy to achieve finer levels of control over its resources.

By migrating the policies to the cloud, we remove the restriction on the number of policy definitions previously possible. The following subsections summarize various policy types.

2.2.1 Access Control Policy Engine

Our access control policy engine authorizes *users* to perform a set of *actions* on the underlying *resources*. Unless authorized through one or more access control policies, these users have no access to any of the resources in the data layer.

There are different kinds of access control policies, which can be grouped into three main classes [8]. These policies differ by the constraints they place on the sets of *users*, *actions* and *objects* (access control models often refer to *resources* as *objects*). These classes are (1) RBAC, which restricts access based on roles; (2) discretionary access control (DAC), which controls access based on the identity of the user; and (3) mandatory access control (MAC), which controls access based on mandated regulations determined by a central authority. The policy engine layer supports many policy engines; therefore, we can support an implementation of each class of access control policy, as well as any extension of a previously defined access control policy.

2.2.2 Policy Resolution policy Engine

```
@prefix foaf:    <http://xmlns.com/foaf/0.1/> .
@prefix rdf:     <http://www.w3.org/1999/02/22-rdf-syntax-ns#> .

<http://cs.utdallas.edu/semanticweb/Prov-AC/agency#employee_1>
        a       foaf:Person ;
        foaf:interest   <http://www.w3.org/2001/sw/> ;
        foaf:mbox_sha1sum  "289d4d44325d0b0218edc856c8c3904fa3fd2875" ;
        foaf:name "John Miller" ;
        foaf:projectHomepage   <http://www.utdallas.edu/> .
```

Figure 2: An Example Resource

A general form of an access control policy is a tuple of the form (*user, resource, authorization*), *users* ∈ *Users*, resource $\in$ *Resource* and *authorization* $=\{+ve,-ve\}$. A $+ve$ authorization implies that the *user* can access the *resource*, while a $-ve$ authorization implies that the *user* is denied access to the *resource*.

Figure 2 is a listing of RDF triples, which we will refer to as G. We will use the triples in G for illustrating different combinations of authorizations next. Let P_{-ve} be a policy with a $-ve$ authorization effect. After evaluating P_{-ve} over the input graph, G, assume that the following graph, G_1, is created:

```
<http://cs.utdallas.edu/semanticweb/Prov-AC/agency#employee_1>
    foaf:interest  <http://www.w3.org/2001/sw/> ;
    foaf:name "John Miller".
```

Likewise, let P_{+ve} be a policy with a $+ve$ authorization effect. After evaluating P_{+ve} over the input graph, G, assume that the following graph, G_2, is created:

```
<http://cs.utdallas.edu/semanticweb/Prov-AC/agency#employee_1>
    foaf:name "John Miller";
    foaf:projectHomepage <http://www.utdallas.edu/> .
```

After the application of policies, P_{-ve} and P_{+ve}, there will be four possible partitions of G, namely G_1, G_2, G_3 and G_4 where, $G_3 = G_1 \cap G_2$, and $G_4 = G - (G_1 \cup G_2)$. Note that G_3 is an example of a conflict, which will require policy engines with logic for handling such a conflict. A policy engine that handles conflict resolution may implement one of many policy resolution schemes; for example, Denials take precedence, Permissions take precedence, Nothing takes precedence, etc.

Similarly, the triples in the graph, G_4, have no predefined authorization and therefore require a policy resolution scheme as well. Two examples of such policy resolution schemes are Denial takes precedence and Nothing takes precedence. The former can be used to ensure that a user does not have the ability to perform unnecessary and potentially harmful actions on the RDF triples in G_4, merely as a side effect of granting access to these triples.

2.2.3 Redaction Policy Engine

Redaction is the process of blocking out (or deleting) the sensitive parts of documents before releasing them to a user. Redaction policies encourage sharing of information, but they can also be used to ensure that sensitive or proprietary information is removed (or obscured) before providing the final RDF graph (referred to as a redacted graph) to a user's query. Our redaction policy engines rely on a graph transformation technique that is based on a graph grammar approach (which is presented in [4, 7] and implemented in [3] for redacting provenance graphs). Basically, there are two steps to applying a redaction policy over a directed labeled RDF graph: (i) Identify a resource (or subgraph) in the original RDF graph that we want to protect. This can be done with a graph query (*i.e.*, a query equipped with regular expressions). (ii) Apply a redaction policy to this identified resource in the form of a graph transformation rule.

2.2.4 Information Sharing Policy Engine

An information sharing policy provides another mechanism to agencies for sharing their information. Note that the discussion so far made no mention of a query requesting information on two or more RDF graphs simultaneously. An information sharing policy plays a vital role when the execution of a query requires a combination of resources from two or more agencies. We illustrate this using the following SPARQL query.

SELECT $\vec{B}$ FROM NAMED uri1 FROM NAMED uri2
WHERE P,

where P is a graph pattern, $\vec{B}$ is a tuple of variables appearing in P and uri1 and uri2 are URIs for two resources, R1 and R2. Agency 1 owns R1 and Agency 2 owns R2. Each of these agencies may define individual policy rules for its respective resources. We define a combined operator $\odot$, so that a combined policy is now evaluated over uri1 $\odot$ uri2. The operator $\odot$ can be implemented as a graph operation over a RDF graph. Note that, $\odot$, could be one of the following operators: $\cap, \cup$ or $-$; furthermore, $\odot$ can be applied as many times to a RDF graph as desired. In order to execute the combined operator, we define a graph recursively as follows.

- ϵ is a graph.

- The set of graphs are closed under intersection, union and set difference. Let G_1 and G_2 be two graphs, then $G_1 \cup G_2$, $G_1 \cap G_2$ and $G_1 - G_2$ are graphs, such that if $t \in G_1 \cup G_2$ then $t \in G_1$ or $t \in G_2$; if $t \in G_1 \cap G_2$ then $t \in G_1$ and $t \in G_2$; or if $t \in G_1 - G_2$ then $t \in G_1$ and $t \notin G_2$.

2.2.5 Provenance Policy Engine

The discussion so far ignores the relationships in a RDF graph (*i.e.*, the history of a data item is along the directed paths formed by the triples). There are cases, however, when the relationships among the RDF triples must be taken into consideration while defining security policies. The three policy types discussed so far fail to address the cases where sensitive information is implicit in the various paths within a RDF graph. The provenance policy engines we implemented focus on definitions of policies that are tailored to the execution of access control and redaction policies over a provenance graph. The theory behind the logic of these policy engines is based on [2], which discusses an access control policy language for provenance and [3], which discusses how to perform redaction over provenance.

2.3 Policy Sequence

A protected resource could have multiple associated policies defined over the different policy types. Each policy type produces a new subgraph of its input RDF graph. Therefore, the original input graph will go through a series of transformations until a final RDF graph is returned to the user. It is important to note that the effect of a policy is directly dependent on the RDF graph it receives as input, and furthermore, the effect may be different from the original effect the policy was intended to achieve. In other words, the success of a policy rule (which is implemented as a SPARQL query) returning a particular set of RDF triples is dependent on the transformation step at which the rule was applied. Let us revisit the structure of a query again, but this time using the CONSTRUCT variation of a SPARQL query:

CONSTRUCT G WHERE P,

The newly constructed graph G contains a set of triples that satisfy condition P in the input graph. For the resource in Figure 2, a policy protecting the triples, when P is

```
<http://cs.utdallas.edu/semanticweb/Prov-AC/agency#employee_1>
    foaf:name "John Miller";
    foaf:projectHomepage <http://www.utdallas.edu/> .
```

will fail if either the name or project home page triples were earlier removed or altered by a previous access control or redaction policy. These considerations motivated us to design a policy precedence feature in the framework. In the user interface layer, an agency determines the ordering of its policies, as well as the ordering of the corresponding policy rules. The policy sequence is then stored in a RDF sequence file (using the "rdf:seq" feature of the RDF specification). When a query is evaluated, the policy framework will in turn invoke each policy (and corresponding policy rule) in the intended order.

2.4 Features of our Policy Engine Framework

In the subsections below, we present some novel features of our policy engine framework.

2.4.1 Policy Reciprocity

*Agency*1 wishes to share its resources if *Agency*2 also shares its resources with it. Current access control and redaction policies do not provide for this reciprocity. Our framework provides information sharing policies, which allow agents to define policies based on reciprocity and mutual interest amongst cooperating agencies.

We present two sample information sharing policies below:

1. $\forall r1 \in Agency1, \forall r2 \in Agency2$, use r1∪r2.
   This policy states that *Agency*1 shares all its resources with any resource of *Agency*2 as a union of the resources (i.e., $\odot \in \{\cup\}$).

2. let $r1_1, r1_2, \ldots, r1_n \in Agency1$, use $r1_1 \cup r2, r1_2 \cap r2$, $\forall r2 \in Agency2$.
   This policy offers a finer level of control and defines the combined operator, $\odot \in \{\cap, \cup\}$.

Policy Symmetry. A consequence of policy reciprocity is to have symmetry in the sharing of policies. For example, *Agency*1 shares its resources with *Agency*2 with a combined operator, $\odot$, if *Agency*2 also shares its resources with *Agency*1 using the same combined operator, $\odot$. We present a sample information sharing policy below:

1. $\forall r1 \in Agency1, \forall r2 \in Agency2$, *Agency*1 uses r1∪r2 if *Agency*2 also uses r2∪r1.

Conditional Policies. Another consequence of policy reciprocity is allowing the use of conditional sharing policies. For example, *Agency*1 shares its resources with *Agency*2 if *Agency*2 does not share *Agency*1's resources with *Agency*3. We present a sample information sharing policy below:

1. $\forall r1 \in Agency1, \forall r2 \in Agency2$, *Agency*1 defines r1∩r2. If $\forall r3 \in Agency3$, then
   - *Agency*2 does not define any sharing policy of the form r1∩r3,
   - or *Agency*2 does not define any sharing policy of the form r1 $\subseteq$ r2 $\odot$r3, where $\odot \in \{\cup, \cap\}$.

2.4.2 Develop and Scale Policies

Agency 1 wishes to extend its existing policies with support for constructing policies at a finer granularity. Our policy engine provides a policy interface that should be implemented by all policies; therefore, we can add newer types

of policies as needed. In addition, our policy framework provides three configurations: (i) a standalone version for development and testing; (ii) a version backed by a relational database; and (iii) a cloud-based version that achieves high availability and scalability while maintaining low setup and operation costs.

Sequencing effects: Agency 1 wishes to vary the result set to a user's query based on the user's credentials. The policy sequence feature can be used to configure different outcomes by permuting the policies and their respective rules.

2.4.3 Justification of Resources

Agency 1 asks Agency 2 for a justification of resource R2. The current commercial access control policies are mainly designed to protect single data items while current redaction policies are designed for redacting text and images. Our policy engine allows agents to define policies over provenance; therefore, Agency 2 can provide the provenance to Agency 1, but protect it by using access control or redaction policies.

3. CONCLUSIONS

We implemented a cloud-centric RDF policy engine that provides a flexible security checkpoint for data resources. The policy engine can be used to extend traditional policies with new kinds of policies, *e.g.*, sharing policies that allow cooperating organizations to securely share information.

4. REFERENCES

[1] U. Braun, A. Shinnar, and M. Seltzer. Securing provenance. In *Proceedings of the 3rd conference on Hot topics in security*, page 4. USENIX Association, 2008.

[2] T. Cadenhead, V. Khadilkar, M. Kantarcioglu, and B. Thuraisingham. A language for provenance access control. In *Proceedings of the first ACM conference on Data and application security and privacy*, pages 133–144. ACM, 2011.

[3] T. Cadenhead, V. Khadilkar, M. Kantarcioglu, and B. Thuraisingham. Transforming Provenance using Redaction. In *Proceedings of the Sixteenth ACM Symposium on Access Control Models and Technologies (SACMAT)*. ACM, 2011.

[4] H. Ehrig. *Fundamentals of algebraic graph transformation*. Springer-Verlag New York Inc, 2006.

[5] G. Klyne and J. J. Carroll. Resource Description Framework (RDF): Concepts and Abstract Syntax. http://www.w3.org/TR/2004/REC-rdf-syntax-20040210/, 2004.

[6] E. Prud'hommeaux and A. Seaborne. SPARQL Query Language for RDF. http://www.w3.org/TR/rdf-sparql-query, 2008.

[7] G. Rozenberg and H. Ehrig. *Handbook of graph grammars and computing by graph transformation*, volume 1. World Scientific, 1997.

[8] P. Samarati and S. de Vimercati. Access control: Policies, models, and mechanisms. *Foundations of Security Analysis and Design*, pages 137–196, 2001.

Practical Risk Aggregation in RBAC Models

Suresh Chari, Jorge Lobo, Ian Molloy
IBM Research TJ Watson
Hawthorne, NY, USA
{schari, jlobo, molloyim}@us.ibm.com

ABSTRACT

This paper describes our system, built as part of a commercially available product, for inferring the risk in an RBAC policy model, i.e., the assignment of permissions to roles and roles to users. Our system implements a general model of risk based on any arbitrary set of properties of permissions and users. Our experience shows that fuzzy inferencing systems are best suited to capture how humans assign risk to such assignments. To implement fuzzy inferencing practically we need the axiom of *monotonicity*, i.e., risk can not decrease when more permissions are assigned to a role or when the role is assigned to fewer users. We describe the visualization component which administrators can use to infer aggregate risk in role assignments as well as drill down into which assignments are actually risky. Administrators can then use this knowledge to refactor roles and assignments.

Categories and Subject Descriptors

D.4.6 [**Operating Systems**]: Security and Protection—*Access Controls*

General Terms

Management, Security, Human Factors

Keywords

access control, RBAC, risk, demonstration

1. OVERVIEW

This paper describes the design rationale and salient features of a system to model the risk of RBAC policies built as a component of a commercially available role and policy modeling product. Our goal was to build a system which was *usable* by non-technical role engineers and policy administrators. To this end, our risk model is general and risk can accrue from arbitrary properties of permissions and users. Further, we aimed to achieve intuitive results for the aggregation of risk in the assignment of permissions to roles and roles to users. Another key requirement for our system was to effectively present to users how risk accrues in the RBAC policy that was being modeled.

Our goal was to find models to mimic what humans naturally assign in terms of risk in role assignments. The most usable method for humans to reason about risk is to assign discrete levels, e.g., high, medium, and low or systems such as color coded Homeland Security Advisory System. Past work [2] has shown that the mathematical models best suited to deal with such notional levels is *fuzzy logic*. Our system can be seen as a practical realization of a fuzzy logic risk inferencing system. The key functions implemented by our component are:

- *Aggregation:* Computing the *aggregate sensitivity* of a group of permissions given the notional sensitivity levels of individual permissions or the *aggregate user access risk level*[1]

- *Inferencing:* Given the assignment of a set of permissions to a set of users via a role, we want to infer the risk of this assignment given the aggregate sensitivity of the role and aggregate user access risk level.

Our system is based on the work of Ni et al. [2] for aggregating risk in policies. We start with this as the core model and identify what it takes to make it a practical usable system which human administrators can use. We modify their model to add a crucial axiom, monotonicity, over assignment risks[2]. While we note that some permissions may be interrelated and may aggregate non-monotonically, these are usually outside the scope of RBAC models. Our modifications to the model of Ni et al. include special handling of the fuzzy set membership and defuzzification functions, which are omitted here due to space limitations.

Key to the usability of our system is a visualization component which allows the role engineer to effectively visualize the risk in an RBAC model. This intuitive interface depicts the components of the assignment and the risk of each of these components. Our interface allows the user to drill down on the components of the assignment which have accrued higher risk as well as to see how the risk components aggregate. This insight can be used to tune the RBAC model by splitting high risk role into smaller pieces where the high risk components can be isolated and those assignments reevaluated for appropriateness.

[1] We found this term to be more accepted by end-users than the traditional security term of *clearance*) of a group of users.
[2] Monotonicity was only present in set membership functions.

2. ARCHITECTURE

Our *Risk Analysis* component is part of a commercially available *Role and Policy Modeling* product [1]. When invoked, it computes the risk level of each role in a given policy by aggregating the sensitivities of permissions assigned to this role, the aggregate user access risk level for users, and infers the overall risk to be assigned to the role. Figure 2 shows a component-wise description of our system.

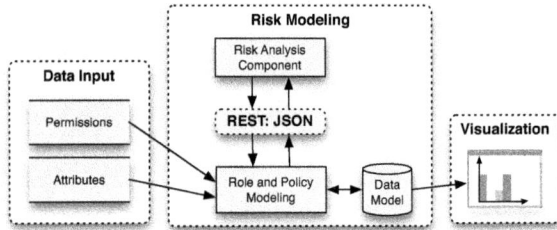

Figure 1: System architecture for Risk Analysis

The inputs to the system consist of users, permissions, and their attributes imported from a variety of sources, e.g., other identity management products or CSV files. The inputs include attributes which mark the sensitivity of individual permissions or the user access risk levels of users. In the current version these are entered as four distinct notional levels High, Elevated, Moderate, and Low or, alternately, an integer value from 1 through 100 where the notional values correspond to $80, 60, 40, 20$ respectively. Typically the sensitivity and access risk levels are determined by other attributes, such as the training levels of users. In this version, these are pre-determined and entered manually as attributes. Future versions will consider defining methods by which these values can be determined automatically from other attributes.

The *Risk Analysis* component is distinct from the *Role and Policy Modeler* product and uses REST APIs to query the underlying data models. When invoked on a set of policies from the core product, the Risk Analysis component computes the aggregate risk levels for each role in the given policy, using the process of aggregation and inferencing, and stores the result back. Due to some idiosyncrasies of the current version of the data model, the component does *not* support functions such as the computation of the user's risk level due to all their assigned permissions (through roles or directly). The results of the risk analysis is stored back as attributes of the role in this policy. This is then used by our visualization component 3 to present the results to the end-user. We note that the risk analysis component does not monitor policy changes and must explicitly be invoked when such changes occur.

3. VISUALIZATION

Central to the usability of our system is the effective visualization of the risk of the policies being modeled. Our goal was to present administrators with an intuitive interface to understand how sensitivity aggregates from the assignment of permissions to a role (and similarly for user access risk level) and to see how risk accrues in this assignment. The functions we wanted to support included: seeing how the sensitivity of the role aggregates from components; seeing how the user access risk level of the users assigned to the role aggregates; and how risk aggregates in the assignment. Due to the underlying data models, some features could not be implemented and are planned for a future version.

Figure 3 shows an excerpt of the report for a set of roles chosen from within a policy that is being modeled by the administrator. In this instance, the sensitivities, user access risk levels and risk are assigned the notional values of High, Elevated, Moderate and Low. This excerpt shows the aggregate sensitivity of the permissions assigned to this role, the aggregate user access risk level of the users this role is assigned to and the resulting aggregate risk. The graphs serve to help the user understand how these aggregate results were obtained. The histograms show the distribution of the sensitivities (and user access risk levels) for this role and serve to illustrate how the aggregate sensitivity was obtained. While it is difficult to depict directly the nuances of fuzzy aggregation at a glance this gives an intuition.

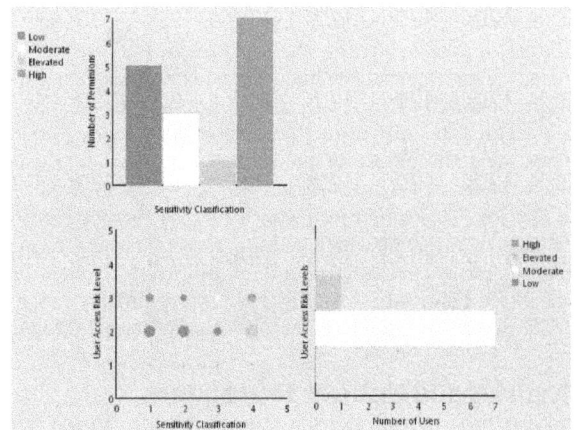

Figure 2: Excerpt from the risk report for role report depicting the aggregation of sensitivity, user access risk level and role risk

The bubble chart is intended to depict the risk in various components of the role. There are potentially 16 bubbles, one for each combination of sensitivity s and user access risk level r, and indicates the assignment risk of this component of the role *i.e* the risk in assigning the subset of permissions in this role with sensitivity s to the users assigned this role with access risk level r. The size of the bubble reflects the weight of this component to the aggregate risk score. In this example we can see that most of the components have low risk but there is a (small) high risk component. The bubble chart instantly allows the administrator to gain insight on how risk is distributed and focus on areas to be potentially address. Other components of this visualization allow the administrator to inspect the users (and permissions) assigned (to) this role and their attributes to further gain insight into the riskiness of the role. This component has been very favorably received by end-users who find it intuitive to visualize the mathematical inferencing models.

4. REFERENCES

[1] Tivoli identity manager. http://www-01.ibm.com/software/tivoli/products/identity-mgr/.
[2] Q. Ni, E. Bertino, and J. Lobo. Risk-based access control systems built on fuzzy inferences. In *ASIACCS*, Apr. 2010.

Towards a Policy Enforcement Infrastructure for Distributed Usage Control

Florian Kelbert
Karlsruhe Institute of Technology
Am Fasanengarten 5
Karlsruhe, Germany
florian.kelbert@kit.edu

Alexander Pretschner
Karlsruhe Institute of Technology
Am Fasanengarten 5
Karlsruhe, Germany
alexander.pretschner@kit.edu

ABSTRACT

Distributed usage control is concerned with how data may or may not be used after initial access to it has been granted and is therefore particularly important in distributed system environments. We present an application- and application-protocol-independent infrastructure that allows for the enforcement of usage control policies in a distributed environment. We instantiate the infrastructure for transferring files using FTP and for a scenario where smart meters are connected to a Facebook application.

Categories and Subject Descriptors

D.4.6 [**Security and Protection**]: Information flow controls; D.4.6 [**Security and Protection**]: Access controls

General Terms

Security

Keywords

Distributed Usage Control, Policy Enforcement, Security and Privacy, Sticky Policies

1. INTRODUCTION

Usage control [8] has been proposed and discussed with the goal to overcome one shortcoming of traditional access control models: the loss of control after access to data has been granted. *Distributed* usage control [4] is concerned with the usage of data in distributed system environments. Policies express what may or may not happen to usage-controlled data [3, 5]. They must be enforced at and across all systems storing, processing, and distributing data. For this reason, an infrastructure is needed that allows for (1) inter-system data flow tracking and (2) the enforcement of both globally and locally enforceable usage control policies. Examples for policies are "do not process my data with application X" and "not more than two instances of document

Y may be opened simultaneously". While the compliance with the former can be enforced locally, this is not the case for the latter, since the document may be opened on different systems at the same time.

We present an infrastructure that supports (1) application- and protocol-independent data flow tracking across different operating system instances, (2) sticking policies to data upon sending it to another system, and (3) policy enforcement at the receiving site. We implement our infrastructure at the operating system layer and focus on TCP/IP and locally enforceable policies. The infrastructure integrates into an existing usage control infrastructure for independent systems [6]. Security aspects, provided guarantees, and the corresponding assumptions are out of the scope of this work.

We show two instantiations of our infrastructure: the File Transfer Protocol (FTP) and a scenario where a smart meter is connected to a Facebook application in order to share energy usage data with online contacts.

2. INFRASTRUCTURE

The core components of our distributed enforcement infrastructure are a distribution-enhanced Policy Information Point (PIP) and a Policy Management Point (PMP). The infrastructure is distributed in that its components must be deployed on any system, i.e. an operating system instance, that is expected to enforce usage control policies. The task of the PIP is to hold the information flow state of the system on which it is deployed, i.e. information about the distribution of data. At the operating system layer this is essentially the information which data is stored in which files [1, 6]. The PMP manages all usage control policies for data entering, leaving, and residing in the respective system. We equipped both the PIP and the PMP with the capability to communicate with their respective counterparts on other systems, therefore allowing for the exchange of usage control relevant information (namely inter-system data flow tracking and usage control policies) once data flows between systems.

Our infrastructure integrates into an existing usage control solution for single independent systems [6]. The latter consists of a Policy Enforcement Point (PEP), a Policy Decision Point (PDP), and a local Policy Information Point (PIP). We will now show how these two infrastructures integrate.

Initially, the PMP deploys the policy in the system (Fig. 1, step 1). In this work we assume policies to be formulated in terms of system calls as described in [3, 6]. The PEP is tailored to one system layer [6] (in our case the operating system); it intercepts attempted and actual events within

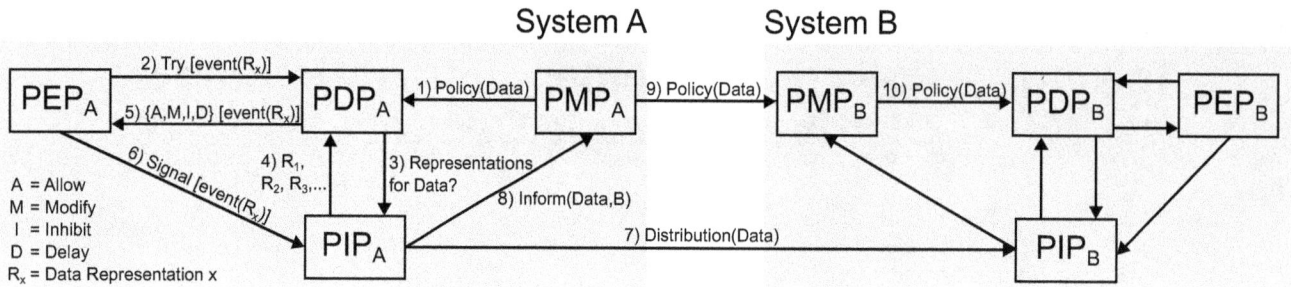

Figure 1: Interplay of the infrastructure's main components.

the layer (at the operating system layer such events have been identified as system calls [1]) and signals them to the PDP (step 2). In order to take a usage control decision, the PDP queries the PIP for additional information about data distribution (step 3). The PIP therefore replies with a list of representations the data has taken (step 4) (e.g., data may be contained in files, pipes, or in some processes' memory). The PDP then decides on the grounds of the policy and data distribution whether to allow, modify, inhibit, or delay the event [5] and sends the decision to the PEP (step 5). The PEP enforces the PDP's decision. If an event actually happened, the PEP signals it to the PIP (step 6) that then updates the system's information flow state.

Likewise any event corresponding to sending usage controlled data to another system over the network is temporarily blocked by the PEP. Our infrastructure then takes care of tracking the inter-system data flow and sticking the corresponding usage control policies to the data.

For example, if PEP_A (X_A denotes component X on system A) intercepts an event of sending data d to system B and if PDP_A decides that releasing data d complies with the policy (otherwise there is no inter-system data flow), then both PIP_A and PMP_A communicate with their respective counterparts on system B: PIP_A communicates to PIP_B that data d is about to be received on a specific network socket (step 7), therefore accomplishing inter-system data flow tracking. PIP_A then informs PMP_A about the data flow to system B (step 8) and PMP_A communicates the usage-control policy associated with data d to PMP_B (step 9), therefore implementing the sticky policy paradigm. PMP_B then deploys the received policy on system B (step 10). After the PIPs and PMPs finished their communication, the original event is unblocked and the actual data transfer proceeds. Once data d is received on system B, its components are already aware of the previous inter-system data flow and the corresponding policy. Consequently they enforce the policy on the received data. Note that the example is analogous if PEP_B intercepts a corresponding event.

3. IMPLEMENTATION

Our implementation leverages an existing PEP for the OpenBSD operating system [1]. This implementation observes and intercepts system calls using the tool *Systrace* [7]. We extended the implementation with TCP/IP-related system calls, the most important ones being *socket*, *accept*, *connect*, and *write* (and all equivalents like *send*). Notably all system calls related to sending data through a TCP connection (*write* and equivalents) are intercepted and handled as described in §2. The remote communication between the PIPs and PMPs has been realized using XML-RPC [9]; though conceptually different, our current implementation bundles the two remote procedure calls for performance reasons.

4. USE CASES

We instantiate our generic infrastructure for FTP in §4.1 and for a smart meter connected to a Facebook application in §4.2. Note that our infrastructure is independent of application-level protocols, applications, and implementations. It may be used with any application building upon TCP/IP. Videos of our use cases are provided online[1].

4.1 File Transfer Protocol (FTP)

In this use case we consider users Alice and Bob on two different operating system instances. Alice owns the usage-controlled file "AlicesFriends.txt" within her home folder; the corresponding policy states that "the content of 'AlicesFriends.txt' may not be opened using the 'mousepad' text editor". Technically, this policy is specified as event-condition-action (ECA) rule [3]:

```
1   <controlMechanism>
2     <id>DenyMousepad</id>
3     <triggerEvent>
4       <id>open</id>
5       <param name="filename" value="/home/alice/
            AlicesFriends.txt" type="dataUsage"/>
6     </triggerEvent>
7     <condition>
8       <XPathEval>
9        /triggerEvent/param[@name='command']/@value='
            mousepad'
10      </XPathEval>
11    </condition>
12    <actions>
13      </inhibit>
14    </actions>
15  </controlMechanism>
```

Therefore, if Alice tries to open the file "AlicesFriends.txt" (or any local copy of it, since the infrastructure for single independent systems tracks local data flows) using mousepad, the corresponding *open* system call is denied and mousepad fails to open the file (cf. Fig. 2).

Then, Alice decides to share this file with Bob and starts an FTP server (we used a standard vsftpd implementation) that is configured to make Alice's home folder readable. Now, Bob runs an FTP client (gftp standard implementation) and logs in to Alice's FTP server. Therefore, Bob is able to list and read the contents of Alice's home folder; he transfers the usage-controlled file "AlicesFriends.txt" to

---

[1]http://zvi.ipd.kit.edu/english/26_422.php

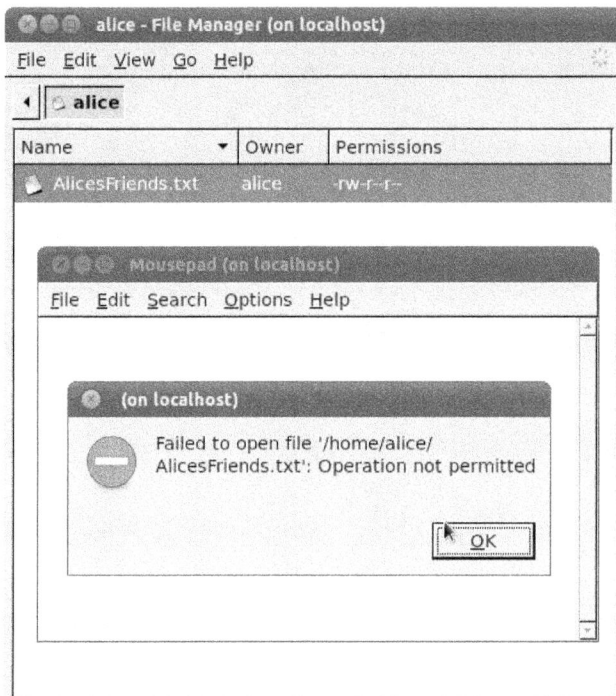

Figure 2: Mousepad fails to open the protected file.

his home folder. Although having read permissions on the transferred file, Bob is not able to open the file, nor any copy of it, using the mousepad text editor.

This is because the PIPs and PMPs of the two systems took care of (i) tracking the inter-system data flow of the content of file "AlicesFriends.txt" through the TCP channel established by FTP and (ii) transferring and deploying the policy to Bob's system before the actual data transfer happened. Note that we didn't modify the implementation of vsftpd, gftp, or mousepad. Any other equivalent tools would behave identically.

4.2 Smart Meter connected to Facebook

Our second use case is an instantiation of our infrastructure to smart meters connected to Facebook [2]. In this scenario, both Alice and Bob have (simulated) smart meters installed in their homes and opted in to a Facebook application that allows for the sharing and comparison of the energy consumption measured by the smart meters.

The smart meters send their readings to a trusted third party (meter reader) that accumulates the data for further services like billing. The meter reader also releases the energy usage data to other services, like the Facebook application, upon receiving appropriate credentials (that must be provided by the corresponding smart meter user). Since both Alice and Bob provided their credentials in the registration phase, the Facebook application is allowed to request their energy usage data and share it for comparison in forms of graphs and avatars. If no usage control policy is specified, data may be used, stored, and shared unrestrictedly once it has been released by the meter reader.

The meter reader gives users the ability to specify usage control policies for their energy usage data. While in our current implementation users have to specify policies as ECA rules, future instantiations of this work may integrate a more user-friendly policy specification tool as described in

[3]. Once Alice decides to deploy the policy "Facebook application must delete all data older than 14 days", the policy is sent to the Facebook application along with the next request of energy usage data. The policy is enforced and the graphs and avatars shown are based on the data of the last 14 days only.

Technically, the meter reader and the Facebook application communicate using HTTP. The meter reader runs a (standard Apache) HTTP server that is queried regularly for the readings by a (simple self-written) script run on the Facebook application server. We instantiated our enforcement infrastructure at both of these sites, therefore expanding data flow tracking and policy enforcement of the energy usage data to the Facebook application once Alice deploys a policy. Each further data request after policy deployment is then temporarily blocked until the meta communication introduced by our infrastructure (between the respective PIPs and PMPs) has finished.

Again, our infrastructure is independent from the applications used.

Acknowledgment. This work was funded by a Google Focused Research Award on Cloud Computing.

5. REFERENCES

[1] M. Harvan and A. Pretschner. State-Based Usage Control Enforcement with Data Flow Tracking using System Call Interposition. In *Proc. 3rd International Conference on Network and System Security*, pages 373–380, Oct. 2009.

[2] P. Kumari, F. Kelbert, and A. Pretschner. Data Protection in Heterogeneous Distributed Systems: A Smart Meter Example. In *Proc. Workshop on Dependable Software for Critical Infrastructures. GI Lecture Notes in Informatics*, Oct. 2011.

[3] P. Kumari and A. Pretschner. Deriving Implementation-level Policies for Usage Control Enforcement. In *Proc. 2nd ACM Conference on Data and Application Security and Privacy*, pages 83–94, Feb. 2012.

[4] A. Pretschner, M. Hilty, and D. Basin. Distributed Usage Control. *Communications of the ACM*, pages 39–44, Sept. 2006.

[5] A. Pretschner, M. Hilty, D. Basin, C. Schaefer, and T. Walter. Mechanisms for Usage Control. In *Proc. 2008 ACM Symposium on Information, Computer and Communications Security*, pages 240–244, Mar. 2008.

[6] A. Pretschner, E. Lovat, and M. Büchler. Representation-Independent Data Usage Control. In *Data Privacy Management and Autonomous Spontaneus Security*, volume 7122 of *Lecture Notes in Computer Science*, pages 122–140, 2012.

[7] N. Provos. Improving Host Security with System Call Policies. In *Proc. 12th USENIX Security Symposium*, June 2003.

[8] R. Sandhu and J. Park. Usage Control: A Vision for Next Generation Access Control. In *Computer Network Security*, volume 2776 of *Lecture Notes in Computer Science*, pages 17–31. 2003.

[9] D. Winer. XML-RPC, http://xmlrpc.scripting.com/, 1998.

SecureBPMN: Modeling and Enforcing Access Control Requirements in Business Processes

Achim D. Brucker
SAP Research
Vincenz-Priessnitz-Str. 1
76131 Karlsruhe, Germany
achim.brucker@sap.com

Isabelle Hang
SAP Research
Vincenz-Priessnitz-Str. 1
76131 Karlsruhe, Germany
isabelle.hang@sap.com

Gero Lückemeyer
Hochschule für Technik Stuttgart
Schellingstr. 24
70174 Stuttgart, Germany
gero.lueckemeyer@hft-stuttgart.de

Raj Ruparel
SAP Research
Vincenz-Priessnitz-Str. 1
76131 Karlsruhe, Germany
raj.ruparel@sap.com

ABSTRACT

Modern enterprise systems have to comply to regulations such as Basel III resulting in complex security requirements. These requirements need to be modeled at design-time and enforced at runtime. Moreover, modern enterprise systems are often business-process driven, i. e., the system behavior is described as high-level business processes that are executed by a business process execution engine.

Consequently, there is a need for an integrated and tool-supported methodology that allows for specifying and enforcing compliance and security requirements for business process-driven enterprise systems.

In this paper, we present a tool chain supporting both the design-time modeling as well as the run-time enforcement of security requirements for business process-driven systems.

Categories and Subject Descriptors

K.6.5 [**Computing Milieux**]: Management of Computing and Information Systems—*Security and Protection*

General Terms

Security, Languages

Keywords

Process Security, SecureBPMN, RBAC, BPMN

1. INTRODUCTION

Security requirements and compliance regulations are a major concern for designing, building, and running business process driven systems. Many software development methods often treat non-functional requirements, such as security, separately. As the functional behavior and the security of a system are, usually, not independent from each other, this separation of concerns makes it difficult to ensure that a given system fulfills its requirements. Thus, we propose a tool supported, model-driven development process that integrates seamlessly the security and compliance requirements across all phases of the system life-cycle, i. e., from the *system design* to *system execution* to *system audit*.

In this paper, we concentrate on the first two aspects: integrating security and compliance requirements into a BPMN-based design phase as well as enforcing these requirements, at run-time, in a workflow management system.

2. THE SECUREBPMN METHODOLOGY

Consider a travel approval process in which the budget and the travel duration need to be approved by different managers. The main window in Figure 1 illustrates such a process. This simple process requires already the following compliance and security requirements (see, e. g., [10] for a more detailed discussion of security requirements for process models):

- *Access Control:* Access to resources as well as actions need to be restricted to certain roles (e. g., clerks, managers) or subjects.

- *Separation of Duty:* More than one subject is required to successfully complete the process.

While modeling several other case studies we identified the following security requirements as particularly important:

- *·Binding of Duty:* The same subject needs to execute several tasks of a process.

- *Need to Know:* A subject should only be able to access the information that is strictly necessary for completing a certain task.

In the following, we discuss how these requirements can be modeled and enforced for business-process-driven systems.

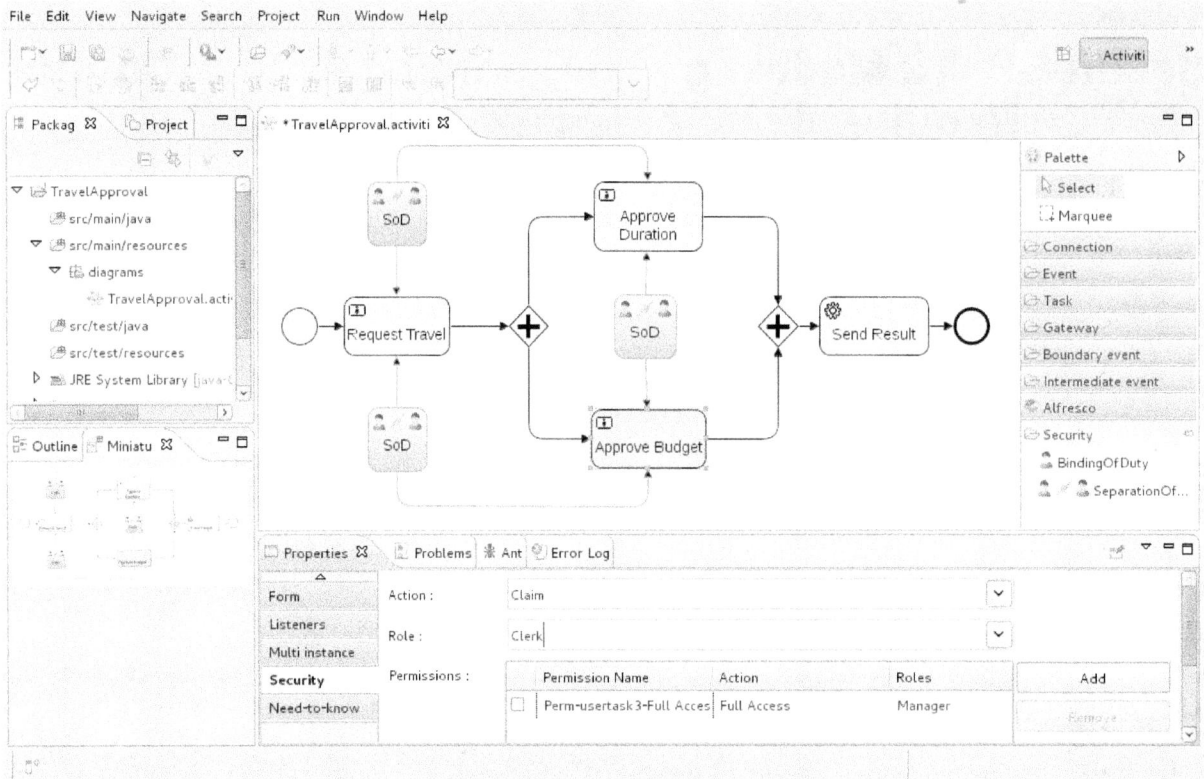

Figure 1: Specifying security requirements diagrammatically as well as using specialized user interfaces.

2.1 Modeling Security Requirements

Modeling compliance and security requirements on the process level requires the extension of the process modeling language with security concepts. In our work, we follow the meta-modeling approach for extending the Business Process Modeling and Notation (BPMN) [9] with a security language, called SecureBPM, that allows for specifying role-based access control (RBAC) [1] as well as the other security and compliance properties. The decision for a meta-model based approach is based on our previous experience in extending UML with RBAC (see [4] for a comparison of the different possibilities for adding domain-specific extensions to an existing modeling language).

Beside the specification of hierarchical, role-based access control (inspired by SecureUML [3]), SecureBPMN supports, e.g., separation of duty and binding of duty constraints. In contrast to standard approaches, our meta-model allows to specify these requirements not on the task level but on the permission level. This supports use cases where separation of duty or binding of duty is only necessary under certain conditions, e.g., the travel request has to be approved by two managers or one senior manager.

Moreover, SecureBPMN also supports the need-to-know principle which restricts the use of resources such as process variables or data objects.

The visualization of these security requirements is another characteristic of our work. They must be embedded in a business process model during the BPMN-based design phase in a well-arranged manner. So, we provide diagrammatic representations as well as specialized user interfaces to avoid crowded diagrams. We decide to depict separation of duty and binding of duty in a diagrammatic way and specify access control and need to know in a domain-specific user interface.

2.2 Enforcing Security Requirements

Naturally, the specified security and compliance requirements need to be enforced at runtime. Integrating security requirements, as first-class citizen, into the process modeling language, allows to easily support modern service-oriented or cloud-based systems. In contrast to traditional monolithic workflow systems, modern systems are usually a composition of many different services and each of these services needs to enforce a subset of the security requirements. Moreover, there are requirements, e.g., separation of duty, that need to be enforced by the workflow management system orchestrating the various services.

To address this challenge, we propose to apply the Model-driven Security (MDS) paradigm, i.e., to generate the necessary artifacts for standard security frameworks from the SecureBPMN model. Generating these artifacts allows for generating all the security configuration for all services from a *single* source—even for services using different security frameworks. For example, the RBAC, separation of duty, and binding of duty requirements can be automatically translated into XACML [8] policies and enforced by one or more Policy Enforcement Points (PEPs). The PEPs are generated from the SecureBPMN model as well and use an XACML Policy Decision Point (PDP) to decide if a certain request should be granted or not. If a request is denied, the PEP in the user interface of the workflow management systems informs the user about the violation of the security policy.

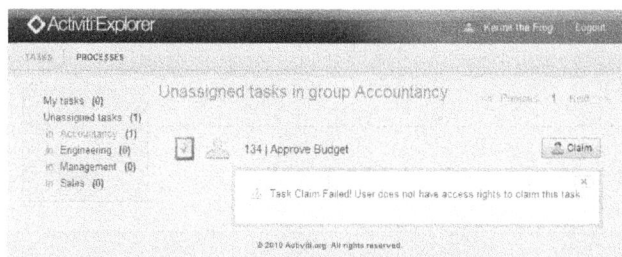

Figure 2: Enforcing SecureBPMN policies at runtime and informing users about violations.

2.3 Implementation

Our prototype uses the Activiti BPMN Platform (`http://www.activiti.org/`). In particular, we extended the Activiti Eclipse Designer and the Activiti Process Engine.

Our extension of the Activiti Designer provides an integrated environment for modeling secure business processes. As we made the experience that many security requirements are too complex to be represented intuitively in a diagrammatic way, we provide diagrammatic extensions of BPMN as well as security specific extension of the user interface:

- For certain requirements, such as separation of duty, we provide a diagrammatic representation, i. e., user can specify separation of duty constraints via drag using the Palette (see the right-hand side of Figure 1),

- For the specification of the role-based access control policies as well as certain details of, e. g., complex separation of duty constraints, we provide specialized user interfaces. For example, the Security Tab for tasks (see the lower part of Figure 1) allows for a table-based specification of access control requirements.

The diagrammatic representation of security requirements and the security-specific user interfaces are two views on the same secure process model. Thus, the user is free to choose the specification approach that best suits his or her needs.

For the access control enforcement, we automatically generate XACML policies as well as XACML compliant PEPs based on SUN's XACML implementation (`http://sunxacml.sf.net/`). Of course, support for other policy languages can be added easily. Moreover, we extended the Activiti Process Engine to use the generated PEPs for enforcing the security policies as well as informing users about certain violations, e. g., the violation of a separation of duty constraint (see Figure 2).

3. CONCLUSION AND FUTURE WORK

We presented a model-based approach for designing and operating business-process-driven systems that integrates security and compliance requirements as first class citizens.

In this paper, we concentrated on the design-time modeling as well as the run-time enforcement of security and compliance requirements. Providing an integrated solutions that ensures the secure and compliant operation of business-process-driven systems, requires, requirements, further extensions in several ways. For example, at design-time we plan to integrate consistency analysis techniques similar to [2] as well as formal security analysis techniques such as [6].

Moreover, the use of model-based test case generation techniques, e. g., similar to [7], allows for ensuring that, on the one hand, access control enforcement infrastructure works correctly and, on the other hand, that externals services adhere to the security requirements as well. Finally, we suggest to integrate policy analysis frameworks such as [5] to cover the system audit phase.

Acknowledgments.
The research leading to these results has received funding from the European Union Seventh Framework Programme (FP7/2007–2013) under grant no. 257930 (Aniketos).

References

[1] *American National Standard for Information Technology – Role Based Access Control.* ANSI, New York, 2004. ANSI INCITS 359-2004.

[2] W. Arsac, L. Compagna, G. Pellegrino, and S. E. Ponta. Security validation of business processes via model-checking. In Ú. Erlingsson, R. Wieringa, and N. Zannone, editors, *ESSoS*, volume 6542 of *LNCS*, pages 29–42. Springer, 2011. doi: 10.1007/978-3-642-19125-1_3.

[3] D. A. Basin, J. Doser, and T. Lodderstedt. Model driven security: From UML models to access control infrastructures. *ACM Transactions on Software Engineering and Methodology*, 15(1):39–91, 2006. doi: 10.1145/1125808.1125810.

[4] A. D. Brucker and J. Doser. Metamodel-based UML notations for domain-specific languages. In J. M. Favre, D. Gasevic, R. Lämmel, and A. Winter, editors, *4th International Workshop on Software Language Engineering (ATEM 2007)*. 2007.

[5] A. D. Brucker and H. Petritsch. A framework for managing and analyzing changes of security policies. In *IEEE POLICY*, pages 105–112. IEEE Computer Society, 2011. doi: 10.1109/POLICY.2011.47.

[6] A. D. Brucker, J. Doser, and B. Wolff. A model transformation semantics and analysis methodology for SecureUML. In O. Nierstrasz, J. Whittle, D. Harel, and G. Reggio, editors, *MoDELS 2006: Model Driven Engineering Languages and Systems*, number 4199 in LNCS, pages 306–320. Springer, 2006. doi: 10.1007/11880240_22.

[7] A. D. Brucker, L. Brügger, P. Kearney, and B. Wolff. An approach to modular and testable security models of real-world health-care applications. In *ACM SACMAT*, pages 133–142. ACM Press, 2011. doi: 10.1145/1998441.1998461.

[8] OASIS. eXtensible Access Control Markup Language (XACML), version 2.0, 2005.

[9] Object Management Group. Business process model and notation (BPMN), version 2.0, 2011. Available as OMG document formal/2011-01-03.

[10] A. Rodríguez, E. Fernández-Medina, and M. Piattini. A BPMN extension for the modeling of security requirements in business processes. *IEICE - Trans. Inf. Syst.*, E90-D:745–752, 2007. doi: 10.1093/ietisy/e90-d.4.745.

Encryption-Enforced Access Control for an RFID Discovery Service

Florian Kerschbaum
Chair of Privacy and Data Security
Technical University Dresden, Germany
florian.kerschbaum@tu-dresden.de

Leonardo Weiss Ferreira Chaves
SAP AG
SAP Research Center Karlsruhe, Germany
leonardo.weiss.f.chaves@sap.com

ABSTRACT

In this demonstration we present a novel encryption scheme for enforcing access control in a Discovery Service. A Discovery Service is a piece of software that allows one to "discover" item-level data which is stored in data repositories of different companies. Such data can be gathered with the help of Radio Frequency Identification or 2D bar codes. Our software allows the data owner to enforce access control on an item-level by managing the corresponding keys. Data remains confidential even against the provider of the Discovery Service. We present three ways of querying data and evaluate them with databases containing up to 50 million tuples.

Categories and Subject Descriptors

D.4.6 [**Operating Systems**]: Security and Protection—*Cryptographic controls*; D.4.6 [**Operating Systems**]: Security and Protection—*Access control*

General Terms

Experimentation, Performance, Security

Keywords

RFID Discovery Service, Visibility Policies, Searchable Encryption, Access Control

1. INTRODUCTION

More and more companies are implementing item-level tracking in their supply chains using Radio Frequency Identification (RFID) [4] or 2D bar codes. Each RFID tag or bar code carries a unique identifier for each good [14]. Companies are collecting information about the items they handle by scanning the identifier and recording it in their data repositories. Each tuple recorded consists of the item identifier, a timestamp, the location and situation-specific data.

The full benefit of this information can be gained when companies exchange their item-level data. For instance, applications like anti-counterfeiting [7] and targeted batch recalls [15] require that the path of each single item is tracked along the supply chain. This cannot be achieved with aggregated data. Despite the potential of such new applications, companies are reluctant to share item-level data [2, 13]. This is because strategic relations or best practices might be inferred from the data. Furthermore, companies may suffer consequences for unfair behavior. Because of that companies need to selectively exchange item-level data with other companies in the supply chain.

There are two main methods of exchanging item-level data: storing data locally at each company (distributed repositories), and storing the data centrally (central repository). These methods are discussed in detail in the following section. In summary, none of these methods is satisfactory:

1. **Distributed Repositories:** When data is distributed, one has to first "discover" which company and thereby which repositories contain data about each item [1]. This makes data access slower. And the discovery itself can reveal sensitive information.

2. **Central Repository:** A central repository does not require discovery. However, the data owner has to relinquish access control to the repository provider.

In this demonstration we present a novel encryption scheme for exchanging item-level data in a distributed data repository. It extends an existing encryption scheme used for central repositories [10, 11]. The modified encryption scheme enables the data owners to enforce access control over their data, prevents observers of the Discovery Service to infer any information and enables efficient queries on the stored data. It thereby reconciliates the conflict between security and performance in item-level data repositories.

2. EXCHANGING ITEM-LEVEL DATA

As already mentioned, there are two main methods of exchanging item-level data: (1) storing data locally at each company, and (2) storing the data centrally. For the sake of completeness, we also consider (3) storing the data on an RFID tag [12].

Distributed Repositories: Item-level data is usually partitioned horizontally and tuples corresponding to one item are spread across a number of repositories, e.g. because each company will store the data it gathers in its own repository.

Nevertheless, the typical query searches for all tuples corresponding to one item (pedigree). Locating the repositories that contain information about one item is difficult. This is because companies usually do not know the complete supply chain of each item, such that they have to "discover" which companies possessed which items [1]. Proposals have been made for discovery servers that contain an index over all repositories [3, 1]. However, they do not provide the appropriate level of security. Furthermore, data access becomes slower since data repositories have to be discovered before data can be queried.

Central Repository: When data is stored centrally, there is no need to locate the repositories. However, the data owner looses the control over who can access his data. He has to trust that the repository provider will enforce the access control as specified. And if the repository is compromised, all data about the whole supply chain might be revealed. Since business critical information can be inferred from this data, companies need to stay in control over their data.

Data-on-Tag: While companies can easily exchange data by storing it on the RFID tags, it poses many security risks. If data is unencrypted, it might be read at any time by any person. If data is encrypted, key management becomes a problem. Furthermore, the information flow is only in one direction, i.e. from manufacturer to consumer, and data cannot be updated after an item leaves your company.

3. OVERVIEW OF OUR DEMO

We target a scenario with a distributed repository using a Discovery Service. Our demonstration extends a previous method [10, 11] designed for central repositories. Our security requirements for the Discovery Service are

1. A party observing the Discovery Service should not be able to track items.

2. A party should be able to enforce fine-grained visibility policies on its items.

The first requirement is important in order to protect against attacks introduced by the use of a Discovery Service. One can imagine an attacker that continuously monitors the Discovery Service and tries to infer as much information as possible. We would like to prevent such an attacker from gaining any information.

The second requirement implies fine-grained access control policies. It is a functional requirement on the security mechanism. A data owner has different trust relationships with different parties and he should be able to set the access control policies accordingly. In particular, we map the policy model of visibility policies to the following levels of access control:

A1: for each tuple

A2: for each party, all tuples corresponding to items that the party possessed

A3: for each party, all tuples corresponding to items that the data owner previously possessed

These levels are a subset of visibility policies [6] which have been defined for mobile physical objects, such as goods in a supply chain, and can be enforced via authentication [8]. The first level A1 allows setting any arbitrary policy on a tuple-level. It allows implementing the full spectrum of attribute-based access control at the cost of managing a large number of keys.

The second level A2 of access control is particularly useful for item-level tracking. It allows restricting the visibility of items to someone who possessed the item without having to set access control to individual items. One can then engage in fair data sharing agreements with other parties without the risk of disclosing information about other supply chain partners – even by inference. This is the basic notion of visibility policies combined with an authorization for a specific party. Without loss of generality let that party be Alice, then we express the access control level A2 as

$$access(s, o) = \text{``}vis\text{''} \in ATTR(s, o) \wedge \text{``}Alice\text{''} \in ATTR(s)$$

Such visibility policies can be implemented using tuple-level access control, but we significantly reduce the number of managed keys.

The third level A3 enables including trusted parties, e.g. outsourced manufacturers or service providers. They get full access to the data of their trusting partner. This level implements access control orthogonal to visibility policies based on the ownership of the data in ones data repository. Using an example, let Alice be the service provider and Bob be the party granting access. Then we express the access control level A3 as

$$access(s, o) = \text{``}Bob\text{''} \in ATTR(o) \wedge \text{``}Alice\text{''} \in ATTR(s)$$

Consider implementing these requirements with traditional cryptography: in both symmetrical and asymmetrical encryption, one key or one key pair would be required for each tuple and for each party. Since an average supply chain produces millions of items with hundreds of supply chain partners, these methods would result in a huge number of cryptographic keys. Furthermore, cryptographic keys would need to be exchanged between parties for each item/tuple produced. Thus, both methods are unpractical.

We follow a different approach: we propose a new cryptographic scheme which only requires a random number for each item, and two cryptographic keys. And it only requires cryptographic keys to be exchanged once, i.e. new items/tuples do not require an exchange of new cryptographic keys. Our cryptographic scheme stores encrypted data in a distributed repository and finds it using a Discovery Service.

Our cryptographic scheme requires tuples containing two values:

- I: a unique identifier for the combination of one item and one party

- D: Information where the actual data lies, i.e. a data endpoint like an URL

Note that I will uniquely identify all data endpoints D corresponding to one or several attributes of the item, therefore it can be used to query all D's from the Discovery Service.

The challenge of our cryptographic scheme is to on the one hand prevent an observer from inferring information about an item or company from I, but on the other hand let legitimate queries efficiently identify the tuples containing I.

We describe our cryptographic scheme following the steps in its basic procedure, cf. Figure 1:

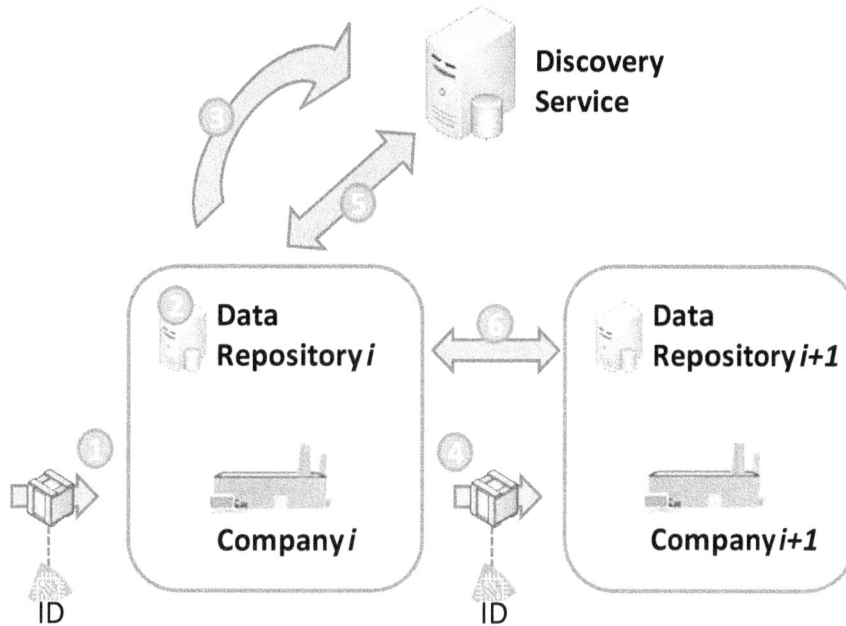

Figure 1: Overview of the basic steps in our cryptographic scheme

1. Company i receives or produces an item which is equipped with an unique ID

2. Company i collects data about this item, encrypts it, and stores it in its own data repository

3. For each attribute corresponding to the item, Company i writes (I, D) to the Discovery Service

4. Company i sells the item, i.e. it sends it to Company $i+1$

5. Later, Company i can query and decrypt the data endpoints of each attribute

6. After that Company i can retrieve the actual data from each data repository

Furthemore, we present three ways of querying our Discovery Service:

- Client-side Computation: For all companies, the querying party will use the public key to calculate I, and then retrieve the corresponding tuple(s) from the repository.

- Server-side Computation: After receiving a query, the Discovery Service will use billinear pairings to calculate which tuple(s) correspond to the query. After that it returns these tuples.

- Chaining: The ID of the tuple of the predecessor (Company $i - 1$) and of the successor (Company $i + 1$) of an item are encrypted and stored in the tuple. This way each party with appropriate access rights can follow the information about each item up and down the supply chain.

4. PERFORMANCE EVALUATION

Our implementation is based on elliptical curves. We use a group $\mathbb{G}_1 = E(\mathbb{F}_p)[\ell]$ where p is a prime number longer than 512 Bit, and ℓ one that is 160 Bit long. The parameters a_i, b_i, c_i and r are also 160 Bit long. Note that the length of the keys is sufficient, since 160 Bit in elliptic curves provides similar security to 1024 Bit RSA. For the encryption of D we use 128-Bit AES.

The parameters influencing the runtime of our cryptographic scheme are: the overall number of companies $|C|$, the number of companies that possessed an item $|L|$, and the number of tuples in the repository $|DB|$. We generate data to mimic a large supply chain, with the maximum size of the parameters being $|C| = 10,000$; $|L| = 100$; and $|DB| = 50\ million$.

Our fully functional prototype was implemented in Java (1.6.0_12, 64-Bit), using $java.math.BigInteger$ as a large number arithmetic library. We executed the code on a Linux server with 64GB RAM, and 4 quad-core 64-Bit CPUs with 2.40GHz. The tuples were stored on a dedicated Linux server with 3GB RAM, a dual-core 32-Bit CPU with 3GHz, running PostgreSql 8.4.

In the demonstration we analyze the following aspects of our prototype:

- Comparison of the overall runtime of all three queries without considering parallelization

- Runtime for fetching tuples from a database with up to 50 million items

- Parallelization of cryptographic computations on the client and on the server

- Environment parameters for which each query type is the fastest

5. CONCLUSIONS

In this demonstration we presented a novel application of encryption for the secure implementation of a Discovery Service. Different levels of fine-grained access control can be enforced, e.g. on each item, without the need to exchange new cryptographic keys. We evaluated three ways of querying the repository: One query that relies on computations on the client side, one that relies on computations on the server side, and one that queries tuples sequentially. We performed a performance evaluation with a database containing up to 50 million tuples.

Acknowledgements

The work presented in this paper was partly funded by the German government (BMBF) through the *Polytos* project.

6. REFERENCES

[1] S. Beier, T. Grandison, K. Kailing, and R. Rantzau. Discovery Services - Enabling RFID Traceability in EPCglobal Networks. In *Proceedings of the 13th International Conference on Management of Data COMAD'06*, 2006.

[2] M. Eurich, N. Oertel, and R. Boutellier. The impact of perceived privacy risks on organization's willingness to share item-level event data across the supply chain. *Electronic Commerce Research*, 10:3–4, 2010.

[3] B. Fabian, O. Günther, and S. Spiekermann. Security Analysis of the Object Name Service. In *Proceedings of the International Workshop on Security, Privacy and Trust in Pervasive and Ubiquitous Computing SECPERU'05*, 2005.

[4] K. Finkenzeller. *RFID Handbook: Fundamentals and Applications in Contactless Smart Cards and Identification.* John Wiley & Sons, Inc., 2003.

[5] F. Kerschbaum. Simple Cross-Site Attack Prevention. In *Proceedings of the 3rd International Conference on Security and Privacy in Communication Networks SecureComm'07*, 2007.

[6] F. Kerschbaum. An Access Control Model for Mobile Physical Objects. In *Proceedings the 15th ACM Symposium on Access Control Models and Technologies SACMAT'10*, 2010.

[7] F. Kerschbaum and N. Oertel. Privacy-Preserving Pattern Matching for Anomaly Detection in RFID Anti-Counterfeiting. In *Proceedings of the Workshop on RFID Security RFIDsec'10*, 2010.

[8] F. Kerschbaum and A. Sorniotti. RFID-Based Supply Chain Partner Authentication and Key Agreement. In *Proceedings of the 2nd ACM Conference on Wireless Network Security WISEC'09*, 2009.

[9] F. Kerschbaum and O. Terzidis. Filtering for Private Collaborative Benchmarking. In *Proceedings of the International Conference on Emerging Trends in Information and Communication Security ETRICS'06*, 2006.

[10] F. Kerschbaum and L. Weiss Ferreira Chaves. Secure Sharing of Item-level Data in the Cloud. In *Proceedings of the 4th IEEE Conference on Cloud Computing CLOUD'11*, 2011.

[11] F. Kerschbaum and L. Weiss Ferreira Chaves. Encrypted Searchable Storage of RFID Tracking Data. In *Proceedings of the 13th IEEE International Conference on Mobile Data Management MDM'12*, 2012.

[12] A. Melski, L. Thoroe, and M. Schumann. Managing RFID data in supply chains. *International Journal of Internet Protocol Technology (IJIPT)*, 2(3/4):176 – 189, 2007.

[13] B. Santos and L. Smith. RFID in the Supply Chain: Panacea or Pandora's Box? *Communications of the ACM*, 51(10):127–131, 2008.

[14] S. Sarma, D. Brock, and D. Engels. Radio frequency identification and the electronic product code. *IEEE Micro*, 21(6):50–54, 2001.

[15] L. Weiss Ferreira Chaves and F. Kerschbaum. Industrial Privacy in RFID-based Batch Recalls. In *Proceedings of the International Workshop on Security and Privacy in Enterprise Computing InSPEC'08*, 2008.

Automating Architectural Security Analysis

Andreas Schaad
SAP Research, Security & Trust
Vincenz-Priessnitz Str. 1
76131 Karlsruhe, Germany
andreas.schaad@sap.com

Alexandr Garaga
University of Trento
Via Sommarive 14
I-38050 Povo, Italy
algaraga@gmail.com

ABSTRACT

In earlier work [1] we had looked at implementing the Microsoft STRIDE methodology in the context of evaluating security properties of FMC/TAM architectural diagrams. However, a major drawback of this approach is that it requires significant manual work to assess all reported potential threats, as well as identify concrete follow-ups. Equally, it is not possible to analyse an architecture from the perspective of the primary assets that require protection. This led us to two questions:

a) whether using interaction information in architecture diagrams, supported by additional security semantics, can reduce the scope of analysis as well as partly automate it;

b) whether using asset-centric and attacker-centric perspectives can complement the software-centric perspective of STRIDE and thus add value to the current threat model.

Categories and Subject Descriptors

D.2.11 [**Software Architectures**]

Keywords

Threat modelling, CORAS, STRIDE, Architecture, TAM, FMC

1 INTRODUCTION

Identifying and resolving security problems as early as possible in the software development life cycle should by now be a conventional wisdom. However, we observe that there is no threat modelling approach suitable for analysing FMC/TAM-based software architecture models. Our earlier work [1] did aim at filling this gap by applying a threat modelling technique called STRIDE [2] to TAM-based software architecture diagrams. We did validate that even little additional security related information on architecture diagrams can yield significant value in a lightweight (automated) security analysis. We implemented and verified our approach by building a tool for threat analysis of software architecture diagrams. Our tool did originate in the RescueIT supply chain security research project [3] and was validated in the context of several large-scale industrial software projects.

Although the tool showed to be useful, it still requires final manual assessment of all reported potential threats, as well as identification of concrete follow-ups by the security analyst. In an attempt to further address this problem of how to automatically

support the elicitation process, this work prototypically discusses new approaches that allow for a more precise description of the application security profile; identifying new types of threats; prioritizing them; looking at the threat modelling process from different perspectives; performing some reasoning based on the interaction between the architecture diagram components; as well as providing a graphical summary of the threat modelling results.

2. BASIC TOOL FEATURES

Based on the earlier motivation and on top of what we have implemented in [1], our tool now supports the following features:

1. Specifying additional security related semantics: The architectural models were enhanced with additional information that captures some of the security aspects of an application in a more precise way. For that, new notions were introduced in the tool, such as security controls, trust boundaries and access controls lists. This allows both better documenting the security of the architecture as well as reducing the scope of analysis, by enabling automated data flow reasoning and facilitating question-based analysis (Figures 1 and 2).

2. Automated data flow analysis of security properties (Figure 2): Based on the specified security objectives and the enriched security semantics, an automated data flow analysis can be performed on the architecture diagram. This analysis verifies the supported security properties against some of the possible threats by taking interaction information on the architecture diagrams into account. The identified issues are displayed graphically on the diagrams.

3. Performing high level threat modelling (Figure 3): We did integrate CORAS diagrams to capture high level security goals, involved parties, threat agents and risks. This provides attacker-centric and asset-centric perspectives, and, at the same time, drives the further threat analysis process by focusing on the most important assets.

4. Using attack trees for high level threat modelling: We did integrate attack tree diagrams, detailing the conditions for the attacker goals to be met. This allows extending the analysis with some application specific threats.

REFERENCES

[1] Andreas Schaad, Mike Borozdin "TAM2 Automated Threat Analysis". ACM Symposium on Applied Computing (SAC), ACM Press, 2012

[2] S. Hernan , Scott Lambert, Tomasz Ostwald, Adam Shostack "Uncover Security Design Flaws Using the STRIDE Approach" http://msdn.microsoft.com/en-us/magazine/cc163519.aspx

[3] Ganna Monakova, Achim D. Brucker and Andreas Schaad. "Security and Safety of Assets in Business Processes." ACM Symposium on Applied Computing (SAC). ACM Press, 2012.

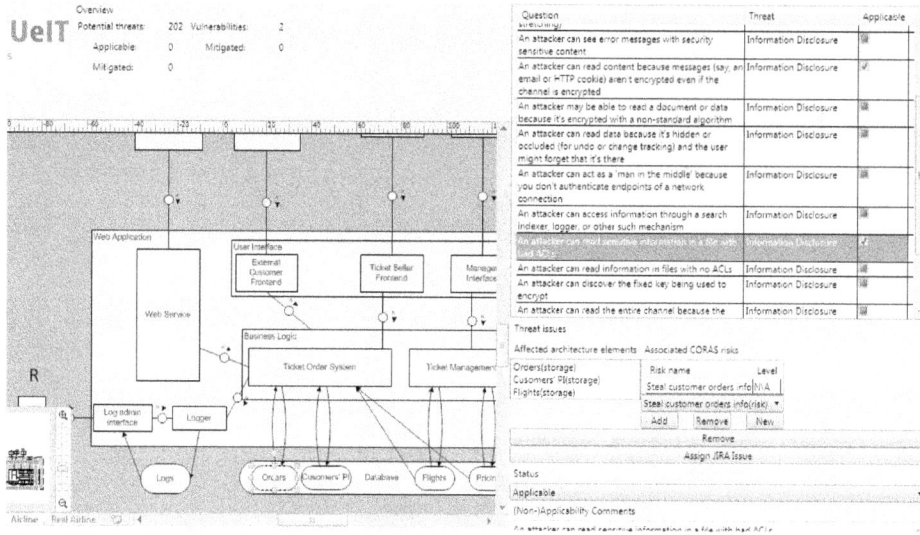

Figure 1: Question-based assessment - CORAS model integration

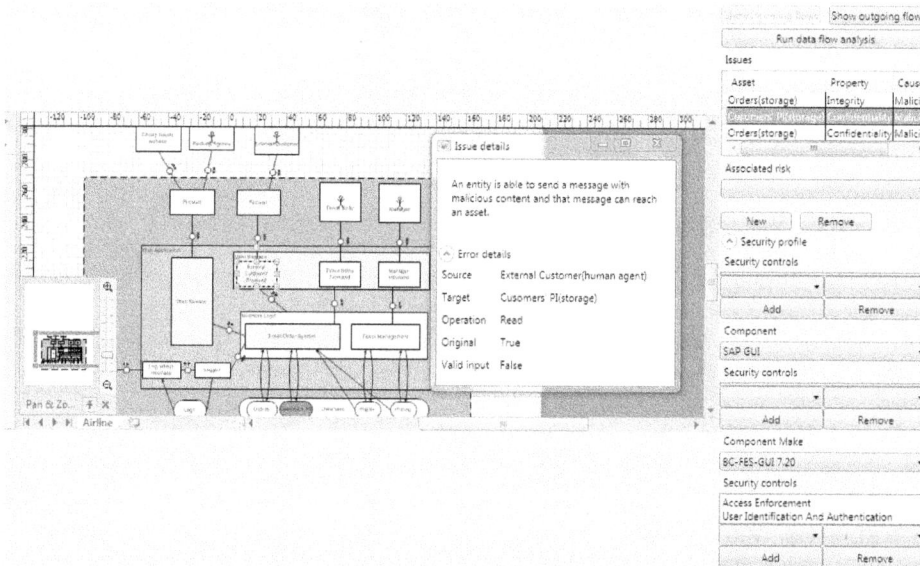

Figure 2: Automatic data flow analysis – Violation of a Confidentiality security property

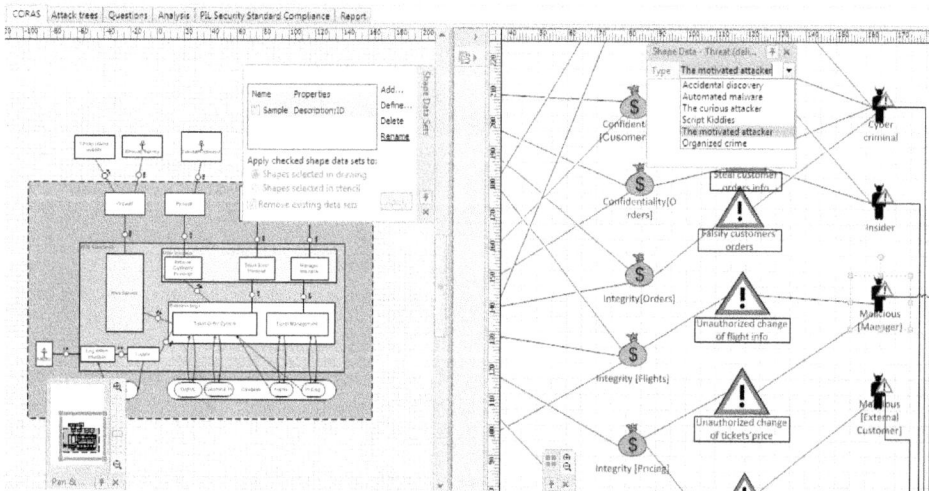

Figure 3: Defining threats in CORAS diagrams

Efficient Privacy Preserving Content Based Publish Subscribe Systems

Mohamed Nabeel, Ning Shang, Elisa Bertino
Dept. of Computer Science
Purdue University
West Lafayette, IN, USA
{nabeel, nshang, bertino}@cs.purdue.edu

ABSTRACT

The ability to seamlessly scale on demand has made Content-Based Publish-Subscribe (CBPS) systems the choice of distributing *messages/documents* produced by *Content Publishers* to many *Subscribers* through *Content Brokers*. Most of the current systems assume that *Content Brokers* are trusted for the confidentiality of the data published by *Content Publishers* and the privacy of the subscriptions, which specify their interests, made by *Subscribers*. However, with the increased use of technologies, such as service oriented architectures and cloud computing, essentially outsourcing the broker functionality to third-party providers, one can no longer assume the trust relationship to hold. The problem of providing privacy/confidentiality in CBPS systems is challenging, since the solution to the problem should allow *Content Brokers* to make routing decisions based on the content without revealing the content to them. The previous work attempted to solve this problem was not fully successful. The problem may appear unsolvable since it involves conflicting goals, but in this paper, we propose a novel approach to preserve the privacy of the subscriptions made by *Subscribers* and confidentiality of the data published by *Content Publishers* using cryptographic techniques when third-party *Content Brokers* are utilized to make routing decisions based on the content. Our protocols are expressive to support any type of subscriptions and designed to work efficiently. We distribute the work such that the load on *Content Brokers*, where the bottleneck is in a CBPS system, is minimized. We extend a popular CBPS system using our protocols to implement a privacy preserving CBPS system.

Categories and Subject Descriptors

H.4 [**Information Systems Applications**]: Miscellaneous; D.2.8 [**Software Engineering**]: Metrics—*complexity measures, performance measures*

General Terms

Design, Protocols, System, Implementation

Keywords

Publish subscribe, Privacy, Confidentiality

1. INTRODUCTION

Many systems, including online news delivery, stock quote report dissemination and weather channels, have been or can be modeled as Content-Based Publish-Subscribe (CBPS) systems. Full decoupling of the involved parties, that is, *Content Publishers* (Pubs), *Content Brokers* (Brokers) and *Subscribers* (Subs), in time, space, and synchronization has been the key [13] to seamlessly scale these systems on demand. Hence, CBPS systems have the huge potential to be enabled over cloud computing infrastructures. In a CBPS system, each Sub selectively subscribes to some Brokers to receive different messages. In the most common setting, when Pubs publish messages to some Brokers, these Brokers, in turn, selectively distribute these messages to other Brokers and finally to Subs based on their *subscriptions*, that is, what they subscribed to. These systems, in general, follow a *push based* dissemination approach, that is, whenever new messages arrive, Brokers selectively distribute the messages to Subs. Figure 1 shows an example CBPS system.

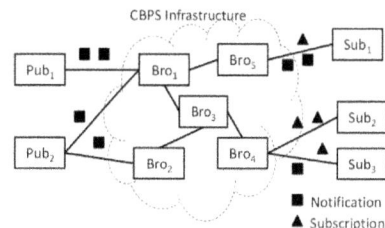

Figure 1: An example CBPS system

It is not feasible to have a private Broker network for each CBPS system and most CBPS systems utilize third-party Broker networks which may not be trusted for the confidentiality of the content flowing through them. Because content represents the critical resource in many CBPS systems, its confidentiality from third-party Brokers is important. Consider the popular example of publishing stock market quotes where Subs pay Pub, that is the stock exchange, either for the types of quotes they wish to receive or per usage basis. In such a domain, whenever a new stock quote, referred to in general as a *notification*, is published, Brokers selectively send such a notification only to authorized Subs. Confidentiality is important here because Pubs want to make sure that only paying customers have access to the quotes. We say that a CBPS system provides *publication confidentiality* if Brokers can neither identify the content of the messages published by Pubs nor infer the distribution of *attribute values* of the message [1]. For the stock quote example, in the absence of *publication confidentiality*, Brokers may collect stock quotes, re-sell to others, and/or sell derived market data without any economic incentive to Pubs.

At the same time, the privacy of subscribers is also crucial for many reasons, like business confidentiality or personal privacy. We say that a CBPS system provides *subscription privacy* if Brokers can neither identify what subscriptions Subs made nor relate a set of subscriptions to a specific Sub. Consider again the stock quote example. Suppose for example that Sub subscribes to some Brokers for receiving stock quotes characterized by certain attribute values (e.g. bid price < 2438, $1000 <$ bid size < 2000, symbol $=$ "MSFT", etc.). In the absence of *subscription privacy*, such a subscription can reveal the business strategy of Sub. Further, Brokers may profile *subscriptions* of each Sub and sell them to third parties.

Current trends in cloud computing technologies are further pushing brokering functions for content distribution to third-party providers. While such a strategy provides economies of scale, it increases the risk of breaches in publication confidentiality and subscription privacy. Breaches may result from malicious insiders or from platforms that are poorly configured and managed, and that do not have in place proper security techniques. It is thus essential that effective and efficient techniques for publication confidentiality and subscription privacy be devised to allow parties involved in the production and distribution of contents to take full advantages from those emerging computing infrastructures.

Privacy and confidentiality issues in CBPS have long been identified [26], but little progress has been made to address these issues in a holistic manner. Most of prior work on data confidentiality techniques in the context of CBPS systems is based on the assumption that Brokers are trusted with respect to the privacy of the subscriptions by Subs [3, 24, 18]. However, when such an assumption does not hold, both publication confidentiality and subscription privacy are at risk; in the absence of subscription privacy, subscriptions are available in clear text to Brokers. Brokers can infer the content of the notifications by comparing and matching notifications with subscriptions since CBPS systems must allow them to make such decisions to route notifications. As more subscriptions become available to Brokers, the inference is likely to be more accurate. It should also be noted that the above approaches restrict Brokers' ability to make routing decisions based on the content of the messages and thus fail to provide a CBPS system as expressive as a CBPS system that do not address security or privacy issues. Approaches have also been proposed to assure confidentiality/privacy in the presence of untrusted third-party Brokers. These approaches however suffer from one or two major limitations [21, 25, 17, 9]: inaccurate content delivery, because of

the limited ability of Brokers to make routing decisions based on content; weak security protocols; lack of privacy guarantees. For example, some of these approaches are prone to false positives, that is, sending irrelevant content to Subs.

In this paper, we propose a novel cryptographic approach that addresses those shortcomings in CBPS systems. To the best of our knowledge, no existing cryptographic solution is able to protect both publication confidentiality and subscription privacy in CBPS systems that address the above shortcomings. A key design goal of our privacy-preserving approach is to design a system which is as expressive as a system that does not consider privacy or security issues. We implement our scheme on top of a popular CBPS system, SIENA [8], and provide several experimental results in order to show our approach is practical.

In summary, our CBPS system exhibits the following properties:

- Notifications and subscriptions are randomized and hidden from Brokers and secure under chosen-ciphertext attacks.

- Both publication confidentiality and subscription privacy are assured as Brokers are able to make routing decisions without decrypting subscriptions and notifications. It is the first system to achieve these properties without sharing keys with Brokers or Subs.

- It supports any type of subscription queries including equality, inequality and range queries at Brokers.

- The computational cost at Brokers are minimized by judiciously distributing the work among Pubs and Subs.

The paper is organized as follows. Section 2 overviews the CBPS model and the protocols supported by our system. Section 3 provides some background knowledge about the main cryptographic primitives used. Section 4 provides a detailed description of the proposed protocols. Section 5 reports experimental results for the main protocols as well as the system developed on top of SIENA using the main protocols. Section 6 discusses related work. Section 7 concludes the paper and outlines future work.

2. OVERVIEW

In this section we give an overview of our proposed scheme by showing the interactions between Pubs, Subs and Brokers, and the trust model. Unless otherwise stated, we describe our approach for one Pub, mainly for brevity. However, our approach can be trivially applied to a system with any number of Pubs. In practice, all the parties in a CBPS system are software programs that act on behalf of real entities like actual organizations or end users, and therefore many of the operations of the protocols we propose are performed transparently to real entities.

Each *notification* is characterized by a set of Attribute-Value Pairs (AVPs). It consists of two parts: the actual message in the encrypted form, which we call the *payload message*, and a set of *blinded AVPs* derived from the payload message. As mentioned in Section 1, a payload message also consists of a set of AVPs. In a blinded AVP, the value is blinded, but the attribute name remains in clear text. The blinding encrypts the value in a special way such that it is computationally infeasible to obtain the value from the

---

[1] We assume that a message consists of a set of attribute-value pairs.

blinded values, and that the blinded values are secure under chosen-ciphertext attacks. The blinded AVPs are placed in the header and the payload message is in the body of the notification. There is a one-to-one mapping between the AVPs in the payload message and the blinded AVPs. Depending on the representation, each attribute name and its corresponding value may be interpreted differently.

In an XML-like syntax, a notification has the following format:

```
<notification>
    <header> -- blinded AVPs -- </header>
    <body> -- enc. payload message -- </body>
</notification>
```

Depending on the representation, each attribute name and its corresponding value may be interpreted differently. For example, the payload could be in a simple property-value format or a complex XML format. If the payload is in XML, attribute names could be the XPaths and values could be the immediate child nodes of XPaths. We use the latter for the examples.

A *subscription* specifies a condition on one of the attributes [2] of the AVPs associated with the notifications. It is an expression of the form $(attr, bval_1, bval_2, bval_3, op)$ where $attr$ is the name of the attribute, $bval_1, bval_2, bval_3$ are the blinded values derived from the actual content v and its additive inverse,[3] and op is a comparison operator, either $\geq$ or $<$. All the other comparison operators are derived from op. Note that our approach supports a wide array of conditions including range queries for numerical attributes and keyword queries for numerical and string attributes.

EXAMPLE 1. *In the stock market quote dissemination system, a payload message, that is, a quote, looks like:*

```
<q>
  <symbol>MSFT</symbol>
    <bid>
       <price>2328</price>
       <size>10000</size>
       ...
    </bid>
    <offer>
       <price>2355</price>
       <size>5000</size>
       ...
    </offer>
</q>
```

The set of AVPs, as a collection of pairs,

$$\left\{ \begin{array}{ll} (\text{"/q/symbol", "MSFT"}), & (\text{"/q/bid/price", 2328}), \\ (\text{"/q/bid/size", 10000}), & (\text{"/q/offer/price", 2355}), \\ (\text{"/q/offer/size", 5000}) & \end{array} \right\}$$

from the payload message is blinded and placed in the header of the notification. The notification for the above quote includes these blinded values and the encrypted quote.

2.1 Interactions

We now present an overview of the protocols proposed in our CBPS system. The motivation behind constructing a set of protocols is that they can easily be implemented on top an existing CBPS infrastructure in order to satisfy privacy and security requirements. In summary, `Initialize` protocol initializes the system parameters. `Register` protocol registers Subs with Pubs. `Subscribe` protocol subscribes Subs to Brokers. `Publish` protocol publishes notifications from Pubs to Brokers. `Match` protocol matches notifications with subscriptions at Brokers. `Cover` protocol finds relationships among subscriptions at Brokers. An important property of the two most frequently used protocols, `Match` and `Cover`, is that they are non-interactive. The following gives more details of each protocol.

`Initialize`:
There is a set of system defined public parameters that all Pubs, Brokers and Subs use. In addition to these parameters, Pubs also generate some public and private parameters that are used for subsequent protocols and publish the public parameters. If there are several Pubs, each Pub generates its own public and private parameters.

`Register`:
Subs register themselves with the Pub to obtain a *private key* and *access tokens*. An *access token* includes Sub's *identity* (id) and allows a Sub to subsequently authenticate itself to the Broker from which it intends to request notifications. An *identity* is a pseudonym that uniquely identifies a Sub in the system. A *private key* allows a Sub to decrypt the payload of notifications.

`Subscribe`:
In order to assure confidentiality and privacy, unlike in a typical CBPS system, Subs need to perform an additional communication step with Pub to get the subscription blinded before submitting the subscription to Broker [4].

After authenticating themselves using access tokens to Pubs, Subs receive the content in their subscriptions blinded by the corresponding Pubs. In this step, Subs perform as much computation as it can before sending the subscriptions to Pub so that the overhead on Pubs is minimized. Further, this overhead on Pubs is negligible as subscriptions are fairly stable and the rate of subscriptions is usually way less than that of notifications in a typical CBPS system. Once this step is done, Subs authenticate themselves to Brokers without revealing their identities and present these blinded subscriptions to Brokers. These subscriptions are blinded in such a way that Brokers do not learn the actual subscription criteria, that is, Brokers cannot decrypt the blinded values. However, they can perform `Match` (or `Filter`),[5] and `Cover` protocols based on the blinded subscriptions. Furthermore, no two subscriptions for the same value are distinguishable by Brokers. In order to prevent Brokers from linking different subscriptions from the same Sub, Subs may request for multiple access tokens such that all these access tokens have the same identity but are indistinguishable. For each subscription, Subs may present these different valid access tokens so that Subs' identities are further protected from Brokers.

`Publish`:
Using the counterparts of the secret values used to blind subscriptions, Pubs blind the notifications and publish them to some Brokers. A blinded notification has a set of blinded AVPs and an encrypted payload message. These notifications are blinded in such a way that Brokers do not learn

---

[2]Note that our approach can easily be extended to subscriptions having multiple attributes.
[3]The additive inverse of a number $v \in \mathbb{Z}_m$ can be represented by the number $m - v$.

[4]Instead of Pub, a trusted third party may be utilized to blind subscriptions in order to reduce the load on Pub.
[5]We use the terms `Match` and `Filter` interchangeably.

actual values in the messages, but can perform Match and Cover protocols based on the subscriptions. Further, no two notifications for the same content are distinguishable by Brokers.

Match:
For each notification from Pubs, Brokers compare it with Subs' subscriptions. If there is a match, that is, the subscription satisfies the notification, Brokers forward the notification to the correct Subs. The outcome of the Match protocol allows Brokers to learn neither the notification nor the publication values. It also prevents Brokers from learning the distribution of the values.

Cover:
For each subscription received from Subs, Brokers check if *covering* relationship holds with the existing subscriptions. A subscription S_1 covers another subscription S_2 if all notifications that match S_2 also match S_1. Finding covering relationships among subscriptions allows to reduce the size of the subscription tables maintained by each Broker, and hence improves the efficiency of matching. Like the Match protocol, the outcome of the Cover protocol does not allow the Brokers to learn the subscription values nor their distribution.

2.2 Trust model

In the system design, we consider threats and assumptions from the point of view of Pubs and Subs with respect to third-party Brokers. We assume that Brokers are honest but curious; they perform PS protocols correctly, but curious to know what Pubs publish and Subs consume. In other words, they are trusted for these PS protocols but not for the content in the notifications and subscriptions nor for the privacy of Subs if they make one or more subscription requests. Further, Brokers may collude. Pubs are trusted to maintain the privacy of Subs. However, our approach can be easily modified to relax this trust assumption. Pubs are also trusted to correctly perform PS protocols and not to collude with any other parties.

3. BACKGROUND

Some of the mathematical notions and the cryptographic building blocks which inspired our approach are described below.

3.1 Pedersen commitment

A cryptographic "commitment" is a piece of information that allows one to commit to a value while keeping it hidden, and preserving the ability to reveal the value at a later time. The *Pedersen commitment* [20] is an unconditionally hiding and computationally binding commitment scheme which is based on the intractability of the discrete logarithm problem.

Pedersen Commitment

Setup A trusted third party T chooses a multiplicatively written finite cyclic group G of large prime order $\mathfrak{p}$ so that the computational Diffie-Hellman problem is hard in G.[6] T chooses two generators g and h of G such that it is hard to find the discrete logarithm of h with respect to g, i.e., an

integer x such that $h = g^x$. It is not required that T know the secret number x. T publishes $(G, \mathfrak{p}, g, h)$ as the system parameters.

Commit The domain of committed values is the finite field $\mathbb{F}_{\mathfrak{p}}$ of $\mathfrak{p}$ elements, which can be represented as the set of integers $\mathbb{F}_{\mathfrak{p}} = \{0, 1, \ldots, \mathfrak{p} - 1\}$. For a party U to commit a value $\alpha \in \mathbb{F}_{\mathfrak{p}}$, U chooses $\beta \in \mathbb{F}_{\mathfrak{p}}$ at random, and computes the commitment $c = g^\alpha h^\beta \in G$.

Open U shows the values α and β to open a commitment c. The verifier checks whether $c = g^\alpha h^\beta$.

3.2 Paillier homomorphic cryptosystem

The *Paillier homomorphic cryptosystem* is a public key cryptosystem by Paillier [19] based on the "Composite Residuosity assumption (CRA)." The Paillier cryptosystem is homomorphic in that, by using public key, the encryption of the sum $m_1 + m_2$ of two messages m_1 and m_2 can be computed from the encryption of m_1 and m_2. Our approach and protocols are inspired by how the Paillier cryptosystem works. Hence, we provide some internal details of the cryptosystem below so that readers can follow the rest of the paper.

Key generation
Set $n = pq$, where p and q are two large prime numbers. Set $\lambda = \text{lcm}(p - 1, q - 1)$, i.e., the least common multiple of $p - 1$ and $q - 1$. Randomly select a base $g \in \mathbb{Z}/(n^2)^\times$ such that the order of g_p is a multiple of n. Such a g_p can be efficiently found by randomly choosing $g_p \in \mathbb{Z}/(n^2)^\times$, then verifying that

$$\gcd(L(g_p^\lambda \pmod{n^2}), n)) = 1, \text{ where } L(u) = (u - 1)/n \tag{1}$$

for $u \in S_n = \{u < n^2 | u = 1 \pmod{n}\}$. In this case, set $\mu = \left(L(g_p^\lambda \pmod{n^2})\right)^{-1} \pmod{n}$. The public encryption key is a pair (n, g_p). The private decryption key is (λ, μ), or equivalently (p, q, μ).

Encryption $E(m, r)$
Given plaintext $m \in \{0, 1, \ldots, n - 1\}$, select a random $r \in \{1, 2, \ldots, n-1\}$, and encrypt m as $E(m, r) = g_p^m \cdot r^n \pmod{n^2}$. When the value of r is not important to the context, we sometimes simply write a short-hand $E(m)$ instead of $E(m, r)$ for the Paillier ciphertext of m.

Decryption $D(c)$
Given ciphertext $c \in \mathbb{Z}/(n^2)^\times$, decrypt c as

$$D(c) = L(c^\lambda \pmod{n^2}) \cdot \mu \pmod{n}. \tag{2}$$

More specifically, the homomorphic properties of Paillier cryptosystem are:

$$D(E(m_1, r_1)E(m_2, r_2) \pmod{n^2}) = m_1 + m_2 \pmod{n},$$

$$D(g^{m_2} E(m_1, r_1) \pmod{n^2}) = m_1 + m_2 \pmod{n},$$

$$D(E(m_1, r_1)^k \pmod{n^2}) = km_1 \pmod{n}.$$

Also note that the Paillier cryptosystem described above is semantically secure against chosen-plaintext attacks (IND-CPA).

In the construction of our CBPS system, the Paillier homomorphic cryptosystem is used in a way that public and private keys are judiciously distributed among Pubs, Subs, and Brokers such that the confidentiality and privacy are assured based on homomorphic encryption. A detailed description of the construction is presented in Section 4.

---

[6] For a multiplicatively written cyclic group G of order q, with a generator $g \in G$, the *Computational Diffie-Hellman problem (CDH)* is the following problem: Given g^a and g^b for randomly-chosen secret $a, b \in \{0, \ldots, q - 1\}$, compute g^{ab}.

4. PROPOSED SCHEME

In this section, we provide a detailed description of the privacy preserving CBPS system we propose. As introduced in Section 2, the system consists of 6 protocols: 1) `Initialize`, 2) `Register`, 3) `Subscribe`, 4) `Publish`, 5) `Match`, and 6) `Cover`.

4.1 Initialize

A trusted party, which could be one of the Pubs, runs a Pedersen commitment setup algorithm [20] to generate system wide parameters $(G, \mathfrak{p}, g, h)$. These parameters have the same meaning and purpose as mentioned in Section 3. The same party also runs a key generation algorithm similar to Paillier [19] to generate the parameters $(n, p, q, g_p, \lambda, \mu)$. Only Pubs know the parameters (p, q, λ). The parameters (n, g_p, μ) are public. Note that unlike in Paillier, μ is public in our scheme. The system parameter l is the upper bound on the number of bits required to represent any data values published, and we refer to it as *domain size*. For example, if an attribute can take values from 0 up to 500 $(< 2^9)$, l should be at least 9 bits long. For reasons that will soon become clear in this section we choose l such that $2^{2l} \ll n$.[7] In addition to these parameters, each Pub has a key pair (K_{pub}, K_{pri}) where K_{pri} is the private key used to sign access tokens of Subs and K_{pub} is the public key used by Brokers to verify authenticity and integrity of them. Each Pub also has a symmetric key K, which it shares only with Subs and is used to encrypt the payload messages. Each Pub computes two pairs of secret values (e_m, d_m) and (e_c, d_c) such that $e_m + d_m \equiv 0 \pmod{\phi(n^2)}$, and $e_c + d_c \equiv 0 \pmod{\phi(n^2)}$, where $\phi(\cdot)$ is Euler's totient function and $e_m \neq e_c$. Note that we have $g^{e_m} g^{d_m} \equiv g^{e_c} g^{d_c} \equiv 1 \pmod{n^2}$. Pub uses e_m to blind Paillier encrypted notifications and d_m, d_c, e_c to blind Paillier encrypted subscriptions.[8] Let s be the largest number $\in \mathbb{Z}$ such that $2^s < n$ and $u \in \mathbb{Z}$ such that $l < u < s - 1$. Finally, each Pub chooses two secret random values $r_m, r_c \in \mathbb{Z}$ such that $1 < r_m, r_c < 2^{u-l}$ and $r_m \neq r_c$. These values are used to prevent Brokers from learning the distribution of the difference of the values that are being matched. In summary, $(G, \mathfrak{p}, g, h, n, g_p, \mu, K_{pub})$ are the public parameters that all the parties know, $(p, q, \lambda, K_{pri}, r_m, r_c, (e_m, d_m), (e_c, d_c))$ are private parameters of Pubs. Note that in a practical implementation, most of these parameters can be auto-generated by a computer program which usually only requires Pub to pre-determine l depending on the domain of the content of notifications.

4.2 Register

As shown in Figure 2, each Sub registers itself with Pub by presenting an id (identity), a pseudonym uniquely identifying Sub. In a real-world system, registration may involve Subs presenting other credentials and/or making payment. Upon successful registration, Pub sends K, the symmetric

key, to Sub.[9] During this protocol, each Sub also obtains its initial access token, a Pedersen commitment signed by Pub.

An access token allows Sub to authenticate itself to Broker from which it intends to request notifications as well as to create additional access tokens in consultation with Pub. To create the first access token, Sub encodes its id as an element $\langle id \rangle \in \mathbb{F}_{\mathfrak{p}}$, chooses a random $a \in \mathbb{F}_{\mathfrak{p}}$, and sends the commitment $com(\langle id \rangle) = g^{\langle id \rangle} h^a$ and the values $(\langle id \rangle, a)$. The Pub signs $com(\langle id \rangle)$ and sends the digital signature $K_{pri}(com(\langle id \rangle))$ back to the Sub.

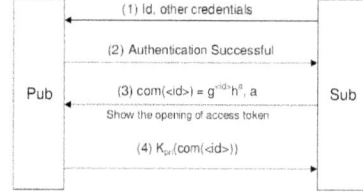

Figure 2: Sub registering with Pub

4.3 Subscribe

During this protocol, Subs inform their interests to Brokers as subscriptions. Before subscribing to messages, as Figure 3 illustrates, Subs must authenticate themselves to Brokers. Sub gives a zero-knowledge proof of knowledge (ZKPK) of the ability to open the commitment $com(\langle id \rangle)$ signed by Pub:

$$ZKPK\{(\langle id \rangle, a) : com(\langle id \rangle) = g^{\langle id \rangle} h^a\}$$

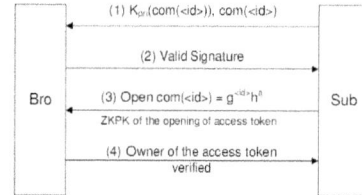

Figure 3: Sub authenticating itself to Broker

Notice that the ZKPK of the commitment opening does not reveal the identity of Sub. Further, Sub may use different access tokens by having different random a values for different subscriptions to prevent Brokers from linking its subscriptions to one access token [10] [11].

---

[7] We use notation $a \ll b$ to denote that "a is sufficiently smaller than b."

[8] The "blind" operation will be introduced in Section 4.3.

[9] We use a symmetric encryption algorithm in the presentation. In practice, Pubs and Subs can choose any encryption scheme, symmetric or not, to hide the payload messages in transmission. In our extended version, we use a fine-grained encryption technique based on broadcast group key management in order to selectively and efficiently encrypt payload messages [22]. Attribute based encryption or proxy re-encryption, as mentioned in Section 6, could be a possible choice as well.

[10] One may use a randomized signature scheme on a committed value [7] to achieve the same objective at the expense of additional computation cost.

[11] Our scheme only provides application level privacy, but

If the ZKPK is successful, Sub may submit one or more subscriptions. Recall that subscriptions are blinded by Pub before sending to Broker. The subscription "blinding" functions, $bval_m$, $bval_{c_1}$, $bval_{c_2}$ are defined as follows:
Let v be the original subscription.

$$E(v) = g_p^v \cdot r_1^n \quad (\text{mod } n^2)$$

$$bval_m(E(-v)) = g^{d_m} \cdot (E(-v))^{r_m \lambda} \quad (\text{mod } n^2) \qquad (3)$$

$$bval_{c_1}(E(-v)) = g^{d_c} \cdot (E(-v))^{r_c \lambda} \quad (\text{mod } n^2) \qquad (4)$$

$$bval_{c_2}(E(v)) = g^{e_c} \cdot (E(v))^{r_c \lambda} \cdot (E(r))^{\lambda} \quad (\text{mod } n^2) \quad (5)$$

where $d_m, e_m, r_m, d_c, e_c, r_c$ are generated during Initialize, r in Formula 5 is a random number such that $r \leq min\{r_c, 2^{(s-1-u)}\}$.

Sub sends $E(v)$ and $E(-v)$, where v is the original subscription for the attribute $attr$, to Pub. Pub sends back the blinded subscription to Sub and Sub sends the tuple $\langle attr, bval_{c_1}(E(-v)), bval_{c_2}(E(v)), bval_m(E(-v)), op \rangle$ to Broker. The first two blinded values in the subscription are used by Broker for Cover protocol and the third one for Match protocol. Note that Sub performs these encryptions to reduced the load on Pubs. It should also be noted that equality filters in our protocols are treated as range filters preventing Brokers from distinguishing equality filters from range filters. For example, in order to subscribe for $v = 5$, Sub subscriber for a range filter where $v \leq 5$ and $v > 4$. Except for range filters, each subscription from the same Sub are treated as disjunctive conditions.

EXAMPLE 2. *Sub wants to get all the notifications with bid price less than 22. The subscription has the format ("/quote/bid/price", 346213, 152311, 453280, <) where the second and third parameters are the blind values of 22 and -22, respectively, for Cover protocol to use, and the fourth is the blinded value of -22 for Match protocol to use.*

4.4 Publish

Using e_m, the counterpart of d_m which is used to blind subscriptions for Match protocol, and other private parameters, Pubs blind the notifications using the function $bval_n$ as defined below.
Let x be one value in the notification.

$$bval_n(x) = g^{e_m} \cdot (E(x))^{r_m \lambda} \cdot E(r)^{\lambda} \quad (\text{mod } n^2)$$
$$= g^{e_m} \cdot E((r_m x + r)\lambda) \quad (\text{mod } n^2),$$

where e_m and r_m are generated during Initialize, r is selected uniformly at random such that $r \leq min\{r_m, 2^{(s-1-u)}\}$.

Pubs publish the blinded notifications to Brokers. A notification has a set of blinded AVPs and an encrypted payload message. For an illustration purpose, let us assume these AVPs are numbered from 1 to t, where t is the number of attributes of the payload message M being considered. The blinded notification looks like $(\langle attr_1, bval_n(x_1) \rangle, \ldots, \langle attr_t, bval_n(x_t) \rangle)$, where $attr_i$ and x_i are the ith attribute name and value respectively.

___

not network level privacy. For example, it does not hide IP addresses. In order to provide network level privacy/anonymity, one needs to utilize other orthogonal techniques such as Tor [12]

Table 1: Matching Decision

diff	Decision
$< n/2$	$x \geq v$
$> n/2$	$x < v$

4.5 Match

For each notification from Pub, Broker compares it with Subs' subscriptions to make routing decisions. We explain the Match operation for one attribute in the message, but it can be naturally extended to perform on multiple attributes. If at least one of the attributes in the message matches, we say that the subscription matches the notification, and in this case Broker forwards the notification to the corresponding Subs. For range filters, the conjunction of two corresponding Match operations is taken.

Let the blinded values be $bval_n(x)$ and $bval_m(E(-v))$ that Broker has received from Pub and Sub, respectively, for an attribute $attr$ with subscription value being v and notification value being x. Broker computes the following value $diff$ and then makes the matching decision based on Table 1.

$$diff = L(bval_n(x) \cdot bval_m(E(-v))$$
$$(\text{mod } n^2)) \cdot \mu \quad (\text{mod } n),$$

,

where L, μ are public parameters derived from Paillier.

Before we show that the above computation gives a $diff$ equal to $r_m \cdot (x - v) + r$, we describe how Match protocol gives the correct matching decision while outputting a (controlled) random $diff$ value to Broker. Recall that in Initialize, the domain of the input values is set to $0 \sim 2^l$. Therefore, $0 \leq x, v \leq 2^l$. Notice that the difference of any two values x and v is either between $0 \sim 2^l$ if the difference is positive, or between $(n - 2^l) \sim n$ if the difference is negative. Also, notice that the range $2^l \sim (n - 2^l)$ is not utilized. In order to randomize the difference, we take advantage of this unused range and multiply the actual difference with a random secret value r_m and add another random value r both selected by Pub. The idea behind r_m and r are to first expand $0 \sim 2^l$ range to $0 \sim 2^u$ and $(n - 2^l) \sim n$ to $n - 2^s \sim n - n_m$, and then expand them to $0 \sim n/2$ and $n/2 \sim n$ respectively. Thus the difference is randomized, yet it allows Broker to make correct matching decisions without resulting in false positives or negatives.

During Match protocol, Broker does not learn the content under comparison. This is achieved due to the fact that without knowing λ, Broker cannot perform decryption freely, but is forced to engage into the protocol described below. Not knowing the values r_m and r, Broker does not learn the exact difference of the two values under comparison as well.

The following shows the correctness of $diff$. Let

$$y = bval_n(x) \cdot bval_m(E(-v)) \quad (\text{mod } n^2).$$

$$y = g^{e_m} \cdot (E((r_m x + r)\lambda) \cdot g^{d_m} \cdot (E(-v))^{r_m \lambda}$$
$$(\mathrm{mod}\ n^2)$$
$$= g^{e_m + d_m} \cdot \{E(r_m x + r)) \cdot E(-r_m v)\}^\lambda \quad (\mathrm{mod}\ n^2)$$
$$= (E(r_m(x - v) + r))^\lambda \quad (\mathrm{mod}\ n^2)$$
$$diff = L(y) \cdot \mu \quad (\mathrm{mod}\ n) = r_m(x - v) + r. \quad (6)$$

4.6 Cover

Subscriptions are categorized into groups based on the covering relationships so that Brokers can perform Match protocol efficiently. For each subscription received from Subs, Brokers check if covering relationship holds within the existing subscriptions. If it exists, they add the new subscription to the group with the covering subscription, otherwise a new group is created for the new subscription.

Notice that we have not used the blinded values $bval_{c_1}(E(-v))$ and $bval_{c_2}(E(v))$ in subscriptions yet. These two values are used in the Cover protocol. In what follows, we explain how the Cover protocol works.

Let S_1 and S_2 be two subscriptions for the same $attr$ and compatible op. Two op's are compatible if either both of them are of the same type. $bval_{c_1}(E(v_1))$ and $bval_{c_2}(E(-v_1))$ refer to the so far unused blinded values of v_1 and of its additive inverse, respectively, of the subscription S_1. The blinded values $bval_{c_1}(E(v_2))$ and $bval_{c_2}(E(-v_2))$ have similar interpretations.

Broker computes one of the following two values in order to decide the covering relationship.

$$diff_1 = L(bval_{c_2}(E(v_1)) \cdot bval_{c_1}(E(-v_2))$$
$$(\mathrm{mod}\ n^2)) \cdot \mu \quad (\mathrm{mod}\ n)$$
$$diff_2 = L(bval_{c_2}(E(v_2)) \cdot bval_{c_1}(E(-v_1))$$
$$(\mathrm{mod}\ n^2)) \cdot \mu \quad (\mathrm{mod}\ n) \quad (7)$$

$diff_1$ and $diff_2$ give results $r_c \cdot (v_1 - v_2) + r$ and $r_c \cdot (v_2 - v_1) + r'$ respectively, where r, r' are random numbers. Broker uses the same matching Table 1 that is used for making matching decision to make the covering decision. The covering decision for range filters is performed in a similar way, but we omit the details due to lack of space. Similar to Match, Brokers do not learn the actual subscription values.

4.7 The Distribution of Load

We now briefly explain the rationale behind the distribution of work load among Pubs, Subs and Brokers. If there are $O(N)$ notifications and $O(S)$ subscriptions, in the worst case, Broker needs to perform $O(NS)$ Match protocols. Thus, Brokers have to perform significantly more work compared to Pubs and Subs in a typical CBPS system. This is one of the key reasons why the performance of Brokers degrades as the number of notifications and/or subscriptions in the system increases. By optimizing for the frequent case, one can achieve a significant overall system improvement. We followed this well-known design principle to redistribute the load on Brokers partly to Pubs and Subs. Notice that there are no exponentiation operations in both Match and Cover protocols. Hence, these protocols can be performed very efficiently. This is made possible at the cost of extra work at Pubs and Subs. Since the protocols at Pubs and Subs are executed less frequently compared to those at Brokers, our

distribution leads to a better overall system performance. The experimental results show that the protocols at Brokers are very efficient and those at Pubs and Subs also run fast.

5. EXPERIMENTAL RESULTS

In this section, we present experimental results for various operations and the two main protocols, Match and Cover, in our system as well as our privacy preserving CBPS (PP-CBPS) system itself which extends an enhanced SIENA system by implementing privacy preserving matching and covering using our protocols. For the protocol experiments, we have built a prototype system in Java that incorporates our techniques for privacy preserving Match and Cover protocols as described in Section 4.

The experiments are performed on an Intel® Core™ 2 Duo CPU T9300 2.50GHz machine running GNU/Linux kernel version 2.6.27 with 4 Gbytes memory. We utilize only one processor for computation. The code is built with Java version 1.6.0. along with Bouncy Castle lightweight APIs [6] for most cryptographic operations including the symmetric-key encryption. The Paillier cryptosystem is implemented as in the paper [19], except that we modified the algorithms to fit our scheme. We first look at the experiments mainly on the two important protocols, Match and Cover, and then describe the system experiments performed on PP-CBPS system.

5.1 Protocol experiments

In our experiments we vary values of n in Paillier cryptosystem and the domain size l, and fix the parameters for Pedersen commitment generation, digital signature generation/verification, zero-knowledge proof of knowledge protocol, and symmetric key encryption/decryption. In all our experiments we only measure computational cost, and assume the communication cost to be negligible. All data obtained by our experiments correspond to the average time taken over 1000 executions of the protocols with varying values for the bit length of n in the Paillier cryptosystem and the domain size l. Appendix B shows the computation time for the general operations.

In the experiment shown in Figure 4, we vary the bit length of n in the Paillier cryptosystem. Figure 4 shows the time to generate blinded subscriptions and notifications whose values are less than 2^l where l, the domain size, is fixed at 100, a reasonably large value. The time to generate blinded values increases as the bit length of n increases, but even for large bit lengths, it takes only a few milliseconds. The time required to blind subscription is split into two tasks with the Sub performing the encryption and the Pub performing the blinding, but to blind notifications, the Pub performs both operations as one task. We remark that the overall computational cost can be reduced by employing well-known caching techniques.

We measure in our experiment the performance impact on blinding when l, the domain size, is changed. We fix n to be of length 1024 bits and measure the time to blind subscriptions and notifications for $l = 10, 20, \cdots, 100$. As shown in Figure 5, the domain size does not significantly affect the performance of the blinding operations. Further, as indicated by both Figure 4 and Figure 5, the time for either component of the subscription blinding is less than that for notification blinding. Since for each subscription, the overhead at the Pub is less compared to the time required to

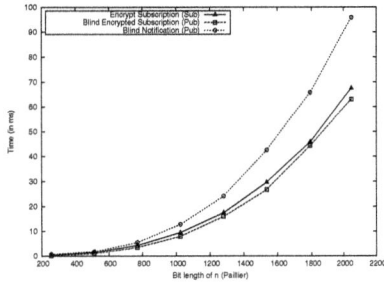

Figure 4: Time to blind subscriptions and notifications for different bit lengths of n

blind a notification, our decision to blind part of the subscription at the Pub is comparable to blinding additional notifications.

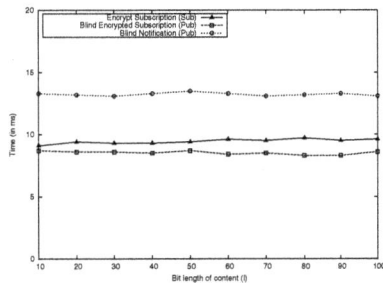

Figure 5: Time to blind subscriptions and notifications for different l

In a CBPS, Match is the most executed protocol. Hence, it should be very efficient so as not to overload Brokers. For each Subscribe protocol, Brokers may need to invoke the Cover protocol and, therefore, we want to have a very efficient Cover protocol as well. In the following two experiments, we observe the time to perform these protocols.

Figure 6 shows the execution time of Match and Cover protocols as the bit length of n in the Paillier cryptosystem is changed while the domain size l is fixed at 100 bits. The time for both protocols increases approximately linearly with the bit length of n. Note that they take only a fraction of a millisecond (less than 100 microseconds) even for large bit lengths of n. This indicates that our Match and Cover protocols are very efficient for large bit lengths of n.

Figure 7 shows the time to execute Match and Cover protocols as the domain size l is changed while the bit length of n is fixed at 1024. Similar to the blind computations, computational times remain largely unchanged for different l values.

An observation made through all our protocol experiments is that the domain size l does not significantly affect the computational time of the key protocols Publish, Subscribe, Match and Cover, but the bit length n of the Paillier cryptosystem does. However, even for large bit lengths of n, our protocols take only a few microseconds or milliseconds and thus they are very efficient and practical.

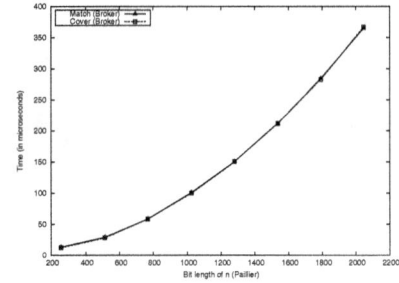

Figure 6: Time to perform match and cover for different bit lengths of n

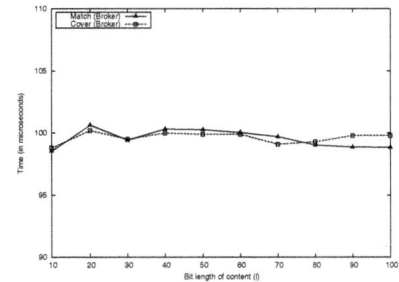

Figure 7: Time to perform match and cover for different l

5.2 System experiments

In this section, we provide the experiments performed on our PP-CBPS system. PP-CBPS is constructed by a freely available popular wide-area event notification implementation SIENA. SIENA provides a pluggable-architecture that allows to incorporate our protocols to provide Match and Cover operations. All the testing data are generated uniformly at random. In all the experiments, the average time to match a notification with a subscription is measured where 1000 notifications are generated each time and the system groups the subscriptions according to the covering relationships at the time of subscription. It should be noted that the matching time does not include the time to create notifications and subscriptions which is measured in our protocol experiments in Section 5.1.

Figure 8 shows the time to perform equality filtering in PP-CBPS (secure matching) and SIENA (plain matching) for different number of subscriptions in the system. Notifications and subscriptions are drown uniformly from 10 bit random integers. We use a small domain size to demonstrate the effect of covering on the overall system with and without security. As can be seen, PP-CBPS performs the matching within 10x of that of SIENA and is still quite efficient to match thousands of subscriptions within 10 ms. In both cases, the increase in matching time with the number of subscriptions is sub-linear since the covering operation groups the similar subscriptions together, reducing the number of Match protocols needs to be executed.

Figure 9 shows the time to perform equality filtering in PP-CBPS for two different domain sizes, 10 and 25 bits, of notifications and subscriptions for different number of subscriptions in the system. It should be noted that SIENA

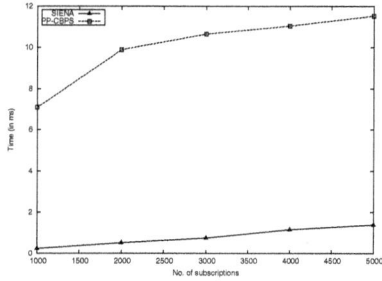

Figure 8: Equality filtering time

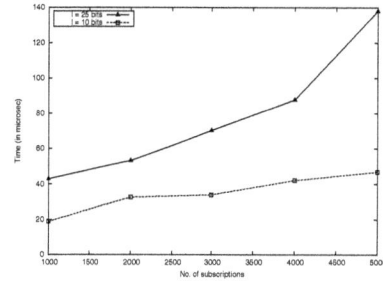

Figure 10: Inequality filtering time for different domain sizes

currently does not support domain sizes larger than 27 bits, but our protocols can work under much larger domains. As can be seen, the matching is more efficient with smaller domains. This is due to the fact that smaller domains create more covering relationships than larger domains and, hence, less matching protocols need to be executed to match a notification against all the subscriptions. Further, observe that the rate of increase of the overall matching cost decreases as the number of subscriptions increases. This, again, is due to the covering protocol.

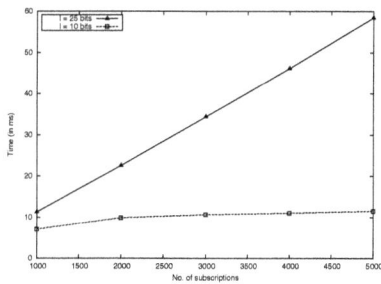

Figure 9: Equality filtering time for different domain sizes

Figure 10 shows the time to perform inequality filtering in PP-CBPS for two different domain sizes, 10 and 25 bits, of notifications and subscriptions for different number of subscriptions in the system. We observe results similar to that of equality filtering in Figure 9. However, notice that the inequality filtering is much more efficient than equality filtering for the same domain size. This is due to the fact that inequality subscriptions create more covering relationships than equality subscriptions requiring much less matching operations.

Even though, according to the protocol experiments in Section 5.1, the time to perform individual `Match` or `Cover` operations remains largely constant for different domain sizes, the overall system performs better with smaller domain sizes. As the domain size is reduced, there is a higher probability of having subscriptions satisfying covering relationships. Hence, the number of matching operations need to be performed reduces considerably leading to a better performance.

6. RELATED WORK

In addition to the research work discussed in Section 1, our work is related to research in proxy re-encryption systems [16, 2], searchable encryption [23, 4, 5], secure multiparty computation [14, 11] and private information retrieval [10, 15].

Proxy re-encryption system.

In a proxy re-encryption system one party A delegates its decryption rights to another party B via a third party called a "proxy." More specifically, the proxy transforms a ciphertext computed under party A's public key into a different ciphertext which can be decrypted by party B with B's private key. In such a system neither the proxy nor party B alone can obtain the plaintext. A direct application of the proxy re-encryption system does not solve the problem of CBPS: with the proxy as the Broker, it does not by default have the capability of selectively making content-based routing decisions. However, it might still be possible to use proxy re-encryption as a building block in the construction of a CBPS system for data confidentiality.

Searchable encryption.

Search in encrypted data is a privacy-preserving technique used in the *outsourced storage model* where a user's data are stored on a third-party server and encrypted using the user's public key. The user can use a query in the form of an encrypted token to retrieve relevant data from the server, whereas the server does not learn any more information about the query other than whether the returned data matches the search criteria. There have been efforts to support simple equality queries [23, 4] and more recently complex ones involving conjunctions and disjunctions of range queries [5]. These approaches cannot be applied directly to the CBPS model.

Secure Multiparty Computation (SMC).

SMC allows a set of participants to compute the value of a public function using their private values as input, but without revealing their individual private values to other participants. The problem was initially introduced by Yao. Since then improvements have been proposed to the initial problem [14, 11]. SMC solutions rely on some form of zero-knowledge proof of knowledge (ZKPK) or oblivious transfer protocols which are in general interactive. Interactive protocols are not suitable for the CBPS model. Hence SMC solutions do not work for the CBPS model. Further, these solutions usually have a higher computational and/or communication cost which may not be acceptable for a CBPS system.

Private Information Retrieval (PIR).

A PIR scheme allows a client to retrieve an item from a database server without revealing which item is retrieved. Approaches of PIR assume either the server is computationally bounded, where the problem reduces to oblivious transfer, or there are multiple non-cooperating servers each having the same copy. Having only two communication parties, PIR schemes are not directly applicable to the Pub-Sub-Broker architecture of the CBPS model. Moreover, similar to SMC solutions, PIR schemes in general have a higher communication complexity which may not be acceptable for a CBPS system.

7. CONCLUSIONS AND FUTURE WORK

We have presented an efficient cryptography-based approach to preserve subscription privacy and publication confidentiality in a CBPS system in which third-party Brokers perform Match and Cover protocols to make routing decisions for subscriptions without learning the actual content of the notifications published by Pubs and the subscriptions made by Subs. The experimental results on both the protocols and the system, in Section 5 show that our techniques are practical and efficient. We believe that our cryptographic techniques have a broader application of performing privacy-preserving third-party comparisons.

We are currently integrating our privacy preserving protocols to Apahce ActiveMQ [1], a popular open source Java message broker middleware.

Acknowledgments

The work reported in this paper has been partially supported by the MURI award FA9550-08-1-0265 from the Air Force Office of Scientific Research.

8. REFERENCES

[1] Apache. ActiveMQ. http://activemq.apache.org/.
[2] G. Ateniese, K. Benson, and S. Hohenberger. Key-private proxy re-encryption. In *RSA '09*, pages 279–294, Berlin, Heidelberg, 2009. Springer-Verlag.
[3] E. Bertino, B. Carminati, E. Ferrari, B. Thuraisingham, and A. Gupta. Selective and authentic third-party distribution of XML documents. *IEEE TKDE*, 16(10):1263–1278, Oct. 2004.
[4] D. Boneh, G. Crescenzo, R. Ostrovsky, and G. Persiano. Public-key encryption with keyword search. In *EUROCRYPT '04*, 2004.
[5] D. Boneh and B. Waters. Conjunctive, subset, and range queries on encrypted data. *Theory of Cryptography*, pages 535–554, May 2007.
[6] Bouncycastle. Bouncy Castle Crypto APIs. http://www.bouncycastle.org/.
[7] J. Camenisch and A. Lysyanskaya. Signature schemes and anonymous credentials from bilinear maps. In *CRYPTO '04*, pages 56–72. Springer-Verlag, 2004.
[8] A. Carzaniga, D. S. Rosenblum, and A. L. Wolf. Design and evaluation of a wide-area event notification service. *ACM TCS*, 19(3):332–383, 2001.
[9] S. Choi, G. Ghinita, and E. Bertino. A privacy-enhancing content-based publish/subscribe system using scalar product preserving transformations. In *DEXA '10*, 2010.
[10] B. Chor, O. Goldreich, E. Kushilevitz, and M. Sudan. Private information retrieval. In *FOCS '95*, pages 41–50, Oct 1995.
[11] I. Damgård, M. Geisler, and M. Kroigard. Homomorphic encryption and secure comparison. *Int. J. on App. Crypto.*, 1(1):22–31, 2008.
[12] R. Dingledine, N. Mathewson, and P. Syverson. Tor: The second-generation onion router. In *Usenix Sec. '04*, 2004.
[13] P. Eugster, P. Felber, R. Guerraoui, and A. Kermarrec. The many faces of publish/subscribe. *ACM Comp. Survey*, 35(2):114–131, 2003.
[14] M. J. Freedman, K. Nissim, and B. Pinkas. Efficient private matching and set intersection. In *EUROCRYPT '04*, 2004.
[15] E. Kushilevitz and R. Ostrovsky. Replication is NOT needed: Single database, computationally-private information retrieval. In *FOCS '97*, pages 364–373, 1997.
[16] T. Matsuo. Proxy re-encryption systems for identity-based encryption. In *PAIRING '07*, pages 247–267, 2007.
[17] K. Minami, A. J. Lee, M. Winslett, and N. Borisov. Secure aggregation in a publish-subscribe system. In *WPES '08*, pages 95–104, New York, NY, USA, 2008. ACM.
[18] M. Nabeel and E. Bertino. Secure delta-publishing of XML content. In *ICDE '08*, pages 1361–1363, April 2008.
[19] P. Paillier. Public-key cryptosystems based on composite degree residuosity classes. In *EUROCRYPT '99*, pages 223–238, 1999.
[20] T. Pedersen. Non-interactive and information-theoretic secure verifiable secret sharing. In *CRYPTO '92*, pages 129–140, London, UK, 1992. Springer-Verlag.
[21] C. Raiciu and D. S. Rosenblum. Enabling confidentiality in content-based publish/subscribe infrastructures. In *SECURECOMM '06*, pages 1–11, 28 2006-Sept. 1 2006.
[22] N. Shang, M. Nabeel, F. Paci, and E. Bertino. A privacy-preserving approach to policy-based content dissemination. In *ICDE '10*, 2010.
[23] D. X. Song, D. Wagner, and A. Perrig. Practical techniques for searches on encrypted data. In *SP '00*, page 44, Washington, DC, USA, 2000. IEEE Computer Society.
[24] M. Srivatsa and L. Liu. Securing publish-subscribe overlay services with eventguard. In *CCS '05*, pages 289–298, New York, NY, USA, 2005. ACM.
[25] M. Srivatsa and L. Liu. Secure event dissemination in publish-subscribe networks. In *ICDCS '07*, page 22, Washington, DC, USA, 2007. IEEE Computer Society.
[26] C. W., A. Carzaniga, D. Evans, and A. Wolf. Security issues and requirements for internet-scale publish-subscribe systems. In *Proceedings of the 35th Annual Hawaii International Conference on System Sciences*, pages 3940–3947, Jan. 2002.

APPENDIX

A. SECURITY ANALYSIS

In this section, we briefly analyze the security of the proposed CBPS system. The proposed system is built upon provably secure cryptographic primitives: digital signatures, Pedersen commitment, Schnorr's zero-knowledge proof protocol, and a modified Paillier homomorphic encryption.

A.1 Privacy-preserving subscription

The subscription protocol is privacy preserving in that it supports anonymous credential authentication of the Subs to Brokers. When a Sub subscribes to a Broker, it shows an access token containing a Pedersen commitment of Sub's identity attribute value $\langle id \rangle$ together with a digital signature from a Pub. The Broker verifies the digital signature using the Pub's public key K_{pub} to make sure that the Pedersen commitment is a valid one approved by the Pub. Due to the unconditional hiding property of the Pedersen commitment scheme, the Broker learns nothing about the value $\langle id \rangle$ from $com(\langle id \rangle) = g^{\langle id \rangle} h^a$. By performing a zero-knowledge proof of knowledge protocol, the Sub can convince the Broker that the Sub knows the values $\langle id \rangle$ and a, thus has the ability to open the commitment, but prevents the Broker from learning the actual values. Without knowing the values $\langle id \rangle$ and a, anyone without valid ownership to the access token cannot open the commitment. This provides a mechanism to defend identity theft. In such a way, the combined use of digital signatures and the ZKPK technique realizes a privacy-preserving authentication.

A.2 Privacy-preserving matching and covering

Match and Cover protocols are privacy preserving in that while Brokers are performing matching and covering operations correctly, they do not learn the actual values in Subs' subscriptions or Pubs' notifications.

To see that Match preserves Pub's and Sub's privacy, we look at the underlying scheme. When Sub subscribes, Broker gets a subscription specified with blinded values $bval_{c_1}(E(v))$, $bval_{c_2}(E(-v))$, and $bval_m(E(-v))$ from which the actual value v cannot be recovered knowing only the public parameters of Paillier and μ [19]. Note that Broker even may not be able to feed these blinded values into formula (1) in an attempt to recover the unblinded values, because in general the blinded values are not in the domain S_n of function $L(\cdot)$ (see Section 3.2). In this way the Broker is forced to follow the Match protocol as specified, obtain $r_m \cdot (x - v) + r$, and make matching decisions using Table 1.

Similarly, in Cover protocol, although Broker is able to perform operation as in formula (7) to obtain $r_c \cdot (v_1 - v_2) + r$ or $r_c \cdot (v_2 - v_1) + r'$, then use Table 1 to make covering decisions, it cannot perform decryption to get either v_1 or v_2 from the blinded values. In this way, Subs' subscription privacy is protected.

Note that since r and r' are selected uniformly at random for each execution of $bval_n$, $bval_{c_1}$ and $bval_{c_2}$ functions, the *diff* values obtained from Cover and Match do not reveal the actual distribution. Even for multiple subscriptions and notifications with the same values, Broker gets different *diff* values due to the randomization. Having said that, however, it should be noted that Match and Cover inherently leaks certain information about subscriptions and notifications even with such randomization. It is hard, if not impossible, to prevent such leakages.

B. STANDARD PROTOCOL EXPERIMENTS

We compare our protocol results with the well established computations to show that our approach is efficient and practical.

Table 2: Average computation time for general operations

Computation	Time (in ms)
Create access token (Sub)	4.21
Open access token (Pub)	4.17
Sign access token (Pub)	4.10
Verify token signature (Broker)	0.36
ZKP of access token (Sub)	4.18
ZKP of access token (Broker)	6.31
Encrypt payload message (Pub)	34.56
Decrypt payload message (Sub)	0.36

Table 2 shows the average running time for various operations for which we kept the system parameters constant. Access token creation, opening, signing are performed during Register protocol and based on Pedersen commitment scheme. Pub signs the access token using SHA-1 and RSA with 1024-bit long private key K_{pri}. Verification of the signature on the access token using the public key K_{pub}, and the ownership proof of the access token via the ZKPK are performed during Subscribe protocol. Zero-Knowledge Proof (ZKP) protocols are generally considered time consuming, but in our approach ZKP computation is comparable to other operations in the system, in that it takes merely a few milliseconds. For the experiments, we set the payload size to 4 Kbytes and used AES-128 as the symmetric key algorithm. These performance results demonstrate that the constructs we use and the computations are very efficient.

Fine-Grained Access Control of Personal Data

Ting Wang
IBM Research
tingwang@us.ibm.com

Mudhakar Srivatsa
IBM Research
msrivats@us.ibm.com

Ling Liu
Georgia Tech
lingliu@cc.gatech.edu

ABSTRACT

The immensity and variety of personal information (e.g., profile, photo, and microblog) on social sites require access control policies tailored to individuals' privacy needs. Today such policies are still mainly specified *manually* by ordinary users, which is usually coarse-grained, tedious, and error-prone. This paper presents the design, implementation, and evaluation of an *automated* access control policy specification tool, XACCESS, that helps non-expert users effectively specify who should have access to which part of their data. A series of key features distinguish XACCESS from prior work: 1) it adopts a role-based access control model (instead of the conventional rule-based paradigm) to capture the implicit privacy/interest preference of social site users; 2) it employs a novel hybrid mining method to extract a set of semantically interpretable, functional "social roles", from both static network structures and dynamic historical activities; 3) based on the identified social roles, confidentiality setting of personal data, and (optional and possibly inconsistent) predefined user-permission assignments, it recommends a set of high-quality privacy settings; 4) it allows user feedback in every phase of the process to further improve the quality of the suggested privacy policies. A comprehensive experimental evaluation is conducted over real social network and user study data to validate the efficacy of XACCESS.

Categories and Subject Descriptors

K6.5 [**Computing Milieux**]: Management of Computing and Information Systems—*Security and Protection*

General Terms

Security, Management

Keywords

Social role, Social Network, Access control

1. INTRODUCTION

This is the era of social networking! Online social networks (OSNs) have become a de facto portal for hundreds of millions of Internet users. For example, FACEBOOK, one representative social network provider, claims that it enjoys over 350 million active users [2]. With the help of these social sites, users share information with their friends, participate in online activities, and get to know more new friends. The unprecedented immensity and diversity of personal information over social networks (e.g., it is estimated that over 3.5 billion pieces of content, including web links, news stories, blog posts, notes, and photo albums, are shared by FACEBOOK users each week), however, is far beyond the development of privacy control enforcement tools. Improper privacy control over personal information tends to lead to severe consequences [4, 1].

So far, users still mainly rely on social network sites to provide privacy control to restrict data sharing with friends, corporate affiliates, or application developers. Nevertheless, the available controls are rather limited. For example, FACEBOOK launched the platform for users to personalize their privacy setting, via manually specifying who (classified into classes such as *public, friends*}) should have access to which parts of their information. Clearly the rigid classification of relevant users into several groups is fairly coarse-grained. For example, for two users belonging to the same category, one may desire to assign different permissions. More flexible control could only be achieved through a manual *custom* setting, such as the "circle" concept in GOOGLE PLUS[1], which leads to the next problem; a full manual setting is usually tedious and error-prone. Consider that right now an average user has 130 friends on FACEBOOK, and the number of friends of friends is typically quadratic. With such a large pool of relevant users, it becomes a non-trivial task for ordinary users to effectively specify their privacy policies.

1.1 State of the Art

In both the database and security communities, intensive research efforts have been dedicated to protecting individuals' privacy in social network data publishing, a problem orthogonal to the scope of this work. In [5, 17, 25], it was shown to be possible to re-identify individuals in the published network data even if explicit identification information, e.g., name, affiliation, and address, has been masked. In [26, 7, 13, 15], countermeasures have been proposed against the re-identification attacks while the adversary possesses various background knowledge regarding the original network, e.g., degree, neighborhood structure, or subgraph in general.

Some initiative research works have recently recognized the importance of enforcing user-specified privacy control over personal information on online social networks. For example, xBOOK [22] attempts to enforce control of what third-party applications can do with the information they receive from social network sites, using an information flow model. PERSONA [6] hides user data

---

[1] https//plus.google.com

with attribute-based encryption (ABE) schemes, allowing users to apply fine-grained, customized policies over who may view their data. Nevertheless, all these works focus on how to enforce user-specified control, with the assumption that the privacy policies are completely and clearly specified.

In a recent work [10], Fang and LeFevre proposed PRIVACY WIZARDS, a *semi-automated* privacy setting recommendation tool that extracts a set of permission assignment rules, based on an active learning paradigm, *uncertainty sampling*. This *rule-based* model, however, suffers from two major drawbacks. First, it implicitly relies on a "lazy user" assumption (users are fully capable of, yet not willing to manually specify the policies), and requires accurate user input on a set of highly ambiguous assignments that, however, are typically the most difficult spots for non-expert users. Second, the discovered permission assignment rules may lack semantic interpretation, and are thus difficult to understand by social site users, which severely limits its applicability.

1.2 Challenges and Contributions

This work presents the design, implementation, and evaluation of an access-control policy specification tool, XACCESS, for social networking platform. To our best knowledge, this is the first *automated* framework that helps ordinary social network users effectively specify customized privacy polices for their personal data. For a social site user, XACCESS suggests a set of high-quality permission assignments for all relevant users. The suggested assignments are semantically meaningful and understandable from the perspective of social activity in that they reflect functional, fine-grained, latent "social roles", e.g., a friend with certain common interest, a co-worker on certain project, etc.

The fundamental assumption of XACCESS is the existence of a set of fine-grained, latent social roles that capture the social functions of the users relevant to the target individual. This concept is in spirit similar to the "role" in role-based access control (RBAC) paradigm [11]. We argue that it makes much more sense to reason about user-permission assignment based on social roles instead of social relationships: first, the social relationship could be fairly vague, and deviates from its semantic meaning, e.g., "friend" may actually mean relative or co-worker; second, an individual may carry multiple social roles, and thus should have the union of permissions associated with these social roles, which could not be captured by a single social relationship.

Unlike conventional RBAC frameworks wherein roles are typically captured by auxiliary structures, e.g., enterprise managerial hierarchies, a social network is, however, inherently "flat", in the sense that no hierarchical structures are available to define social roles. To address this challenge, we introduce a novel hybrid mining method that combines graph mining (over social network structure) and event mining (over historical social activities of users). Based on the identified social roles, confidentiality setting of personal information, and predefined user-permission assignments (optional and may contain inconsistency), XACCESS matches relevant users to their potential social roles, and social roles to their associated permissions. Moreover, XACCESS allows user feedback in every phase of the process to further improve the quality of suggested user-permission assignments. The main framework of XACCESS is illustrated in Figure 1.

Our contributions can be summarized as follows. First, we highlight and articulate the problem of helping ordinary social site users understand and specify privacy control policies over their personal data. Second, we propose a novel hybrid mining method that discovers semantically meaningful social roles from both social network structure data and historical activity data. Third, based on the

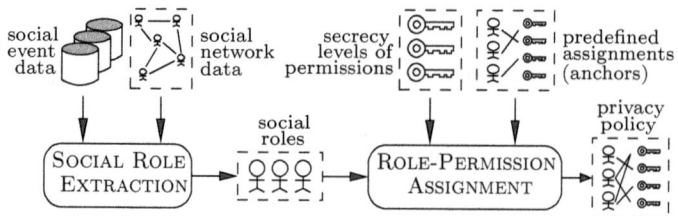

Figure 1: Framework of xAccess.

social role mining method, we construct a fully *automated* access control policy specification tool, XACCESS, for social networking platforms. Finally, we validate the analytical models and the efficacy of XACCESS over real social network and user study data.

The remainder of the paper will be organized as follows. Section 2 introduces the fundamental concepts of XACCESS. Section 3 and 4 detail the design and implementation of XACCESS, with possible extensions discussed in Section 5. An empirical evaluation of the proposed solution is presented in Section 6. The paper is concluded in Section 7.

2. MODELS AND CONCEPTS

A social network is modeled as a graph $G = (\mathcal{V}, \mathcal{E})$, with $\mathcal{V}$ and $\mathcal{E}$ representing the set of users and their social relationships, respectively. In this paper, we focus on deriving the access control policies for a specific user $v \in \mathcal{V}$, and thus introduce a variant of this definition:

DEFINITION 1 (VIEWPOINT NETWORK). *We define the h-hop viewpoint network of user v as the subgraph $G_h^v = (\mathcal{V}_h^v, \mathcal{E}_h^v)$ of G which consists of the users within h hops of v (including v) in G and the social relationships among them.*

By limiting h to a small number (typically 2 or 3), we focus on the set of users socially local to v, which is sufficient for most social sites. In the following, when the context is clear, we omit the referred target user v in the notations.

A permission is an access privilege to certain personal information. Its concrete definition depends on social sites and applications (e.g., access one's photo album or comment on one's microblog), and is orthogonal to the scope of this work. We assume a set of predefined permissions. The permissions may be structurally related; later, we will discuss how such structure impacts the setting of privacy policy.

The problem of specifying access control policies for user v is essentially equivalent to identifying a proper permission assignment ϕ_u for each user $u \in \mathcal{V}_h^v \setminus \{v\}$ (with respect to v's personal information). Henceforth, we refer to u and v as the source and target, respectively. The focus of this work is to alleviate the burden of social site users by suggesting *informative*, *personalized* policy settings. Instead of relying solely on static information (e.g., hop distance or relationship type) as currently adopted by most social sites, we construct the recommendation framework atop the notion of *social role*.

DEFINITION 2 (SOCIAL ROLE). *A social role [24] is a set of connected behaviors as conceptualized by individuals with a given social connection to the target individual.*

A social role specifies the expected social functions, thereby implying the expected access rights of individuals with a given social connection to the target user, which makes it an ideal bridge between users and permissions. To capture the social role of the source u (relative to the target v), one needs to consider (i) u's social connection to the target v as reflected in the social network structure, and (ii) u's social behaviors as reflected in the social activities in which u and v participate. Motivated by this observation, we propose a novel hybrid mining method that extracts a set of semantically interpretable roles from social network and social activity data. To our best knowledge, this is the first in its category.

3. SOCIAL ROLE EXTRACTION

Next, we present our hybrid mining method that exploits both social network structure (for social connection) and historical social activity (for social behavior), with details presented in Section 3.1 and 3.2, respectively.

3.1 Social Network Structure

The social connection between the source and the target may not be solely determined by their hop distance or their relationship type; rather, it involves all relevant users. As an example, consider three friends u_i, u_j, u_k of v, while u_i and u_k are also friends, which may indicate a stronger connection between u_i and v than u_j. We introduce the concept of *social proximity* to capture this notion, which measures the overall strength of a social connection.

Ideally, if two individuals share many common neighbors with close relationships, or they belong to a small and tight community, their social proximity would be high. A variety of measures have been proposed [23] to capture the notion of network proximity, including *Katz measure*, *hitting time*, and *escape probability*. In our implementation, we adopt the measure of *random walk with restart* (RWR), one of the most popular proximity metrics in graphs [18], which is empirically proved to perform the best in our experiments. Specifically, in a RWR, starting from node v, at each step, the walk moves to one of its current neighbors with probability proportional to the corresponding edge weight, or returns to v with a restart probability $(1 - c)$. This process can be analogized to the spread of an ink drop on paper. The network proximity between u and v can be defined as the steady-state probability that the walk appears at u. If we stack the proximity scores into a vector $\mathbf{p}$, the definition of RWR is given by:

$$\mathbf{p} = cW\mathbf{p} + (1 - c)\mathbf{e} \qquad (1)$$

where W represents the column normalized adjacent matrix of the viewpoint network G_h^v (details referred to Appendix A), and $\mathbf{e}$ is the starting vector for v. In the following, we use $P(u)$ to denote the proximity score of user u (relative to v).

For clarity of presentation, we temporarily assume the network structure to be static, which may not hold for real social networking sites. Later, we will lift this assumption and take into account the impact of network dynamics in specifying access control policies.

3.2 Historical Social Activity

While the network structures reflect the relatively static social connection between two users, the social activities capture their dynamic social interactions. Right now, most social sites support myriad online activities (e.g., join online communities, comment on others' microblogs, play online games), which makes it feasible to understand such interactions by extracting semantically meaningful patterns from the activity data.

Without more detailed information, we can model an activity using (i) the set of users who have participated in it, and (ii) its activity type[2] (from a finite set $\mathcal{A}$), which indicates its nature (e.g., photo

---

[2]Without ambiguity, in what follows, we use a to denote both an activity and its associated activity type.

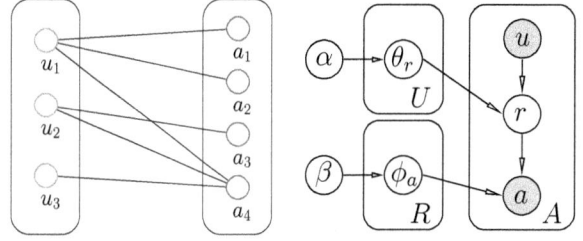

Figure 2: User-activity bipartite graph and user-role-activity generative model.

sharing or game playing). Particularly, since we intend to model the social roles of relevant users with respect to target v, we focus on the set of activities participated by v. We can organize the set of users and activities in a bipartite-like graph, as shown in the left plot of Figure 2.

To extract the set of social roles from such activity data, we introduce a probabilistic user-role-activity generative model. We assume that each user u is associated with a conditional multinomial distribution $P(r|u)$ over a set of roles $r \in \mathcal{R}$ ($\mathcal{R}$ is latent), measuring the degree that u carries each role r; further, each role r is associated with a multinomial distribution $P(a|r)$ over the set of activity types $a \in \mathcal{A}$, indicating the likelihood that an individual with role r participates in an activity of type a. Conceptually, the event that user u participates in an activity of type a is generated in two steps: 1) u picks a role r (sample a role r from $P(r|u)$); 2) with role r, u participates in a (sample an activity a from $P(a|r)$). In this model, we have one focused objective, that is identifying the number of latent roles and the association between each user and each role.

The Bayesian network of this general generative model is shown in the right plot of Figure 2: θ_r and ϕ_a denote the Dirichlet priors, parameterized by α and β, while U, R, and A represent the number of users, roles, and activities in the data, respectively. The conditional distribution of parameters for given user and activity is calculated as:

$$P(\theta_r, \phi_a, r|a, u, \alpha, \beta) = \frac{P(\theta_r, \phi_a, r, a, u|\alpha, \beta)}{\sum_a \sum_u P(\theta_r, \phi_a, r, a, u|\alpha, \beta)} \qquad (2)$$

where the joint distribution $P(\theta_r, \phi_a, r, a, u|\alpha, \beta)$ can be calculated using

$$P(a|\phi_a, r)P(\phi_a|\beta)P(r|u, \theta_r)P(\theta_r|\alpha)P(u)$$

In our implementation, we apply *Gibbs sampling* [19] to estimate all the parameters, and *perplexity* measure to select the optimal number of roles (details referred to Appendix B). After the parameters are estimated, we can easily identify the association between each user u and each role r, as reflected in the conditional distribution $P(r|u)$ computed as $P(r|u) = P(r|u, \theta_r)P(\theta_r|\alpha)$.

3.3 Computing Role Score

Recall that from the social network structure, we extract a prior distribution $P(u)$ over all the users, while from the dynamic social activities, we obtain a conditional distribution $P(r|u)$. We can therefore use the joint distribution $P(u, r) = P(r|u)P(u)$ (role scores) to measure the probability that user u with role r consumes information from v. In what follows, let $\theta_{u,r}$ denote the score $P(u, r)$. We organize $\{\theta\}$ as a $U \times R$ matrix with the u-th row, r-th column element being $\theta_{u,r}$. For a given role r^*, one can rank all the users according to their role scores θ_{u,r^*}, i.e., the r^*-

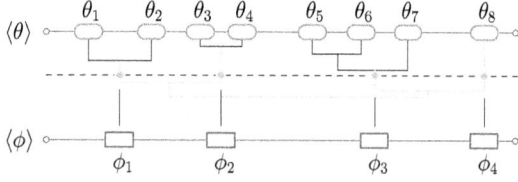

Figure 3: User-permission assignment based on agglomerative clustering.

th column, which serves as the cornerstone for the user-permission assignment, as discussed next.

4. USER-PERMISSION ASSIGNMENT

In this section, we present the step of bridging users and permissions via social roles. One key feature of XACCESS lies in its consideration of the structure of permissions. For ease of presentation, we assume that the set of permissions $\{\phi\}$ correspond to a single (unknown) social role r^*, and are pair-wise comparable: $\phi_i \prec \phi_j$, if and only if the grant of ϕ_j implies that of ϕ_i, i.e., the confidentiality levels of two permissions are comparable. We will allow the more general case that permissions correspond to multiple social roles, and are not pair-wise comparable (not monotonically sortable) in Section 5. Here, without loss of generality, we assume that $\{\phi\}$ is sorted in a monotonic list $\langle\phi\rangle$.

Intuitively, we are given two measures, role scores $\langle\theta\rangle$ (with respect to a specific role r^*) and permissions $\langle\phi\rangle$. We intend to match each θ_u[3] to certain ϕ. Let $M(\cdot)$ denote the mapping of indices, such that θ_u is mapped to $\phi_{M(u)}$. We dictate that the mapping must be: (1) *Monotonic*. If $\theta_{u_i,r^*} < \theta_{u_j,r^*}$, then $M(u_i) \leq M(u_j)$; that is, for given two users, their assigned permissions and role scores should follow the same order. (2) *Complete*. $\forall u, \exists M(u)$; that is, for every user, there must exist an assigned permission, but may not vice versa. We attempt to match users and permissions while obeying their orders.

We distinguish the case that each permission is associated with a quantitative confidentiality score (e.g., via automated mining [16]) indicating its privacy level, and the more general case that only the ordering information is given. Here, for clarity of presentation, we only consider the latter general case, and the former case is discussed in Appendix C. Next, we start with the case that no predefined user-permission assignments (called "anchors") are given, and later consider the case that the user supplies a set of anchors.

4.1 Matching without Anchors

In the case that no anchors are given, we attempt to provide assistance for the most non-expert users. We therefore rely on the intrinsic structure of the series $\langle\theta\rangle$ to identify the optimal mapping between $\langle\phi\rangle$ and $\langle\theta\rangle$. Without further information, it is impossible to identify the latent role r^* underlying $\langle\phi\rangle$; hence, we evaluate user u based on its marginal role score $\theta_u = \sum_r \theta_{u,r}$.

We assume that both series have been sorted in non-decreasing orders. Intuitively, we consider that two individuals with similar role scores should be assigned similar permissions; the question is thus to find a partition of $\langle\theta\rangle$ into a set of subsets, where the number of subsets is unknown. Clearly, an unsupervised partitioning method is suitable for our purpose. To this end, we apply an agglomerative hierarchical clustering method, which intuitively creates a hierarchy of clusters, called dendrogram, with leaves as the series of role scores, non-leaf nodes as clusters, and root corre-

sponding to the entire collection of users. To construct the dendrogram, one starts at the leaves, and successively merges the closest clusters together, until all the users are included. This process is illustrated in Figure 3. Clearly, one critical measure is the similarity of two consecutive clusters; in out implementation, we adopt the average Manhattan distance as the similarity metric. Cutting the hierarchy at a given height generates a partition at a selected precision. We use a parameter λ to control the precision: the partition continues only if the number of clusters is larger than the number of permissions, or there exist two consecutive clusters with similarity above λ.

After the cluster generation, one may follow a *conservative* (starting from the permission with the lowest confidentiality level, assign a distinct permission to each cluster in an increasing order), *open* (starting from the highest confidentiality level, assign a distinct permission to each cluster in a decreasing order), or *random* (arbitrarily pick the same number of permissions as clusters, and assign them to the clusters following their order) strategy.

4.2 Matching with Anchors

It is possible that the target user may have a set of predefined user-permission assignments, called "anchors", that, in our setting, is equivalent to a set of role score-permission match. More formally,

DEFINITION 3 (ANCHOR). *An anchor is a user predefined role score θ to permission ϕ match ($\theta - \phi$).*

Anchors provide important implications regarding the target user's expected permission assignment: that is, users with similar role scores to an anchor should be assigned similar permissions. The challenge lies in, however, that the anchors may also introduce inconsistency into the matching process. By inconsistency, intuitively, we mean that for two given anchors, their assigned permissions disobey the order of their associated role scores. Next, we discuss how to incorporate anchors to improve the quality of assignment, and how to detect and resolve potential inconsistency in anchors.

Detecting Inconsistent Anchors

We first introduce the formal definition of *inconsistency*.

DEFINITION 4 (INCONSISTENCY). *An inconsistency is a pair of anchors $(\theta_{u_i} - \phi_{M(u_i)})$ and $(\theta_{u_j} - \phi_{M(u_j)})$, such that $\theta_{u_i,r^*} < \theta_{u_j,r^*}$ and $\phi_{M(u_i)} \succ \phi_{M(u_j)}$.*

To identify the subset of inconsistent anchors, we resort to the principle of *minimal causations* [21]. Intuitively, it states that the best explanation of a given set of data features the minimum set of causes. Based on this principle, we propose the following detection scheme. For each role $r \in \mathcal{R}$ (each dimension of $\langle\theta\rangle$), we check if any inconsistency exists, i.e., if $\exists(\theta_{u_i} - \phi_{M(u_i)})$ and $(\theta_{u_j} - \phi_{M(u_j)})$, $\theta_{u_i,r} < \theta_{u_j,r}$ and $\phi_{M(u_i)} \succ \phi_{M(u_j)}$. If positive, r is added to an initially empty set $\mathcal{R}^I$. If all the dimensions contain inconsistency (i.e., $\mathcal{R} = \mathcal{R}^I$), we regard the dimension (role) r containing the minimum number of inconsistencies as r^*, and proceed to resolving the inconsistency (see below); otherwise, we rank users based on their role scores along the dimensions $\mathcal{R} \setminus \mathcal{R}^I$: $\theta_u = \sum_{r \in \mathcal{R} \setminus \mathcal{R}^I} \theta_{u,r}$. In this case, we can consider the provided anchors as a set of ground-truth role score-permission assignment, $\langle\theta_u, \phi_{M(u)}\rangle$.

This set of anchors slice the two sequences $\langle\theta\rangle$ and $\langle\phi\rangle$ into pieces. Consider two consecutive anchors (in terms of θ values), $\langle\theta_{u_i}, \phi_{M(u_i)}\rangle$ and $\langle\theta_{u_j}, \phi_{M(u_j)}\rangle$. We are left with aligning the two sub-sequences, $\langle\theta_{u_{i+1}}, \ldots, \theta_{u_{j-1}}\rangle$ and $\langle\phi_{M(u_i)}, \ldots, \phi_{M(u_j)}\rangle$,

---

[3]For simplicity, we use θ_u as a short version of $\theta_{u,\cdot}$.

$\langle\theta\rangle$ θ_1 θ_2 θ_3 θ_4 θ_5 θ_6 θ_7 θ_8

$\langle\phi\rangle$ ϕ_1 ϕ_2 ϕ_3 ϕ_4 ϕ_5 ϕ_6 ϕ_7

(a)

$\langle\theta\rangle$ θ_1 θ_2 θ_3 θ_4 θ_5 θ_6 θ_7 θ_8

$\langle\phi\rangle$ ϕ_1 ϕ_2 ϕ_3 ϕ_4

(b)

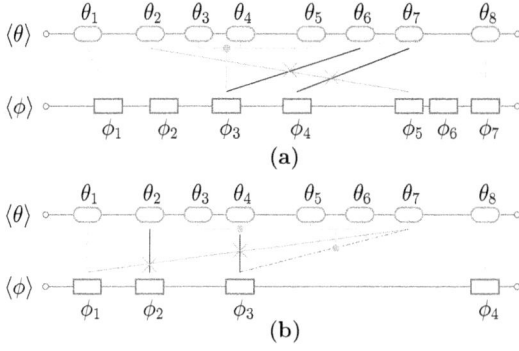

Figure 4: User-permission matching under inconsistent anchors (solid lines): (a) exceptionalization (b) multi-assignment.

which can be easily solved following the paradigm introduced in Section 4.1.

Resolving Inconsistent Anchors

Next we show how to resolve the inconsistency introduced by the anchors, i.e., the permissions of the anchors disobey the order of the associated social role scores. In general, we solve such inconsistency using two mechanisms, *exceptionalization* and *multi-assignment*. Intuitively, exceptionalization allows the cases that some users have exceptional trust (or distrust) by the target user, not reflected in their social relationships and activities; while multi-assignment accommodates the cases that the anchors only reflect certain aspects of the "true" assignments for some users, who essentially should be given certain other permissions. More formally,

DEFINITION 5 (EXCEPTIONALIZATION). *An exception is an anchor $(\theta_u - \phi_{M(u)})$ that encodes special trust (or distrust) to user u by the target, which should not be used in the assignment process to provide general guidance.*

We apply exceptionalization to identify the set of anchors that would result in inconsistency and should be considered as exceptions, and suspend them from providing guidance for permission assignment for the rest users.

DEFINITION 6 (MULTI-ASSIGNMENT). *For a given anchor $(\theta_u - \phi_{M(u)})$, multi-assignment identifies potentially missing permission assignment for u other than $\phi_{M(u)}$.*

We apply multi-assignment to identify the set of anchors that should be accompanied by certain other permissions, and remove the original permission assignments from the matching process. Multi-assignment is especially meaningful when incomparable permissions are taken into consideration, and users tend to feature multiple social roles, e.g., both friend and co-worker, as viewed from different perspectives; in such cases, a single user may be associated with multiple permissions along different dimensions (i.e., multiple roles).

Our approach of matching role score and permission under anchors with possible inconsistency is sketched in Algorithm 1: 1) check if inconsistency exists in the set of anchors; 2) identify the minimum subset of anchors (exceptions), whose absence removes inconsistency; 3) depending on its intersection with other anchors, apply either multi-assignment or exceptionalization to each exception; 4) apply time-warping-based (for permissions associated with confidentiality scores) or clustering-based matching to sub-series of permissions and role scores, as partitioned by the anchors.

Input: proximity set Θ, permission set Φ, anchor set Ψ
Output: permission assignments for all $\theta \in \Theta$
```
// consistency check
```
$\Psi^e, \Psi^r \leftarrow \emptyset$;
for *each anchor $\psi \in \Psi$* **do**
    $n_\psi \leftarrow$ number of intersected anchors;
    if $n_\psi > 0$ **then** add ψ to Ψ^e;
end
```
// inconsistency removal
```
if $\Psi^e \neq \emptyset$ **then**
    sort $\psi \in \Psi^e$ according to n_ψ;
    while *inconsistency exists* **do**
        pop up ψ from Ψ^e to Ψ^r;
        adjust the order of Ψ^e;
    end
    $\Psi \leftarrow \Psi \setminus \Psi^r \cup \Psi^e$;
    for *each $\psi \in \Psi^r$* **do**
        if $\exists \psi' \in \Psi, \theta(\psi) > \theta(\psi')$ *and* $\phi(\psi) \prec \phi(\psi')$ **then**
            multi-assignment;
        else
            exceptionalization;
        end
    end
end
```
// proximity-permission matching
```
for *two consecutive anchors $(\theta_i, \phi_{m_i}), (\theta_j, \phi_{m_j}) \in \Psi$* **do**
    if *permissions associated with confidentiality* **then**
        match $\theta_{i+1} : \theta_{j-1}$ and $\phi_{m_i} : \phi_{m_j}$ using time warping;
    else
        if $j - i > m_j - m_i$ **then**
            match $\theta_{i+1} : \theta_{j-1}$ and $\phi_{m_i} : \phi_{m_j}$ using clustering;
        else
            conservative, aggressive, or arbitrary matching;
        end
    end
end

Algorithm 1: Role-permission matching under (possibly inconsistent) anchors.

While the overall framework is clear, we still need to answer several challenging questions: first, how to identify the minimum set of exceptions? second, whether to apply multi-assignment or exceptionalization, when both are possible? Following, we answer these questions in the case of pair-wise comparable permissions, and the more general permission structures will be discussed in Section 5. For simplicity, we use ψ to denote an anchor, and $\theta(\psi)$ and $\phi(\psi)$ as its associated role score and permission.

Q1: how to find the minimum set of exceptions? We have the following theorem regarding the complexity of finding the minimum set of anchors that result in inconsistency (exceptions).

THEOREM 1. *Identifying the minimum set of anchors responsible for inconsistency is NP-Hard.*

PROOF. The problem can be re-formulated as the following *Set Cover* problem. Let $\mathcal{S}$ be the set of intersection points of anchors, and $\mathcal{A}$ be the set of anchors involved in the intersections. We intend to find the minimum subset of $\mathcal{A}$ that "covers" all the intersection points in $\mathcal{S}$, which is an instantiation of the classical set cover problem, known to be NP-Hard. □

Hence, instead of attempting to find the minimum set, we apply a greedy approach: at each step, we identify the anchor that causes

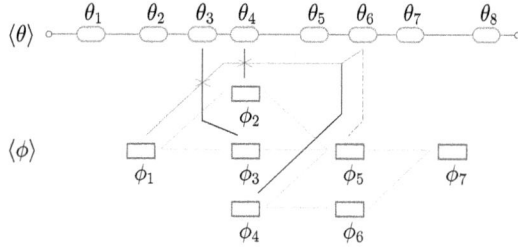

Figure 5: Role-score-permission matching under partially ordered permissions.

the largest number of inconsistencies in the current anchor set, and remove it as an exception. The intuition behind this scheme is that an anchor in conflict with a larger number of others tends to be an exception with higher possibility. It can be derived that this greedy approach achieves an approximation ratio of $H(s)$, where s is the largest number of intersections on a single anchor, and $H(n)$ the n-th harmonic number.

Q2: exceptionalization or multi-assignment? After identifying the set of exceptions, the anchors are divided into two sets: the exceptions Ψ^e and the rest Ψ^r, the next step is to apply exceptionalization or multi-assignment to handle each $\psi \in \Psi^e$. Conceptually, both mechanisms remove ψ from the matching process; while, in addition, multi-assignment also attempts to find any missing permission assignments potentially neglected by the user. We distinguish the cases that ψ intersects with "up-stream" anchors, i.e., $\exists \psi' \in \Psi^r$, $\theta(\psi) < \theta(\psi')$ and $\phi(\psi) \succ \phi(\psi')$, as shown in Figure 4(a), or with "down-stream" ones, i.e., $\exists \psi' \in \Psi^r$, $\theta(\psi) > \theta(\psi')$ and $\phi(\psi) \prec \phi(\psi')$, as shown in Figure 4(b). We claim that in the case of pair-wise comparable permissions, only one case is possible, with the following theorem.

THEOREM 2. *For pair-wise comparable permissions, each exception can only exclusively intersect with either up-stream or down-stream anchors.*

PROOF. Without loss of generality, consider an exception ψ that intersects with an "up-stream" anchor, i.e., $\exists \psi' \in \Psi^r$, $\theta(\psi) < \theta(\psi')$ and $\phi(\psi) \succ \phi(\psi')$. Assume that it also intersects with certain "down-stream" one, i.e., $\exists \psi'' \in \Psi^r$, $\theta(\psi) > \theta(\psi'')$ and $\phi(\psi) \prec \phi(\psi'')$. We have $\theta(\psi'') < \theta(\psi')$ and $\phi(\psi'') \succ \phi(\psi')$, i.e., an exception, which is a contradiction to that Ψ^r is exception-free. $\square$

Hence, multi-assignment makes sense only when ψ intersects with "down-stream" anchors; that is, an additional permission ψ^* with higher confidentiality level ($\phi(\psi^*) \succ \phi(\psi)$) is assigned. Without further information, we set the additional permission ϕ^* as the *minimum* one that does not cause any inconsistency in Ψ^r: $\psi^* = \max\{\phi(\psi') : \psi' \in \Psi^r \text{ and } \theta(\psi') < \theta(\psi)\}$. An example is shown in Figure 4(b) where the exception ($\theta_7 - \phi_1$) intersects with two down-stream anchors ($\theta_2 - \phi_2$) and ($\theta_4 - \phi_3$), and an additional permission ϕ_3 is assigned to θ_7.

Also note that the multi-assignement policy bears the nature of "suggestion"; it is possible that an exception encodes certain special "distrust" preference by the target user. In such cases, only exceptionalization will be applied.

5. EXTENSION

In the discussion so far, we have made two simplification assumptions: 1) the set of permissions are pair-wise comparable, i.e.,

a totally ordered set; 2) the target user provides sufficient information (e.g., social network structures, historical social activities, anchors), for XACCESS to perform privacy setting recommendation. Now we lift these simplifications and consider the cases that 1) the set of permissions form a partially ordered set, i.e., not every pair of permissions are comparable, which is fairly common in access control literatures and practice [9], and 2) the information supplied by the target user is insufficient to make informative recommendation; we can, however, gain valuable insights into the reasonable privacy setting by examining the settings of his/her peers. Further, we discuss the problem of semantically labeling a social role, thereby making it interpretable by users.

5.1 Partially Ordered Permissions

Assume that the set of permissions form a partially ordered set (i.e., lattice) according to their confidentiality levels. Now, a pair of permissions can be one of the following relationships, $\succ$, $\prec$, $=$, and *incomparable*; therefore, the techniques in Section 4 is not directly applicable. One can, however, apply *linear extension* [8] over the set of permissions, which generates a *topological ordering* of the permissions, compatible with the original partial ordering. In particular, we are interested in a classed representation of the ordering information, where the permissions in each class are equal or incomparable to each other, and can be considered as having equivalent confidentiality level. For example, in Figure 5, the set of permissions can be grouped into four classes $\{\phi_1\}$, $\{\phi_2, \phi_3, \phi_4\}$, $\{\phi_5, \phi_6\}$, $\{\phi_7\}$. Note that these classes are totally ordered, and it holds that for every two consecutive classes Φ_i and Φ_j, $\forall \phi \in \Phi_i$, $\exists \phi' \in \Phi_j$, $\phi \prec \phi'$. Such classification can be obtained following a breadth-first search paradigm, as sketched in Algorithm 2 (we define two permissions ϕ and ϕ' as predecessor and successor, respectively, if and only if $\phi \prec \phi'$).

Input: set of permissions Φ
Output: classification of Φ
$\mathcal{C} \leftarrow \emptyset$;
$C \leftarrow$ set of permissions with no successors;
$C' \leftarrow \emptyset$;
while C *is non-empty* **do**
    add C to $\mathcal{C}$;
    for *each permission* $\phi \in C$ **do**
        for *each direct predecessor* ϕ' *of* ϕ **do**
            delete relationship $\phi' \prec \phi$;
            if ϕ' *has no successor* **then**
                add ϕ' to C';
            end
        end
    end
    $C \leftarrow C'$;
end

Algorithm 2: Linear extension of partially ordered set.

Now we can perform role-score permission assignment on the level of permission classes. In the case that no anchors are provided, we apply agglomerative clustering to the set of social roles scores, generate a partition, and match each class of role scores (i.e., users) with a distinct permission class, following their orders. Such class-to-class mapping is then presented to end users for further refinement.

Given the non-comparability of permissions, it is likely that for one social score θ_u, the target user may provide multiple anchors, $\{\psi^u\}$. As an example, in Figure 5, θ_6 is assigned two permissions ϕ_1 and ϕ_4. We assume that each pair of $\phi(\psi_i^u)$ and $\phi(\psi_j^u)$ are incomparable; otherwise, one can remove the one with lower confidentiality level, without affecting the overall capacity.

We consider that such multiple anchors correspond to multiple social roles; that is, each $\psi_i^u \in \{\psi^u\}$ is associated with a role. Conceptually, two anchors ψ_i^u and $\psi_j^{u'}$ associated with the same role should be consistent; hence, we intend to find a permission-role mapping such that the number of inconsistencies could be minimized. After that, one can perform user-permission assignment along each dimension (role) independently, solve the possible inconsistency, and finally collect and merge the exception-free anchors. Exception handling is similar to that in Section 4.2, except that the selected additional permission ϕ^* should be a successor of the permissions associated with conflicting anchors, i.e., their least common ancestor (LCA). One then merge the set of exception-free anchors and the identified missing permission assignment to form the anchor set for proximity-permission matching. For example, in Figure 5, $(\theta_6 - \phi_1)$ conflicts with anchors $(\theta_3 - \phi_3)$ and $(\theta_4 - \phi_2)$; the LCA of θ_2 and θ_3, θ_5, is identified as the missing permission, which is then merged with another assignment ϕ_4, with ϕ_5 as the final assignment for ϕ_6.

5.2 Collaborative Privacy Setting

The privacy settings by his/her peers provide valuable information for determining the best access control policy for a specific user, especially when the information associated with the user (e.g., social activities, anchors, etc.), is insufficient for XACCESS to perform informative recommendation. Here, we discuss how to leverage such information in suggesting reasonable privacy setting.

The most straightforward solution is based on the principle of *mutual equivalence*: a pair of individuals tend to demonstrate similar trust/distrust inclination in information sharing with each other; hence, one can "mirror" the setting of a peer: given two individuals u and v, let $\phi(u \rightsquigarrow v)$ denote the permission assigned by u to v; v can simply copy this setting as $\phi(v \rightsquigarrow u) = \phi(u \rightsquigarrow v)$. This solution, though simple, considers only the information of the specific peer when determining his/her access level. A more comprehensive solution is based on the paradigm of *collaborative filtering*. Given two individuals u and v, for the sets of users relevant to u and v, $\mathcal{V}_u$ and $\mathcal{V}_v$, one creates a mapping (let $M_{uv}(w)$ be the counterpart of w of $\mathcal{V}_u$ in $\mathcal{V}_v$), based on the social role scores of $\mathcal{V}_u$ and $\mathcal{V}_v$ with respect to u and v, respectively. The setting of $w \in \mathcal{V}_u$ can be calculated as: $\phi(u \rightsquigarrow w) = \arg\min_\phi \prod_v f(\phi(v \rightsquigarrow M_{uv}(w)), \phi)$, where $\phi(v \rightsquigarrow M_{uv}(w))$ is the actual assignment to $M_{uv}(w)$ by v, and $f(\phi(v \rightsquigarrow M_{uv}(w)), \phi)$ is the *cost* function of assigning ϕ to $M_{uv}(w)$ by v. Various instantiations are possible, L^1 norm for example, $f(\phi(v \rightsquigarrow M_{uv}(w)), \phi) = |\phi(v \rightsquigarrow M_{uv}(w)) - \phi|$.

5.3 Labeling Social Roles

To make the extracted social roles interpretable, it is imperative to attach "semantic tags" to them. Back to our discussion in Section 3.2, we assume that each activity type a is associated with a set of descriptive terms, from a finite set $\mathcal{W}$. We can extend the generative model in Section 3.2 by including another observable w, i.e., the terms of an activity type a, associated with multinomial distribution ψ_w parameterized by γ. Now, the joint distribution is given by $P(w, a, r, u | \alpha, \beta, \gamma)$, which can be estimated following that sketched in Section B. From the joint distribution, one can derive the conditional distribution $P(w|r)$.

We can extract a set of candidate labels using frequent pattern mining. For each candidate label l, we evaluate its semantic relevance to a role r, $S(l, r)$. More formally, let $l = w_0^l w_1^l \ldots w_m^l$, we can estimate its semantical relevance to a role r using multiple

metrics, the simplest case, for example:

$$S(l, r) = \log \frac{P(l|r)}{P(l)} = \sum_{i=0}^{m} \log \frac{P(w_i^l|r)}{P(w_i^l)} \tag{3}$$

alternatively, the negative KL divergence of $\{P(w|r)\}$ and $\{P(w|l)\}$ over $w \in \mathcal{W}$ could also be used.

6. EMPIRICAL EVALUATION

In this section, we present an empirical evaluation of the efficacy of XACCESS over two real-life social network and user study datasets. The experiments are specifically designed centering around the following metrics: 1) the efficacy in capturing individuals' implicit privacy preference for relevant users, 2) the effectiveness in incorporating users' predefined preference to improve the quality of privacy setting, 3) the scalability with respect to the scale of underlying social network and the volume of historical activity data.

6.1 Datasets and Experimental Design

In the first set of experiments, we apply XACCESS to analyzing a publicly available speed dating dataset [12] from a study conducted by Fishman et al. [12]. It involves 530 participants and consists of data regarding 4,150 dynamic "dates" arranged between pairs of participants. For each participant, the demographic information (e.g., age, race, zipcode, etc.) and the information of hobby activities (e.g., entertainment, museum, hiking, etc.) the participants usually take part in is also collected. After the date, the satisfaction of each participant regarding his/her partner is recorded with a score on a scale from 1 to 10, which we regard as the implicit privacy preference indicated by the participant. For each individual, we apply XACCESS to extracting the roles of his/her partners, based on the structure of dating arrangement (as the static network structures) and the description of their hobbies (as the dynamic social activities), and match it against the set of permissions (the set of integers over $[1, 10]$). We compare the predicated results with that given by the participants in the dataset.

In the second set of experiments, we analyze the social network of a subset of IBM employees who participated in the Small Blue project [14] and the archive of bookmarks tagged by these social users (as the dynamic activity data), to predict individuals' information sharing behavior. The dataset corresponds to the social network as of January 2009, which involved 41,702 IBM employees. The personal information regarding each individual includes his/her (i) work location, (ii) managerial position, and (iii) social connections with other employees. The associated bookmark archive consists of the webpages tagged by the individuals appearing in the first dataset, collected by DOGEAR [3], a personal bookmark management application that as well supports sharing the community's bookmarks. The archive contains 20,870 bookmark records, relevant to 7,819 urls. Attributes of interest to us are listed in Table 1; in particular, *email* and *url* uniquely identifies a user and a webpage, respectively, and *tags* encode the semantics of the object. We regard the volume of email sent from an individual to his/her relevant user (note this communication is directional) as a quantitative indication of his/her intension of information sharing, and evaluate the result predicted by XACCESS against it.

In the last set of experiments, we implement and deploy XACCESS on the platform of FACEBOOK and conduct a concrete user study on helping everyday users specify their privacy policies. For a given FACEBOOK user u, we consider the following types of social activities of u's friends with respect to u's FACEBOOK page: *comment* (post), *like* (page, post, status), and *tag* (photo).

Additionally we consider the following set of private data items

Attribute	Description
email	email address of user s (identifier of subject)
url	url o bookmarked by s (identifier of object)
tags	bookmark tags made by s regarding o
time	time-stamp that s accesses o

Table 1: Attributes and descriptions of Dogear dataset.

Structure	Permission order
total order	$(4) > (5) > (7) > (8) > (2) > (6) > (3) > (9) > (10) > (11) > (12) > (1)$
partial order	$\{(4)\} > \{(5),(7),(8)\} > \{(2),(6),(3),(9)\} > \{(10),(11),(12)\} > \{(1)\}$

Table 2: Alternative structures of permission order.

(permissions): *(1) About me, (2) Personal Info, (3) Birthday, (4) Religious and Political Views, (5) Family and Relationship, (6) Education and Work, (7) Photos and Videos of Me, (8) Photo Albums, (9) Posts by Me, (10) Allow to post on my Wall, (11) Posts by Friends, (12) Comments on Posts.* We consider alternative access structures of these permissions (e.g., totally ordered set, partially ordered set) as listed in Table 2. We then collect the privacy settings regarding these permissions by 23 volunteers, and compare the privacy settings suggested by XACCESS with that manually labeled by the participating users.

We use all three datasets in the experiments, aiming at capturing the influence of factors such as activity types and user characteristics. The algorithms are implemented using Python, and all the experiments are conducted on a workstation with 1.6GHz Pentium IV and 2GB memory, running Windows XP.

6.2 Experimental Results

Capture of Privacy Preference

This set of experiments are designed to evaluate the efficacy of XACCESS (denoted by X) in capturing social users' implicit preference of information sharing with relevant users. In particular, we intend to examine the contributions by different features (i.e., static social network structure, dynamic historical activities) in capturing such implicit reference. Let $\phi^*(\cdot)$ and $\phi^r(\cdot)$ be the access control level set manually by the user, and suggested by a recommendation method, respectively. We measure the quality of recommendation using the metric of *recommendation accuracy*,

$$1 - \frac{\sum_{i \in \mathcal{I}} |\phi^*(i) - \phi^r(i)|}{|\mathcal{I}| \cdot |\Phi|}$$

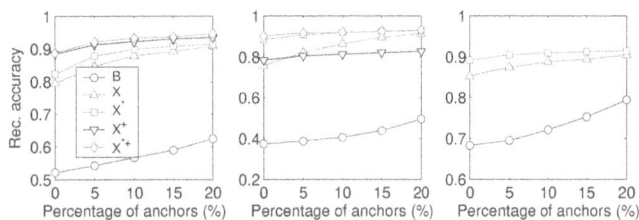

Figure 6: Recommendation accuracy of XACCESS and baseline approach with respect to the number of correct and false anchors. From left to right, the three columns correspond to the speed dating, small blue, and facebook datasets, respectively.

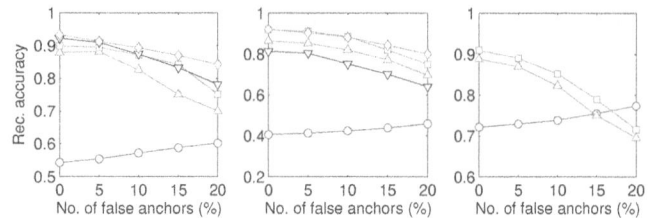

Figure 7: Robustness of XACCESS and baseline approach against false anchors.

where $\mathcal{I}$ and Φ are the set of individuals, distinct access levels, respectively. Further, we construct a baseline bayesian approach (denoted by B) that makes recommendation solely based on hop distance, i.e., *friend, friend-of-friend*, and minimizes the recommendation error, i.e., a unique setting ϕ_h^r for all users with hop distance h to the target individual that satisfies

$$\phi_h^r = \arg\min_{\phi_h} \sum_{i \in \mathcal{I}_h} |\phi^*(i) - \phi^r(i)|$$

where $\mathcal{I}_h$ is the set of users with hop distance h. We also consider the possibility of leveraging the possible quantitative confidentiality levels associated with permissions (detailed discussion in Section C). Overall, we implemented four versions of XACCESS, X, X*, X+, and X*+, where the symbols * and + indicates that the version considers dynamic social activities and confidentiality scores, respectively.

	B	X	X*	X+	X*+
speed dating	0.522	0.795	0.823	0.884	**0.887**
small blue	0.374	0.758	0.885	0.785	**0.902**
facebook	0.683	0.853	**0.892**	N/A	N/A

Table 3: Accuracy of privacy settings suggested by XACCESS and baseline approach.

Table 3 shows the accuracy of the four versions of XACCESS and the baseline approach with respect to the three datasets. It is observed that, for all three datasets, over the baseline approach, XACCESS achieves approximately $1.3 \sim 2.4$ times higher recommendation accuracy. It is noted that the incorporation of dynamic social behavior significantly boots the accuracy, especially for the small blue dataset (17.4% increase). This can be explained by that bookmarks well capture users' interests and preferences, and the behavior of recommending bookmarks is a good indicator of user's will of information sharing. Also, the incorporation of quantitative confidentiality information of permissions further improves the quality of recommendation, which is especially evident for the speed dating dataset. This is explained by that the social network structure in this dataset is much simpler (mainly composed by 1-hop neighbors), while the social activity data includes 11 attributes, and contains much semantically richer information.

Incorporation of User Input

In this set of experiments, we take into account user predefined permission assignment (anchor). Specifically, we measure the recommendation accuracy of XACCESS and the baseline approach with respect to varying percentage of anchors (over the total number of assignments), where the anchors are randomly selected.

The result is shown in Figure 6. First notice that, as the number of provided anchors grows, the accuracy of all the models increase; intuitively, the anchors provide valuable clues regarding

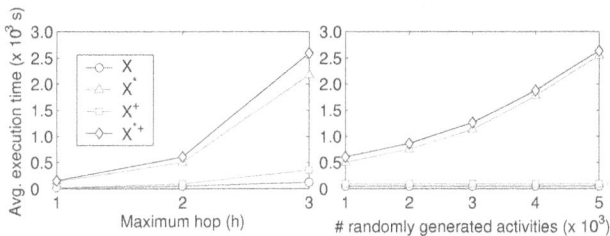

Figure 8: Average execution time (per user) of xAccess **versus the maximum hop and the volume of social activity data.**

users' implicit preference. Also notice that xAccess (all four versions) demonstrates higher effectiveness in leveraging such hints to improve the quality of assignment; for example, for the small blue dataset, even the basic version X achieves accuracy approximately 0.87 when 10% of the assignments are provided as anchors, compared with approximately 0.42 of B. This is explained by the fact that xAccess leverages the anchors as "structural clues" for aligning social role measures and permissions, which improves the overall quality of the alignment, in contrast to the point-wise improvement by the baseline approach.

To evaluate the impact of the inconsistency possibly existing in the anchors, we randomly generate a set of "false" anchors, in addition to the anchors provided by users. With the percentage of "correct" anchors fixed as 5%, we measure the accuracy of xAccess with respect to the varying percentage of false anchors (note that the baseline approach treats anchors as point-wise information, therefore is not affected by the false anchor). The result is shown in Figure 7: on all three datasets, the accuracy of xAccess is fairly stable under the influence of false anchors, mainly attributed to the exceptionalization mechanism.

Efficiency and Scalability

Now, we proceed to evaluating the operation efficiency of xAccess. In particular, we intend to capture the influence of two factors: the scale of the underlying social network, and the volume of historical activity data. We use the small-blue dataset in this set of experiments, given its large scale.

First, we measure the wall execution time of xAccess as a function of the maximum hop h of the viewpoint networks. The result is illustrated in the left plot of Figure 8. Overall, it is noticed that X and X^+ are fairly efficient, even though the number of relevant users grows approximately quadratically. This is attributed to the fact that extracting the social proximity measure from the social network only involves solving a linear equation system, typically featuring polynomial complexity for sparse matrices. While the extraction of social roles in X^* and X^{*+} is costly; their overall execution efficiency, however, is fairly reasonable, considering the scale of the small blue social network (over 40K individuals).

Further, in addition to the activities (bookmarks) in the dataset, we randomly injected in a set of user-activity pairs to evaluate the scalability of xAccess against the size of activity data. The right plot of Figure 8 demonstrates how the volume of activity data affects the efficiency of xAccess (with h fixed as 2), which exhibits even less significant impact over the performance of xAccess, compared with the scale of social network (note that X and X^+ are not affected). This can be attributed to that 1) Gibbs sampling and the optimization of entropy filtering significantly reduces the overall complexity of social role mining; and 2) the number of social activities usually grows quadratically with the scale of the underlying social network.

7. CONCLUSION

This work presents a systematic study on the problem of specifying access control policies over personal data on social sites. We proposed xAccess, a novel automated policy specification tool that can help ordinary social site users understand, specify, and diagnose their privacy settings. Compared with prior work, xAccess highlights itself with three distinct features: 1) it adopts a role-based access control model, instead of the conventional rule-based one, which leads to privacy policies semantically interpretable by users; 2) it exploits both static social network structures and dynamic social activities in extracting the underlying social roles; 3) it considers potential inconsistency in user input permission assignments, and proposes effective countermeasure against such inconsistency. Extensive experiments over real social network data have been conducted to validate the efficacy of xAccess.

Acknowledgements

Research was sponsored by the Army Research Laboratory and was accomplished under Cooperative Agreement Number W911NF-09-2-0053. The views and conclusions contained in this document are those of the authors and should not be interpreted as representing the official policies, either expressed or implied, of the Army Research Laboratory or the U.S. Government. The U.S. Government is authorized to reproduce and distribute reprints for Government purposes notwithstanding any copyright notation here on. This work is also partially supported by grants from NSF NetSE, CyberTrust, an IBM faculty award and a grant from Intel ISTC.

8. REFERENCES

[1] British spy chief's cover blown on Facebook: http://www.reuters.com/article/idustre56403820090705.

[2] facebook - Press Room: http://www.facebook.com/press.

[3] Lotus Connections - Dogear: http://www.ibm.com/dogear.

[4] Teacher fired over Facebook sues district: http://www.cbsatlanta.com/news/21573759/detail.html.

[5] L. Backstrom, C. Dwork, and J. Kleinberg. Wherefore art thou r3579x?: anonymized social networks, hidden patterns, and structural steganography. In *WWW*, 2007.

[6] R. Baden, A. Bender, N. Spring, B. Bhattacharjee, and D. Starin. Persona: an online social network with user-defined privacy. In *SIGCOMM*, 2009.

[7] S. Bhagat, G. Cormode, B. Krishnamurthy, and D. Srivastava. Class-based graph anonymization for social network data. *Proc. VLDB Endow.*, 2(1):766–777, 2009.

[8] T. Cormen, C. Leiserson, R. Rivest, and C. Stein. *Introduction to algorithms*. MIT Press, Cambridge, MA, USA, 2001.

[9] D. E. Denning. A lattice model of secure information flow. *Commun. ACM*, 19(5):236–243, 1976.

[10] L. Fang and K. Lefevre. Privacy wizards for social networking sites. In *WWW*, 2010.

[11] D. F. Ferraiolo, R. Sandhu, S. Gavrila, D. R. Kuhn, and R. Chandramouli. Proposed nist standard for role-based access control. *ACM Trans. Inf. Syst. Secur.*, 4(3):224–274, 2001.

[12] R. Fisman, S. S. Iyengar, E. Kamenica, and I. Simonson. Gender differences in mate selection: Evidence from a speed dating experiment. *The Quarterly Journal of Economics*, 121(2):673–697, 2006.

[13] M. Hay, G. Miklau, D. Jensen, D. Towsley, and P. Weis. Resisting structural re-identification in anonymized social networks. *Proc. VLDB Endow.*, 1(1):102–114, 2008.

[14] C.-Y. Lin, N. Cao, S. X. Liu, S. Papadimitriou, J. Sun, and X. Yan. Smallblue: Social network analysis for expertise search and collective intelligence. In *ICDE*, 2009.

[15] K. Liu and E. Terzi. Towards identity anonymization on graphs. In *SIGMOD*, 2008.

[16] K. Liu and E. Terzi. A framework for computing the privacy scores of users in online social networks. In *ICDM*, 2009.

[17] A. Narayanan and V. Shmatikov. De-anonymizing social networks. In *SP*, 2009.

[18] J.-Y. Pan, H.-J. Yang, C. Faloutsos, and P. Duygulu. Automatic multimedia cross-modal correlation discovery. In *KDD*, 2004.

[19] C. P. Robert and G. Casella. *Monte Carlo Statistical Methods (Springer Texts in Statistics)*. Springer-Verlag New York, Inc., 2005.

[20] M. Rosen-Zvi, T. Griffiths, M. Steyvers, and P. Smyth. The author-topic model for authors and documents. In *UAI*, 2004.

[21] H. Shaklee and B. Fischhoff. Discounting in Multicausal Attribution: The Principle of Minimal Causation. *SSRN eLibrary*, 1905.

[22] K. Singh, S. Bhola, and W. Lee. xbook: Redesigning privacy control in social networking platforms. In *SECURITY*, 2009.

[23] H. H. Song, T. W. Cho, V. Dave, Y. Zhang, and L. Qiu. Scalable proximity estimation and link prediction in online social networks. In *IMC*, 2009.

[24] R. Stark. *Sociology*. Cengage Learning, 2006.

[25] G. Wondracek, T. Holz, E. Kirda, and C. Kruegel. A practical attack to de-anonymize social network users. In *SP*, 2010.

[26] L. Zou, L. Chen, and M. T. Özsu. k-automorphism: a general framework for privacy preserving network publication. *Proc. VLDB Endow.*, 2(1):946–957, 2009.

APPENDIX

A. RANDOM WALK WITH RESTART

We assume that each relationship type is associated with a weight, indicating its strength. We use w_{ij} to denote the weight of the relationship $\overline{ij}$ (between two direct friends i and j). Specifically, in RWR, at each step, the walk moves from a user j to one of its friends k with probability proportional to the weight w_{jk}, and returns to j (restart) with probability $(1 - c)$ (c is a parameter). More concretely, let $\mathcal{N}_j$ be the set of friends of j. The transition probability from j to $k \in \mathcal{N}_j$, p_{jk}, is given as:

$$p_{jk} = \frac{w_{jk}}{\sum_{k' \in \mathcal{N}_j} w_{jk'}} \qquad (4)$$

where the parameter c controls the probability of returning to the original node. Stacking p_{ij} into a matrix, column-wise, which produces the column, normalized adjacent matrix W.

B. PARAMETER ESTIMATION

To obtain parameter estimates for the generative model, we employ Gibbs Sampling, a Markov chain Monte Carlo (MCMC) algorithm, as it provides a simple method of performing parameter estimation for Dirichlet priors and allows combinations of estimates from several local maxima of the posterior distribution.

Instead of estimating the model parameters directly, we first evaluate the posterior distribution on role r, then use the results to infer θ_r and ϕ_a. For each activity, the role of users who participate in it

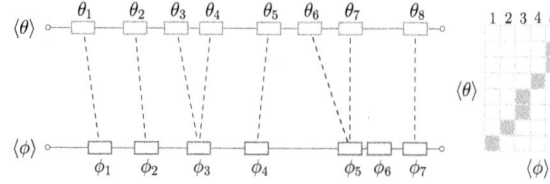

Figure 9: User-permission matching (with quantitative confidentiality scores) using dynamic time warping.

(role assignment) is sampled from the following term:

$$P(r_i = j | a_i = m, u_i = k, \mathbf{r}_{-i}) \propto \frac{C_{mj}^{AR} + \beta}{\sum_{m'} C_{m'j}^{AR} + B\beta} \frac{C_{kj}^{UR} + \alpha}{\sum_{j'} C_{kj'}^{UR} + R\alpha}$$

where $r_i = j$ represents the assignment of the i-th activity, and $a_i = m$ and $u_i = k$ represent that the observation that the user k participates in the i-th event of activity type m; A, B, R, U are the number of activity types, activities, roles, and users, respectively; C_{mj}^{AR} is the number of times that an activity of type m is associated with a social role j, similar for C_{kj}^{UR}; $\mathbf{r}_{-i}$ represents the all the role assignment except the i-th activity. From these count matrices, one can easily estimate the parameters θ_r and ϕ_a as:

$$\phi_{mj} = \frac{C_{mj}^{AR} + \beta}{\sum_{m'} C_{m'j}^{AR}} \qquad \theta_{kj} = \frac{C_{kj}^{UR} + \alpha}{\sum_{j'} C_{kj'}^{UR} + R\alpha}$$

Further, in this process, we use *entropy filtering* to filter non-informative trash activities to improve efficiency. Specifically, after N (a user-specified parameter) iterations of sampling, we start to ignore the set of non-informative activities (trash activities). In our implementation, we measure the informativeness of activities using the entropy of the variable C^{AR}. Particularly, we ignore the i-th activity a_i if the i-th row of C^{AR} has entropy above a threshold ω.

The remaining question is how to select the optimal number of latent roles. We employ the perplexity measure, a standard measure of estimating the performance of a probabilistic model. We run the Gibbs sampling using perplexity score as the termination condition; the number of roles is determined by using the minimum number of roles that leads to the near maximum perplexity. More details are referred to [20].

C. PERMISSIONS WITH CONFIDENTIALITY SCORES

Here we consider the case that each permission is associated with a quantitative confidentiality level[4].

Intuitively, we intend to match the shapes of the entire series $\langle \theta \rangle$ and $\langle \phi \rangle$ to the maximum extent; that is, if the difference between θ_i and $\theta_{i'}$ is (non)significant, so should be the case for ϕ_{m_i} and $\phi_{m_{i'}}$. We can formalize this notion as follows:

$$\min_{m_{(\cdot)}} \sum_i \Delta(\theta_i, \phi_{m_i}) \qquad (5)$$

where $\Delta(\theta_i, \phi_{m_i})$ is the distance between θ_i and ϕ_{m_i}; its concrete definition depending on the definitions of θ and ϕ.

We assume that both series $\langle \theta \rangle$ and $\langle \phi \rangle$ have been properly normalized to the interval of $[0, 1]$ (e.g., via linear interpolation), and $\Delta(\theta, \phi)$ may simply be the absolute value of their difference. Essentially, the optimization problem of Eq. 5 can be re-formulated

---

[4] Here we abuse the notation a little bit, and use ϕ to denote both the permission and its associated confidentiality level (if available).

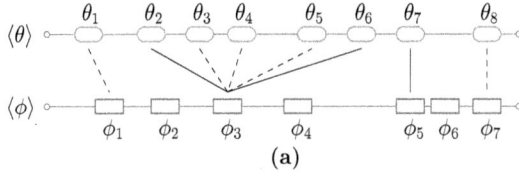

Figure 10: User-permission matching under consistent anchors (solid lines): (a) permissions with confidentiality levels.

as computing the minimum *time warping distance* between $\langle\theta\rangle$ and $\langle\phi\rangle$, $\Delta(\langle\theta\rangle,\langle\phi\rangle)$, with definition given as:

$$\min \begin{cases} \Delta(head(\langle\theta\rangle), head(\langle\phi\rangle)) + \Delta(rest(\langle\theta\rangle), rest(\langle\phi\rangle)) \\ \Delta(\langle\theta\rangle, rest(\langle\phi\rangle)) \end{cases}$$

where $head(\cdot)$ is the first element of a series, and $rest(\cdot)$ is the sub-series without the first element. Specifically, we have

$$\Delta(\langle\rangle,\langle\rangle) = 0 \qquad \Delta(\langle\theta\rangle,\langle\rangle) = \infty \qquad \Delta(\langle\rangle,\langle\phi\rangle) = 0$$

This time warping distance defines a path in the matrix composed of the elements of (θ_i, ϕ_j), corresponding to the alignment of θ_i and ϕ_j, i.e., $m_i = j$, as shown in the right plot of Figure 9. This path represents an optimal mapping between $\langle\theta\rangle$ and $\langle\phi\rangle$. Given the mapping $m_{(\cdot)}$, users with social proximity score θ_i are assigned permission ϕ_{m_i}. The computation of minimum time warping distance can be approached using dynamic programming.

In the case of consistent anchors, we perform piece-wise time-warping distance matching for each piece-pair $\{\theta_{i^*+1}, \ldots, \theta_{j^*-1}\}$ and $\{\phi_{m_{i^*}}, \ldots, \phi_{m_{j^*}}\}$. An example is shown in Figure 10, where the solid lines represent anchors, and the dashed ones derived matches. Note the difference of the match for θ_5 from that in Figure 9. In the case of permission without confidentiality levels,

A Calculus for Privacy-friendly Authentication

Patrik Bichsel
IBM Research – Zurich
pbi@zurich.ibm.com

Jan Camenisch
IBM Research – Zurich
jca@zurich.ibm.com

Dieter Sommer
IBM Research – Zurich
Technische Universität
Darmstadt,
FB Informatik/FG SIT
dso@zurich.ibm.com

ABSTRACT

Establishing authentic channels has become a common operation on the Internet and electronic commerce would not be possible without it. Because traditionally authentication is based on identifying users, the success of electronic commerce causes rapid erosion of their privacy. Privacy-friendly authentication, such as group signatures or anonymous credential systems, could mitigate this issue minimizing the information released during an authentication operation. Unfortunately, privacy-friendly authentication systems are not yet deployed. One reason is their sophistication and feature richness, which is complicating their understanding. By providing a calculus for analyzing and comparing the requirements and goals of privacy-friendly authentication systems, we contribute to a better understanding of such technologies. Our calculus extends the one by Maurer and Schmid [18], by introducing: (1) pseudonyms to enable pseudonymous authentication, (2) a pseudonym annotation function denoting the information an entity reveals about itself, and (3) event-based channel conditions to model conditional release of information used for privacy-friendly accountability.

Categories and Subject Descriptors

C.2 [**Computer Systems Organization**]: Communication/Networking and Information Technology—*Network-level security and protection*

General Terms

Security, Design, Algorithms

Keywords

Authentication, accountability, privacy, security, secure channel modeling, anonymous credential systems

1. INTRODUCTION

Electronic communication networks such as the Internet have an enormous merit when it comes to the ease of distributing information. However, the lack of physical presence requires the communication partners to establish mutual trust using mechanisms

such as authentication. Today, most service providers use a simple authentication approach in which a user shows knowledge of a username/password combination. The use of such simple authentication mechanisms poses severe security risks [15, 23]. Furthermore, the fact that service providers require users to release excessive amounts of (user-provided) personal information upon their first visit erodes privacy. Authentication mechanisms based on technologies such as anonymous credential systems, originally proposed by Chaum [12], provide strong authentication while requiring a user to disclose only the minimal information necessary in a specific context. The drawback of such technologies is that their complexity makes them hard to understand, explain, and compare with traditional approaches. This seems to be an important factor hindering practical deployment so far.

In this paper, we provide a calculus for describing the establishment of secure, i.e., authentic and confidential, channels. We focus on the properties that are particularly important to privacy-friendly authentication. We envision that the improved understanding will contribute in convincing decision makers to adopt privacy-enhancing technology. As a basis we use the model and channel derivation calculus proposed by Maurer and Schmid [18, 19]. Their calculus analyzes the functionality provided by standard cryptographic primitives, i.e., their requirements and security properties when bootstrapping a secure channel. We extend the Maurer-Schmid calculus to model privacy-friendly authentication and accountability. More concretely, we model *pseudonymous authentication*, *attribute-based statements*, and *conditional release* of information.

First, pseudonymous authentication is a basic concept in privacy-friendly authentication. It allows a user to be known to her communication partner only by a pseudonym instead of her unique identity. Consequently, a user can have several unlinkable connections to the same party allowing her to separate different contexts at her discretion. Second, attribute-based statements enable a user to release attributes selectively or even to reveal only a statement about an attribute and thereby fulfill the authentication requirements in a privacy-optimal manner. As an example, consider a liquor store, which is required to verify the age of its customers by regulation. Through attribute-based statements the store can verify the age of customers without requesting any further information. Conversely, in today's practice, the store would request the date-of-birth attribute as contained in an appropriate credential such as an identity card. Third, conditional release of information to a third party is a feature enabling privacy-friendly accountability. It ensures that attributes become available under well-defined circumstances, such as a user abusing the terms and conditions, to designated parties. Conditional release of information can also help in attaining better privacy in general business processes assuming the existence of a mutually trusted party. For instance, when buying a book, a user could release the payment information only to her bank who uses it to bill her. While the service provider can make sure that the user provides the appropriate payment information to her bank, it does not learn this information. Similarly, the shipping information can only be released to the delivery company, which allows the user to have a pseudonymous connection to the book seller itself. Such processes would relieve service providers from knowledge of sensitive personal information, mitigating the risks associated with possession of the latter.

Related Work.

In the area of modeling security of authentication and communication channels, numerous recent papers are available. Typically, they focus on formally verifying security properties of protocols in an automated fashion. Backes, Maffei, and Unruh [3] have integrated zero-knowledge proofs, a major building block of privacy-friendly authentication, into an automated verification tool. Mödersheim and Vigano [20] have later put forth a formal model of pseudonymous channels. Following their approach of modelling pseudonyms, we could aim at a more formal model of attribute-based statements and conditional release of information. However, we want to focus on the intuition and consider a rigorous formalization to be an interesting future contribution. Notable work addressing pseudonymous authentication channels that provides a formal model and tool-based verification of a subset of the idemix protocols has been published by Camenisch, Mödersheim, and Sommer [10].

Regarding semi-formal models of authentication, Maurer and Schmid [19] have introduced a simple, yet expressive, notation allowing for analyzing and comparing protocols that establish secure channels based on standard cryptographic technologies available at the time. This model represents the starting point for various recent formal approaches towards modeling cryptographic functionality [16, 17]. In our paper, we have the same goals as the original model, but for substantially more complex protocols, the properties of which are harder to grasp and only understood by a small group of privacy or cryptography researchers. In contrast to the aforementioned proposals [3, 10, 20] that use more complex and less intuitive notation for achieving their protocol specification and automated verification goals, our model extends the intuitive notation of the model of Maurer and Schmid while retaining its basic concepts and simplicity. Our model can, like Maurer and Schmid's, be used for comparing and analyzing security properties, especially for today's authentication protocols. In addition, our calculus can act as a teaching model for the goals and properties of complex protocols and thereby contribute to a wider understanding of privacy-friendly authentication and accountability technologies and their future deployment. Therefore, our work closes the gap in the space of semi-formal models of expressing cryptographic schemes for privacy-friendly authentication with an intuitive yet formalized method. In this respect our work is orthogonal to the results in the space of formal protocol verification that have been presented before.

Our extension for attribute-based authentication requires authentication properties to be expressed in a suitable language. Sommer [22] presents a logic-based requirements language and dual specification language for attribute-based authentication supporting advanced schemes such as the idemix anonymous credential system. A closely-related language for specifying attribute-based authentication requirements has been put forth by Camenisch et al. [9]. Both contributions allow for combining anonymity of transactions with user accountability based on the ideas originally put forth by Backes et al. [2].

Structure of this Paper.

We start in Section 2 by introducing the main concepts of privacy-friendly authentication. In addition, we provide a brief overview of the channel calculus proposed by Maurer and Schmid [18]. In Section 3 we introduce our extensions to Maurer and Schmid's model. In the same section we extend the set of channel derivation rules to accommodate our extensions. We show in Section 4 how our extended model applies to the examples of standard X.509 certificates, the privacy-enhanced idemix authentication protocols, and the general example of privacy-friendly accountability. Finally, we conclude with a discussion of the merits of our model and future directions in Section 5.

2. PRELIMINARIES

In this section we introduce the most relevant aspects of privacy-friendly authentication and accountability. In addition, we discuss the Maurer-Schmid model that we extend such that it allows for modeling privacy-friendly authentication and accountability.

2.1 Privacy-friendly Authentication

In recent years, numerous cryptographic systems that allow for the protection of a user's privacy have been proposed [4, 5, 6, 8]. An important feature thereby is the ability of a user to authenticate pseudonymously. As outlined in the introduction, we may use privacy-enhanced protocols for fine-grained control of information to be released. Namely, when a user orders a book, the delivery information is only needed by the delivery company and the payment information is only used by the user's bank. However, the entity requesting the authentication (in our example the book shop) has a legitimate interest in getting security assurances. Group signature schemes [4, 5, 13] or anonymous credential systems [6, 8, 12] are examples of technologies that achieve strong authentication guarantees in combination with substantial privacy guarantees. We will focus on anonymous credential systems as they provide the most general set of features.

Anonymous Credential Systems.

Anonymous credential systems allow a user to obtain a certification of attributes from an issuing party, called the *issuer* or *identity provider*. The attributes can be arbitrarily chosen and may include identity attributes (e.g., name, date of birth) or access rights. We refer to the set of certified attributes as the *credential* and to the protocol for obtaining a credential as the *issuing protocol*. Note that privacy protection can be achieved as the issuer does not necessarily learn all the information contained in a credential, i.e., he may not learn all attribute values. After a user has obtained a credential, she can use it to selectively reveal the certified attributes or prove statements about those attributes. As the recipient of such proof usually offers a service in exchange for the proof, we name it a *service provider*, *verifier*, or *relying party* and we call the protocol for proving statements over attributes the *proving protocol*. A main merit of anonymous credentials is that a proof can be done anonymously or pseudonymously, i.e., it does not leak any information that can be linked to the issuing protocol. Some systems, such as the Identity Mixer (idemix) library [21], even allow a user to unlinkably issue proofs based on one credential any number of times. Furthermore, a user can release any subset of the certified information. For instance, a user with an anonymous credential containing her name, address, and birth date, may use this credential to prove that she is older than 21 years without revealing any further information.

In our model we distinguish three components offered by anonymous credential systems that improve privacy: pseudonymous authentication, attribute-based information disclosure, and conditional attribute release.

Pseudonymous Authentication. Systems such as idemix enable a user to choose a pseudonym when authenticating. Whenever a user authenticates using the same pseudonym, the service provider may link the information related to the different transactions. In addition, a service provider may require that one user can only have one pseudonym for a specific domain.

Attribute-based Information Disclosure. While selectively revealing attributes already provides an improvement over standard certification technology w.r.t. the privacy of a user, proving statements about attributes goes even further. Anonymous credentials allow a user to only reveal a statement about attributes instead of the attribute value itself. Such statements include equalities among attributes, or inequalities between attributes or constants.

Conditional Attribute Release. To prevent abuse of the privacy granted to users, service providers may want to ensure that users are accountable for their actions. For example, if a user wants to rent sports equipment, the rental agency does not need any information about the user. Still, in case the user damages or does not return the equipment, the agency wants to have the identity or billing information to claim the damages. In such a situation the user could issue a verifiable encryption containing its identity information on behalf of the local government. As the encryption is verifiable, the agency can verify that it indeed contains the identity information of the user as claimed without learning the specific attribute values. Attached to the verifiable encryption would be the condition that decryption is to be done only if the equipment is damaged or has not been returned at all. The agency as well as the user do trust in the local government to decrypt in case the indicated condition is fulfilled, and only in that case. The example shows how verifiable encryption [1, 11] allows a relying party to attain accountable transactions. During authentication, the relying party requires the user to release a verifiable encryption containing the desired attributes. The encryption to a mutually trusted entity can be verified by the relying party. In addition, the parties agree on a condition defining when the message may be decrypted. The relying party trusts the third party to actually decrypt in case the condition is met and the user trusts it to only decrypt in this case. This assures the relying party that it will learn certain attributes if the user does not act as agreed.

2.2 Formal Model of Secure Channels

Maurer and Schmid [18] define a simple and expressive formal framework for comparing security properties of cryptographic protocols. They propose a channel calculus to compare security properties achieved by standard cryptographic primitives. The capabilities of cryptographic protocols are modeled using channel transformations. Maurer and Schmid highlight the capabilities of their framework by modeling the channel transformations that can be implemented with symmetric-key encryption, message authentication codes, public-key encryption or digital signature schemes. As a further capability, their model simplifies reasoning about trust relations and the transformations enabled through trusted entities. This enables, e.g., the expression of a public key infrastructure in their model.

Maurer and Schmid model two security properties called *authentication* and *confidentiality*. Let us summarize their authentication definition using entities A and B. Informally, if party A is authenticated to party B, the latter is assured that it actually communicates with party A. In other words, if B is convinced that it communicates with a well-defined, unique party A, then there cannot be a

party A' that fakes messages to look as if A had sent them. The confidentiality property is dual to the authentication property, thus, a party B knows that her messages can only be read by a party A (and not A') if it has a confidential channel to A.

$$A \longrightarrow B \quad (1) \qquad A \longrightarrow\!\!\!\bullet\, B \quad (3)$$
$$A \,\bullet\!\!\!\longrightarrow B \quad (2) \qquad A \,\bullet\!\!\!\longrightarrow\!\!\!\bullet\, B \quad (4)$$

Maurer and Schmid use the notation (1) for an insecure channel from A to B, (2) for an authentic channel where A is authentically known to B, and (3) for a confidential channel where A is sure that its messages can be only read by B. A secure channel fulfills the authentication and confidentiality properties of the respective channel endpoints and is denoted as in (4). In their notation a bullet denotes a security property, i.e., either authentication or confidentiality of the respective channel endpoint.

When it comes to channel transformations achieved by using cryptographic protocols, the time at which a channel is available is of importance. Thus, the model defines a channel over which a message, fixed or chosen at time t_1, can be sent at time t_2 to be denoted as $A \bullet\!\!\xrightarrow{t_2[t_1]} B$, where $t_2 > t_1$ must hold. For example, (5) shows that a message can only be forwarded from a party A to C if the time t_3 at which the relaying party B can choose its message is after the time it has received the original message from party A.

$$A \xrightarrow{t_2[t_1]} B, \ B \xrightarrow{t_4[t_3]} C, \ t_3 > t_2 \ \implies A \xrightarrow{t_4[t_1]} C \quad (5)$$

Maurer and Schmid conclude that, using the basic cryptographic primitives they discuss, a security property (i.e., a bullet) at one end of a channel can be re-established at time t_2 using an insecure channel given a bullet on the same side of the channel at time t_1, given $t_2 > t_1$. However, they state that two things cannot be achieved through cryptographic protocols: (1) bullets cannot be created, and (2) bullets cannot be moved from one side of the channel to the other.

3. FORMAL CHANNEL MODEL

We present multiple extensions to Maurer and Schmid's approach of modeling secure channels, which has recently been used for more formal treatments of cryptographic methods [16, 17]. Our extensions aim at modeling privacy-friendly authentication and accountability. First, we extend the notion of authentication such that a party can have multiple different names, denoted as *pseudonyms*. This enhancement accounts for the fact that cryptographic schemes allow a user to authenticate pseudonymously. Second, we enable parties to make *statements about their attributes*. We use those statements to model attribute-based authentication, where the service provider merely learns attributes or predicates about attributes. This allows us to model situations where, e.g., a party presents a statement derived from anonymous credentials. Finally, we use *generic conditions* instead of time semantics to denote when a message has to be chosen by the sender and when a message is sent. Using this generalization allows us to model channels established trough events, which build the basis for privacy-friendly accountability. We now present the extensions to the model of Maurer and Schmid in detail and provide the definitions we build upon.

3.1 Extensions to the Maurer-Schmid Model

We start with presenting the foundations of our model and put it in context with the approach taken by Maurer and Schmid in their work. As Maurer and Schmid, we use channels to model that parties may exchange information and we use a bullet to annotate a security assurance. More concretely, a bullet at the source of a channel denotes an authenticated communication partner and a bullet at the destination stands for a confidential channel. A channel without bullet annotations does not have any security assurances and is called an insecure channel.

3.1.1 Pseudonyms

In the original Maurer-Schmid model, a party is assumed to have a unique, system-wide identifier. Technology-wise, such an identifier can, e.g., be implemented by the unique public key of the party in a system where each party has exactly one public key. In each authentic or confidential channel, the party with the security annotation (i.e., the bullet) is known to its communication partner by this unique identifier. This is a core property of the model, based on which channels can be composed to obtain a target channel. A major drawback of this modeling approach is that it cannot reflect the capabilities of today's privacy-enhanced authentication technologies. We overcome this limitation by allowing parties to have and act under multiple pseudonyms. Therefore, we define channels to connect two pseudonyms instead of the parties themselves. Intuitively, a cryptographic pseudonym can be seen as the equivalent of a public key in that it (provably) can be related to a secret key. However, a party A can generate an arbitrary number of pseudonyms using a single secret key. Note that a party knowing a set of pseudonyms (without the corresponding secret information) cannot distinguish whether or not they have been generated using the same user secret. Thus, we denote pseudonyms to be *unlinkable*.

More formally, given a set of user secrets $\mathfrak{S}$ and a set of parties $\mathfrak{P}$, each party $P \in \mathfrak{P}$ is assigned a secret $s_i \in \mathfrak{S}$ using a function $f : \mathfrak{P} \to \mathfrak{S}$. Note that extending this situation to using several secrets per user is straightforward. Let us assume a function $nym(\cdot, \cdot)$ that takes a user secret and a randomization factor as input and outputs a pseudonym $n_i \in \mathfrak{N}$. First, we assume that pseudonyms are unique, i.e., $(\forall s_1, s_2 \in \mathfrak{S} \; \forall n_1, n_2 : n_1 = nym(s_1, \cdot), n_2 = nym(s_2, \cdot)) : n_1 \neq n_2$. Second, the unlinkability property of pseudonyms n_1, n_2 is defined as follows: Let $\mathfrak{B}_j = \{nym(s_j, \cdot)\}$ be the set of all pseudonyms based on secret s_j, for $j \in \{1, 2\}$. Unlinkability of n_1 and n_2 is equivalent to the following cases (1) $n_1 \in \mathfrak{B}_1, n_2 \in \mathfrak{B}_2$ and (2) $n_1, n_2 \in \mathfrak{B}_1$ being (computationally or information-theoretically) indistinguishable. As suggested by the analogy of pseudonyms with public keys, a party P with secret $s_p = f(P)$, and pseudonym $n_i = nym(s_p, r)$ can prove to a communication partner that she is the legitimate owner of n_i (i.e., that she knows the secrets s_p and r corresponding to n_i). Because of the uniqueness of pseudonyms we can define a mapping function $p(\cdot)$ using a pseudonym as input and providing the corresponding party as output. We denote with $P = p(n_i)$ that party P is the holder of pseudonym n_i, i.e., $n_i = nym(s_p, \cdot)$. This mapping function p between parties and their pseudonyms is needed for expressing our channel composition rules. More concretely, we use this function to compose channels with different pseudonyms, where the composition requires the party having generated those pseudonyms being the same. Note that this function is not available to parties within the system since this would invalidate the unlinkability property.

In our channel model we use a more intuitive notation, where we denote a pseudonym of a party A in a communication as $\mathcal{A}_i$ instead of n_i. Note that this notion closely relates to what is denoted as $[A]_i$ by Mödersheim and Vigano [20]. However, our unlinkability property of pseudonyms goes further than their perspective in which pseudonyms model *sender invariance*, where a recipient is assured to be communicating with the same sender (e.g., through the use of an unauthenticated public key). In any prac-

tical system, pseudonyms can be realized through cryptographic mechanisms, e.g., using a commitment scheme as in anonymous credential systems [8]. A user may generate a polynomial number of pseudonyms $\mathcal{A}_i$ such that uniqueness of the pseudonyms is attained with overwhelming probability. Depending on the cryptographic scheme, the unlinkability can hold computationally or even information-theoretically.

Note that certain scenarios merit from a party having a unique pseudonym. As an example, a well-known service provider may profit from having only one pseudonym and it does not benefit from the privacy that multiple pseudonyms offer. In such cases we use *public pseudonyms*, i.e., for a party I we would denote the public pseudonym as $\mathcal{I}$, omitting the index.

3.1.2 Authentication and Confidentiality

As we specify channels between pseudonyms that parties act under, and not between parties themselves, we need to appropriately define authentication for our model.

DEFINITION 1 (PSEUDONYM AUTHENTICATION). *An entity A acting under pseudonym $\mathcal{A}_b$ is pseudonym authenticated towards an entity B acting under pseudonym $\mathcal{B}_a$ if B is assured that it communicates with the entity legitimately holding pseudonym $\mathcal{A}_b$.*

The intuition behind this definition is aligned with the original model, with the difference that B is assured that it communicates with a party holding the pseudonym $\mathcal{A}_b$ instead of being assured that it communicates with party A known under its unique identifier. The difference articulates in the situation where a party A repeatedly communicates with another entity. In such case, we can see that using the different pseudonyms $\mathcal{A}_i$ and $\mathcal{A}_{\bar{i}}$ allows A to maintain two authenticated but unlinkable communication channels with her communication partner. Consequently, parties are only linkable when using the same pseudonym on several channels. Note that the definition does not touch on information that is released through the channel, in particular, it does not specify attributes that B knows about the pseudonyms, i.e., about the parties holding them.

In the Maurer-Schmid model, the dual property to authentication is confidentiality. In analogy, we introduce the notion of pseudonym confidentiality.

DEFINITION 2 (PSEUDONYM CONFIDENTIALITY). *A channel between an entity A acting under pseudonym $\mathcal{A}_b$ and an entity B acting under pseudonym $\mathcal{B}_a$ is pseudonym confidential if A can be ensured that only the party holding pseudonym $\mathcal{B}_a$ has access to the messages sent on this channel.*

Clearly, authentication and confidentiality as modeled by Maurer and Schmid are a special case of our extended model where every party is constrained to one unique, system-wide identifier. How our changes affect the model can be most easily expressed using the examples of the basic channels, i.e., *insecure*, *authenticated*, *confidential*, and *secure* channel.

Insecure Channel.

We start with an insecure channel from A acting under pseudonym $\mathcal{A}_b$ to B acting under pseudonym $\mathcal{B}_a$. We model this similarly to the Maurer-Schmid model, with the difference that not parties but pseudonyms are denoted as communication partners. Thus, we denote such insecure channel as

$$\mathcal{A}_b \longrightarrow \mathcal{B}_a \ . \tag{6}$$

Note that the index of a pseudonym denotes the *intended* communication partner, e.g., $\mathcal{A}_b$ for A communicating with B.

We can look at the channel in two different ways. First, it visualizes the security information (authentication or confidentiality) available to the communicating parties. From this point of view, the entity $A = p(\mathcal{A}_b)$ may be any party in the system. This results from the fact that the pseudonym does not have a security annotation (i.e., a bullet). $\mathcal{A}_b$ here is simply a name used to refer to the *intended channel endpoint*. Party $B = p(\mathcal{B}_a)$ learns only the unauthenticated pseudonym about its communication partner. This is what we define as an insecure channel: similarly to using an unauthenticated public key, the pseudonym does not imply communication with the party legitimately holding the pseudonym. Second, an insecure channel denotes the availability of a channel. For our channel transformations we often use insecure channels between two pseudonyms to denote that the parties holding the pseudonyms have access to a communication channel.

Authentic Channel.

An example of a channel from A, the holder of $\mathcal{A}_b$, to B, the holder of $\mathcal{B}_a$, where the pseudonym $\mathcal{A}_b$ is authenticated is denoted as

$$\mathcal{A}_b \bullet\!\longrightarrow \mathcal{B}_a \quad . \tag{7}$$

Note that B does not know which party holds the pseudonym $\mathcal{A}_b$. This results from the unlinkability of pseudonyms as well as the fact that parties within the system do not have access to the function p. Party A can send messages authenticated as $\mathcal{A}_b$ to $\mathcal{B}_a$ over this channel where the former does not have any (authentic) information on the pseudonym it sends its messages to. By extension, A does not have any information on the party $B = p(\mathcal{B}_a)$. This is the natural notation of a pseudonym authenticated channel based on the notation of an authenticated channel in the model of Maurer and Schmid where authentication is defined in a more restrictive way through a party authenticating under its system-wide identifier.

Confidential Channel.

We generalize confidential channels similarly to authentic channels. Instead of knowing that the channel is established with an entity specified by a unique identifier, the message recipient of a pseudonym confidential channel is known to be a party holding a specified pseudonym. In an example, we denote a pseudonym confidential channel from a pseudonymous party $\mathcal{A}_b$ to a party B holding $\mathcal{B}_a$ as

$$\mathcal{A}_b \longrightarrow\!\bullet \mathcal{B}_a \quad . \tag{8}$$

In this example, only the pseudonym $\mathcal{B}_a$ comprises an assurance.

Secure Channel.

A secure channel between the pseudonyms $\mathcal{A}_b$ and $\mathcal{B}_a$ assures the parties $A = p(\mathcal{A}_b)$ and $B = p(\mathcal{B}_a)$, holding the pseudonyms $\mathcal{A}_b$ and $\mathcal{B}_a$, that their communication partner is the party holding the denoted pseudonym. We denote a secure channel as

$$\mathcal{A}_b \bullet\!\longrightarrow\!\bullet \mathcal{B}_a \quad . \tag{9}$$

Note that we simplify the notation in the remainder of the paper by saying that a pseudonym $\mathcal{A}_b$ having a channel to a pseudonym $\mathcal{B}_a$ as shorthand notation for the party $A = p(\mathcal{A}_b)$, i.e., party A holding pseudonym $\mathcal{A}_b$, having a channel to party $B = p(\mathcal{B}_a)$.

3.1.3 Attribute-based Pseudonym Annotations

For modeling privacy-friendly authentication we not only need to model pseudonymous communication but also the exchange of attributes. This goes well beyond what Maurer and Schmid can express in their model where authentication is a binary property indicated through the bullet and the authentication information remains implicit. Due to the importance of attribute-based authentication in today's information systems and application scenarios, we make an extension to the Maurer-Schmid model to capture this concept.

We implement this by annotating the pseudonyms with a formula ϕ that expresses the attribute statements a party makes.

DEFINITION 3 (ATTRIBUTE-BASED ANNOTATION). *An attribute-based annotation of a pseudonym $\mathcal{A}_b$ held by an entity A is defined as the statements ϕ about $\mathcal{A}_b$ being released to the communication partner.*

This definition means that the party B learns attribute statements as defined by ϕ, which are expressed as a logic-based formula. In case the pseudonym is annotated with a bullet, this allows its communication partner to derive that the statements are about a *given* pseudonym, e.g., $\mathcal{A}_b$ in the definition. Without a bullet, the statement is purely a declaration about an (unverified) pseudonym. Consequently, the presence or absence of a bullet annotation of a pseudonym making an attribute-based statement plays the crucial role of defining whether the statement is about the indicated pseudonym or not. Note that the direction of the channel between $\mathcal{A}_b$ and $\mathcal{B}_a$ is orthogonal to the attribute-based pseudonym annotation. That is, we assume the attributes can be learnt by the communication partner even if the channel direction does not suggest so.

Channel Syntax.

To express that $\mathcal{A}_b$ has a pseudonym authenticated channel to $\mathcal{B}_a$ with pseudonym annotation ϕ we use the notation

$$\mathcal{A}_b{}^\phi \bullet\!\longrightarrow \mathcal{B}_a \quad . \tag{10}$$

That is, entity $B = p(\mathcal{B}_a)$ is ensured that it has a channel with the party holding pseudonym $\mathcal{A}_b$ and in addition learns attribute information as specified by ϕ about this party. Note that we often annotate the formula to illustrate the pseudonymous entity that is described, e.g., $\phi_{\mathcal{A}_b}$ in case the information is about $\mathcal{A}_b$.

We naturally extend this notion to a secure channel by providing an annotation also at the recipient pseudonym of a channel, the syntax being as follows:

$$\mathcal{A}_b{}^{\phi_{\mathcal{A}_b}} \bullet\!\longrightarrow\!\bullet{}^{\phi_{\mathcal{B}_a}} \mathcal{B}_a \quad . \tag{11}$$

In addition to the properties of the channel before, this channel ensures that it is pseudonym confidential to $\mathcal{B}_a$ and the party holding $\mathcal{A}_b$ learns the attribute statement $\phi_{\mathcal{B}_a}$. As noted previously, we mean the parties holding the pseudonyms when we talk about pseudonyms exchanging information.

Annotation Formula.

For defining how the attribute annotations relate to the channel transformations, we introduce our approach of expressing the annotation formula ϕ and provide an intuition on how it expresses statements.

The simple approach of expressing attribute statements by modeling them as a set of attribute-value pairs is not powerful enough for expressing data-minimizing statements about parties. Concretely, it is lacking the following features: (1) Revealing partial information about an attribute value, (2) grouping of attributes, and (3) relating attributes without revealing them. Feature (1) is necessary for making data-minimizing statements, e.g., revealing that the date of birth attribute is less than a given reference date to establish a minimum age of a user. Feature (2) can be used to make statements about attributes that conceptually belong together, e.g., about the number and expiration date of a specific credit card of a person. Feature (3) allows for specifying that an attribute of one attribute collection is in a relation with an attribute of another collection. For instance, the last name of a party's driver's license can be expressed to be the same as the one on its eID card. For realizing those features, we decided to model a pseudonym annotation as a formula ϕ in a logic as explained next.

We start with the basic concept of a *credential* used to group attributes into attribute collections, which was done eralier by Camenisch et al. [9] and Sommer [22], where the attributes can be certified using a suitable technology, or remain uncertified. Suitable technologies for certification are, e.g., X.509 attribute certificates [14], anonymous credential systems such as idemix [21] or U-Prove [7], or identity federation schemes with an online identity provider. A possible example for a credential is one of type Electronic Identity Card (eID Card), issued by the Swiss Government using idemix anonymous credential technology. Such credential could, e.g., comprise the attributes first name, last name, and date of birth of the credential's holder. By referring to the attributes of credential c using the "."-notation, as for example in c.a, we can address attributes of credentials, in this example attribute a of credential c.

To make statements about attributes of credentials, we use *predicates*. A predicate can make a statement about an attribute and a constant or about two attributes. For example, the $Eq(\cdot, \cdot)$-predicate expresses equality between its two arguments, where the arguments may be attributes of credentials or constants. Another example is the $Leq(\cdot, \cdot)$-predicate expressing the relation "less than or equal" between the first and second argument. The predicate

$$Eq(\text{c}.dateOfBirth, 1978\text{-}12\text{-}01)$$

expresses, e.g., that the attribute *dateOfBirth* of credential c is equal to the constant date value 1978-12-01.

With privacy-friendly authentication we want to express, e.g., a predicate specifying that the attribute *dateOfBirth* of credential c is less than or equal to the constant date value 1991-06-20 to establish that an entity has an age greater than or equal to 21 years, when being considered on 2012-06-20. This predicate expresses a statement over an attribute, providing less information compared to releasing its value. Such information is sufficient for many scenarios, e.g., where only a minimum age has to be established.

$$Leq(\text{c}.dateOfBirth, 1991\text{-}06\text{-}20)$$

We abstract in our syntax from using different predicate terms depending on the argument types, e.g., for expressing equality on strings and integers, but overload those into a single predicate term to simplify the notation without loss of expressiveness. Not all predicates are defined for all argument types due to constraints of the cryptographic proof system of idemix and other protocols. The inequality predicates $Leq(\cdot, \cdot)$, $Lt(\cdot, \cdot)$, $Geq(\cdot, \cdot)$, and $Leq(\cdot, \cdot)$ can by applied to attribute types with a total order (e.g., integers or dates) with their usual semantics. The Eq-predicate is applicable to arguments of any type supported by the underlying technology.

Multiple predicates can be connected with the operators $\wedge$ and $\vee$ as is standard in logic to obtain a sentence or formula ϕ expressing attribute statements:

$$\phi_0 = Eq(\text{c}.lastName, \text{Doe}) \wedge$$
$$Eq(\text{c}.dateOfBirth, 1978\text{-}12\text{-}01) \wedge$$
$$Eq(\text{c}.type, \text{eID\_Card}) \ .$$

The formula ϕ_0 expresses values of the attributes of credential c by relating the values with the constants through Eq-predicates. A formula like this can be used to specify the attribute values of a credential of a party as being certified by an identity provider, e.g., for an anonymous credential the party obtains as an eID card.

Our language for expressing ϕ is based on a fragment of the logic of [22] for modeling identity statements with a focus on privacy-preserving identity management through the data minimization features, though we omit multiple features that are not relevant for our model.

As in standard logic we can derive new formulae from an existing formula, e.g., a formula ϕ_1 from a formula ϕ_0, which is denoted as $\phi_0 \vdash \phi_1$. Continuing the example from before, the holder of credential c specified through ϕ_0 can derive a formula ϕ_1 that comprises partial information about the credential's attribute values and is "consistent" with the statements in ϕ_0. Using appropriate technology such as an anonymous credential system, a party can prove this formula correct, i.e., consistent with the issued anonymous credential, to a recipient party.

$$\phi_1 = Leq(\text{c}_1.dateOfBirth, 1991\text{-}06\text{-}20) \wedge$$
$$Eq(\text{c}_1.type, \text{eID\_Card})$$

The credential must be renamed to prevent undesired linkability of formulae, e.g., c is renamed to c_1 in the above example.

3.1.4 Channel Conditions

The timing annotation $t_2[t_1]$ of a channel in the model of Maurer and Schmid has the semantics that the message has to be fixed at time t_1 and can be sent at time t_2 over the channel where $t_2 > t_1$ must always hold. We extend this purely time-based semantics with *event-based semantics* for modeling more general *conditions*. The original timing semantics is a special case of our extended notion. This extension particularly allows for realizing conditional release of data, e.g., to model privacy-friendly accountability. Events are specified through monotone formulae in a generic manner.

We define the function $\tau(c)$ for specifying the time at which the event or event formula c occurs. For event formulae c_1 and c_2, we recursively define for $c = c_1 \wedge c_2$, $\tau(c) = \text{Max}(\tau(c_1), \tau(c_2))$, and for $c = c_1 \vee c_2$, $\tau(c) = \text{Min}(\tau(c_1), \tau(c_2))$. For an atomic event c, $\tau(c) = t$ for a constant time value t from a totally-ordered set that indicates the time the event occurs. This defines the function $\tau(c)$ recursively for all monotone formulae for specifying events. Extracted time components of event formulae can be compared using the binary relations $=, <, \leq, \geq$ and $>$ as in the Maurer-Schmid model. For example, $\tau(c_3) > \tau(c_2)$ expresses that the event formula c_3 must have been fulfilled strictly after c_2. An event can model fulfillment of any condition, e.g., a condition used for modeling conditional release as in Section 4.3 or a simple time condition for specifying times.

A channel symbol in our model is annotated with $c_2[c_1]$ where the message on the channel needs to be fixed before $\tau(c_1)$ and the message is sent over the channel at $\tau(c_2)$. In the following example we can see how the general conditions naturally extend the time-based notion of Maurer and Schmid, where we generalize the conditions using the example introduced in Equation (5).

$$\mathcal{A}_b \xrightarrow{c_2[c_1]} \mathcal{B}_a, \quad \mathcal{B}_c \xrightarrow{c_4[c_3]} \mathcal{C}_b, \quad p(\mathcal{B}_a) = p(\mathcal{B}_c), \quad \tau(c_3) > \tau(c_2)$$
$$\implies \mathcal{A}_b \xrightarrow{c_4[c_1]} \mathcal{C}_b$$

Thus, we can see that if we assume $B = p(\mathcal{B}_a) = p(\mathcal{B}_c)$ to be reliable, then $\mathcal{A}_b$ attains a channel to $\mathcal{C}_b$. A reliable party, as in the original model, states that a party forwards the received messages. We assume that all parties are reliable. When it comes to the events of the resulting channel, we can see that messages have to be fixed by $\mathcal{A}_b$ before $\tau(c_1)$ such that they can be sent via B. Still, the target channel only is ready to transmit the message after $\tau(c_4)$, i.e., at the time the channel from $\mathcal{B}_c$ to $\mathcal{C}_b$ becomes available. Note that in the originating channels we require that B can select the message sent to C_b only after having received the message from A_b.

All previously discussed examples can be extended with channel conditions to express the conditions under which the message has been fixed or can be sent over the channel in a straightforward manner. Consequently, whenever there are no specific requirements on channel conditions we omit them for simpler notation. An example for such a situation being that the only requirement on the conditions is that the message on the target channel cannot be fixed before the last message of any source channel has been sent.

3.2 Channel Transformations

We have to define the transformation rules with annotated channels as per our extension to obtain a sensible channel transformation algebra. All transformation rules of Maurer and Schmid can be carried over to our model and they need to be adapted to our notation. We refer to those transformations as basic channel transformations and provide some examples of how we change the original rules to the setting of our model. Additionally, we show how attribute-based annotations are transformed when we apply channel transformations. The rule set comprising the basic channel transformation rules and the new rules presented in this section are the basis for our extended Maurer-Schmid channel composition algebra. This small rule set is sufficient for the channel derivation calculus we propose and is minimal.

3.2.1 Basic Channel Transformations

Let us show by the example of a transformation enabled through public-key cryptography how we amend the transformations of Maurer and Schmid.

$$\mathcal{A}_b \bullet \xrightarrow{c_2[c_1]} \mathcal{B}_a, \ \mathcal{A}_b \xleftarrow{c_4[c_3]} \mathcal{B}_a, \ \tau(c_3) > \tau(c_2)$$
$$\implies \mathcal{A}_b \bullet \xleftarrow{c_4[c_3]} \mathcal{B}_a$$

The example transformation rule specifies that an authenticated channel from $\mathcal{A}_b$ to $\mathcal{B}_a$ over which a message fixed when condition c_1 holds and sent when c_2 holds, can be used to create a confidential channel from $\mathcal{B}_a$ to $\mathcal{A}_b$.

We use the same notion of *trust* as Maurer and Schmid, i.e., if we say that $\mathcal{R}$ trusts $\mathcal{I}$ we mean that $R = p(\mathcal{R})$ trusts $I = p(\mathcal{I})$ to correctly authenticate entities. In an example where $\mathcal{B}_a$ trusts $\mathcal{I}$, an authenticated channel can be built from two authenticated channels using $\mathcal{I}$ to forward the message from one channel to the other.

$$\mathcal{A}_i \bullet \xrightarrow{c_2[c_1]} \mathcal{I}, \ \mathcal{I} \bullet \xrightarrow{c_4[c_3]} \mathcal{B}_a, \ \mathcal{B}_a \text{ trusts } \mathcal{I}, \ \tau(c_3) > \tau(c_2) \quad (12)$$
$$\implies \mathcal{A}_i \bullet \xrightarrow{c_4[c_1]} \mathcal{B}_a$$

Similarly as in these examples, all transformations due to Maurer and Schmid can be adapted by denoting channels between pseudonyms as well as adapting the time constraints to generic constraints. As stated previously, we use the notion of *reliability* as in the Maurer-Schmid model, i.e., a reliable party dependably forwards received messages. Thus, reliability can be seen as a weak form of trust, which we assume to hold for all parties.

3.2.2 Attribute-based Transformations

A main aspect of our model is to allow parties to provide attribute information through the pseudonym annotation function ϕ. We next present channel transformation rules that define how attribute-based pseudonym annotations are propagated between channels. Note that those rules are orthogonal to the rules about the propagation of security annotations (i.e., bullets). This is relevant as channels with both, security and pseudonym, annotations are the most common ones in practice.

Combining Pseudonym Annotations.

A basic rule defines how pseudonym annotations of two channels between the same entities can be combined. This is relevant in a scenario where two parties A and B repeatedly communicate using the same pseudonyms $\mathcal{A}_b$ and $\mathcal{B}_a$.

$$\mathcal{A}_b \xrightarrow{\phi_1} \mathcal{B}_a, \ \mathcal{A}_b \xrightarrow{\phi_2} \mathcal{B}_a$$
$$\implies \mathcal{A}_b \xrightarrow{\phi_3} \mathcal{B}_a, \ \phi_3 = \phi_1 \wedge \phi_2$$

The intuition behind this rule is that statements about a party A acting under a pseudonym $\mathcal{A}_b$ with a party $\mathcal{B}_a$ over different channels can be combined into a new channel revealing a statement that is the conjunction of both statements. To the best of our knowledge, no cryptographic protocols that would combine ϕ_1 and ϕ_2 with other operations than conjunction exist. This rule can, like any other rule, be applied recursively to combine security properties from $k > 2$ channels into a single newly-created channel.

Connecting Pseudonym-annotated Channels.

Another new rule specifies how annotations propagate to a new channel that is created through a party connecting two channels. For example, similar to the trust-based rule in Equation (12) that allows for propagation of a security annotation, trust enables propagation of pseudonym annotations.

$$\mathcal{A}_i \xrightarrow{\phi_1 \ c_2[c_1]} \mathcal{I}, \ \mathcal{I} \bullet \xrightarrow{c_4[c_3]} \mathcal{B}_a, \ \mathcal{B}_a \text{ trusts } \mathcal{I}, \ \tau(c_3) > \tau(c_2)$$
$$\implies \mathcal{A}_i \xrightarrow{\phi_1 \ c_4[c_1]} \mathcal{B}_a$$

The rule shows how a pseudonym annotation of $\mathcal{A}_r$ can be transferred from the first channel to the target channel, using a party $\mathcal{I}$ as trusted intermediary. A noteworthy aspect of this rule is that the second prerequisite channel of the rule needs a bullet annotation on the side of $\mathcal{I}$ because otherwise the trust relation does not have any meaning as the pseudonym could be employed by any party.

K-fold Transfer of Certified Information.

Let us investigate the transformation required to model a setting of an identity provider I issuing certificates, e.g., anonymous credentials. The parties receiving the credentials use them to authenticate to other entities releasing attribute statements. In particular, we focus on a situation where several credentials are used to generate one attribute-based annotation.

The following transformation rule allows a party $A = p(\mathcal{A}_b)$ to use the authentications with k parties $\mathcal{I}_i$ with $1 \leq i \leq k$ to establish a new channel to $B = p(\mathcal{B}_a)$ with the pseudonym annotation comprising a combination of the annotations of the channels with $\mathcal{I}_i$.

$$\left(\mathcal{A}_i \xrightarrow{\phi_i \ \bullet c_{i_2}[c_{i_1}]} \mathcal{I}_i, \mathcal{I}_i \bullet \xrightarrow{c_{i_4}[c_{i_3}]} \mathcal{B}_i, \right.$$
$$\left. \tau(c_5) > \tau(c_{i_2}), \tau(c_5) > \tau(c_{i_4}), \mathcal{B}_i \text{ trusts } I_i \right)_{\forall 1 \leq i \leq k}$$
$$\left(p(\mathcal{A}_i) = p(\mathcal{A}_b), p(\mathcal{B}_i) = p(\mathcal{B}_a) \right)_{\forall 1 \leq i \leq k}$$
$$\mathcal{A}_b \xrightarrow{\phi' \ c_6[c_5]} \mathcal{B}_a, \ \left(\bigwedge_{i=1}^{k} \phi_i \right) \vdash \phi'$$
$$\implies \mathcal{A}_b \bullet \xleftarrow{\phi' \ c_6[c_5]} \mathcal{B}_a$$

This rule models establishing an attribute-based authentication of $\mathcal{A}_b$ with $\mathcal{B}_a$ where the attribute statement ϕ' is composed from multiple attribute statements ϕ_i. The latter are the annotation functions A has established using possibly different pseudonyms with parties $\mathcal{I}_i, 1 \leq i \leq k$. Note that this rule is atomic and cannot be derived from the basic rule and composition of channel rules because in this case it would be only possible to have $\phi' = \bigwedge_{i=1}^{k} \phi_i$. However, this would not be in line with privacy-preserving attribute statements. The above rule reflects what technologies such as the idemix credential system can achieve. Namely, they allow for stating relations between attributes enclosed in the credentials a party holds, not only their combination.

The above procedure can be integrated with public key infrastructures such that there need not exist a direct authenticated channel between $\mathcal{I}_i$ and $\mathcal{B}_i$, but between $\mathcal{I}$ and a certification authority $\mathcal{C}$ as well as $\mathcal{C}$ and $\mathcal{B}_c$ such that $\mathcal{C}$ is taking the role of a trust mediator for ensuring authenticity of the public keys of $\mathcal{I}_i$. We can model this derivation following the standard channel transformation rules of the Maurer-Schmid model.

4. EXAMPLES

In this section we illustrate the expressivity of our extensions with several examples. First, we discuss how to model the issuing and use of a standard X.509 certificate. Second, we extend the first example to one using a privacy-friendly anonymous credential, e.g., using idemix or U-Prove. Finally, we show how we model privacy-friendly accountability achieved by verifiable encryption.

4.1 X.509 Certificates

A standard X.509 certificate gets issued by an identity provider I to a user A. The identity provider uses a public pseudonym $\mathcal{I}$ and the user creates a pseudonym $\mathcal{A}_i$ that it only uses in this transaction. After having received the certificate, A may use the cryptographic token to present the certified attributes to a relying party R. The latter uses its public pseudonym $\mathcal{R}$.

Certificate Issuing.

The requirements for issuing a standard certificate using technology such as X.509 must allow the identity provider I to verify that $\mathcal{A}_i$ possesses the attributes $\phi_{\mathcal{A}_i}$ it will certify. In addition it will need a channel to $\mathcal{A}_i$ to send the certificate. The confidentiality of the target channel can be achieved using public-key cryptography as described in Section 3.2.1.

$$\mathcal{I} \longleftarrow\bullet^{\phi_{\mathcal{A}_i}} \mathcal{A}_i,\ \mathcal{I} \longrightarrow \mathcal{A}_i \implies \mathcal{I} \longrightarrow\bullet^{\phi_{\mathcal{A}_i}} \mathcal{A}_i$$

Through the available channels, the recipient does not get any security assurance about the issuer. In real world scenarios an identity provider, e.g., a state or a bank, may base the issuing of a credential on a strongly identifying transaction where the user needs to physically visit the issuer. Through such visit, the user authenticates the identity provider. Even if the authentication is not strictly necessary, the user may want to only provide her attributes after establishing a confidential channel, i.e., $\mathcal{I}\longleftarrow\bullet\mathcal{A}_i$. Using public-key cryptography, such a confidential channel can be transferred into an authentic one. Consequently, in a setting where the user wants the assurance of revealing its attributes to and getting a credential from $\mathcal{I}$, issuing would be modeled as shown next.

$$\mathcal{I}\bullet\longleftarrow \mathcal{A}_i,\ \mathcal{I}\longleftarrow\bullet^{\phi_{\mathcal{A}_i}}\mathcal{A}_i,\ \mathcal{I}\longrightarrow\mathcal{A}_i \implies \mathcal{I}\bullet\longrightarrow\bullet^{\phi_{\mathcal{A}_i}}\mathcal{A}_i$$

Release of Certified Attributes.

After having received a certificate, the user A can release the certified attributes to a relying party R. Using certification technology such as X.509 forces A to release all the certified information as the certificate can otherwise not be verified. In our channel model this corresponds to A not being able to change the endpoint annotation function $\phi_{\mathcal{A}_i}$ after the issuing process. The channel modeling the release of certified information from A to R is denoted

by $\mathcal{A}_i{}^{\phi_{\mathcal{A}_i}} \bullet\longrightarrow \mathcal{R}$. If the user wants confidentiality of her data, as in the issuing process, she would need an authenticated channel $\mathcal{A}_i \longleftarrow\bullet \mathcal{R}$ and use public key cryptography (see Section 3.2.1). For the verification of the statement $\phi_{\mathcal{A}_i}$ the relying party needs an authentic channel with the identity provider.

$$\mathcal{I} \longrightarrow\bullet^{\phi_{\mathcal{A}_i}} \mathcal{A}_i,\ \mathcal{I} \bullet\longrightarrow \mathcal{R},\ \mathcal{A}_i{}^{\phi_{\mathcal{A}_i}} \longrightarrow \mathcal{R}, \mathcal{R} \text{ trusts } \mathcal{I}$$
$$\implies \mathcal{A}_i{}^{\phi_{\mathcal{A}_i}} \bullet\longrightarrow \mathcal{R}$$

We can see that due to the authentication of $\mathcal{A}_i$ at the identity provider and the authentic channel to $\mathcal{I}$, the relying party achieves the authentication of $\mathcal{A}_i$. For the same reason, the statement $\phi_{\mathcal{A}_i}$ can be transferred to the resulting channel. While we can see how attribute statements can be transferred to new channels, we do not see the full flexibility of our model due to limitations of X.509 credentials.

4.2 Anonymous Credentials

Anonymous credential systems such as the ones proposed by Brands [6] or Camenisch and Lysyanskaya [8] provide the features for demonstrating the flexibility of our model. Indeed, modeling such systems was the reason for extending the model in the first place. We will discuss two main features of anonymous credential systems. First, we model that transactions of issuing an anonymous credential and release transactions of attribute values of this credential are all unlinkable. We visualize this feature using a distinct pseudonym for each transaction. To create channel transformations we need to make sure that pseudonyms belong to the same party. We use the function p to attain this goal. Second, we capture the capability of selectively revealing the certified attributes. To model this possibility, we allow the recipient of an anonymous credential to change the endpoint annotation function ϕ.

Selective Release of Attributes.

Let us start with the selective release of attributes. Similar to standard certification technology, the issuer uses a pseudonym authenticated channel to assert that the recipient $A = p(\mathcal{A}_i)$ holds the attributes $\phi_{\mathcal{A}_i}$ it will certify. In contrast to the example discussed in Section 4.1, the technology allows A to select a pseudonym $\mathcal{A}_r$, *different* from the pseudonym used in the issuing process, when releasing the information. Note that the transformation is only possible if both pseudonyms belong to the same entity, i.e., $p(\mathcal{A}_i) = p(\mathcal{A}_r)$. Furthermore, anonymous credentials allow a user to only reveal a subset of its certified attributes. Consequently, the relying party learns $\phi_{\mathcal{A}_r}$, which is a statement derived from $\phi_{\mathcal{A}_i}$. Therefore, the issuing and use of an anonymous credential can be modeled as presented next.

$$\mathcal{I} \longrightarrow\bullet^{\phi_{\mathcal{A}_i}} \mathcal{A}_i,\ \mathcal{I} \bullet\longrightarrow \mathcal{R},\ \mathcal{A}_r{}^{\phi_{\mathcal{A}_r}} \longrightarrow \mathcal{R},$$
$$\mathcal{R} \text{ trusts } \mathcal{I},\ \phi_{\mathcal{A}_i} \vdash \phi_{\mathcal{A}_r},\ p(\mathcal{A}_i) = p(\mathcal{A}_r) \tag{13}$$
$$\implies \mathcal{A}_r{}^{\phi_{\mathcal{A}_r}} \bullet\longrightarrow \mathcal{R}$$

The semantics of the resulting channel is that using, (1) the authentic connection between $\mathcal{R}$ and $\mathcal{I}$, (2) the authentic connection between the identity provider and the $\mathcal{A}_i$, as well as (3) the trust of $\mathcal{R}$ in $\mathcal{I}$, allows $\mathcal{R}$ to create a pseudonym authenticated channel with $\mathcal{A}_r$. The statements $\phi_{\mathcal{A}_r}$ need to be derived from the original statements under which the party A has been authenticated to $\mathcal{I}$. Consequently, we can model that the relying party does not get all certified statements but only the part that is relevant for the given purpose.

Similar to the X.509 example, the need for an authenticated channel between $\mathcal{I}$ and $\mathcal{R}$ can be met using a public key infrastructure. Concretely, using the channels $\mathcal{I} \bullet\!\!\!\longrightarrow \mathcal{C}$ and $\mathcal{C} \bullet\!\!\!\longrightarrow \mathcal{R}$ as well as trust of $\mathcal{R}$ in $\mathcal{C}$, we can derive the channel $\mathcal{I} \bullet\!\!\!\longrightarrow \mathcal{R}$.

4.3 Conditional Release of Information

As already mentioned, modern cryptographic primitives allow a user A to release attributes such that they become available to a recipient party R only if a well-defined condition is fulfilled. Technically, this is achieved by the user verifiably encrypting attributes under the public key of a trusted entity T. The user needs to trust T that it will only decrypt the attributes if the condition is fulfilled. The recipient R of the verifiable encryption can verify the correctness of its content and it has to trust T to provide the information in case the condition holds. Clearly, the user and the relying party have to agree on the mentioned condition. Assuming that the condition is fulfilled, T decrypts the attributes and sends them to R to finalize the conditional release. In such a conditional release setting it may happen that the condition is never reached and the verifiably encrypted information is not learnt by R. Assuming that R only communicates the encrypted information in case the condition holds, the trusted party T does not learn the values either.

Consider as example a customer A who wants to rent a car from a car rental agency. The car rental agency acts as relying party R in a selective attribute disclosure transaction with A. Conversely to how such a transaction is carried out today, where R would require A to release personal data such as her name, address, or driver's license number, the rental agency will only request the attributes that are strictly necessary for renting a car. That is, it will require a proof that A has a valid driver's license to drive the car she wants to rent as well as information that allows R to bill A. Note that the latter could be released in a way that does not leak information about the user A, e.g., through anonymous e-cash. For simplicity we only consider an attribute statement based on the driver's license in the remainder of this scenario. Using the rule for k-fold transfer of certified information as stated in Section 3.2.2, we can easily generalize this setting to information from multiple identity providers. Through the release of a proof of owning a valid driver's license combined with the use of anonymous payment, the agency does not learn the identity of A. In fact, the transaction is carried out anonymously with R only learning required attributes of A.

However, in case of a violation of the terms and conditions of the car rental agency as well as if the user commits illegal actions (e.g., violation of traffic regulations), the agency wants to ensure accountability of A, e.g., by being able to obtain her name and address information. This goal is achieved by A creating a verifiable encryption towards the mutually-trusted entity T (e.g., the local government or a notary service) and R checking its correctness without learning the encrypted information. The encryption has a (cryptographically-associated) condition attached under which T should decrypt and provide the information to R.

We can model such scenario as follows: Let A be the party acting under pseudonyms $\mathcal{A}_i$, $\mathcal{A}_r$, and $\mathcal{A}_t$ with the other parties. Further, let R be the relying party acting under public pseudonym $\mathcal{R}$, the identity provider I acting under public pseudonym $\mathcal{I}$, and the trusted party T acting under $\mathcal{T}$. The channel $\mathcal{I}\longrightarrow\!\!\bullet^{\phi_{\mathcal{A}_i}} \mathcal{A}_i$ models the issuing of an anonymous credential from the identity provider $\mathcal{I}$ to party A. The authentic channel $\mathcal{I} \bullet\!\!\!\longrightarrow \mathcal{R}$ models that R has obtained the authentic public key of $\mathcal{I}$ and is therefore able to authenticate attribute statements made by the identity provider $\mathcal{I}$. Finally, the channel $\mathcal{A}_r^{\phi_{\mathcal{A}_r}}\!\!\longrightarrow\mathcal{R}$ models the release of attribute statements $\phi_{\mathcal{A}_r}$ to $\mathcal{R}$. As in example (13), we can derive a channel modeling the release of certified attributes from A to R and becoming authenticated under a pseudonym $\mathcal{A}_r$.

The channel $\mathcal{A}_t^{\phi_{\mathcal{A}_t}} \xrightarrow{c_{\mathrm{dec}}}\!\!\bullet \mathcal{T}$ models the conditional release of attributes $\phi_{\mathcal{A}_t}$ from $\mathcal{A}_t$ to $\mathcal{T}$, conditioned on c_{dec}. This is the crucial channel for modeling the conditional release of identifying attributes $\phi_{\mathcal{A}_t}$ from $\mathcal{A}_t$ to $\mathcal{T}$, which only happens once condition c_{dec} is satisfied. Thus, such channel exactly models the trusted party obtaining the conditionally released information. After T receives the information it will use an authentic channel to transfer it to R. Consequently, conditional release of information can be modeled as follows:

$$\mathcal{A}_t{}^{\phi_{\mathcal{A}_t}} \xrightarrow{c_{\mathrm{dec}}}\!\!\bullet \mathcal{T}, \ \ \mathcal{T} \bullet\!\!\!\longrightarrow \mathcal{R}, \ \ \mathcal{R} \text{ trusts } \mathcal{I},$$
$$p(\mathcal{A}_r) = p(\mathcal{A}_t), \ \phi_{\mathcal{A}_i} \vdash \phi_{\mathcal{A}_t} \implies \mathcal{A}_r{}^{\phi_{\mathcal{A}_t}} \xrightarrow{c_{\mathrm{dec}}} \mathcal{R} \ \ .$$

One crucial step in privacy-friendly accountability is not yet taken care of. Namely, $\mathcal{R}$ does not attain any guarantees about the attribute statements $\phi_{\mathcal{A}_t}$ that it learns. The use of an anonymous credential in combination with conditionally revealing information solves such issue. Using a sequence of channel transformation rules, we can obtain the target channels $\mathcal{A}_r{}^{\phi_{\mathcal{A}_r}} \bullet\!\!\!\longrightarrow \mathcal{R}$ and $\mathcal{A}_r{}^{\phi_{\mathcal{A}_t}} \xrightarrow{c_{\mathrm{dec}}}\mathcal{R}$. Those channels model both the attributes released directly to R, i.e., $\phi_{\mathcal{A}_r}$, and the ones that have been conditionally released, namely $\phi_{\mathcal{A}_t}$.

$$\mathcal{I} \longrightarrow\!\!\bullet^{\phi_{\mathcal{A}_i}}\mathcal{A}_i, \ \ \mathcal{I} \bullet\!\!\!\longrightarrow \mathcal{R}, \ \ \mathcal{A}_r{}^{\phi_{\mathcal{A}_r}} \longrightarrow \mathcal{R},$$
$$\mathcal{A}_t{}^{\phi_{\mathcal{A}_t}} \xrightarrow{c_{\mathrm{dec}}}\!\!\bullet \mathcal{T}, \ \ \mathcal{T} \bullet\!\!\!\longrightarrow \mathcal{R}, \ \ \mathcal{R} \text{ trusts } \mathcal{I},$$
$$p(\mathcal{A}_i) = p(\mathcal{A}_r) = p(\mathcal{A}_t), \ \phi_{\mathcal{A}_i} \vdash \phi_{\mathcal{A}_r}, \ \phi_{\mathcal{A}_i} \vdash \phi_{\mathcal{A}_t}$$
$$\implies \mathcal{A}_r{}^{\phi_{\mathcal{A}_r}} \bullet\!\!\!\longrightarrow \mathcal{R}, \ \mathcal{A}_r{}^{\phi_{\mathcal{A}_t}} \bullet\!\!\xrightarrow{c_{\mathrm{dec}}} \mathcal{R}$$

This example nicely shows the capabilities of our model to express privacy-friendly authentication and accountability. We strongly believe that transactions as shown in this example, where a user may remain pseudonymous as long as she complies with rules and regulations, while being accountable in case of well-defined misbehaviour, will be important for the future of the Internet.

For a scenario of conditionally releasing information, we next relate the concrete information flow in a system realized with cryptographic protocols and the idealized model of the functionality as presented. Technically, the verifiable encryption towards T is sent from the user A to R. The latter can verify the encrypted attributes w.r.t. attributes certified in credentials and make sure that the user can be held accountable in case of misconduct. Once the decryption condition is fulfilled, R may request the decryption of the encrypted attributes from T. Note that in a system based on verifiable encryption, the relying party may send the verifiable encryption to T already when it receives it or it may wait until c_{dec} is fulfilled. Both flows realize the same semantics under our assumption that the trusted party T follows its protocol. Thus, this difference in the message flow in a system is not reflected in our model.

Relating this discussion to the car rental scenario, the channel $\mathcal{A}_r{}^{\phi_{\mathcal{A}_r}} \longrightarrow \mathcal{R}$ conveys the attribute statements that the user has a valid driver's license for the car intended to rent. The channel $\mathcal{A}_t{}^{\phi_{\mathcal{A}_t}} \xrightarrow{c_{\mathrm{dec}}}\!\!\bullet \mathcal{T}$ models the communication of the conditionally-released identity attributes to $\mathcal{T}$ to allow for user accountability. As mentioned before, the actual flow of information in a system, when using verifiable encryption as technical mechanism, is from A to the relying party $\mathcal{R}$ and not to the trusted party $\mathcal{T}$ itself which reflects the intended functionality. The target channels are a combination of the channel conveying the directly revealed statement and the conditional channel releasing the identity attributes once c_{dec} is fulfilled. The latter channel can thus only be derived in the case of a need to hold the user accountable and obtain her conditionally-released identity information. This is exactly what realizes the accountability feature of a transaction in which normally a user can be known only under some attribute statement, while under a well-defined condition her identity can be obtained and the target channel be derived.

5. CONCLUSION

We have presented a simple and intuitive model for expressing the semantics of privacy-friendly authentication and accountability technologies such as anonymous credential systems and verifiable encryption. It allows for expressing the precise relations as well as the authentication and accountability properties between parties.

The concepts we cover with our model comprise pseudonyms, attribute-based authentication, as well as conditional release of information. As a result, our model can express the relevant primitives for privacy-preserving authentication and accountability at the same time.

A formalization of our model, similar to the work aiming at a more formal treatment of the Maurer-Schmid calculus [16, 17], is an interesting piece of future work. Through such formal approach, one may be able to express more precisely the functionality of cryptographic protocols and analyze, e.g., their composability.

6. REFERENCES

[1] G. Ateniese. Efficient verifiable encryption (and fair exchange) of digital signatures. *Proc. 6th ACM CCS*, p.138–146. Nov. 1999.

[2] M. Backes, J. Camenisch, and D. Sommer. Anonymous yet accountable access control. *Proceedings of ACM WPES 2005*, November 2005.

[3] M. Backes, M. Maffei, and D. Unruh. Zero-knowledge in the applied pi-calculus and automated verification of the direct anonymous attestation protocol. *IEEE Symposium on Security and Privacy*, p.202–215, 2008.

[4] P. Bichsel, J. Camenisch, G. Neven, N. P. Smart, and B. Warinschi. Get shorty via group signatures without encryption. *SCN '10*, v.6280 of *LNCS*, p.381–398. Sept. 2010.

[5] D. Boneh, X. Boyen, and H. Shacham. Short group signatures. *CRYPTO '04*, v.3152 of *LNCS*, p.41–55. 2004.

[6] S. Brands. *Rethinking Public Key Infrastructures and Digital Certificates: Building in Privacy*. MIT Press, 2000.

[7] S. Brands and C. Paquin. U-prove cryptographic specification v1.0, Mar. 2010.

[8] J. Camenisch and A. Lysyanskaya. Efficient non-transferable anonymous multi-show credential system with optional anonymity revocation. *EUROCRYPT '01*, v.2045 of *LNCS*, p.93–118. 2001.

[9] J. Camenisch, S. Mödersheim, G. Neven, F.-S. Preiss, and D. Sommer. A card requirements language enabling privacy-preserving access control. *Proceedings of SACMAT 2010*, p.119–128, 2010.

[10] J. Camenisch, S. Mödersheim, and D. Sommer. A formal model of identity mixer. *FMICS 2010*, LNCS. 2010.

[11] J. Camenisch and V. Shoup. Practical verifiable encryption and decryption of discrete logarithms. *CRYPTO '03*, v.2729 of *LNCS*, p.126–144, 2003.

[12] D. Chaum. Untraceable electronic mail, return addresses, and digital pseudonyms. *Comm. of the ACM*, 24(2):84–88, Feb. 1981.

[13] D. Chaum and E. van Heyst. Group signatures. *EUROCRYPT '91*, v.547 of *LNCS*, p.257–265. 1991.

[14] D. Cooper, S. Santesson, S. Farrell, S. Boeyen, R. Housley, and W. Polk. Internet X.509 Public Key Infrastructure Certificate and Certificate Revocation List (CRL) Profile. RFC 5280 (Proposed Standard), May 2008.

[15] B. Ives, K. R. Walsh, and H. Schneider. The domino effect of password reuse. *Comm. of the ACM*, 47:75–78, Apr. 2004.

[16] U. Maurer. Constructive cryptography – a new paradigm for security definitions and proofs. *Theory of Security and Applications (TOSCA 2011)*, v.6993 of *LNCS*, p.33–56. Apr. 2011.

[17] U. Maurer, A. Rüedlinger, and B. Tackmann. Confidentiality and integrity: A constructive perspective. *Theory of Cryptography — TCC 2012*, LNCS. 2012.

[18] U. Maurer and P. Schmid. A calculus for security bootstrapping in distributed systems. *Journal of Computer Security*, 4(1):55–80, 1996.

[19] U. M. Maurer and P. E. Schmid. A calculus for secure channel establishment in open networks. *ESORICS '94*, v.875 of *LNCS*, p.173–192. Nov. 1994.

[20] S. Mödersheim and L. Viganò. Secure pseudonymous channels. *Proceedings of Esorics'09*, number 5789 in LNCS, p.337–354. 2009.

[21] Security Team, IBM Research Zurich. Specification of the identity mixer cryptographic library. IBM Research Report RZ 3730, IBM Research Division, Apr. 2010.

[22] D. Sommer. Architecture. *Digital Privacy: PRIME – Privacy and Identity Management for Europe*, LNCS Volume 6545. 2011.

[23] J. Yan, A. Blackwell, R. Anderson, and A. Grant. Password memorability and security: Empirical results. *IEEE Security and Privacy*, 2:25–31, Sept. 2004.

A Trust-and-Risk Aware RBAC Framework: Tackling Insider Threat

Nathalie Baracaldo
University of Pittsburgh
School of Information Sciences
nab62@pitt.edu

James Joshi
University of Pittsburgh
School of Information Sciences
jjoshi@sis.pitt.edu

ABSTRACT

Insider Attacks are one of the most dangerous threats organizations face today. An insider attack occurs when a person authorized to perform certain actions in an organization decides to abuse the trust, and harm the organization. These attacks may negatively impact the reputation of the organization, its productivity, and may produce losses in revenue and clients. Avoiding insider attacks is a daunting task. While it is necessary to provide privileges to employees so they can perform their jobs efficiently, providing too many privileges may backfire when users accidentally or intentionally abuse their privileges. Hence, finding a middle ground, where the necessary privileges are provided and malicious usage are avoided, is necessary. In this paper, we propose a framework that extends the role-based access control (RBAC) model by incorporating a risk assessment process, and the trust the system has on its users. Our framework adapts to suspicious changes in users' behavior by removing privileges when users' trust falls below a certain threshold. This threshold is computed based on a risk assessment process that includes the risk due to inference of unauthorized information. We use a Coloured-Petri net to detect inferences. We also redefine the existing role activation problem, and propose an algorithm that reduces the risk exposure. We present experimental evaluation to validate our work.

Categories and Subject Descriptors

K.6.5 [**Management of Computing and Information Systems**]: Security and Protection

Keywords

Trust, risk management, insider threat, role-based access control, inference threat

1. INTRODUCTION

According to the Computer Crime and Security Survey, insider attacks accounted for 33% of the total incidents reported in 2010 [19]. An insider attack is performed by people who are legitimately authorized in the system to per-

form certain tasks. The consequences of insider attacks may be devastating, and may include monetary losses, negative impact on the reputation, loss of customers, among others. According to [22], the monetary losses due to insider attacks ranged from five hundred dollars to tens of million dollars, around 75% of the organizations had a negative impact to their business operations, and 28% experienced a negative impact to their reputations.

Some of these attacks could be avoided if access control systems were able to react when a user is performing actions that are not appropriate for their normal job functions. These attacks are typically preceded by *technical precursors* that include download and use of hacker tools, unauthorized access of customers' or coworkers' systems, system access after termination, inappropriate Internet access at work, and the setup or use of backdoor accounts [22]. Hence, if the system is able to identify such inappropriate behaviors, it is possible to mitigate the missuse of permissions. For this reason, having an access control system integrated with an appropriate monitoring system can significantly help reduce potential insider attacks. The monitoring module can alert the access control module of a user's suspicious behavior, so that it can react by restricting privileges to the suspicious user.

Although Role Based Access Control (RBAC) model has proved to be a promising approach for different types of organizations [26], it is not able to cope with the changing behavior of the users. As long as a user is authorized to a role, the system grants him access. RBAC is appropriate in environments where users are well-behaved, where they can be trusted to perform actions according to their roles. Unfortunately, as the statistics show, insiders do perform attacks! Moreover, even if the users could be trusted, malware can be inadvertently installed and a user account be compromised. Thus, it is necessary to include the behavior of the users in the access control loop. The trust the system has on a user should be updated according to the user's behavior. When a user's behavior falls out of the expected pattern in a suspicious fashion, the trust the system has on him should be reduced. If a user is no longer trusted, the system should react by denying access to key resources. Several researchers have recognized the advantages of adding trust to access control models, e.g.,[9, 15, 14, 24]. Adding trust to RBAC helps the system react to changes in the behavior of users. A trust threshold is typically used to limit the access resources. However, these works do not present a comprehensive analysis of the way in which trust thresholds should be assigned, nor do they include the separation of duty constraints or hybrid hierarchy. They also do not specify how to enforce such policies or reduce the risk exposure automatically.

In this paper, we propose a framework that integrates RBAC with the notion of *risk* and *trust*. Our trust-and-risk aware RBAC approach differs from existing ones in that it allows the integration of the risk assessment results in the access control policy. This permits the establishment of a threshold that represents the minimum amount of trust the system needs to have on a user in order to acquire the permissions associated with a particular role, as well as the risk of inference of unauthorized information. Our model also supports cardinality and separation of duty constraints [2], as well as the hybrid hierarchy [28]. Including these components of RBAC allows us to inherit their well-known advantages. The main contributions of this paper are as follows:

1. We propose a model that includes risk and trust in RBAC systems that reacts to anomalous and suspicious changes in users' behavior.

2. We present a comprehensive way in which the risk values can be associated with permissions and roles. In particular, we introduce the notion of inference of unauthorized permissions when calculating the risk of activation of a set of roles. For this purpose, we present a formulation of a Coloured Petri-net [20] to identify when a particular user may infer unauthorized permissions, and subsequently adjust the trust threshold required to activate needed roles.

3. We define an optimization problem to enforce the policy, reduce the risk exposure of the organization, and ensure that all constraints are respected. To the best of our knowledge this is the first work that attempts to reduce the risk exposure in this way.

4. We present a role activation algorithm to solve the optimization problem, and evaluate its performance using well-formed policies.

The rest of the paper is organized as follows. In Section 2, we overview RBAC, risk, trust and Coloured Petri-nets. In Section 3, we present the requirements of the system. We present the proposed model in Sections 4 and 5. The formal definition of the role activation problem and the proposed algorithm is presented in Sections 6 and 7, respectively. We present the related work in Section 8 and the conclusions in Section 9.

2. PRELIMINARIES AND NOTATION

2.1 RBAC, Constraints and Hybrid Hierarchy

Our work is based on Role Based Access Control (RBAC) model [16], because of its benefits. It encompasses discretionary and mandatory access control models and supports organization or user-specific requirements. In addition, RBAC uses roles which are a natural abstraction for most organizations, and it provides organizations with economic benefits due to the reduction on the administration cost [26].

In RBAC, *permissions* are assigned to *roles*, and roles are assigned to *users*. In order to obtain the permissions authorized for a role, users need to *activate* the role in a *session*. Sets U, R, and P represent the set of users, roles and permissions in the system, respectively. The separation of duty constraints (SoD) are used to avoid fraudulent activities within an organization by preventing a unique user from assuming two or more conflicting roles. There are two types of SoD constraints: Static (SSoD) and the Dynamic (DSoD).

SSoD restricts the authorization of users to conflicting roles [2]. Each constraint is denoted as $ssod(RS, k) \in SSoD$, where $RS \subseteq R$ with $2 \leq k \leq n$. This constraint states that a user can be *authorized* to at most $k-1$ roles in RS. Similarly, a DSoD constraint $dsod(RS, k) \in DSoD$ states that a user can *activate* at most $k-1$ roles in RS simultaneously.

We consider two types of cardinality constraints in our model. An *activation cardinality constraint* restricts the number of users that can *activate* a particular role in a system simultaneously. To denote that a role r can be activated at the same time by at most $k-1$ users, we use the notation $card(r, k)$. An *assignment cardinality constraint* restricts the number of users that can be assigned to a role. This is denoted as $card_A(r, k)$.

Roles can be hierarchically organized using *hybrid hierarchy* [28]. Roles r_1 and r_2 can be hierarchically related in one of the following ways. (1) **I-hierarchy** ($r_1 \geq_I r_2$) where r_1 inherits the permissions of r_2. (2) **A-hierarchy** ($r_1 \geq_A r_2$) where users assigned to r_1 can activate r_2. (3) **IA-hierarchy** ($r_1 \geq_{IA} r_2$), in this case, r_1 is I-senior and A-senior of r_2. The hybrid hierarchy allows the enforcement of different types of policies such as DSoD when roles are hierarchically related [28]. For this reason, we incorporate it into our model. We use function $P_{au}(r \in R)$ to denote the set of permissions that can be acquired through r; this includes the permissions directly assigned to r and those inherited through I and IA hierarchical relations. Similarly, $P_{au}(R_c \subseteq R)$ returns the authorized permissions of all the roles in R_c. Function $authorized(u \in U)$ returns the roles in R that are authorized for u (if u is authorized for role r, it means he can activate r). Function $activated(r \in R)$ returns the number of sessions that contain role r.

2.2 Risk and Trust

We adopt the following trust definition: *"Trust is a subjective expectation an agent has about another's future behavior based on the history of their encounters"* [23]. Trust may depend on the *context* in which the interaction between entities takes place. We denote the set of contexts as C. For instance, the type of service and the network connection used by the user may define a context.

Risk is defined by the likelihood of a hazardous situation and its consequences if it occurs. The likelihood of occurrence can be reduced through the implementation of controls and mechanisms in the system that aim to mitigate threats. The risk exposure after all the controls and mechanisms are in place is called *residual risk*, and ideally, it is the risk that the organization is willing to accept. Risk can be calculated using the expected value formula [8], where the probability of occurrence is multiplied by the cost of the event.

2.3 Coloured Petri-net (CP-net)

We model the history of access as a *Coloured Petri-net* (CP-net) [20]. Here, we provide the basic concepts of CP-nets, and in Section 5.2.1, we present the proposed CP-net. A CP-net is a bipartite graph that contains two types of nodes *places* (W) and *transitions* (T). Places and transitions are connected through *arcs* $(F \subseteq (W \times T) \cup (T \times W))$. No arc can exist between two nodes of the same type. *Tokens* (V) live in places, and move around in the CP-net when transitions fire. Usually, tokens represent objects and their attributes which are called colors or types. Not all types of tokens are accepted in all the places. $\Upsilon(w \in W)$ denotes the type of accepted tokens in place w. Each transition $t \in T$ has a boolean guard that evaluates a condition based on tokens $V' \subseteq V$ located in the input place; a guard is represented by $G(t \in T, V' \subseteq V)$. If the guard evaluates to true, the transition fires. Otherwise, the transition does not fired. If a transition fires, it consumes the tokens that made the guard evaluate to true and collocates a new token in the output place(s). This is represented by the function $\lambda : t \in T \times V' \subseteq V \rightarrow v_o \in V$, where $G(t, V') = true$ and v_o is the token produced by the transition. We use m_o to denote the initial placing of tokens in the CP-net. Finally, a CP-net in its initial state is defined by tuple $\langle W, T, F, V, \Upsilon, \lambda, m_o \rangle$.

3. REQUIREMENTS

The proposed framework aims to reduce the attacks and missuses performed by insiders. We identify the following requirements.

1. The system should allow the specification and enforcement of SoD and cardinality constraints.

2. The system should detect suspicious activities. This process should be automatic and should be able to establish to which level each user is trusted by the system.

3. It should be possible to associate different trust values for a user depending on the user's and system's *context*.

4. Since different permissions may have different risk associated with them, the system should be able to react to suspicious changes in behavior of users by removing access to riskier permissions quickly, and if the misuse continues to other permissions as well.

5. The system should determine the risk associated with the activation of a set of roles by a particular user. The risk associated should include the imminent risk associated with the permissions acquired through the roles, and the risk due to inference of unauthorized objects. The risk exposure should be automatically reduced, minimizing the impact of possible attacks.

Requirement 1 can significantly reduce the risk of insider attacks [17]. When organizations pay close attention to the way responsibilities are divided some of the potential attacks are mitigated. For instance, it may require two or more employees to collude to launch an attack.

In this paper, we focus on requirements 1, 3, 4 and 5. For requirement 2, solutions such as those proposed in [5, 12] can be used to monitor the behavior of users and calculate how trusted they are based on monitored data.

4. OVERVIEW OF THE MODEL

We consider RBAC systems with hybrid hierarchy, cardinality and SoD constraints. We extend this model by adding the following components (a detailed explanation of each of them is provided in Section 5).

- Each user is associated with a *trust value* that is a function of his behavior under a particular context. We denote this as $trust(u \in U, c \in C)$.

- Each permission is assigned a *risk value* within a particular context. We denote this as $rs(p \in P, c \in C)$.

- The policy contains a set of inference tuples $\mathcal{I}$, which allows the calculation of the risk exposure due to inference of unauthorized information.

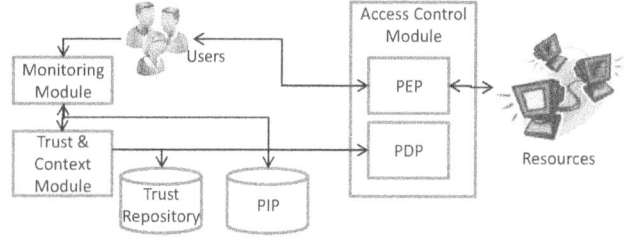

Figure 1: System architecture.

- When a set of roles RS is to be activated, first its combined risk value is computed ($rs(RS \subseteq R, c \in C, u \in U)$) based on *(i)* the permissions it is authorized for, *(ii)* the inference risk associated with those permissions, *(iii)* the context, and *(iv)* the user trying to activate the roles.

- Similarly, when a set of roles RS is to be activated simultaneously by a user, a *trust threshold* is computed based on the risk of RS. This threshold is denoted as $\tau(RS \subseteq R, c \in C, u \in U)$.

A user can activate a set of roles in a session if *(i)* he is assigned to all the roles in the set, *(ii)* their activation does not violate any constraint, and *(iii)* he possesses a trust value greater or equal than the trust threshold required for those roles. We formalize this notion in Section 6. In RBAC, only the first two conditions need to be fulfilled for a user to be able to activate a role. In our model, we also consider the trust value of the user, which allows the system to react to misbehaving users.

The system architecture is shown in Figure 1. The *Monitoring Module* monitors the users in the system. The *Trust and Context Module* (TCM) uses the monitored information to identify the context, and calculate the trust value of each of the users accordingly. These trust values are stored in the *Trust Repository*. The *Access Control Module* has three components, the *Policy Enforcement Point* (PEP), the *Policy Decision Point* (PDP), and the *Policy Information Point* (PIP). The policy of the system is stored in the PIP. An access request consists of the set of permissions a user wants to acquire. The PEP intercepts all these requests, and ensures that the resources of the system can be accessed only if the policy authorizes it. The access requests are intercepted by the PEP, which sends them to the PDP. The PDP evaluates the policy according to the trust the system has on the user, and the context. In case the trust value of a user decreases, the TCM sends a notification to the PDP, which re-evaluates whether the privileges the user is exercising should be revoked. In this way, the system is able to deny access to misbehaving users before they can perform extensive damage to the system.

5. RISK AND TRUST THRESHOLDS

In this section, we present the proposed methodology to calculate the risk exposure of an organization. We show how the risk is calculated for different roles that a user wants to activate based on the risk of the permissions they can acquire. Finally, we show how to compute the trust threshold.

5.1 Risk of Permissions

A permission is a tuple $\langle obj, act \rangle$ where the *obj* is an asset in the organization such as a file or other resource, and the *act* corresponds to the action that a user can perform on the object. Objects are susceptible to different threats. Among these are object's *loss of integrity*, *loss of confidentiality*, and *loss of availability*. Intuitively, different objects have different security requirements that depend on the business functions of a particular organization. For instance, some objects require that their integrity be well guarded, other objects are sensitive (their leakage would result in a lot of damage to the business), while others may be critical and sensitive simultaneously. Hence, the risk exposure of the organization depends on the action that is performed on the object and the relevance of the object.

The risk value of a permission p is the likelihood that p is misused multiplied by the corresponding damage cost. We are interested in the residual risk which means that the likelihood of a particular misuse depends on the mitigation mechanisms and controls that the organization has in place to reduce the vulnerabilities that can lead to the misuse.

DEFINITION 1. *The risk of permission* $p = \langle obj, act \rangle \in P$ *in context* $c \in C$, *written as* $rs(p,c)$, *is defined as follows:*

$$rs(p,c) = \sum_{x_p \in MaliciousUsage} Pr[x_p|\,c\,] * cost(x_p)$$

Where MaliciousUsage is a set of possible events in context c *that can lead to a misuse of object obj through the action act,* $Pr[x_p|\,c\,]$ *is the probability of occurrence of a particular malicious usage of object obj through action act given* c, *and* $cost(x_p)$ *is its associated cost.*

EXAMPLE 1. *For simplicity, in this example we only consider one context: users are accessing the system through the intranet. Consider an organization that produces soaps. In order to calculate the risk associated with permission* $p_1 = \langle listProviders, read \rangle$, *the organization performs the following analysis. The provider's list is considered to be sensitive, as its information provides the organization a competitive advantage. The organization calculates that its leakage would cost around \$30,000. According to their system's configuration, the probability of occurrence of this event is 0.1. This results in a total risk of \$3,000. Permission* p_2, *corresponds to writing the number of orders to be placed. The concern related to this object is its integrity. In case this number is overwritten maliciously, the organization would face problems. They may either run out of materials before planned or they would be paying for a large unnecessary inventory. The company estimates that having a large inventory would cost them around \$500 and a insufficient inventory \$2,000, for a total cost of \$2,500. The probability of those events is 0.1. Therefore, the total risk of* p_2 *is \$250. Permission* p_3 *allows halting the machines that produce soaps. If this permission is maliciously used, the entire factory would be stopped and serious consequences may occur. The organization may not be able to fulfil its contracts, may lose money, and in the worst case, clients. The cost of this event is estimated to be \$20,000. However, in order to use it, three administrators need to authorize the operation. Hence, the probability of this misuse is estimated to be very low: 0.005, for a total risk of \$100.*

5.2 Risk Associated with Role Sets

Intuitively, the risk associated with a set of roles is a function of the risk of the permissions that can be accessed through those roles. When calculating such risk values, we include the risk of the permissions that can be explicitly acquired through those roles, as well as those that can be inferred from them. We first show how we model the inference problem, and then we present how to calculate the risk of activating a set of roles.

5.2.1 Inference Threat and Activation History

An *Inference threat* exists when a user is able to infer unauthorized sensitive information through what seems to be innocuous data he is authorized for.

DEFINITION 2. *An Inference Tuple* $\langle PS, p_x \rangle$ *consists of a set of permissions* $PS \subset P$, *and an inferred permission* $p_x = \langle x, read \rangle \in P$, *for which the following conditions hold:*

1. *PS does not contain the inferred permission:* $p_x \notin PS$.
2. *Once a user has acquired all the permissions in PS, he has all the information required to infer object* x.
3. *The set PS is the minimum set of permissions required to infer object* x.

We denote the set of all inference tuples by $\mathcal{I}$.

Several inference tuples may exist in the system. For instance, it may be possible to infer object x through two different set of permissions PS_1 and PS_2; which results in two inference tuples: $\langle PS_1, p_x \rangle$ and $\langle PS_2, p_x \rangle$. It is also possible that the same set of permissions can be used to infer different objects, e.g $\langle PS_3, p_i \rangle$ and $\langle PS_3, p_j \rangle$. These inference tuples can be automatically found using techniques such as those described in [11, 32]. We use the following terminology to refer to the components of $\mathcal{I}$.

DEFINITION 3. *We define the set of* risk inference objects $\mathcal{O}_\mathcal{I}$, *and* inference permissions $\mathcal{P}_\mathcal{I}$ *as follows:*

$$\mathcal{O}_\mathcal{I} = \{o \mid \langle PS, \langle o, r \rangle \rangle \in \mathcal{I}\} \quad and \quad \mathcal{P}_\mathcal{I} = \bigcup_{\langle PS, p \rangle \in \mathcal{I}} PS$$

To determine when a user has activated all the roles needed to infer a particular object, we model the role activation history using a CP-net. The inference tuples in $\mathcal{I}$ determine the specific structure of the CP-net. The general structure of the proposed CP-net is presented in Figure 2a.

In the following discussion, we assume that each inference tuple in $\mathcal{I}$ has been enumerated from 1 to k. That is, there are k inference tuples in the system, and $\langle PS_i, p_{xi} \rangle_i$ refers to the inference tuple i. For each inference tuple $\langle PS_i, p_{xi} \rangle_i$, two transitions $BelongToTuple_i$ and $CompletedTuple_i$, and a place β_i are created. Each user has tokens positioned in different places of the CP-net; the placement of tokens reflect the access history of each user. We use function $tokensAt(u \in U, w \in W)$ to retrieve the set of tokens of user u at place w. In what follows, we formally define the CP-net and then explain how it works.

DEFINITION 4. *An Inference CP-net* $\mathcal{H} = \langle W, T, F, V, \Upsilon, \lambda, m_o \rangle$ *is defined as follows:*

1. **Places (W):** *For each* $\langle PS_i, x_i \rangle_i \in \mathcal{I}$, *a place* β_i *is created. Let* $B = \{\beta_1, ..., \beta_k\}$, *then:* $W = \{w_s, w_f, w_{end}\} \cup B$.

2. **Transitions (T):** *For each* $\langle PS_i, x_{pi} \rangle_i \in \mathcal{I}$, *a pair of transitions* $BelongToTuple_i$ *and* $CompletedTuple_i$ *are created. Let* $D_1 = \{BelongToTuple_1, ..., BelongToTuple_k\}$, $D_2 = \{CompletedTuple_1, ..., CompletedTuple_k\}$. *Then:* $T = \{InitialSetup\} \cup D_1, \cup D_2$.

3. **Arcs (F):** *Let* $E = \{\langle BelongToTuple_i, \beta_i \rangle : \forall i\ 1 \le i \le k\} \cup \{\langle \beta_i, CompletedTuple_i \rangle : \forall i\ 1 \le i \le k\}$. *Then,* $F = \{\langle w_s, InitialSetup \rangle, \langle InitialSetup, w_f \rangle\} \cup \{w_f\} \times D_1 \cup E \cup D_2 \times \{w_{end}\}$

4. **Token Types (V):** *Let* $u \in U$, $R' \subseteq R$, $P_{R',\mathcal{I}} \subseteq \mathcal{P}_\mathcal{I}$, *and* $p_x \in \mathcal{P}_\mathcal{I}$, *we have:* $V = \{\langle R', u \rangle, \langle P_{R',\mathcal{I}}, R', u \rangle, \langle u, p_x \rangle\}$.

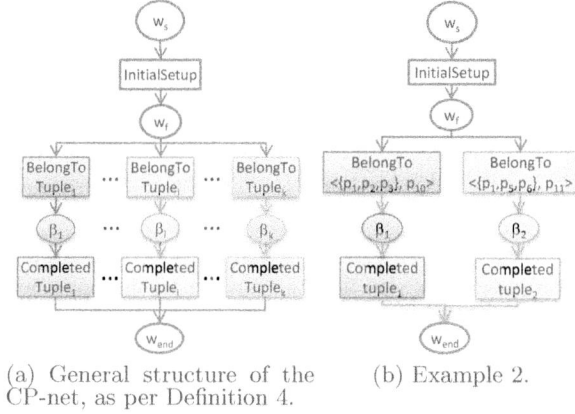

(a) General structure of the CP-net, as per Definition 4.

(b) Example 2.

Figure 2: CP-net graphical representation.

5. **Accepted Types of Tokens (Υ)**: $\Upsilon(w_s) = \langle R', u \rangle$, $\Upsilon(w_f) = \Upsilon(\beta_i) = \langle P_{R', \mathcal{I}}, R', u \rangle$, for all $1 \leq i \leq k$ $\Upsilon(w_{end}) = \langle u, p_x \rangle$.

6. **Firing rules (G and λ)**:
InitialSetup: Given token $\langle R', u \rangle$ place at w_s:
$G(InitialSetup, \langle R', u \rangle) = true$
$\lambda(InitialSetup, \langle R', u \rangle) = \langle P_{R', \mathcal{I}}, R', u \rangle$,
where $P_{R', \mathcal{I}} = [P_{au}(R') \cap \mathcal{P}_\mathcal{I}]$

BelongToTuple$_i$ ($1 \leq i \leq k$): Given token $\langle P_{R', \mathcal{I}}, R', u \rangle$ place at w_f, and tuple $\langle PS_i, p_{xi} \rangle_i$:
$G(BelongToTuple_i, \langle P_{R', \mathcal{I}}, R', u \rangle) = [(PS_i \cap P_{R', \mathcal{I}}) \neq \emptyset \wedge p_{xi} \notin P_{au}(authorized(u))]$
$\lambda(BelongToTuple_i, \langle P_{R', \mathcal{I}}, R', u \rangle) = \langle P_{R', \mathcal{I}}, R', u \rangle$

CompletedTuple$_i$ ($1 \leq i \leq k$): Given a set of tokens $V' = tokensAt(u, \beta_i)$ of type $\langle P_{R', \mathcal{I}}, R', u \rangle$:
$G(CompletedTuple_i, V') = [\bigcup_{\langle P_{R', \mathcal{I}}, R', u \rangle \in V'} P_{R', \mathcal{I}}] = PS_i$
$\lambda(CompletedTuple_i, V') = \langle u, p_{xi} \rangle$, where p_{xi} is the inferred permission of tuple i.

7. **Initial State (m_0)**: Initially, no tokens have been placed.

The CP-net works as follows. When a user u initially tries to activate a set of roles $R' \subseteq R$ for which he is authorized, a token $\langle R', u \rangle$ is placed in w_s. Then, transition *InitialSetup* fires, consuming the token in w_s and placing a token of a different color at w_f. Changing colors enables us to keep track of relevant attributes. In this case, it is important to know which of the permissions acquired through R' would allow an inference. We denote this set of permissions as $P_{R', \mathcal{I}} = P_{au}(R') \cap \mathcal{P}_\mathcal{I}$. Hence, when *InitialSetup* fires, token $\langle P_{R', \mathcal{I}}, R', u \rangle$ is placed at w_f. Tokens placed at w_f are evaluated in parallel by the *BelongToTuple* transitions. A transition *BelongToTuple$_i$* fires when at least one of the permissions in $P_{R', \mathcal{I}}$ belongs to the corresponding set of inference PS_i, and when the user cannot legitimately acquire p_{xi}. If the transition fires, the token at w_f is consumed and a token is placed at β_i. Note that it is possible that a token placed at w_f fires several transitions of the type *BelongToTuple$_i$*. If at some point of time, a place β_i contains all the tokens that for the same user complete the entire set of permissions PS_i required to infer object x_i, transition *CompletedTuple$_i$* fires. In other words, *CompletedTuple$_i$* is triggered when a user has acquired all the permissions in

PS_i of inference tuple $\langle PS_i, p_{xi} \rangle_i$. Transition *CompletedTuple$_i$* consumes *all* the tokens that show user u has acquired enough information to infer p_{xi}, and places token $\langle u, p_{xi} \rangle$ at w_{end}.

The history of accesses is provided by the places where the tokens are stored in the CP-net; as roles are activated by users, the tokens move around the CP-net. We use the notation $\mathcal{H}.tokensAt(u, w_s)$ to obtain the tokens at place w_s of user u in CP-net $\mathcal{H}$. The purpose of using CP-net is to identify whether the activation of a set of roles R' by user u, would allow the user to infer new information. In order to identify if this is the case, before adding the tokens of activation, the current inferred permissions of the user are stored $M = \mathcal{H}.tokensAt(u, w_{end})$. Thus, M contains the set of tokens inferred by user before activating R'. Then, we place one token in $\langle R', u \rangle$ at w_s. After the transitions fire, and all tokens are in a place different than w_s, we check the state of the CP-net. We denote this new state as $\mathcal{H}'$. Letting $N = \mathcal{H}'.tokensAt(u, w_{end})$, we can identify whether user u would be able to infer new information. If $N \neq M$, the user has completed a new inference tuple. In which case, the set of new tokens at w_{end} is given by $Q = N \setminus M$, and the set of new inferred permissions is given by $P' = \{p_x \mid < u, p_x > \in Q\}$. Considering the previous discussion, and letting u be the user that is going to activate the set of roles R', we define function $inferred(\mathcal{H}, u, R')$ which returns P'.

5.2.2 Calculating The Role Set Risk

The risk exposure of providing access to a set of roles $R' \subseteq R$ to a user u depends on the state of the CP-net. The following formula provides the risk exposure.

Definition 5. *The risk exposure of the system if user u activates a set of roles $R' \subseteq R$ in context c is given by*

$$rs(R', c, u) = \sum_{p \in \wp} rs(p, c)$$

where $\wp = P_{au}(R') \cup inferred(\mathcal{H}, u, R')$.

When no inference occurs due to the activation of R', $inferred(\mathcal{H}, u, R') = \emptyset$; and the risk exposure is given by the risk of the authorized permissions $P_{au}(R')$. On the contrary, when one or more roles in R' allow the user to infer unauthorized information, the risk includes the risk of directly acquired permissions and the risk of the inferred permissions in $inferred(\mathcal{H}, u, R')$.

Example 2. *Suppose $\mathcal{I}$ is given by tuples $\langle \{p_1, p_2, p_3\}, p_{10} \rangle$, and $\langle \{p_1, p_5, p_6\}, p_{11} \rangle$. The corresponding CP-net is shown in Figure 2b; initially there are no tokens. User u_1 activates roles $R_1 = \{r_1, r_2\}$ for which $P_{au}(R_1) = \{p_1, p_2, p_8, p_9, p_{15}\}$. A token $v_1 = \langle u_1, \{r_1, r_2\} \rangle$ is placed at w_s. After transition InitialSetup fires, v_1 is consumed and a token $\langle u_1, \{p_1, p_2\}, \{r_1, r_2\} \rangle$ is placed at w_f. Since R_1 acquires p_1 which is part of both inference tuples and u_1 is not authorized for p_{10} or p_{11}, the token at w_f is removed, and two tokens are placed at β_1, and β_2. The tokens placed contain this information: $\langle u_1, \{p_1, p_2\}, \{r_1, r_2\} \rangle$. Since none of the inference tuples is completed by R_1, there are no new tokens at w_{end}, and $inferred(\mathcal{H}, u_1, R_1) = \emptyset$. Thus, in context c, $rs(R_1, c, u_1) = rs(p_1, c) + rs(p_2, c) + rs(p_8, c) + rs(p_9, c) + rs(p_{15}, c)$, which does not contain any inferred risk. We denote the new state of the CP-net by $\mathcal{H}'$. After a while, assume u_1 activates role r_3, where $P_{au}(r_3) = \{p_3, p_4\}$. Token $\langle u_1, \{r_3\} \rangle$ is placed at w_s. Transition BelongTo$\langle \{p_1, p_2, p_3\}, p_{10} \rangle$ fires and token $\langle u_1, \{p_3\}, \{r_3\} \rangle$ is placed at β_1. At that point, transition CompletedTuple$_1$ fires because two tokens that belong to u_1, and complete the inference tuple are at β_1. This* time $inferred(\mathcal{H}', u_1, \{r_3\}) = \{p_{10}\}$. *Hence, the risk in context c of $rs(r_3, c, u_1) = rs(p_3, c) + rs(p_4, c) + rs(p_{10}, c)$, which includes the risk of the inferred permission p_{10}.*

5.3 Trust Thresholds Associated with Role Sets

The trust threshold associated with a set of roles represents how trusted a user needs to be in order to use those roles. Intuitively, this threshold needs to reflect the risk exposure of the organization when the roles are activated by a user. We define the trust threshold as follows.

DEFINITION 6. *The trust threshold of the set of roles $R' \subseteq R$, in context c for user u is defined as follows:*

$$\tau(R', c, u) = \frac{rs(R', c, u)}{\sum_{p \in P}(rs(p, c))}$$

Where $0 \leq \tau(R', c, u) \leq 1$. When $\tau(R', c, u) = 0$, it means that user u does not need to be trusted to activate R' in context c; when $\tau(R', c, u) = 1$ means that user u needs to be completely trusted in order to activate R' in context c.

5.4 Trust of Users

We assign each user in the system a trust level. The trust for a user u in context c is denoted by $trust(u, c)$ and is defined in the interval $[0, 1]$, where 1 means the user is fully trusted and 0 means the user is totally untrusted. The *Trust and Contexts Module* in Figure 1 considers the behavior of users over time and the context to calculate the trust value for each user; e.g., if the user is using an untrusted connection, the trust in the user may be reduced. The details of this process are out of the scope of this paper. Solutions such as [5, 12] can be used to construct profiles and latter calculate a trust value based on the behavior of a user.

6. MINIMIZING THE RISK EXPOSURE

To make sure that our system enforces a policy correctly, we provide the definition of a *well-formed policy* that establishes a baseline of the types of accepted policies.

DEFINITION 7. *A well-formed policy is defined as follows:*

1. *The elements in $\mathcal{I}$ comply with Definition 2.*
2. *No roles in a DSoD constraint are allowed to have any I or IA-seniors:*
   $\forall r \in R, dsod(RS, k) \in DSoD \, [\nexists r' \in R : (r' \geq_I r) \vee (r' \geq_{IA} r)]$
3. *User to role assignments should respect SSoD:*
   $\forall u \in U, ssod(RS, k) \in SSoD : |authorized(u) \cap RS| < k$
4. *User to role assignments should respect the cardinality constraints:*
   $\forall u \in U, card_A(r, k) \in CARD_A : |authorized(u) \cap RS| < k$

Condition 2 states that the roles involved in a DSoD constraint may only have A-senior roles. As explained in [28], this condition allows the system to enforce DSoD constraints. Condition 3 establishes that all SSoD constraints are enforced in presence of hybrid hierarchy. Finally, condition 4 ensures that the user assignment fulfills the cardinality constraints. When a policy fulfills all these conditions, it is possible to enforce it during runtime.

6.1 Trust-and-Risk Aware Role Activation

The role activation process is instrumental in our framework. It is in charge of identifying when a user should be denied to activate roles due to lack of trust, user assignments or other constraints. It also allows us to minimize the risk exposure by selecting the roles that have less risk in the system. First, we provide the problem statement.

Problem Statement: A user u in context c with a trust value $trust(u, c)$ requests the system to activate a permissions set $PS \subseteq P$ in a single session. The system responds to the user's request by either accepting it and determining the proper roles to be activated or rejecting it. If the access is granted, the roles selected to be activated should *minimize the risk* exposure of the organization.

A request of a user $u \in U$ in context c for permissions $PS \subseteq P$ is granted if a set of roles $R_q \subseteq R$ can provide the permissions in PS, and the following conditions hold: (1) The user is authorized for all the roles in R_q. (2) The user's trust level ($trust(u, c)$) is greater or equal to the trust threshold of the set of roles R_q. (3) The DSoD and cardinality constraints are not violated when roles in R_q are activated simultaneously. The following optimization problem captures the Trust-and-Risk Role Activation problem.

DEFINITION 8. *The Trust-and-Risk Aware Role Activation Optimization Problem for a query $q = \langle u, PS, c \rangle$, consists of finding a solution, R_q, such that:*

$$\min_{R_q \subseteq authorized(u)} rs(R_q, c, u)$$

$$s.t. \, \forall \, dsod(RS_i, k_i) \in DSoD : |R_q \cap RS_i| < k_i$$
$$\forall \, card(r_c, k) \in CARD \wedge r_c \in R_q : activated(r_c) + 1 \leq k - 1$$
$$trust(u, c) \geq \tau(R_q, c, u)$$
$$P_{au}(R_q) \supseteq PS$$

The system grants a request only if the entire set of requested permissions can be authorized to the user, as we assume that the permissions in PS need to be used simultaneously. In addition, we only require that $P_{au}(R_q) \supseteq PS$. This means that the selected roles may provide additional permissions than those requested by the user. We argue that selecting the roles that minimize the risk is better than providing the roles that minimize the number of extra permissions. To see why, let us consider two possible solutions. The first solution contains one role that provides one additional permission, with a risk of \$10, whereas the second solution contains a role that provides two extra permissions with a risk of \$1. In this cases, the algorithm selects the second solution, as, even though the number of additional permissions is higher, the total risk exposure is reduced.

6.2 Role Activation Algorithm

We propose Algorithm 1 to find a solution for the Trust-and-Risk Aware Role Activation Problem. Our algorithm assumes that the policy is well-formed, as per Definition 7. The algorithm first removes from the search space the roles that cannot be activated due to trust issues (line 4). The current best solution is stored in the set R_q, which initially is empty. The function $selectRoles(P_{rem}, R_{avail}, R_{sel}, u, c)$ finds candidate solutions, and compares them to select the best one. This function is recursive and it starts by checking the base case. This occurs when a candidate solution provides all the permissions requested (line 16). If the candidate solution is less risky than the current best solution, it becomes the new best solution. If both solutions have the same risk, the algorithm selects the one that has lesser number of roles. Otherwise, it keeps the original solution. Before the algorithm reaches the base case, it prunes the search space by removing the roles that cannot be activated due to DSoD and cardinality constraints (lines 25 and 28).

Algorithm 1 Trust-and-Risk Aware Role Activation

```
1: findTrusAndRiskAwareActivationSet(u, PS, c)
2:   R_avail ← authorized(u) {Candidate roles}
3:   for all r ∈ R_avail do
4:     if τ(r, c, u) > trust(u, c) then
5:       R_avail ← R_avail \ r {Pruning based on user's trust}
6:   R_sel ← ∅ {Selected roles so far}
7:   P_rem ← PS {Set of permissions that haven't been found}
8:   R_q ← ∅ {Global variable, stores the best found solution}
9:   selectRoles(P_rem, R_avail, R_sel, u, c)
10:  if R_q ≠ ∅ then
11:    return R_q {Request accepted, activate R_q}
12:  else
13:    return ∅ {Request denied}
14: ──────────────────────────────────────
15: selectRoles(P_rem, R_avail, R_sel, u, c)
16:  if P_rem = ∅ then
17:    if R_q = ∅ then
18:      R_q ← R_sel
19:    else
20:      if rs(R_q, c, u) > rs(R_sel,c,u) then
21:        R_q ← R_sel
22:      else if (rs(R_q, c, u) = rs(R_sel, c, u)) ∧ | R_q | > | R_sel | then
23:        R_q ← R_sel
24:    return {Found candidate solution}
25:  for all dsod(RS, t) ∈ DSoD do
26:    if | R_sel ∩ RS | = (k − 1) then
27:      R_avail ← R_avail \ [RS \ (R_sel ∩ RS)]
28:  for all card(r_c, k) ∈ CARD ∧ r_c ∈ R_q do
29:    if activated(r_c) + 1 = k − 1 then
30:      R_avail ← R_avail \ r_c
31:  for all r_i ∈ R_avail do
32:    if P_rem ∩ P_au(r_i) = ∅ then
33:      R_avail ← R_avail \ r_i
34:  if R_avail = ∅ then
35:    return
36:  r_best ← nextRole(P_rem, R_avail, H, u, R_sel)
37:  R_avail ← R_avail \ r_best
38:  selectRoles(P_rem \ P_au(r_best), R_avail, (R_sel ∪ {r_best}), u, c)
39:  selectRoles(P_rem, R_avail, R_sel, u, c)
```

Ratio of roles to number of users	1:1
Ratio of roles to number of users assigned to roles	6:1
Ratio of roles to directly assigned permissions	1:5
Ratio of roles to constraints	5:1
Ratio of roles to inference tuples	10:1
Ratio of requested permissions to maximum user assignment multiply by directly assigned permissions per role	1:2
Maximum number of junior roles	3
Number of contexts	1

Table 1: Experiment Parameters

Roles that do not provide the missing permissions in the candidate solution, are also removed (line 32). These pruning steps take place before any role is added to a candidate solution, ensuring that candidate solutions do not contain roles that violate the constraints of the policy. In case no candidate roles are left after the pruning (line 34), the algorithm backtracks as that search path did not lead to a valid solution. Otherwise, the next role to be added to the candidate set is chosen in line 36; this function only selects a role r if adding it to R_{sel} fulfils $\tau(R_{sel} \cup \{r\}, c, u) \leq trust(u, c)$. We evaluate two heuristics to perform this step in Section 7. After that, the selected role is added to the candidate solution and the function is invoked again with the updated parameters (line 38). The algorithm also evaluates the solution that does not contain the role selected in line 36, invoking the function without the selected role in line 39.

7. IMPLEMENTATION RESULTS

In order to evaluate the proposed algorithm, we generated synthetic *well-formed policies*, as per Definition 7. The policies were generated randomly according to the ratios shown in Table 1. The risk assigned to each permission in the pol- icy was randomly assigned a value in the interval [0,100] using a uniform distribution. The users' trust thresholds were also randomly assigned using a uniform distribution. Each point in our figures represents the average time of running the algorithm for 30 different policies. Requests were randomly generated. The time required to process requests that could not be granted was very low. For this reason, we only present the results for granted requests.

Comparing Selection Heuristics: Our first experiment contrasts the performance of the algorithm under two different heuristics to select the next role in line 36. Heuristic 1 selects a role that provides the minimum risk (*min risk*), and heuristic 2 selects a role that provides the maximum number of permissions in the request set that have not been covered by previously selected roles (*max perm*). In order to compare these heuristics, the same policy and requests were used for both algorithms. The performance of the heuristics depends on the proportion of *I, IA* and *A-hierarchy* relations. As shown in Figure 3a, when all the hierarchical relations were of type *IA*, the *max perm* heuristic is faster. Figure 3b presents the results of having all the relations of type *I*. There, 61% of the times the *max perm* heuristic behaved better than the other heuristic. In contrast, when all the relations in the hierarchy are of type *A*, as shown in Figure 3c, the results of the two heuristics are equivalent. We also compared the results for policies that contain the same number of *I, A* and *IA* relations. Figure 3d shows that *min risk* heuristic is slower for all the policy sizes. Our results suggest that when the amount of *A-hierarchy* relations is greater than the other two types of hierarchical relations, the two heuristics behave similarly. However, when the proportions are different, the *max perm* heuristic is consistently faster than the *min risk* heuristic. In all the experiments, the *min risk* heuristic never outperformed the *max perm* heuristic. For that reason, in the following experiments we only present the results for the *max perm* heuristic.

The time required to find a solution for policies of the same size, but with different proportions of *I, A,* and *IA* hierarchical is very similar for policies with less than 75 roles (it took less than 0.2 millisecond in all cases). For bigger policies the results change. The time required for finding a solution for policies where all relations are of type *I*, is smaller than for policies with all hierarchy relations of type *A*. This difference occurs because the number of roles users can activate increases when the hierarchy relations are of type *A* (e.g., the search space includes the roles the user is assigned to and all their junior roles). In contrast, when all the relations are of *I*-type, the number of roles users can activate are uniquely those directly assigned to them. When all the relations are of type *IA*, the algorithm takes more time than when they are all of type *I*, but it takes less time than when the relations are all of type *A*. The time required to find a solution when all the relations are of type *IA* is very similar to the cases where the proportion of the three hierarchy types is the same.

Comparing Percentage of Granting Requests for Different Proportions of Misbehaving Users: This ex-

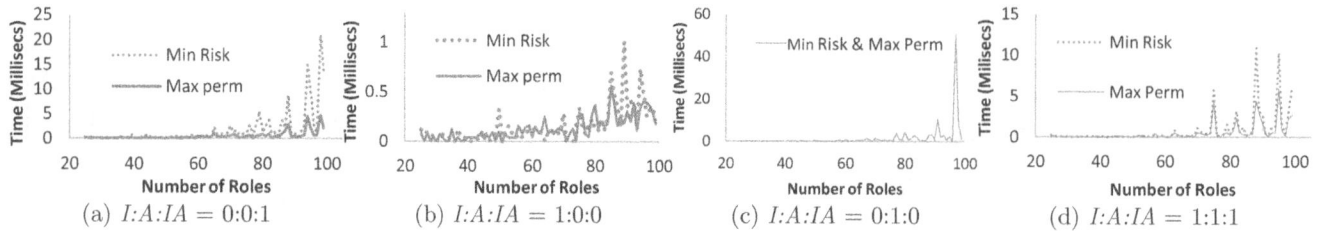

(a) $I{:}A{:}IA = 0{:}0{:}1$ (b) $I{:}A{:}IA = 1{:}0{:}0$ (c) $I{:}A{:}IA = 0{:}1{:}0$ (d) $I{:}A{:}IA = 1{:}1{:}1$

Figure 3: Comparison of selection heuristics for different types of hierarchy proportions.

periment shows how the system behaves as the percentage of users that misbehave increases, and their trust thresholds are reduced. Initially, we randomly generated policies, and requests that were all granted. This is represented by the line of 0% users misbehaving in Figure 4. For the same policies and requests, we randomly selected some users, and reduced - randomly again - their trust thresholds; then we ran the experiments again to see how many requests were denied because of decreases in trust of some users. The results for 20%, 40% and 60% of users misbehaving are shown in Figure 4. As the number of misbehaving users increases, the number of requests granted decreases. The lines are not flat, as the number of requests denied depends on the trust threshold of the selected roles, as well as the random reduction of the user's trust value. The results of this experiment show that our framework is able to deny access to misbehaving users, thus adapting to prevent possible insider attacks.

Comparing Objective Functions: We compared the risk exposure when two different objective functions are used to select the roles to be activated. The objective functions compared are as follows. (1) Our proposed objective function: minimize the risk which is presented in lines 20 to 23; we refer to it as *objective min risk*, and (2) The traditional objective function used in RBAC systems which consists on minimizing the number of roles to be activated; we refer to it as *objective min num roles*. When all the hierarchical relations are of type IA, the *objective min num roles* always found riskier solutions, as shown in Figure 5. Similarly, when the ratios of I, A and IA hierarchies were proportional, 95% of the time the *objective min num roles* provided riskier solutions. The *objective min num roles* was also riskier in 51% of the cases when all the relations were of type I. Interestingly, for policies in which all the hierarchical relations were of type A, the risk of the solutions found by both objective functions were the same. This is because there are no permissions directly acquired by any role that can reduce the number of roles to be selected. The time required to find a solution for both objective functions were very similar, and the number of roles selected by both approaches were always the same for all hierarchy ratios. Hence, we believe our objective function and the proposed algorithm is appropriate, as it reduces the risk and does not augment the number of selected roles. Finally, our results suggest that the time required to answer an authorization query is acceptable.

8. DISCUSSION AND RELATED WORK

We identify three branches of related work. The first one is related to risk assessment methodologies, the second with inference threat, and the third one is related to RBAC, risk and trust.

Risk Assessment Methodologies and Our Framework: Our framework requires an administrator to provide the risk values associated with each permission in the sys-

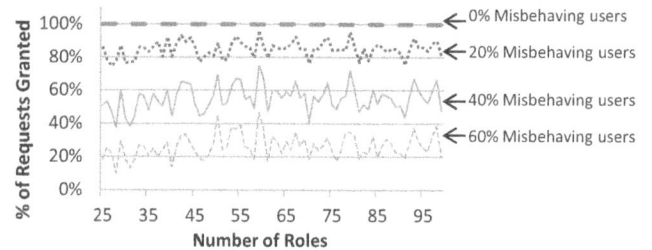

Figure 4: Comparison of granted requests for different percentage of misbehaving users.

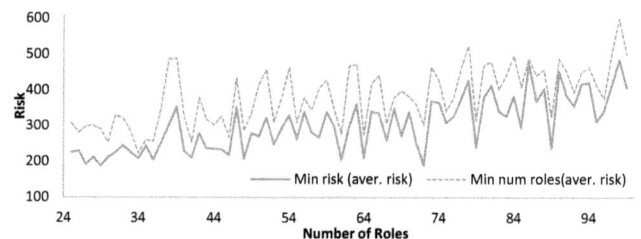

Figure 5: Risk exposure using our algorithm (min. risk) compared to the risk of traditional role activation algorithm (min. num. of roles) when all relations are of type IA.

tem. At first glance, this may seem like a lot of work. However, we believe that organizations that need to use this type of scheme also are expected to utilize some type of risk assessment methodology. Several risk assessment methodologies such as the ones provided by NIST [30], Octave [3], Aagedal *et. al* [1], among others, allow organizations to identify threats and evaluate their risks to determine an appropriate course of action (i.e., to mitigate the threat, or to accept it). It is possible to leverage these risk assessment approaches to specify the policy of our system. This is the case even when the methodology used is a qualitative one (e.g., [30]), where the risk is usually a function of qualitative levels (e.g., high, medium, low). These risk levels can easily be assigned probability values, and impact values to obtain a risk value for the permissions as is done in [30].

In addition, according to [33], big organizations typically have from 10 to 12 key services. This implies that it is possible to simplify the specification of the policy to include uniquely the permissions that are more important in the system, while leaving the risk of non-relevant permissions set to a default small value.

Inference Threat: In [7, 13, 6], when a user is about to infer some information, the system prevents it by either denying access or providing scrambled data. In contrast, we assume that real organizations may need to provide access to roles to a single employee even if they allow inference. For instance, an organization may not have enough employees making it impossible to assign roles without allowing inference. We believe that the risk of inference can be attenuated by increasing the trust threshold necessary to get the roles that complete an inference tuple. Our solution does not deny the access to those inference channels, but taxes their utilization with a higher trust threshold.

RBAC, Risk and Trust: Although RBAC has several benefits, it has a static nature that avoids the system to revoke access to users that are not behaving properly. For this reason, several approaches have incorporated *trust* [9, 15, 14]. In [9], roles are associated with trust intervals, and trust intervals are assigned to users. Users are assigned to roles according to their trust levels. This model does not capture the intuitive nature of RBAC systems in which users are assigned to roles according to their organization's functions, not trust levels. In [15], users are assigned to roles based on trustworthiness and context information. A similar approach was proposed in [14], where role thresholds are a function of the risk of the operations. If the trust of the user offsets the risk of the action, the access is granted. However, none of these works provide a clear framework to find trust thresholds, reduce the risk the organization faces during runtime, and do not consider SoD and cardinality constraints.

In [21], each role is assigned a minimum level of confidence and each user a clearance level. Based on these values, the risk associated with a user activating a role is calculated. Objects and actions are assigned a value according to their importance and criticality. Our model differs form this work in that the trust level of users depends on their behavior, not in a static value. In addition, [21] does not consider role hierarchy, inference risk, and does not present experiments.

In [24, 4, 10], the main focus is also to reduce the risk exposure. In [24] a risk based analysis is proposed to ensure that system administrators assign permissions to the roles considering the risk inherent to those permissions. Each permission is assigned a risk value, and the role hierarchy is organized based on these risk values. This may not be appropriate, as it is more intuitive to organize the role hierarchy according to the employee's structure. In contrast, our approach respects an organization's hierarchy and reduces the risk exposure of the organization during the role activation process. In [4], a model that modifies the policy to minimize the risk exposure as systems evolve is proposed. This model results in a difficult to manage policy in which the administrator does not know the current status of the policy; making it cumbersome and prone to errors to modify it. In contrast, our system reduces the risk exposure during the role activation process without modifying the policy. Chen *et. al* [10] propose a model in which the risk associated with a role is calculated using the trustworthiness of the user, the degree of competence he has to activate a role, and the degree of appropriateness of the permission-role assignments. Each permission is assigned a mitigation strategy, which is a list of risk thresholds and an associated obligation pairs. When a user wants to obtain a set of permissions, the role with minimum risk is selected (no algorithm is proposed for this purpose, however). Then, the system consults the mitigation strategy to see which action is more appropriate: e.g., deny access or allow access and impose an obligation. Our proposal differs from this work in several ways. Firstly, Chen *et. al* do not consider SoD constraints, which is crucial for addressing insider attacks. Secondly, our model accounts for the context as an important component to define which risk threshold should be enforced; such context-based risk is not considered in [10]. Thirdly, we consider the inference

threat, while [10] does not. Chen *et. al* use the appropriateness of permission to role assignment as part of the risk computation. We believe this makes the semantics of permission to role assignment complex, as the appropriateness value becomes a functional input for such assignments. This may result in too many inappropriate assignments -although they will likely be captured through risk computation. By not including this in our approach, we reduce the complexity of administration of the policy. We propose an algorithm to enforce the policy while reducing the risk exposure of the system, and evaluate its performance experimentally; in contrast, [10] does not provide such algorithm.

In [27] costs of access are assigned to permissions depending on the risk of their operations, and each user is assigned a budget. Users are assigned to roles, but being assigned or not does not necessarily determine whether a user can activate a role. If the user accesses permissions that he can obtain through an authorized role, the cost is reduced. In case he is not authorized to a role, the cost of activating it is *taxed*. Nonetheless, if the user has enough budget to make the operation, he can access the permissions. Salim *et. al* [27] claim that this mechanism incentives the users to spend their budget cautiously, activating low cost (low risk) roles. However, this scheme may lead to several problems. Users can use their budget to perform unauthorized access without being detected; e.g., if a disgruntled employee wants to quit the organization, he would not mind to expend all the budget performing a malicious action. In addition, leaving to users the management of the budget is risky. We believe that our proposed system automatically reduces the risk exposure, enforces constraints, is more user friendly (users do not need to manage their budget) and overall is more effective mitigating insider threats.

Many commercial products also incorporate risk in their solutions; e.g., SAP [29], Oracle [25], IBM [18] and Beta Systems [31]. These products mitigate risk by closely monitoring and auditing the usage of risky permissions. The risk values, however, are not used to make access control decisions. In contrast, our solution performs access control decisions using the trust value that the system has on the users, and the trust threshold of the requested permissions under a particular context. It is worth noting that our solution could be integrated to the ones offered by commercial products to improve the accountability in the system.

To the best of our knowledge, none of the related work has provided an analysis of the way the roles should be activated. This paper is the first to introduce the Trust-and-Risk Aware Activation Problem. In addition, we acknowledge the fact that sometimes the risk of activating several roles is higher than the addition of the risks of the permissions they acquire, as in the case of the inference threat.

9. CONCLUSIONS

In this paper, we have presented an approach to perform access control considering the behavior of the users, and the risk exposure that an organization is ready to accept when granting access to certain roles in the system. Our approach reacts to negative behaviors of users by denying access to permissions whose misuse would negatively impact an organization. In this way, our approach is able to deter possible attacks when there are technical precursors that indicate a user is behaving maliciously. In order to reduce the risk exposure further, we have also defined an optimization problem, and an algorithm that reduces the risk exposure. We have presented experimental results for different types of policies. We believe the features offered by our framework make it difficult for the insider attackers to misuse the privileges. As future work, we plan to investigate in detail the integration of the work presented here with the *Monitoring Module*, and *Trust and Context Module*.

Acknowledgment

We thank the anonymous reviewers for their helpful feedback. This research has been supported by the US National Science Foundation award IIS-0545912.

10. REFERENCES

[1] J. O. Aagedal, F. d. Braber, T. Dimitrakos, B. A. Gran, D. Raptis, and K. Stølen. Model-based risk assessment to improve enterprise security. In *Proc. of the 6th International Enterprise Distributed Object Computing Conference*, 2002.

[2] G.-J. Ahn and R. Sandhu. Role-based authorization constraints specification. *ACM Trans. Inf. Syst. Secur.*, 3:207–226, November 2000.

[3] C. Alberts, S. Behrens, R. Pethia, and W. Wilson. Operationally critical threat, asset, and vulnerability evaluation (octave), 1999.

[4] B. Aziz, S. N. Foley, J. Herbert, and G. Swart. Reconfiguring role based access control policies using risk semantics. In *Journal of High Speed Networks: Special Issue on Managing Security Policies, Modelling Verification and Configuration*, 2006.

[5] E. Bertino, E. Terzi, A. Kamra, and A. Vakali. Intrusion detection in rbac-administered databases. In *Computer Security Applications Conference, 21st Annual*, dec. 2005.

[6] J. Biskup. History-dependent inference control of queries by dynamic policy adaption. In *Proc. of the 25th annual IFIP WG 11.3 conference on Data and applications security and privacy*, DBSec'11, pp. 106–121, Berlin, Heidelberg, 2011. Springer-Verlag.

[7] A. Brodsky, C. Farkas, and S. Jajodia. Secure databases: constraints, inference channels, and monitoring disclosures. *Knowledge and Data Engineering, IEEE Transactions on*, 2000.

[8] E. Celikel, M. Kantarcioglu, X. Li, and E. Bertino. A Risk Management Approach to RBAC. *Risk and Decision Analysis*, 1(2), November 2009.

[9] S. Chakraborty and I. Ray. Trustbac: integrating trust relationships into the rbac model for access control in open systems. In *Proc. of the 11th ACM symposium on Access control models and technologies*, SACMAT '06, pp. 49–58, New York, NY, USA, 2006. ACM.

[10] L. Chen and J. Crampton. Risk-aware role-based access control. In *Proc. of the 7th International Workshop on Security and Trust Management.*, 2001.

[11] Y. Chen and W. Chu. Protection of database security via collaborative inference detection. *Knowledge and Data Engineering, IEEE Transactions on*, 20(8):1013–1027, aug. 2008.

[12] C. Y. Chung, M. Gertz, and K. Levitt. Demids: A misuse detection system for database systems. In *Proc. of the Integrity and Internal Control in Information System*, pp 159–178, 1999.

[13] H. S. Delugach and T. H. Hinke. Using conceptual graphs to represent database inference security analysis. *Jour. Computing and Info. Tech.*, 4(4):291–307, 1994.

[14] N. Dimmock, A. Belokosztolszki, D. Eyers, J. Bacon, and K. Moody. Using trust and risk in role-based access control policies. In *In Proc. of the 9th ACM Symposium on Access Control Models and Technologies SACMAT'04*. ACM Press, 2004.

[15] F. Feng, C. Lin, D. Peng, and J. Li. A trust and context based access control model for distributed systems. In *Proc. of the 2008 10th IEEE International Conference on High Performance Computing and Communications*, HPCC '08, pp 629–634, Washington, DC, USA, 2008. IEEE Computer Society.

[16] D. F. Ferraiolo, R. Sandhu, S. Gavrila, D. R. Kuhn, and R. Chandramouli. Proposed nist standard for role-based access control. *ACM Trans. Inf. Syst. Secur.*, 4:224–274, August 2001.

[17] V. D. Gligor and C. S. Chandersekaran. Surviving insider attacks: A call for system experiments. In S. J. Stolfo, S. M. Bellovin, A. D. Keromytis, S. Hershkop, S. W. Smith, and S. Sinclair, editors, *Insider Attack and Cyber Security*, volume 39 of *Advances in Information Security*, pp. 153–164. Springer US, 2008.

[18] IBM. Resource access control facility (racf), 2012. www-03.ibm.com/systems/z/os/zos/features/racf/.

[19] C. S. Institute. Csi computer crime and security survey, 2010.

[20] K. Jensen. Coloured petri nets. In W. Brauer, W. Reisig, and G. Rozenberg, editors, *Petri Nets: Central Models and Their Properties*, volume 254 of *Lecture Notes in Computer Science*, pp. 248–299. Springer Berlin / Heidelberg, 1987.

[21] J. Ma, K. Adi, M. Mejri, and L. Logrippo. Risk analysis in access control systems. In *Privacy Security and Trust (PST), 2010 Eighth Annual International Conference on*, pp. 160 –166, aug. 2010.

[22] A. Moore, D. Cappelli, and T. R. The "big picture" of insider it sabotage across u.s. critical infrastructures, 2008. CERT, http://www.cert.org/insider_threat.

[23] L. Mui and M. Mohtashemi. A computational model of trust and reputation. In *Proc. of the 35th Hawaii International Conference on System Science (HICSS)*, 2002.

[24] N. Nissanke and E. J. Khayat. Risk based security analysis of permissions in rbac. In *Proc. of the 2 nd International Workshop on Security In Information Systems, Security In Information Systems*, pp. 332–341. INSTICC Press, 2004.

[25] Oracle. Application access controls governor, 2012. http://www.oracle.com/us/solutions/corporate-governance/access-controls/index.html.

[26] Q. M. S. Osborn, R. Sandhu. Configuring role-based access control to enforce mandatory and discretionary access control policies. In *ACM Transaction on Information and System Security*, 2000.

[27] F. Salim, J. Reid, E. Dawson, and U. Dulleck. An approach to access control under uncertainty. In *Availability, Reliability and Security (ARES), 2011 6th International Conference on*, pp. 1 –8, 2011.

[28] R. Sandhu. Role activation hierarchies. In *In Proc. of 3rd ACM Workshop on Role-Based Access Control*, pp. 33–40. ACM, 1998.

[29] SAP. Access risk management, 2012. www.sap.com/solutions/sapbusinessobjects/large/governance-risk-compliance/accessandauthorization.

[30] G. Stoneburner, A. Goguen, and A. Feringa. Risk management guide for information technology systems, recommendations of the national institute of standards and technology, 2002.

[31] B. Systems. Identity and access governance, 2012. www.betasystems.com/en/portfolio/identityaccessgovernance

[32] R. Yip and E. Levitt. Data level inference detection in database systems. In *Computer Security Foundations Workshop, 1998. Proc. 11th IEEE*, pp. 179 –189, 1998.

[33] L. Young and J. Allen. Security risk assessment using octave ® allegro, podcast's transcripts, 2008.

Analyzing Temporal Role Based Access Control Models

Emre Uzun
Rutgers University
emreu@rutgers.edu

Vijayalakshmi Atluri
Rutgers University
atluri@rutgers.edu

Shamik Sural
Indian Institute of Technology
shamik@cse.iitkgp.ernet.in

Jaideep Vaidya
Rutgers University
jsvaidya@business.
rutgers.edu

Gennaro Parlato
University of Southampton
gennaro@ecs.soton.ac.uk

Anna Lisa Ferrara
University of Bristol
anna.lisa.ferrara@bristol.ac.uk

P. Madhusudan
University of Illinois at
Urbana-Champaign
madhu@illinois.edu

ABSTRACT

Today, Role Based Access Control (RBAC) is the de facto model used for advanced access control, and is widely deployed in diverse enterprises of all sizes. Several extensions to the authorization as well as the administrative models for RBAC have been adopted in recent years. In this paper, we consider the temporal extension of RBAC (TRBAC), and develop safety analysis techniques for it. Safety analysis is essential for understanding the implications of security policies both at the stage of specification and modification. Towards this end, in this paper, we first define an administrative model for TRBAC. Our strategy for performing safety analysis is to appropriately decompose the TRBAC analysis problem into multiple subproblems similar to RBAC. Along with making the analysis simpler, this enables us to leverage and adapt existing analysis techniques developed for traditional RBAC. We have adapted and experimented with employing two state of the art analysis approaches developed for RBAC as well as tools developed for software testing. Our results show that our approach is both feasible and flexible.

Categories and Subject Descriptors

H.1.0 [**Information Systems Models and Principles**]: General

General Terms

Design, Security, Verification

Keywords

Access Control, Temporal RBAC, Safety Analysis

1. INTRODUCTION

Providing restrictive and secure access to resources is a challenging and socially important problem. Role-based access control (RBAC), which allocates permissions to users via roles, is one of the primary access control models. It has been successfully incorporated in a variety of commercial systems, and has become the norm in many of today's organizations for enforcing security.

One major advantage with RBAC is that, unlike in discretionary access control (DAC) where users can grant access privileges at their own discretion, organizations have central control over its resources. For large organizations, it is normal to have roles in the order of thousands and users in the order of tens of thousands. Typically, security administration is performed by a system security officer (SSO) and is decentralized by delegating administrative activities as it is overwhelming for a single SSO to administer all roles. Administrative RBAC (ARBAC) [14], is a comprehensive model of using RBAC to administer RBAC, by introducing administrative roles and associated privileges. Administrative activities of ARBAC include user-role assignment (URA), permission-role assignment (PRA) and role-to-role assignment (to specify the role hierarchies).

While decentralized RBAC administration enhances the flexibility and scalability, an obvious side effect of it is reduced organizational control over its resources. Therefore, certain security guarantees are essential to ensure controlled delegation and to retain the desired level of control. Such guarantees can only be ensured through a formal analysis of the security properties of the RBAC system. A study of the formal behavior of RBAC models helps organizations gain confidence on the level of control they have on the resources they own. Moreover, security analysis helps them set policies so that owners do not unknowingly lose their control on resources, and aids them make to changes to the policies only if the analysis yields no security policy violations.

Several extensions to RBAC have been proposed for implementation in different domains such as geospatial, mobile and temporal. Noted examples include: temporal RBAC (TRBAC) [2], generalized temporal RBAC (GTRBAC) [10], and Geo-RBAC [3].

In this paper, we limit our focus to the temporal extensions of RBAC. In temporal RBAC, it is possible to specify that a role can be enabled only during a certain time interval (fixed or periodic), or a role can be enabled as long as another role is enabled. In advanced temporal RBAC models there are additional constraints that introduce the notion of role activation, temporal validity on the user-to-role and permission-to-role assignments. Bertino et al. [2] propose a model for TRBAC which has temporal constraints on role activation and deactivation, periodic role enabling and disabling. Later, Joshi et al. [10] propose a generalized version of TRBAC (GTRBAC) that has temporal constraints on user and permission assignments, in addition to the existing temporal constraints on TRBAC.

The main goal of this paper is to offer formal analysis of TRBAC. In order to accomplish this, we first define an administrative model for TRBAC (called ATRBAC). In conventional RBAC systems, where administration is done by users with specific administrative privileges (separation of duty), a separate administrative model in which, the policies to control role assignments, role revocations and other possible operations are declared. These policies are often represented by *can-assign* and *can-revoke* rules, which allow administrative users to assign or revoke roles for users that satisfy certain preconditions, or assign or revoke permissions from roles. Therefore, the assignment / revocation operations are limited to the extent covered by the policies.

The first comprehensive administrative model for RBAC is called ARBAC97 [14], which introduces the notion of an administrator role (AR) with administrative permissions (AP). ARBAC97 has three components: URA97 (user-role assignment), PRA97 (permission-role assignment) and RRA97 (role-role assignment) dealing with the different aspects of RBAC administration. URA97 and PRA97 are exact duals of each other, and are based on the notions of prerequisite conditions and role ranges. They use *"can_assign"* and *"can_assignp"* rules for role and permission assignments, respectively. These rules use the notions of (1) the role range that an administrator role has authority over, and (2) the prerequisite role (or prerequisite condition) needed to exercise that authority. Later, several other administrative models are proposed by Crampton and Loizou [4], Kern et al. [11], Li and Mao [12], Dekker et al. [5] and Bertino et al. [1] to cover more advanced administrative structures.

The temporal constraints can be considered as an additional layer of preconditions to the access control policies, but they are not limited to them. There are two different ways to embed temporal constraints in RBAC. The role assignments can have a temporal dimension, denoting the time intervals (we denote them as *role schedules*) in which the role assignment is valid, or the administrative rules can have a temporal dimension denoting the time intervals (we denote them as *rule schedules*) in which a particular rule is executable. The former restricts the time intervals that the users assume a given role, whereas the latter restricts the time intervals that the administrators execute an administrative rule in the system.

The safety problem, first identified by Harrison, Ruzzo and Ullman [8] can be formulated as testing the following: "Whether there exists a reachable authorization state in which a particular subject possesses a particular privilege for a specific object". Stoller et al. [15] have developed a fixed parameter tractable algorithm to perform security analysis for a simplified version of RBAC. Another security analysis on RBAC using reduction based algorithms is proposed by Li and Tripunitara [12]. Jha et al. [9] compared the use of model checking and first order logic programming for the security analysis of RBAC, and concluded that model checking is a promising approach for security analysis. Ferrara et al. [7] propose an RBAC reachability analysis which exploits abstraction techniques as used in program verification. Their approach reduces the RBAC model into a program and makes a sound analysis to prove whether a particular state is unreachable. While none of the above work address the TRBAC analysis, recently, a timed automata based analysis of GTRBAC is proposed by Mondal et al. [13]. Since it assumes continuous time model, the cost of analysis has been shown to be very expensive; in this paper, we tackle the problem by considering discrete time intervals.

Specifically, we make the following contributions in this paper. (1) We propose an administrative model for the TRBAC that governs the access control rights of the users. (2) We propose a novel approach for security analysis of TRBAC. The main strategy we use while performing the security analysis is to decompose the TRBAC analysis problem into multiple subproblems similar to RBAC. Essentially, we split the problem into simpler RBAC subproblems so that deciding whether a particular target state is reachable or not can be potentially simpler. Additionally, it lends itself to employ the analysis techniques developed for traditional RBAC.

We present two different decomposition strategies – (1) Decomposition using rule schedules and (2) Decomposition using role schedules. Though we can employ any RBAC reachability analysis method, in this paper, we have used the approach developed by Stoller et al. [15] and Ferrara et al. [7], where the latter method can perform multi-user analysis.

The rest of the paper is organized as follows. In Section 2, we review the preliminaries. In Section 3, we introduce the temporal constraints and propose our administrative model for TRBAC. In Section 4, we discuss our two different decomposition strategies that map the TRBAC into a series of subproblems. In Sections 5 and 6, we present the details of the methodologies along with their experimental results. In Section 7, we provide a discussion to compare these two strategies and introduce an approach to analyze the multi-user case. In Section 8, we give our concluding remarks and future work.

2. PRELIMINARIES

In this section, we review the definition of our administrative model for TRBAC. Since we reduce the problem of analyzing administrative TRBAC systems to that of administrative RBAC, we also recall the definition of RBAC and administrative RBAC.

2.1 RBAC and Administrative RBAC

A RBAC policy [6] is a tuple $\langle U, R, PRMS, UA, PA \rangle$ where U, R and $PRMS$ are finite sets of *users*, *roles*, and *permissions*, respectively, $UA \subseteq U \times R$ is the *user-role assignment* relation, $PA \subseteq PRMS \times R$ is the *permission-role assignment* relation. A tuple $(u, r) \in UA$ represents that user u belongs to role r. Similarly, $(p, r) \in PA$ represents that members of role r are granted permission p.

The *Administrative RBAC* (ARBAC) [14] model specifies rules to modify an RBAC system. It is composed of three modules URA user-role administration, PRA permission-role administration, and RRA role-role administration. In this paper we focus on administrative permissions to assign users to roles, therefore, we will only describe the URA component.

The URA policy allows to make changes to the user-role assignment relation UA by using assignment/revocation rules performed by administrators. Administrators are those users that belong to administrative roles. We denote the set of administrative roles as AR. Some policies consider the set AR to be disjoint from the set of roles R. Those policies are said to meet the *separate administration* constraint [15]. We assume that the set of administrative roles AR is included in the set of roles R, unless differently specified. A user can be assigned to a role if she satisfies the precondition associated to that role. A *precondition* is a conjunction of literals, where each literal is either in positive form r or in negative form $\neg r$, for some role r in R. Following [7], we represent preconditions by two sets of roles *Pos* and *Neg*. A user u satisfies a precondition (Pos, Neg) if u is member of all roles in *Pos* and does not belong to any role of *Neg*.

Rules to assign users to roles are specified by the set:

$$can\_assign \subseteq AR \times 2^R \times 2^R \times R.$$

A can-assign tuple $(admin, Pos, Neg, r) \in can\_assign$ allows a member of the administrative role $admin$ to assign a user u to roles r provided u's current role memberships satisfies the precondition (Pos, Neg).

Rules to revoke users from roles are specified as follows:

$$can\_revoke \subseteq AR \times R.$$

If $(admin, r) \in can\_revoke$, a member of the administrative role $admin \in AR$, can revoke the membership of any user from role $r \in R$.

A URA system can be seen as a state-transition system defined by the tuple $\mathcal{S} = \langle U, R, UA, can\_assign, can\_revoke \rangle$. A *configuration* of $\mathcal{S}$ is any user-role assignment relation $UR \subseteq U \times R$. A configuration UR is *initial* if $UR = UA$. Given two $\mathcal{S}$ configurations $c = UR$ and $c' = UR'$, there is a *transition* (or *move*) from c to c' with rule $m \in (can\_assign \cup can\_revoke)$, denoted $c \xrightarrow{\tau_m} c'$, if there exists an *administrative* user ad and administrative role $admin$ with $(ad, admin) \in$ UR and a user $u \in U$, and one of the following holds:

[**can-assign move**] $m = (admin, P, N, r)$, $P \subseteq \{r' \mid (u, r') \in UR\}$, $N \subseteq R \setminus \{r' \mid (u, r') \in UR\}$, and $UR' = UR \cup \{(u, r)\}$;

[**can-revoke move**] $m = (admin, r)$, $(u, r) \in UR$, and $UR' = UR \setminus \{(u, r)\}$.

A *run* (or *computation*) of $\mathcal{S}$ is any finite sequence of $\mathcal{S}$ transitions $\pi = c_1 \xrightarrow{\tau_{m_1}} c_2 \xrightarrow{\tau_{m_2}} \ldots c_n \xrightarrow{\tau_{m_n}} c_{n+1}$ for some $n \geq 0$, where c_1 is the *initial* configuration of $\mathcal{S}$. An $\mathcal{S}$ configuration c is *reachable* if c is the last configuration of a run of $\mathcal{S}$.

Reachability Problem: Given an URA system $\mathcal{S}$ over the set of roles R and a role goal $\in R$ and a user u, the *role-reachability problem* asks whether a configuration c with $(u, goal) \in c$ is reachable in $\mathcal{S}$.

2.2 Temporal RBAC

We consider a TRBAC model which is a simplified version of prior work [2, 10]. Temporal RBAC enriches the definition of RBAC by associating to each component a schedule that enables users to assume roles only in certain time intervals. Let T_{MAX} be a positive integer. A *time slot* of *Times* is a pair $(a, a + 1)$, where a is an integer, and $0 \leq a < a + 1 \leq T_{MAX}$. A time slot $(a, a + 1)$ represents the set of all times in the set $[a, b)$, i.e., $\{t \mid a \leq t < b\}$. We use a *time interval*, consisting of a pair (a, b) where a, b are two integers and $0 \leq a < a + 1 \leq T_{MAX}$, to represent the set of corresponding time slots $\{(a, a + 1), (a + 1, a + 2), \ldots (b - 1, b)\}$ succinctly. A *schedule* over T_{MAX} is a set of time slots.

For instance, consider a hospital that works for 24 hours with three shifts (between 8 am and 4 pm, between 4 pm and 12 am, and between 12 am and 8 am). If we want to have the precision of hours, we choose $T_{MAX} = 24$, and a schedule s that covers shifts 8 am–4 pm and 4 pm–12 am is represented as $s = \{(8, 9), (9, 10), \ldots, (23, 24)\}$. The schedule definition is a simplified version of the Calendar definition in Bertino et al. [2], where we have simpler periodic constraints and do not have duration constraints. We assume that the system is periodic, thus the schedules repeat themselves after any T_{MAX}; in the hospital example above, time intervals are repeated each 24 hours. Given a schedule s over T_{MAX} and a real number t, we say that t belongs to s, denoted $t \in s$, if there is a time interval $(a, b) \in s$ such that $t' \in [a, b)$, where $t' = t \mod T_{MAX}$.

Let S be the set of all possible schedules over T_{MAX}. A TRBAC policy over T_{MAX} is a tuple $M = \langle U, R, PRMS, TUA, PA, RS \rangle$ where U, R and $PRMS$ are finite sets of *users*, *roles*, and *permissions*, respectively. $TUA \subseteq (U \times R \times S)$ is the *temporal user-role assignment* relation, $PA \subseteq (PRMS \times R)$ is the *permission-role assignment* relation, and $RS \subseteq (R \times S)$ is the *role-status* relation. A tuple $(u, r, s) \in TUA$ represents that user u is a member of the role r only during the time intervals of schedule s. During the life time of the system, a role can be either enabled or disabled. A tuple $(r, s) \in RS$ imposes that role r is *enabled* only during the time intervals of s (and therefore it can be assumed to be a member of r only at these times), and *disabled* otherwise. As in classical RBAC, a tuple $(p, r) \in PA$ means that permission p is associated to role r. Thus, a user u is granted permission p at time $t \in [0, T_{MAX}]$ provided that there exists a role $r \in R$ such that $(u, r, s_1) \in TUA$, $(r, s_2) \in RS$, $(p, r) \in PA$, and $t \in (s_1 \cap s_2)$, for some time intervals s_1 and s_2.

Throughout the paper, we assume that relation RS for each role $r \in R$ contains always exactly one pair with first component r. Similarly, the relation TUA contains exactly one tuple for each pair in $U \times R$. Thus, if a role r is disabled in any time interval, we require that RS relates r with the empty schedule. Similarly, if a user u does not belong to a role r in any time interval, the pair (u, r) is associated to the empty schedule by the relation TUA.

In the next section we introduce our administrative model.

3. ADMINISTRATIVE TRBAC

In temporal RBAC, it is important to decide on the extent to which the notion of time is embedded into the system. Theoretically, if one wants to capture complete behavior of the system at every piece of time instance, then a continuous time model should be built and for the analysis, continuous time models like timed automata should be used. However, continuous time analysis adds extra complexity to the model, since in real life systems, temporal decisions on access control are usually handled in discrete time intervals. For instance, the access control schemes may change depending on predefined intervals like day-time hours and night-time hours, weekdays and weekends (in both cases we have two discrete intervals), or even hourly (24 discrete intervals). Thus, it is sufficient to analyze the behavior of the system in only these intervals rather than having a continuous time analysis.

In the following, we propose an administrative model that allows administrators to make changes to the role-status relation RS and the temporal user-role assignment relation TUA by using respectively enable / disable and assignment / revocation rules. More specifically, the goal of an enable/disable (respectively, assignment/revocation) rule for a role r (for a user u and a role r, resp.) is that of updating the time intervals of the current schedule s associated to each pair $(r, s) \in RS$ (respectively, each triple $(u, r, s) \in TUA$).

In the following, we describe a Temporal URA system (TURA) as a state-transition system. A TURA system is a tuple $\mathcal{S}_T = \langle M, can\_enable, can\_disable, t\_can\_assign, t\_can\_revoke \rangle$ where $M = \langle U, R, PRMS, TUA, PA, RS \rangle$ is a TRBAC policy over T_{MAX}, and can_enable, $can\_disable$, t_can_assign, $t\_can\_revoke \subseteq (R \times S \times 2^R \times 2^R \times S \times R)$.

A *configuration* of $\mathcal{S}_T$ is a pair (ER, TUR) where $ER \subseteq (R \times S)$ is an enabled-role assignment relation and $TUR \subseteq (U \times R \times S)$ is a user-role assignment relation. A configuration (ER, TUR) is *initial* if $ER = RS$ and $TUR = TUA$. Given two $\mathcal{S}_T$ configurations $c = (ER, TUR)$ and $c' = (ER', TUR')$, we describe below the conditions under which there is a *transition* (or *move*) from c to c' at time $t \in \mathbb{N}$ with rule $m \in \mathcal{M}_{ALL} = (can\_enable \cup can\_disable \cup t\_can\_assign \cup t\_can\_revoke)$, denoted $c \xrightarrow{(\tau_m, t)} c'$.

Before defining the transition relation, we first describe the components of move $m = (admin, s_{rule}, Pos, Neg, s_{role}, r)$. Move m can be executed only by a user, say ad, belonging to the *administrative role* $admin \in R$. The times t in which ad can execute m are all those in which ad is assumed to be a member of role $admin$, and furthermore, t must also belong to the schedule s_{rule} which denotes the time intervals when m can be fired (or we say *valid*): $t \in (s_{ad} \cap s_{admin} \cap s_{rule})$ where $(ad, admin, s_{ad}) \in TUR$ and $(admin, s_{admin}) \in ER$. In the rest of the section we say that m can be *executed* at time t whenever t fulfills the above condition. The component s_{role} is used to update the schedule of a role, or the membership of a user to a role, depending on the kind of rule of m. The pair of disjoint role sets (Pos, Neg) is called the *precondition* of m whose fulfillment depends by the kind of the rule m.

The fulfillment of the precondition of a can-enable and can-disable rule depends on the current status of the other roles. Let $\hat{s} \subseteq s_{role}$. A can-enable or can-disable rule $m = (admin, s_{rule}, Pos, Neg, s_{role}, r)$ satisfies its precondition (Pos, Neg) w.r.t. candidate schedule $\hat{s}$, if for every time slot $\alpha \in \hat{s}$, if 1) for every role $pos \in Pos$, $\alpha \subseteq s_{pos}$ where $(pos, s_{pos}) \in ER$, 2) for every role $neg \in Neg$, $\alpha \cap s_{neg} = \emptyset$, where $(neg, s_{neg}) \in ER$, and 3) α satisfies all preconditions. In other words, a candidate schedule $\hat{s} \subseteq s_{role}$ satisfies a precondition only if each time slot $\alpha \in \hat{s}$ satisfies the precondition individually. Let $(r, s) \in ER$.

[Enabling Rules] A can-enable rule adds a new schedule to a specific role. A tuple $(admin, s_{rule}, Pos, Neg, s_{role}, r) \in can\_enable$ allows to update the tuple $(r, s) \in RS$ to $(r, s \cup \hat{s})$ for some schedule $\hat{s}$, provided that m can be executed at time t and also satisfies its precondition. Formally, rule m is executable at time t, m satisfies its precondition (Pos, Neg) w.r.t. schedule $\hat{s}$, $ER' = (ER \setminus \{(r, s)\}) \cup \{(r, s \cup \hat{s})\}$, and $TUR' = TUR$.

[Disabling Rules] A can-disable rule removes a schedule from a designed role. A tuple $m = (admin, s_{rule}, Pos, Neg, s_{role}, r) \in can\_disable$ allows to update the tuple $(r, s) \in RS$ to $(r, s \setminus \hat{s})$, for some schedule $\hat{s}$, provided that m can be executed at time t, and satisfies its precondition. Formally, m is executable at time t, m satisfies its precondition (Pos, Neg) w.r.t. schedule $\hat{s}$, $ER' = (ER \setminus \{(r, s)\}) \cup \{(r, s \setminus \hat{s})\}$, and $TUR' = TUR$.

The next two rules are similar to those given above with the difference that we now update the schedules associated to each element of the user-role relation. Another difference is that can-assign and can-remove rules have a different semantics to fulfill their preconditions. A user $u \in U$ satisfies a precondition (Pos, Neg) w.r.t. a schedule $\hat{s}$ if for every time slot $\alpha \in \hat{s}$, 1) for every $(u, pos, s_{pos}) \in TUR$ with $pos \in Pos$, $\alpha \subseteq s_{pos}$, 2) for every $(u, neg, s_{neg}) \in TUR$ with $neg \in Neg$, $\alpha \cap s_{neg} = \emptyset$, and 3) α satisfies all preconditions. Let $(u, r, s) \in TUR$.

[Assignment Rules] A tuple $(admin, s_{rule}, Pos, Neg, s_{role}, r) \in t\_can\_assign$ allows to update the user-role assignment relation for the pair (u, r) as follows. Let $\hat{s}$ be a schedule over T_{MAX} with $\hat{s} \subseteq s_{role}$. Then, if m can be executed at time t, and user u satisfies the precondition (Pos, Neg) w.r.t. schedule $\hat{s}$, then the tuple (u, r, s) is updated to $(u, r, s \cup \hat{s})$, i.e. $TUR' = (TUR \setminus \{(u, r, s)\}) \cup \{(u, r, s \cup \hat{s})\}$, and $ER' = ER$.

[Revocation Rules] A tuple $(admin, s_{rule}, Pos, Neg, s_{role}, r) \in t\_can\_revoke$ allows to update the user-role assignment relation for the pair (u, r) as follows. Let $\hat{s}$ be a schedule over T_{MAX} with $\hat{s} \subseteq s_{role}$. Then, if m can be executed at time t, and user u satisfies the precondition (Pos, Neg) w.r.t. schedule $\hat{s}$, then the tuple (u, r, s) is updated to $(u, r, s \setminus \hat{s})$, i.e. $TUR' = (TUR \setminus \{(u, r, s)\}) \cup \{(u, r, s \setminus \hat{s})\}$, and $ER' = ER$.

Reachability problems: A *run* (or *computation*) of $\mathcal{S}_T$ is any finite sequence of $\mathcal{S}_T$ transitions $\pi = c_1 \xrightarrow{(\tau_{m_1}, t_1)} c_2 \xrightarrow{(\tau_{m_2}, t_2)} \dots c_n \xrightarrow{(\tau_{m_n}, t_n)} c_{n+1}$ for some $n \geq 0$, where c_1 is an *initial* configuration of $\mathcal{S}_T$, $t_1 = 0$, and $t_i \leq t_{i+1}$ for every $i \in [n-1]$. An $\mathcal{S}_T$ configuration c is *reachable within time t*, if there exists a run π in which $c_{n+1} = c$ and $t_n \leq t$. Furthermore, c is simply *reachable* if c is reachable within time t, for some $t \geq 0$.

Let $\mathcal{S}_T$ be a TURA system over T_{MAX}, u and r be a user and a role of $\mathcal{S}_T$, respectively, and s be a schedule over T_{MAX}. Given a time t, the *timed reachability problem* for $(\mathcal{S}_T, u, r, s, t)$ asks whether there is a reachable configuration within time t of $\mathcal{S}_T$ in which user u is a member of role r in the schedule s. Similarly, the *reachability problem* for $(\mathcal{S}_T, u, r, s)$ is defined as above where there is no constraint on time t.

In our analyses, we assume Separate Administration, in which there is an administrative user who is assigned to the required administrative roles which are enabled all the time. Hence, the times to fire a rule is only restricted by s_{rule}.

EXAMPLE 1. Let us now consider an example of a TR-BAC system deployed in a hospital. Assume that there are 7 different roles, namely, Employee (*EMP*), Day Doctor (*DDR*), Night Doctor (*NDR*), Practitioner (*PRC*), Nurse (*NRS*), Secretary (*SEC*) and Chairman (*CHR*). Hospital works for 24 hours and there are three different shifts (time slots) from 8 am to 4 pm (Time Slot 1), 4 pm to 12 am (Time Slot 2) and 12 am to 8 am (Time Slot 3). Only the Chairman role (*CHR*) has administrative privileges.

1. $(CHR, \{(0,2)\}, \{DDR\}, \emptyset, \{(0,1)\}, PRC) \in can\_enable$: At time slots 1 and 2, a chairman can enable the role *Practitioner* for the first time slot if the role *Day Doctor* is also enabled during this time slot.

2. $(CHR, \{(0,3)\}, \{EMP, NDR\}, \{(2,3)\}, NRS) \in can\_disable$: At time slots 1, 2 and 3, a chairman can disable the role *Nurse* for the third time slot if the roles *Employee* and *Night Doctor* are enabled at this time slot.

3. $(CHR, (0,2), \{EMP\}, \{NRS\}, (0,2), DDR,) \in t\_can\_assign$: At time slots 1 and 2, a chairman can assign the role *Day Doctor* for the first and the second time slots to any user that has *Employee* role and does not have *Nurse* role during these time slots.

4. $(CHR, \{(2,3)\}, \{EMP\}, \{NRS\}, \{(2,3)\}, NDR) \in t\_can\_assign$: At time slot 3, a chairman can assign the role *Night Doctor* for the third time slot to any user that has *Employee* role and does not have *Nurse* role during this time slot.

5. $(CHR, \{(0,2)\}, \{EMP\}, \{DDR, NDR\}, \{(0,3)\}, NRS) \in t\_can\_assign$: At time slots 1 and 2, a chairman can assign the role *Nurse* for all time slots of any user that has *Employee* role and does not have *Day Doctor* and *Night Doctor* role during these time slots.

6. $(CHR, \{(0,2)\}, \{DDR\}, \emptyset, \{(0,1)\}, PRC) \in t\_can\_assign$: At time slots 1 and 2, a chairman can assign the role *Practitioner* for the first time slot of any user that has *Day Doctor* role during this time slot.

7. $(CHR, \{(0,3)\}, \{NDR\}, \emptyset, \{(2,3)\}, PRC) \in t\_can\_assign$: At time slots 1, 2 and 3, a chairman can assign the role *Practitioner* for the third time slot to any user that has *Night Doctor* role during this time slot.

8. $(CHR, \{(0,3)\}, \emptyset, \emptyset, \{(0,3)\}, SEC) \in t\_can\_revoke$: At time slots 1 and 2, a chairman can revoke the role *Secretary* for all time slots of any user that has *Secretary* role assigned in these slots.

In short, the TRBAC system has *t_can_assign* and *t_can_revoke* rules for users and *can_enable* and *can_disable* rules for roles. Using this distinction, we can analyze the system by two separate subsystems, since *t_can_assign* - *t_can_revoke* rules and *can_enable* and *can_disable* rules are mutually exclusive. Suppose that a rule is used to assign a role to a user. This assignment process and the schedule update operation can be done even though the role is not enabled at that moment. This implies that the user has the rights to assume the role with respect to the given schedule in the future only if the role is enabled at that time. The preconditions for the *t_can_assign* rules only check the presence of role assignments, not the enabled / disabled state of the roles. Enabling/disabling operation on roles

is a completely separate procedure handled by *can_enable* / *can_disable* rules. Hence, for a complete reachability analysis, first we need to trace the roles assigned to a particular target user and then we need to trace the time periods that a particular role (a set of roles) can be enabled. Since the latter is similar to the former, in the analysis, we only consider *t_can_assign*/*t_can_revoke* rules.

Our TRBAC administrative model and analysis assume a static set of users, permissions, roles and administrative rules and only cover the user to role assignments without any role hierarchies.

In the next two sections, we propose two alternative strategies to perform security analysis on TRBAC systems.

4. PROPOSED TRBAC ANALYSIS STRATEGIES

As outlined in Section 1, security analysis is essential to understand the implications of the policies and changes to them. The typical analysis questions in a TRBAC related to safety, liveness and mutual exclusion include the following:

1. Safety:

   (a) Will there be no reachable state in which a user u is assigned to a role r at time t?

   (b) Will an enabled role r eventually be disabled?

   (c) Will a user u ever assigned to a role r?

2. Liveness:

   (a) Will an enabled role remain enabled at time t?

   (b) Will a user u eventually be assigned to a role r?

3. Mutual Exclusion: Will a user u be assigned to roles r_1 and r_2 at the same time (i.e., do the time intervals during which u is assigned to roles r_1 and r_2 overlap?

The reachability analysis of TRBAC that we do in this paper can be easily modified to answer all the above questions. Our main idea for performing the reachability analysis is to use a divide and conquer strategy. Since the time dimension is discrete, we decompose the TRBAC analysis problem into multiple subproblems, so that each instance can be treated similar to an RBAC system. We employ two different alternative decomposition strategies – the *rule schedule strategy* and the *the role schedule strategy*. In the following, we explain these two strategies in detail, and we provide computational complexity analysis and the results of the computational experiments in Sections 5 and 6.

4.1 Rule Schedule Strategy

Under this strategy, we split the problem into smaller subproblems with respect to the schedules associated with the rules (s_{rule}) and analyze them serially with respect to time.

Let $m \in \mathcal{M} \subseteq \mathcal{M}_{ALL}$ be a subset of all rules in the system. A *constant region* $\mathcal{C}(a, b, \mathcal{M})$ is a bounded time interval between $t = a$ and $t = b$, $a \leq b$ such that $\forall m \in \mathcal{M}$, $(a, b) \subseteq s_{rule}^m$ and $\nexists m' \notin \mathcal{M}$ such that $s_{rule}^{m'} \subseteq (a, b)$. Informally, if a rule m is included in a constant region $\mathcal{C}$ then it should be valid in all time slots $\alpha \in (a, b)$, and there should not be any other rule m' that is valid in some but not all of the time slots of (a, b). In the rule schedule approach, we split the timeline from 0 to T_{MAX} into non overlapping constant regions $\mathcal{C}_i$ w.r.t the s_{rule} of the roles. Because the rules are static in each $\mathcal{C}_i$, it can be treated similar to an RBAC system. Then, we trace the state space in each constant region serially w.r.t time. In order to control the expansion of the state space, we provide a Sub-schedule assumption to restrict the number of states generated. This assumption and the other details of this decomposition is explained in Section 5.

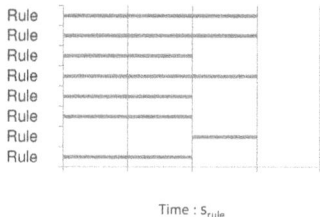

Figure 1: Rule Schedules

EXAMPLE 2. Now, let us consider the hospital example given in Section 3. There are eight different administrative rules with different valid periods as depicted in Figure 1, where the bars indicate their respective rule schedules. As can be seen from the figure, the set of valid rules does not change in interval (0,2) $\mathcal{C}_1$ and (2,3) ($\mathcal{C}_2$). More specifically, the valid rules for $\mathcal{C}_1$ are 1, 3, 4, 5, 6, 7, 8 and the valid rules for $\mathcal{C}_2$ are 2, 5, 7, 8. Essentially, we decompose the analysis problem of TRBAC into two subproblems which are similar to RBAC problems pertaining to these *constant regions*.

4.2 Role Schedule Strategy

Under this strategy, we decompose the TRBAC analysis problem into multiple subproblems using schedules associated with the roles (s_{role}).

Let $\mathcal{T}(\alpha, \mathcal{M})$ be a subproblem for time slot $\alpha \in (0, T_{MAX})$, where a rule $m \in \mathcal{M}$ if $\alpha \subseteq s_{role}^m$. Informally, a subproblem for a time slot contains all of the rules that is valid w.r.t its role schedule (i.e.: the rules that is authorized to change ER and TUR relations for that particular time slot). The details of this decomposition is explained in Section 6.

EXAMPLE 3. Consider Figure 2, which shows the role schedules of the rules in the hospital example given in Section 3. Here, we have three distinct time slots (Time Slot 1: (0,1), Time Slot 2: (1,2), Time Slot 3: (2,3)) with different rules. The rules for Time Slot 1 are Rule 1, 3, 4, 6, and 8; for Time Slot 2 are Rule 1, 3, and 8; for Time Slot 3 are Rule 2, 3, 5, 7, and 8.

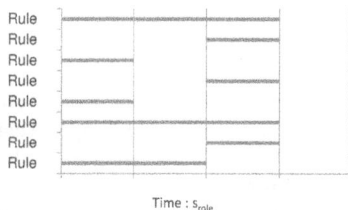

Figure 2: Role Schedules

5. REACHABILITY ANALYSIS USING RULE SCHEDULE STRATEGY

As noted earlier, in this strategy, we split the TRBAC analysis problem into multiple RBAC analysis problems using the rule schedules. In order to handle the RBAC problems, we have adapted the ideas from Stoller et al. [15] and modified them to suit to the temporal case.

In the analysis, we keep track of different configurations c that can be reachable from an initial state c_0. Since we only consider t_can_assign and t_can_revoke rules and one target user, c is composed of $(\widehat{TUR})$ where $\widehat{TUR} \subseteq R \times S$. Hence in each configuration, we track $(role, s_{role})$ pairs. In the algorithm, we trace *constant regions* $\mathcal{C}_1, \mathcal{C}_2, ...$ serially with respect to time. These regions can be seen as separate RBAC systems. However, $\mathcal{C}_{i+1}$ depends on $\mathcal{C}_i, \forall i$, which implies the output of an RBAC reachability analysis at $\mathcal{C}_i$ is an input (or initial configuration) to $\mathcal{C}_{i+1}$. Since an RBAC analysis could result in multiple configurations, then, in each *constant region*, a separate RBAC analysis should be performed for each configuration generated by the analysis done in the previous *constant region*. Moreover, there are other issues related to role schedules that are assigned by the rules. Recall that all of the rules have a role schedule which denotes the time intervals that the role can be assigned. But, according to the rule definitions, the administrators are free to choose a sub schedule of the role schedule and assign/revoke the role only for some of the designated time intervals. This further complicates the reachability analysis, since in a serial fashion, one should keep all of the possible schedule combinations for the subsequent time intervals. Therefore we make the following assumption to simplify the algorithm:

Sub-schedule Assumption: For each t_can_assign and t_can_revoke rule, the assignment and revocation operations are performed using the entire schedule s_{role}. In other words, assume that a schedule s_{role} covers all time slots. This means that an administrator may use this rule to assign the associated role r to a user u, all of the subsets of the schedule s_{role} (as long as the preconditions are satisfied). In our analysis, we assume that s_{role} is assigned or revoked completely - no sub schedule assignments are allowed. Hence, this assumption ensures that a rule can generate only one (new) configuration, which is actually similar to the non temporal analysis.

Here we provide a sketch of the algorithm. The TRBAC reachability analysis starts with an initial configuration c_0 and *constant region* $\mathcal{C}_1$. The state space is expanded using Stoller's algorithm and the rules that are valid at time $t = 0$. At the end of this step, a set of reachable configurations, $\mathcal{S}_1 = \{c_1, c_2, ..., c_M\}$ are obtained. Afterwards, the analysis moves to $\mathcal{C}_2$. For each distinct configuration obtained so far, Stoller's algorithm is used to expand these configurations using the valid rules in this constant region. At the end of this step, we obtain an updated set of reachable configurations $\mathcal{S}_2 \supseteq \mathcal{S}_1$. The algorithm then moves to $\mathcal{C}_3$ and the trace goes in this fashion for a specified number of cycles P of length T_{MAX} (The algorithm returns to $\mathcal{C}_1$ whenever T_{MAX} is reached). Since TURA tuple S_T is finite and since the iterations are bounded by the number of cycles, the algorithm is guaranteed to terminate. However since this approach is a greedy heuristic, we are not guaranteed to get an optimal solution.

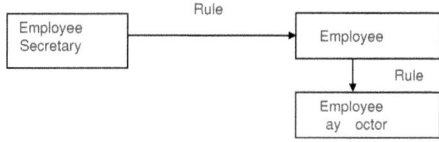

Figure 3: State diagram for the first constant region.

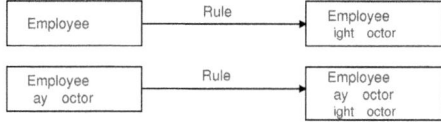

Figure 4: State diagram for the second constant region.

EXAMPLE 4. Now, suppose we are interested in checking whether a particular part time employee, Alice, with TUA records (Alice, EMP, (1,3)) and (Alice, SEC, (1,2)) would eventually get "Day Doctor" and "Practitioner" roles at the same time. In the configuration c_0, only the roles Employee and Secretary exist with the schedules (1,3) and (1,2), respectively (The other roles have an empty schedule). Then implementing the Stoller's algorithm in the first *constant region* results two new configurations, c_1 and c_2 (Figure 3). In the next *constant region*, the search starts with two configurations, and implementing Stoller's algorithm on these configurations separately results (any duplicate configuration is discarded) two new configurations c_3 and c_4. 4. Revisiting the first and the second *constant regions* does not generate new configurations. Hence the possible reachable configurations of this TRBAC system is c_1, c_2, c_3, c_4. Afterwards, one should trace the *can_enable* and *can_disable* rules in the same fashion to conclude on the enabled roles on each constant region. Since there are no configuration that "Day Doctor" and "Practitioner" appear together, we can conclude that the goal is unreachable.

The complexity of the algorithm depends not only on the number of roles and rules but also depends on the number of time slots, and the schedules (rule-role) that are assigned to the roles. The state space that is generated by this algorithm tends to be exponential in the worst case since it is a brute force state space exploration algorithm. We have implemented our algorithm with C programming language and have run it on a computer with 3 GB RAM and Intel Core2Duo 3.0 GHz processor running Debian Linux operating system. In the experiments, the initial state is set to be an empty state (meaning that none of the roles are assigned), and the rules and the goal are created randomly by the code with respect to the corresponding parameter values for the number of rules, number of roles, number of time slots and the number of cycles. The parameter settings are shown on Table 1. 10 replications are done for each parameter setting and their average is reported. The results are in Figure 5(a),5(b) and 5(c).

According to the results obtained, the run time performances of the algorithms do not tend to be exponential, especially for the number of roles. A possible explanation to this situation is that the datasets are generated randomly.

Table 1: Parameter Settings

Number of Roles $|R|$	100, 500, 900
Number of Rules $|\mathcal{M}_{ALL}|$	100, 500, 900
Number of Time Slots T_{MAX}	100, 500, 900
Number of Cycles P	30 for all cases

Hence there does not exist any "pattern" among the rules. We mean pattern in the sense that, the components that determine the usability of the rules, i.e., all of the precondition relations, rule and role schedules of the moves are generated randomly – so it might become probabilistically harder to satisfy all of these conditions. Nevertheless, the results give some insight about how the algorithm is likely to behave under different parameter settings.

The effect of number of rules while all other parameters are constant is more significant and tends to be an increasing relationship as number of rules increases (See Figure 5(b)). Moreover, the increasing tendency becomes more significant as the number of roles and number of time slots increase. Furthermore, there is a noticeable group formation between the fixed parameters (number of roles and number of time slots). The groups are formed by different number of time slots values indicating that the effect of number of roles is comparably smaller. Finally, Figure 5(c) denotes the relationship between different values of number of time slots parameter when the other two parameters are kept constant. The results show that for the majority of the cases, there is a linearly increasing relationship with the increasing number of rules.

6. REACHABILITY ANALYSIS USING ROLE SCHEDULE STRATEGY

In this approach, we split the TRBAC problem into smaller RBAC subproblems using the role schedules of the rules. The main idea is to generate subproblems $\mathcal{T}(\alpha, \mathcal{M})$ for each time slot $\alpha \in (0, T_{MAX})$ with nontemporal administrative rules, so that the system can be treated like an RBAC. In order to achieve nontemporal administrative rules, (and hence an RBAC system for each time slot), we need to remove two components: Rule schedules and Role Schedules and we need show the inter-time slot independency.

The removal of the role schedules follows the definition of subproblems $\mathcal{T}(\alpha, \mathcal{M})$. For the rule schedules, we observe the Long Run Behavior property of the administrative model that we propose.

Long Run Behavior: In the long run, rule schedules of the rules can be neglected, if the system is periodic.

Here we give the intuition of this result. Rule schedules restrict the times that a particular rule can be fired. This means that if a rule m is valid in at least one time slot and if the assignment/revocation (or enabling/disabling) operation that is going to be performed m is necessary for the other rules m', one can wait until m becomes valid, and perform the necessary operation. The other rules m' can be fired next time when the system periodically repeats itself. For example, suppose that we have two roles, r_1 and r_2 and two t_can_assign rules $(..., (4,10), r_1, ...)$ and $(..., (1,3), \{r_1\}, r_2, ...)$. The first rule states that we can use it only within $(4,10)$; the second rule states that we can only use it within $(1,3)$. Notice that if the rules are serially applied with respect to time, then since the second rule has

183

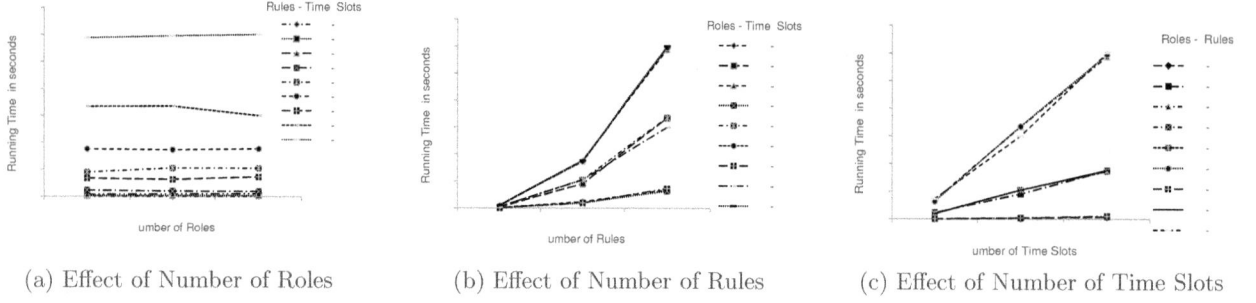

(a) Effect of Number of Roles   (b) Effect of Number of Rules   (c) Effect of Number of Time Slots

Figure 5: Rule Schedule Approach

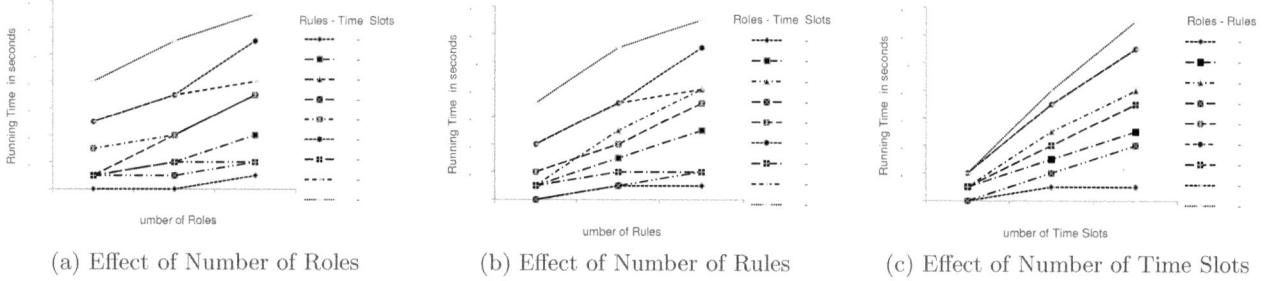

(a) Effect of Number of Roles   (b) Effect of Number of Rules   (c) Effect of Number of Time Slots

Figure 6: Role Schedule Approach

a precondition of r_1, we cannot fire second rule if we do not have r_1 already assigned. It means that first we need to wait until first rule becomes valid (until $t = 4$) and assign r_1. Then we should wait until the system restarts from $t = 0$ (since it is periodic) to fire second rule. Then the Long Run Behavior property ensures that for the reachability analysis purposes, if one waits sufficient amount of time then the effects of these kind of rule conflicts can safely be neglected. This property allows us to treat all of the rules valid on the entire time line. Hence, the s_{rule} restrictions can be relaxed from the rules.

In order to handle the independency issues among different time slots, we need to consider preconditions. Recall that in Section 3, we define the preconditions as (Pos, Neg) relationships to be satisfied in order to fire a rule. Now consider a rule $m \in \mathcal{M}$ which belongs to $\mathcal{T}(\alpha, \mathcal{M})$, and $\hat{s} = \alpha$. In order to fire m, the precondition relations declared by (Pos, Neg) of m must be satisfied for $\hat{s}$. For each role $pos \in Pos$ ($neg \in Neg$, resp.) $\hat{s} \subseteq s_{pos}$ ($\hat{s} \cap s_{pos} = \emptyset$, resp.) must be satisfied, which simply depends on the corresponding (single) time slot in s_{pos} (s_{neg}, resp.). Then it is sufficient to check the schedule only for time slot α for each rule. This implies that the preconditions do not depend on other time slots, hence the time slots are independent.

So, using the Long Run Behavior property and the independency of time slots, one can perform an RBAC reachability analysis using the rules $m \in \mathcal{M}$ for time slot α. Then, the whole TRBAC system can be analyzed by a series of independent RBAC systems $\mathcal{T}_i$ traced separately. This reduction provides usability of any RBAC reachability analysis procedure proposed in the literature.

The computational complexity of the algorithm depends on the RBAC analyzer. Suppose that the RBAC analyzer has the complexity $O(\cdot)$ then our approach yields a complexity of $O(T_{MAX} \cdot)$ since we utilize the RBAC analyzer

for each time slot (Totally we have T_{MAX} of them). Since the algorithm runs for T_{MAX} iterations and given that the RBAC analyzer terminates, our algorithm is guaranteed to terminate.

We perform computational experiments of this approach under the same parameter and hardware setup as the rule schedule approach. We again report the average run time of 10 replications for each parameter setting. We use the RBAC analyzer by [15]. According to the results obtained, there is a linear and increasing relationship with 100, 500 and 900 roles in the system while all other parameters are constant (See Figure 6(a)). The effect of number of rules while all other parameters are constant is very similar to the effect of roles. There is an increasing relationship in the running time as the number of rules increases (See Figure 6(b)).

Finally, Figure 6(c) denotes the relationship between different values of number of time slots parameter when the other two parameters are kept constant. The results show that there is a linearly increasing behavior as the number of time slots increase. This result is expected since the complexity of the algorithm linearly depends on this parameter.

7. DISCUSSION

The procedures that we propose have certain advantages and disadvantages to be considered. The advantage of using the rule schedule approach is that it simulates the system in a serial fashion until a given time in the future. This is crucial, since it can determine exactly when the goal state is reachable, so it can answer many of the security questions like, will the system be safe at the end of a specified amount of time? On the other hand, the algorithm has an exponential complexity, so running this algorithm for large number of time slots can explode the state space, which may lead to scalability issues. This is depicted in Figure

7, where the number of states that should be considered in subsequent constant regions simply explodes. Lastly, this algorithm tracks the assignments on only one target user.

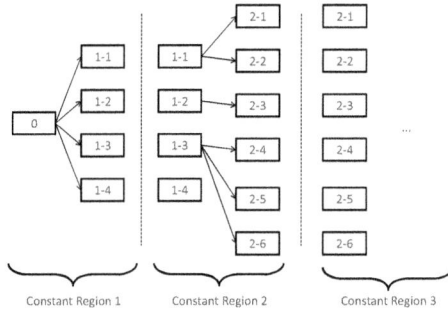

Figure 7: Depicting the Complexity of the Rule Schedule approach

The advantage of the role schedule approach is that it determines the worst case scenarios in the long term by simply running the algorithm for the number of time slots T_{MAX}. Moreover, it provides a direct mapping from TRBAC to a series of independent RBAC problems so that the user is flexible to choose the RBAC analyzer that she wants to use. The performance of this approach will completely depend on the underlying RBAC analyzer. Since the overall complexity depends linearly on the number of time slots, this approach is more scalable than the prior one. The disadvantage of this approach is that, the algorithm only outputs whether the goal state is reachable or not, but it does not output the exact moment when it becomes reachable. In this case, certain security queries, that can be answered by the rule schedule approach, cannot be answered by this approach. An example query can be: "Will there be no reachable state in which a user u is assigned to a role r at time t?". Furthermore, the approach does not work if the time slots are not independent, meaning that the precondition relations require tracking the system status in the other time slots.

From the experimental results, it is clear that the running time of the rule schedule approach grows faster than that of the role schedule approach. Hence, if the security question of interest only covers a short amount of time, then rule schedule approach is useful, but for large number of slots, there might be computational problems related to state space. Role schedule approach is better for these problems but it fails to answer certain time-specific security questions as noted above.

Multi-user Reachability Analysis: In real life systems, where there is no separate administration, there might be certain relations between users in such a way that they might obtain administrative privileges and could use these privileges to assign roles to other users. Our reachability analyses (presented in Sections 5 and 6), that track one target user, cannot capture these specific instances. Hence, the analyses should also support multiple target user tracing to be fully applicable in more realistic scenarios.

EXAMPLE 5. Consider once again the hospital example given in Section 3. Suppose that we have two additional t_can_assign rules as follows: (SEC, (1,3), {EMP}, {CHR, SEC} ,(0,3), $ASST$) and (CHR, (0,3),{}, {$ASST$}, (1,3),

SEC) where the role "ASST" stands for "Assistant Chair". Now suppose that we have a target user "John" who has a TUA record ("John", EMP,(0,3)) and one initial administrative user, "CHR". Given these rules, in order for John to get "Assistant Chair" role, there must be a separate user who is a secretary. Otherwise, the goal is always unreachable. Hence, multiple user reachability analysis is crucial to capture a possible security breach in this scenario.

The approach of Ferrara et al. [7] can perform RBAC reachability analysis with multiple target users. Since our role schedule approach has the flexibility to utilize any of the existing RBAC analyzing techniques without altering the algorithm, we extend our analysis using the RBAC analyzer of Ferrara et al. [7]. We perform reachability analysis under the same hardware configuration with different number of users having random initial role assignments. The parameters used are on Table 2. According to the experiments, the results in Figure 8 are obtained. It can be seen that the running time is significantly longer when the analysis involves multiple users.

Number of Roles, Rules, Time Slots	Number of Users
100-100-100	50,100,200
500-500-500	50,100,200
900-900-900	50,100,200

Table 2: Parameters used in the experiments

Finally, in Figure 9, we compare the runtime performance of all three cases, (i) the rule schedule approach, (ii) the role schedule approach with single target user, and (iii) the role schedule approach with multiple target users. As can be seen, the runtime performance of single target user cases are significantly faster than multiple user cases. Furthermore, the role schedule approach is faster than the rule schedule strategy especially when the number of time slots is higher.

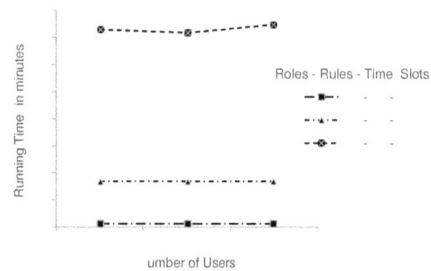

Figure 8: The results of the Role Schedule approach via the RBAC algorithm by Ferrara et al.

8. CONCLUSIONS

Several different extensions of RBAC systems are proposed to cover different requirements or constraints including temporal and geospatial. Although RBAC and its extensions provide a more manageable environment, security analysis is essential to capture any unforeseen security breaches. In this paper, we propose an administrative model for a TRBAC system, and present two different strategies for performing the security analysis of TRBAC that enable one to employ the already existing traditional RBAC analysis techniques. The results of our computational studies indicate that the algorithms are scalable and flexible.

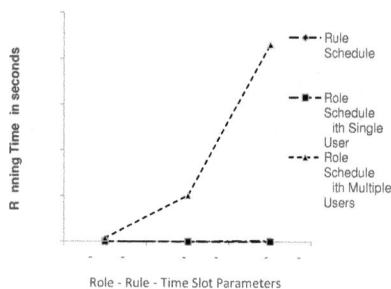

Figure 9: Comparison of all three cases

Although the administrative model that we propose is capable of handling many temporal access control scenarios, it does not cover some of the characteristics such as role hierarchies. We also assume a static environment so that no new rules, roles, users and permissions are introduced to the system. Hence the administrative model does not have rules such as *can create*. As a future work, the model can be extended by including such components to fully represent real life access control systems. The reachability analysis strategies, especially role schedule strategy is flexible enough to handle these additional components without any significant change in the algorithm as long as the RBAC analyzer that is being used supports them. Our computational analysis can be extended to observe the behavior of the strategies by implementing rules derived from real life access control data. In addition, we plan to explore the analysis problem in spatio-temporal RBAC models.

9. ACKNOWLEDGMENTS

The work of Uzun and Sural is supported in part by NSF under grant number 1018414 and the work of Madhusudan is supported in part by NSF grant number 1018182. The work of Atluri is supported through the IR/D by the National Sceince Foundation.

10. REFERENCES

[1] E. Bertino, C. Bettini, E. Ferrari, and P. Samarati. Decentralized administration for a temporal access control model. *Information Systems*, 22(4):223–248, 1997.

[2] E. Bertino, P. Bonatti, and E. Ferrari. TRBAC: A temporal role based access control model. *ACM Transactions on Information and System Security*, 4(3):191–233, 2001.

[3] E. Bertino, B. Catania, M. Damiani, and P. Perlasca. GEO-RBAC: A spatially aware RBAC. *ACM Symposium on Access Control Models and Tecnologies*, pages 29–37, 2005.

[4] J. Crampton and G. Loizou. Administrative scope: A foundation for role-based administrative models. *ACM Transactions on Information and System Security*, 6(2):201–231, 2003.

[5] M. Dekker, J. Crampton, and S. Etalle. RBAC administration in distributed systems. *ACM Symposium on Access Control Models and Technologies*, pages 93–102, 2008.

[6] D. Ferraiolo and R. Kuhn. Role-based access control. In *15th NIST-NCSC National Computer Security Conference*, pages 554–563, 1992.

[7] A. L. Ferrara, P. Madhusudan, and G. Parlato. Security analysis of access control policies through program verification. In *25th IEEE Computer Security Foundations Symposium*, 2012.

[8] M. Harrison, W. Russo, and J. Ullman. Protection in operating systems. *Communications of the ACM*, 19(8), 1976.

[9] S. Jha, N. Li, M. Tripunitara, Q. Wang, and W. Winsborough. Towards formal verification of role based access control policies. *IEEE Transactions on Dependable and Secure Computing*, 5(4):242–255, October 2008.

[10] J. Joshi, E. Bertino, U. Latif, and A. Ghafoor. A generalized temporal role based access control model. *IEEE Transactions on Knowledge and Data Engineering*, 17(1):4–23, 2005.

[11] A. Kern, A. Schaad, and J. Moffett. An administration concept for the enterprise role-based access control model. *ACM Symposium on Access Control Models and Technologies*, pages 3–11, 2003.

[12] N. Li and Z. Mao. Administration in role-bsed access control. *ACM Symposium on Informationi Computer and Communications Security*, pages 127–138, 2007.

[13] S. Mondal, S. Sural, and V. Atluri. Towards formal security analysis of GTRBAC using timed automata. In *ACM Symposium on Access Control Models and Technologies*, pages 33–42, 2009.

[14] R. Sandhu, V. Bhamidipati, and Q. Munawer. The ARBAC97 model for administration of roles. *Proceedings of the 14th ACM conference on Computer and communications security*, 2(1):105–135, 1999.

[15] S. Stoller, P. Yang, C. Ramakrishnan, and M. Gofman. Efficient policy analysis for administrative role based access control. *ACM*, pages 445–455, 2007.

A Framework Integrating Attribute-based Policies into Role-Based Access Control *

Jingwei Huang, David M. Nicol, Rakesh Bobba and Jun Ho Huh
Information Trust Institute, University of Illinois at Urbana-Champaign
1308 W. Main St., Urbana, IL 61801, USA
{jingwei,dmnicol,rbobba,jhhuh}@illinois.edu

ABSTRACT

Integrated role-based access control (RBAC) and attribute-based access control (ABAC) is emerging as a promising paradigm. This paper proposes a framework that uses attribute-based policies to create a more traditional RBAC model. RBAC has been widely used, but has weaknesses: it is labor-intensive and time-consuming to build a model instance, and a pure RBAC system lacks flexibility to efficiently adapt to changing users, objects, and security policies. Particularly, it is impractical to manually make (and maintain) user to role assignments and role to permission assignments in industrial context characterized by a large number of users and/or security objects. ABAC has features complimentary to RBAC, and merging RBAC and ABAC has become an important research topic. This paper proposes a new approach to integrating ABAC with RBAC, by modeling RBAC in two levels. The aboveground level is a standard RBAC model extended with "environment". This level retains the simplicity of RBAC, supporting RBAC model verification/review. The "underground" level is used to repre-

*This material is based upon research sponsored by the U.S. Department of Energy under Award Number DE-OE0000544, and by the U.S. Air Force Research Laboratory and the U.S. Air Force Office of Scientific Research, under agreement number FA8750-11-2-0084. Neither the United States Government nor any agency thereof, nor any of their employees, makes any warranty, express or implied, or assumes any legal liability or responsibility for the accuracy, completeness, or usefulness of any information, apparatus, product, or process disclosed, or represents that its use would not infringe privately owned rights. Reference herein to any specific commercial product, process, or service by trade name, trademark, manufacturer, or otherwise does not necessarily constitute or imply its endorsement, recommendation, or favoring by the United States Government or any agency thereof. The views and opinions of authors expressed herein do not necessarily state or reflect those of the United States Government or any agency thereof. The U.S. Government is authorized to reproduce and distribute reprints for Governmental purposes notwithstanding any copyright notation thereon.

sent security knowledge in terms of attribute-based policies, which automatically create the simple RBAC model in the aboveground level. These attribute-based policies bring to RBAC the advantages of ABAC: they are easy to build and easy to adapt to changes. Using this framework, we tackle the problem of permission assignment for large scale applications. This model is motivated by the characteristics and requirements of industrial control systems, and reflects in part certain approaches and practices common in the industry.

Categories and Subject Descriptors

D.4.6 [**Security and Protection**]: [Access controls]

Keywords

RBAC, Attribute-Base Access Control, Role Engineering, Industrial Control Systems

1. INTRODUCTION

A recent study [18] shows that the adoption of role-based access control (RBAC) [7, 19] is quickly growing, and that RBAC has become the most popular access control model. RBAC is simple, reflects organizational structure, and is easy to administer and review. However, it also has weaknesses: it is difficult and costly to build a good RBAC instance, and a pure RBAC system lacks flexibility to efficiently adapt to changing users, objects, and security policies. Particularly, it is impractical to manually make (and maintain) user to role assignment and role to permission assignment for dynamic applications and/or large scale applications with a large number of users or objects. Recently introduced attribute-based access control (ABAC) has features that are complimentary to RBAC. It is straightforward to use ABAC to represent policy based on the attributes of users, objects, and the access environment, and it is easy to revise policy to adapt to a changing application; however, ABAC is typically more complex than RBAC w.r.t. policy review. Researchers are exploring ways to integrate RBAC and ABAC [1, 11, 12, 15, 16].

We propose a new approach that integrates attribute-based policies into RBAC, designed for supporting RBAC model building for large scale applications. We model RBAC in two layers. One layer, called the "aboveground" level, is a traditional RBAC model extended with environment constraints. This layer retains the simplicity of RBAC, and allows routine operations and policy review. In a second layer, called the "underground layer", we focus on how to construct attribute-based policies to automatically create the primary RBAC model on the aboveground level. This second layer takes the advantages of ABAC, eases the difficulty of RBAC model building, particularly for large scale applications, and brings flexibility to adapt to dynamic applications. In this way, the proposed approach combines the advantages of both RBAC and ABAC.

Prior work (e.g. [1, 11]) focuses on rule-based automatic user-role assignment, thereby addressing the difficulty in user-role assignment when there is a large dynamic population of users. We extend this by defining attribute-based policies for both user-role assignment and role-permission assignment. This extension addresses the challenge posed by a large number of security objects observed in the context of industrial control systems (ICS), by automated role-permission assignment. Many existing research only considers the attributes of users; we consider the attributes of users, roles, objects, and the environment.

This work is motivated by characteristics of ICS and the requirements for a large scale RBAC model for the same [22]. However, the model we propose is generic.

The contents are organized as follows: §2 briefly discusses the related research; §3 presents the aboveground level of RBAC model; §4 presents the underground level of RBAC model; §5 presents the application of this proposed framework in ICS; §6 further discusses our model by comparing it with most relevant previous work; §7 gives a summary and the directions for future research.

2. RELATED RESEARCH

Kuhn et al [12] suggested that combining the best features of RBAC and ABAC can provide effective access control for distributed and changing applications. They compared the strength and weakness of RBAC and ABAC with respect to simplicity of security administration, easiness of reviewing permissions assigned to users, and flexibility to adapt to rapid changing applications; then they presented a spectrum of possible ways to combine RBAC and ABAC; finally, they revealed that standards organizations are developing a policy-enhanced RBAC standard to accommodate attribute-based features. They presented a very interesting picture of the landscape of combining RBAC and ABAC. However, the attributes they considered are limited to user-centered attributes. The attributes of objects and environment are also important to access control, and should be considered.

Earlier, Al-Kahtani and Sandhu [1] proposed a model of rule-based automatic user-role assignment for RBAC, called RB-RBAC, to overcome the difficulty of manual user-role assignment for service-providing enterprises which typically have a huge number of users. In this model, users are dynamically assigned roles by using rules, based on users' attributes. This model also has the limitation of considering only the attributes of users; furthermore, attributes are expressed in propositional logic, thus being less expressive than what we permit (first order logic). In addition their approach to representing mandatory access control is to create roles of *read* and *write* for every node in a security lattice. This approach can lead to a large number of roles; more importantly, the roles are created based on the general security classification lattice rather than specific job functions; this makes it difficult to realize the principle of least privilege.

Similar to [1], Kern and Walhorn [11] also adopted a rule-based approach to user-role assignment, supporting auto-mated administration of roles in large organizations. They pointed out that dynamic user-role assignment as in [1] creates difficulties in reviewing permission assignments and in evaluating the impact of a new rule or revision of rules. To overcome these problems, they proposed static user-role assignment. In this way, the rule-based user-role assignment is separated from run-time RBAC system. This approach has been applied in a bank and identity management solution of an IT service provider.

OASIS issued a standard RBAC profile for XACML [16]. They adopted an approach of representing roles as an attribute rather than entities or subjects of access. Their focus is on using standard XACML [17] to represent the standard (core and hierarchical) RBAC [2], rather than to combine the strength of RBAC and ABAC.

Most recently, Ni and Bertino [15] proposed a new access control language *xfACL*, attempting to combine the benefits of XACML and RBAC, and emigrate their drawbacks. Their focus is on language specification.

In the context of access control for relational databases, Giuri and Iglio [8] introduced the concept of "restricted privilege" to extend a privilege with a condition, called "privilege restriction", under which the object(s) can be accessed with the access mode specified in a privilege. A restricted privilege is a triple of: an access mode (operation type), a single object / or an object collection of the same object type, and a privilege restriction; a privilege restriction is a logic expression on the attributes of an object in the object collection or the context, and if the logic expression is true, then the single object or the objects in the collection satisfying that condition can be accessed in the specified access mode. So, a privilege is a single permission or a group of permissions of the same access mode (operation type) on a set of objects selected by the privilege restriction. Further, they introduced "parameterized privilege" to allow a privilege restriction to contain variables; then, they extend concept of role into "role template" which contains parameterized privileges. A striking feature of their approach is that the concepts of *parameterized privileges* and *role template* allow them capture the common access control patterns over different attribute values, and represent roles and associated permissions in a compact manner. This model can be regarded as a standard hierarchical RBAC model extended with attribute-based constraints on permissions.

Chae and Shiri [4] proposed a variant of RBAC to categorize objects in hierarchical classes (more exactly, groups), to enable association of an object group rather than an individual object with an operation in a permission, and to allow authorization propagation through object group hierarchy. Different from [1, 11, 12], this model deals with the difficulty of handling a large number of objects. Jaeger et al [9] also proposed aggregating objects into groups however their aggregation of objects and operations into groups was based on similarities of objects (e.g., objects with similar operations) and similarities of operations (e.g., operations corresponding to common operative types such as read).

RBAC has been extended in serval directions, particularly with the context or environment of access. Examples include: temporal RBAC [10], location sensitive RBAC [6], context constrained RBAC [14], and others. They provide us clues in modeling the context of access.

With respect to access control in ICS, Bertino [3] discussed the requirements and possible approaches for critical infras-

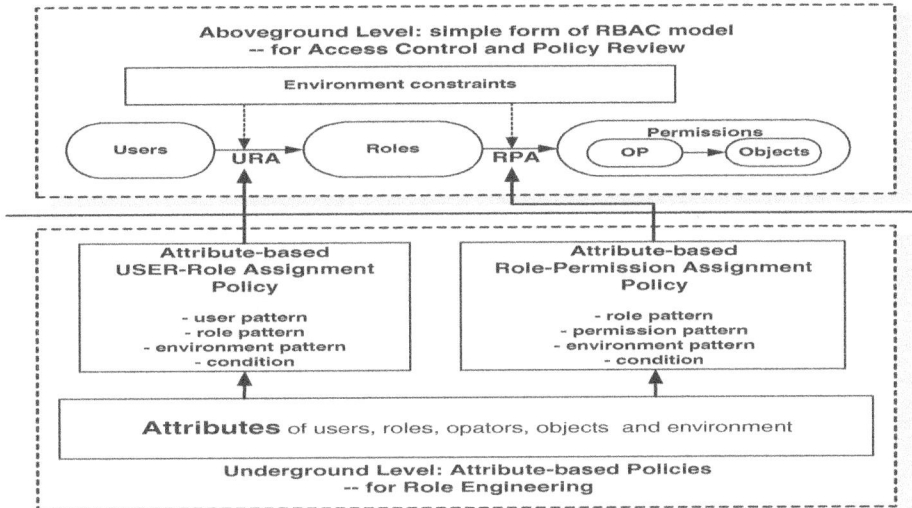

Figure 1: A two-layered framework integrating Attribute-based policies into RBAC

tructures, particularly addressed the need of attribute-based and context based user-role assignment.

Another area of relevant research is "role engineering", an approach to defining roles and assigning permissions to those roles [5]. Role engineering can be regarded as the process of building a RBAC model instance, including role definition, structuring roles, permission definition, assignment of permissions to roles, and identification of constraints. There are two basic approaches of role engineering: top-down and bottom-up [5, 13, 24]. In the top-down approach, to define roles, role engineers, together with business administration staff, analyze business processes in an organization, identify job functions in business process, decompose job functions into smaller units, identify actions and objects of operations in each work step, identify constraints, finally assign permissions to roles. Top-down approach can be labor-intensive, time-consuming, and expensive. To overcome the problems with top-down approach, the bottom-up approach is developed [13, 24], using machine learning technologies to automatically discover roles from the existing user-permission assignments, so called "role mining". However, the bottom-up approach also has some significant limitations: 1) as commonly recognized, the meaning of the roles discovered by role mining are difficult to interpret with respect to business processes, thus making it difficult to manage and maintain such roles; 2) each role mining algorithm developed so far typically requires user-permission association data in some form, and lacks flexibility to consider various constraints and attributes of interest; 3) the outcome of role mining is not guaranteed to be completely consistent with the existing access control policies; 4) because the outcome of role-mining depends on the input user-permission associations, it is necessary to review (and revise) the input data to make it represent expected access control policy. So, even though roles can be identified automatically, the process to collect, review and revise input data can be labor-intensive and time-consuming as in the case of the top-down approach.

In our specific context of RBAC modeling, the application we target has a very large number of security objects (order of millions), and that there are complex policies beyond the concept of role applied to the access of those objects. There-

fore, on one hand, it is impractical to assign each permission (an operation on an object) to a role manually; on the other hand, role mining approach appears insufficient to meet the complex needs of the domain.

3. ABOVEGROUND LEVEL: TABLES

In this paper, we mainly use first order logic to make formal descriptions, and follow the convention that all unbound variables are universally quantified in the largest scope. The aboveground level is a simple and standard RBAC model, but extended with constraints on attributes of the "environment". We use the notion of environment to represent the context of a user's access, such as the time of access, the access device, the system's operational mode, and so forth.

The model is formally described as a tuple,

$$\mathcal{M} = (U, R, P, O, OP, EP, URA^e, RPA^e),$$

where U is a set of *users*. A user could be either a human being or an autonomous software agent; R is a set of *roles*. A role reflects a job function, and is associated with a set of permissions; O is a set of *objects*. Objects are the resources protected by access control; OP is a set of *operators*. An operator represents a specific type of operations; P is a set of *permissions*. A permission is defined by a legitimate operation, which comprises an operator and an object; EP is a set of predefined *environment state patterns*. We use *environment state* to model the context of an user's access. Each environment state pattern (*environment pattern*, hereafter) defines a set of environment states; URA^e is the extended *user-role assignment* relation, which is basically a mapping from users to roles, associated with certain environment patterns; RPA^e is the extended *role-permission assignment* relation, which is basically a mapping from roles to permissions, also associated with certain environment patterns. All sets are finite. In the following, we give some further formal description of *environment*.

3.1 Environment

We represent the context of access as environment, and model an environment as a vector of *environment attributes*, each of which is represented by an environment variable (called an attribute name) associated with an attribute value in a domain. An environment is defined by n attributes, let $v_i \in D_i, i = 1, ..., n$, be the ith environment variable, where D_i is the domain of that environment variable; then a vector $(v_1, ..., v_n)$, in which all variables are instantiated is called an *environment state* (also denoted as s.) The set of all possible environment states is denoted by E. Choice of environment attributes (and hence environment state) is domain dependent. Environment attributes, particularly the dynamic attributes, are gathered by an access control engine at runtime.

Example (environment state): Assume that the environment is defined by three attributes: mode, access location and access time; then mode = "normal" and access_location = "station 1" and access_time = "8:00AM Monday" is an environment state.

An *environment pattern*, denoted as e, is treated as an individual in domain EP, but is semantically defined by a first-order logical expression of assertions involving environmental attributes. An environment pattern defines a set of environment states, in which every environment state satisfies the environment pattern, i.e.

$$\{(v_1, ..., v_n) | e(v_1, ..., v_n)\}.$$

Hereafter sometime we directly use e to denote the set of environment states defined by the environment pattern.

Examples (environment pattern): $Access\_location = station\_1$ and $access\_time \in [8 : 00, 22 : 00]$ is an environment pattern, which defines the set of all the environment states, having any mode, $access\_location$ at $station\_1$, and $access\_time$ between 8:00AM and 10:00PM.

We say that an environment state s matches environment pattern e, iff: $e(s)$ is true. An environment pattern can be empty, denoted by ϕ, which is most general; every state matches ϕ. We say that e_1 is subsumed by e_2, iff: the set of all environment states that match e_1 is a subset of the set that match e_2. That is, $subsume(e_2, e_1)$, iff: $\{s | e_1(s)\} \subseteq \{s | e_2(s)\}$. The relation is reflexive, transitive, and anti-symmetric.

3.2   User-role assignments

A particular user-role assignment associates a user, a role, and an environment pattern :

$$URA^e \subseteq U \times R \times EP, \qquad (1)$$

where EP is the set of all environment patterns that have been defined for the system of interest.

The semantics of a user-role assignment, $(u, r, e) \in URA^e$, is defined as:

$$match(s, e) \rightarrow has\_role(u, r), \qquad (2)$$

which states that if the real environment state s matches the given environment pattern e, then user u is assigned to role r. We assume that the RBAC engine could understand the semantics of each environment pattern as defined.

Basic RBAC models define user-role assignments simply as a mapping from users to roles,

$$URA \subseteq U \times R. \qquad (3)$$

We have extended this notion with a dependency on the environment, as a means to integrate certain extended RBAC

features of context and constraints. The environment pattern associated with a user-role assignment is the environment-dependent condition which is sufficient for the assignment. This feature can be regarded as constrained user-role assignment. If there are no constraints on user-role assignments, the associated environment patterns are simply empty, so the model becomes the common one.

In this model, the relation between URA^e and URA is:

$$(u, r) \in URA \leftrightarrow (\exists e, (u, r, e) \in URA^e). \qquad (4)$$

User-Role assignments may be expressed in tabular form. Table 1 shows an example, with an environment extension.

3.3   Role-permission assignments

A role-permission assignment associates a role, a permission, and an environment pattern. Thus the set of all such assignments is a subset

$$RPA^e \subseteq R \times P \times EP. \qquad (5)$$

The semantics of a role-permission assignment, $(r, p, e) \in RPA^e$, is defined as:

$$match(s, e) \rightarrow has\_permission(r, p), \qquad (6)$$

which states that if the real environment state s matches the pattern e, then permission p is assigned to role r.

Similar to user-role assignments, we've extended the common role-permission assignment with environment patterns. The relation between RPA^e and RPA is:

$$(r, p) \in RPA \leftrightarrow (\exists e, (r, p, e) \in RPA^e). \qquad (7)$$

As with user-role assignments, the role-permission assignment may also be organized in tabular fashion.

4.   UNDERGROUND LEVEL: POLICIES

The underground level of RBAC model focuses on the security policies used to construct the aboveground level of RBAC model. Those security policies are a formalism of a role engineers' tacit knowledge about access control based on the attributes of users, roles, objects, and the environment, and the relation among them. We attempt to explicitly represent the implicit knowledge used to construct a RBAC model, and to integrate the extensions to standard RBAC models in an attribute-based paradigm.

In the following, we treat all users, roles, permissions, operators, and the security objects as "*objects*" (in the sense of the object-oriented design) and each of which has certain attributes. Notion $obj.attr$, or equivalently $attr(obj)$, denotes the attribute $attr$ of object obj.

The attributes needed in RBAC are typically domain dependent, and need to be customized for each specific target system. Some examples of attributes are as follows. The attributes of users may include "id", "department", "security clearance", "knowledge domain", "academic degree" or "professional certificate". A role may have attributes such as "name"; "type" reflecting job function types such as "manger", "engineer", and "operator"; "security level"; "professional requirements"; "direct superior roles" and "direct subordinate roles" (if role hierarchy is modeled). Objects may have attributes such "id", "type", "security level", "state". Operators may have attributes like "name", and "type". The environment attributes may include "access time", "access location", "access application", "system mode", "target value", and so forth.

Table 1: Extended User-Role Assignment Table

User Id	Role Id	Environment Pattern
com:ab:zn1:amy	Manager.Zone1	Device = "Station_1.2" & Time = "Weekday"
com:ab:zn1:ben	Engineer.Zone1	Device = "Station_1.2" & Time = "Weekday" & Mode = "normal"
com:ab:zn1:jim	Engineer.Zone1	Mode = "emergency"
com:ab:zn1:bob	Operator.Zone1	Device = "Station_1.2" & Time = "Weekday" & Mode = "normal"
...	...	...

4.1 Role-Permission Assignment Policy

The role-permission assignment policy is a set of rules. Each rule has the following structure:

```
rule_id {
   target {
     role_pattern;
     permission_pattern {
        operator_pattern;
        object_pattern;
     };
     environment_pattern;
   }
   condition;
   decision.
}
```

where, all of the *patterns* and the *condition* are FOL (First Order Logic) expressions; an *environment pattern*, as presented in § 3.1, defines a set of environment states; similarly, a *role pattern* defines a set of roles by specifying their common attributes; a *permission pattern*, consisting of an operator pattern and one object pattern, defines a set of permissions by specifying their common features w.r.t. the attributes of the operator and the object in a permission; an *operator pattern* defines a set of operators (or operation types); each *object pattern* defines a set of objects; the *target*, which is, formally, the Cartesian product of the above sets of roles, permissions, and environment patterns, defines *the range of (role, permission, environment_pattern) triples to which this rule applies*; the *condition* is a logical expression defining a relation among the attributes of both the roles, the permissions (operators and objects), and the environment. This expression is the *condition under which a role-permission assignment can be made*; the *decision* is the role-permission assignment. This form of rules states that when the condition is true, a role covered by the role pattern can be assigned with a permission covered by the permission pattern in the specified environment pattern.

Let $pattern^R(r)$ denote a role pattern, refereing the role as r, e.g. r.type="engineer"; $pattern^P(op, o)$ denote the general form of a permission pattern, referring to permissions of form $p(op, o)$. A permission pattern actually consists of zero or one operator pattern and zero or one object pattern; $pattern^E(\varepsilon)$ represents a predefined environment pattern ε; $condition(r, p(op, o), \varepsilon)$ denotes a logical expression, describing a relation among the attributes of role r, object o, and environment ε.

The semantics of a role-permission assignment rule is defined as follows.

$$(\forall r, op, o)(pattern^R(r) \wedge pattern^P(p(op, o)) \wedge pattern^E(\varepsilon)$$
$$\wedge\ condition(r, p(op, o), \varepsilon) \supset (r, p(op, o), \varepsilon) \in RPA^e) \quad (8)$$

which states that for any role r, satisfying the given role pat-
tern $pattern^R(r)$, for any permission $p(op, o)$, satisfying permission pattern $pattern^P(p(op, o))$, if $condition(r, p(op, o), \varepsilon)$ is true, then role r is assigned with permission $p(op, o)$ in environment pattern ε.

A pattern can be empty, ϕ. An empty pattern defines the most general pattern, which every element in a domain matches. For example, if role pattern is empty, then the defined role-permission assignment rule is applied to all of the roles in R. Therefore, if the target of a rule is empty, then the rule is most general and applicable to all combination of role, permission, and environment; on the other hand, a rule is most specific, (i.e. only applicable to a single specific combination,) if the target of the rule is defined most specifically, i.e. the role pattern is exactly defined as a specific role instance, the permission pattern is exactly defined as a specific permission/operation, and the environment pattern is also most specific. Generally, the target of a rule defines a specified range of (role, permission, environment) triples to which the rule applies.

In this framework, a role could be defined based on a role template. Different from the concept of "role" in RBAC, a role template is associated with a set of permission patterns rather than permissions. The idea is developed to address scaling issues that arise in the ICS domain. We will give detailed discussion on role template and "proto-permission" (a specific form of permission pattern) in §5.

Examples of attribute-based RPA policies are given in §5 paragraph (f).

For simplicity, we only use positive rules. If (r, p, e) is in RPA^e, then role r is assigned with permission p in environment e; if not, by the close world assumption, we conclude that role r does not have permission p in environment e.

In role engineering, the defined role-permission assignment policy (rule set) is applied to all possible combinations of (role instance, permission, environment pattern), and if a combination can be inferred by any rule, then it is included in the RPA^e on the aboveground level of RBAC model.

4.2 User-Role Assignment Policy

User-role assignment is highly dependent on business rules and constraints. In our view, the task of assigning users to roles can be approached like the role-permission assignment problem, in terms of policies that enforce those rules and constraints. Such policies would be formulated in terms of user and role attributes, and would be crafted to enforce things like Separation of Duty. However, unlike role-permission assignment, user assignment may have to balancing competing or conflicting policy rules against each other. Correspondingly a complete policy oriented formulation will need to specify how to combine rules and arrive at a final assignment decision. In what we present below, an attribute based user-role assignment policy is used only to identify *po-*

tential assignments. A rule-combining algorithm is used for making the final assignments.

Similar to role-permission assignment rule, the user-role assignment rule consists of:

```
rule_id {
    target {
        user_pattern;
        role_pattern;
        environment_pattern;
    }
    condition;
    decision.
}
```

where, similarly, an user/role/environment pattern defines a set of users/roles/environment_states by specifying the common attributes; all of the *patterns* and the *condition* are expressions in first order logic; differently, the *decision* of a rule is *to mark an (user,role,environemt_pattern) triple as a potential assignment*.

Let $pattern^U(u)$ denote a user pattern, referring to user u; $pattern^R(r)$ denote a role pattern, referring to role r; $pattern^E(\varepsilon)$ denote the specification of an environment pattern; $condition(u,r,\varepsilon)$ denote a logical expression, describing a relation among the attributes of user u, role r, and environment pattern ε.

The semantics of a user-role assignment rule is defined as follows.

$$(\forall u, r)(pattern^U(u) \wedge pattern^R(r) \wedge pattern^E(\varepsilon)$$
$$\wedge\, condition(u,r,\varepsilon) \rightarrow (u,r,\varepsilon) \in temp\_URA^e), \quad (9)$$

which states that for any user u satisfying $pattern^U(u)$, any role r satisfying $pattern^R(r)$, if the condition that states a relation among the attributes of u, r, and ε is true, then $(u,r,\varepsilon) \in temp\_URA^e$, which means that according to this rule, u can be assigned to r in environment ε.

Example:

```
rule:{
    target:{
        role_pattern(r): r.type = "chemical engineer";
        environment_pattern(e):{
            Device = "Station_1.2"
            and Time = "Weekday"
            and Mode = "Normal" }
    }
    condition:{
        knowledge_match(u,r);
        security_req_match(u,r);
        u.base_plant = "Houston";
    }
    decision: add (u,r,e) in URAe.
}
```

In this rule, knowledge_match(u,r) is a function which returns true if the professional knowledge of user u matches the knowledge requirements of role r; security_req_match(u,r) is a function which returns true if the user meets the security requirements of role r. A necessary condition for considering assigning a user u to role r is that the user work at the Houston plant (where presumably one finds Station_1.2.)

The rule has no filter on the users it considers. The rule applies to roles with job_type attribute "chemical_engineer". Now suppose that there is a role "Engineer.Zone.1.2" designed to work in Zone 1, on Station_1.2, on weekdays; this role has job_type attribute chemical_engineer, requires pro-

fessional knowledge in Chemical Engineering, and at least a Bachelor's degree in that field. Going through employees one finds John, who works at the Houston plant; John has a Bachelor degree on Chemical Engineering; and suppose that John sufficiently meets the security requirements for role "Engineer.Zone.1.2". The patterns for user and role cover these instances, the condition of the rule is true, and so the assignment of John to that role will be marked as possible. Of course, there may be other roles that John is suitable for, and there may be other employees suitable for role "Engineer.Zone.1.2", so a later step is needed to select among all assignments marked as possible, by considering some constraints such as separation of duty.

The following is the pseudo-code of rule combining algorithm.

```
rule_combining(temp_URAe) {
    for (i = 0; i < constraints.length(); i++){
        if ( ! satisfy(temp_URAe, constraints[i])){
            add i in conflictList;
        }
    }
    if ( conflictList.length() == 0) {
        URA^e = temp_URAe;
    } else {
        if (constraintConflictResolution(temp_URAe,
                    conflictList, temp2_URAe))
            URAe = temp2_URAe;
        else
            notify(temp_URAe, conflictList);
    }
}
```

Note that the constraint conflict resolution algorithm is dependent on constraints, which in turn are domain-dependent, so it is difficult to give a general algorithm for constraint conflict resolution. If conflict cannot be resolved by algorithm, the algorithm will inform RBAC administrator, and the conflict resolution needs to be performed manually (or with tools we have not identified) by the role-engineer.

5. CASE STUDY : LARGE SCALE ICS

This section presents how the proposed framework might be applied to construct a RBAC model for industrial control systems (ICS). Our knowledge of these systems is informed by close collaboration our institute has with vendors of commercial ICS systems.

Problems: The target application domain of ICS has the following features. There is a very large number of security objects (order of millions) with complex relations among them; on the other hand, many objects and operations applied on them are similar, and there are patterns to follow; security objects are organized in hierarchical structures; each role or security object may have a security level; users dynamically change over time as business changes; security objects also change over time due to device replacement or maintenance; access to control processes and devices is through some Human-Machine Interfaces and software applications; each protected point of access to a control system, called "*point*", or "control blocks", contains information about the status of a control process or device, and is used to set target control values or control parameters; all those points are important parts of the security objects to be protected by the target access control system; runtime operation environment (with dynamic attributes), e.g. access location and/or access time, is a sensitive / important factor in access control; different zones have similar structure, i.e. roles, operations and objects are similar in different zones; zones and devices may have operation "modes"; control stations play an important role in access control.

A specific challenge we face is to construct an RBAC framework that is compatible with access control mechanisms used in the modern ICS, which are a mixture of different mechanisms including station-based, group-based, attribute-based, and (simplified) lattice-based. The underlying reason for the compatibility requirement is to recognize the practical need for an incremental transition path. Another major challenge is how to define roles and assign fine-grained permissions to roles for a large scale application effectively, efficiently, and in an automated fashion as much as possible.

5.1 RBAC Model Building Process

In the following, we briefly present how to apply the proposed framework in building RBAC model instance for ICS. More detailed discussion and design of RBAC for ICS can be found in [23].

(a) **Identify security objects and object hierarchy**: In a plant, security engineers identify devices and points to be protected by RBAC as a set of security objects, and organize those objects in hierarchical structures (an acyclic graph, generally). In ICS, it is common to find that the control devices and other assets involved in monitoring and controlling the physical process and in overall management of a plant are organized in an hierarchical and modular manner as per ISA-88 and ISA-95 standards. This hierarchical structure grouping objects is called "object hierarchy" in this paper.

(b) **Identify operation types**: All types of the operations applied to each security object are identified, e.g. a specific type of control parameter may have the types of operations such as "read" and "reset". Minimally, an operation type could be defined by just an *operator*; generally, an operation type could be defined by a *permission pattern*.

(c) **Identify *role templates***: ICS tend to have very well defined job functions, with well defined access needs, to monitor and control the physical processes. For example, "Operator" and "Engineer" are very well understood job functions in the ICS community even though there might be some variations in their functions across different types of ICS. In the world of electric power "operator" is actually a licensed position. Such well-defined job functions with well defined access needs are good candidates to define "roles". However, in practice users performing these well defined job functions are limited in scope to either a particular sub-process or a particular geography in accordance with the organization of the plant. In other words, the job functions identified in ICS, such as 'Operator" and "Engineer", perform certain types of operations; what objects those operations can apply to are dependent on the attributes of users and those objects. From this point of view, we defined in our previous work [23, 22]: *role template* and *proto-permission* that leverage some common characteristics of ICS to simplify the creation and management of roles. Here we show how our framework can be used to represent these concepts and realize a manageable RBAC solution for ICS. Different from a permission that comprises a pair of *operator* and *object*, a *proto-permission* consists of an *operator* and the object type of the operand. So, a *proto-permission* represents just an operation type, rather than a specific operation on a specific

object. Proto-permission is a specific form of permission pattern. Different from the concept of "role" in RBAC, a *role template* is associated with a set of *proto-permissions*. Therefore, a *role template* tells what types of operations can be performed by a role created from the role template. Let RT denote the set of all role templates; PP denote the set of proto-permissions. Every *role template* has an attribute (or equivalently function) of *proto-permission set*, denoted as pps; every proto-permission has an attribute (or function) of *operator*, and an attribute (or function) of object type, denoted as *objType*. These can be formally described as follows.

$$pps : RT \to 2^{PP}; \tag{10}$$

$$op : PP \to OP; \tag{11}$$

$$objType : PP \to TYPES. \tag{12}$$

We use concept *role template* to formally represent each well defined job function in ICS, and use *proto-permission* to represent each allowed operation type associated with a role template. Assume that the plant has a number of basic types of job functions such as "Operator", "Engineer", and "Manager". They are identified as role templates. Each of them associates with a set of operation types, e.g. "Engineer" has operation type "reset_parameter" on objects of type "XYZ", "Manager" has operation type "view_schedule" on "System", et al. All identified operation types should be covered by role templates.

(d) **Identify *roles* and their *privilege ranges***: Based on business workflow analysis, a number of roles can be identified for each role template. Each role has an assigned working (access) environment pattern such as access through station B in zone 1 on daytime. Furthermore, as discussed earlier, in practice each role only has access to a range of objects; this range of objects accessible to a role is called the *privilege range* of the role. Formally,

$$pr : R \to 2^O. \tag{13}$$

Privilege range is used to define the boundary of objects for which a role is responsible, and is used as constraints in role-permission assignment. A role has access to an object only if the object is within the role's *privilege range*. If the *privilege range* is not concerned, then it can be simply set as the whole set of objects.

Privilege range can be defined over *object hierarchy*. An *object hierarchy* (denoted as OH) is simply a subset of the power set of all *objects* considered, i.e. $OH \subseteq 2^O$. A node in the *object hierarchy* is called an "*object group*", which is a subset of the *objects*, i.e. og $\in 2^O$. In an *object hierarchy*, that an *object group* is a child of another in OH means that the former is a subset of the latter.

For example, the privilege range of an instantiated role "engineer_A.1.2.1" might be defined as:

$$pr(\text{"engineer\_A.1.2.1"}) =$$
$$objectgroup(A.1.2.1) \cup objectgroup(C.1.2)$$
$$- objectgroup(C.1.2.1.3)$$
$$- \{x \mid x.type = \text{"XXX"} \wedge x.Security\_level > 100\}. \tag{14}$$

A label such as C.1.2.1.3 describes a node (object group) identified by a path through a hierarchy. Starting at node C, one selects an immediate child labeled "1" with respect to C's parentage, having parentage C, from that node one selects the node labeled "2" with respect to $C.1$'s parentage, having parentage $C.1$ and so on. This scheme reveals immediately that $C.1.2$ is higher up in the hierarchy than $C.1.2.1.3$ as one passes through the former node to reach the latter. In the above example, the subtracted sets are "exceptions", which can be a single node in an object hierarchy, or a set which is defined by a logical expression as needed.

Back to the task of role identification, as an example, a role called "Engineer_Chem_Zone1_Daytime" may be created, based on role template "Engineer". This role has privilege range that covers all Chemical engineering related objects in zone 1, and this role works in a predefined environment pattern called "Daytime_Zone1". There could be other "Engineer" roles such an on electrical engineering, in zone 2, and working in evening shift, and so forth;

(e) **Analyze security policies and identify attributes**: The security engineers analyze all security policies and requirements applied to the plant, and list all of the concerned attributes of users, roles, objects, and access environment. For example, *privilege range* is a critical attribute of a role. There are many other attributes that may be of concern, as the examples given in §4. A particular attribute that needs to be considered is "security level". It is common to assign a security object a "security level", requiring a subject of access to have a corresponding security level.

(f) **Develop** *attribute-based policies*: The security engineers construct the underground level of RBAC model by developing attribute-based policies for role-permission assignment and user-role assignment.

First, let us consider a simple yet general case: (1) a role can only perform the types of operations, specified by the proto-permissions of the role's template; (2) privilege range constraint: a role can access an object only if that object is within the privilege range of that role; (3) security level constraint: to access an object, the role's security level needs to be greater than or equivalent to the one of the object. This can be represented with the attribute-based policy for role-permission assignment:

```
rule:{
    target:{}
    condition:{
        memberOf(o, r.pr);
        r.securityLevel >= o.securityLevel;
        memberOf(pp, r.template.pps)
            and op = pp.op and o.type = pp.objType;}
    decision: add (r, p(op,o), \phi) in RPAe.
}
```

The formal semantics of this rule is as follows:

$$(\forall r, pp, op, o)(memberOf(o, r.pr)$$
$$\wedge\ r.securityLevel \geq o.securityLevel$$
$$\wedge\ memberOf(pp,\ r.template.pps)$$
$$\wedge\ op = pp.op \wedge o.type = pp.objType$$
$$\rightarrow (r, p(op, o), \phi) \in RPA^e), \quad (15)$$

which states that for all *role r*, *proto-permission pp*, *operator op*, and *object o*, if o is within the privilege range of role r, the security level of r is greater than or equivalent to the one of o, *proto-permission pp* is within r's *role template*'s *proto-permission set*, and op is the *operator* specified in pp, as well as the type of o is the object type specified in pp, then role r is assigned with permission (instance) $p(op, o)$ without

any environment constraints (where environment pattern is empty).

Nevertheless, in reality, role-permission assignment must satisfy more constraints. Let us look at the example below. (1) using role template, "*Engineer*", and using a proto-permission that allows to perform "*reset_parameter_T*" type of operations on objects of type "ObjectType_YYY" ; (2) privilege range constraint: a role can access an object only if that object is within the privilege range of that role; (3) security level constraint: to access an object, the role's security level needs to be greater than or equivalent to the one of the object; (4) environment constraint: the operation must be performed in the mode of "normal"; (5) environment constraint: access time must be in daytime shift; (6) environment constraint: the operation must be performed from station "station_X"; (7) station privilege range constraint: the object to be accessed must be within the privilege range of the operation station; (8) parameter range constraint: the target value of the parameter to be set must be within a specified interval [68,73]; (9) professional domain constraint: the role's professional domain must match with the object's domain. These security requirements can be represented as an attribute-based rule as follows:

```
rule: {
    target: {
        role_pattern(r): r.template.id = "Engineer";
        operator_pattern(op): op = "reset_parameter_T";
        object_pattern(o): o.type = "ObjectType_YYY";
        environment_pattern(e): {
            e.mode = "Normal";
            e.accessTimeStart = 8AM;
            e.accessTimeEnd = 16PM;
            e.station = "Station_X";
            e.targetValueInf = 68;
            e.targetValueSup = 73;
        }
    }
    condition: {
        memberOf(o, r.pr);
        memberOf(o, e.station.pr);
        r.securityLevel >= o.securityLevel;
        r.profDom = o.profDom;
    }
    decision: add (r, p(op,o), e) in RPAe table.
}
```

The role-permission assignment policy consists of a set of rules like the one above. As stated earlier, we use only positive rules, therefore, a permission is assigned to a role if any rule grants the assignment.

User-role assignment rule can be specified based on the attributes of users and roles in a similar manner, as shown in §4.2.

(g) **Create RBAC assignment tables**: Use the specified attribute-based policies to create role-permission assignment and user-role assignment in the aboveground level.

This task can be illustrated by considering how the above example rule is used to make role-permission assignment. For each pair of role and permission, if the pair or the role's assigned working environment does not match the target of the rule, then skip this pair; otherwise, continue to evaluate the condition part of the rule. If the condition is true, then assign the permission to the role in that assigned environment, in the role-permission assignment table of the aboveground level. Consider role "Engineer_Chem_Zone1_Daytime", and a permission "reset_parameter_T" on object "point_1.2.7" (saying it represents the 7th point in zone 1 sector 2), in the environment pattern as stated in the example rule. This (role, permission) pair is within the target; assume that object "point_1.2.7" is within the privilege ranges of the role and the access station; the role's security level dominates the object's; the professional domains match; then the permission is assigned to the role in the specified environment pattern. For another role, saying, "Engineer_Chem_Zone2_Daytime", having privilege in zone 2 which does not cover "point_1.2.7", thus that permission cannot be granted.

(h) **Verify/review RBAC model**: Formally verify / review the RBAC policy represented by the aboveground level of RBAC model instance against security policies and requirements by using logic [21]. Detailed description on policy review will be presented in another paper.

(i) **Repeat the process**: If the above logical verification and review fail, go back to an earlier step to revise the RBAC model, and then verify and review again.

Detailed role engineering process for ICS is out of the scope of this paper, and will be discussed in another paper.

5.2 Discussion on Case Study

Migration to RBAC from a legacy system could be a great challenge for ICS. The proposed framework could support building RBAC model for ICS and the migration. We highlight some major features as follows.

Expressibility: The proposed framework is general enough to cover the required features of the targeted access control systems in ICS; [20]; User groups are modeled by *role template*; the types of operations conducted by a user roup is modeled by *proto-permission*; station-based access constraints, access application constraints, temporal constraints, "mode" constraints, "parameter range' constraints, and others are modeled as environment constraints.

Support for role engineering: Role engineering is widely recognized as difficult; it becomes even more challenge for ICS due to the large scale and dynamic features. The proposed framework enables automatic user-role assignment and role permission assignment, through attribute-based polices. This approach could largely help to overcome the problems of manual user-role assignment and role-permission assignment for large scale applications in ICS.

Simplicity: The proposed framework can integrate the existing mechanisms and concepts in ICS uniformly, in the form of attribute-based policies; thus avoiding complexity caused by ad hoc representation and management. Attribute-based policies can express security policies and requirements in a straightforward manner; thus easier to construct and maintain. The simplicity of the aboveground level eases RBAC model review.

Flexibility: The attribute-based policies have flexibility to adapt to the dynamically changing users, objects, security policies and requirements, and even business processes.

Verifiability: The logic representation of the attribute-based policies provides a basis for formal verification of the RBAC model.

6. FURTHER DISCUSSION

In our approach to RBAC modeling, in the underground level, we develop attribute-based policies for user-role assignment and role-permission assignment separately, and use these policies to create the aboveground level of RBAC in a simple and standard form. The policy form of role defi-

nition and user-role assignment makes the model easier to build and easier to change for dynamic applications. The simple form of RBAC in the aboveground makes the model easy to operate and easy to perform access review. In this way, this proposed framework combines the advantages of both ABAC and RBAC.

In the following, we clarify our contributions with respect to prior art. Our framework of combining ABAC with RBAC is new compared to all of the strategies summarized by Kuhn et al in the table 1 of [12] and other research presented in Section 2. Using the mapping notion of [12], our framework has a 2-level and 2-step architecture: (1) underground level: $U, A^U, A^R, E \rightarrow R$; $R, A^R, A^O, E \rightarrow perm$; (2) aboveground level: $U, E \rightarrow R$; $R, E \rightarrow perm$, where $A^U/A^R/A^O$ is the set of attributes of users/roles/objects. In addition, past research tends to focus on the attributes of users (including [12]), but our model considers the attributes of all relevant entities including users, roles, objects, and the environment.

Al-Kahtani and Sandhu's research [1] and Kern and Walhorn's work [11] focused on addressing the difficulty of user-role assignment. We move further to provide a solution for the problems of role-permission assignment in large scale applications with millions of objects.

Chae and Shiri [4] addressed the problem of dealing with large number of objects in a manner somewhat similar to ours. They proposed to organize objects in "classes" (more exactly, groups) with hierarchal structure; a permission is defined as association of an operation (operation type) with a "class" (group) of objects, and a role having that permission can perform that operation over all objects in that "class" (group). In our model, a proto-permission is defined as association of an operation type and an object type; a role having a proto-permission can perform a specified type of operations over the objects of a specified type in the privilege range of that role; a privilege range can be defined arbitrarily as needed, typically based on an existing object group in the object hierarchy and modified with "exceptions" defined with relevant attributes. The main advantage of our model is that we are not only able to support a object hierarchy but also deal with exceptions to inheritance in that hierarchy.

Our research is also relevant to role engineering. As discussed in §2, role engineering is a difficult task. One of the reasons underlying the difficulty of role engineering is that the simplicity of RBAC transforms the complex access control knowledge into the tacit knowledge owned by role engineers who define roles. We envision that the explicit representation of that knowledge will ease the difficulty of RBAC system building, enable to formally verify RBAC model, and make it easy to adapt to the changes. Our approach to RBAC model building can be regarded in the stream of the "top-down" approach of role engineering. A top-down approach mainly includes role name identification from business process analysis, permission identification, and role-permission assignment, and the approach is typically carried out manually; we assume that from business process analysis, role names, role templates (or types of roles), proto-permission (or types of operations), and the attributes concerned are identified manually; then we develop the attribute-based policies and use the policies to automatically create user-role assignment and role-permission assignment. In the course of using RBAC, some security requirements or regulations may change. It is commonly recognized that it is difficult to change a RBAC model instance, particularly a large one. By using our framework, role engineers can more easily change the attribute-based policies, then use the updated policies to generate the user-role assignment and role-permission assignment in the aboveground level.

Finally, we find that no single existing RBAC model readily meets all needs of the ICS domain, such as unifying all access mechanisms in use and automatic role-permission assignment. Our proposed framework could work well in the context, as discussed in §5.2.

Although motivated by ICS, our proposed framework is generic, and can be used in other areas, such as health information networks, military and government information management. Particularly, access control for cloud-based information and computing services across security domains is a great challenge; our proposed framework can be used in a unified form of attributed-based policies to combine RBAC with traditionally used mandatory access control, including non-hierarchical caveats, and other security polices; the framework also helps to deal with a great number of security objects, including both information and cloud services.

7. CONCLUDING REMARKS

This paper proposed a new approach to combining ABAC and RBAC, that brings together the advantages of both the models. We developed our model in two levels: aboveground and underground. The aboveground level is a simple and standard RBAC model extended with environment constraints, which keeps the simplicity of RBAC, and supports straightforward security administration and review; in the underground level, we explicitly represent the knowledge for RBAC model building as attribute-based policies, which are used to automatically create the simple RBAC model in aboveground level. The attribute-based policies bring the advantages of ABAC: they are easy to build and easy to change for a dynamic application. We showed how the proposed approach can be applied to RBAC system design for large scale ICS applications. Regarding future work, we will continue to make formal analysis of the the properties of the proposed model, further explore approaches of formal verification of a RBAC model instance against security requirements and higher level of policies, and work out the proposed framework based role engineering process. Another direction to go is to extend the proposed model to cover more features such as operations with multiple objects.

Acknowledgments

We would like to thank Tom Markham, Julie Hull, Alex Chernoguzov, Kevin Staggs, and Himanshu Khurana for their valuable discussion and insight.

8. REFERENCES

[1] M. A. Al-Kahtani and R. Sandhu. A model for attribute-based user-role assignment. ACSAC '2002.

[2] ANSI. *American National Standard for Information Technology - Role Based Access Control.* 2004.

[3] E. Bertino. Policies, access control, and formal methods, 2012. Chapter in Handbook on Securing Cyber-Physical Infrastructure (in print).

[4] J. H. Chae and N. Shiri. Formalization of rbac policy with object class hierarchy. In *Proceedings of the 3rd international conference on Information security practice and experience*, ISPEC'07, pages 162–176, Berlin, Heidelberg, 2007. Springer-Verlag.

[5] E. J. Coyne and J. M. Davis. *Role Engineering for Enterprise Security Management.* Artech House, Inc., Norwood, MA, USA, 1st edition, 2008.

[6] M. L. Damiani, E. Bertino, B. Catania, and P. Perlasca. Geo-rbac: A spatially aware RBAC. *ACM Trans. Inf. Syst. Secur.*, 10(1), 2007.

[7] D. F. Ferraiolo and D. R. Kuhn. Role-based access control. In *Proceedings of the NIST-NSA Conference*, pages 554–563, 1992.

[8] L. Giuri and P. Iglio. Role templates for content-based access control. RBAC '97, pages 153–159, New York, NY, USA, 1997. ACM.

[9] T. Jaeger, A. Prakash, J. Liedtke, and N. Islam. Flexible control of downloaded executable content. *ACM Trans. Inf. Syst. Secur.*, 2:177–228, May 1999.

[10] J. B. D. Joshi, E. Bertino, U. Latif, and A. Ghafoor. A generalized temporal role-based access control model. *IEEE Trans. on Knowl. and Data Eng.*, 17:4–23, January 2005.

[11] A. Kern and C. Walhorn. Rule support for role-based access control. SACMAT '2005, pages 130–138. ACM, 2005.

[12] D. R. Kuhn, E. J. Coyne, and T. R. Weil. Adding attributes to role-based access control. *Computer*, 43(6):79 –81, June 2010.

[13] I. Molloy, H. Chen, T. Li, Q. Wang, N. Li, E. Bertino, S. Calo, and J. Lobo. Mining roles with multiple objectives. *ACM Trans. Inf. Syst. Secur.*, 13:36:1–36:35, December 2010.

[14] G. Neumann and M. Strembeck. An approach to engineer and enforce context constraints in an rbac environment. SACMAT '03, pages 65–79. ACM, 2003.

[15] Q. Ni and E. Bertino. xfacl: an extensible functional language for access control. SACMAT '11, pages 61–72. ACM, 2011.

[16] OASIS. Core and hierarchical role based access control (RBAC) profile of XACML v2.0, Feb. 2005.

[17] OASIS. eXtensible Access Control Markup Language (XACML) version 2.0, OASIS standard, 2005.

[18] A. C. O'Connor and R. J. Loomis. 2010 economic analysis of role-based access control, nist report, 2010.

[19] R. S. Sandhu, E. J. Coyne, H. L. Feinstein, and C. E. Youman. Role-based access control models. *Computer*, 29:38–47, February 1996.

[20] UIUC-ITI. RBAC driven least privilege architecture for control systems solution requirements specification, July 2011. Technical Documentation.

[21] UIUC-ITI. RBAC policy audit and review, Nov. 2011. Technical Documentation.

[22] UIUC-ITI. An RBAC specification for industrial control systems, Oct. 2011. Technical Documentation.

[23] UIUC-ITI and Honeywell Labs. Towards an RBAC for distributed control systems, Apr. 2012. Technical Report, http://users.crhc.illinois.edu/pvt/rbac-for-dcs-tr.pdf.

[24] J. Vaidya, V. Atluri, and Q. Guo. The role mining problem: A formal perspective. *ACM Trans. Inf. Syst. Secur.*, 13:27:1–27:31, July 2010.

A Framework for Verification and Optimal Reconfiguration of Event-driven Role Based Access Control Policies

Basit Shafiq
Computer Science Dept.
LUMS
DHA, Lahore, Pakistan
basit@lums.edu.pk

Jaideep Vaidya
MSIS Dept. and CIMIC
Rutgers University
1 Washington Park, Newark,
NJ 07102, USA
jsvaidya@rbs.rutgers.edu

Arif Ghafoor
School of ECE
Purdue University
465 Northwestern Ave. West
Lafayette, IN 47907, USA
ghafoor@ecn.purdue.edu

Elisa Bertino
Computer Science Dept.
Purdue University
305 N. University Street, West
Lafayette, IN 47907, USA
bertino@cs.purdue.edu

ABSTRACT

Role based access control (RBAC) is the de facto model used for advanced access control due to its inherent richness and flexibility. Despite its great success at modeling a variety of organizational needs, maintaining large complex policies is a challenging problem. Conflicts within policies can expose the underlying system to numerous vulnerabilities and security risks. Therefore, more comprehensive verification tools for RBAC need to be developed to enable effective access control. In this paper, we propose a verification framework for detection and resolution of inconsistencies and conflicts in policies modeled through event-driven RBAC, an important subset of generalized temporal RBAC applicable to many domains, such as SCADA systems. We define the conflict resolution problem and propose an integer programming based heuristic. The proposed approach is generic and can be tuned to a variety of optimality measures.

Categories and Subject Descriptors

D.4.6 [**Operating Systems**]: Security and Protection—*Access Controls*

General Terms

Security

Keywords

Access control, conflict resolution, policy verification

1. INTRODUCTION

Role based access control (RBAC) has generated great interest in the security community for its inherent richness and flexibility in modeling a wide range of access control policies [7, 10]. Several beneficial features such as policy neutrality, support for least privilege, and efficient access management, are associated with RBAC models [7]. The concept of role is associated with the notion of functional roles in an organization and hence RBAC models provide intuitive support for expressing organizational access control policies.

However, the size and complexity of typical organizational policies make it difficult to ensure their consistency. Indeed, the interplay of various RBAC constraints such as hierarchy, separation of duty (SoD), dependency, and triggers may introduce inconsistencies and conflicts in the underlying access control policy. If these conflicts are not detected and resolved, they can expose an organization to numerous vulnerabilities and risks pertaining to security and privacy of organizational data and resources. Therefore, any comprehensive access control model requires tools for consistency verification and conflict resolution.

In this paper, we formalize the conflict resolution problem for event driven RBAC, and propose a solution to resolve conflicts equitably. We focus on event-driven RBAC, since it is an important subset of generalized temporal RBAC, which is applicable to many domains, such as industrial control systems (e.g., SCADA) and financial workflow management systems. In such systems occurrence of some events may trigger certain actions that need to be executed by authorized users. For example, consider an industrial process control system in which the authorization for changing the steam valve settings from a remote terminal is available to an on-duty supervisor *only if* an operator has logged on to the local terminal for monitoring the process status.

For resolving policy conflicts, we present an integer programming (IP) based technique that can be applied with different optimality measures. Note that while our conflict resolution technique is presented in the context of event-driven RBAC, our results are also relevant to a large variety of existing and next generation access control models [10, 11]. Indeed, our conflict resolution technique is quite general, and extends beyond access control. For example, since event driven RBAC can be mapped to the policy specifications of networks [14], conflicts in network policy can easily be resolved using a modification of the same technique.

The rest of this paper is organized as follows. Section 2 briefly overviews the event-driven RBAC model. Section 3 presents our approach. An illustrative example is presented in Section 4. We discuss related work in Section 5. Finally, Section 6 concludes the paper and discusses future work.

2. OVERVIEW OF EVENT-DRIVEN RBAC

The RBAC model [7], consists of the following four basic components: a set U of users, a set R of roles, a set P of permissions, and a set S of sessions. A key aspect of RBAC is the use of role hierarchies to simplify management of authorizations. The original RBAC model supports only inheritance or usage hierarchy, which allows users of a senior role to inherit all permissions of junior roles. In order to preserve the principle of least privilege, RBAC model has been extended to include activation hierarchy which enables a user to activate one or more junior roles without activating senior roles [10]. From this point onward, we will use the notations I and A, to refer to inheritance and activation hierarchies, respectively. The symbols $\geq_I^*$ and $\geq_A^*$ are used to express I and A hierarchy relationship between two roles, respectively. Accordingly, $r_i \geq_f^* r_j$, where $f \in \{I, A\}$ implies that role r_i is senior to r_j and the hierarchical relationship between them can be either inheritance only, or activation only. If role r_i is immediately senior to role r_j then the superscript $*$ is omitted from the symbol $\geq_f^*$.

Separation of duty (SoD) policies have been found to be crucial for securing many commercial and business applications. Role-based models provide a convenient way for expressing and enforcing such policies. In the event-based RBAC formalism presented in this paper, the majority of the SoD constraints identified in the literature [7, 10] can be composed from the following basic SoD constraints:

1. *Role-specific SoD:* a role-specific SoD disallows activation of conflicting roles by same user in the same session or in concurrent sessions.

2. *User-specific SoD:* a user-specific SoD prohibits conflicting users of a role from activating/accessing that role concurrently.

2.1 Dependency Constraints

The event dependency relationship semantics is incorporated in the RBAC formalism by introducing event triggers. We define two types of dependency constraints, namely: *strong dependency* represented by the symbol $\rightarrow\rightarrow$ and *weak dependency* denoted by the symbol $\rightarrow$. These constraints can be used to model a variety of dependence and workflow based constraints. In the following, we first define different types of event expressions and then introduce event triggers for implementing dependency constraints.

Simple Role Event Expression: A simple role event expression is of the form $activate(u_i, r_j)$, where $u_i \in U$, $r_j \in R$, specifying that user u_i has activated role r_j. All the role-related events can be specified in terms of activation of a role by some user. To represent the enabling (disabling) event of a role r_j, a special user u_{ej} (u_{dj}) is assigned to role r_j. Activation of r_j by u_{ej} (u_{dj}) corresponds to the enabling (disabling) of role r_j. To prevent simultaneous activations of r_j by u_{ej} and u_{dj} a user-specific separation of duty constraint is specified between u_{ej} and u_{dj}.

Event Triggers: Event triggers are used to model the dependence and ordering relationship between events. We distinguish two types of triggers based on strong and weak dependency semantics.

Strong Dependence Trigger: A strong dependence trigger is of the form: $E_1 * \ldots * E_n \rightarrow\rightarrow E$, where E_i ($i = 1, \ldots, n$) and E are simple role event expressions and $*$ represents logical conjunction or disjunction. Event E occurs if and only if the body of the trigger is true.

For instance, in the industrial control system example mentioned in the introduction, the availability of authorization to on-duty supervisor for remotely changing the steam valve settings depends on the operator to log into the local terminal for process monitoring. This can be modeled as strong dependency trigger: *activate(localOperator, processMonitoringRole)* $\rightarrow\rightarrow$ *activate(u_{ej}, remoteValveSettingRole)*. Accordingly, when the local operator activates the *process monitoring role* from local terminal, the *remote valve setting role* is enabled. Assuming the on-duty supervisor is assigned to this remote valve setting role, he or she gains the authorization to change the valve settings remotely by activating this role. Moreover, this authorization cannot be acquired if the body of trigger is false (i.e., no local operator is monitoring the process status).

Weak Dependence Trigger: A weak dependence trigger is of the form: $E_1 * \ldots * E_n \rightarrow E$, where E_i ($i = 1, \ldots, n$) and E are simple role event expressions and $*$ represents logical conjunction or disjunction. In case of weak dependence, event E occurs if the body of the trigger is true. However, it can also occur independently of E_is.

2.2 Graph-based Specification Model

The RBAC policy and associated event-based constraints can be specified using a graph based model. Thus, users, roles and permissions are represented as nodes and the edges of the graph describe the association and constraints between different nodes. Nodes in a RBAC graph cannot be connected arbitrarily. The type graph shown in Figure 1(a) defines all possible edges that may exist between different nodes. An edge between a user node u and a role node r indicates that role r is assigned to user u. The hierarchy relationship between roles are modeled by self-edges labeled with I and A. In the type graph, *I-hierarchy* and *A-hierarchy* are represented by solid and dashed edges, respectively. There can be edges between role and permission nodes. A permission is a pair (*object, accessmode*) specifying which objects can be accessed and in which mode (read, write, execute, approve, etc). Permission is represented as a square in type graph of Figure 1(a). The graph model also supports specification of various separation of duty (SoD) constraints. A Role-specific SoD constraint between two roles is represented by a double headed arrow between corresponding nodes. To represent conflicting users u_i and u_j for role r_k, a double headed edge with a label r_k is drawn between the user nodes u_i and u_j. The label r_k specifies that the corresponding users are conflicting for role r_k and cannot access r_k simultaneously. An event trigger in the graph-based model is represented by a bold edge labeled with the trigger expression TE. The trigger edge originates from all role nodes, listed in the body of the trigger, and terminates at the role node defined in the head of the trigger. A single trigger may have more than one edge because of the presence of multiple terms in the body of the trigger; however, all such edges are labeled with the same trigger expression.

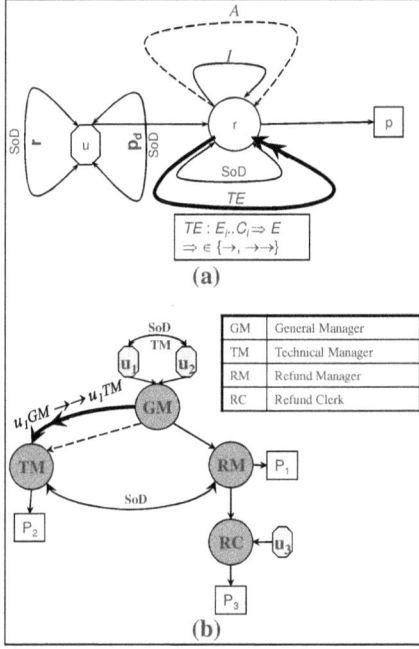

Figure 1: (a) Type graph of event-driven RBAC. (b) Example of an event-driven RBAC policy.

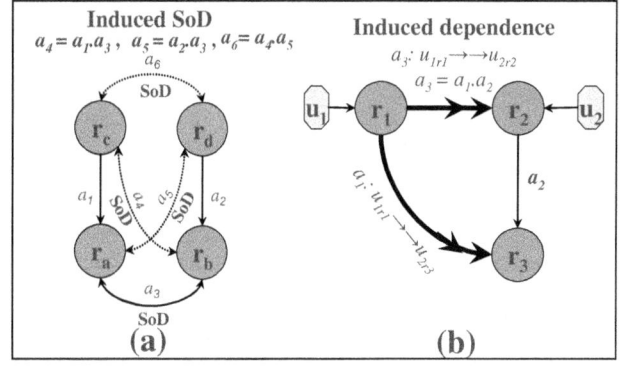

Figure 2: (a) Induced SoD constraint. (b) induced dependence constraint.

Figure 1(b) shows an instance of the event driven RBAC policy graph consisting of four roles: General Manager (GM), Technical Manager (TM), Refund Manager (RM), and Refund Clerk (RC). There are three users: u_1, u_2, and u_3; and three permissions: P_1, P_2, and P_3. Users u_1 and u_2 are assigned the role GM and u_3 is assigned the role RC. The permissions P_1 and P_2 are assigned to role RM and TM, respectively, while the permission P_3 is assigned to role RC. The inheritance hierarchy relationship $GM \geq_I RM \geq_I RC$ enables user u_1 and u_2 to acquire the permissions of junior roles RM and RC by activating the senior role GM. On the contrary, activation of role GM does not entitle u_1 or u_2 to inherit all the permissions of role TM without activating TM. Role TM is junior to GM in the *A-hierarchy semantics*, $GM \geq_A TM$. This *A-hierarchy* relationship permits u_1 and u_2 to activate role TM. A role-specific SoD constraint is defined between role TM and RM, implying that these roles cannot be accessed by same user simultaneously. The double headed arrow between the user nodes u_1 and u_2 defines the user specific SoD constraint between these two users for role TM, meaning that users u_1 and u_2 cannot activate role TM concurrently. The strong dependency constraint, $u_{1GM} \longrightarrow\rightarrow u_{1TM}$, defined between the role nodes GM and TM, implies that user u_1 can activate the role TM only if u_1 has activated the role GM.

2.3 Induced Constraints

Induced Constraints are added to the event-driven RBAC policy because of incomplete specification and without their addition the original constraints in the policy may not be enforced consistently within the intended semantics of the RBAC model. There are two types of induced constraints: i) induced SoD and ii) induced dependence.

i) Induced SoD. The *I-hierarchy* semantics of RBAC requires that conflicting role-set of a senior role includes the conflicting role-set of all its junior roles that are related to the senior role by *I-hierarchy*. Conflicting role-set of a role r is the set of all roles that have a role-specific SoD constraint with r. Induced SoD constraints are recursively defined from junior roles to senior roles in the following manner.

Consider a role-specific SoD constraint a_3 between two roles r_a and r_b as shown in Figure 2(a). Let roles r_c and r_d be related to r_a and r_b with *I-hierarchy* constraints $a_1 : r_c \geq_I r_a$ and $a_2 : r_d \geq_I r_b$. Induced SoD constraints $a_4 = (a_1)(a_3)$ is added between r_c and r_b, $a_5 = (a_2)(a_3)$ is added between r_d and r_a, and $a_6 = (a_4)(a_5)$ is added between r_c and r_d. Similarly, the induced SoD constraint a_6 propagates upward in the hierarchy. Note that an induced SoD constraint is defined between two roles only if such roles do not have a previous role-specific SoD constraint. The product of constraints in the definition of induced SoD constraint implies that if the original SoD constraint between junior roles is removed, the induced SoD constraint becomes invalid.

ii) Induced dependence. The strong dependence semantics in an event trigger requires that the triggered event cannot occur without the occurrence of triggering event. An incomplete constraint specification may violate this dependence. For instance, in the event-driven RBAC policy shown in Figure 2(b), it is possible that user u_2 accesses role r_3 by activating the senior role r_2 without the activation of role r_1 by u_1. This is a violation of the dependence constraint $a_1; u_{1r_1} \longrightarrow\rightarrow u_{2r_3}$. In order to preserve the strong dependency implied by a_1, a strong dependency constraint of the form $u_{1r_1} \longrightarrow\rightarrow u_{2r_2}$ needs to be defined. Like induced SoDs, induced dependence constraints are recursively defined from junior roles to senior roles. The recursive definition of induced dependence is given below.

For the dependency constraint $a_1 : \vee_{C_i}(\wedge_{u_x \in C_i} u_x) \longrightarrow\rightarrow u_{ir_j}$, if there exists a role r_k such that $a_2 : r_k \geq_I r_j$ and user u_i is authorized for r_k, then a dependency constraint $a_3 : \vee_{C_i}(\wedge_{u_x \in C_i} u_x) \longrightarrow\rightarrow u_{ir_k}$ is induced by a_1 and a_2. The induced dependency a_3 is related to a_1 and a_2 by the equation $a_3 = (a_1)(a_2)$, implying that the a_3 becomes ineffective if any of the constraints a_1 or a_2 is dropped.

3. PROPOSED APPROACH

Formal specification of security requirements and access constraints is the first step in designing access control policy. The next step is to identify and resolve any policy conflicts. Conflicts in an event-driven RBAC policy may not be explicit and may occur because of the interplay between various constraints embedded in the policy. For instance, the RBAC policy shown in Figure 1(b) becomes inconsistent when user u_1 activates role GM. The strong dependency trigger defined between GM and TM constrains u_1 to either activate both roles GM and TM or none at all. By activating the role of GM, u_1 also acquires permission over the junior role RM because of the inheritance hierarchy relationship. This leads to a violation of the role-specific SoD constraint defined between TM and RM. One of the following solutions resolves this conflict: i) Disallow u_1 to activate the role GM. ii) Drop the strong dependence constraint between GM and TM. iii) Remove the SoD constraint between TM and RM. iv) Remove the hierarchical relationship between GM and RM. The first solution restricts the accessibility of u_1 to GM and all other junior roles and may cause deadlock if there is no other user to access these roles. The last three solutions correspond to conflict resolution by constraint relaxation. However, relaxing a constraint in an arbitrary manner may produce significant deviations from the original policy and may not yield optimal resolution. Instead, we would like to formally define the policy conflict resolution problem, so that we can methodically select the solution that best fits our situation.

[Policy Conflict Resolution Problem]: Given a set of k policies $P_1, \ldots, P_k$, that are inconsistent with each other, pick the constraints (from each policy) that must be dropped to make the modified policies consistent overall, while optimizing the global collaboration objective.

Here, the global collaboration objective could be defined in several ways: for example, one may want to maximize the accessibility of roles and permissions. Alternatively, we may want to remove hierarchy edges with the least priority or weight, etc. Different objectives lead to different variants of the problem. [8] shows that a special case of the above problem is NP-hard. Thus, finding an optimal solution to our problem is also NP-hard. Therefore, we must look for efficient heuristics.

We now describe a 0-1 integer programming (IP) based approach to solve this problem. The authorizations produced by the resulting policy are always deterministic. The proposed approach primarily uses constraint relaxation strategy. All the constraints that can be relaxed are assigned a weight according to their importance and a conflict free policy is generated by selecting all the non-conflicting constraints that yield an optimal value of the objective function. The proposed approach is generic in the sense that it can work for a variety of optimality measures such as maximizing accessibility, minimizing the set of relaxed constraints, and maximizing prioritized accesses and constraints. Changing the optimality measure in our formulation only requires changing the weight in the objective function.

3.1 IP Formulation of Event-Driven RBAC

The event-driven RBAC policy can be formulated as the following 0-1 integer programing problem:

maximize $c^T [a \ u_r]$
subject to: $A[a \ u_r \ pu_r] \leq b$
$\forall a_i \in a, \ a_i = 0$ or $1, \ \forall u_{ir_j} \in u_r, \ u_{ir_j} = 0$ or $1,$
$\forall pu_{ir_j} \in pu_r, \ pu_{ir_j} = 0$ or 1

Where a is a vector whose elements correspond to the policy authorizations including role assignment, role-hierarchy;

or constraints including, SoD, and event dependency constraints. u_r is a vector defining the user-role activations and pu_r is a vector defining the role activations for proxy users. Proxy users (discussed in next section) are not the actual users specified in the original access control policy and are included in the IP formulation to create a problem instance in which all the constraints can be evaluated. In the IP formulation of an RBAC policy, all the constraints are defined using algebraic equations / inequalities. The elements of matrix A correspond to the coefficients of terms used in the equations / inequalities defining the constraints. All the variables used in above IP formulation are binary variables, i.e., they can only take a value of '0' or '1'.

In the solution to the IP problem, if the value of a variable a_i equals '1' then the corresponding authorization or constraint is retained in the final policy; otherwise, it is dropped. The user role variable u_{ir_j} defines the activation of role r_j by user u_i. If u_i is not authorized for role r_j then $u_{ir_j} = 0$ is specified as an IP constraint.

c is the cost/weight vector defining the optimality criterion. This optimality criterion could be: maximizing the total number of access, minimizing the number of constraints relaxed, minimizing the number of additional constraints or minimizing deviation from the original policy, among others. The cost of each constraint is application dependent and in some cases certain accesses have a higher priority than others. In this case, an application requiring a certain workflow task executed with a high priority can assign a higher cost to the relevant constraints. The IP constraints described above are used to define security requirements of event based RBAC policies.

For instance, consider the conflicting authorizations of a user u over roles r_1, r_2, r_3, and r_4. These authorizations are represented by the authorization variables: a_1 (u's authorization for r_1), a_2 (u's authorization for r_2), a_3 (u's authorization for r_3), and a_4 (u's authorization for r_4). Let c_1, c_2, c_3 and c_4, respectively, denote their costs or weights. Suppose the following rules specify the relative priorities of these authorizations: i) a_1 supersedes each of the individual authorizations a_2, a_3, and a_4, implying that either a_2 or a_3 or a_4 can be removed in favor of a_1. ii) a_1 also supersedes $a_2 + a_3$, implying that if there is a choice of retaining the single authorization a_1 or two authorization a_2 and a_3, then a_1 is retained and both a_2 and a_3 are removed. iii)$a_2 + a_4$ and $a_3 + a_4$ supersede the authorization a_1, implying that the single authorization a_1 can be removed in favor of joint authorizations a_2 and a_4 or a_3 anda_4. iv) a_4 supersedes the individual authorizations a_2 and a_3. The weight assignment corresponding to this priority specification is given by: $c_4 > max\{c_2, c_3\}$ and $max\{c_4, c_2 + c_3\} < c_1 < min\{c_2 + c_4, c_3 + c_4\}$.

3.1.1 IP Constraint Transformation Rules

The rules for transforming the policy constraints into IP constraints are listed in Tables 2 and 3. The predicates and functions used in these transformation rules are given in Table 1.

The transformation rules are grouped into following categories: hierarchy and assignment, enabling, SoD and dependency triggers. Rules for each of these categories are separately defined for actual users specified in the original event-driven RBAC policy and for proxy users created to evaluate all possible authorizations and constraints in the

Predicate / Function	Description
$reachable(u, r)$	Returns True if the role node r in the event-driven RBAC graph is reachable from the user node u This reachability implies that user u can activate/access the role r.
$u\_assign(u, r)$	Returns True if the user u is assigned to the role r.
$active\_proxy(u, r)$	Returns the active proxy users of user u for role r.
$passive\_proxy(u, r)$	Returns the passive proxy users of user u for role r.

Table 1: Predicates and functions used in the IP transformation rules

underlying IP problem. Table 2 lists the rules for the users defined in the original policy.

Hierarchy and assignment. Rules 1-3 ensure that in any feasible solution of the IP, if a user accesses a role then the user should have proper authorization for the role being accessed. A user u is authorized for a role r if either u is assigned to r or u is assigned to senior role r' such that there is a path from r' to r that consists of *I-hierarchy* and/or *A-hierarchy* edges in the RBAC policy graph.

Role enabling. The role enabling rules (4 and 5) imply that a role can only be accessed / activated in the enabled state. For defining the event corresponding to enabling of role r_j a special user u_{ej} is assigned to r_j. $u_{ej r_j} = 1$ implies that r_j is in enable state.

SoD Rule 6 represents the role-specific SoD constraint and Rule 7 represent the user-specific SoD constraint in mathematical form using the corresponding user-role binary decision variable.

Dependency triggers. Rules 8 and 9 defines the event trigger dependency implying that whenever the body of the event trigger becomes true, the event listed in the head of the corresponding dependency constraint is triggered. For a strong dependency constraint the dependent event çannot occur if the body of the corresponding trigger is false. The events in the trigger are represented as role event expressions discussed in Section 2.1.

3.1.2 Proxy Users

The solution to the IP problem with actual user-role and constraint variables may yield an instance in which not all policy constraints are evaluated. Omission of these constraints from IP evaluation can be attributed to SoD constraints and event triggers that derive the policy to a single instance out of many other legal policy instances. Because of this omission, it is quite possible that some conflicting constraints may remain undetected and unresolved in the final policy derived from the IP solution. For example in the RBAC policy graph shown in Figure 3(a), the dependency constraints $a_3 : u_{1r_1} \rightarrow\rightarrow u_{3r_2}$ and $a_4 : u_{2r_1} \rightarrow\rightarrow u_{3r_3}$ jointly conflict with the SoD constraint a_5 defined between roles r_2 and r_3. An IP problem derived from the rules given in Table 2 for the RBAC policy graph of Figure 3(a) may yield a solution in which this conflict may remain unresolved. For instance, the assignment $a_1 = a_2 = a_3 = a_4 = a_5 = u_{4r_1} = 1$, and $u_{1r_1} = u_{2r_1} = 0$ is a feasible solution to the

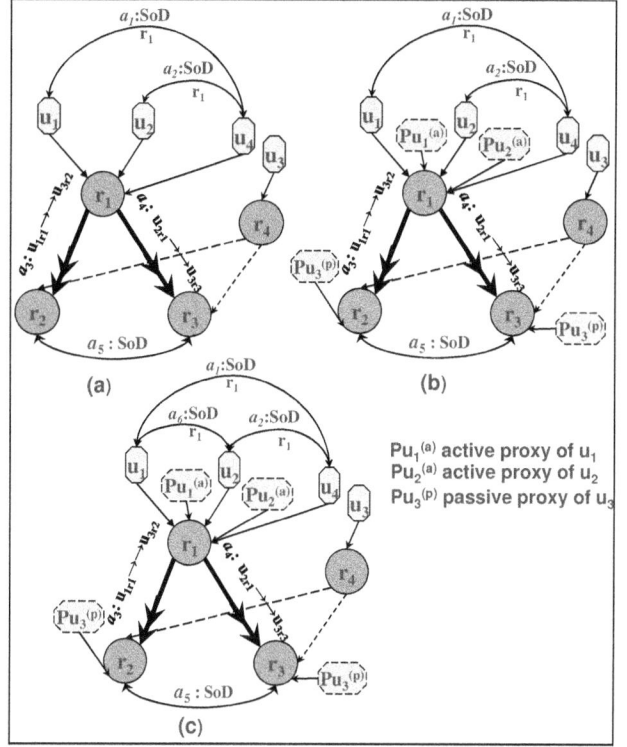

Figure 3: (a) RBAC graph without proxy user assignment leading to undetected conflicts. (b) RBAC graph with proxy users to evaluate policy conflicts. (c) RBAC graph with SoD constraint a_6 preventing conflicting authorizations to constraints a_3, a_4, a_5.

IP problem corresponding to Figure 3(a). In this solution, the policy is evaluated without considering the activation of role r_1 by u_1 and u_2, and so the conflicting constraints a_3, a_4, and a_5 remain undetected. In order to include all the legal authorizations and constraints, we expand the IP problem to include proxy user-role variables. Additional constraints are defined between the actual users and proxy users in such a way that all access rules and constraints are evaluated in the policy instance generated by the expanded IP problem. There are two types of proxy users: *active proxy* and *passive proxy*. An *active proxy* user upon activation of a role triggers the activation of another role for a *passive proxy user*, provided an event trigger is defined for such activation.

Below are the rules for proxy user assignment.

1. Given a dependency constraint $C_1 \vee \ldots \vee C_n \Rightarrow activate$
   (u_x, r_y), where each C_i is of the form $activate(u_{i_1}, r_{i'_1}) \wedge$
   $\ldots \wedge activate(u_{i_m}, r_{i'_m})$. and $\Rightarrow \in \{\rightarrow\rightarrow, \rightarrow\}$. For
   each predicate $activate(u_{i_j}, r_{i'_j})$ in C_i, assign an *active proxy user* $pu_{i_j}^{(a)}$ to role $r_{i'_j}$. For the simple role event expression $activate(u_x, r_y)$ in the trigger head, assign a *passive proxy user* $pu_x^{(p)}$ to role r_y.

2. If a user u_i assigned to role r_j then assign an *active proxy user* $pu_i^{(a)}$ to role r_j.

3. Let user u_i be assigned to role r_j or any role r_k such

Cate-gory	No.	Rule	Explanation	Example (from Figure 3(b))
Hierarchy and assignment	1	$\neg reachable(u_i, r_j) \Rightarrow u_{ir_j} = 0$	if there is no access path from a user node u_i to role node r_j then u_i cannot access / activate r_j.	$u_{3r_1} = 0$
	2	For an *I-hierarchy* constraint $a_m : r_j \geq_I r_k$ and for any user $u_i \in U$, $a_m u_{ir_j} - u_{ir_k} \leq 0$	Any user u_i activating/accessing role r_j also accesses role r_k if the constraint $a_m : r_j \geq_I r_k$ is retained in the final policy.	
	3	Let $U_{\neg AK} = \{u \mid \neg u\_assign(u,r) \wedge (r = r_k \vee r \geq_A^* r_k)\}$ and $R_{IK} = \{r_j \mid$ there is a role hierarchy constraint $a_j : r_j \geq_I r_k\}$ then $$\forall u \in U_{\neg AK}, \sum_{r_j \in R_{IK}} a_j u_{r_j} - u_{r_k} \geq 0$$	Any user u not assigned to role r_k or any of its senior role in the *A-hierarchy* sense can access r_k only if u is able to access at least one role in the set R_{IK}. The set R_{IK} includes all the roles that are senior to r_k in the *I-hierarchy* sense.	
Role enabling	4	$\forall u \in U, \forall r_j \in R,$ $$u_{r_j} - u_{ejr_j} \leq 0$$	Any role can only be accessed in enable state. For defining the event corresponding to enabling of role r_j a special user u_{ej} is assigned to r_j. $u_{ejr_j} = 1$ implies that r_j is in enable state.	$u_{3r_4} - u_{e4r_4} \leq 0$
	5	Let $A_u = \{u \mid reachable(u,r_j)\},$ $$\sum_{u \in A_u} u_{r_j} - u_{ejr_j} \geq 0$$	For any role in enabled state, at least one of the authorized users must access that role in any feasible solution.	$u_{1r_1} + u_{2r_1} - u_{e1r_1} \geq 0$
SoD	6	For a role specific SoD constraint a_m between r_j and r_k, $\forall u \in U,$ $$a_m(u_{r_j} + u_{r_k}) \leq 1$$	Conflicting roles cannot be accessed by the same user simultaneously.	$a_5(u_{3r_2} + u_{3r_3}) \leq 1$
	7	let U_r^{SoD} be the set of conflicting users for role r and a_m be the corresponding SOD constraint, $$a_m \sum_{u \in U_r^{SoD}} u_r \leq 1$$	Conflicting users for a given role r cannot access r concurrently.	$a_1(u_{1r_1} + u_{4r_1}) \leq 1$
Dependency triggers	8	For a strong dependency constraint a_m represented as $C_1 \vee \ldots \vee C_n \rightarrow\rightarrow activate(u_x, r_y)$, where each C_i is of the form $activate(u_{i_1}, r_{i'_1}) \wedge \ldots \wedge activate(u_{i_m}, r_{i'_m})$. $\forall C_i, a_m \prod_j u_{i_j r_{i'_j}} - u_{x_{r_y}} \leq 0$; $a_m \sum_{C_i} \prod_j u_{i_j r_{i'_j}} - u_{x_{r_y}} \geq 0$ where $u_{i_j r_{i'_j}}$ is the user-role variable corresponding to the predicate $activate(u_{i_j}, r_{i'_j})$ in C_i	The event corresponding to the head of the trigger can occur only if the body of the trigger is true. These events are represented in the trigger as role event expressions discussed in Section 2.1.	$a_3(u_{1r_1}) - u_{3r_2} \leq 0$; $a_3(u_{1r_1}) - u_{3r_2} \geq 0$
	9	For a weak dependency constraint a_m represented as $C_1 \vee \ldots \vee C_n \rightarrow activate(u_x, r_y)$, where each C_i is of the form given in rule 8. $$\forall C_i, a_m \prod_j u_{i_j r_{i'_j}} - u_{x_{r_y}} \leq 0$$	Whenever the body of the trigger becomes true, the event in the head of the trigger is forced to occur. The events in the trigger are represented as role event expressions discussed in Section 2.1.	

Table 2: IP transformation rules for actual users specified in the policy

Cat.	No.	Rule	Explanation and example
Hierarchy and assignment	11	$\neg reachable(pu_i, r_j) \Rightarrow pu_{ir_j} = 0$	If no access path from pu_i to r_j then pu_i cannot access r_j. (**Example from Fig. 3(b).** $pu_{3r_4}^{(p)} = pu_{3r_1}^{(p)} = 0$)
	12	For an *I-hierarchy* constraint $a_m : r_j \geq_I r_k$ and for any proxy user pu_i, $a_m pu_{ir_j} - pu_{ir_k} \leq 0$	Any proxy user pu_i activating/accessing role r_j also accesses role r_k if the constraint $a_m : r_j \geq_I r_k$ is retained in the final policy.
	13	Let $PU_{\neg AK} = \{pu \mid \neg u\_assign(pu, r) \wedge (r = r_k \vee r \geq_A^* r_k)\}$ and $R_{IK} = \{r_j \mid \text{there is a role hierarchy constraint } a_j : r_j \geq_I r_k\}$ then $$\forall pu \in PU_{\neg AK}, \sum_{r_j \in R_{IK}} a_j pu_{r_j} - pu_{r_k} \geq 0$$	Any proxy user pu not assigned to role r_k or any of its senior role in the *A-hierarchy* sense can access r_k only if pu is able to access at least one role in the set R_{IK}. The set R_{IK} includes all the roles that are senior to r_k in the *I-hierarchy* sense.
	14	For a user u_i with an active proxy $pu_i^{(a)}$ authorized to access role r_j, $u_{ir_j} + pu_{ir_j}^{(a)} = 1$	Either an authorized user or its active proxy (but not both) must access role r_j in any feasible solution of the underlying IP problem. (**Example from Fig. 3(b).** $u_{1r_1} + pu_{1r_1}^{(a)} = 1$; $u_{2r_1} + pu_{2r_1}^{(a)} = 1$)
	15	For a user u_i with a passive proxy $pu_i^{(p)}$ authorized to access role r_j, $u_{ir_j} + pu_{ir_j}^{(p)} \leq 1$	In any feasible solution role r_j may be accessed by the authorized user u_i or its passive proxy $pu_i^{(p)}$ but not both. (**Example from Fig. 3(b).** $u_{3r_2} + pu_{3r_2}^{(p)} \leq 1$; $u_{3r_3} + pu_{3r_3}^{(p)} \leq 1$)
Dependency triggers	16	Given a dependency constraint a_m represented by $C_1 \vee \ldots \vee C_n \Rightarrow activate(u_x, r_y)$, where each C_i is of the form $activate(u_{i_1}, r_{i_1'}) \wedge \ldots \wedge activate(u_{i_m}, r_{i_m'})$. and $\Rightarrow \in \{\rightarrow\rightarrow, \rightarrow\}$. $$a_m [1 - \sum_{C_i} \prod_j u_{i_j r_{i_j'}}] - pu_{x_{r_y}}^{(p)} \leq 0$$ where $u_{i_j r_{i_j'}}$ is the user-role variable corresponding to the predicate $activate(u_{i_j}, r_{i_j'})$ in C_i and $pu_x^{(p)}$ is the passive proxy user of u_x for role r_y	In case the body of the dependency trigger a_m is false, the passive proxy user of u_x for role r_y (i.e., $pu_x^{(p)}$) can access r_y. This ensures that all authorizations related to dependency constraints are checked in the final solution of IP. (**Example from Fig. 3(b).** $a_3(1 - u_{1r_1}) - pu_{3r_2}^{(p)} \leq 0$; $a_4(1 - u_{2r_1}) - pu_{3r_3}^{(p)} \leq 0$)
	17	If the constraint a_m given in Rule 15 is a strong dependency constraint, then $$a_m \sum_{C_i} \prod_j pu_{i_j r_{i_j'}}^{(a)} - pu_{x_{r_y}}^{(p)} \geq 0$$ Where for the predicate $activate(u_{i_j}, r_{i_j'})$ in C_i, $pu_{i_j r_{i_j'}}^{(a)}$ is the binary variable corresponding to the activation / access of role $r_{i_j'}$ by the *active proxy* of user u_{i_j}. $pu_{x_{r_y}}^{(p)}$ is the binary variable corresponding to the activation of role r_y by the *passive proxy* of user u_x	For strong dependency constraint, Rules 15 and 16 jointly imply that the passive proxy user of u_x for role r_y (i.e., $pu_x^{(p)}$ can access r_y if and only if the body of the trigger a_m is 'False' with the actual user-role variables. However, the body of the trigger evaluates 'True' when the actual user-role variables are substituted with the corresponding *active proxy user* variables. (**Example from Fig. 3(b).** $a_3(pu_{1r_1}^{(a)}) - pu_{3r_2}^{(p)} \geq 0$; $a_4(pu_{2r_1}^{(a)}) - pu_{3r_3}^{(p)} \geq 0$)
SoD	18	For a role specific SoD constraint a_m between r_j and r_k, $\forall u \in U$, and for all the active ($pu^{(a)}$) and passive proxies ($pu^{(p)}$) of u for r_j and r_k, $a_m[u_{r_j} + pu_{r_k}^{(a)}] \leq 1$, $a_m[pu_{r_j}^{(a)} + u_{r_k}] \leq 1$, $a_m[pu_{r_j}^{(a)} + pu_{r_k}^{(a)}] \leq 1$, $a_m[u_{r_j} + pu_{r_k}^{(p)}] \leq 1$, $a_m[pu_{r_j}^{(p)} + u_{r_k}] \leq 1$, $a_m[pu_{r_j}^{(p)} + pu_{r_k}^{(p)}] \leq 1$, $a_m[pu_{r_j}^{(a)} + pu_{r_k}^{(p)}] \leq 1$, $a_m[pu_{r_j}^{(p)} + pu_{r_k}^{(a)}] \leq 1$	In any feasible solution of the underlying IP problem, the conflicting roles r_j and r_k cannot be concurrently accessed by any user u and/or its active/passive proxy users. (**Example from Fig. 3(b).** $a_5[u_{3r_2} + pu_{3r_3}^{(p)}] \leq 1$; $a_5[pu_{3r_2}^{(p)} + u_{3r_2}] \leq 1$; $a_5[pu_{3r_2}^{(p)} + pu_{3r_3}^{(p)}] \leq 1$)
	19	Let a_m represent a user-specific SoD constraint between users u_i and u_j for role r_k. Also, let $pu_x^{(a)} = active\_proxy(u_x, r_k)$ and $pu_x^{(p)} = passive\_proxy(u_x, r_k)$, where $u_x \in \{u_i, u_j\}$. $a_m[u_{ir_k} + pu_{jr_k}^{(a)}] \leq 1$, $a_m[pu_{ir_k}^{(a)} + u_{jr_k}] \leq 1$, $a_m[pu_{ir_k}^{(a)} + pu_{jr_k}^{(a)}] \leq 1$, $a_m[u_{ir_k} + pu_{jr_k}^{(p)}] \leq 1$, $a_m[pu_{ir_k}^{(p)} + u_{jr_k}] \leq 1$, $a_m[pu_{ir_k}^{(p)} + pu_{jr_k}^{(p)}] \leq 1$, $a_m[pu_{ir_k}^{(a)} + pu_{jr_k}^{(p)}] \leq 1$, $a_m[pu_{ir_k}^{(p)} + pu_{jr_k}^{(a)}] \leq 1$,	In any feasible solution of the underlying IP problem, role r_k cannot be accessed simultaneously by conflicting users and/or their active/passive proxy users. (**Example from Fig. 3(b).** $a_1[u_{1r_1} + pu_{4r_1}^{(a)}] \leq 1$; $a_1[pu_{1r_1}^{(a)} + u_{4r_1}] \leq 1$; $a_1[pu_{1r_1}^{(a)} + pu_{4r_1}^{(a)}] \leq 1$)

Table 3: IP transformation rules for proxy users

Algorithm 1 ConfRes

Input: Event-driven RBAC Policy graph G_{in}
Output: A consistent and conflict free policy Graph
1: $G \leftarrow G_{in}$
2: Add all the proxy users in G according to the proxy user assignment rules given in Section 3.1.2
3: Add the objective function based on the desired criterion

4: Solve the IP problem for optimal solution
5: Remove all the constraints from the policy graph G_{in} for which the corresponding constraint variable $a_m = 0$ in the solution
6: **return** the modified policy graph G_{in}

---

that $r_j \geq_A^* r_k$ and $\neg(r_j \geq_I^* r_k)$, assign an *active proxy user* $pu_i^{(a)}$ to role r_k.

Figure 3(b) shows the policy instance of 3(a) with proxy user assignment according to the above rules.

Table 3 lists the rules for defining IP constraints involving proxy users. The hierarchy and assignment rules (Rules 11-13) for proxy users are similar to the hierarchy and assignment rules (Rules 1-3) for actual users in Table 2. In addition, there is a constraint (Rules 14 and 15) that a role can be accessed by either an authorized actual user or its active/passive proxy but not both. Rule 15 in Table 3 ensures that if the event (activation of a role) in the head of the trigger cannot occur for an actual user (because the body of the trigger evaluates to False), then the event occurs for the passive proxy of the corresponding user. Rule 16 enforce the strong dependency constraint on top of Rule 15. These two rules jointly imply that event (activation of a role) in the head of the trigger can only occur for a passive proxy user if the body of the trigger evaluates to False for actual users but it evaluates to "True" when the actual user-roles variables are substituted with the corresponding active proxy user variables. Rules 17 and 18 specify the role-specific and user-specific SoDs for proxy users.

3.2 Conflict Resolution

The IP transformation rules described in the above section are used to represent the constraints embedded in the underlying access control policy. Once the policy constraints are transformed into IP constraints, an optimal resolution can be achieved by solving the IP problem described in Section 3.1. The optimality measure is embedded in the objective function of the corresponding IP problem. Each decision variable in the objective function is assigned a weight and an optimal solution maximizes the over all weight of the objective function. These weights may be assigned based on the priority of the underlying constraints and accesses.

The procedure *ConfRes* for optimal resolution of conflicts in the event-based RBAC policy is given in Algorithm 1. *ConfRes* takes as input an event-driven policy graph G_{in} and returns a consistent and conflict-free policy graph. *ConfRes* first generates proxy user to role and special user to role assignment as discussed in the IP transformation rules. It then transforms the updated set of policy constraints into IP constraints using the transformation rules described in the above section. Next the objective function is defined based on the desired optimality criterion and the IP problem is solved for an optimal solution. Finally, all the

constraints for which the corresponding constraint variable $a_m equals 0$ in the optimal solution are removed from given policy graph.

The policy derived through the procedure *ConfRes* will be consistent as proved in Appendix. Note that, in presence of dependence triggers leading to activation of conflicting roles, if the original policy has additional user-specific SoD constraints to stop violation of any role constraint, our procedure may not be able to identify that the policy is consistent, and may instead unnecessarily relax some constraint(s) from it. For example constraints a_3, a_4, and a_5 are conflicting in Figure 3(b) – u_1 and u_2 activating role r_1 simultaneously will result in activation of roles r_3 and r_4 by u_3 which is a violation of the SoD constraint a_5. With the addition of a user specific SoD constraint between u_1 and u_2 for r_1 in Figure 3(c), a_3 and a_4 will not be effective at the same time making the policy consistent. However, our procedure will identify the conflict among a_3, a_4, and a_5, and will simply resolve it by the removal of one of the three (based on utility). It is possible to resolve this more effectively by traversing the RBAC policy graph to identify dependency triggers that results in activation of conflicting roles by same user and then ensuring that such triggers will not be effective simultaneously. However, to keep the solution procedure focused, we take the simple approach for now, and plan to formally address this problem in the future.

4. ILLUSTRATIVE EXAMPLE

We now illustrate the proposed conflict resolution technique by considering an event-based RBAC policy that models a workflow and the associated policy constraints. An important aspect highlighted in this example is the resolution of policy conflicts that may arise because of the interplay between workflow execution constraints and the organizational constraints restricting the accessibility of users over certain roles and permissions.

Figure 4(a) shows a graphical representation of an event-driven RBAC policy modeling the workflow of the tax refund process of Figure 4(b). The RBAC graph in Figure 4(a) consists of nine roles: General Manager (GM), Technical Manager (TM), Refund Manager (RM), Refund Clerk (RC), Issue Void Check (IVC), Prepare Check (PC), Approve/disapprove Check 1 (ADC_1), Approve/disapprove Check 2 (ADC_2), and Summarize Decision (SD). Amongst these roles, the last five roles (IVC, PC, ADC_1, ADC_2, and SD) are activated for each invocation of the workflow. Each of these five roles correspond to a workflow task depicted in Figure 4(b). We therefore refer to these roles as *workflow-specific roles*. These workflow specific roles are linked to the relevant organizational roles using the activation hierarchy semantics. This means that any user assigned to the organizational role can perform the corresponding workflow task by activating the appropriate workflow-specific role in the given session.

In the policy graph of Figure 4(a), there are five users: u_1, u_2, u_3, u_4, and u_5. Users u_1 and u_2 are conflicting users for role GM (constraint a_2), u_1, u_2, and u_3 are conflicting for TM (constraint a_1), and u_2 and u_4 are conflicting for RM (constraint a_4). The strong dependency constraint a_5 : $u_{1GM} \rightarrow\rightarrow u_{1TM}$ implies that user u_1 can activate role TM only if u_1 has activated the role of GM. Similarly the event trigger a_6 : $u_{2GM} \rightarrow\rightarrow u_{2RM}$ prevents u_2 to activate the role RM without activating the role GM.

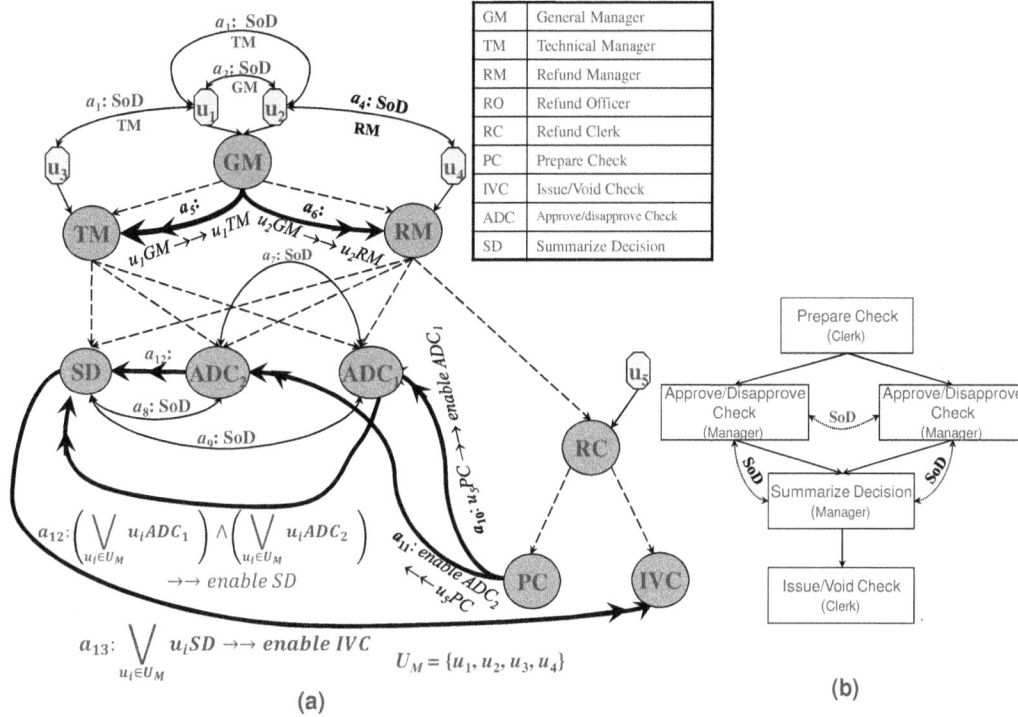

Figure 4: (a) policy graph modeling access control policy related to tax refund process. (b) Tax refund process workflow.

The tax refund workflow shown in Figure 4(b) is represented in the policy graph using the workflow-specific roles and event dependency triggers. Since a check needs to be approved by two separate managers, this task is modeled as activation of two separate roles ADC_1 and ADC_2. The event triggers defined on workflow-specific roles define the execution semantics of the workflow. First a refund clerk (RC) prepares a check which needs to be approved by two separate managers for further processing. These constraints are represented in the graph by the triggers $a_{10} : u_5 PC \rightarrow\rightarrow enableADC_1$ and $a_{11} : u_5 PC \rightarrow\rightarrow enableADC_2$. Enabling of the roles ADC_1 and ADC_2 imply that the users authorized for the manager roles can now activate these roles to approve or disapprove the refund.

The condition that the check must be approved by two different managers is enforced by defining a role-specific SoD a_7 between ADC_1 and ADC_2. After the checks are approved or disapproved, a decision summary is prepared. This is done by activating the role SD. This role can only be activated by a user authorized for some Manager role who has not approved or disapproved the check. The event trigger: $a_{12} : (\vee_{u_i \in U_M} u_i ADC_1) \wedge (\vee_{u_i \in UM} u_i ADC_2) \rightarrow\rightarrow enable(SD)$, where $UM = \{u_1, u_2, u_3, u_4\}$, implements this workflow dependency by enabling the role SD. The role-specific SoD constraints (a_7, a_8, a_9) among SD, ADC_1, and ADC_2 prevent a single user activating some manager role(s) to perform more than one operation on a given check. Once any user activating Manager role prepares decision summary by activating SD, the refund check needs to be issued or voided. This workflow dependency is represented by the event trigger $a_{13} : (\vee_{u_i \in U_M} u_i SD) \rightarrow\rightarrow enable(IVC)$. Enabling of the role IVC implies that any authorized user by activating

IVC can issue or void the refund check depending on the summary decision.

The policy graph shown in Figure 4(a) may also lead to conflicting authorizations. For instance, the dependency constraint a_5 and user-specific SoD constraint a_1 becomes conflicting by activation of role GM by u_1 and activation of TM by u_2 or u_3. Conflicts in the event-driven RBAC policy shown in Figure 4(a) are resolved by applying the conflict resolution algorithm $ConfRes$. The IP constraint transformation process produces almost 550 constraints with 130 variables for the event-driven RBAC policy of Figure 4(a). The resulting IP problem can be solved with different optimality criteria. One optimality criterion could be retention of maximum number of constraints specified in the original policy. The objective function for this optimality criterion is Maximize $\sum_{i=1}^{13} a_i$. An optimal solution with this criterion is to remove the user-specific SoD constraints a_1 and a_4 from the final policy graph. a_1 prevents users u_1, u_2, and u_3 from activating the role TM concurrently in a given workflow instance; similarly, a_4 prevents users u_2 and u_4 from activating the role RM concurrently. This solution yields an objective function value of 11 implying that 11 out of a total of 13 constraints are retained in this resolution.

5. RELATED WORK

The related work can be categorize into two categories: i) policy conflict resolution; and ii) workflow satisfiability.

Policy conflict resolution. There is a lot of work devoted to this topic in the context of access control policies [12, 3, 4, 6]. The resolution techniques proposed earlier can be classified into three classes: resolution by priority [13, 1,

6], resolution by constraint/rule relaxation [9], and resolution by restriction [4, 9].

In the priority-based techniques each authorization / prohibition is assigned a priority and lower priority authorizations / prohibitions are overridden in case of conflict. Priorities can either be explicitly assigned to each individual authorization / prohibition [6] or can be derived based on the administrative scope of the grantor, the specificity and the modality of the authorization [12]. For the latter case in [12], an administrative hierarchy is used to determine the authorization privileges of the granters. This resolution strategy is more suitable for systems that are managed by multiple administrators who may specify contradictory rules for access to a particular resource. Conflict resolution based on the specificity of authorization assumes the existence of an object oriented hierarchy relating the targeting objects and subjects. However, such a hierarchy may not exist. For instance, in RBAC models there is no assumption as to how the underlying objects are related. For all practical purposes, the target objects can be considered as atomic entities. The strategy that negative authorization takes precedence may resolve policy conflicts but decreases flexibility [12] and may produce deadlocks in case there are other authorizations dependent on the denied authorization. Other priority-based resolution techniques [1, 10] resolve policy constraints at runtime and do not consider a global optimality measure for conflict resolution. Restriction-based resolution strategy prevents conflicting accesses at the expense of restricting accessibility. Some of the conflict resolution techniques that belong to this group include the event-action constraint cancellation technique proposed by Chomicki et al. [4], the well-formed model authorization set, and the stable model authorization set with pessimistic reasoning [2]. The restricted access semantics in these approaches may significantly reduce accessibility and may lead to a deadlock.

[13] uses an integer programming-based approach for resolving interoperation conflicts among organizations that employ RBAC policies. However, their conflict resolution strategy is applicable to only static RBAC policies that do not include event-driven constraints.

Workflow satisfiability. The existing work on workflow satisfiability deals with determining whether a workflow can be completed under the given authorization constraints. Crampton [5] proposed a model for speccifying workflow authorization constraints. Based on this model, an algorithm is given for checking workflow satisfiability. Wang et al. [15] have studied the complexity of workflow satisfiability problem. They have proposed a role-and-relation-based access control (R^2BAC) model and shown that workflow satisfiability is NP-complete for R^2BAC as well as for any workflow model that supports certain simple types of constraints (e.g., SoD). None of these papers [5, 15] address the issue of resolving inconsistencies and conflicts in underlying access control policies that hinder completion of the workflow.

6. CONCLUSION

In this paper, we have examined the problem of conflict identification and resolution in the context of event-driven RBAC policies. We have developed an integer programming based framework to solve this problem. Appropriate constraints are created for each policy using the IP transformation rules, and the modeled problem is solved using standard IP solvers to give an optimal solution. Our solution is practical, efficient, and generalizable. In the future, we plan to extend our work beyond event driven RBAC. We also plan to examine this problem for more complex context based access control policies.

7. ACKNOWLEDGMENTS

The work of Shafiq is supported in part by the LUMS Departmental Research Grant and the work of Ghafoor is supported in part by the National Science Foundation under Grant No. IIS-0964639.

8. REFERENCES

[1] E. Bertino, P. A. Bonatti, and E. Ferrari. Trbac: A temporal role-based access control model. *ACM Trans. Inf. Syst. Secur.*, 4:191–233, August 2001.

[2] E. Bertino, F. Buccafurri, E. Ferrari, and P. Rullo. A logical framework for reasoning on data access control policies. In *IEEE Computer Security Foundations Workshop*, pages 175 –189, 1999.

[3] E. Bertino, E. Ferrari, and V. Atluri. The specification and enforcement of authorization constraints in workflow management systems. *ACM Trans. Inf. Syst. Secur.*, 2:65–104, February 1999.

[4] J. Chomicki, J. Lobo, and S. Naqvi. Conflict resolution using logic programming. *IEEE Trans. on Knowl. and Data Eng.*, 15:244–249, January 2003.

[5] J. Crampton. A reference monitor for workflow systems with constrained task execution. In *SACMAT '05*, pages 38–47, 2005.

[6] F. Cuppens, N. Cuppens-Boulahia, and M. B. Ghorbel. High level conflict management strategies in advanced access control models. *Electron. Notes Theor. Comput. Sci.*, 186:3–26, July 2007.

[7] D. F. Ferraiolo, R. Sandhu, S. Gavrila, D. R. Kuhn, and R. Chandramouli. Proposed nist standard for role-based access control. *ACM Trans. Inf. Syst. Secur.*, 4:224–274, August 2001.

[8] L. Gong and X. Qian. Computational issues in secure interoperation. *IEEE Trans. Software Eng.*, 1996.

[9] P. Hein, D. Biswas, L. A. Martucci, and M. Muhlhauser. Conflict detection and lifecycle management for access control in publish/subscribe systems. In *IEEE HASE*, pages 104 –111, nov. 2011.

[10] J. Joshi, E. Bertino, U. Latif, and A. Ghafoor. A generalized temporal role-based access control model. *IEEE TKDE*, jan. 2005.

[11] A. Lazouski, F. Martinelli, and P. Mori. Usage control in computer security: A survey. *Computer Science Review*, 4(2):81 – 99, 2010.

[12] E. Lupu and M. Sloman. Conflicts in policy-based distributed systems management,. *IEEE Transactions on Software Engineering*, nov. 1999.

[13] B. Shafiq, J. Joshi, E. Bertino, and A. Ghafoor. Secure interoperation in a multidomain environment employing rbac policies. *IEEE TKDE.*, 2005.

[14] M. Sloman and E. Lupu. Security and management policy specification. *Network, IEEE*, 16(2), 2002.

[15] Q. Wang and N. Li. Satisfiability and resiliency in workflow authorization systems. *ACM Trans. Inf. Syst. Secur.*, Dec. 2010.

APPENDIX

The policy derived through the procedure $ConfRes$ is consistent as proved in the following Theorem.

Theorem. Given an acyclic event driven RBAC policy graph G_{in}. Let G be the final policy graph after applying the $ConfRes$ algorithm over G_{in}. In the final policy graph G, there are no hierarchy or event dependency constraints that violates any: i) role-specific SoD, and ii) user-specific SoD.

Proof. We will prove this separately for role-specific SoD and user-specific SoD.

Role-specific SoD. Consider a role-specific SoD constraint a_c. Any indirect access that may lead to violation of the role-specific SoD constraint a_c will fall into one of the four cases shown in Figure 5

Case 1: In this case a user accesses two conflicting roles by activating a senior role that is related to both conflicting roles through an *I-hierarchy*. This is depicted in Figure 5(a) in which roles r_x and r_y have a SoD constraint a_c and role r_z is a senior role linked to r_y through an *I-hierarchy*. Assume that the policy graph G after conflict resolution contains a sub-graph isomorphic to the graph shown in Figure 5(a). This implies that in the final solution to the IP $a_c = 1$ and all the variables a_i, corresponding to *I-hierarchy* edges that link r_z to r_x and r_y, are assigned a value of one. As a result of the inheritance path from r_z to r_x and r_y, any authorized user by activating r_z accesses r_x and r_y (Rules 2 and 3). Rules 5 and 14 ensure that at least one regular user or proxy user accesses role r_z. Without Loss of generality, assume that u_i is such user. Therefore, in any feasible solution $u_{ir_x} = 1$ and $u_{ir_y} = 1$. However, the IP constraint $a_c(u_{ir_x} + u_{ir_y}) \leq 1$, derived from Rules 6 and 18, imply that either $a_c = 0$ or there is no inheritance from r_z to r_x or from r_z to r_y. Hence G does not contain a role that is linked to two conflicting roles through an *I-hierarchy*.

Case 2: This case captures the role-specific SoD violations because of the existence of inheritance path and dependency constraint. The inheritance path from r_z to r_y enables a user assuming the role r_z to access r_y (Rules 2 and 3). An induced SoD constraint a_n (see Section 2.3) is defined between r_z and r_x because of the role specific constraint a_c and the inheritance path from r_z to r_y. $a_n = a_c \prod a_i$, where a_i corresponds to an *I-edge* in the path from r_z to r_y. Similar to case 1, Rules 5 and 14 ensure that at least one regular user or proxy user accesses role r_z in any feasible solution to the underlying IP problem Let u_i be such user. The dependency constraint a_d in Figure 5(b) causes u_i to access role r_x, whenever the body of the dependency trigger becomes true. Rules 8, 9, 16, and 17 imply that in any feasible solution either u_i or its passive proxy accesses r_x.

In addition SoD constraint with the corresponding proxy variables are added in the underlying IP problem (Rule 18). Moreover, the IP constraints derived from Rule 6 for the induced SoD constraint a_n imply that in any feasible solution, if $a_n = 1$, then the conflicting roles r_z and r_x cannot be accessed by u_i and/or its proxies concurrently. This contradicts with the authorizations for u_i derived from Rules 2 and 3 in conjunction with Rules 5 and 14 as explained above. Therefore, in any feasible solution either $a_d = 0$ or $a_i = 0$ or $a_c = 0$. Hence, G does not contain a role-specific SoD constraint that conflicts with a dependency constraint because of *I-hierarchy*, as shown in Figure 5(b).

Case 3: Figure 5(c) depicts a generic scenario in which

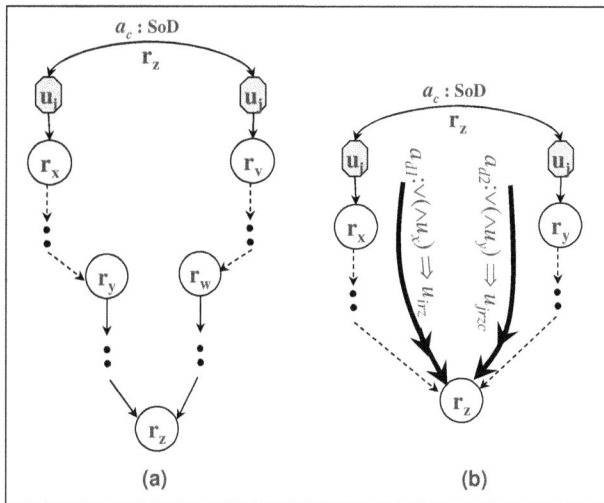

Figure 6: Cases of user-specific SoD violation

a role-specific SoD conflicts with a dependency constraint. The nature of conflict between the role-specific SoD constraint a_c and the dependency constraint a_d in this case is similar to the conflict between the induced SoD a_n and the dependency constraint a_d in Case 2. Using reasoning similar to Case 2, we can show that one of the constraint a_c or a_d cannot be present in the final policy graph G.

Case 4: In this case two dependency constraints jointly conflict with a role-specific SoD constraint as shown in Figure 5(d). If we assume that the graph G contains the graph shown in Figure 5(d) as a sub-graph then in any feasible solution of the underlying IP problem, either u_i or its passive proxy activate the conflicting roles r_x and r_y simultaneously (Rules 8, 9, 14 and 15).

Rule 18 adds SoD constraints involving u_i and its proxies to the underlying IP problem. In addition, the IP constraints derived from Rule 6 for the SoD constraint a_c imply that in any feasible solution, if $a_c = 1$, then the conflicting roles r_x and r_y cannot be accessed by u_i and/or its proxies concurrently. This contradicts with the authorizations for u_i derived from Rules 8, 9, 14, and 15 as explained above. Therefore, in any feasible solution either $a_c = 0$ or $a_{d1} = a_{d2} = 0$. Hence, G does not contain a role-specific SoD constraint that conflicts with dependency constraints, as shown in Figure 5(d).

User-specific SoD. Consider a user-specific SoD constraint a_c. Any indirect access that may lead to violation of the user-specific SoD constraint a_c will fall into one of the two cases shown in Figure 6.

Case 1: This case covers all the scenarios in which the existence of inheritance path(s) leads to the violation of user-specific SoD as shown in Figure 6(a). In Figure 6(a), users u_i and u_j have a user-specific SoD constraint a_c for role r_z. For the generic case, the relationship between the roles shown in Figure 6(a) is given by: $((r_x \geq_A^* r_y) \vee (r_x = r_y)) \wedge (r_y \geq_I^* r_z) \wedge ((r_v \geq_A^* r_w) \vee (r_v = r_w)) \wedge ((r_w \geq_I^* r_z) \vee (r_w = r_z))$

In any feasible solution of the IP problem formulated for the policy graph of Figure 6(a), either u_i or its proxy (u_j or its proxy) activates role r_y (r_w), which causes the corresponding users to access role r_z because of the inheritance

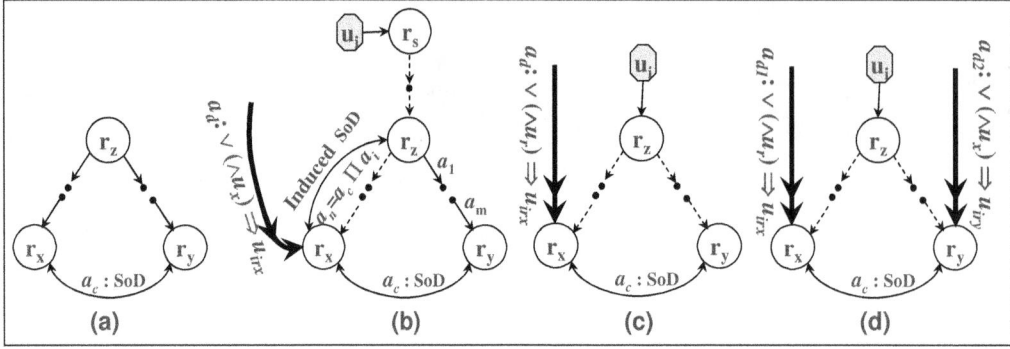

Figure 5: Cases of role-specific SoD violation

paths from r_y to r_z and from r_w to r_z. The constraint a_c implies that the role r_z cannot be simultaneously accessed by u_i and u_j. Rule 7 ensures this for actual users. In addition, Rule 19 adds SoD constraints involving the corresponding proxy variables for a_c in the underlying IP problem. This contradicts with the authorizations for u_i and u_j derived from Rules 2 and 3 in conjunction with Rules 5 and 14. Therefore in any feasible solution of the underlying IP problem either $a_c = 0$, or there is no inheritance from r_y to r_z and from r_w to r_z. Hence, G does not contain a user specific SoD constraint that conflicts with any inheritance path.

Case 2: In this case two dependency constraints jointly conflict with a user-specific SoD as shown in Figure 6(b). In this figure, users u_i and u_j have a user-specific SoD a_c for role r_z. For the generic case, the relationship between the roles shown in Figure 6(b) is given by: $((r_x \geq_A^* r_z) \vee (r_x = r_z)) \wedge ((r_y \geq_A^* r_z) \vee (r_y = r_z))$

Because of the dependency constraint a_{d1} (a_{d2}) depicted in Figure 6(b), either u_i or its proxy (u_j or its proxy) activates role r_z. The constraint a_c implies that the role r_z cannot be simultaneously activated by u_i and u_j. The IP constraints derived from Rule 7 and Rule 19 for the user specific SoD constraint a_c imply that in any feasible solution, if $a_c = 1$, then both u_i and u_j and or their respective proxies cannot access role r_z concurrently. This contradicts with the authorizations for u_i and u_j derived from transformation rules for dependency constraints (Rules 8, 9, 16, and 17) in conjunction with Rule 14. Therefore in any feasible solution of the underlying IP problem either $a_c = 0$, or $a_{d1} = 0$ or $a_{d2} = 0$. Hence, G does not contain a user specific SoD constraint that conflicts with any dependency constraint.

A Model-Based Approach to Automated Testing of Access Control Policies

Dianxiang Xu, Lijo Thomas, Michael Kent
National Center for the Protection of the Financial
Infrastructure, Dakota State University
Madison, SD 57042, USA
+1 605 256 5694

{dianxiang.xu, lthomas, mjkent}@dsu.edu

Tejeddine Mouelhi, Yves Le Traon
Interdisciplinary Centre for Security, Reliability and
Trust, University of Luxembourg, Campus Kirchberg
L-1359, Luxembourg, Luxembourg
+352 46 66 44 5840

{tejeddine.mouelhi, Yves.LeTraon}@uni.lu

ABSTRACT

Access control policies in software systems can be implemented incorrectly for various reasons. This paper presents a model-based approach for automated testing of access control implementation. To feed the model-based testing process, test models are constructed by integrating declarative access control rules and contracts (preconditions and post-conditions) of the associated activities. The access control tests are generated from the test models to exercise the interactions of access control activities. Test executability is obtained through a mapping of the modeling elements to implementation constructs. The approach has been implemented in an industry-adopted test automation framework that supports the generation of test code in a variety of languages, such as Java, C, C++, C#, and HTML/Selenium IDE. The full model-based testing process has been applied to two systems implemented in Java. The effectiveness is evaluated in terms of access-control fault detection rate using mutation analysis of access control implementation. The experiments show that the model-based tests killed 99.7% of the mutants and the remaining mutants caused no policy violations.

Categories and Subject Descriptors

D.2.5 [**Testing and debugging**]: Testing tools (e.g., data generators, coverage testing). D.4.6 [**Security and protection**]: Access Controls

General Terms

Reliability, Security, Verification.

Keywords

Access control, software testing, model-based testing, Petri nets, mutation analysis.

1. INTRODUCTION

Access control is a fundamental mechanism for providing security-intensive software with first-level security by regulating user access to resources. An access control policy is usually expressed in terms of declarative rules, defining the conditions to which the access to resources can be granted and to whom.

Although the specification of an access control policy can be supported by powerful verification techniques, the specified policy and its mechanism may not be implemented correctly for various reasons, such as programming errors, omissions, and misunderstanding of the policy specification. The flaws in an incorrect implementation may result in serious violations of access control policy, such as unauthorized accesses and escalation of privileges. Therefore, it is important to reveal the potential discrepancy between the policy specification and the actual implementation.

Software testing is a major means for software quality assurance. It aims at finding errors by executing a program with test cases, including test inputs and test oracles (expected results). To reveal access control violations, one approach is to devise test cases for individual access control rules. The main issue of testing individual rules, however, is that it cannot see the forest for the trees because access control rules are often related to each other. In a library management system, for example, access control rules may be defined for such activities as borrow and return, where a precondition of return is that there is a borrowed book. Testing the individual borrow and return rules would lead to duplicated tests – testing the return activity typically involves a borrow activity. In addition, it is difficult to cover all the interactions among access control activities by testing individual rules.

To address the above issue, this paper presents a model-based approach to testing access control policies. Model-based testing uses models of a system under test (SUT) for generating test cases. It is an appealing approach to software testing because of several potential benefits [1]. First, the modeling activity helps clarify requirements and enhances communication between developers and testers. Without a good understanding about the SUT, testers would not be able to perform effective testing. Second, automated test generation enables more test cycles and assures the required coverage of test models. Third, model-based testing can help improve fault detection capability due to the increased number and diversity of test cases [2]. Nevertheless, studies have shown that the tester's ability to build quality models or required expertise in rigorous modeling is a major barrier to the effective application of model-based testing [3]. There is little work on how to build access control test models in a structured, repeatable process. Existing literature typically focuses on what modeling notation is used and how tests are generated and executed. Another issue is that abstract tests generated from models need to be transformed into concrete tests for execution, which can be a time-consuming process. As will be detailed in the related work section, these two issues remain largely open.

The approach in this paper generates executable access control tests from a MID (Model-Implementation Description) specification, which consists of an access control test model and a MIM (Model-Implementation Mapping) description. The underlying test model, represented by a Predicate/Transition (PrT) net [4][5][6], is constructed from the given access control rules and functional requirements according to which the SUT is designed and implemented. PrT nets are high-level Petri nets, a well-studied formal method for system modeling and verification. We use contracts (preconditions and post-conditions) to construct test models for two considerations. First, design by contracts [7] is a widely accepted approach to functional specification. Second, access control rules as security constraints on system functionality cannot be tested without involving system functionality. Access control testing requires understanding of the preconditions and post-conditions of the related activities. Consider testing the rule that a student is allowed to return books on working days. The test cannot be performed unless the functional precondition *"book is borrowed"* is satisfied. The accurate test oracle cannot be determined without knowing its post-condition *"book becomes available"*. For test generation purposes, we integrate declarative access control rules and contracts into an operational PrT net. For code generation purposes, we create the MIM description by mapping the elements in a test model to the implementation constructs based on the SUT's programming interface. The generated code can then be executed with the SUT.

Our approach has been implemented in MISTA (formerly ISTA)[1], a framework for automated generation of test code in a variety of languages, including Java, C, C++, C#, and HTML/Selenium IDE (a Firefox plugin for testing web applications) [6][8]. We have conducted case studies using two Java applications, LMS (a library management system) and ASMS (an auction sale management system) [9][10]. To assess the fault detection capability of our approach, we applied mutation analysis of access control implementation. Mutants were created by seeding faulty rules in policy implementation. A mutant is said to be killed or detected if a failure is reported during at least one test execution. Mutation analysis is a widely applied method for evaluating the effectiveness of software testing techniques. Since the injected faults would represent the defects that likely occur in software implementation, the percentage of mutants killed by the test cases created from a testing technique is often a good indicator of how effective the testing technique is (For further information on mutation testing, a survey can be found in [11]). For each case study, we constructed the access control test models in the subject program, generated executable tests from the test models, and executed the tests against the mutants. Our experiments show that our approach is highly effective in detecting policy violations since the generated tests killed a large percentage of mutants.

The contribution of this paper is threefold. First, we formalize several desired characteristics of role-based access control rules (consistency, non-redundancy, and completeness) and deal with incomplete specification of access control rules. Incompleteness of specification is a norm in real-world software development and the undefined situations more likely lead to security holes in the implementation. Second, we present an automated process for constructing operational test models by integrating declarative access control rules and contracts into PrT nets. The test models can cover all access control rules and contexts. Third, we generate

executable test code automatically to cover the access control rules and their contexts. Once the MID specification is completed, test generation and execution would need no human intervention. To the best of our knowledge, none of the above aspects has been addressed in the literature on model-based access control testing.

The remainder of this paper is organized as follows. Section 2 introduces the role-based access control model used in this paper, formalizes the desired characteristics of access control rules, and deals with incomplete access control rules. Section 3 describes how test models are constructed from access control rules and contracts. Section 4 discusses how executable test code is generated from test models. Section 5 presents the case studies. Section 6 reviews and compares our approach to the related work. Section 7 concludes this paper.

2. The Role-Based Access Control Model

2.1 Role-based Access Control

Our approach is based on role-based access control (RBAC) extended with the contexts and prohibition rules. An access control policy consists of the following elements:

- A set of roles R,
- A role hierarchy H,
- A set of objects (or resources) O,
- A set of contexts C,
- A set of operations A (called activities in this paper),
- A set of authorization types *{Permission, Prohibition}*,
- A set of subjects (human users or computer agents) *Sub*,
- A role assignment $Sub \rightarrow 2^R$ (one subject may play a set of roles), and
- A set of role-based access control rules $\Re$. $\Re(r)$ is the set of access control rules defined for role r.

Definition 1 (Access control rule). An access control rule is a 5-tuple $<r, o, a, c, \tau>$, where $r \in R$, $o \in O$, $a \in A$, c is a Boolean expression representing the policy's context, and $\tau \in \{Permission, Prohibition\}$. It means that role r's activity a on object o is permitted (when $\tau = Permission$) or prohibited (when $\tau = Prohibition$) when context c holds.

Table 1. Access control rules for borrower in LMS

No	Object	Activity	Context	Auth_Type
1	Book	GiveBackBook	day(HD)	Prohibition
2	Book	BorrowBook	day(HD)	Prohibition
3	Book	BorrowBook	day(WD)	Permission
4	Book	GiveBackBook	day(WD)	Permission
5	Book	ReserveBook	day(HD)	Prohibition
6	Book	ReserveBook	day(WD)	Permission

A role hierarchy $H \subseteq R \times R$ is a partial-order relation on R. Given $(r', r) \in H$, r' is said to be a direct super-role of r, and r is a direct sub-role of r'. Role r is called a primitive role if r is a leaf in the role hierarchy. In LMS, for example, the set of roles is *{student, teacher, director, secretary, admin, borrower, personnel}*, the role hierarchy is *{<borrower, student>, <borrower, teacher>, <personnel, director>, <personnel, secretary>}* (*borrower* is the super-role of *student* and *teacher*, whereas *personnel* is the super-role of *director* and *secretary*), the set of objects is *{book, borrowerAccount, personnelAccount}*, and the set of activities is

[1] The beta release of MISTA can be downloaded at:

http://www.homepages.dsu.edu/dxu/research/MBT.html.

{BorrowBook, ReserveBook, GiveBackBook, AdminActivity, ManageAccess, CreateAccount, Modify Account, DeliverBook, FixBook, ConsultBorrowerAccount}. Table 1 shows the rules specified for the *borrower* role. *day(HD)*, *day(WD)*, and *day(MD)* denote holiday, working day, and maintenance day, respectively. *day(HD)* can also be interpreted as *day(d) ∧ d=HD*, where *d* is a variable. According to rule 1, a borrower is not allowed to give back books on holidays. According to rule 3, a borrower is allowed to borrow books on working days.

In a role hierarchy, each role inherits all rules from its super roles. According to this semantics, we can flatten a role hierarchy. For each primitive role $r \in R$, the set of all defined access control rules with respect to r, denoted by $\wp(r)$, includes and only includes the access control rules defined for role r and its super roles in $\Re$. If roles are allowed to override the inherited rules, the overriding can also be handled in the flattening process. Therefore, without loss of generality, this paper focuses on the access control rules of primitive roles after the hierarchy is flattened. In LMS, *student*, as a sub-role of *borrower*, inherits all the access control rules in Table 1. Suppose there is no other rule defined with respect to the *student* role in $\Re$. The rules in Table 1 are all the rules defined for *student*, i.e., $\wp(student)$ ={rules 1-6 in Table 1}.

2.2 Characteristics of Access Control Rules

In the following, we formalize several characteristics required of a good access control policy. They provide a basis for building sound test models.

Definition 2 (Consistency). A set of access control rules $\wp$ is said to be consistent if, for any $r \in R$, there do not exist conflicting rules in $\wp(r)$. Two rules for the same role, object, and activity, $<r, o, a, c_1, \tau_1>$ and $<r, o, a, c_2, \tau_2>$, are said to conflict with each other if $\tau_1 \neq \tau_2$ (one of τ_1 and τ_2 is *Permission* and the other is *Prohibition*) and $c_1 \wedge c_2$ is satisfiable (may evaluate to true).

For example, *<student, book, borrow, day(WD), Permission>* and *<student, book, borrow, true, Prohibition >*are inconsistent. The former implies that student is allowed to borrow books on working days. The latter says that student is prohibited from borrowing books on any day.

Definition 3 (Non-redundancy). A set of access control rules $\wp$ is said to be non-redundant if there do not exist two rules for the same role, object, and activity such that one rule's context subsumes the other rule's context. Formally, there do not exist two rules $<r, o, a, c_1, \tau>$and $<r, o, a, c_2, \tau>$ in $\wp(r)$ such that $c_1 \rightarrow c_2$. (c_1 implies c_2)

For example, *{<student, book, borrow, true, Permission>, <student, book, borrow, day(WD), Permission>}* is redundant because the first rule subsumes the second one.

Definition 4 (Completeness). A set of access control rules $\wp$ is said to be complete if and only if $\wp$ provides an authorization definition for any role, object, activity, and context. Formally, for any $r \in R$, $o \in O$, $a \in A$, $\wp(r)$ must contain one or more rules, say $<r, o, a, c_1, \tau_1>,..., <r, o, a, c_k, \tau_k>(k \geq 1)$, such that $c_1 \vee ... \vee c_k$=*true* (tautology).

Consider rules 2 and 3 in Table 1. They are the only rules related to activity *BorrowBook* for *student*. Their contexts are *day(HD)* and *day(WD)*. They do not cover maintenance days (*MD*). *day(HD) ∨ day(WD)* is not tautology. In other words, *¬day(HD) ∧ ¬day(WD)* is satisfiable: *¬day(HD) ∧ ¬day(WD) = day(MD)*. Thus, the rules in Table 1 are incomplete.

Consistency, non-redundancy, and completeness can be checked automatically. Dealing with inconsistent and redundant specifications is beyond the scope of this paper. In the following, we discuss how to deal with incomplete rules.

2.3 Dealing with Incomplete Rules

Given a set of access control rules $\wp$, we obtain a complete set of access control rules $\wp'$ as follows.

- We extend the authorization types from *{Permission, Prohibition}* to *{Permission, Prohibition, Undefined}*. "*Undefined*" means that authorization is not defined for the given role, activity, object, and context. We also initialize $\wp'$ as $\wp$.

- For each $r \in R$, $o \in O$, $a \in A$, if there is no such rule $<r, o, a, c, \tau> \in \wp(r)$, then we add rule $<r, o, a, true, Undefined>$ to $\wp'(r)$

- For each $r \in R$, $o \in O$, $a \in A$, if $\wp(r)$ contains k ($k \geq 1$) consistent rule(s), $<r, o, a, c_1, \tau_1>,..., <r, o, a, c_k, \tau_k>$, such that $c_1 \vee ... \vee c_k$ is not tautology or $\neg c_1 \wedge ... \wedge \neg c_k$ is satisfiable, we add rule $<r, o, a, \neg c_1 \wedge ... \wedge \neg c_k, Undefined>$ to $\wp'(r)$

We can prove that the addition of these new rules does not cause inconsistency or redundancy if $\wp$ is consistent and non-redundant. In LMS, because borrowing books on a maintenance day is not defined, we add rule *<student, Book, BorrowBook, day(MD), Undefined>* to $\wp'(student)$. This is similar for *ReserveBook* and *GiveBackBook*. Therefore, we have rules 7-9 in Table 2. Consider *FixBook* for *student*. $\wp(student)$ does not contain any rule for *FixBook* under any context. So we add rule *<student, Book, FixBook, day(d), Undefined>* to $\wp'(Student)$. Here *day(d)* is true for any $d \in \{HD, WD, MD\}$. This is similar for *DeliverBook*. Therefore we have rules 10-11 in Table 2. Here we apply all activities to each role. It may require a large number of access control rules to complete the specification. To deal with complex models, our approach allows tests to be generated with respect to various coverage criteria and can reduce the search space by using partial ordering and pairwise combination techniques. This will be discussed in Section 4.1.

Table 2. Access control rules added to $\wp'(student)$

No	Object	Activity	Context	Auth_Type
7	Book	BorrowBook	day(MD)	Undefined
8	Book	ReserveBook	day(MD)	Undefined
9	Book	GiveBackBook	day(MD)	Undefined
10	Book	FixBook	day(d)	Undefined
11	Book	DeliverBook	day(d)	Undefined

According to the security design principle "secure by default", a secure system should prohibit the activity from being performed under an unspecified context. If this security principle is followed, the effect of an activity under an unspecified context is similar to prohibition. This paper takes a more general approach - we differentiate the undefined contexts from prohibition contexts so that test models can be independent of implementation choices. In LMS and ASMS, for example, prohibition due to a prohibition context and prohibition due to an undefined context have different effects. The attempt of an activity under an undefined context will lead to an exception of *UndefinedSecuritPolicyException*, whereas the attempt of a prohibited activity will result in *SecuritPolicyViolationException*.

3. Construction and Analysis of Test Models

In this section, we first give an introduction to the PrT nets used in this work. Then, we describe how to integrate access control rules and contracts into PrT nets. We also discuss how test models can be analyzed through simulation and verification.

3.1 PrT Nets

The PrT nets in this paper, as in the previous work [5][8], are a lightweight version of the original PrT nets [4]. They have both operational and declarative semantics. The operational semantics refers to removal and addition of tokens when transitions are fired. The declarative semantics interprets each transition as a first-order logic formula and transition firing as logical inference. The declarative semantics ensures the correctness of transforming declarative access control rules and contracts (preconditions and post-conditions in first-order logic) into a PrT net. The operational semantics provides a basis for the generation of test sequences (firing sequences) from PrT nets.

A PrT net consists of places (data and conditions), transitions (activities), normal and bidirectional arcs between places and transitions (input and output conditions of activities), inhibitor arcs from places to transitions (negative input conditions), and initial markings (states). A transition can be associated with a guard condition. An arc can be labeled by a list of arguments (constants and variables). If an arc is not labeled, the default label is the zero-argument tuple <>. In Figure 1, *available*, *day*, and *borrowed* are places (circles); *BorrowBook* and *GiveBackBook* are transitions (rectangles). The guard condition of *BorrowBook* is *d=WD*. An arrow (e.g., from *available* to *BorrowBook*) represents a normal arc. A bi-directional arc (arc without arrow) between *n1* and *n2* represents two arcs: one from *n1* to *n2* and the other from *n2* to *n1*. A marking is a set of tokens in all places. A token in *p* is a tuple of constants $<X1, ..., Xn>$, also denoted as $p(X1, ..., Xn)$. The zero-argument tuple is denoted as <>. For token <> in *p*, we also denote it as *p*. We associate a transition with a list of variables as formal parameters, if any. Multiple initial states can be associated with the same net for generating multiple test suites.

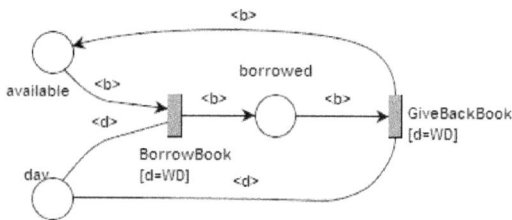

Figure 1. A simple net

Place *p* is called an input (or output) place of transition *t* if there is a normal or bi-directional arc from *p* to *t* (or from *t* to *p*). *p* is called an inhibitor place if there is an inhibitor arc between *p* and *t*. Let *x/V* be a variable binding (variable *x* is bound to value *V*). A substitution is a set of variable bindings. For example, {*b/B1*, *d/WD*} is a substitution where *b* and *d* are bound to *B1* and *WD*, respectively. Let θ be a substitution and *l* be an arc label. l/θ denotes the tuple (or token) obtained by substituting each variable in *l* for its bound value in θ. For instance, if *l* = $<b>$ and θ = {*b/B1*, *d/WD*}, then l/θ = $<B1>$.

Transition *t* is enabled by substitution θ under a marking if the following conditions are satisfied:

- Each input place *p* has a token that matches l/θ, where *l* is the label of the input arc from *p* to *t*;

- Each inhibitor place *p* has no token that matches l/θ, where *l* is the label of the inhibitor arc between *p* and *t*;

- The guard condition evaluates to true according to θ.

Suppose {*available(B1)*, *day(WD)*, *day(MD)*} is an initial marking for the net in Figure 1. A simple net *BorrowBook* is enabled by θ ={*b/B1*, *d/WD*} because token $<B1>$ in the input place *book* matches $<b>/\theta$, token $<WD>$ in the input place *day* matches $<d>/\theta$, and the guard *d=WD* is true according to θ. Only enabled transitions can be fired.

Firing an enabled transition *t* with substitution θ under marking M_0^k removes the matching token from each input place and adds new token l/θ to each output place, where *l* is the label of the arc from *t* to the output place. This leads to new marking M_1^k.

We denote a firing sequence as $M_0^k [t_1\theta_1> M_1^k ... [t_n\theta_n> M_n^k$, where $t_i(1 \leq i \leq n)$ is a transition, $\theta_i(1 \leq i \leq n)$ is the substitution for firing t_i, and $M_i^k (1 \leq i \leq n)$ is the marking after t_i fires, respectively.

A marking *M* is said to be reachable from M_0^k if there is such a firing sequence that transforms M_0^k to *M*.

The PrT nets can be interpreted in terms of logic formulas and inference. Given a net, each input (output) place *p*, together with the associated arc label $<x_1, ...x_n>$ is corresponding to an input (output) predicate $p(x_1, ...x_n)$; each inhibitor place *p*, together with the associated arc label $<x_1, ...x_n>$, is corresponding to a negative predicate $\neg p(x_1, ...x_n)$ (called inhibitor predicate). Each transition can be captured by logic formula $P \rightarrow Q$, where precondition *P* is the conjunction of the inhibitor predicates, input predicates, and guard condition, and post-condition *Q* is the conjunction of the output predicates and negation of each input predicate. *P* and *Q* are universally quantified. For *BorrowBook* in Figure 1, *P*= *available (b)* ∧ *day(d)* ∧*d=WD* and *Q*=¬*available(b)*∧ *borrowed(b)*∧*day(d)*. This lays a theoretical foundation for the transformation of access control rules and contracts.

3.2 Construction of Test Models

Contracts are in the form of *precondition* → *post-condition*. Suppose *available(b)* means book *x* is available and *borrowed(b)* means book *b* is borrowed. The contract of *GiveBackBook(b)* is for *any b*, *borrowed(b)* → *available(b)*. An activity can be associated with multiple contracts, representing different situations. A general precondition in the disjunctive form $P_1 \lor ... \lor P_n$ can be represented by multiple contracts $P_1 \rightarrow Q_1...,$ $P_n \rightarrow Q_n$. For example, the contract of *BorrowBook(b)* is for any *b*, *available(b)* → *borrowed(b)*∧ ¬*available(b)* or for any *b*, *reserved(b)* → *borrowed(b)*∧ ¬*reserved(b)*, where *reserved(b)* means book *b* is reserved. In this paper, the preconditions and post-conditions are not necessarily accurate specifications of activity's semantics. They may represent ordering constraints for testing the activities involved in access control rules.

The process for transforming access control rules together with the contracts of relevant activities is as follows. First, we partition the complete rule set $\wp'$ into a number of subsets in terms of roles and relevant activities so that a PrT net will be constructed for each subset. In LMS, *student* and *teacher* are independent roles although they have similar activities. So we group the access control rules for *student* and *teacher* into different subsets. Second, each subset together with the contracts of the relevant activities is integrated into a PrT net. This is done by converting each rule and the contract of the corresponding activity into a net and composing the nets of all rules into a single net. Third, we define test data and system settings as initial markings of the PrT net so that it can be analyzed for correctness and then used for test generation.

Suppose the access control rules with respect to activity $a \in A$ are $\langle r, o, a, c_1, \tau_1 \rangle, \langle r, o, a, c_2, \tau_2 \rangle, ..., \langle r, o, a, c_m, \tau_m \rangle$ and $p_1(x_1) \wedge ... \wedge p_n(x_n) \rightarrow q_1(y_1) \wedge ... \wedge q_k(y_k) \wedge \neg p_1(x_1)...$ is a contract of activity a. Here $m>0$ because $\wp'(r)$ is a complete set of access control rules. We handle each rule $\langle r, o, a, c_i = r_1 \wedge ... \wedge r_u, \tau_i \rangle$ $(1 \le i \le m)$ as follows:

- If $\tau_i = Permission$, we first convert the contract into a net with one transition named after activity a. Generally, predicates $p_1(x_1),... , p_n(x_n)$ in the precondition are corresponding to the input places of the transition if they are not built-in functions such as arithmetic and relational operations (e.g., $z=x+y$ and $x>y$). Built-in predicates are transformed into part of the transition's guard condition. Predicates $q_1(y_1),...,q_k(y_k)$ in the post-condition are corresponding to the output places of the transition. The input/output arcs are labeled by the arguments of the corresponding predicates. The input arc for p_j is bi-directional if its negation $\neg p_j$ does not appear in the post-condition. As the context in an access control rule is an additional precondition of the activity in the rule, the predicates $r_1,...,r_u$ in the context lead to additional input places for the transition. The arc labels depend on the corresponding arguments. If $r_i(z_i)$ does not have negation and z_i is a variable, then the arc label is $\langle z_i \rangle$. If $r_i(Z_i)$ does not have negation and Z_i is a constant, then the arc label is $\langle z_i \rangle$, and $z_i = Z_i$ is added to the guard condition of the transition[2]. If $r_i(Z_i)$ is a negative predicate and Z_i is a constant, then the arc label is $\langle z_i \rangle$, and $z_i \neq Z_i$ is added to the guard condition of the transition. The arcs are bi-directional unless the activity negates the context. Figure 2 shows the net, where the arc between p_1 and a is directed because $p_1(x_1)$ is negated in the post-condition; the arc between p_n and a is bi-directional as we assume that $\neg p_n(x_n)$ does not appear in the post-condition.

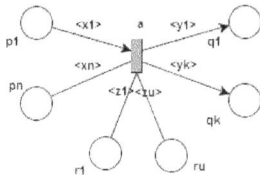

Figure 2. PrT net for a permission rule

- If $\tau_i = Prohibition$, we convert the precondition of the contract into a net with one transition named Pa ("P"

---

[2] $r_i(Z_i)$ is equivalent to $r_i(z_i) \wedge z_i = Z_i$. Alternatively, $\langle Z_i \rangle$ can be used directly as the arc label, with no change to the guard condition.

denotes "prohibition"). The post-condition of the contract is not used because the activity is prohibited. The predicates in the precondition are corresponding to input places and the arcs are labeled by the corresponding arguments. The arcs are all bidirectional because, when the prohibited activity is attempted under the specified context, it should not change the system's state. The context is handled in the same way as $\tau_i = Prohibition$. Figure 3 shows the net.

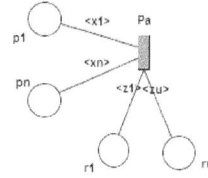

Figure 3. PrT net for a prohibition rule

- If $\tau_i = Undefined$, the transformation is similar to that for $\tau_i = Prohibition$. The only difference is that the transition is named as Ua ("U" denotes "$Undefined$").

Consider rules 2, 3, and 7 in Tables 1 and 2. For contract $available(b) \rightarrow borrowed(b) \wedge \neg available(b)$ of *BorrowBook*, we transform rule 2, together with the contract, into transition *BorrowBook*, as shown in Figure 4(A). Its input places are *available* (resulted from the precondition) and *day* (resulted from the context in rule 2), its output places are *borrowed* (resulted from the post-condition) and *day* (resulted from the context in rule 2), and its guard condition is $d=WD$ (resulted from the context in rule 2). Then we transform rule 3, together with the precondition of the contract, into transition *PBorrowBook*. Its input and output places are *available* (resulted from the precondition) and *day* (resulted from the context in rule 3) and its guard condition is $d=HD$. Likewise, we transform rule 7 into transition *UBorrowBook*.

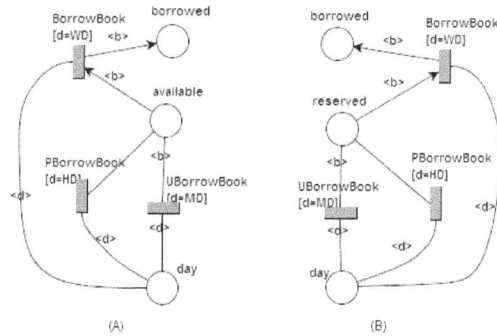

Figure 4. Composition of nets

Similarly, $reserved(b) \rightarrow borrowed(b) \wedge \neg reserved(b)$, with rules 2, 3, and 7, can be transformed into the net in Figure 4 (B). It is the same as (A) except that *available* is replaced by *reserved*. We compose multiple nets into one net through place fusion - places with the same name in different nets become one place in the composed net. However, transitions with the same name in different nets become different transitions in the composed net (each of them is assigned a unique internal identity). In Figure 4 (A) and (B) share places *borrowed* and *day* after they are composed. The resultant net can further be composed with the nets obtained from other access control rules and contracts. Figure 5 shows the net that covers all the rules in Tables 1 and 2. For clarity, an annotation is used to specify *day* as a global predicate, meaning that there is a bidirectional arc between *day* and each transition

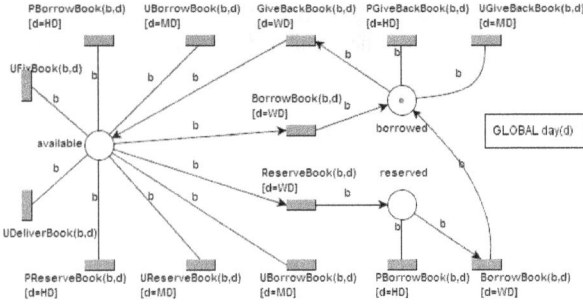

Figure 5. Access control model of the student role

According to the semantics of the PrT nets, we can prove that the above transformations have preserved the semantics of contracts and access control rules. For the sake of simplicity, the above discussion focuses on rules for individual roles. We can build a test model that involves multiple roles. The transformation of access control rules into a net essentially depends on the given subset of access control rules and the contracts of involved activities. If the given rules involve different roles, then the net captures the behaviors of different roles. In this case, we enhance the net with a new place, named *role*, new arcs from place *role* to each transition labeled with $<r>$, and additional guard condition for each transition (e.g., *r=Student*). In essence, this is to use *role(r)* as an additional precondition for each activity. In ASMS, for example, the complete auction process involves various activities (e.g., creation of a sale, change of the state of a sale for auction, comments and bids by buyers) performed by different roles (e.g., *seller*, *admin*, and *buyer*). We can build the test models based on the auction process, rather than individual roles.

3.3 Analysis of Test Models

After the structure of a PrT net is constructed, we define its initial markings by specifying test data (e.g., actual arguments of the activities) and test configurations (e.g., system settings and contexts in the access control rules). Consider the net in Figure 5. Let $M_0=\{m_0\}$, where $m_0=\{available(B1),\ day\ (WD),\ day(HD),\ day(MD)\}$. The net and M_0 form a test model for the *student* role. In m_0, test data *available(B1)* can reach the activities of *BorrowBook*, *ReserveBook* and *GivebackBook*. *day(WD)*, *day(HD)*, and *day(MD)* represent all possible contexts in the rules so that the test model can cover all the contexts.

Our approach provides three techniques for analyzing and debugging the specifications of test models – verification of transition reachability, verification of state reachability, and model simulation. In a test model, each transition is corresponding to an access control rule under a certain condition of the involved activity. Thus, all transitions should be reachable from some initial state. If there is one transition that is unreachable from the given initial states, then the transition will not be covered by any tests to be generated from the specified test model. In this case, either the net or the initial states is specified incorrectly. Suppose $M_0=\{m_1\}$, where $m_1=\{available(B1),\ day(WD),\ day(MD)\}$. *UBorrowBook* is not reachable from m_1 in the net in Figure 5. In this case, M_0 is not specified properly.

If a goal state is known to be reachable (or unreachable), but the verification reports that it is unreachable (or reachable), then the net or the initial states is specified incorrectly. For example,

$\{reserved(B1)\}$ is a state reachable from $m_0=\{available(B1),\ day(WD),\ day(MD),\ day(HD)\}$. It can be reached by transition firings *ReserveBook(b/B1, d/WD)*. However, if the arc from transition *ReserveBook* to place *reserved* is missing, the verification would report that the above state is not reachable.

Our approach also provides an animator for stepwise simulation of test models. At each state, the animator shows the number of tokens in each place and highlights the enabled transitions. The user can choose to manually fire one enabled transition at a time or continuously fire randomly selected enabled transitions. This can help find out whether the expected behaviors are specified correctly in a test model. Suppose $M_0=\{m_1\}$, where $m_1=\{available(B1),\ day(WD),\ day(MD),\ day(HD)\}$ for the net in Figure 5. We choose to fire *BorrowBook(b/B1, d/WD)* under m_1, which results in $=\{borrowed(B1),\ day(WD),\ day(MD),\ day(HD)\}$. At this state, the animator should highlight three enabled transitions: *GiveBackBook*, *PGiveBackBook*, and *UGiveBackBook*. If any one of them is not highlighted, we can check if the transition's associated arcs are described correctly.

4. Generation of Access Control Tests

In this section, we first describe how MISTA generates model-level access control tests from a test model. Then we discuss how to create a MIM specification so that executable test code can be generated.

4.1 From Transition Firings to Access Control Tests

Definition 5 (Model-level access control test). Given an access control test model represented by a PrT net, a test case is a firing sequence $< M_0^k\ [t_1\theta_1> M_1^k,\ ...,\ [t_n\theta_n> M_n^k >$ in the PrT net, where

- M_0^k is the initial setting of the test,

- Transition firings $t_1\theta_1,...,t_n\theta_n$ are ***test inputs***, i.e., calls to the activities in access control rules. Suppose transition t_i is corresponding to activity $a(x_1,...,x_m)$ and substitution $\theta_i=\{x_1/u_1,\ ...,\ x_m/u_m\}$. Then $t_i\theta_i$ $(1\leq i\leq n)$ represents component call $a(u_1,...,u_m)$, where u_j $(1\leq j\leq m)$ is x_j' actual argument.

- $M_1^k,...,M_n^k$ are ***test oracles*** for respective test inputs $t_i\theta_i$ $(1\leq i\leq n)$. For each place $p\in P$ and each token $<v_1,...,v_m>\in M_i^k(p)$, proposition $p(v_1,...,v_m)$, when used as an ***oracle value***, is expected to evaluate to true in the SUT.

For example, m_0, *Reserve(b/B1, d/WD)*, m_1, *Borrow (b/B1, d/WD)*, m_2, *UGiveBackBook(b/B1, d/HD)*, m_3 is a firing sequence in the test model in Figure 5. Access control model of the student role where $M_0=\{m_0\}$ and $m_0=\{available(B1),\ day(WD),\ day(HD),\ day(MD)\}$. Thus:

$m_1=\{reserved(B1),\ day(WD),\ day(HD),\ day(MD)\}$,

$m_2=\{borrowed(B1),\ day(WD),\ day(HD),\ day(MD)\}$

$m_3=\{borrowed(B1),\ day(WD),\ day(HD),\ day(MD)\}$

The firing sequence is a test case that exercises three access control rules: reserve books on working days (permitted), borrow books on working days (permitted), and give back books on holidays (prohibited). The states of book *B1*, *reserved(B1)*, *borrowed(B1)*, and *borrowed(B1)*, represent the expected results of these activities. We assume that a prohibited activity, such as *PGiveBackBook(b/B1, day/HD)*, should not change the system state. Here *day(WD), day(HD), day(MD)* are not used as test oracles because they represent different system settings for access control contexts.

Therefore, test generation from a test model in our approach is to produce firing sequences from the test model according to a certain strategy (e.g., to achieve a coverage criterion). MISTA supports automated test generation for several coverage criteria, such as reachability tree coverage, state coverage, and transition coverage. In an access control test model, a transition is corresponding to one access control rule. A test suite is said to meet transition coverage if each transition is covered by at least one test. A test suite is said to meet state coverage if each state is covered by at least one test. A test suite is said to meet reachability tree coverage if each edge in the reachability graph (i.e., each transition firing under each reachable marking) is covered by at least one test. Reachability tree coverage subsumes transition coverage and state coverage because the reachability tree includes each reachable transition and each reachable state. The case studies in this paper use the reachability tree coverage.

In MISTA, test cases are structured as a test tree, where each path from an initial marking to a leaf is corresponding to a firing sequence (i.e., test case). Figure 6 shows portion of the test tree generated for the reachability tree coverage of the test model in Figure 5. Node "*1 new*" represents the initial marking, i.e., the initial setting of each test. The path *1→1.1→1.1.2* exercises two access control rules. It first borrows book *B1* on a working day, which should be permitted, and attempts to return the book on a holiday, which should be prohibited.

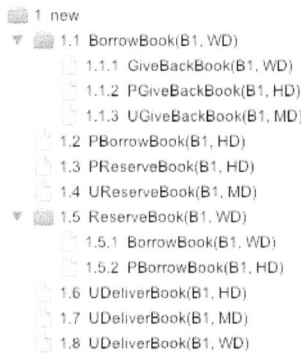

```
    1 new
    ▼    1.1 BorrowBook(B1, WD)
             1.1.1  GiveBackBook(B1, WD)
             1.1.2  PGiveBackBook(B1, HD)
             1.1.3  UGiveBackBook(B1, MD)
         1.2 PBorrowBook(B1, HD)
         1.3 PReserveBook(B1, HD)
         1.4 UReserveBook(B1, MD)
    ▼    1.5 ReserveBook(B1, WD)
             1.5.1  BorrowBook(B1, WD)
             1.5.2  PBorrowBook(B1, HD)
         1.6 UDeliverBook(B1, HD)
         1.7 UDeliverBook(B1, MD)
         1.8 UDeliverBook(B1, WD)
```

Figure 6. Portion of a test tree

In order to represent tests generated from multiple initial markings that represent different sets of test data and system settings, the test tree uses an invisible root node whose child nodes are corresponding to the initial markings. The test tree for reachability tree coverage is constructed as follows. The nodes of initial markings are put into a stack (if depth-first search is used) or queue (if breadth-first search is used) for expansion. When a node is expanded, all possible transition firings (including all substitutions for each transition) under the current marking are computed and a child node is created for each possible firing. The child node will also be expanded if the new marking has not expanded before. Due to the combinatorial nature of transition firings, the test tree for a complex model may have a large number of tests. MISTA provides two effective techniques for reducing the number of tests: partial ordering and pairwise combination. The total ordering of n $(n>1)$ independent or concurrent transition firings yield $n!$ sequences, where the partial ordering only

produces one sequence. When there are more than two inputs, the pairwise technique covers all pairs of inputs, rather than all combinations of inputs. Suppose each of 10 input variables has 10 values. There are 10^{10} combinations of these variables. In MISTA, however, 120 combinations can cover all pairs of the variables.

4.2 Building MIM Specification for Test Code Generation

The model-level tests in *Definition 5* are not executable because they are generated solely from a given test model, which can be independent of the SUT. The test model of *student* does not specify how *BorrowBook* can be performed against the SUT. In our approach, a MIM specification for a test model can be created so that all model-level tests can be converted into test code automatically. A MIM specification maps the elements in a test model into corresponding constructs in the SUT. It consists of the following main components: object function f_o, method function f_c, accessor function f_o, mutator function f_m, a list of setting predicates l_s, and helper code function f_h. Table 3 presents an example of these components in LMS.

Object function f_o maps objects in the test model to objects in the SUT. In LMS, book *B1* in the test model of *student* is corresponding to a named constant, referring to a book titled "Software Security". Method function f_c maps activities in the test model to test operations in the SUT. For example, the implementation of *BorrowBook* is a method *doPermittedBorrow*. Accessor function f_a maps predicates in the test model to accessors in the SUT. It is used for verifying oracle values. For example, book *b* is borrowed on day *d* in a test case, i.e., *borrowed(b, d)*, can be verified by method *isBookBorrowed(b)*. Mutator function f_a maps the system setting predicates in l_s to operations in SUT so that the SUT can be configured to a specific state. For example, predicate *day* in LMS is a system setting. As an access control precondition, it must be set correctly because the individual activities can be called. Setting LMS to a working day, i.e., making *day(WD)* true, can be done by the following statement: *ContextManager.currentContext=Context Manager. workingday;* Helper code function f_h includes header code (e.g., package and import statements in Java), constant and variable declarations, setup, teardown, and methods for testing individual activities. All of this code will be included in the test code. The methods for testing individual activities depend on how the SUT is implemented, e.g., what types of security exceptions will be reported. In the case studies, the exceptions for prohibited activities and undefined activities are *SecuritPolicyViolationException* and *UndefinedSecuritPolicyException*, respectively. Thus, a test for a permitted activity fails if the SUT throws an exception of *SecuritPolicyViolationException* or *UndefinedSecurit PolicyException*. A test for a prohibited activity fails if no exception is thrown or the thrown exception is not *SecuritPolicyViolationException*. A test for an undefined activity fails if no exception is thrown or the thrown exception is not *UndefinedSecuritPolicyException*.

Table 3. Sample MIM specification

MIM	Model element	Implement ation element	Notes
f_o	B1	Book1Title	Book1Title is a named constant in the helper code

f_c	BorrowBook(b,d)	doPermitedBorrow(b)	doPermittedBorrow is a test method in the helper code. It fails if an exception is thrown.
f_o	borrowed(b,d)	isBookBorrowed(b)	isBookBorrowed is a query method for verifying whether the status of the book is borrowed by the borrower
f_m	day(WD)	ContextManager.current Context = ContextManager.working day;	It sets the concurrent context to working day.
l_s	day		day is a system setting
$f_h(PACKAGE)$	package com.library.test.software.m odeltest;		Helper code for the package statement of Java test code
$f_h(CODE)$	private final String Book1Title = "Software security"; …		Declarations and methods to be included in the test code

Given a complete MID specification (i.e., test model and MIM), the executable test code for all model-level tests can be generated automatically. Each model-level test is corresponding to a test method. For the aforementioned test: m_0, ReserveBook(b/B1, d/WD), m_1, BorrowBook(b/B1, d/WD), m_2, PGiveBackBook(b/B1, d/HD), m_3, the Java test method is as follows:

```
public void test12() throws exception {
    System.out.println("Test 12");
    ContextManager.currentContext=ContextManager.workingday;
    doPermittedReserve(Book1Title);
    assertTrue(isBookReserved(Book1Title));
    ContextManager.currentContext = ContextManager.workingday;
    doPermittedBorrow(Book1Title);
    assertTrue(isBookBorrowed(Book1Title));
    ContextManager.currentContext = ContextManager.holiday;
    doProhibitedGiveBack(Book1Title);
    assertTrue(isBookBorrowed(Book1Title));
}
```

5. EMPIRICAL STUDIES

5.1 Experiment Setup

Our case studies are based on two Java programs, LMS and ASMS [9][10]. Table 4 presents the main parameters, where R is the number of roles, PR is the number of primitive roles, O is the number of objects, A is the number of activities, and RL is the total number of specified rules for the primitive roles. The mutants of the access control rules were created by the MutaX tool[3] using five types of mutation operators [9][10]: replacing permission rule with prohibition, replacing prohibition rule with permission, changing role, changing context, and adding a rule. They were created before this work was initiated. To evaluate the proposed approach, the following mutants were excluded:

- Mutants related to non-implemented activities are not used because the tests could not be performed.

- Mutants with inconsistent access control rules are not used because our approach assumes that the given

access control rules are consistent. These mutants are typically created by the operator that adds new rules..

- Equivalent mutants, which have the same behavior as the original version because of the implementation issues in the original version (e.g., some access control contexts, hard-coded in the implementation, are not affected by mutation of access control rules).

Table 4. Subjects in the empirical studies

	LOC	Classes/Methods	R	PR	O	A	RL
LMS	3,204	62/335	7	5	4	12	33
ASMS	10,703	134/797	8	6	6	23	107

The protocol of our experiment is as follows. First, we specify the contracts of the activities involved in access control rules, and construct and analyze the test models. Second, we create the MIM specification for each test model as described in Section 4. Thus complete MID specifications are obtained for test code generation. Third, we use MISTA to generate test code from the MID specifications. Fourth, we execute the generated test code against the original version such that no test fails (the original version is considered as the correct version). If there is a failure, then the previous steps need to be repeated. Finally, we run the test code against each mutant.

5.2 Results

The results of our experiments are summarized in Table 5, where T is the total number of transitions, P is the total number of places (they reflect the complexity of test models), TC is the number of test cases, LOC is the number of lines of code generated, M is the total number of mutants, K is the number of mutants killed by the test, and FDR is the fault detection rate (i.e., number of mutants killed/total mutants tested also called mutation score).

Table 5. Results of the empirical studies

	Models		Tests		Mutation Analysis		
	T	P	TC	LOC	M	K	FDR
LMS	73	27	207	3,086	243	233	95.9%
ASMS	126	30	179	4,680	914	914	100%

For LMS, 207 test cases in 3,086 lines of non-comment code were generated. They killed 233 out of 243 mutants, with an overall detection rate of 95.9%. The 10 remaining mutants not killed by the tests have the same nature – they contain a new rule created by the adding-rule operator but can never cause security problems because the functional precondition of the activity in the added rule is not satisfiable. These mutants do not violate the required security policies. Consider a mutant with the following added rule that allows the *admin* role to return books on any day: *(admin, Book, GiveBackBook, true, Permission)*. According to the required access control policies, none of the *Borrower*'s activities, *BorrowBook*, *ReserveBook*, and *GiveBackBook*, is intended for use by the *admin* role (no access control rules with respect to these activities are specified for *admin*). The above rule can never enable the *admin* role to return books because the precondition of *GiveBackBook*- "the book is borrowed" (by the same person) - is unsatisfiable. This precondition can only be fulfilled by *BorrowBook*. In the mutant, however, *Admin* is not able to borrow

---

[3]https://sites.google.com/site/servalteam/tools/mutax

books (*BorrowBook* is undefined for *admin*). It is worth pointing out that our approach killed the mutant with the following added rule that allows *admin* to borrow books: *(admin, Book, BorrowBook, true, Permission)*. In ASMS, 179 tests in 4,680 lines of code were generated. They killed all of the 914 mutants.

There are two main reasons for the near-perfect mutation scores in our case studies. First, our approach for dealing with incomplete access control specification makes it possible to reveal all undefined situations. The tests generated to cover these situations are not only necessary but also powerful for revealing potential policy violations in an implementation. Second, the tests generated for the reachability graph coverage can cover all access controls, objects, activities, and contexts. This was feasible thanks to the automation of both test generation and test execution. In comparison, transition coverage (or rule coverage) has a low fault detection capability. As an initial experiment, the application of transition coverage to the *student* role in LMS only killed about 50% of the mutants. The reason was that many objects and contexts were not exercised. Thus, we decided not to continue the empirical evaluation of the transition coverage.

5.3 Threats to Validity

The main result of the case studies is that our approach is highly effective in detecting violations of access control rules. The key aspects that have led to this result include the access control model, the formalization of contracts, generation of access control tests with the reachability tree coverage, generation of executable test code, and mutation analysis of access control rules. In the following, we discuss how these aspects can be affected when our approach is applied to real-world software where access control is an important security mechanism.

First, our approach focuses on testing of access control rules. It does not cover every aspect of RBAC, such as role assignment and session management. Second, due to the small sizes of the subject programs, we were able to generate tests to cover all rules and combinations of objects, resources, and contexts. Generation of such comprehensive tests may not be feasible for complex or large-scale software systems where access control is involved in very large state space. In order to deal with such systems, testers may try to divide the system to several small components/modules and apply our approach to each one in an independent way. This will reduce the complexity and the testing effort. Since our technique was not applied to such systems, we cannot evaluate the effectiveness of this strategy. Third, we were able to generate executable test code by completing the MIM specifications of the test models. In the MIM specifications, invocations to individual activities and verification of test oracles are programmed. For real-world software, the individual activity tests and the test oracles may not be completely programmable. Fourth, although our approach is applicable to a variety of languages and applications (Java, C, C++, C#, VB, HTML/Selenium IDE) supported by MISTA, the subject programs were limited to Java applications. Finally, the evaluation of fault detection capability is based on the mutation analysis of access control rules. Although the mutants were created by five different operators, they do not necessarily represent all possible access control flaws in real-world software.

6. RELATED WORK

Software security testing involves two different perspectives - testing of security policies and performing security attacks (penetration testing) to identify vulnerabilities. This paper focuses on policy testing.

In recent years, Le Traon's group have investigated various issues of testing access control policies, such as test criteria of access control policies [9], test generation from access control models [10], mutation analysis of access control policies [12], and selection and transformation of functional tests for policy testing [13]. In the above work, test generation was not automated. Pretschner, in collaboration with Le Traon's group, has proposed a model-based approach [14], where the access control model consists of a role hierarchy, a permission hierarchy, and a context hierarchy. They use a combinatorial testing technique to derive test targets, i.e., combinations of roles, permissions, and contexts. Each test target is relevant to one access control rule. In comparison, this paper focuses on automatic test code generation from models that capture the interactions of access control rules. A test is usually a sequence of access control requests for exercising multiple access control rules.

Masood et al. [15][16] have investigated a state-based approach to test generation for RBAC policies. They first construct a finite state machine (FSM) of the RBAC policy and then derive tests from the FSM. This model essentially captures the behaviors of role assignment, rather than access control rules. Different from FSMs, PrT nets can capture both control flows and data flows (e.g., test data and contexts). Based on the Assurance Management Framework (AMF), Hu and Ahn have proposed an approach to the generation of conformance tests of access control policies through constraint verification [17]. Test cases are derived through verification by either removing or negating the security constraints. Our approach focuses on test generation with respect to coverage criteria and transformation of model-level tests into executable code. Mallouli et al. proposed a model-based approach for integrating OrBAC (Organizational Based Access Control) rules into an initial functional model represented by an extended finite state machine [18]. Test sequences generated from the integrated model will be able to exercise the OrBAC rules. Different from this approach, we do not assume the availability of the full functional model. We integrate the access control rules with the contracts of the activities involved in the given rules. This integration can handle incomplete specification of access control rules. Jürjens has developed an approach for testing security-critical systems based on UMLsec models [19]. Test sequences for access control properties are generated from UMLsec models to test the implementation for vulnerabilities. Li et al. proposed an approach to test generation from security policies specified as OrBAC rules [20]. It focuses on generation of test purposes from individual OrBAC rules. In comparison to these two approaches, our work integrates access control rules into an operational model and generates tests to cover different access control rules. Julliand et al. have proposed an approach to generating security tests in addition to functional tests by re-using the functional test model together with a new model of security properties defined by a security engineer [21]. The security properties describe tortuous situations that could violate security policies. They did not use an explicit access control model. Different from this work, our approach not only provides a process for building the model of access control rules, but also generates tests to exercise all access control rules and contexts. Generally, the above model-based approaches focus on generating model-level tests, not executable tests. Our approach can produce executable test code by using a flexible mechanism that maps modeling elements into implementation constructs.

Martin et al. have investigated techniques for test generation from access control policy specifications written in XACML [22][23]. They have defined policy coverage criteria and developed a mutation-testing framework for XACML policies. To generate tests from policy specifications, they synthesize inputs to a change-impact analysis tool. Different from this work, our approach does not focus specifically on XACML and targets both PDP (policy decision point, where access control decisions are made) and the enforcement mechanisms inside the system.

7. CONCLUSIONS

We have presented a new model-based approach for automated testing of access control policies. It provides a tool-supported process for building access control test models from contracts and access control rules. Access control tests can then be generated and converted into executable code based on a MIM specification that maps the modeling elements into implementation constructs. By using mutation analysis of access control implementation, our empirical studies have demonstrated that our approach is highly effective in detecting violations of access control policies.

In the case studies, tests were generated using the reachability tree coverage, which subsumes both transition coverage and state coverage. In addition, this paper has focused on access control rules, which define role and permission authorization. When a role is involved in a test case, a subject is created and assigned to that role. Our future work will deal with other RBAC features, such as role assignment and session management.

8. ACKNOWLEDGMENTS

This work was supported in part by NSF under grants CNS 1004843 and CNS1123220.

9. REFERENCES

[1] Pretschner, A., Prenninger, W., Wagner, S., Kühnel, C., Baumgartner, M., Sostawa, B., Zölch, R. and Stauner, T. 2005. One evaluation of model-based testing and its automation. In *Proc. of the 27th International Conf. on Software Engineering (ICSE'05)*, 392-401.

[2] Pretschner, A., Slotosch, O., Aiglstorfer, E. and Kriebel, S. 2004. Model-based testing for real - The inhouse card case study. *J. Software Tools for Technology Transfer* 5(2-3): 140-157.

[3] Zander, J., Schiefewrdecker, I., and Mosterman, P. J. (eds.). 2011. *Model-Based Testing for Embedded Systems*, CRC Press.

[4] Genrich, H.J. 1987. Predicate/transition nets. *Petri Nets: Central Models and Their Properties*, 207–247.

[5] Xu, D. and Nygard, K.E. 2006. Threat-driven modeling and verification of secure software using aspect-oriented Petri nets, *IEEE Trans. on Software Engineering*, vol. 32, no. 4, 265-278.

[6] Xu, D. 2011. A tool for automated test code generation from high-level Petri nets. In *Proc. of Petri Nets'11*, LNCS 6709, 308-317, Newcastle upon Tyne, UK, June 2011.

[7] Meyer, B. 1997. *Object-Oriented Software Construction*, 2nd Edition, Prentice-Hall PTR.

[8] Xu, D., Tu, M., Sanford, M., Thomas, L., Woodraska, D., and Xu, W. 2012. Automated security test generation with formal threat models. *IEEE Trans. on Dependable and Secure Computing*. In press.

[9] Le Traon, Y., Mouelhi, T., Pretschner, A., and Baudry, B. 2008. Test-driven assessment of access control in legacy applications. In *Proc. of the First IEEE International Conference on Software, Testing, Verification and Validation (ICST'08)*, Norway, 238-247.

[10] Mouelhi, T., Fleurey, F., Baudry, B., and Le Traon, Y. 2008. A model-based framework for security policy specification, deployment and testing. In *Proc. of the ACM/IEEE 11th International Conf. on Model Driven Engineering Languages and Systems (MODELS'08)*, Toulouse, France.

[11] Jia, Y. and Harman, M. 2010. An analysis and survey of the development of mutation testing. *IEEE Trans. on Software Engineering*, vol. 37, no. 5, 649-678.

[12] Le Traon, Y., Mouelhi, T., and Baudry, B. 2007. Testing security policies: going beyond functional testing. In *Proc. of the IEEE International Symposium on Software Reliability Engineering (ISSRE'07)*, Sweden.

[13] Mouelhi, T., Le Traon, Y., and Baudry, B. 2009. Transforming and selecting functional test cases for security policy testing. In *Proc. of the Second International Conf. on Software Testing Verification and Validation (ICST'09)*. Denver, USA.

[14] Pretschner, A. Le Traon, Y., and Mouelhi, T. 2008. Model-based tests for access control policies. In *Proc. of the First IEEE International Conference on Software, Testing, Verification and Validation (ICST'08)*. Norway.

[15] Masood, A. Bhatti, R., Ghafoor, A., Mathur, A. 2009. Scalable and effective test generation for role-based access control systems. *IEEE Trans. on Software Engineering*, vol. 35, no. 5, 654-668.

[16] Masood, A., Ghafoor, A., Mathur, A. 2010. Conformance testing of temporal role-based access control systems. *IEEE Trans. on Dependable and Secure Computing*, vol. 7, no. 2, 144-158.

[17] Hu, H. and Ahn, G. 2008. Enabling verification and conformance testing for access control model. In *Proc. of the 13th ACM Symposium on Access Control Models and Technologies (SACMAT'08)*, 195–204.

[18] Mallouli, W., Orset, J.M., Cavalli, A., Cuppens, N., Cuppens, F. 2007. A formal approach for testing security rules. In *Proc. of the 12th ACM Symposium on Access Control Models and Technologies (SACMAT'07)*, 127-132.

[19] J. Jürjens, 2008. Model-based security testing using UMLsec. *Electronic Notes in Theoretical Computer Science (ENTCS)*, 220(1): 93-104.

[20] Li, K., Mounier, L., Groz, R. 2007. Test generation from security policies specified in Or-BAC. In *Proc. of the 31st Computer Software and Applications Conference (COMPSAC'07)*, 255-260.

[21] Julliand, J., Masson, P.A., Tissot, R. 2008. Generating security tests in addition to functional tests. In *Proc. of the Workshop on Automation of Software Test (AST'08)*, 41–44.

[22] Martin, E. and Xie, T. 2006. Defining and measuring policy coverage in testing access control policies. In *Proc. of the 8th International Conference on Information and Communications Security*, 139-158.

[23] Martin, E. and Xie, T. 2007. A fault model and mutation testing of access control policies. In *Proc. of WWW'07*, 667-676.

PlexC: A Policy Language for Exposure Control

Yann Le Gall and Adam J. Lee
Department of Computer Science
University of Pittsburgh
Pittsburgh, PA, USA
{ylegall, adamlee}@cs.pitt.edu

Apu Kapadia
School of Informatics and Computing
Indiana University Bloomington
Bloomington, IN, USA
kapadia@indiana.edu

ABSTRACT

With the widespread use of online social networks and mobile devices, it is not uncommon for people to continuously
broadcast contextual information such as their current location or activity. These technologies present both new opportunities for social engagement and new risks to privacy, and
traditional static 'write once' disclosure policies are not well
suited for controlling aggregate *exposure* risks in the current
technological landscape.

Therefore, we present *PlexC*, a new policy language designed for exposure control. We take advantage of several
recent user studies to identify a set of language requirements
and features, providing the expressive power to accommodate information sharing in dynamic environments. In our
evaluation we show that *PlexC* can concisely express common policy idioms drawn from survey responses, in addition
to more complex information sharing scenarios.

Categories and Subject Descriptors

H.4.0 [**Information Systems Applications**]: General

Keywords

Privacy, Exposure, Policy Languages

1. INTRODUCTION

The popularity of online social networks has contributed
to an unprecedented amount of personal information sharing. Moreover, the widespread use of mobile devices encourages the broadcast of *contextual* information from any location. For example, smart phone users can send their current
location to social networks such as Facebook Places [25],
Google+ [14], and Foursquare [13]. Furthermore, technologies such as CenceMe [19] can infer the current activity (e.g.,
running or dancing) from a smart phone's onboard sensors.
With so many ways to share personal contextual information, the task of protecting individual privacy is becoming
more challenging. One important challenge is to maintain

the utility of information sharing without sacrificing personal privacy. To achieve this equilibrium individuals need
to do more than simply define a static disclosure policy once
and for all. They must be able to specify flexible and adaptive policies that can manage the disclosure of personal information in the face of both typical and atypical access
patterns. We refer to such policies as *exposure-aware*.

Motivation. Over the years, a large body of research literature has explored a variety of access control mechanisms
and their policy language encodings. Existing policy languages have incorporated powerful features to group princi-
pals into functional roles [16, 17, 27], delegate authorization
decisions across security domains [2, 4], and even manage
state changes during policy evaluation [3, 21]. However, few
sharing systems or policy languages have drawn upon large
user studies to inform their design. As a consequence, the resulting languages and systems offer a variety of interesting
features, yet may not provide users with the functionality
needed to address their real-world exposure concerns. By
contrast, we carefully consider findings from several recent
user studies within the exposure space [5, 24, 28] and leverage a variety of findings from these studies to provide insight
into exposure perception and control.

For example, Schlegel et al. highlighted the importance of
exposure feedback through an intuitive interface [28]. Additionally, Patil et al. discovered that certain factors, like the
frequency with which location requests occur, are more important to users than other common factors, like the current
time of the location request [24]. This is quite interesting, as
few existing systems allow for controlling the frequency of requests, while several [18, 26, 30] provide policy constructs for
controlling disclosures based upon the day of week or time
of day. Another important outcome of this study was the
identification of several common concerns and policy idioms
that are not typically associated with social engagement purposes, such as only sharing location during emergencies or
with law enforcement personnel.

Our Contributions. Findings from these recent user
studies reveal several ways to address shortcomings in current information sharing systems and their respective policy languages. To summarize a few, location sharing systems and their disclosure policy languages must be flexible
enough to support users with diverse privacy concerns [5].
Furthermore, it is important to provide unobtrusive, ambi-
ent feedback about how users' data are being shared without necessarily revealing the identity of the requester [28].
Finally, policies should provide the ability to manage disclo-

sure based on more than just common factors, such as the identity of the requester, but more complex policies may not be easily expressed [24]. To address these concerns we propose a new policy language *PlexC* whose functionality is based in large part on the needs voiced by the human subjects who participated in these studies. In doing so we make the following contributions:

1. We survey the recent research literature for human subjects' data regarding contextual information sharing and exposure control. Based on these findings we develop policy language and system requirements necessary for servicing the exposure control needs of users;

2. We develop a general system model for contextual information sharing systems that represents the features of existing logically centralized systems and is capable of modeling more user-centric systems that may appear;

3. We design a novel policy language, *PlexC*, that addresses the limitations identified in recent user studies and specify its syntax and semantics. We further discuss the query resolution procedure used by *PlexC*;

4. To evaluate the utility of *PlexC* we demonstrate that it is both capable of expressing a range of common policy idioms and can encode interesting real-world information sharing constraints specified by the subjects of several survey studies.

Paper outline. We start by defining the exposure problem and by identifying a set of language requirements that are motivated by recent user studies in §2. Next we discuss related work in §3. The syntax of *PlexC* is described in §4. In §5 we evaluate the expressivity of our policy language against real user policies, interpret the findings, and discuss future work in §6. Finally, we conclude in §7.

2. BACKGROUND AND REQUIREMENTS

In this section, we first define the concept of *exposure* and introduce the relevant research challenges. Next we highlight the results of several recent user studies that explore aspects of the exposure-control problem space. We conclude this section by enumerating a set of exposure-control policy language features the need for which is highlighted by these studies and other works in the research literature.

2.1 The exposure problem

Before describing our system model and how it addresses the exposure problem, we first explain what we mean by "exposure". Intuitively, a user's ideal policy for controlling access to their personal data is a moving target that is, at best, approximated by the policies and controls that the user puts in place to protect their information. To paraphrase an example by Schlegel et al. [28], a user may initially set a policy allowing her co-workers to access her location during normal work hours to facilitate in-person meetings. However, if she later finds that her boss is accessing her location every 5 minutes to ensure that she remains in-office, she may become uncomfortable. This disconnect between the employee's model of permissible sharing and the level of sharing allowed by the protections that she put in place leave her more *exposed* to external queries and analysis than she had anticipated.

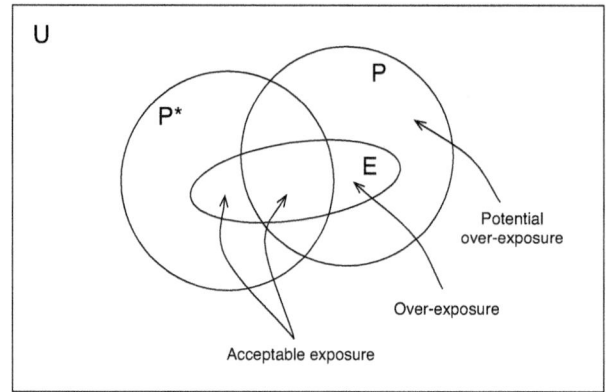

Figure 1: The exposure control problem.

The problem of exposure control is non-trivial, as exposure can be viewed as a function over a multi-dimensional space expressing a human sentiment. Some of these inputs may be unknown a priori as many contextual factors may influence a user's perception of exposure. For example, someone's notion of exposure may be influenced by the time of day, their current location, whom they are with, how many requests they have received, and so on. We propose that trying to control such a complex and dynamic property requires an adaptive process in which disclosure policies are continuously specified, enforced, and revised.

A semi-formal view of the exposure problem is captured in Figure 1. In this depiction U represents the universe of all access traces to a user's personal data. These traces describe sequences of queries to a user's data, which may be dependent on system and user context (location, activity, etc.), as well as other past queries. $P^\star$ represents the user's ideal model of data sharing—which is unlikely to be captured correctly due to the complexities of managing the myriad contextual facets of the exposure control problem—while P represents the access traces permitted by the user's deployed policies. E represents the access traces that have actually been made to the user's data and represents the user's *exposure*. $E \cap P^\star$ represents the user's *acceptable exposure*, whereas $E \cap P \setminus P^\star$ represents the user's *over-exposure*. $P \setminus P^\star \setminus E$ represents the user's *potential over-exposure*.

The complexities of properly capturing $P^\star$ lead us to envision an *exposure control loop* in which a policy is specified and deployed, and feedback on the allowed access traces is periodically provided to the user. This exposure feedback can then be used by the user to revise their policy over time, resulting in a sequence of policies allowing trace sets $P_1, P_2, \ldots, P_n$ that aims to minimize potential over exposure and avoid further over-exposure. In the following sections we describe the design of the *PlexC* system and how it accommodates and encourages the exposure control loop.

2.2 Recent Studies

Our work is grounded in a series of recent user studies relating to exposure control. Here we describe each study in more detail and explain how their findings are relevant to exposure control. The results of these studies contribute to many of the requirements discussed in Section 2.3.

When Privacy and Utility are in Harmony: Towards

Better Design of Presence Technologies. In this study, Biehl et al. explored user sentiment about presence data collection and sharing with an emphasis on workplace settings [5]. Another goal was to explore the utility of receiving various types of presence information. They conducted a survey of 32 participants representing a wide range of ages, professions, and geographic regions across the US.

This study is relevant to exposure control because it measured how comfortable participants felt as a function of many variables, including the type of data collected (e.g., location, activity), the recipient of the data (e.g., boss, coworker, friend), the setting in which the data collection occurred (e.g., office, work event, home), and the format, owner, and location of the data collected. Also, the authors measured how comfort levels changed based on perceived utility for the recipient.

One important finding of this study was that comfort levels across different sensing technologies were bimodal. In other words there is no one-size-fits-all privacy policy that addressed all users' privacy needs. Thus, information sharing systems must be flexible. Another finding was the strong correlation between how comfortable users were with sharing information by granularity and their perceived utility of receiving information from others at that granularity.

Eyeing Your Exposure: Quantifying and Controlling Information Sharing for Improved Privacy. In this study, Schlegel et al. address the problem of location exposure feedback and control in a game-based simulated lab study [28]. They develop and compare two different smart-phone interfaces: (i) a so-called "detailed information interface" that shows the number of requests in the last hour from different categories of people (e.g., friends, family, strangers), and (ii) a so-called "eyes interface" that shows the user a number of cartoon eyes on the main screen of the app in which each eye represents location requests from a single person, and the size of the eye grows depending on the number of requests and the social relationship.

This study is relevant because it quantifies the role of frequency in exposure control and embraces the notion that informative *feedback* is an important part of controlling exposure. However, with too much detail feedback interferes with querier anonymity. Likewise, if feedback is too frequent or obtrusive, then it may annoy the user. The findings of this study suggest that it is possible to benefit from feedback without sacrificing querier anonymity or usability.

My Privacy Policy: Exploring End-User Specification of Free-Form Location Access Rules. In this online study Patil et al. asked over a hundred participants to write location-sharing policy rules using everyday English [24]. In addition participants were asked to rate and rank the importance of a number of factors that might influence location sharing, such as the identity of the recipient, the current location, the frequency of requests, and the like.

The research questions addressed in this work are also very pertinent to the domain of exposure control. The notion of exposure varies across individuals and across many other dimensions. This study measured the preferences of a large sample of individuals and allowed them to freely identify factors that contribute to over-exposure. Furthermore, the ratings and rankings suggest which factors might require more attention than others.

There were a number of interesting findings. Unexpect-edly, participants indicated that the 'time of day' and the 'day of the week' of location requests were less important than the 'frequency of receiving requests'. Furthermore, in general people had difficulty expressing coherent policies that controlled for all of the factors that they rated as being important. Finally, the authors identified several common themes in the free-form policies. Some of these include complete manual mediation of requests, temporary blocking, and sharing only for emergencies.

2.3 Language Requirements

Here we describe a series of language features that are important for the efficient and accurate expression of exposure control policies. These requirements are motivated by past work as well as the recent user studies previously described.

Disclosure Negotiation. In open distributed systems it is impossible to specify the trust relationship between all pairs of individuals a priori. Negotiation allows strangers to build trust by exchanging credentials, information, etc. Negotiation has been identified as an important feature and used in several policy languages [4,12,29]. Negotiation is also important for understanding the reasons for which a request was made, and individuals are more likely to feel comfortable sharing their location if they believe it will be useful to the requester [5]. An example of this type of policy idiom is given below: *Share my city-level location with anonymous requesters, but if the requester is willing to reveal his identity then also share my street-level location.*

Polymorphism. Here we use polymorphism to describe a policy whose requirements change based on the user's degree of over-exposure. Schlegel et al. explore ways of estimating and representing this metric [28]. The following policy illustrates the utility of exposure polymorphism: *Share my exact location with family only when my current over-exposure level is low; Otherwise if my over-exposure is high, only share my city-level location.*

Side Effects. Side effects appear in policy rules and specify transactions that modify the authorization state of the system when the rule is satisfied. Side effects are appropriate in large dynamic systems where maintaining ACLs is inefficient [21]. Furthermore, role-based policy languages typically require updates to the authorization state as users activate roles. However, most modern authorization languages do not explicitly provide constructs to express state changes, so management of state changes must be hard-coded into system resource guards [3]. An example of a policy that would be more easily expressed with side-effects might be: *The first 3 location requests from an individual require my explicit approval, but subsequent requests do not.*

Aggregate Operations. Aggregate operators can provide users with summary information about the set of accesses to their personal information (the region labeled "E" in Figure 1). This often includes operations such as SUM, COUNT, or MAX, over sets and multisets of tuples [20]. Frequency-based policies rely on the ability to aggregate records in the audit log, and Patil et al. showed that individuals believe that the frequency of requests is an important factor to consider [24]. Furthermore, it is demonstrated by Dell'Armi et al. that aggregate operators can increase the modeling power of disjunctive logic programming languages and provide concise knowledge representation [11]. A typical use of this feature would be the use of aggregation to limit the frequency of location disclosures, e.g.: *Do not share my location more than 10 times per day.*

Querier Privacy. "Querier privacy" often refers to anonymous access of resources, but, in general, it is not limited to protecting the identity of the requester. Querier privacy has been identified as an important feature in large online social networks (OSNs), especially those that have been used to organize protests and share sensitive documents [1]. Interestingly, Tsai et al. showed that users of the location-sharing technology *Locyoution* felt more comfortable sharing their location when they were given feedback about who requested their location. The ability to provide users with exposure feedback might seem to be incompatible with querier anonymity, but Schlegel et al. demonstrated intuitive feedback interfaces that accomplish this [28].

Delegation. Delegation allows disclosure decisions to be passed on to a trusted authority. The utility of this feature is apparent in the following policy rule: *Share my location with the same people with whom my friends share their location.* Delegation is an important feature of many authorization languages [2,4,10,12,16,17]. In large decentralized systems preexisting trust relationships often do not exist between authorizer and requester. Thus, delegation allows the authorizer to make decisions based on trusted third parties. Delegation also simplifies policies in hierarchical systems.

Groups and Roles. In role-based access control (RBAC), subjects are assigned to one or more roles (or groups), and permissions are assigned based on their roles, e.g.: *Family members can always see my exact location, but colleagues can view my location only during work hours.* RBAC greatly simplifies permissions management, is well suited for large organizations in the commercial and government sectors [27], and is supported in most modern policy languages [5,24].

Time and Location-based Rules. Time-based rules control disclosure based on the current time. Similarly, location-based rules control disclosure based on the current location of the policy owner or the requester. As an example of a location-based rule, the owner might define a number of 'named regions' as a coordinate pair and a radius, and associate regions with a sharing policy: *Share my location with family only if I am at the hospital.*

Time intervals and named regions are natural ways to specify policies that accommodate daily schedules and routines, and previous work has demonstrated that users of OSN's are comfortable expressing policies using these features [30]. Furthermore the current time and location of an individual influence the type of information that she is willing to share [5], e.g.: *Share my location only between 9am and 5pm.* As previously shown, policy rules that are based on the frequency of requests can also be implemented by combining features that allow access to the current time and audit log. Patil et al. observed that frequency-based rules may have a greater importance than time-based rules [24].

Disclosure Levels. In a policy language that supports multiple disclosure levels, the policy owner can specify the degree of information to disclose. For example, in response to a location request, the policy owner might choose to disclose only the name of the current city. This feature would accommodate many of the challenges identified by Biehl et al. [5]. They found people were more comfortable sharing

detailed location information at work and less detailed information outside of work. Therefore, comfort with different disclosure levels is highly influenced by current location.

3. RELATED WORK

The body of literature describing access control policy languages and policy idioms is extensive. Researchers have developed role-based abstractions [17,31] to simplify the management of user rights, trust management approaches [6,7] that combine the management of policies and trust relationships, and distributed logic-based approaches [4,12] that can concisely and compactly manage very complex policies. While some of these approaches have a logical syntax and semantics, others are based on XML [31] or object-oriented paradigms [10]. In this section we survey several recent and feature-rich policy schemes and illustrate that none of these schemes supports the full set of features outlined in Section 2.3 (Table 1 summarizes the features of these schemes).

Li et al. introduced the RT framework, which consists of a family of related languages for specifying distributed authorization policies [17]: RT is a role-based trust management language in which policies are constructed using four simple rule types that assign users to roles, represent delegations, and structure roles into hierarchical relationships; RT_1 extends this basic framework with support for parameterized roles; RT^T provides syntax for specifying policies that require thresholding and separation of duty; and RT^D introduces constructs for constrained delegation. RT has both a set-based semantics and a Datalog-based semantics, and policies can be efficiently evaluated via translation into a Datalog program.

Park and Sandhu introduced $UCON_{ABC}$, a family of models for usage control (UCON) [22, 23]. UCON is a conceptual framework that provides a comprehensive approach to managing access control, Digital Rights Management (DRM), and trust management. It can express a wide variety of policies by applying different combinations of authorizations, obligations, and conditions to digital objects. For example, basic RBAC can be expressed using authorization rules alone, whereas DRM can be expressed using a combination of authorization rules, conditions, and obligations. UCON also explores the complexities that arise when data consumers become data producers, if, for example, a client's personal information is logged during transactions.

Damianou et al. introduced Ponder, an access control language for a variety of applications such as firewalls, operating systems, and databases [10]. In addition to traditional features such as roles and delegation, Ponder supports policies that require actions to be taken after being triggered by a certain event. Unlike many other authorization languages, Ponder is described as a declarative, strongly typed, object-oriented language.

DeTreville presents Binder, a security language for distributed systems, which is based on Datalog [12]. However, unlike basic Datalog, Binder programs can securely communicate with other Binder programs across distributed environments using signed certificates.

Becker et al. developed Cassandra, which is built upon Datalog with constraints (Datalog$_C$ [4]). Cassandra provides role-based trust management in distributed domains with credential retrieval, separation of duty, and role activation/deactivation. Additionally, Cassandra rules may contain a constraint c drawn from a constraint domain C that

	negotiation	exposure polymorphism	side effects	aggregation	tunable querier privacy	roles & delegation	time rules	location rules*	tunable disclosure granularity
RT	no	no	no	no	no	yes	no	no	yes
Cassandra	yes	no	no	yes	no	yes	yes	no	yes
SecPal	no	no	no	yes	no	yes	yes	no	yes
SMP	no	yes	yes	no	no	yes	no	no	no
Ponder	no	no	yes	no	no	yes	yes	no	yes
Binder	no	no	no	no	no	yes	no	no	yes
UCON	yes	no	yes	no	no	roles	yes	yes	no
PlexC	yes	yes	yes	yes	yes	yes	yes	yes	yes

Table 1: Comparison of language features.
*While other languages were not designed with location sharing in mind, they may be able to support location via minor extensions.

can be tuned to provide different tradeoffs between computational complexity and expressivity. Becker et al. then build upon the extensibility of Cassandra in SecPal [2]. Sec-Pal has a high-level natural syntax and its design features include delegation, constraints, and negation in queries. Sec-Pal policies can also be compiled into Datalog$_C$ programs.

The State Modifying Policies framework [3] can be used to extend policy languages based on distributed logics with concepts from Transactional Datalog [8]. This provides support for the use of policies that are capable of adding/retracting facts to/from the policy's logic program at runtime. This is useful, e.g., for supporting policies that can augment and examine their own audit logs.

Recently, Gunter et al. described an idiom called "Experience-Based Access Control" (EBAM) [15]. Briefly, EBAM is a set of models, tools, and techniques to reconcile the differences between ideal policies and the operational policies enforced by the underlying system. A typical approach for realizing EBAM may include maintaining and analyzing an access log to suggest ways to update and improve existing rules. This iterative process is similar to the exposure feedback loop discussed previously; however, *PlexC* focuses on the human perception of exposure.

Collectively, these policy languages introduce an impressive assortment of paradigms, idioms, and features for expressing security policies in different contexts. However, no single policy language provides support for all of the features identified in Section 2.3 as being important to the management of end-user exposure (see Table 1). This is not surprising, as exposure management was not a primary goal during the development of this prior work. In the next section we describe *PlexC*, a policy language for exposure control that was designed not only to meet all of the needs identified in Section 2.3, but also to take into account the findings of recent user studies in the domain of exposure control.

4. PLEXC: SYSTEM AND SYNTAX

We now describe the system model assumed by *PlexC* including its components, interfaces, and assumptions. We then develop the *PlexC* exposure control language, which is based on transactional extensions to Datalog.

4.1 System Model

PlexC is a system that acts as a protection layer around a set of resources. It has four main components: an external query interface, an evaluation engine, a set of local knowledge bases, and a component that manages sending feedback to the user. This high-level structure is shown in Figure 2.

In a typical workflow, an application requests access to some resource, say, Alice's location. This request goes

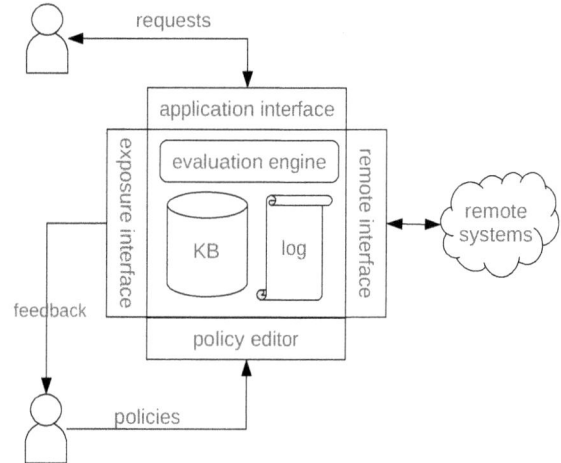

Figure 2: The general *PlexC* system model.

through the external query interface, which limits and controls ways in which external applications can interact with the system. The query is then processed by a policy evaluation engine, which determines if the requester should be granted access to the resource. This decision might be based on information from several sources. In addition to evaluating disclosure policies, the evaluation engine may examine audit logs and the authorization state stored in local knowledge bases, and it may even request information from remote *PlexC* systems. Finally, the disclosure decision is written to the system audit log, and the feedback component may decide to notify Alice about this interaction.

Communication between knowledge bases. When the resource engine evaluates Alice's disclosure policies, communication with other system components may be necessary. For example, Alice may choose to reveal her location only if very few requests have been made in the past hour. This policy rule would require that the evaluation engine communicate with the local database, which maintains a log of transactions. Furthermore, Alice's disclosure policies might depend upon Bob's policies. For instance, Alice might only reveal her location to members of a volunteer group organized by Bob. Consequently, the policy engine would communicate with Bob's knowledge base to verify that the requester is a member of the appropriate group. In order to enable this type of behavior, knowledge bases can communicate with each other via an *exported interface* that allows users to reference each other's disclosure rules.

Storage of disclosure policies. Users store their exposure control policies in a knowledge base composed of facts and rules. Notice that the system model shown in Figure 2 caters to the principles of the exposure control loop by explicitly providing a path by which feedback information can flow from the system to the policy owner. Furthermore, this general system design lays the groundwork to support a rich set of features that are important for controlling exposure. We discuss these features in the next section.

4.2 Datalog Overview

Datalog is a logic programming language for deductive databases. Because of its well-defined declarative semantics and efficient query evaluation algorithms, it provides a nice environment within which to express authorization policies. Indeed, many policy languages—including *PlexC*—are based on Datalog or can be translated into Datalog programs (e.g., [2–4, 12, 17]). We now provide a brief review of the terminology, syntax, and semantics of Datalog.

Datalog is a syntactic subset of Prolog, and programs are composed of *facts* and *rules*. A *rule* is a statement of the form $q :- p_1, p_2, ..., p_n$, where q and each p_i for $1 \leq i \leq n$ are *literals*. Intuitively, this rule can be read as "p_1 and p_2 and ... and p_n imply q". q is referred to as the *head* of the rule, and the *body* is composed of each p_i. A *fact* is a rule that contains only a head and no body.

A *literal* has the form $P(x_1, x_2, ..., x_m)$ where P is a predicate name followed by a tuple with arity m, and each x_i for $1 \leq i \leq m$ is a *variable* or *constant*.

Consider the following example that demonstrates a simple Datalog program:

```
parent('alice','bob').
parent('carol','alice').
ancestor(?X,?Y) :- parent(?X,?Y).
ancestor(?X,?Z) :- ancestor(?X,?Y),ancestor(?Y,?Z).
?-ancestor(?X,'bob').
```

Here we denote variables as strings prefaced by a question mark, "?", and string literals are surrounded by quotes. In this example, the first two statements are ground facts. These are sometimes stored in a physically separate database called the *Extensional Database* or EDB. The next two statements are rules, which are stored in the *Intensional Database* or IDB. The EDB and IDB contain disjoint sets of predicates; as such, predicates defined in the EDB may only appear in the body of rules, and may not appear in the head of any rule. The last statement above is a query that seeks to find all bindings of ?X such that ?X is an ancestor of 'bob'. In the above program, the tuples `ancestor('alice','bob')` and `ancestor('carol','bob')` satisfy this query.

4.3 PlexC

We now describe the set of extensions distinguishing *PlexC* from pure Datalog. First, we discuss the interface across which external applications communicate with our system. We then explain how transactional updates to the system state can be expressed and how policy authors can both create rules that are based on changes in the system audit log and rules that are sensitive to user feedback. Finally, we list additional built-in predicates and functions.

External Interface. External applications, such as location- or presence-sharing applications, communicate with the *PlexC* system to determine if a certain resource of a user should be disclosed to the requester. This communication occurs through an *external interface* exposed to these types of applications that is composed of a set of predicates described below:

System defined:.

- `get(?Q,?U,?R,?L) :- U.canAccess(?Q,?R,?L)` ⊗ `+log(?Q,?U,?R,?L,NOW);` `get()` is a system predicate that is invoked when user Q requests resource R at granularity L belonging to user U. Successful evaluation of this predicate inserts a record into the audit log.

- `over-exposure(?U,?E)` binds the current exposure of user U to the free variable E. The current exposure could be estimated by a user-defined function that runs over the audit log. For example, a user's exposure might be HIGH if the audit log shows a large number of accesses in the past hour.

User defined:.

- `canAccess(?Q,?R [, ?L])` is true if the requester, Q, can access the desired resource, R, at the (optional) level of granularity, L.

- `isMember(?U,?R)` is true if user U is currently a member of role R.

- `canQuery(?U,?P)` is true if the policy author allows another user U to reference predicate P in her policy rules.

By creating a set of policy rules, the policy author is free to define the conditions satisfying the predicates in the external interface. However, the system is responsible for defining the `get` predicate, which retrieves the user's personal information, such as the current location or activity.

When personal information is disclosed via the `get` predicate, a transaction occurs in which a record of the access is inserted into the system audit log. The record contains information about the requester, the resource disclosed, the time of disclosure, and the level of detail (granularity) of the disclosure. Prior research has explored incorporating transactions into Datalog. Transaction Datalog (TD) is an extension to Datalog for executing transactions that modify the database as rules are evaluated. TD supports the classical ACID properties as well as other properties like transaction hierarchies, concurrency, and cooperation [8].

PlexC also supports the notion of *state effects* as introduced by Becker and Nanz [3]. Effects can be composed by the sequential transaction operator "⊗" from Transactional Datalog [8]. This feature allows users to express policies that require role activation, separation of duty, or other state-dependent operations. For example, the following rule allows requesters to access an individual's location only once:

Example 4.1
```
canAccess(?X,LOCATION) :- not seen(?X,LOCATION)
⊗ +seen(?X,LOCATION);
```

Here, the sequential transaction operator, ⊗, is used to specify the facts to be inserted to or deleted from the database (denoted by a "+" or "−" respectively), if all conditions in the body are satisfied.

Built-in Constants. *PlexC* also includes a number of constants that refer to resources that the user is not responsible for defining:

- NOW refers to the current time;
- TODAY is a string representing the current date;
- MYLOC represents the current location of the user, stored as a point (coordinate pair), and a radius;
- LOCATION is a constant used to identify location resources;
- CITY is a constant used to specify the city-level of granularity for location resources;
- ANYONE is a placeholder that matches any user when scanning the audit log;
- TRUE represents the positive truth value;
- FALSE represents the negative truth value.

User Policies. Users can define facts and rules to control disclosure. As with basic Datalog this allows the easy creation of groups and roles. Example 4.2 demonstrates a set of basic facts and rules that a user might create.

Example 4.2
```
canAccess('bob', LOCATION);
canAccess(?X, LOCATION) :- isMember(?X,
'friend');
```

The first statement is a fact that explicitly gives Bob access to Alice's location information. In the next statement, Alice also allows her friends to view her location. Thus we see that with basic Datalog syntax we can easily implement a simple, static role-based access control model.

Remote predicates. Users can also specify *remote predicates* by providing an identifier as a prefix before the predicate name. With this feature we can encode policies that require delegation. In the following example, Alice delegates disclosure decisions to Bob:

Example 4.3
```
canAccess(?X, LOCATION) :- bob.canAccess(?X,
LOCATION);
```

Similarly, with these features we can express basic forms of disclosure negotiation and other rules that are *quid pro quo*. In the following example, Alice only allows another user to access her location if she can access his location:

Example 4.4
```
canAccess(?X, LOCATION) :- ?X.canAccess('alice',
LOCATION);
canAccess(?X, LOCATION, CITY) :-
?X.canAccess('alice', LOCATION, CITY);
```

Additionally, *PlexC* allows policy authors to constrain the information in the knowledge base that is visible to other users. This is achieved with the built-in predicate, canQuery(?U,?P), which allows another user U to query the predicate, P. For example, the registrar at a university might allow a teacher, T, to query the list of students enrolled in courses that he teaches.

Example 4.5
```
canQuery(?T, enrolled) :- teaches(?T, ?C),
enrolled(?U, ?C);
```

Handling Exposure. Users have the ability to write policies that depend on the current exposure conditions. Aggregation is an important prerequisite for achieving this

behavior [28], and Mumick et al. investigate extending Datalog with aggregate operators [20]. They show that Datalog can be efficiently extended with aggregate operators using magic sets and semi-naive evaluation algorithms, which provide good heuristics over the naive, bottom-up approach. In order to ensure the termination of Datalog programs, aggregate operators are subject to restrictions such as stratification [11]. In our case we provide special built-in predicates that are restricted to aggregating over a logically separated set of facts and predicates. This restriction is sufficient for our purposes, as it allows *PlexC* policies to aggregate over the audit log, for example. The following demonstrates how aggregation over the audit log can be used to limit the frequency of location sharing to no more than 5 times per day:

Example 4.6
```
canAccess(?X,LOCATION) :- accessCount(?X, ?N, 1,
00:00, 23:59), ?N <= 5;
```

Here, accessCount(?X, ?N, ?D, ?T_1, ?T_2) invokes a search of the audit log for the number of accesses N by requester X between times T_1 and T_2 over the past D days.

In addition to aggregation over the audit log, users can write rules that depend on their current exposure. Prior research suggests that several factors contribute highly to an individual's notion of exposure, such as the social relation of the requester [28], the frequency of requests [24], and the surroundings at the time of request [5]. *PlexC* provides the access to this information through built-in functions, predicates, and language features, making it easy to define custom exposure functions. For example, a user might define exposure levels to be HIGH if the number of requests by strangers in the audit log exceeds a certain threshold.

Example 4.7
```
canAccess(?X,LOCATION) :- exposure(?E), ?E <
MEDIUM;
canAccess(?X,LOCATION,CITY) :- exposure(?E), ?E
>= MEDIUM;
```

Keeping the User in the Loop. In the study by Patil et al. many participants expressed the desire to mediate all requests for their personal information [24]. To this end we introduce a built-in function prompt(?X,?R) that prompts the current user to give requester X permission to access resource R. Other participants simply wanted to be notified for each request, so we define a similar function notify(?X,?R), which notifies the user that requester X has accessed resource R.

Additional Features. There have been a number of extensions to pure Datalog, some of which *PlexC* incorporates. These include built-in predicates, functions, and negation [9]. *PlexC* includes support for basic equality, comparison, and arithmetic operators. These can be viewed as infix predicates except that the operands correspond to terms, and the result of the atom is evaluated by the underlying implementation and does not depend on facts in the local knowledgebase. The following rule demonstrates both a built-in function to test if the current day is a weekday, as well as the built-in greater-than operator, and stipulates that location requests are only permitted on weekdays between 9am–5pm:

Example 4.8
```
canAccess(?X, LOCATION) :- weekday(TODAY), NOW >
9:00, NOW < 17:00;
```

```
program     : statement*
statement   : (fact | rule | query) ';'
rule        : literal ':-' literals ['⊗' effects]
fact        : atom
query       : '?' literals
literals    : atom (',' atom)*
literal     : 'not'? atom
effects     : effect (',' effect)*
effect      : ('+'|'-') atom
atom        : [identifier '.'] identifier tuple
tuple       : '(' terms ')'
terms       : term (',' term)*
term        : function | variable | constant |
              string | number
variable    : '?' constant
function    : identifier tuple
```

Figure 3: The formal grammar of *PlexC*.

PlexC also supports several predicates to create *named regions*, which are essentially locations on a map with an associated radius. The region(?NAME,?LAT,?LON,?R) predicate defines a region *NAME* centered at the coordinate (*LAT*,*LON*) with radius *R*. The predicate inRegion(?L,?NAME) tests if the location *L* is within the region, *NAME*. Example 4.9 only allows members of a *student* group to access location when the user is on campus:

Example 4.9
```
region('campus', 40.2, -100.2, 1km);
canAccess(?X,LOCATION) :- inRegion(MYLOC,
'campus'), member(?X, 'student');
```

Furthermore, *PlexC* supports a limited form of negation. Pure Datalog does not allow negation, which can threaten the evaluation safety of programs. Typically, negation is handled using *stratification* or the *closed world assumption* (CWA). Stratification imposes an evaluation order on rules where negated body predicates must be evaluated before predicates in the rule head. CWA allows the inference of negative ground facts if they do not appear in the EDB [9]. *PlexC* uses the CWA to handle negation.

Example 4.10 demonstrates a rule that uses negation to implement an exclusion policy:

Example 4.10
```
canAccess(?X,LOCATION):- not
member(?X,'enemies');
```

Finally, we support a set of built-in functional-symbols that may depend on the deployment environment. For example, a location-sharing application might contain a set of functional-symbols to perform distance calculations, e.g. within(?L1,?L2,?D) would return true if *L1* and *L2* are within distance *D*. Similarly, functions that provide reverse geocoding would be useful, such as cityOf(?L), which would return the city of the location coordinate *L*.

Figure 3 shows the grammar production rules for *PlexC*.

4.4 Rule Evaluation

In typical Datalog systems extensional facts are applied to rules in the intensional database to generate new facts until no new facts can be generated (a fixed point). This bottom-up approach is straightforward and can occur before handling queries. However, more expressive languages do not take this approach to evaluate queries. One of the reasons is that certain special predicates and function symbols cannot be computed prior to receiving queries. For example, some predicates and constants depend on current time and location (e.g., accessCount, many types of rules defining the canAccess relation), while others require the user's interaction (e.g., prompt).

Therefore, instead of using bottom-up strategies, modern expressive policy languages employ memoized, top-down evaluation algorithms that combine the efficiency of goal-oriented approaches while avoiding the non-termination issues of standard SLD resolution used in Prolog [4].

Consider the following example:

Example 4.11
```
canAccess(?X, LOCATION) :- weekday(TODAY),
    bob.member(?X,'friend'),
    accessCount(?X,?N,1,00:00,23:59), ?N <= 5
```

Access to the current user's location is contingent upon several factors. First, the date is obtained and tested as a parameter of weekday. Next, the second literal is a remote predicate indicating that the requester needs to be a friend of Bob. A query is therefore sent to Bob's exported predicates interface, and if Bob allows the current user to query this predicate, and the requester belongs to the friend role, then a positive result is returned. The accessCount predicate invokes a query on the audit log and binds the number of accesses by the requester (in the current day) to the free variable *N*, and the last item tests that *N* is no more than 5.

5. EVALUATION

In this section we give an informal evaluation of the expressiveness of *PlexC*. First, we show how *PlexC* meets all of the language requirements outlined in Section 2.3. We then show how a variety of common policy idioms can be represented in *PlexC*. Finally, we use *PlexC* to encode some of the more interesting policies gathered from free-response questions in the study conducted in [24].

5.1 Meeting All Language Requirements

Here we show how *PlexC* achieves all of the requirements outlined in Section 2.3.

- **Groups and Roles:** Example 4.2 demonstrates how to define roles and limit access based on group membership. Policy authors can create different roles and assign membership relations using the natural Datalog syntax.

- **Delegation:** Example 4.3 shows how delegation is possible in *PlexC*. Delegation requires the evaluation of a relation whose records are not contained in the local knowledge base.

- **Disclosure Negotiation:** Example 4.4 relies upon the evaluation of remote predicates to exchange information between the policy author and the requester until the conditions for disclosure are satisfied.

- **Side Effects:** Example 4.1 shows how *PlexC* draws upon existing syntax [3,8] to specify changes to the authorization state during the evaluation of rules.

- **Disclosure Levels:** The amount of detail in a disclosure can be controlled by specifying the appropriate resource identifier. For instance, Example 4.7 shows how the granularity of information to be disclosed can be adjusted.

- **Time and Location rules:** Time-based rules can be expressed using the built-in constants that represent the current time and day as shown in Example 4.8 and Example 4.9, respectively.

- **Aggregate Operations:** *PlexC* provides support for aggregation over the system audit log via special predicates. This functionality can be seen in Example 4.6.

- **Polymorphism:** In Example 4.7 we encode a policy whose behavior is dependent on the target user's current level of over-exposure.

5.2 Encoding Free-form Policies

Here we demonstrate the expressiveness and utility of *PlexC* by encoding some interesting and complex policies taken from participant free responses gathered during the study detailed by Patil et al. [24].

A number of participants expressed the desire for complete mediation of all requests for their location. For example, one such policy was: *Keep my location private and ask every time someone wants to know my location.* This policy would have the following implementation in *PlexC*:

Example 5.1
```
canAccess(?X,LOCATION) :- prompt(?X,LOCATION);
```

Another common response was that users wanted to be notified after every location disclosure, but didn't necessarily need to know who had accessed their location. For example, one user stated *"Any time anyone views my location, I must get a notification."* This rule is similar to the previous example, but does not require direct interaction from the user. One interpretation of this policy is that access should be allowed to everyone as long as there is a notification:

Example 5.2
```
canAccess(?X,LOCATION) :- TRUE ⊗
notify(?X,LOCATION);
```

Another interpretation might be to modify any existing rules by adding a notification upon success, in which case the `notify()` predicate can be appended to the existing rules.

Location-based rules were also among the more unique responses. For example, one participant wrote, *"Allow users to see when I am within a particular radius of them."* An interesting implication of this is that the user wants to share her location only when it could possibly be of use to the recipient. This would be implemented in the following way:

Example 5.3
```
canAccess(?X, LOCATION) :- get(?X, LOCATION,
?L1), within(MYLOC, ?L1, 1km);
```

Many participants also indicated that they would not want to share their location for social engagement purposes. However, many of these otherwise unwilling users of location-based services indicated that they *would* share their location during emergency situations, e.g.: *I would only want someone to know my physical location in an emergency situation.* This introduces the difficult problem of determining when the user is experiencing an emergency. However,

one response provided some intuition: *"only if I'm missing for 24+ hours"*. This policy could be approximated in the following way:

Example 5.4
```
canAccess(?X,LOCATION) :- member(?X,'emergency'),
accessCount(ANYONE, ?N, 1, NOW-24:00, NOW), ?N
= 0;
```

By this encoding access is granted only if the requester belongs to the 'emergency' role and the audit log shows that nobody has received the user's location in the past 24 hours.

6. DISCUSSION AND FUTURE WORK

Implementation. We are currently implementing *PlexC* as part of a larger location-sharing application. We have already implemented several major components of the system, including a mobile application to track current location and view the locations of others, a web interface for managing policies and carrying out more complex queries, and a server application to store data and manage social relations. *PlexC* will be used as the fundamental access control component to manage the information flow between the other system components. We plan to use this testbed to better understand the utility of *PlexC*, as well as to explore the system design tradeoffs present in this space.

Validation of User Studies. The design of *PlexC* is motivated by the collection of recent user studies described in Section 2.2. However, these studies share a common limitation: because these studies are based on user surveys, they reveal only the *perceived* preferences and needs of participants in an artificial environment. In other words, although the participants in these studies are likely to have given truthful answers to the surveys, there is a chance that they would behave differently in a real-world scenario. While it is not possible to completely account for all sources of response bias in a lab setting, a field study of a fully functional system would be able to mitigate these effects and support or challenge the findings upon which *PlexC* is based.

Usability of Policy Creation. *PlexC* allows users to create concise policies for exposure management, and it inherits many desirable traits from Datalog (e.g., unambiguous semantics and tractable evaluation). However, we do not expect the average user to write rules in *PlexC* directly. *PlexC* was developed, instead, to represent a formal semantics for exposure-aware policies. While it is possible to write *PlexC* policies directly, we envision that most users will interact with their policies via some form of structured policy editor. We believe that a form-based rule editor would simplify the creation of *PlexC* rules that are easy for users to understand, while still taking advantage of the power of *PlexC*. Striking a good balance between usability and expressive power will be an interesting research challenge.

7. SUMMARY

In this paper we address the development of *PlexC*: a policy language for exposure control. The concept of *exposure* denotes the extent to which an individual's personal data is shared, and addresses the individual's resulting concern for privacy. Given the complexity of this design space, we first articulate requirements for policy languages for exposure control by analyzing the findings of several recent survey studies addressing various facets of the exposure problem. Not surprisingly, existing *access control* policy languages are shown to be insufficient for meeting the *exposure control* needs voiced by participants in these studies. We present *PlexC* as a solution to meet the needs of these participants. After describing the details of *PlexC*, we show that it is both suitable for meeting the needs of users in modern context-sharing systems, as well as capable of encoding a variety of historically useful policy idioms. Although *PlexC* was derived by examining surveys of users' perceived exposure-control needs, further evaluation work is still required. In particular our team plans to explore the development of usable policy-management interfaces and user studies of *PlexC*-based contextual sharing systems.

Acknowledgements. This research is supported by NSF grants CCF-0916015, CNS-1016603, & CNS-1017229, and US DHS grant 2006-CS-001-000001, under the auspices of the Institute for Information Infrastructure Protection (I3P). The contents of this paper do not necessarily reflect the views of the sponsors.

8. REFERENCES

[1] M. Backes, M. Maffei, and K. Pecina. A security api for distributed social networks. In *NDSS*, Feb. 2011.

[2] M. Y. Becker, C. Fournet, and A. D. Gordon. SecPAL: Design and semantics of a decentralized authorization language. *Journal of Computer Security*, 2009.

[3] M. Y. Becker and S. Nanz. A Logic for State-Modifying Authorization Policies. *ACM TISSEC*, 13:20:1–20:28, July 2010.

[4] M. Y. Becker and P. Sewell. Cassandra: Distributed Access Control Policies with Tunable Expressiveness. In *POLICY*, pages 159–168, June 2004.

[5] J. T. Biehl, E. Rieffel, and A. J. Lee. When Privacy and Utility are in Harmony: Towards Better Design of Presence Technologies. *Personal Ubiquitous Computing*, in press, Feb. 2012.

[6] M. Blaze, J. Feigenbaum, and A. D. Keromytis. KeyNote: Trust Management for Public-Key Infrastructures. In *Infrastructures (Position Paper). LNCS 1550*, pages 59–63, 1998.

[7] M. Blaze, J. Feigenbaum, and J. Lacy. Decentralized Trust Management. In *In Proceedings of the 1996 IEEE Symposium on Security and Privacy*, pages 164–173, May 1996.

[8] A. J. Bonner. Transaction Datalog: a Compositional Language for Transaction Programming. In *In Proceedings of the International Workshop on Database Programming Languages*, 1997.

[9] S. Ceri, G. Gottlob, and L. Tanca. What you always wanted to know about datalog (and never dared to ask). *IEEE TKDE*, 1:146–166, March 1989.

[10] N. Damianou, N. Dulay, E. Lupu, and M. Sloman. The ponder policy specification language. In *POLICY*, pages 18–38, 2001.

[11] T. Dell'Armi, W. Faber, G. Ielpa, N. Leone, and G. Pfeifer. Aggregate functions in disjunctive logic programming: semantics, complexity, and implementation in dlv. In *Proceedings of the 18th international joint conference on Artificial intelligence*, pages 847–852, 2003.

[12] J. DeTreville. Binder, a logic-based security language. In *Proceedings of the IEEE Symposium on Security and Privacy*, pages 105–113, May 2002.

[13] Foursquare. http://www.foursquare.com/.

[14] Google+. https://plus.google.com/.

[15] C. A. Gunter, D. M. Liebovitz, and B. Malin. Experience-based access management: A life-cycle framework for identity and access management systems. *IEEE Security & Privacy Magazine*, 9(5), September/October 2011.

[16] A. J. Lee, T. Yu, and Y. L. Gall. Effective trust management through a hybrid logical and relational approach. In *ASIACCS*, Apr. 2010.

[17] N. Li and J. C. Mitchell. RT: A role-based trust-management framework. In *Proceedings of the DARPA Information Survivability Conference and Exposition (DISCEX III)*, pages 201–212, Apr. 2003.

[18] Locaccino. http://locaccino.org/.

[19] E. Miluzzo, N. D. Lane, K. Fodor, R. Peterson, H. Lu, M. Musolesi, S. B. Eisenman, X. Zheng, and A. T. Campbell. Sensing meets mobile social networks: the design, implementation and evaluation of the CenceMe application. In *SenSys*, pages 337–350, 2008.

[20] I. S. Mumick, H. Pirahesh, and R. Ramakrishnan. The magic of duplicates and aggregates. In *VLDB*, pages 264–277, 1990.

[21] L. E. Olson, C. A. Gunter, and P. Madhusudan. A formal framework for reflective database access control policies. In *CCS*, pages 289–298, 2008.

[22] J. Park and R. Sandhu. Towards usage control models: beyond traditional access control. In *SACMAT*, pages 57–64, 2002.

[23] J. Park and R. Sandhu. The uconabc usage control model. *ACM TISSEC*, 7(1):128–174, Feb. 2004.

[24] S. Patil, Y. L. Gall, A. J. Lee, and A. Kapadia. My Privacy Policy: Exploring End-user Specification of Freeform Location Access Rules. In *Proceedings of the Workshop on Usable Security (USEC)*, Mar. 2012.

[25] Facebook places. http://www.facebook.com/places/.

[26] N. Sadeh, J. Hong, L. Cranor, I. Fette, P. Kelley, M. Prabaker, and J. Rao. Understanding and Capturing People's Privacy Policies in a Mobile Social Networking Application. *Personal and Ubiquitous Computing*, 13:401–412, August 2009.

[27] R. Sandhu, E. J. Coyne, H. L. Feinstein, and C. E. Youman. Role-based access control models. *IEEE Computer*, 29(2):38–47, Feb. 1996.

[28] R. Schlegel, A. Kapadia, and A. J. Lee. Eyeing your Exposure: Quantifying and Controlling Information Sharing for Improved Privacy. In *SOUPS*, July 2011.

[29] K. E. Seamons, M. Winslett, T. Yu, B. Smith, E. Child, J. Jacobson, H. Mills, and L. Yu. Requirements for policy languages for trust negotiation. In *POLICY*, pages 68–79, 2002.

[30] J. Y. Tsai, P. Kelley, P. Drielsma, L. F. Cranor, J. Hong, and N. Sadeh. Who's viewed you?: the impact of feedback in a mobile location-sharing application. In *ACM CHI*, pages 2003–2012, 2009.

[31] W. Yao, K. Moody, and J. Bacon. A Model of OASIS Role-Based Access Control and its Support for Active Security. In *SACMAT*, pages 171–181, 2001.

Author Index

www.ingramcontent.com/pod-product-compliance
Lightning Source LLC
Chambersburg PA
CBHW082110220326
41598CB00066BA/6157